AESOPIC CONVERSATIONS

MARTIN CLASSICAL LECTURES

The Martin Classical Lectures are delivered annually at Oberlin College through a foundation established by his many friends in honor of Charles Beebe Martin, for forty-five years a teacher of classical literature and classical art at Oberlin.

John Peradotto, *Man in the Middle Voice: Name and Narration in the Odyssey*

Martha C. Nussbaum, *The Therapy of Desire: Theory and Practice in Hellenistic Ethics*

Josiah Ober, *Political Dissent in Democratic Athens: Intellectual Critics of Popular Rule*

Anne Carson, *Economy of the Unlost (Reading Simonides of Keos with Paul Celan)*

Helene P. Foley, *Female Acts in Greek Tragedy*

Mark W. Edwards, *Sound, Sense, and Rhythm: Listening to Greek and Latin Poetry*

Michael C. J. Putnam, *Poetic Interplay: Catullus and Horace*

Julia Haig Gaisser, *The Fortunes of Apuleius and the Golden Ass: A Study in Transmission and Reception*

Kenneth Reckford, *Recognizing Persius*

Leslie Kurke, *Aesopic Conversations: Popular Tradition, Cultural Dialogue, and the Invention of Greek Prose*

AESOPIC CONVERSATIONS

POPULAR TRADITION, CULTURAL DIALOGUE,
AND THE INVENTION OF GREEK PROSE

LESLIE KURKE

PRINCETON UNIVERSITY PRESS
PRINCETON AND OXFORD

Copyright © 2011 by Princeton University Press

Published by Princeton University Press, 41 William Street, Princeton, New Jersey 08540

In the United Kingdom: Princeton University Press, 6 Oxford Street, Woodstock, Oxfordshire OX20 1TW

press.princeton.edu

All Rights Reserved

Library of Congress Cataloging-in-Publication Data

Kurke, Leslie
  Aesopic conversations : popular tradition, cultural dialogue, and the invention of Greek prose / Leslie Kurke.
    p. cm. — (Martin classical lectures)
  Includes bibliographical references and index.
    ISBN 978-0-691-14457-3 (hardcover : alk. paper) — ISBN 978-0-691-14458-0 (pbk. : alk. paper)
    1. Greek prose literature—History and criticism. 2. Fables, Greek—History and criticism. 3. Aesop's fables. 4. Aesop—Influence. 5. Popular culture—Greece—History—To 146 B.C. 6. Popular culture and literature—Greece—History—To 146 B.C. 7. Literary form—History—To 1500. 8. Literature and society—Greece—History—To 146 B.C. I. Title.
PA3257.K87 2010
886′.0109—dc22   2010006842

British Library Cataloging-in-Publication Data is available

This book has been composed in Sabon

Printed on acid-free paper. ∞

Printed in the United States of America

10 9 8 7 6 5 4 3 2 1

*For my students
and in memory of NCBK*

κοὐκ ἐμὸς ὁ μῦθος, ἀλλ' ἐμῆς μητρὸς πάρα

CONTENTS

LIST OF ILLUSTRATIONS   xi

ACKNOWLEDGMENTS   xiii

ABBREVIATIONS   xvii

INTRODUCTION
I. An Elusive Quarry: In Search of Ancient Greek Popular Culture   2
II. Explaining the Joke: A Road Map for Classicists   16
III. Synopsis of Method and Structure of Argument   46

PART I: Competitive Wisdom and Popular Culture   51

CHAPTER 1
Aesop and the Contestation of Delphic Authority   53

I. Ideological Tensions at Delphi   54
II. The Aesopic Critique   59
III. Neoptolemus and Aesop: Sacrifice, Hero Cult, and Competitive Scapegoating   75

CHAPTER 2
Sophia before/beyond Philosophy   95

I. The Tradition of Sophia   95
II. Sophists and (as) Sages   102
III. Aristotle and the Transformation of Sophia   115

CHAPTER 3
Aesop as Sage: Political Counsel and Discursive Practice   125

I. Aesop among the Sages   125
II. Political Animals: Fable and the Scene of Advising   142

CHAPTER 4
Reading the *Life:* The Progress of a Sage and the Anthropology of *Sophia*   159

I. An Aesopic Anthropology of Wisdom   160
II. Aesop and Ahiqar   176
III. Delphic Theōria and the Death of a Sage   185
IV. The Bricoleur as Culture Hero, or the Art of Extorting Self-Incrimination   191

viii CONTENTS

CHAPTER 5
The Aesopic Parody of High Wisdom   202
   I. Demystifying Sophia: *Hesiod, Theognis, and the Seven Sages*   204
   II. Aesopic Parody in the Visual Tradition?   224

PART II: Aesop and the Invention of Greek Prose   239

CHAPTER 6
Aesop at the Invention of Philosophy   241
Prelude to Part II: The Problematic Sociopolitics of Mimetic Prose   241
   I. Mimēsis and the Invention of Philosophy   244
   II. The Generic Affiliations of Sōkratikoi logoi   251

CHAPTER 7
The Battle over Prose: Fable in Sophistic Education and Xenophon's *Memorabilia*   265
   I. Sophistic Fables   268
   II. Traditional Fable Narration in Xenophon's Memorabilia   288

CHAPTER 8
Sophistic Fable in Plato: Parody, Appropriation, and Transcendence   301
   I. Plato's Protagoras: *Debunking Sophistic Fable*   301
   II. Plato's Symposium: *Ringing the Changes on Fable*   308

CHAPTER 9
Aesop in Plato's *Sōkratikoi Logoi:* Analogy, *Elenchos,* and Disavowal   325
   I. Sophia into Philosophy: Socrates between the Sages and Aesop   326
   II. The Aesopic Bricoleur and the "Old Socratic Tool-Box"   330
   III. Sympotic Wisdom, Comedy, and Aesopic Competition
      in Hippias Major   344

CHAPTER 10
Historiē and Logopoiia: Two Sides of Herodotean Prose   361
   I. History before Prose, Prose before History   362
   II. Aesop Ho Logopoios   370
   III. Plutarch Reading Herodotus: Aesop, Ruptures of Decorum,
      and the Non-Greek   382

CHAPTER 11
Herodotus and Aesop: Some Soundings   398
   I. Cyrus Tells a Fable   400

II. Greece and (as) Fable, or Resignifying the Hierarchy of Genre   404
III. Fable as History   412
IV. The Aesopic Contract of the Histories: *Herodotus Teaches His Readers*   426

BIBLIOGRAPHY   433

INDEX LOCORUM   463

GENERAL INDEX   478

ILLUSTRATIONS

FIGURE 4.1. The end of *Vita* G and beginning of the fable collection in Morgan ms M.397, folio 67ᵛ (late tenth or early eleventh century CE). 195

FIGURE 5.1. Aesop(?) in conversation with a fox. Vatican, Museo Etrusco Gregoriano inv. no. 16552. Interior of Attic red-figure cup, attributed to the Painter of Bologna 417, ca. 450 BCE. 226

FIGURE 5.2. Oedipus in conversation with the Sphinx. Vatican, Museo Etrusco Gregoriano inv. no. 16541. Interior of Attic red-figure cup, attributed to the Oedipus Painter, ca. 470 BCE. 227

FIGURE 5.3. Oedipus in conversation with the Sphinx. Museum für Regionalgeschichte und Volkskunde, Schloss Friedenstein Gotha, no. 80. Interior of Attic red-figure cup, attributed to the Veii Painter, 470–460 BCE. 228

FIGURE 5.4. Wall paintings of the Seven Sages, Terme dei Sette Sapienti, Ostia III x 2, Room 5, ca. 100–120 CE. Detail of Chilon, showing barrel vault, all three registers of the wall painting, and doorway. 231

FIGURE 5.5. Wall paintings of the Seven Sages, Terme dei Sette Sapienti, Ostia III x 2, Room 5, ca. 100–120 CE. Detail of Thales and sitting man below. 232

FIGURE 5.6. Wall paintings of the Seven Sages, Terme dei Sette Sapienti, Ostia III x 2, Room 5, ca. 100–120 CE. Detail of Chilon and sitting men below. 233

ACKNOWLEDGMENTS

I HAVE BEEN THINKING ABOUT and writing this book for a very long time, during which I've benefited from innumerable conversations, formal and informal, with generous and inspiring interlocutors. So if this book is obsessed with the idea of dialogue, the meaningful back-and-forth of different voices and traditions over time, that is because such a process has been essential to its own making. So first, let me thank those interlocutors at the more formal end. To all the students who participated in two graduate seminars I taught on this material—one entitled "The Invention of Greek Prose" at Berkeley in Fall 1999, and a second on the Greek wisdom tradition at Princeton in Spring 2004—I owe a debt of gratitude. Thanks also to the faculty and students who attended the series of four Martin Classical Lectures based on this material at Oberlin in spring 2005—with special gratitude to my hosts, Tom Van Nortwick, Kirk Ormand, and Benjamin Lee, and to the remarkable undergraduates of Oberlin.

At the more informal end, I have been incredibly fortunate in my colleagues and students; their ongoing challenges, support, provocations, conversations, and reading of endless drafts have integrally shaped and enriched my arguments, while many aspects of this project were inspired originally by their ideas, questions, and projects. Thanks in particular to Pavlos Avlamis, Tamara Chin, Carol Dougherty, Page duBois, Kate Gilhuly, Mark Griffith, Deborah Kamen, James Ker, Kathy McCarthy, Boris Maslov, Richard Neer, Lauri Reitzammer, Laura Slatkin, and Håkan Tell. Additional thanks to Vicky Kahn for inviting me to contribute to a special issue of *Representations* and for forcing me to realize that mimesis was a key issue.

Following on the trail of Aesop and the Aesopic, I have in the course of writing this book transgressed many disciplinary boundaries and poached from foreign territories—for example, venturing into folklore studies, Roman wall painting, the Pāli tradition of the *Jātakas*, and the domain of ancient philosophy for the Sophists, Xenophon, and Plato. In this last case especially I am acutely aware of how limited and inadequate my reading of the relevant scholarship has been (which I can do no more than acknowledge here as the necessary concomitant of this kind of project). But one of the great pleasures of such disciplinary poaching is the serendipitous help furnished by colleagues in other fields. Special thanks to those who provided guidance and insight as I was struggling to come to grips with Plato and the ancient philosophical tradition: Alan Code, G.R.F. Ferrari, Andrew Ford, Tony Long, Wolfgang Mann, David Sedley, and Christian Wildberg. Thanks also to a whole host of other scholars in different fields who gave me help or advice along the way: Danielle Allen,

Mary Beard, Robin Fleming, Billy Flesch, Andrew Garrett, Rupert Gethin, Chris Hallett, Todd Hickey, Mike Jameson, François Lissarrague, Nikolaos Papazarkadas, Ted Peña, Laura Quinney, Alex von Rospatt, Ken Rothwell, Nancy Ruttenburg, Seth Schwartz, and Brian Stock. Even when the ground was more familiar (for example, in working on Herodotus), I have had my thinking shaped and changed by the advice, conversation, and generous reading of several thoughtful and broad-minded interlocutors: for that, thanks to Carolyn Dewald, Paul Kosmin, Nino Luraghi, Emily Mackil, and Chris Pelling. I am also indebted to those scholars who shared unpublished material with me: Benjamin Acosta-Hughes, Sara Forsdyke, Wolfgang Mann, Deborah Steiner, Håkan Tell, and Nancy Worman.

Finally, I owe a special debt of gratitude to Richard Martin, who has been unfailingly supportive of this project and whose interventions were particularly crucial at the beginning and at the end. Thanks to Richard and to William Hansen, both of whom provided remarkably thoughtful, attentive, and generous readings of a large and unwieldy manuscript. Thanks also to Jared Hudson and Boris Maslov for their meticulous and energetic editorial work in the final stages of the manuscript preparation. In addition, I am grateful to my editor at Princeton University Press, Rob Tempio, for his consistent support, encouragement, and patience throughout the process. Lauren Lepow provided wonderfully thoughtful, sharp-eyed, and sympathetic copyediting; Blythe Woolston professional help with the Index; and David Crane assistance with the Index Locorum.

I have been writing this book for so long that I cannot possibly reconstruct all the places I have presented pieces of it in talks, but I would like to single out, for special thanks for inviting and hosting me, Greg Nagy at the Center for Hellenic Studies in fall 2003, and Peter Wilson and Oliver Taplin at Oxford that same fall. In addition, I must here record the financial and institutional support that has enabled the writing of this book over ten years: for the first half of its long gestation period, I had the benefit of a John D. and Catherine T. MacArthur Fellowship. In spring 2004, I enjoyed a semester's support from the Humanities Council in Princeton and in fall 2007 another semester as Mary L. Cornille Visiting Professor in the Humanities at Wellesley College. I am grateful for unstinting financial as well as intellectual support from the University of California, Berkeley throughout this whole period—for a Humanities Research Fellowship in fall 2003, for ongoing COR funds, and, starting in 2007, for the support of the Richard and Rhoda P. Goldman Distinguished Professorship in the Arts & Humanities.

This book is dedicated to the memory of my mother, Nancy Charlotte Booth Kurke, who died in November 2002, and to generations of my students—the former, because she was the most Aesopic character I ever knew; the latter because they have over the years helped me understand what that meant and how to think about it.

An earlier version of part of chapter 1 appeared as "Aesop and the Contestation of Delphic Authority" in the volume *The Cultures within Ancient Greek Culture: Contact, Conflict, Collaboration* (Cambridge University Press, 2003). An earlier version of parts of chapters 6 and 9 appeared in the form of an article entitled "Plato, Aesop, and the Beginnings of Mimetic Prose" in *Representations* 94 (2006): 6–52. For permission to reprint that material here I am grateful to Cambridge University Press and the University of California Press, respectively.

Finally, a word about translations. The translations offered in the text are a combination of my own translations and those of other scholars; where not otherwise indicated, the translations are my own. But here, I confess, I have stayed within my "comfort zone": I have offered my own translations for all Greek poetry, Herodotus, the *Life of Aesop*, some Plato, some Plutarch, and bits of Aristotle, but I have relied on other scholars' translations for much late material (e.g., the Second Sophistic), and where I wanted to be sure of accurately capturing philosophical nuances (e.g., for some Plato, the Sophists, and Aristotle). My own translations aim not at elegance, but at an accurate rendition of the Greek within the limits of English syntax. Readers may find them awkward and overliteral in places, and too colloquial in others. All I can say in their defense is that my aim was demystification and defamiliarization; I have tried to capture in translation different generic and stylistic levels, as well as the pervasive strangeness of Greek texts. Thus it seemed best to translate the *Life of Aesop* (for example) colloquially, while I have tried to convey the rich texture and sudden stylistic shifts of Herodotus in English.

ABBREVIATIONS

Abbreviations generally follow the standard list in the *Oxford Classical Dictionary* (*OCD*), third edition, ed. S. Hornblower and A. Spawforth, 1996. The following list includes some works frequently cited, and some departures from the usage of the *OCD* (where I have provided English rather than Latin titles for Greek works). For Greek authors, inscriptional and papyri collections, see also the list in Liddell-Scott-Jones, *A Greek-English Lexicon* (LSJ), ninth edition with Supplement, 1968.

Ancient Authors and Works

Aelian	
VH	*Varia Historia*
Aesch.	Aeschylus
Ag.	*Agamemnon*
Prom.	*Prometheus Bound*
Aristoph.	Aristophanes
Arist.	Aristotle
Met.	*Metaphysics*
NE	*Nicomachean Ethics*
Poet.	*Poetics*
Pol.	*Politics*
Rhet.	*The Art of Rhetoric*
[Arist.] *Ath. Pol.*	ps.-Aristotle, *Athenaiōn Politeia*
Call.	Callimachus
Clem. *Strom.*	Clement of Alexandria, *Stromateis*
Dem.	Demosthenes
D.L.	Diogenes Laertius
D.S.	Diodorus Siculus
Eur.	Euripides
Andr.	*Andromache*
Heracl.	*Heracleidae*
IA	*Iphigeneia in Aulis*
IT	*Iphigeneia in Tauris*
Or.	*Orestes*
Suppl.	*Suppliants*
Hdt./Hdt	Herodotus
Hes.	Hesiod

Th.	*Theogony*
WD	*Works & Days*
Homer	
Il.	*Iliad*
Ody.	*Odyssey*
Iambl. *VP*	Iamblichus, *On the Pythagorean Way of Life*
Isoc.	Isocrates
Paus.	Pausanias
Pindar	
I.	*Isthmian*
N.	*Nemean*
O.	*Olympian*
P.	*Pythian*
Phil.	Philostratus
Apoll.	*Life of Apollonius of Tyana*
VS	*Lives of the Sophists*
Photius *Bibl.*	Photius *Bibliotheca*
Plato	
Alc. I	*Alcibiades* I
Apol.	*Apology*
Euthyd.	*Euthydemus*
Gorg.	*Gorgias*
Hipparch.	*Hipparchus*
Hipp. Mai.	*Hippas Major*
Hipp. Min.	*Hippias Minor*
Phd.	*Phaedo*
Phdr.	*Phaedrus*
Prot.	*Protagoras*
Rep.	*Republic*
Soph.	*Sophist*
Sym.	*Symposium*
Tht.	*Theaetetus*
Plut.	Plutarch
Alex.	*Life of Alexander*
Banq.	*Banquet of the Seven Sages*
Dem.	*Life of Demosthenes*
Div.Veng.	*On the Delays of the Divine Vengeance*
Lyc.	*Life of Lycurgus*
Mal.Hdt.	*On the Malice of Herodotus*
Mor.	*Moralia*
Sol.	*Life of Solon*
Them.	*Life of Themistocles*
Quint.	Quintilian, *Institutio Oratoria*

Schol. *ad*	Scholiast to ...
Soph.	Sophocles
Ant.	*Antigone*
Them. *Or.*	Themistius, *Orations*
Theophr.	Theophrastus
Char.	*Characters*
Thgn.	Theognis
Thuc.	Thucydides
Tzetzes *Chil.*	John Tzetzes, *Chiliades*
Xen.	Xenophon
Cyr.	*Cyropaedia*
HG	*History of Greece*
Mem.	*Memorabilia*
Sym.	*Symposium*

Editions, Reference Works, and Journals

Add.²	T. H. Carpenter, T. Mannack, and M. Mendonça, eds. 1989. *Beazley Addenda*. 2nd ed. Oxford.
Adler	A. Adler, ed. 1928–38. *Suidae Lexicon*. 5 vols. Leipzig.
AJP	*American Journal of Philology*
ARV²	J. D. Beazley. 1963. *Attic Red-figure Vase-painters*. 2nd ed. Oxford.
BCH	*Bulletin de Correspondance Hellénique*
CA	*Classical Antiquity*
CID	*Corpus des inscriptions de Delphes*
CJ	*Classical Journal*
CP	*Classical Philology*
CQ	*Classical Quarterly*
CR	*Classical Review*
DK	H. Diels and W. Kranz, eds. 1966–67. *Die Fragmente der Vorsokratiker*. 12th ed. Berlin.
FGrH	F. Jacoby, ed. 1954–69. *Die Fragmente der griechischen Historiker*. Leiden.
Gigon	Olof Gigon, ed. 1987. *Aristotelis Opera*. Vol. 3, *Librorum deperditorum fragmenta*. Berlin.
GRBS	*Greek, Roman, and Byzantine Studies*
HSCP	*Harvard Studies in Classical Philology*
HTR	*Harvard Theological Review*
JHS	*Journal of Hellenic Studies*
KA	R. Kassel and C. Austin, eds. 1983–. *Poetae Comici Graeci*. Berlin.

Kock	T. Kock, ed. 1880–88. *Comicorum Atticorum Fragmenta*. 3 vols. Leipzig.
Latte	Kurt Latte, ed. 1953–56. *Hesychii Alexandrini Lexicon*. 2 vols: A-O. Copenhagen.
Leutsch-Schneidewin	E. L. Leutsch and F. G. Schneidewin. 1958. *Corpus Paroemiographorum Graecorum*. Hildesheim.
LSJ	H. G. Liddell, R. Scott, and H. S. Jones. 1968. *A Greek-English Lexicon*. 9th ed., with Supplement. Oxford.
MH	*Museum Helveticum*
MW	R. Merkelbach and M. L. West. 1967. *Fragmenta Hesiodea*. Oxford.
N²	A. Nauck, ed. 1964. *Tragicorum Graecorum Fragmenta*. 2nd ed. Hildesheim.
*Para.*²	J. D. Beazley. 1971. *Paralipomena: Additions to Attic Black-Figure Vase-Painters and to Attic Red-Figure Vase-Painters*. 2nd. ed. Oxford.
P.Berol.	Berlin Papyri, a series published under different editors
PCPS	*Proceedings of the Cambridge Philological Society*
Perry *Test.*	B. E. Perry, ed. 1952. *Aesopica: A Series of Texts Relating to Aesop or Ascribed to Him or Closely Connected to the Literary Tradition that Bears his Name*. Vol. 1. Urbana, Ill., *Testimonium*.
Pfeiffer	Rudolf Pfeiffer, ed. 1949–53. *Callimachus*. 2 vols. Oxford.
PMG	D. L. Page, ed. 1962. *Poetae Melici Graeci*. Oxford.
P.Oxy.	*The Oxyrhynchus Papyri*, a series published under different editors
P.Ross.Georg.	G.Zereteli, O. Krüger, and P. Jernstedt, eds. 1925–35. *Papyri russischer und georgischer Sammlungen*. Tiflis.
PSI	*Papiri greci e latini* (Pubblicazioni della Società italiana per la recerca dei papiri greci e latini in Egitto)
QS	*Quaderni di Storia*
QUCC	*Quaderni Urbinati di Cultura classica*
Radt	S. Radt, ed. 1977. *Tragicorum Graecorum Fragmenta*. Vol. 4, Sophocles. Göttingen. OR S. Radt, ed. 1985. *Tragicorum Graecorum Fragmenta*. Vol. 3, Aeschylus. Göttingen.
RE	G. Wissowa, ed. 1894–1980. *Paulys Realencyclopädie der classischen Altertumswissenschaft*. Munich.

REG	*Revue des Études Grecques*
RhM	*Rheinisches Museum*
Rose	V. Rose, ed. 1966. *Aristotelis qui ferebantur librorum fragmenta.* Stuttgart.
*SIG*³	W. Dittenberger, ed. 1982. *Sylloge Inscriptionum Graecarum.* 3rd ed. Hildesheim/Zurich/New York.
SM	B. Snell and H. Maehler, eds. 1970. *Bacchylidis carmina cum fragmentis.* 10th ed. Leipzig. OR B. Snell and H. Maehler, eds. 1975. *Pindarus. Pars II. Fragmenta. Indices.* 4th ed. Leipzig.
Spengel	L. Spengel, ed. 1853–56. *Rhetores Graeci.* 3 vols. Leipzig.
TAPA	*Transactions of the American Philological Association*
W	M. L. West, ed. 1989–92. *Iambi et Elegi Graeci.* 2 vols. 2nd ed. Oxford.
Wachsmuth-Hense	Kurt/Curtius Wachsmuth and Otto Hense, eds. 1884–1912. *Ioannis Stobaei Anthologium.* Berlin.
WJA	*Würzburger Jahrbücher für die Altertumswissenschaft*
ZPE	*Zeitschrift für Papyrologie und Epigraphik*

AESOPIC CONVERSATIONS

INTRODUCTION

LET ME BEGIN WITH A FABLE about fable. In his second/third-century CE biography of the sage Apollonius of Tyana, Philostratus stages a miniature philosophical debate about the relative merits of mythological poetry and Aesopic fable. Philostratus's protagonist has just expounded his reasons for preferring humble Aesopic beast fable to the grandiloquent mythic lies of the poets, and then adds a fable by way of coda:[1]

> My own mother, Menippus, taught me a tale about Aesop's wisdom, when I was very young. Aesop, so she said, was once a shepherd, and was tending his flock near a sanctuary of Hermes, and being a passionate lover of wisdom, he prayed the god to be given it. Many others visited Hermes with the same request, and dedicated gold, silver, an ivory herald's baton, or something equally dazzling. Aesop, however, was not in a position to possess anything like that, and was thrifty with what he did have. So he used to pour out for the god as much milk as a sheep yields at a milking, and to bring to the altar a honeycomb large enough to fit his hand, and he would think himself to be regaling the god with myrtle when he offered just a few roses or violets. 'Why should I weave crowns, Hermes,' he used to say, 'and neglect my sheep?'
>
> But when the worshipers came on a day appointed for the distribution of wisdom, Hermes as a lover of wisdom and of profit said 'You may have philosophy' to the one whose offering was no doubt the largest. 'You may join the ranks of the orators,' he said to the one next in generosity, 'while *your* place is astronomy, *yours* is music, *yours* is epic poetry, *yours* is iambic poetry.' But despite all his great shrewdness he used up all the branches of wisdom without noticing, and forgot Aesop by mistake. But then he recalled the Seasons (*Hōrai*) who had raised him on the peaks of Olympus, and how, once when he was in his cradle, they had told him about a cow, and how this cow had conversed with a human about itself and the world. In this way they had set him to lusting after Apollo's cows. Accordingly he gave storytelling to Aesop, the last thing left in the house of wisdom, saying 'You may have what I learned first.' (Phil. *Apoll.* 5.15; trans. Jones 2005; translation slightly modified)

I begin with this late text because, in its rich, overdetermined alignment of different hierarchical systems, it adumbrates a whole set of themes connected with Aesop, Aesopic fable, and ancient Aesopica with which I will concern myself here. Aesop's biography and his fables are squarely located within a competition or hierarchical system of wisdom (*sophia*), wherein Aesop represents the lowly

---

[1] This story of the forgetful Hermes seems deliberately to echo Protagoras's fable of Prometheus, Epimetheus, and Hermes dividing up the gifts to animals and men in Plato's *Protagoras*. For discussion of Protagoras's fable, see chapters 7 and 8 below.

and common versus the wealth of ranked valuables (gold, silver, ivory); animals versus human wisdom; tales told by females versus authoritative male speech genres; and traditions that belong to childhood (both Apollonius's and Hermes') versus grown-up poetry and philosophy. Apollonius's fable also implies the opposition of Apollo and Hermes, gift and theft, and problematic sacrifice in its final coy suggestion that it was a beast fable that "set [the baby Hermes] to lusting after Apollo's cows."[2] Finally, although Apollonius paradoxically valorizes fable, his tale constitutes a clear hierarchy of literary genres as subspecies of *sophia*: in ranked order (aligned with the value of precious gifts offered) philosophy, oratory, heroic poetry, iambic, and (below them all) beast fable.

And by virtue of its multiple, overdetermined ranked systems, Apollonius's aetiological fable also makes clear that this hierarchy of literary genre and decorum is inseparable from (at least a notional) sociopolitical hierarchy. Aesopic fables are humble in content and style, just as Aesop himself is poor, lowly, and marginal. My concern throughout this book will be precisely that linked literary and sociopolitical hierarchy for what it can reveal to us about the interaction of popular and high cultural forms in Greek antiquity, and ultimately about the complex and problematic origins of ancient Greek prose writing.

I. An Elusive Quarry: In Search of Ancient Greek Popular Culture

With that preamble, I would like to sketch out the stakes, goals, and methods of my argument in a way that is accessible to a nonspecialist audience.[3] To that end, I start with a broad and concise summary, while deferring to section II below the complicated philological detail and survey of previous scholarship that justify and ground my procedures. These latter elements are absolutely essential as a road map for classicist readers, since the material related to Aesop (unusually within the field of classics) is not already familiar to most professionals. A colleague in English once observed to me that his experience at classics lectures always reminded him of the joke about the joke-writers convention. That is, since classicists by and large take for granted a common canon with which we are all familiar (we've all read the *Aeneid*), we conduct much more of our discussion in a kind of shared code, at once more elliptical and more intimate. In the case of the Aesop materials, I confront the situation of an ancient tradition whose parameters and transmission are fiendishly compli-

---

[2] This seems to be a reference to the tradition preserved in the *Homeric Hymn to Hermes*, that the newborn Hermes stole cattle belonging to his brother Apollo and used them to perform what is usually taken to be an unconventional sacrifice (see *Homeric Hymn to Hermes* 94–175).

[3] I borrow the phrase "An Elusive Quarry" applied to the popular culture of an earlier historical period from Burke 1978.65.

cated and difficult, and simultaneously largely unfamiliar to most professional classicists. So it's not just that the joke has to be told in full, but that the whole backstory and what makes it funny has to be laid out first. (Needless to say, this ponderous amount of necessary detail is very likely to kill the humor.) At the same time (as I am painfully aware) this kind of technical discussion can be particularly bewildering and off-putting to nonspecialist readers who might otherwise be interested in an argument about the figure of Aesop, the conversation of high and low traditions, and the invention of mimetic or narrative prose in Greek antiquity. Such readers are encouraged to skip directly from section I to section III of this introduction. For classicist readers, this will necessarily entail some repetition between sections I and II, as the same points of argument recur with the deepening or ballast of ancient references and modern philological and scholarly argument.

I started out looking for ancient Greek popular culture, or at least for difference and diversity within the tradition. It is a sad fact of the study of antiquity that we have preserved less than 5 percent of the literary production of any period—and that entirely the work of an elite of birth, wealth, and education. And while we may catch rare glimpses of the conditions of life for the nonelite through the finds of archaeology, nonliterary texts like papyrus documents, lead curse tablets, and funerary inscriptions, our reconstructions of antiquity are still overwhelmingly based on the literary self-representations of the elite. How to escape the apparent tyranny of this single hegemonic view? How to get access to a fuller range of voices or positions from the ancient past? A separate but related impetus for this project was my desire to extend downward to prose and to the beginnings of Greek prose writing the sociopolitical analysis of the ancient literary hierarchy of genre and decorum to which I had already devoted many years of my research life.[4] Thus this project was conceived and animated by a dual interest in issues of sociological context and of literary form—indeed, by a conviction of their necessary interimplication in the ancient world.

This cluster of interests led me originally to Aesop and to fable. For from his first appearances in Greek literature and art of the fifth century BCE, Aesop is marked as low—a slave, non-Greek, hideously ugly, and already in trouble (unjustly killed by the angry Delphians).[5] Likewise fable as a form is also markedly low in its pattern of occurrence within the hierarchical system of genre and decorum of archaic Greek poetry. Thus beast fable never occurs in the heroic epic of Homer, but does figure in the middling, didactic epic of Hesiod. And fable proliferates particularly in archaic iambic, the genre that ranks at the bottom of the hierarchy of poetic forms in style, content, and tone, while it is much more sparingly used or only alluded to in the higher poetic forms of elegy and

---

[4] See (e.g.) Kurke 1991, 1992, 1994, 1999, 2000.
[5] Cf. Hdt. 2.134–35, Aristoph. *Wasps* 1446–48, and tondo of cup in the Vatican Museum (on which, see Lissarrague 2000 and discussion in chapter 5, section II below).

choral lyric (and entirely absent from monodic lyric).[6] Throughout the classical and Hellenistic periods and later within the Greek tradition, this cordoning-off of Aesop and fable continues: both are represented as sociologically low, low-class, and base, and therefore properly distinct from the genres of high Greek poetry and prose, once it develops.[7] Thus the figure of Aesop and the form of fable are at least represented by the Greeks themselves as "popular," low, and abject, and so potentially a good starting point for my inquiry.

The figure of Aesop led me in turn to the anonymous tradition of the *Life of Aesop*, preserved in several different manuscript versions and fragments of papyri ranging from (perhaps?) the first to the thirteenth century of our era, but based on much older oral lore that circulated in the Greek world.[8] Among the versions of the *Life* is the remarkable text of "*Vita* G" (as it was called by one of its modern discoverers, Ben Edwin Perry). In 1929, Elinor Husselman and Ben Edwin Perry discovered among the manuscripts of the Pierpont Morgan Library a unique exemplar of the prose *Life of Aesop*. On careful examination, they identified the codex as a tenth- or eleventh-century manuscript that was known once to have existed in the Basilian monastery of Grottaferrata ("known to have existed" because it had been described by a scholar in a letter of 1789, but had then disappeared from the monastery's holdings during the Napoleonic occupation).[9] After this exciting philological detective story of a manuscript lost and (after 150 years) found, Ben Edwin Perry made available this unique longer, fuller exemplar of the *Life* (which he called "G" after its original monastery home) for the first time in his monumental *Aesopica* in 1952. *Vita* G is a fascinating document, which is likely to represent an older, fuller *Life of Aesop* than any other manuscript version (its composition tentatively dated by Perry to the first century CE).

Let me pause at this point to summarize briefly the late and little-known *Life of Aesop*, since some knowledge of its contents is essential for my argument. The fullest preserved version of the *Life of Aesop* (Perry's *Vita* G) begins in medias res, with a detailed description of the protagonist as hideously ugly, a slave, and—most significantly—mute. After the slave Aesop, toiling in the countryside, assists a lost priestess of Isis, he is rewarded by Isis and the Muses with the restoration of his voice and skill "in the invention, weaving, and making of

---

[6] On Homer/Hesiod: Crusius 1920, Lasserre 1984; for Hesiod's didactic as accommodating a much wider range of material, see Martin 1992. On the stylistic and generic hierarchy of iambic, elegy, and melic, see West 1974; Bowie 1986; Kurke 1991, 1992, 1999, 2000; on the distribution of fable within these forms, Nøjgaard 1964.446–49, Lasserre 1984, Rothwell 1995.

[7] Cf. Rothwell 1995, building on Crusius 1920, Meuli 1975b. I will elaborate on this system of genre and decorum and the place of fable within it in chapters 3, 6, 9, and 10 below.

[8] I defer to section II below a full discussion of the different manuscripts and papyrus versions and their relations to one another.

[9] For the narrative of this (re)discovery of what is now Morgan *Codex* 397, see Perry 1952. xiv–xvi.

Greek fables" (ch. 7). He is thereupon sold to a slave-trader, who eventually transports him to Samos, where he is purchased by the pompous philosopher Xanthus (chs. 22–27). The bulk of the *Life*—the Samian portion (chs. 21–100)— then details Aesop's comic, picaresque, and occasionally obscene adventures, mainly showing up the stupidity and incompetence of his philosopher master and the malice and lust of the master's wife. The long Samian portion of the text culminates in a sequence in which Aesop secures his freedom as the precondition for interpreting an ominous bird omen before the entire Samian people. Aesop interprets the omen as portending an imminent threat of conquest by a king or potentate and—lo and behold—his sign reading is immediately confirmed by the arrival of ambassadors from Croesus, king of Lydia, demanding that the Samians become his tribute-paying subjects. Aesop, just freed, goes willingly as an emissary/hostage to the court of Croesus; wins the king over with his apposite use of fables and his skillful rhetoric; and thereby saves Samos from Croesus's domination. The grateful Samians dedicate a monument to Aesop, and Aesop departs to travel the world. Eventually, he arrives in Babylon, where he becomes adviser and vizier to Lycurgus, the king of Babylon, and assists him in a high-stakes contest of wisdom with Nectanebo, pharaoh of Egypt. Finally, after defeating Nectanebo, Aesop wishes again to travel the world, giving displays of his wisdom. This he does until he ends up in Delphi, where he abuses the Delphians for their worthlessness and servile origins. In response, the Delphians plant a golden bowl in Aesop's luggage as he's leaving town, arrest him, and condemn him to death. Eventually, Aesop, unable to persuade the Delphians of his innocence, curses them and hurls himself off a cliff. As a result of their impious treatment of Aesop, the Delphians are then visited with plague, as well as punishment by a military coalition of "Greece, Babylon, and the Samians," mobilized to avenge "the doom of Aesop" (chs. 124–142). There *Vita* G ends, although other traditions tell us that the Delphians "dedicate a temple and stele to Aesop" (*Vita* W) or "build an altar where he fell and offer sacrifices to him as a hero" (*P.Oxy.* 1800).

This relatively new, old version of the *Life of Aesop* is a text that is very difficult to pin down, since everything about it is a mystery—author, date, place of composition, intention, audience. Within the discipline of classical scholarship, this text (and the broader tradition it represents) were initially diseased with all this uncertainty, and so still kept in quarantine—either they were not read at all, or, if read, rarely allowed to interact with canonical texts. Even today, the *Life of Aesop* almost never figures in undergraduate or graduate classics curricula in the United States, and even professional classicists rarely read it (although, happily, this is beginning to change).[10] When they are read, the *Life* and the fables are still often set apart in scholarship and treated as a world unto

---

[10] For a selective account of scholarship on the *Life of Aesop* tradition and the text of *Vita* G, see section II below.

themselves.[11] But I would contend that precisely because of its almost unique and mysterious status, the weird, marginal text (and tradition) of the *Life of Aesop* urgently needs to be read with and against other ancient texts and cultural products of all kinds. For contestations of meaning and cultural resonances emerge from the reading together or juxtaposition that cannot emerge from reading the individual texts or artifacts separately. The project of this book is such a reading together, in which I will be concerned with all the various traditions of Aesopica, but with the *Life of Aesop* as the core or centerpiece of analysis.

But I must acknowledge at the outset that the text of *Vita* G is itself a mystery or a paradox that presents a problem for any simplistic reading as popular literature. Insofar as it offers us a protopicaresque narrative of the comic adventures of an ugly, low-class, non-Greek "hero" in an apparently colloquial and limited style of *koinē* Greek, it has all the hallmarks of what we would identify as "popular literature."[12] And yet the very fact that it is committed to writing at any point in the ancient world precludes its being genuinely "popular" or "nonelite," given the extreme limitations on literacy and the expense of writing materials and book production throughout the ancient world.[13] Further, the situation with *Vita* G is even more extreme than with other versions of the *Life* that survive from antiquity. For *Vita* G represents a version of the text that is by and large lower and more colloquial in style than other recensions, but also (not infrequently) higher, incorporating more poetic words, literary allusions to authors like Homer and Menander, and artful descriptions or *ekphraseis*.[14] All these factors make it impossible to postulate an author who is not a member of an elite of wealth and education.

And yet two factors encourage an approach to the texts of the *Life of Aesop* (*Vita* G and others) as late fixations or instantiations that may include or embed long-lived popular oral traditions. First, there is the fact that our earliest extant references to Aesop in fifth-century BCE literary texts imply a familiar narrative of the Life of Aesop already in circulation that conforms in certain lineaments *and* details to the much later written versions. Thus Herodotus (2.134)

---

[11] Thus for most of the twentieth century, the *Life* and fables of Aesop have suffered the same kind of segregation and marginalization within the field of classics that duBois 2003.3–31 describes for the topic of ancient slavery and specialized studies thereon by those she characterizes as "slaveologists." Nor is this parallel accidental, since Aesop and fable share the same low, degraded status as slavery and (I would suggest) the same simultaneous ubiquity and invisibility that duBois describes for ancient slaves.

[12] For *Vita* G's initial reception in the scholarship as a *Volksbuch* or "popular literature," see section II below. For the arguments in this paragraph and accompanying bibliography, I am indebted to the excellent discussion of Avlamis 2010a.

[13] See Harris 1989, Bowie 1994, Stephens 1994.

[14] For low, colloquial stylistic elements in *Vita* G, see Perry 1936.16, 22–24; Tallmadge 1938; Birch 1955; Hostetter 1955; Shipp 1983; Haslam 1992; for high elements, see Perry 1936.13–14, Mignogna 1992, Hunter 2007; for both, see the excellent concise summary in Karla 2001.53–57.

already knows of Aesop as the slave of a Samian master, victimized and impiously executed by the Delphians. And Aristophanes (*Wasps* 1446–48) shows that certain fables already had a fixed place in the tradition of the *Life*, since he cites the fable of the "eagle and the dung beetle" in the context of Aesop's fatal adventures at Delphi (where it still appears in the much later texts of the *Life*, dated at the earliest to the first or second century CE).[15] Second, all the manuscript *Lives* and papyri versions together read like nothing so much as various transcriptions of popular jokes or anecdotes: the versions differ substantially in diction and in the expansion and contraction of speeches, use of direct versus indirect speech, description, and other circumstantial detail. Whole episodes cycle in and out of the texts, and sometimes occupy different positions within the structure of the work. This striking feature suggests that the traditions about Aesop were perceived by their ancient readers/authors (who were in this case one and the same) to have a different status from high, canonical literary texts, which had to be treated with greater care and respect and transmitted in pristine form. It would be a mistake to correlate this different status of text with a distinct sociological class/status of readers/authors, and yet it does justify a different kind of reading of this tradition from the approach to reading a single known author who composes a closed written work at a precise historical moment.[16]

The first of these features suggests a long-lived and robust oral tradition (or better, traditions) about Aesop; the second implies that even once some version of these traditions was committed to writing, the ongoing work of fashioning and refashioning tales about Aesop continued, probably through a lively interaction between oral traditions and highly permeable written versions. And here we should probably posit for the ancient world conditions akin to those described by Peter Burke in his account of popular culture in early modern Europe (1500–1800), where "popular culture" is itself a misnomer. Adapting the anthropologist Robert Redfield's model of "great and little traditions," Burke suggests that in the early modern period, the "little tradition" was simply the common culture in which all—elite and nonelite alike—participated, while "elite culture" or the "great tradition" was an exclusive minority culture of the privileged, the literate, and the educated:

> There were two cultural traditions in early modern Europe, but they did not correspond symmetrically to the two main social groups, the elite and the common people.

---

[15] For the fixation of the tradition of the *Life* with embedded fables already by the fifth century, see Wiechers 1961.13, Nagy 1979.282–83; this is true whether or not we accept the idea of a written *Life of Aesop* already in the fifth century. In favor of a written *Life*: Perry 1936.24n. 35, 25n. 1; West 1984.122–24; against: La Penna 1962.282–84, Jedrkiewicz 1989.67n. 108. See detailed discussion below, section II.

[16] For the open, unstable status of the tradition, cf. Haslam 1980.54, 1986.152; Winkler 1985.279; Hansen 1998.xxi–xxii. For the fallacy of correlating a low-style text and an open tradition with a specific class or status of author/readers, cf. Jedrkiewicz 1989.171–82, 208–12; Hopkins 1993.11–12n. 15; Avlamis 2006, 2010a, 2010b.

The elite participated in the little tradition, but the common people did not participate in the great tradition. This asymmetry came about because the two traditions were transmitted in different ways. The great tradition was transmitted formally at grammar schools and at universities. It was a closed tradition in the sense that people who had not attended these institutions, which were not open to all, were excluded. In a quite literal sense, they did not speak the language. The little tradition, on the other hand, was transmitted informally. It was open to all, like the church, the tavern, and the market-place, where so many performances occurred. Thus the crucial cultural difference in early modern Europe . . . was that between the majority, for whom popular culture was the only culture, and the minority, who had access to the great tradition but participated in the little tradition as a second culture.[17]

Under analogous circumstances in the ancient world, the individual authors/readers/redactors of the written *Lives* (themselves necessarily "elite") could serve as mediators or middlemen for elements of a broader "popular culture," even while (as we must always bear in mind) they had their own specific local interests and purposes in the incorporation of free-floating, ambient oral material.[18]

The result of all this: we must conceptualize a text like the *Life of Aesop*, as one late moment—or several—of textual fixation within an ongoing oral tradition spanning centuries of time and a wide geographic area.[19] This process eventually generated a strange kind of text—a narrative whose written surface is stratified, fissured, and uneven. This is a text that does not represent a single "symbolic act" by a single (postulated) agent or author, but the accretion of multiple acts and agents, in a written work that itself already contains a centuries-long conversation of "great" and "little" traditions.[20]

---

[17] Burke 1978.28, modifying Redfield 1956.67–104.

[18] As Burke 1978.28 characterizes these elite participants in the common culture, "They were amphibious, bi-cultural, and also bilingual. Where the majority of people spoke their regional dialect and nothing else, the elite spoke or wrote Latin or a literary form of the vernacular, while remaining able to speak in dialect as a second or third language. For the elite, but for them only, the two traditions had two different psychological functions; the great tradition was serious, the little tradition was play." It is an interesting question whether there was a development within the ancient world akin to that which Burke charts for the end of the early modern period in Europe, as elites pulled away from the common culture and then nostalgically invented "the *Volk*" and "popular culture" as a separate romanticized sphere (see Burke 1978.3–22, 244–86). While I would contend that elites throughout the ancient world maintained their connections to the common informal culture of the tavern and the marketplace, there were certain times and places like (e.g.) Hellenistic Alexandria where the educated elite seems to have taken a special interest in documenting and imitating the "little tradition" in artful written texts (e.g., Theocritus 15, Herondas, Machon). Avlamis 2010a, 2010b suggests a similar phenomenon for Greek elites within the high Roman empire.

[19] Cf. Hopkins 1993.3, 11 with n. 14.

[20] I draw from Jameson 1981 the concept of narrative as a socially consequential "symbolic act" within the ongoing contest of culture; and from Nehamas 1981, 1987 the fundamental insight that

Robert Darnton offers an early modern parallel that may help us imagine this process. Darnton describes the complex interaction of written and oral versions of what were originally peasant folktales in prerevolutionary France that eventually got set down in writing as fairy tales or tales of "Mother Goose." Thus Charles Perrault, a powerful figure at the court of Louis XIV, published the first printed edition of his *Contes de ma mère l'oye* in 1697, tales probably originally derived from his son's nurse, but touched up for his audience of "salon sophisticates."[21] But even after Perrault's publication of these tales, traditional oral versions continued to circulate, told by peasants among themselves and carried by servants and wet nurses as mediators from the "little tradition" of the village to the kitchens and nurseries of the houses of the elite, to be imbibed by them "with their milk." In addition, the popular *Bibliothèque bleue*, a series of primitive and inexpensive paperbacks, recirculated a simplified form of Perrault's written version, which itself might in turn be read aloud at peasant gatherings. Darnton's conclusion:

> It would be a mistake to identify [Perrault's] meager Mother Goose with the vast folklore of early modern France. But a comparison of the two points up the inadequacy of envisaging cultural change in linear fashion, as the downward seepage of great ideas. Cultural currents intermingled, moving up as well as down, while passing through different media and connecting groups as far apart as peasants and salon sophisticates.[22]

We cannot simply transpose this model to the ancient world, since we have no print culture and no *Bibliothèque bleue*; nonetheless one could posit similar ongoing interactions between written versions of the *Life of Aesop* as transcriptions and transformations of (some) popular tales and oral versions. Thus we might imagine stories about Aesop continuing to circulate orally as "old wives' tales" or popular tales told at festivals, while the written text in turn might even be read aloud in other public contexts where different social strata mixed (like Burke's "tavern" or "marketplace").[23]

Of course, postmodernist literary theory would assert that all texts are seamed and riven with other voices, resistances, and inconsistencies, and that the notion of a pure, unproblematized "hegemonic voice" is itself a fantasy. And while I subscribe to that position, such critical orthodoxy should not blind us to the very real differences among different kinds of texts based on the materiality and ideology of their production, circulation, and reception. In their permeability

---

the "author" is always an agent and source of meaning postulated and back-formed from the interpretative processes of reading.

[21] Darnton 1984.11–13.

[22] Darnton 1984.62–63; quotations taken from p. 63. For discussion of the various middlemen or mediators between great and little traditions in early modern Europe, see also Burke 1978.65–77.

[23] Cf. Avlamis 2006, 2010a on ancient "barbershop reading."

and openness to this kind of ongoing conversation, the texts of the *Life of Aesop* are nearly unique among the material we have preserved from the ancient world.[24] Even if this is not about the status of author/audience, it is about the status of the text, which is perceived as open, fluid, anybody's property—authored by no one and so authored by each one who writes it down. Finally, I would link this openness and fluidity of the tradition to the *purpose* of the text, rather than to a particular socioeconomic status of author/audience.

For in another way, the *Life of Aesop* is entirely unique. As Keith Hopkins observes, it is the only extended "biography of a slave to survive from the ancient world," and as such is a mystery or paradox of another kind. We must assume that this comic or satirical text was read and enjoyed by slave owners in a slave society, who were solicited thereby to sympathize and identify with Aesop, the clever slave who consistently outwits and shows up his master until he ultimately wins his freedom.[25] How are we to make sense of this paradox? Or more simply, why Aesop? What is the motivation for and enduring appeal of these narratives about Aesop? We might attempt to answer these questions by comparison with the clever slaves of Roman comedy, repeatedly portrayed at the center of public, state-supported dramatic festivals in Republican Rome. Kathleen McCarthy has recently offered a brilliant account of the psychological appeal of a fantasized identification with the clever slave of comedy by an audience constituted largely of masters.[26] On McCarthy's reading, within the elaborate and complex hierarchies of Roman culture, almost every member of the audience is superior to some, but subordinate to others. And insofar as they are subordinate, audience members derive pleasure from the identification with the clever slave as comic hero and with the peculiar kind of fantasized freedom he enjoys because he does not acknowledge or acquiesce in the master's worldview and values. McCarthy also observes that the clever slave is most prominent in Roman comedy's "farcical mode," which, in contrast to its "naturalistic mode," engages in slapstick and play for its own sake, while its artificiality and world-turned-upside-down antics expose the arbitrariness of the existing order. The narrative of the *Life of Aesop* is certainly closer to the "farcical

---

[24] Cf. Hansen 1998.xxi–xxiii on "textual fluidity" as a "common trait of Greek popular literature." Other examples of this kind of text from antiquity: *The Alexander Romance* and fluid collections like *Philogelos* and the late fable collections attributed to Aesop. For discussions of the complex ms history and interrelations of the fable collections, see Perry 1936.71–230, Jedrkiewicz 1989.15–34, Adrados 1999.48–138, Holzberg 2002.84–104, and see section IIC below.

[25] Hopkins 1993 (quotation taken from p. 10). This is not to deny the possibility of different readers' complex, multiple, and shifting identifications—for which, see the excellent remarks of Hopkins 1993.10n. 13.

[26] McCarthy 2000. By this comparison of themes and ideology, I do not mean to imply a specific intertextual relationship between the *Life of Aesop* and Greek or Roman New Comedy. Holzberg 1992b argues for such a relationship, but his arguments often seem to me to attribute too narrowly to the influence of New Comedy what are in fact general characteristics of narrative in the *Life*. For connections between the *Life* and New Comedy, see also Jouanno 2005, 2006.38–43.

mode" in McCarthy's account, and we might posit the same pleasures and gratifications for an audience of slave owners who feel themselves oppressed or subordinated in other ways within the social hierarchy.[27]

Thus McCarthy's notion of the possibility of cross-status identification is important and useful for our reading of Aesop. But there is one notable difference from the pattern of New Comic plots that should impact our reading of the Aesop tradition's fantasized pleasures and gratifications. As McCarthy astutely notes, the clever slave at play in the farcical mode of Roman comedy never works in his own interest and never achieves freedom (indeed, he does not even seem to aspire to manumission). At the end of the play, the clever slave has perhaps won a day's pass from punishment, but nothing has changed and the status quo ante is reinstated.[28] In contrast, Aesop in the *Life of Aesop* works persistently and methodically to gain his freedom and ultimately succeeds, even against his master's intention, by complex public manipulation.[29] He then goes on to serve as valued adviser to peoples and potentates, before losing his life on an ill-fated trip to Delphi. I think it matters that Aesop's struggle for freedom is a mainspring of the plot, and that he dramatically ascends the social scale and wins fantastic honors in exotic locales, for this suggests a different structure of identificatory effects and ideological work the character serves.

We might say that Aesop, like folktale tricksters in many different cultures, enables the articulation in public of elements of what the political theorist James Scott calls the "hidden transcript," the counterideology and worldview developed by the oppressed when they are "offstage"—that is, free from the public world whose performances are largely scripted by the dominant. For the Aesop tradition exhibits simultaneously two characteristic forms of "political disguise" Scott identifies as enabling the speaking of opposition or resistance from the hidden transcript in the public world: anonymity of the messenger and indirection or obliquity of the message.[30] For the former: it is clear that many anecdotes about Aesop and fables circulated anonymously, and we might explain the anonymity of the written *Life* itself as a form of political disguise (rather than merely the accident of transmission). For the latter: the *Life of Aesop* itself articulates a theory of fable as an indirect or disguised message to the powerful, a theory we find paralleled in many other ancient characterizations of Aesopic discourse and known already, I will argue, to Herodotus in the fifth century BCE.[31] The combination of these two characteristic forms of "political disguise" endows the *Life* and other Aesop traditions with a trademark duality: simultaneously parodic and ambiguous, verbally aggressive and flattering to the powerful. But

---

[27] McCarthy 2000.3–31.
[28] See esp. McCarthy 2000.12–15, 212–13.
[29] For the detailed argument laying out this pattern, see chapter 4, section IV below.
[30] Scott 1990.136–66.
[31] For explicit articulation of the theory, see *Vitae* G + W, ch. 93, Phaedrus Bk 3.*Prol*. 33–37, Julian *Orations* 7.207. Full discussion (including Hdt) in chapters 3 and 11 below.

this also accounts for Aesop as a kind of culture hero of the oppressed, and the *Life* as a how-to handbook for the successful manipulation of superiors.

I am not thereby claiming that Aesop represents the veiled fantasies of actual slaves in the ancient world (like Brer Rabbit for slaves in the antebellum South)—although it is possible that the figure did serve this function in strands of the oral tradition largely unrecoverable to us. I would suggest rather that already by the fifth century BCE the figure of Aesop had floated free from any particular context and passed into the common discursive resources of the culture, available as a mask or alibi for critique, parody, or cunning resistance by any who felt themselves disempowered in the face of some kind of unjust or inequitable institutional authority. That is to say, starting in the fifth century and for centuries thereafter, "Aesop" was a readily available cipher or "ideologeme" for all kinds of parody or critique from below.[32] Thus already in the classical period, as I will argue in the first chapter, Aesop serves as a handy vehicle for a civic critique of Delphic control of oracular access and the extortionate sacrificial exactions that attended it, while in the first or second century CE, another shaping strand of the written *Life* seems to be parody of those at the apex of the educational rhetorical and philosophical hierarchy by their underlings within the system (what we might call "graduate-student literature").[33] It is my contention that many of these different appropriations have left their traces in the written *Lives* of Aesop, as the layered bricolage of multiple symbolic actions and agents within the dialectical formation of culture over centuries and a wide geographic area.

The serviceability of this figure for all kinds of resistances within the tradition generated in turn repeated attempts to disarm and domesticate "Aesop," especially within elite philosophical, rhetorical, and educational structures

---

[32] I borrow the concept of "ideologeme" from Jameson (1981.87): "The ideologeme is an amphibious formation, whose essential structural characteristic may be described as its possibility to manifest itself either as a pseudoidea—a conceptual or belief system, an abstract value, an opinion or prejudice—or as a protonarrative, a kind of ultimate class fantasy about the 'collective characters' which are the classes in opposition." In these terms, we might think of the figure of Aesop as itself an ideologeme—or perhaps, better, as a bundle of ideologemes, which can exist in narrative form or as explicit critique. Thus Aesop enables the narrativization of political critiques of local sacrificial practices; of mantic authority; of authority claimed through the wisdom tradition; as well as the narrativization of issues of slavery and freedom, at both the individual and collective levels.

[33] For a reading of *Vita* G along these lines, see section II below. We may find support for this model of the presumptive context of the writing of *Vita* G in the comparatively gentle, farcical humor of the Samian portion of the *Vita*, in contrast with the life-and-death struggles of Aesop at Delphi (in the Samian portion, Aesop occasionally torments his master, but nobody is ever in any real danger). We might read this contrast in relation to Scott's argument that an institutionalized system of violent domination and inequality tends to foster a commensurately violent fantasized response from the oppressed (Scott 1990.36–44, 108–35); the absence of such aggression from the Samian portion of the *Vita* perhaps confirms this reading of it as "student literature." To suggest a modern analogy: our graduate students might want to replace us, but they generally don't want to kill us—one hopes.

ranging from the fifth-century BCE Sophists to Plutarch and the late *Progymnasmata*.[34] We can detect the same pressure of domestication within some strands of the Aesop tradition itself, where (for example) different late, shortened versions of the *Life* mute Aesop's concerted campaign to win his freedom or entirely reconfigure him as the ideal loyal slave.[35] Indeed, we might see these same efforts at domestication informing modern moralizing readings of the narrative arc of the *Life* as a tragic plot wherein Aesop is punished for his hubris, or the justice of his death underwritten by the divine sanction of Apollo.[36]

These ongoing conversations in the Aesop tradition that have seamed and marked the texts of the *Lives* will be my topic. For the purpose of recovering such cultural dialogue, we must clearly acknowledge that by and large the object of reading and interpretation is not the *text* of the *Life of Aesop*, but the *traditions* that lie behind it—traditions variously instantiated in the manuscript versions, papyrus fragments, brief references in high literary texts, and other Aesopica.[37] This reading at one remove—for a penumbra of traditions through a patchwork of textual fragments—means that my interpretations will always be speculative and often sketchy or schematic. Still, it bears emphasizing that, insofar as I am reconstructing agents or sources from ideological positions or values deduced from our texts, I am engaging in precisely the same process that all historicizing readings do.[38]

Thus my topic is "Aesop" as a mobile, free-floating figure in ancient culture, the narrative of whose life, discourses, and death remained endlessly available and adaptable for all kinds of resistance, parody, and critique from below. Whether Aesop "really existed" as a non-Greek slave on sixth-century Samos or not, we will probably never know. Indeed, I am agnostic on this point, and I would contend that it is irrelevant for the purposes of my argument.[39] All we can

---

[34] For a general account of such a repeated process of domestication or recuperation, see Jameson 1981.85–87; for its specific application to Aesop, see Jedrkiewicz 1989.82, 157–82, 208–15; Patterson 1991.31–42; and see chapters 5 and 7 below.

[35] For the former, see *Vita* W, chs. 83–85, which attributes Aesop's preventing his master's suicide to his being *philodespotos* (thereby effacing his careful manipulation of Xanthus to win his freedom, on which see chapter 4, section IV below). For the latter, see Perry 1952.211, *Vitae Minores* 1 (the brief *Life* that serves as proem to the fable recension Ia). I am indebted to the discussion of Avlamis 2010a for this point about the latter *Life*—see his further discussion of its transformations of the legend and its presumptive milieu. And cf. Gasparov 1967, Jouanno 2006.50–52. (I am indebted to Boris Maslov for providing me with an English summary of Gasparov's Russian article.)

[36] For the former reading, see Jedrkiewicz 1989.94–107, 157–60, 182; Holzberg 1992b, 1993, 1996, 2002.78–84; for the latter reading, see Hopkins 1993.25–26. For extended arguments against such moralizing readings of the end of the *Life*, see chapters 1 and 4 below.

[37] In this sense, everything in Perry's *Aesopica* (Perry 1952) is relevant source material for this project; Perry includes the Greek and Latin *Lives* of Aesop, testimonia culled from literary texts, *sententiae*, proverbs, and the Greek and Latin fables.

[38] Cf. Hägg 1997.184.

[39] Debate on the real existence of Aesop still rages in the scholarship: see (e.g.) Perry 1962b, Luzzatto 1988, Jedrkiewicz 1989.41–48.

say is that by the mid-fifth century BCE, to judge from visual evidence as well as literary references, Aesop and many of the traditions about him were already familiar in Athens (and probably elsewhere in the Greek world as well).[40]

And I emphasize that my topic is Aesop also in order to clarify what my topic is *not*. For fable is not coextensive with Aesop, nor the figure of Aesop with fable. As for fable: as the ancients themselves recognized, fables existed in the Greek tradition long before the lifetime of Aesop, occasionally narrated in Hesiod's *Works & Days* and proliferating in archaic iambic, especially in the poetry of Archilochus. As M. L. West has observed, it is in fact only in the course of the fifth century that we can chart the gradual attachment of fables to Aesop.[41] Thus I will not be concerned with the prehistory of fable—whether fable migrated to Greece from the ancient Near East and/or India, and whether the Greeks themselves were aware of that genealogy—although at times later, individual intercultural exchanges of fable and narrative will impinge on my topic.[42] Nor will I be directly concerned with the early history of fable in Greek poetry, especially its proliferation in archaic iambic, although early instantiations of fable and allusions to fable in archaic Greek poetry will occasionally figure in my argument as significant comparanda.[43] But mainly I will be concerned with fables only insofar as they figure in the traditions of the *Life* or are otherwise associated with Aesop.

As for the second half of my formulation ("Aesop" is not coextensive with fable): careful consideration of the *Life of Aesop* and other Aesop traditions will suggest that fable is only a piece of a characteristically Aesopic discursive system or weaponry that is better understood through something like James Scott's notion of veiled or disguised forms of political critique. That is to say, Aesop in the tradition is identified with signature ways of speaking that include different strategic uses of fable but also extend beyond them. I am interested in describ-

---

[40] Scholars generally assume that traditions and stories about Aesop developed first in Ionia/East Greece (specifically Samos): thus Aly 1921.159–60; Zeitz 1936.239–42; Nøjgaard 1964.449–58; Momigliano 1971.35; West 1984.117–19, 123–24, 128; Jedrkiewicz 1989.42–47; Adrados 1999.271–74.

[41] For ancient acknowledgments of the chronological priority of Hesiod and Archilochus to Aesop, see Quint. 5.11.19, Theon II.73 Spengel (= Perry *Test.* 65). For the attachment of fables to Aesop as a fifth-century phenomenon, see West 1984; cf. Nøjgaard 1964.454–63, although Nøjgaard's theory of Ionian versus Athenian fable traditions seems somewhat too rigid and complicated.

[42] For discussion of Greek fables deriving from Near Eastern models and the degree of Greek consciousness thereof, see Nøjgaard 1964.431–41; West 1978.23–25; 1984.109–11, 1997.319–20, 502–5; Adrados 1999.287–366. I will consider the Ahiqar narrative embedded in the *Life of Aesop* in chapter 4 below; and the migration to Greece of an Indian fable ("The Dancing Peacock") in chapter 11 below.

[43] For narrative of and allusion to fable in early Greek poetry, see Lasserre 1984, van Dijk 1997.124–269; for particular focus on the uses of fable in early iambic, see also Steiner 2008. For discussion of certain fables and allusions to fable in the poetry of Solon, see chapter 3, section II below.

ing and catching the multifarious deployments of this broader Aesopic "voiceprint" in a range of ancient texts.

And this inquiry in turn will lead me in the second half of the book to an alternative or supplemental genealogy of the beginnings of mimetic narrative prose in the Greek tradition. This historical narrative is still generally framed in terms of the triumphal march "from *muthos* to *logos*," where written prose emerges together with the slow dawning of rationality from the fancies of the poets, assisted by the invention of writing that helps liberate the Greeks from the mnemonic constraints of rhythm and song. This is, of course, a very old-fashioned teleological narrative that takes prose for granted as the logical and inevitable end point of development (since that is what prose is for us)—a default transparent medium for the communication of rational thought and argument. And yet studies of the beginnings of prose in other eras and traditions have effectively questioned and estranged these assumptions, demonstrating that the emergence of prose is hardly inevitable or unproblematic.[44] Within the Greek tradition, I will argue for a significant Aesopic strand twisting through the beginnings of narrative or mimetic prose—both prose philosophy (the Sophists, Plato, Xenophon) and prose history (Herodotus). And, insofar as Aesop and fable are consistently marked throughout the ancient literary tradition as generically and sociologically low (as I noted above), this affiliation vexes the traditional triumphalist account of the beginnings of Greek prose, suggesting a more complicated story of genre trouble, potential status taint, and ruptures of decorum behind the birth of mimetic prose.

This reading of Aesopic elements lurking behind our earliest mimetic narrative prose in the Greek tradition starts from the fact that both Herodotus and Plato, our first extant authors of extended narrative prose in the historical and philosophical traditions, respectively, acknowledge Aesop as a precursor for their prose forms, even while both go to some trouble to disavow or distance themselves from the low fable-maker. Thus this second half of my argument will focus more narrowly on a single historical moment (ca. 450–350 BCE) when fables were getting attached to Aesop; Aesopic fable was strongly identified with prose (in Herodotus and Plato); and mimetic or narrative prose was first crystallizing as a written form. It is my claim that this is a significant conjuncture of elements that merits our close attention, and that should impinge on our narrative of the invention of Greek prose.

But before I can turn to an account of my methodology and the sequencing of the argument chapter by chapter, I must pause for some basic exposition and definitions of the Aesop tradition, ancient fables, and other Aesopica (the "road map" for classicists I promised at the outset). That will constitute the substance of the next section before I resume this introductory account of my argument in section III.

---

[44] See (e.g.) Godzich and Kittay 1987, Spiegel 1993.

II. Explaining the Joke: A Road Map for Classicists

At this point, I want to offer a more detailed account of the different traditions and instantiations of the *Life* and fables of Aesop we have preserved, their interrelations, the theoretical presuppositions of my readings, and the main scholarly approaches to the *Life* since the discovery and publication of *Vita* G in the mid-twentieth century.

IIA. Background on the Life of Aesop

As I've already mentioned, *Vita* G was first identified in 1929 as a unique exemplar of an older, fuller *Life of Aesop* than any then known. Two other traditions of the *Life* were already known at that point: one that in comparison to the newly found version reads like an epitome (although divergences between the two preclude taking it merely as an abridgment of the newly discovered version), first published in modern times by Anton Westermann in 1845. A second version, attributed in several medieval manuscripts to the Byzantine scholar Maximus Planudes (ca. 1255–1305 CE) as editor, was first printed by Bonus Accursianus in 1479. Whether or not it was actually composed by Planudes, this version is adapted fairly closely from one strand of the epitome version but written in a more elegant, classicizing Greek style. Ben Edwin Perry made available the complete text of *Vita* G in his *Aesopica* of 1952, together with the more substantial *Life* represented by the two other traditions, which he called *Vita* W (after Westermann, its first modern editor).[45] The third version, the Byzantine revision attributed to Planudes, is not included in Perry's *Aesopica*; the standard text of the Accursiana or Planudean *Life* remains that of Alfred Eberhard, published in 1872.[46]

Since Perry's time, further work on the manuscripts of what he called *Vita* W has revealed two separate recensions (with some contamination between them).

---

[45] For the relation of the older *Life of Aesop* (Perry's *Vita* G) to Westermann's text of the *Life* and the Accursiana or Planudean version, see Perry 1936.4–24, 217–28, 1952.1–2, 10–16; for useful summaries of the mss traditions, see Holzberg 2002.72–76 and the summary statement of Hansen 1998.106–7: "Two early recensions of the novel survive, called by scholars *Vita* G and *Vita* W. Although additions, deletions, and other modifications characterize both branches of the tradition, *Vita* G generally remains closer to the original. It is much the longer of the two (G runs to forty-three pages and W to twenty-seven pages in Perry's edition of the Greek text) and is written in a more popular language. The two recensions fortunately have a complementary relationship to some extent in that matter missing from one can sometimes be supplied from the other, but ultimately they are not reconcilable and, like different performances of a folktale or of an oral epic, must each be accepted as valid expressions of the story in their own right." All of these remain useful formulations, even though it is now generally recognized that what Perry called *Vita* W in fact represents two separate, slightly different Byzantine recensions; see discussion below.

[46] Eberhard 1872. Scholars still debate the Planudean authorship of this *Life* (Hausrath 1901, 1937 versus Perry 1936.217–28), but that is irrelevant for my argument.

Thus Manolis Papathomopoulos in his 1999 reedition of *Vita* W grouped the manuscripts as MRNLo and SBPTh, while Grammatiki Karla in 2001 refined that grouping as MORN and BPThSA, concluding that these represented two different early Byzantine recensions, the former somewhat longer and fuller than the latter.[47]

In addition, both before and after the discovery and publication of the manuscript text of *Vita* G, finds of papyri ranging in date from the late second to the seventh century CE have supplemented the manuscript tradition and confirmed the continuing circulation of the ancient *Life*.[48] In 1936, Perry meticulously reedited the four papyri then known (*P.Berol.* inv. 11628, *PSI* II 156, *P.Oxy.* XVIII 2083, *P.Ross.Georg.* I 18) and compared them to the texts of *Vita* G and *Vita* W; two more papyrus fragments derived from a single text (*P.Oxy.* 3331 and 3720) were published by Michael Haslam in 1980 and 1986, respectively.[49] Some of the papyri, when compared with the manuscript texts, are closer to G, others closer to W; still others (like *P.Oxy.* 3720) appear to offer a fuller version of which both G and W read like abridgments.[50] But even those papyri that pattern with one or the other manuscript tradition differ substantially in diction and in the expansion and contraction of speeches, description, and other circumstantial detail. The papyri thus confirm the fluidity and permeability of the tradition of the *Life*, wherein, within a fairly stable framework of narrative episodes, each copyist/redactor feels free to paraphrase and adapt his own version.

Traditional classical scholarship had neither the tools nor the inclination to engage very deeply with this kind of anonymous, morphing, fluid tradition.

---

[47] See Papathomopoulos 1999.31–35, Karla 2001.19–67, and, for the ms sigla, Perry 1952.29–32. In fact, Perry had already anticipated these findings, noting two subbranches within the mss of *Vita* W (see esp. Perry 1966.285–90).

[48] Scholars often point to the papyri as evidence of the enduring "popularity" of the *Life* (e.g., Haslam 1986.151, Hopkins 1993.11, Hägg 1997.178), but in fact this is somewhat misleading. Given that there are only six papyri fragments representing five separate texts currently known, the *Life of Aesop* is distinctly less "popular" than Homer, Demosthenes, Thucydides, Herodotus, and a whole host of other high literary Greek texts between the first and sixth centuries CE in Egypt; for discussion of the distribution and relative popularity of different texts and authors as represented by the papyri evidence (including the *Life of Aesop*), see Stephens 1994.

[49] For the papyri texts, see Perry 1936.37–70 with references to earlier editions; Haslam 1980, 1986. The various papyri are dated by their respective editors as follows: *P.Berol.*—late second or early third c. CE; *P.Oxy.* 3331 and 3720 (fragments from the same papyrus text, according to Haslam)—third c. CE; *PSI* 156—fourth c. CE; *P.Oxy.* 2083—late fourth or early fifth c. CE; *P.Ross. Georg.*—seventh c. CE.

[50] Thus, as Haslam 1986.152 notes, the text represented by *P.Oxy.* 3720 actually seems fuller than that of *Vita* G, although not padded with extraneous material. This may mean (as Holzberg 1992.38 contends) that this papyrus text is then closer to the "archetype" of the *Life* than *Vita* G; or perhaps it is better with this kind of tradition not to attempt to reconstruct a single "source" or "origin," but to treat each text as an equally legitimate, independent version, to be read on its own terms (thus Hansen 1998.106–7, quoted in n. 45 above).

Earlier generations of scholars had judged the version of the *Life* then known a shapeless, incoherent patchwork, of no literary merit, so it was little read.[51] Even with Perry's publication of the longer, fuller *Vita* G, almost everything remains uncertain about this text: date, authorship, even the Greek text itself at many points. For the first: different scholars have suggested dates ranging from the first century BCE to the second century CE for the text of *Vita* G (in fact, the only thing that provides a secure terminus ante quem is the oldest of the papyri, *P.Berol.* inv. 11628, dating to the late second or early third century CE).[52] The text is, of course, anonymous, but Perry himself had suggested, based on the prominence of Egyptian elements and Latin loanwords, that *Vita* G was written (or rewritten) in Roman Egypt, perhaps by an Egyptian, nonnative speaker of Greek.[53] Alternatively, Antonio La Penna contended that the text as we have it was composed in second-century CE Syria.[54] More recently, Francisco Rodríguez Adrados and Thomas Hägg have argued that the substance of *Vita* G, or at least significant portions thereof, took shape in the Hellenistic period.[55] As for the Greek text itself, it is massively corrupt, apparently written originally in late bad *koinē* and then subject to all the ravages of survival in a single manuscript.[56] As edited by Perry, *Vita* G has several episodes missing, several doublets and intrusive elements, with textual emendations that in Perry's continuous numeration run to 679 over forty-three large pages. In the 1990s, Manolis Papathomopoulos undertook the reediting of *Vita* G and *Vita* W, and in 1997, Franco Ferrari produced a new edition of *Vita* G with facing

---

[51] For a sampling of the extremely negative assessments of earlier scholars, see Holzberg 2002.76–77.

[52] Perry 1936.24–26 offers the range 100 BCE to 200 CE; Perry 1952.5 inclines more to the first century CE because of the large number of Latin loanwords in *Vita* G. But as Hopkins 1993.11n. 14 and Hägg 1997.180–81 note, all these dates are guesses; only the earliest papyrus provides a firm terminus ante quem for the text fixation of the *Life*.

[53] Perry 1952.2–5; Perry's conjecture as to the text's Egyptian provenance is endorsed by Haslam 1986.150, Dillery 1999. Note also the important observation of Hopkins 1993.15n. 22, 25 that the use of the term *stratēgos* for a local district magistrate is confined to "Egypt under Greek and Roman rule"; the term occurs in both G and W, ch. 65.

[54] La Penna 1962.272–73; La Penna's argument is based on the different geographical references in G and W's differing versions of the final fable Aesop tells in ch. 142 (what the girl within the fable says to her father who has just raped her). On the basis of these references, he posits G as a Syrian/Eastern recension and W as a Sicilian/Western recension of the story. I'm not sure, however, that La Penna's arguments make sense: in both instances, the point of the girl's geographical comparison is that she would rather wander the distant ends of the earth than be subjected to her father's violence; we cannot therefore take the places she names as specifications of where the respective text versions were themselves composed.

[55] Adrados 1979, 1999.647–83; Hägg 1997, esp. 182–83. The former's argument is based largely on what he takes to be the pervasiveness of Cynic elements in *Vita* G, whereas the latter argues for the Samian portion of the *Life* as largely Hellenistic (but probably not earlier).

[56] On the Greek of *Vita* G, see Tallmadge 1938, Birch 1955, Hostetter 1955, Shipp 1983, Haslam 1992.

Italian translation. And while these editions offer many improvements on Perry's editio princeps, many passages remain hopelessly corrupt.[57]

But perhaps the greatest mystery of all is the status of the *Life* itself: how did it come to be a written text? And can we treat it as genuinely "popular"? Before *Vita* G appeared on the scene, much older scholarship on the *Life of Aesop* (especially German) regularly conceived the text as deriving from an anonymous Ionian *Volksbuch* of the sixth or fifth century BCE. This was anachronistically to borrow a term from the European early modern period, when printing and inexpensive chapbooks and broadsheets enabled much wider dissemination of popular images and texts.[58] The fantasy of a sixth- or fifth-century *Volksbuch* was already decisively critiqued by Perry, who noted how unlikely it was that a text on such a topic aimed at a popular audience could have been composed at this time:

> So far as we know, books written in early Greek prose dealt always with serious matters of an historical, scientific or philosophical nature, which were committed to writing rather as a record to be consulted by other thinkers and by posterity, than as literature meant to be read by Everyman for his edification or entertainment. Histories were written about nations and the world at large, and we know of no personal biography except what was narrated incidentally within the framework of a national or a universal history. In that age no individual, however important he might be historically, was likely to be made the subject of an entire book written in prose, and least of all a comic individual like Aesop. Prose literature was not so trivial, nor its orientation so particularized.[59]

And yet when *Vita* G was first discovered, Perry himself heralded it as "one of the few genuinely popular books that have come down from ancient

---

[57] See Papathomopoulos 1989, 1990, 1999 (with reviews by Haslam 1992, van Dijk 1994) and Ferrari 1995 (textual notes) and 1997 (bilingual Greek-Italian edition). Like many scholars writing on the *Life of Aesop*, I will in general cite the text of Perry 1952 for G and W. Occasionally, where there are lacunae in G, I supplement these from W, and on other occasions, I diverge from Perry's text, following instead Papathomopoulos and/or Ferrari; in all these cases, I will note my divergences from Perry's text in the individual discussions.

[58] For the *Life of Aesop* conceived as an ancient *Volksbuch*, see (e.g.) Hausrath 1909 coll. 1711–14; Crusius 1920.XVI–XVIII; Schmid and Stählin 1929.672–76; Zeitz 1936.242–45; Wiechers 1961.1, 29. For changed conditions of printing and production that enabled the circulation of *Volksbücher* in the early modern period in Europe, see Burke 1978.250–59; for discussion of the problems and inaccuracy of the term *Volksbuch* even for the later period, see Classen 1995.

[59] Perry 1959.31; cf. Perry 1952.5. Perry concludes: "The publication in the fifth or sixth century of a book about the doings of Aesop was as unlikely and as contrary to literary propriety as would have been the publication of a collection of novellae in the style of Boccaccio; although abundant material for either kind of book was ready at hand. Novellae, fables, and short stories unconnected with saga could appear in the literature of that time only as something incidental and subordinate in the context of a larger work dealing with some significant subject, as in Herodotus." Very important here—though rarely acknowledged—is the issue of "literary propriety" and Perry's insightful juxtaposition of that issue with Herodotus; for more on all this, see chapters 10 and 11 below.

times."[60] Perry noted that, in contrast to such written, learned appropriations of popular traditions as *The Contest of Homer and Hesiod*, the *Lives* of Homer, or Plutarch's *Banquet of the Seven Sages*, the *Life of Aesop* "is more naïve and romantic. It gives us the portrait of a wise man as seen through the eyes of the poor in spirit, at the same time enlivened by a spontaneous and vigorous, if somewhat homely, wit."[61] Here Perry himself seems to succumb to the same anachronistic, romantic model he was later to critique in arguing against the theory of the *Volksbuch*, simply transposing it to a later period of antiquity. For, as I have noted, the very fact that we have written texts at all would seem to preclude their being genuinely "popular" or low, given everything we know about the limited literacy and cost of book production at any period in the ancient world. And yet Perry is responding to something significant in the written form and style of the *Life of Aesop*. It simply does not read like any of the comparison texts he names: it is looser, more colloquial, and more vulgar. It is a fallacy, however, to assume that we can simply and unproblematically correlate style and form with the socioeconomic status of author and/or audience. As recent work on the ancient novel has demonstrated, even texts whose style seems "popular" and whose form and content align them with modern trashy or popular novels must be understood as the province of an elite of wealth and education.[62]

Together with the general rejection of the *Volksbuch* model, a few scholars have proposed theories for a different kind of textual fixation of the *Life of Aesop* fairly early on. Thus M. L. West suggests that there may already have existed in the fifth century BCE a written narrative of the "life and death . . . wit and wisdom" of Aesop, with fables and parables embedded in it. West regards the existence of a fifth-century book as a necessary conclusion based on a single passage of Aristophanes. In the *Birds*, Pisthetaerus, before launching into the fable of the lark who buried her father in her own head, reproaches the chorus of birds for their ignorance of the story:

ἀμαθὴς γὰρ ἔφυς κοὐ πολυπράγμων, οὐδ' Αἴσωπον πεπάτηκας,
ὃς ἔφασκε λέγων κορυδὸν πάντων πρώτην ὄρνιθα γενέσθαι,
(*Birds* 471–72)

For you are naturally ignorant and incurious, nor have you spent a lot of time on Aesop, who was always saying, when he told the story, that the crested lark was the first of all the birds . . .

---

[60] Perry 1936.2; still treated as popular by (e.g.) Winkler 1985.279–91; cf. Haslam 1980.54: "The Life of Aesop resembles other quasi-biographical specimens of folk-literature such as the Alexander Romance in that its text had no fixed constitution."

[61] Perry 1936.1–2.

[62] See Bowie 1994, Stephens 1994 on the readership and status of the ancient novel; see also Jedrkiewicz 1989.171–82, 208–12 and Avlamis 2006, 2010a on the fallacy of correlating the peculiar style and status of the *Life of Aesop* with a specific socioeconomic group in antiquity.

Everything depends on how we understand the verb πεπάτηκας here. West, following Morten Nøjgaard, insists that the verb must signify something more active than mere "listening to stories," and cites the parallel use of the same verb in Plato's *Phaedrus* (273a), where it clearly refers to careful study of a written text.[63] But I am not so sure that we can confidently invoke Plato's later usage to establish the meaning of this verb in Aristophanes. It is equally possible that it means simply "you have spent a lot of time on Aesop" (as an Aristophanic scholiast glosses it), referring to careful attention to oral tales.[64] However that may be, for West this written text circulating before 415 BCE is not a *Volksbuch*, but perhaps a Sophistic composition comparable to the later *Contest of Homer and Hesiod* by Alcidamas and the pseudo-Herodotean *Life of Homer*.[65] A different theory of early textual fixation is offered by Ben Edwin Perry. Perry insists that there is no good evidence for a fifth-century written text, but suggests that Demetrius of Phaleron in the volume of Αἰσωπείων λόγων συναγωγαί attributed to him by Diogenes Laertius (D.L. 5.80), might have prefaced a collection of prose fables with a short *Life*, based like the fables on popular anecdotes circulating orally at the time.[66]

Either of these scenarios is possible; I am frankly agnostic. For even if we posit such early textual fixation in one or another form, it cannot adequately account for the texts of the *Life of Aesop* we have. For as Perry already noted (and as I noted above), the *Lives* of Aesop are not really comparable in form, verbal texture, and level of style to such Sophistic texts as the *Contest of Homer and Hesiod*, the pseudo-Herodotean *Life of Homer*, or what we might imagine for a composition by Demetrius of Phaleron. Whether or not we posit early textual fixation, the only way to account for these factors is to assume ongoing, robust oral traditions about Aesop that regularly interact with and impinge on

---

[63] West 1984.121–22, following Nøjgaard 1964.474. Cf. LSJ s.v. πατέω II.2, "hast not thumbed Aesop."

[64] Cf. Dunbar 1995.325–26, who quotes the scholiast (τὸ πατῆσαι ἴσον ἐστὶ τῷ ἐνδιατρῖψαι) and finds the literary references to Aesop in Aristophanes and Plato "inconclusive" on the question of whether or not any Aesopica already existed in written form in the fifth century. Indeed, I would argue that Aristophanes' use of πολυπράγμων and the iterative ἔφασκε are more likely to point to the *oral* circulation of tales.

[65] West 1984.122–28, following Jacoby 1933.10. While I am skeptical about the existence of a fifth-century written text of something that looks more or less like the *Life*, I find West's notion of a "sophistic composition" useful and suggestive for a later period; see below, chapter 4. Note that it is West's speculation that Aristophanes refers not just to a written text, but to a text that looks more like the *Life of Aesop* (a connected narrative of Aesop's life and death, with embedded fables) rather than simply a collection of disconnected fables. Other scholars use Aristophanes' reference as evidence for a written collection of prose fables with no narrative frame: thus (e.g.) Nøjgaard 1964.473–75.

[66] Thus Perry 1959.31–36, 1962a.332–34, 1966.286–87n. 2. As Perry notes, Demetrius of Phaleron's one-volume work is the earliest written collection of prose fables known to us from antiquity; see section IIC below.

various textual instantiations over centuries.[67] Thus we may say that as written texts, the *Lives* of Aesop cannot be "popular" in any authentic and unmediated way; but that as elite instantiations, they carry elements of the popular within them, mediated and transformed.

Indeed, in contrast to older approaches to the *Life* that assumed that it was genuinely and unproblematically "popular," more recent scholarly treatments have come to more or less the opposite conclusion, recognizing in *Vita* G (or parts thereof) a unitary literary work whose sole author or adapter must have been a member of the educated elite.[68] These readings, then, are more generally focused on what is distinctive in *Vita* G as the intervention of an educated individual in the tradition at a particular moment in time. But what tends to get lost in this more recent approach is an acknowledgment of the unique status of a text like the *Life*, which seems to emerge from and remain in continuing interaction with popular oral traditions over centuries. It is this strange permeable, unstable quality of the text that the earlier scholarly models of *Volksbuch* or "folk-literature" aimed to come to grips with.

IIB. *Theoretical Assumptions and Critique of Previous Scholarship*

So if we must read the written *Lives* as elite mediations and transformations of popular oral traditions, how do we sort out popular from elite elements—figure from ground (as it were)? Is this simply hopeless? The methods of cultural historians like Peter Burke and Robert Darnton, who work on the interaction of popular and elite cultures in later periods of European history, suggest that this is not a hopeless endeavor.[69] This is so, first, because still in these periods (as throughout the ancient world), the "little tradition" exists as a common culture in which both nonelites and elites participate. For a period in which we can posit such a common culture, Burke offers a set of indirect or oblique methods for accessing the popular through fragmentary cultural remains and the mediation of elite texts and appropriations, consisting of three elements: reading for "iconology"; the regressive method; and the comparative method.[70] First, fol-

---

[67] This is thus akin to the argument offered by La Penna 1962.282–84 against the theory of the *Volksbuch*, that early textual fixation is unlikely given the sheer number of divergent and different traditions about Aesop proliferating from an early date. That is to say, this proliferation of different traditions suggests either that there was no written text, or that the written text simply made no difference and oral traditions continued to proliferate and develop on their own, informing and feeding back into written sources. Notice that this is precisely the same pattern of dual (oral and written) circulation most scholars postulate for the fables (see section IIC below).

[68] Thus Holzberg 1992, 1993, 1996, 2002.76–84; Ferrari 1997.5–39; Hägg 1997; Jouanno 2006.27–32; Hunter 2007; Avlamis 2010a.

[69] Burke 1978, Darnton 1984.

[70] Burke 1978.77–87. Of course, as Burke 1978.77–79 notes, these three indirect or oblique methods supplement the historian's basic tool kit of reading sources critically to screen for distortion.

lowing Erwin Panofsky, Burke defines "iconology" as "the diagnosis of the attitudes and values of which works of art are the symptoms"; what contemporaries "did not know about themselves—or at any rate, did not know they knew."[71] Burke contends that this style of reading can be applied to popular imagery and artifacts as well as to high works of art. Second, Burke borrows from the great *Annaliste* historian Marc Bloch "the regressive method," used to reconstruct historical phenomena by working backward from periods when our evidence is fuller to earlier periods when it is more fragmentary. This is essentially a structuralist model of constituting connections among a constellation of elements, rather than applying a positivist model of reading that treats each detail separately and assumes that we can date each detail only by its earliest appearance in a text. Finally, the comparative method seeks to supplement a fragmentary record by comparison with a more fully preserved structural or typological system in another culture.

I will throughout be applying *structuralist* methods of reading that are analogous to aspects of Burke's approaches, although I will also be drawing on more literary methodologies for the nuanced reading and interpretation of texts. To be adequate to the material we have and the goal envisioned, we must craft a methodology that starts from cultural history, anthropology, and structuralist and poststructuralist literary and cultural theory. As such, our approach will read for *dialectics*—dialectics within culture, dialectics between texts and culture, between texts and traditions, and within texts—and for *ideology*. In order to elucidate what I mean by these three key terms (structuralism, dialectic, ideology), I begin with a set of axioms and definitions:

1. I take it as axiomatic that culture is not homogeneous, but is instead a domain of contest. All cultures are comprised of many disparate subgroups or subcultures, whose identity and existence are constantly shifting and realigning, whose rituals, beliefs, and practices alternately compete and collaborate. Culture is articulated at several levels—reflected in language, embodied in customs and traditions—and is constantly under negotiation. It will contain both residual strains of its earlier iterations and emergent seeds of change and potential resistance. Following important reconceptualizations of culture by Antonio Gramsci, Pierre Bourdieu, and Michel de Certeau, scholars in various disciplines have shifted their emphasis from culture as a (single, coherent) system to culture as (multiple, diffuse) practices—or, better, to culture as the *dialectic* of

---

Thus he acknowledges the even more basic approach of studying the attitudes of the nonelite through the witness of the elites who shared their common culture. To some extent, this applies to the whole of the text of the *Life of Aesop*, which mobilizes an abject outsider's perspective to critique various institutions and cultural practices.

[71] Burke 1978.79. Similar to Burke's reading for "iconology" is Darnton's analysis of the implicit values encoded in French peasant tales (see esp. Darnton 1984.29–62).

system and practice.[72] Thus I am following the lead of recent theoretical work in cultural studies—work that understands cultural formations as complex, disparate, improvisatory, and diverse—very much in contrast to the monolithic "Greek culture" traditionally imagined by the field of classics.[73]

2. Texts stand in a complex relation to culture as a domain of contest or negotiation. A text does not merely reflect some reified, preexistent culture, but is instead a part of culture—is culture—a "symbolic act" that responds to determinate historical conditions, but also in its turn affects the broader social and culural landscape.[74] That is to say, texts and culture stand in a dialectical relation to each other. And as a symbolic act, each text participates in the contestation of culture through which power and status are negotiated. Thus texts of all kinds offer us the sedimented residue of moments in a dynamic process of struggle or contestation.

3. Issues of power or contestation entail ideology as an essential part of culture. Following Althusser, I define ideology as "the imaginary relationship of individuals to their real conditions of existence"; as such, as Althusser also notes, "there is no outside to ideology."[75] But, as more recent poststructuralist theorists have argued, ideology is itself not monolithic—it is incoherent, layered, and inconsistent. There are at any given time competing ideologies, and there are historical residues of older ideologies.[76] And insofar as ideology is itself a symbolic system—a kind of language—the symbolic systems of texts, especially narratives, are a privileged site for the inscription of ideologies, and therefore also for the inscription of the incoherences, rifts, and blind spots of ideology. Such rifts or seams in a text enable a "symptomatic" reading for the pressures and equivocations of ideology and between coexisting ideologies—the tensions and stresses that the culture can express to itself only in the form of narrative; its "political unconscious."[77] This symptomatic reading for ideology and for competing ideologies within a text is akin to Burke's "iconological method."

4. A structuralist approach to texts and culture reads individual elements relationally as parts of a system; within the system, each element must be motivated. Where weird or anomalous elements occur that cannot be accounted for within the synchronic system postulated, we need another account of motivation. Thus these elements may be parts of a different synchronic system, or they

---

[72] Thus (e.g.) Sahlins 1985, Sewell 1999.

[73] In addition to Bourdieu and de Certeau, I have found the following most useful for my project: Stallybrass and White 1986; Scott 1990; Bell 1992.

[74] Jameson 1981.

[75] Althusser 2001; quotations from pp. 109 and 107, respectively.

[76] For the incoherence of all ideologies, see Macherey 1978.75–101, Belsey 1980.101–24; for the synchronic coexistence of multiple, competing ideologies, see Smith 1988; for the layered residue of different historical ideologies, see Jameson 1981, esp. 93–102.

[77] For such symptomatic reading, see esp. Macherey 1978, Jameson 1981; for the concept of the "political unconscious" of texts, Jameson 1981.

may justify diachronic explanation, as remnants or residue of an older system that has otherwise been erased or overwritten within a cultural formation or within a text.

These are all general axioms about culture, texts, and ideology, but given a text like the *Life of Aesop* that contains within its boundaries a complex dialectic of oral traditions and multiple textual fixations, all these axioms apply a fortiori. For this text is not a single "symbolic act" by an individual postulated author or agent; it is instead the layered bricolage of multiple acts and agents in conversation or contest over hundreds of years. Thus the reading for ideological conflicts within culture that would normally require the aggregation of several texts over an extended period here finds its analogue in the analysis of the all-too-visible seams and rifts of this single strange text. Or put the other way round, narrative incoherences that reveal different interests and emphases may allow us to access different diachronic layers of cultural and ideological contestation.

Insofar as my goal is to read the *Lives* of Aesop and other Aesopica symptomatically for ideologies and for cultural contestation, I am following the lead of two excellent recent discussions of the *Life of Aesop* influenced by cultural studies—those of Jack Winkler and Keith Hopkins. Both Winkler and Hopkins read for ideology—for the tensions and ambiguities articulated and negotiated in such an open text in dialogue with a long-lived oral tradition.[78] For Winkler, the *Life of Aesop* participates in a popular critique of the pretensions of Roman imperial philosophers, scholastici, and rhetors, while Hopkins finds in this narrative a complex engagement with the issues and contradictory ideologies of slavery, for the delectation of slave owners. And while these two provide rich and suggestive readings of how such a narrative works within culture, they do so by mainly limiting their analyses synchronically to the end of a long process: for both Winkler and Hopkins, the *Life of Aesop* is only a Roman imperial text and nothing more. I would like to try a different kind of historicizing approach, reading the *Life* (or at least certain strands in the *Life*) in a way that is simultaneously diachronic and focused on ideology. I start from the assumption that stories about Aesop circulated for centuries, with different elements doing complex ideological work at different points. Thus, in what resembles a three-dimensional chess game, I want to try to take different synchronic slices or snapshots, and, at each point, put the elements in dynamic relation to their cultural and historical context.

---

[78] Winkler 1985.279–91, Hopkins 1993. For the text of the *Life* deriving from a long-lived, ongoing tradition, see esp. Winkler 1985.288–89 ("The *Life of Aesop* can thus be interpreted as a witness to a submerged, largely unwritten and unlettered cultural tradition in which the Deformed Man speaks both comically and seriously against the tyranny of conventional wisdom") and Hopkins 1993.3, 11n. 14 (characterizing the *Life* as "an anonymous accretive novella, composed and revised, as I suspect, over centuries, as a vehicle for comedy and manners"; different elements in the text "suggest multiple sites, origins, and fantasies").

But it should be acknowledged that the readings of Winkler and Hopkins are very much the exception within the scholarly literature on the *Life of Aesop*. To date, most scholarly approaches to the *Life* have been informed by traditional literary and philological methods; this is equally true of older diachronic or *Quellenforschung* approaches and of the more synchronic formal readings that have recently replaced them. As such, these approaches are susceptible to critique based on their (often unexamined) nineteenth-century foundations and assumptions. I will therefore survey the main trends in scholarship on the *Life* since Perry's publication of *Vita* G in 1952, and critique each method in turn. My discussion of the scholarship will be selective rather than comprehensive, attempting to lay out broad trends and focusing on those arguments with which I will most engage (whether to agree or disagree) in the chapters that follow.[79] I will then summarize what I take to be general usable findings before proceeding to lay out my own methodology briefly in positive form in section III.

One might have expected more interest in the text when Perry first published *Vita* G, but after an initial flurry of studies (mainly by Perry's students) on the manuscript, language, and syntax of the *Life*, attention largely subsided.[80] *Vita* G was translated into English for the first time by Lloyd Daly in 1961, published together with English translations of all the fables contained in Perry's *Aesopica* in a volume entitled *Aesop without Morals*.[81] The late 1980s and 1990s saw a marked increase in critical interest in the *Life* and fables of Aesop, as oral and popular cultures, cultural contact, and ancient multiculturalism emerged as significant issues within the field of classics.[82] It is symptomatic of this new interest that Daly's 1961 English translation of the *Life* was republished and made more readily available in William Hansen's *Anthology of Ancient Greek Popular Literature* (1998). And yet this newer surge of interest in the noncanonical and the marginal was often paradoxically shackled to traditional disciplinary subdivisions or as yet unexamined nineteenth-century methodologies and reading strategies. Thus one approach tended to segregate the *Life* and fables from other ancient literature, setting them apart as low forms or "folklore."[83] Alternatively,

---

[79] For a comprehensive analytic bibliography on the *Life of Aesop*, see Beschorner and Holzberg 1992, updated in Holzberg 2002.93–95.

[80] Tallmadge 1938, Birch 1955, Hostetter 1955.

[81] Daly 1961 (republished in Hansen 1998). To my knowledge, there is only one other English translation of *Vita* G available—done by Lawrence M. Wills and published as the appendix to Wills 1997. Daly's translation is generally excellent, but on occasion, I disagree with his interpretation; I will therefore provide my own translations for the passages of *Vita* G quoted and discussed throughout. See also the recent French translation of Jouanno 2006.

[82] E.g., Adrados 1979, 1999; Winkler 1985; Jedrkiewicz 1989, 1997; Papathomopoulos 1989, 1990, 1999; Holzberg 1992, 1993, 1996, 2002; Hopkins 1993; Ferrari 1997; Hägg 1997; Papademetriou 1997; van Dijk 1997; Dillery 1999; duBois 2003; Finkelpearl 2003.

[83] E.g., Karadagli 1981, Zafiropoulos 2001. For more cross-cultural, comparative folklore approaches to the *Life of Aesop* since the publication of *Vita* G, see Papademetriou 1997; Hansen 1998.108, 2002.49–54, 234–40; Konstantakos 2006, 2008.

when the *Life of Aesop* was set in relation to other forms of literary and cultural production from antiquity, this reading together was still largely predicated on methods derived from nineteenth-century *Quellenforschung* or "source criticism," originally developed to analyze the interrelations of fixed texts.

Traditional *Quellenforschung* often assumed that the *Life* was an incoherent patchwork with no synchronic unity, and proceeded to analyze it piecemeal. It attempted to excavate the "sources" that flowed into the *Life of Aesop* tradition and to isolate the oldest core or "original" substrate. According to this line of scholarship, what we have is a core of dim reminiscences of the First Sacred War (dating from ca. 590 BCE) and aetiological myths linked to scapegoat ritual, overlaid with Socratic influences, Cynic influences, the poorly integrated Eastern *Story of Ahiqar*, and Egyptian accretions of the Roman imperial period.[84]

In general, such traditional "source criticism" is open to critique at several levels. First, it focuses on individual details, not system, and once it has identified the "original" detail, all the rest are dismissed or ignored. That is to say, most versions of *Quellenforschung* are prestructuralist. Second, it is a method originally designed to analyze written texts; as a result, the process of interaction of texts with other texts or with their context is here imagined on a bookish or written model as a onetime operation of "influence" or "borrowing" at a fixed moment in time. This model of the static interaction of book with book was partly enabled by the old-fashioned theory of a sixth- or fifth-century BCE *Volksbuch*. Indeed, the *Quellenforschung* approach was at its height together with the heyday of the *Volksbuch* theory, but, oddly, it has endured in the scholarship on the *Life* long after the *Volksbuch* model was rejected and abandoned. In this model, there is no time-depth or history, and often no concept of culture surrounding and interacting with texts. Third, this kind of traditional *Quellenforschung* assumes that influence or borrowing only ever goes one way—from the top down; from the products of elite culture to the popular. This assumption is partly justified by the presumed lateness of the text of the *Life of Aesop*, but even those scholars who imagine a sixth- or fifth-century written text usually adhere to this one-way model. Why is this? I suspect it derives from a subliminal conviction that the "popular" can only be derivative and parasitic on high culture, not creative in its own right. That is to say, this model recognizes no dialectic between the common culture and elite culture, or between oral traditions and textual instantiations. But given such a long-lived, ongoing oral tradition, we must reconceptualize the process of text fixation and, with it, the relation to other texts and contexts. We must imagine the Aesop texts we have as emerging from a constant, ongoing set of exchanges—a dialogue or conversation between

---

[84] For these different layers analyzed diachronically, see (e.g.) Zeitz 1936; Wiechers 1961; La Penna 1962; Adrados 1979, 1999.647–85; Nagy 1979.125–26, 279–91, 302–8; Luzzato 1988; Jedrkiewicz 1989.41–215; Dillery 1999. Among these treatments, Zeitz 1936 still offers many useful insights, and Jedrkiewicz 1989 provides a thoughtful and judicious synthesis of much earlier scholarship.

different traditions taking place over a long period of time, of which our texts represent the sedimented residue.

Finally, when such *Quellenforschung* approaches connect texts with a determinate social or historical context, they tend to posit a world without ideology and no gap between texts and world. By "a world without ideology," I mean a static and monolithic model of culture, with no rifts or power struggles within. "No gap between texts and world" represents a model of textual reflectionism in extreme form, in which all that exists in the world is presumed to be reflected accurately and without distortion in our preserved texts. Given such assumptions, how can one motivate the presence and persistence of particular features in texts and traditions? This model never even raises the question of motivation; instead it posits a bizarrely Parmenidean order in which all that is spoken in texts must exist (there is no room for fantasy or biased, interested reporting), while all that is not explicitly mentioned in texts is presumed not to exist. Such an approach cannot adequately account for the workings of oral traditions *or* the fixation of written texts. For the former: studies of oral tradition suggest that a tale or account is very much the collaborative product of teller and audience together, so that we must imagine an oral tale as the work of a whole group or community.[85] Coordinate with this, we must account for why oral traditions and tales get preserved—why they continue to be told at all. Jan Vansina, a great pioneer in the practice and methodology of oral history, observes that oral tradition is always a selective process, which adapts narratives of the past to the needs of the present: without some kind of present anchor to locality, religious practice, political hierarchy, or group identity, tales cease being told and retold and simply disappear.[86] For the latter: we might suppose that fixation in writing could preserve details of much older material, even when it became disconnected from the needs and interests of a particular community and entirely irrelevant. And this might be the case for a written tradition that was fixed and closed from its inception, but can hardly be presumed for the kind of fluid, open tradition the *Lives* represent. While we must postulate some pressure in

---

[85] For the general model for oral traditions, see Vansina 1985.12, 34, 54–56, 108–9; for different applications to classical material, see Nagy 1996 (poetic/epic traditions), Maurizio 1997 (verse oracles as oral traditions). Note that for Vansina this collaborative process of teller and audience applies particularly to nonpoetic tales that require no special expertise in composition (vs Nagy/Maurizio): "From the point of view of the historian the form is important, as some categories such as poetry require a composition by a single author. . . . Improvisation on an existing stock of images and forms is the hallmark of fictional narrative of all sorts. Such tales develop during performance. They never are invented from scratch, but develop as various bits of older tales are combined, sequences altered or improvised, descriptions of characters shifted, and settings placed in other locales. Unlike poetry and its sisters there is no moment at which a tale is composed" (Vansina 1985.11–12).

[86] Still, Vansina rejects a model of perfect and complete homeostasis between every element in a tale and the present social order, noting that "the presence of archaisms in various traditions gives homeostasis the lie" (1985.121). I would suggest that the presence of archaisms, fixed in writing at different points, makes it possible to read for more than one layer or stratum within the Aesop tradition.

the tradition to respect and preserve the general lineaments of a story about Aesop (as we shall see below), it is clear that individual authors/redactors felt a great deal of freedom in reshaping the details they inherited.

This is a bare-bones schematic critique of traditional *Quellenforschung*. Let me offer a few specific examples to concretize this critique. In a short monograph published in 1961, Anton Wiechers focused on the Delphic episode at the end of the *Life*, generally acknowledged to be the oldest core of the tradition (since specific elements of it figure already in the texts of Herodotus and Aristophanes). Reading the Delphic portion of the *Life* against many other dispersed and fragmentary sources on Delphic history and ritual aetiologies, Wiechers offered a three-part argument:

1. Elements of the condemnation and death of Aesop at Delphi parallel elements in preserved accounts of the causes and results of the First Sacred War (early sixth century BCE), when (supposedly) a league of cities allied to Delphi conquered and destroyed the neighboring city of Cirrha or Crisa; therefore the narrative of the death of Aesop functions as an aetiology for the First Sacred War.
2. Elements of the condemnation and death of Aesop closely parallel elements of the Thargelia *pharmakos* ritual as we know them from other parts of Greece (especially Ionia); therefore the narrative of the death of Aesop is actually the aetiology for a Delphic *pharmakos* ritual (otherwise entirely unattested).
3. Elements of the condemnation and death of Aesop parallel traditions of the death of Neoptolemus at Delphi; therefore Neoptolemus, like Aesop, is a mythological version of a *pharmakos* and his story again provides an aetiology for a Delphic *pharmakos* ritual (otherwise entirely unattested).

Wiechers's argument is closely followed by Gregory Nagy, who accepts all three parts and adds to it the notion that both Neoptolemus and Aesop are also recipients of hero cult (the former as a warrior, the latter as a "poet"), locked in the same relationship of "ritual antagonism" with the god of Delphi. As Nagy explains, "antagonism between hero and god in myth corresponds to the ritual requirements of symbiosis between hero and god in cult."[87]

Both Wiechers's original argument and Nagy's additions to it are still frequently cited with approval by other scholars writing on traditions about Aesop and the *Life*.[88] But Wiechers's account exhibits several of the methodological problems I've identified for traditional *Quellenforschung*. Thus, for example, focus on details rather than system: Wiechers collects a fascinating dossier of sources that comment on and critique Delphic sacrificial practices, some dating back to the archaic and classical periods.[89] But in the end, Wiechers derives his

[87] Nagy 1979.121.
[88] Thus (e.g.) Adrados 1979, 1999.277, 280–81; West 1984.117, 124; Winkler 1985.286–88; Ogden 1997.38–40; duBois 2003.174; Finkelpearl 2003; Compton 2006.19–40. For scholars who do not simply accept Wiechers's argument, see Jedrkiewicz 1989.99–107, Rothwell 1995, Rosen 2007.98–104.
[89] Wiechers 1961.16–17.

entire argument about reminiscences of the First Sacred War in the Aesop story from a single report in a scholion to Aristophanes' *Wasps* that Aesop "mocked the Delphians because they did not have land from which to support themselves by agricultural labor." Since the First Sacred War was supposedly fought over possession of the fertile plain of Crisa below Delphi, this account is therefore privileged as the genuine "original" story, and all the references to problematic Delphic sacrifice are simply ignored. But a structuralist method would insist that this pattern of references, too, must signify *something*; as I will argue in chapter 1 below, these references may in fact give us a better purchase on the story of Aesop at Delphi as ideological critique.

More problematic still is Wiechers's assumption that memories of the early sixth-century First Sacred War would have endured in the Aesop tradition centuries after the utter destruction of Cirrha/Crisa and throughout a much broader geographic territory. Of course, what makes this assumption credible for Wiechers is his belief in a sixth- or fifth-century *Volksbuch* of the *Life of Aesop*, which, once committed to writing, preserved the most archaic material inert and unchanged. But once we have laid the ghost of the *Volksbuch* model, how are we to imagine the workings of such preservation? Both for an oral tradition and for a fluid or permeable written tradition, there must be some motivation for stories to be told and retold—and this gets us to the level of ideology and contestations within culture. Why should the Aesop story preserve memories of the causes of the First Sacred War? Whose interests are served thereby? Wiechers's account never even attempts to answer these questions, since his positivist history sees only material causes and material effects in the world and in the texts that passively reflect it. The First Sacred War happened, and so it must have been remembered. In fact, we should note that some scholars question the very existence of the First Sacred War. Thus Noel Robertson argues that it was simply an invented tradition of the fourth century BCE, in response to Philip of Macedon's manipulations of the Delphic Amphictyony. It may be that Robertson's skepticism is too extreme, but at least he recognizes the fact that stories about the First Sacred War would only be told and preserved when it was in someone's interest to do so in a context of competing ethnic and political claims to territory.[90]

---

[90] Robertson 1978. For a balanced and judicious evaluation of Robertson's argument from the archaic perspective, see Morgan 1990.135–36; Morgan thinks something like the First Sacred War must have occurred at some point in the archaic period, even if traditions about it, who participated, and what the causes were, were much elaborated in the fourth century BCE because of analogous contemporary conditions.

Similar criticisms can be leveled against Wiechers's theory that the Aesop legend preserves a deeply archaic aetiology for *pharmakos* ritual at Delphi. As Wiechers himself acknowledges in a footnote (1961.42n. 24), we have absolutely no evidence for a Thargelia festival at Delphi, although we are very well provided with information on the Delphic cult of Apollo in the historical period. Wiechers's response is that the Delphians abandoned and suppressed the festival "on the threshold

In like manner, religious models dependent on Wiechers presuppose religion—and culture—as entirely static, monolithic, unified systems without any possibility for historical change or human agency. In these models, a reified "religion" or "tradition" often takes over the "author function," thereby suppressing any serious consideration of human motivation or contestation. So, for example, Gregory Nagy, discussing the death of Neoptolemus at Delphi (to which he then assimilates the death of Aesop at Delphi) asserts: "For we see here a striking illustration of a fundamental principle in Hellenic religion: antagonism between hero and god in myth corresponds to the ritual requirements of symbiosis between hero and god in cult." But what is the status of this "fundamental principle"? What are these "ritual requirements"? Does the principle apply to all gods and heroes, or only to certain gods (e.g., Hera, Apollo) at certain times and places in relation to certain heroes (e.g., Heracles, Achilles, Neoptolemus)? More importantly, whose principle is it; whose interests does it serve; and why does such a model develop and subsist (if it does)? That is to say, what social work is this religious structure performing? By establishing this "principle" as axiomatic, Nagy makes of "Hellenic religion" a closed system that is somehow not motivated by or answerable to the domain of social work and social effects. More particularly: Nagy's assimilation of conflict to "symbiosis" in a two-tiered system preempts in advance any attempt to correlate conflict or tension within a narrative tradition with forms of real conflict or contestation within society at large.[91]

Let me offer one final example of the enduring imprint of *Quellenforschung* arguments on the way we read the ancient Aesop tradition. In 1962, Ben Edwin Perry argued that, because Herodotus never explicitly connects Aesop with the Seven Sages or with Croesus, these elements of the tradition simply did not exist in the fifth century BCE, but only got invented in the fourth. Indeed, Perry credits the invention of these traditions to Demetrius of Phaleron, in the brief

---

of the historical period," when the ritual killing of a human scapegoat became offensive to their more highly evolved sensibilities. But by what logic would the aetiology for scapegoat ritual be preserved in oral tradition long after the ritual itself was renounced and abandoned? Again, whose interest is served by the story's continuing to be told? This is partly also a problem of taking our sources too literally or too much at face value, rather than reading them through the mediation of structuralist system. Thus it might be better to imagine that the Aesop tradition mobilizes elements of *pharmakos* ritual as part of a shared religious code through which competing ideological claims are contested. For such modified use of Wiechers's argument, cf. Parker 1983.260-61, Jedrkiewicz 1989.99-107, Rothwell 1995.234, and chapter 1 below.

[91] Quotation from Nagy 1979.121. That is to say, Nagy's model is preeminently structuralist, but lacks any notion of ideology or contestation within culture or religion. Similarly Robertson 2003 argues that Aesop aligns with the primordial Titan Mnemosyne and her daughter Muses against Olympian Apollo, but never offers any explanation for why this should be so; that is, there is no acknowledgment that *people* make religion and myth. The same arguments apply to Compton 2006, who follows Nagy closely.

account he contends Demetrius prefaced to his collection of fables.[92] Perry's argument has proven influential for several more recent treatments of early and late elements in the *Life of Aesop*, but in fact its premises are dubious.[93] There is a fair amount of scattered fourth-century evidence (some even prior to Demetrius) for Aesop as a political sage publicly advising the Samian demos, and for Aesop associated with Solon or the Seven Sages in general.[94] In addition, I would contend, at least one fifth-century visual representation of Aesop by its iconography locates him squarely within the domain of *sophia*.[95] Given such a scattershot pattern of evidence within what I take to be a connected "semantic field" of archaic wisdom traditions, it would perhaps be better to employ something akin to Burke's "regressive method," positing a connection among Aesop, the Seven Sages, and Croesus already in popular traditions of the fifth century BCE, based on isolated earlier evidence and a more complete later pattern.[96] In contrast to this method, Perry's model fragments and reads piecemeal the little evidence we have, while it imagines that only an elite individual author can innovate within the tradition.

Finally, of course, it is a fallacy to suppose that Herodotus must set down in writing every single thing he knows, so that if he does not explicitly articulate some tradition or connection, it must be assumed not to exist. Even leaving aside the fact that Herodotus's text is not endless and therefore cannot be assumed to be coextensive with the world (for every text entails a process of selection), such an argument *ex silentio* fails to acknowledge the pressures of literary decorum and of ideology on the formation of texts. In contrast, I will argue that there is in fact an anomalous constellation of features in Herodotus's text that suggests that he knew of traditions of Aesop interacting with the Seven Sages at

[92] Perry 1962a.313n. 27, 332–34; cf. Perry 1959.31n. 52. In fact, Wilamowitz-Moellendorff 1890.218 had already asserted that it was Ephorus in the fourth century who first linked Aesop and Solon together on the basis of Plut. *Sol.* 28 (which in fact never mentions Ephorus, but bears some resemblance to an anecdote told in D.S. Book 9, generally thought to derive from Ephorus).

[93] For scholars who follow Perry's argument that there is no link between Aesop and the Seven Sages or Croesus before the fourth century, see Hägg 1997.183; Adrados 1999.273–75, 652–54. Holzberg 1992b.63–69, 2002.81 takes an even more extreme position (on which, see discussion below).

[94] For Aesop addressing the Samian demos, see Arist. *Rhet.* 2.20 (= Perry *Test.* 41 and fable no. 427); for Aesop and Solon, Alexis fr. 9 KA (= Perry *Test.* 33); for Aesop and the Seven Sages, there is a report of a statue group of Aesop and the Sages by the fourth-century sculptor Lysippus in an epigram by Agathias (*Palatine Anthology* 16.332 = Perry *Test.* 50). For fuller discussion of these sources, see chapters 3, 4, 5, and 9 below.

[95] See discussion of this image in chapter 5 below.

[96] Martin 1998 offers a similar structuralist argument for the antiquity of Greek traditions about the Seven Sages, countering thereby the extreme positivist skepticism of Fehling 1985, who contends that because Plato is the first extant Greek author to mention the Seven Sages, he actually invented the tradition. Martin's argument is an important foundation for my own—in both its substance and its methodology.

the court of Croesus, but deliberately suppressed them for his own reasons. In this reading, I will be drawing on the methods of structuralism and various versions of poststructuralist literary theory to describe a distinctive shape of absence and an ideologically motivated dialectic of presence and absence within our preserved texts.[97]

More recently, scholars have taken a different approach to the *Life*, explicitly or implicitly assuming an elite author and a unitary text. Much has been gained by the careful attention to the text and texture of *Vita G* of these more charitable literary readings; nonetheless, many of the problematic assumptions of the older *Quellenforschung* approaches endure unexamined. Thus paradoxically, these newer unitary readings often invert the particular findings of *Quellenforschung*—for example, what is taken to be early and late, high and low in the tradition—without ever challenging the problematic grounds and assumptions on which the older method was built. Or in other terms, we might say that each method overvalues one element in the dialectic of text and tradition, but that the two approaches tend thereby to produce readings that look very similar because of their common assumptions (and especially because the older method of source criticism treated fluid traditions as static, monolithic, and inert *texts* all along).

The pioneer and leading proponent of this synchronic style of reading is Niklas Holzberg, who in 1992 published with a group of other scholars a collection of literary essays on *Vita G*, whose centerpiece was an extended formal analysis of the text by Holzberg himself. Based on certain aspects of formal patterning ("three-step action sequences" and "strategic variation" in the kinds of *logoi* Aesop deploys in different parts of the narrative), Holzberg argues for the conscious, artful construction of the entire text by the G author/redactor.[98] In addition, in contrast to older (mainly German) scholarship that regarded Aesop as a political sage as one of the oldest elements in the tradition, Holzberg contends that there is no early evidence for Aesop advising the Samian demos or interacting with Croesus (*Vitae* G + W, chs. 92–100). From this he concludes that the *Story of Ahiqar* adaptation (*Vitae* G + W, chs. 101–23), traditionally treated as a late, poorly integrated intrusion into the *Life*, was in fact the source of inspiration for the anonymous Roman imperial author of G, on the basis of which he fashioned the earlier sequence of Aesop's sage advising to peoples and potentates.[99] Holzberg's conclusion:

---

[97] For the articulation of such a methodology for reading literary texts in general, see Macherey 1978, Jameson 1981; for other examples of the application of this methodology to ancient Greek texts in particular, see Kurke 1995, 1999.

[98] Holzberg 1992b.41–75; cf. Holzberg 2002.78–84 for a brief summary of the findings of the earlier essay in English. Quotations taken from Holzberg 2002.79.

[99] Holzberg 1992b.63–69, 2002.80–81, rejecting the model of Aesop as political sage of (e.g.) Hausrath 1909; Schmid and Stählin 1929.672–78, 682–83; Zeitz 1936—because it is part of an older theory of an Ionian or Samian *Volksbuch*. But this older model, while developed together with the

34   INTRODUCTION

> Regarding the anonymous author's handling of source material: the original version of the *Aesop Romance*—written in the imperial age—did not simply comprise a string of loosely connected episodes, but was conceived as a homogeneous narrative unit. Its author was inspired in no small measure by the *Ahiqar Romance*, and in fact most of the *facta* and *dicta* attributed here to the fabulist are drawn from other lives; the subjects of these were great minds comparable to Aesop—Hesiod, the "Seven Sages," Socrates, and Diogenes of Sinope, to name the most frequently used instances. Relatively little material, by contrast, was adopted from the existing biographical tradition for Aesop. Our anonymous author, we may therefore conclude, did not just take his pick from the available stock and merely adapt this compilation to suit prevalent tastes. Rather, he transposed the motifs he had borrowed, thus forming new episodes which he then assembled according to a carefully devised plan. The result: a new literary work.[100]

But this is to throw out the baby with the bathwater. While I agree wholeheartedly with Holzberg's insistence that we read *Vita* G as "a homogeneous narrative unit," "a new literary work" unified by formal patterns, such a claim in no way entails the complete writing-out of older Aesop traditions that Holzberg here derives from it. In general, it is a fallacy to assume, as Holzberg does, that the synchronic unity of the final product precludes its artful reuse and synthesis of much older material.[101] Specifically, as I have already noted, there is plenty of evidence (although it is dispersed and fragmentary) stretching back at least to the fourth century BCE—and, I would contend, to the fifth—for Aesop as a political sage, advising the Samian demos, interacting with the canonical Seven Sages and with Croesus.[102] Indeed, without this earlier tradition, Holzberg's own account makes no sense: why should the Roman imperial author of G be inspired to assimilate Aesop, the ugly, non-Greek slave, to the honored vizier

---

Volksbuch theory, does not in fact require it; as I shall argue below, we could well imagine oral traditions (especially circulating in East Greece and Samos) of Aesop as sage.

[100] Holzberg 2002.78–79; cf. Holzberg 1992a.XIII.

[101] In contrast, Alter 1981 offers a nuanced reading in a different tradition (the Hebrew Bible) of the complex interaction of diachronic and synchronic, of a long-lived tradition with the artful shaping hand of a redactor. In fact, even the patterns Holzberg claims as the distinctive work of the G author are somewhat questionable. In the first place, "threefold-action sequences" have long been identified as a characteristic of oral folklore narrative, so we should not necessarily see them as the handiwork of one individual (thus Olrik 1965, "the Law of Three," cited by Burke 1978.138; cf. Usener 1903). As for the "strategic" deployment of different kinds of Aesopic *logoi*, the symmetry of Holzberg's model is already critiqued by van Dijk 1995; I would contend that an alternative explanation for Holzberg's "pattern" is the deferral of fable to climactic scenes of public advising or abuse (see below, chapters 1, 3 and 4, and cf. Kamen 2004, Hunter 2007.54–56).

[102] For detailed discussion of this earlier evidence, see chapters 3, 4, 10, and 11 below. Indeed, Holzberg himself (2002.81) acknowledges the existence of this earlier evidence by his citation of Perry's *Testimonia* 33–38, 41, but he attempts to downplay its significance in order to support his own revisionist claim.

Ahiqar in the first place? The instigation for this assimilation—which could have happened as early as the fifth or fourth century BCE or any time thereafter—was surely that there was already a strand in the tradition of Aesop as a sage and political adviser.[103] Holzberg himself, in his list of alternative sources, unwittingly acknowledges this—for how else are Hesiod, the Seven Sages, Socrates, and Diogenes "comparable to Aesop"? Thus, rather than evacuating the biographical tradition of Aesop of any imaginable content, we should treat the parallels between Aesop's story and those of other representatives of the Greek wisdom tradition as clues to what the Aesop legend may have contained. What else would this fantasized lost "biographical tradition for Aesop" then consist of, if not his competition in *sophia* with other figures, texts, and traditions over hundreds of years? That is to say, what Holzberg posits as the onetime borrowing of a determinate author would perhaps be more appropriately thought of as an ongoing conversation of traditions—a conversation in which the Aesop legend not only reacts to traditional lore about other wise men (Hesiod, the Seven Sages), but may influence in turn the representation of figures like Socrates and Diogenes.[104]

Another important argument for significant innovations by the G author/redactor is offered by Franco Ferrari. Starting from the fact that the G recension alone offers a consistent leitmotif of Aesop-Apollo antagonism entirely lacking from W, Ferrari contends that this theme is the late imposition on the legend of the G author/redactor (whom he takes to be later than the anonymous author of the first/second-century CE *Life*.)[105] Perry, who had already noted this unique strand in G, took it to be one of the oldest elements in the tradition of the *Life*, closely linked to Aesop's persecution and death at Delphi, and he has been followed in this by most subsequent scholars.[106] Linked to this "new" theme of Aesop-Apollo antagonism, according to Ferrari, is the unique prominence of the Muses in G, closely associated with Aesop at key points throughout the text. Thus in G it is the Muses together with Isis who restore Aesop's voice and endow

---

[103] Greek knowledge of the *Story of Ahiqar* may date to the fifth century BCE, if we accept Clement of Alexandria's report (*Strom.* 1.15.69) that Democritus copied from a "Stele of Akikaros." The text whose existence Clement attests is often rejected by scholars as a Hellenistic or later "pseudo-Democritean" interpolation (thus DK 68 B 299; West 1969.142, 1984.127). Nonetheless, it seems that the *Story of Ahiqar* was known to the Greeks by the fourth century BCE at the latest, since Diogenes Laertius credits Theophrastus with a volume entitled "Akicharos" (D.L. 5.50). Various scholars date the assimilation of Ahiqar and Aesop to the fifth century BCE (thus Adrados 1979) or to the Hellenistic period (thus West 1984). For more extended discussion of the relation of the *Story of Ahiqar* to the *Life*, see chapter 4 below.

[104] Cf. Gigon 1959.176–80, Winkler 1985.289n. 23, Jedrkiewicz 1989.114 for a similar suggestion (Aesop as a model for the portrayal of Socrates).

[105] Ferrari 1997.12–20.

[106] Perry 1936.15–16, 1952.2–4; followed by Wiechers 1961.44–49; Gasparov 1967; Nagy 1979.279–97; Jedrkiewicz 1989.83–107; Jouanno 2006.39–40, 46, 50.

him with skill in inventing and fashioning Greek fables (*Vita* G, ch. 7; in the two strands of W, this function is performed by *Tuchē* or *Philoxenia*); and Aesop twice honors the Muses with statues erected together with his own statue (*Vita* G, chs. 100, 123; no statues of Muses in W).[107] In addition, Ferrari notes that the G author twelve times has various characters in the novel use the oath "by the Muses" in their speech (*Vita* G, chs. 8, 25, 32, 35, 47, 48, 52, 53, 60, 62, 65, 88), an oath that never occurs in the W recension.[108]

Ferrari's is a bold and innovative theory, but ultimately (like Holzberg's) one that evacuates the older Aesop tradition of too much of its content. To demonstrate this, I will (in the first instance) evaluate separately the two thematic strands Ferrari links together: Apollo-Aesop antagonism and Aesop's close affiliation with the Muses as his patron deities (although these two strands are unquestionably connected). For the former: I would contend that there is independent evidence in other Greek sources as far back as the fourth century BCE, even if this evidence does not take the form of an explicit statement of hostility between the oracular god and the low fabulist. Instead, we can identify a pattern of Aesop-Apollo opposition informing the *structure* of several different Socratic dialogues by Plato and Xenophon (Plato *Alcibiades* I, *Phaedo*, *Protagoras*; Xenophon *Memorabilia*), as well as the Platonist Plutarch's later imitation thereof (*Banquet of the Seven Sages*).[109] In addition, Ferrari offers no explanation for why the late author/redactor of G should want to impose this theme of Aesop's anti-Apolline stance onto a preexisting "story in search of a meaning" (as Ferrari has it).[110] In contrast, I will argue in chapter 1 for a sociopolitical

---

[107] For the text of *Vita* G, ch. 100, I follow Papathomopoulos 1990/Ferrari 1997, rather than Perry 1952 (that is, assuming that Aesop sets up a statue of *himself* together with the Muses). For detailed discussion of this passage, see chapter 4 below.

[108] Ferrari 1997.17–20, followed by Braginskaia 2005; this prominence of the Muses in G compared to their complete absence from W was already noted by Perry (1936.14–16, 1952.11–12) and again assumed by him to be an old element in the tradition. Ferrari claims as proof that all these elements are late the fact that only "late" papyri pattern with G, whereas earlier papyri lack telltale connections with the Muses or the oath "by the Muses" where the G ms has them. But in fact the papyrus evidence is simply not probative either way. Only three of the six preserved papyrus fragments overlap with relevant bits of the text at all; of these, *P.Ross.Georg.* I.18 (seventh c. CE) patterns with G and preserves mention of Apollo's hostility to Aesop, while *P.Berol.* inv. 11628 (late second/early third c. CE) patterns with W, mentioning only an honorific statue of Aesop set up by the Babylonian king Lykoros (with no statues of the Muses). The only papyrus that otherwise patterns with G but seems to lack the telltale oath "by the Muses" is the fourth–fifth c. CE *P.Oxy.* 2083 (incorrectly dated by Ferrari 1997.20 as third–fourth c. CE). But even on this papyrus, an oath "by the gods" intrudes where G has no oath at all (l. 17), whereas in the one spot where G has an oath "by the Muses," the papyrus has a lacuna ending in—ς, whose length would accommodate an oath "by the Muses" slightly better than one "by the gods" (hence Perry's proposed supplement at Perry 1936.46, line 5). Thus the papyri really give us no help in settling this issue.

[109] See chapter 7, n. 98 below.

[110] Ferrari 1997.5. Note that there are three problematic assumptions here akin to those that inform older *Quellenforschung*: (1) The long-lived oral tradition on Aesop is assumed to have no social

context that could motivate the narrative theme of Aesop-Apollo antagonism, possibly as far back as the classical era but continuing for centuries thereafter (and again, supported by independent sources that relate to a whole cluster of issues around Delphic Apollo).

As for Aesop's close association with the Muses as a distinctive element of the G recension, here Ferrari is on firmer ground, but even here the evidence is not as entirely black-and-white as he contends. Perry long ago pointed out that G ch. 134 seems to preserve an older tradition when it has Aesop take asylum in *a shrine to the Muses* at Delphi rather than the temple of Apollo itself (as in W). For the fable Aesop tells when the Delphians mercilessly drag him from the shrine—of the hare that takes refuge with the dung beetle against the eagle—is explicitly predicated on the eagle's contempt for the "littleness" of the beetle, which Aesop emphatically analogizes to his own situation at the end of the fable narrative: "Likewise also you, men of Delphi, do not dishonor this shrine to which I fled, even if the temple is little" (*Vita* G, ch. 139; similar sentiment in W). As Perry noted, this must be the original version of the narrative, since we know from independent sources that there was a small shrine to the Muses at Delphi, whereas it makes no sense for Aesop to describe the magnificent temple of Apollo as "little." And since Aristophanes already refers to Aesop telling this very fable to the Delphians after the discovery of the sacred phiale planted in his luggage (*Wasps* 1446–48), this whole episode must presumably already have figured in the Aesop tradition as far back as the fifth century BCE.[111] That is to say, the author/redactor of G may have added many elements that link Aesop closely to the Muses throughout the story, but he did so on the basis of a connection that already existed in the tradition in some form.

Thus it may be that the G author/redactor added the Muses to the story of Aesop's supernatural initiation as a fabulist (*Vita* G, ch. 7), although, given the parallels with the stories of the poetic initiations of Hesiod and Archilochus, I suspect that this is in fact an old element in the tradition.[112] What we could say, following Ferrari, is that the author/redactor of Vita G is particularly

---

or cultural function or motivation ("a story in search of a meaning"); (2) That meaning can only be imposed or provided by the individual author G; (3) No reason or motivation is offered for G's supposed innovation.

[111] Perry 1936.16. Ferrari 1997.17–18 attempts to counter Perry's compelling conclusions by claiming that the W version is original and preserves a memory of the more modest pre-Alcmeonid temple of Apollo at Delphi. But I find it highly implausible that oral tradition (which we must assume as the medium of transmission from the sixth century to the fifth) would have preserved an accurate memory of the smaller size of the old temple of Apollo long after all traces of it had disappeared.

[112] For the Muses as (potentially) an old element in this episode, see Perry 1936.12–14, Winkler 1985.286, Compton 2006.22–23; for thorough discussion of the cultural logic of Isis participating in this episode as well, see Dillery 1999, Finkelpearl 2003, Kamen 2005, Hunter 2007. In contrast, the two strands of the W recension offer two alternative abstractions—*Tuchē* and *Philoxenia*—both of which seem like fairly vacuous stopgaps.

interested in elaborating a strand that already exists in the tradition, of Aesop's preeminence in ever more consequential contests of *sophia*, often flagged as such by explicit mention of the Muses. Thus specifically, in three passages Ferrari does not discuss (*Vita* G, chs. 36, 78, 88), the Muses are mentioned climactically in contexts where Aesop defeats an opponent or opponents in a competition of wisdom.[113] In addition, I would agree with Ferrari that the oath "by the Muses" is a distinctive element of the G author/redactor's "voiceprint," which he uses as a kind of verbal tic throughout the narrative. If that is the case, this oath may itself give us a hint as to the identity of the G author/redactor. I would suggest that he is someone writing from within the sophistic/rhetorical education system, consciously aligning himself with the Muses, even if he feels himself to be oppressed or downtrodden within that tradition. (Hence my—only somewhat facetious—analogy in section I to "graduate student literature.")[114]

But if the oath "by the Muses" is an identifiable verbal tic of the G author/redactor, it is also worth noting where it does *not* occur in the *Life*: not at all in the Ahiqar section (chs. 101–23) or the Delphi section (chs. 124–42), and only once in the sequence of Aesop's performances as a political sage (chs. 87–100). As I have already noted, the scholarly consensus is that the Delphi episode is the oldest core of the Aesop tradition; the absence of the telltale oath "by the Muses" perhaps suggests that the two other sequences that immediately precede the *Vita*'s Delphic denouement are also old narrative units of the tradition, inherited by the G author/redactor and not so thoroughly reworked by him. I believe that there are independent reasons for regarding (at least) the narrative sequence of Aesop as a political sage as deeply traditional, as I will argue in detail in the chapters below.

The general conclusion I would draw from this critique of Holzberg and Ferrari is that we must assume some important continuities in the Aesop tradition, even while we give credit to the G author/redactor for distinctive features and final shaping.[115] Just as the diachronic, *Quellenforschung* approaches considered above tend to underestimate the pressure of changing audiences through time that requires motivation and relevance for different elements to survive in the tradition, the advocates of G as artful innovator or sole creator tend to under-

---

[113] Cf. Holzberg 1992b.47–48, who notices the first two of these passages and links them to Aesop's successful deployment of *logos*. For full discussion of the pattern, see chapter 4 below.

[114] Thus also Jedrkiewicz 1989.177–181, 208–15 (what he refers to as the "goliardic" matrix of the *Life*) and Hopkins 1993.11 ("the Life makes jokes about academic pedantry and the respect due from children to their professors, which may indicate its origins or circulation among students"). Cf. also Jouanno 2006.14.

[115] Thus also I would reject Ferrari's division between a first–second c. CE anonymous and G (presumed to be much later). Since, as I've noted, the papyrus evidence does not bear out such a division, it seems uneconomical to proliferate anonymi. I will instead use "G" throughout to signify the final shaping hand of the longer version of the *Life*.

estimate the pressure of ongoing tradition in shaping authorial uses and audience expectations for a story about Aesop. In these terms, it might be better to conceive the ongoing interaction of ambient oral traditions and individual written instantiations as akin to something like a biofeedback mechanism or symbiotic loop—because Aesop is strongly identified with certain features from early on, these elements tend to be intensified and replicated in written versions; then textual fixation in turn contributes to their further proliferation and dissemination.[116] Alternatively, we might apply the structuralist linguistic model of *langue* and *parole* to the Aesop tradition. In linguistic terms, *langue* represents the whole language system, which is necessarily social or supraindividual, while *parole* signifies individual utterances as instantiations thereof. Such a linguistic model registers the social level that generates and constrains the tradition, but it also allows space for individual users to formulate new and distinctive "utterances" out of the elements of a shared cultural system.[117]

At the same time, this model of symbiotic loop or cultural *langue* and *parole* should give us a better purchase on the tradition and its contents. If we can identify general elements that all or many scholars across a range of approaches have detected in the *Life*, these should be promising starting points for a reading of the dialectic of text and tradition. But where synchronic readings have seen these elements as specific to the text of *Vita G*, we may need to assume some provocation and greater time-depth in the oral traditions behind the text. Thus, for example, several scholars have noted the importance of *logos* and suggested that a progressive development of Aesop's verbal skills or distinctive styles of speaking is central to the text/tradition. We have already briefly considered Holzberg's argument that a complex pattern of different types of Aesopic *logoi* structures *Vita G*. For Franco Ferrari, what is left as the "historic substrate," once all the elements of Aesop-Apollo antagonism and the Muses' special favor have been removed, is Aesop's gradual development from inability to speak to speech as literalization, to complex forms of figured speech like puzzle solving, mantic utterances, and finally fables and political discourse. Ferrari suggests that this pattern of Aesop's individual verbal development represents the core of the Aesop tradition inherited and reshaped by the G author/

---

[116] Cf. the helpful formulation of Winkler 1985.279: "Like other folk-books, the *Life of Aesop* has a different kind of history from a text written by an author. From papyri we know that the *Life of Aesop* had achieved written form by the second century C.E., but before that we have to posit a repertoire of episodes, featuring Aesop as a fixed character, that undergoes continuous adaptation, contraction, and expansion at the hands of numerous storytellers. *The fact that Aesop stories are an inherited tradition, widely known by audiences in all ages, serves as a check on the freedom with which his life may be retold*" (my italics).

[117] For a succinct summary of the linguistic model of *langue* and *parole*, see Culler 1975.6–10, and cf. Jameson's appropriation of the Saussurian *langue-parole* distinction for his "second semantic horizon": "Now the individual text will be refocused as a *parole*, or individual utterance, of that vaster system, or *langue*, of class discourse" (Jameson 1981.85).

redactor.[118] Richard Hunter has recently picked up on and extended Ferrari's argument, noting a significant pattern distinctive to *Vita* G that evokes a species-level "anthropology" of the development of human speech through Aesop's individual verbal ascent. I regard both these interpretations as compelling and (together) a good example of the dialectic our readings should aim to capture, although I would characterize these two strands slightly differently. As an analogue to Ferrari's progression I would identify an old tradition of Aesop's development as a political sage with his own distinctive style of *sophia* still shaping or informing much of the structure of the written *Vitae*. And I would concur with Hunter's notion that an anthropology of human speech is a distinctive feature of *Vita* G, although I would characterize this more broadly as a Sophistic/philosophical "anthropology of *sophia*" superimposed by the G author (or some predecessor) on an older tradition of the life cycle of a sage. But in order to illuminate these two levels properly and to map their interaction, I must lay out the cultural system of traditional *sophia* before and beyond philosophy. We will have to consider how this system gets appropriated and transformed into philosophy as an elite, minority discourse, even as the older tradition of nonphilosophical *sophia* remains broadly diffused through ancient culture. That is to say, we must chart how this layering occurs in culture in order to see how it is reenacted and inscribed within the text of the *Life*.[119]

In like manner, many scholars across a spectrum of approaches have read the figure of Aesop and the text of the *Life* as satiric or parodic in intent. For some scholars, the object of parody is the pretentions of academic philosophers and rhetors; for others, the arbitrariness and ideological paradoxes of the slave system; still others detect a scathing Cynic critique of all kinds of conventional values.[120] For most scholars, this is a phenomenon of the text of *Vita* G, located synchronically at the end point of a long tradition.[121] But again, in order to explain what would motivate such use of the Aesop story, I would suggest that this element of parody is somehow central to the Aesop tradition from very early on, linked to Aesop's scurrilous, abject, outsider status. This is Aesop as an "ideologeme" for critique from below, as I have suggested—an alibi for "speaking truth to power," endlessly available to those who want to assume the mask, however playfully or seriously. And while these elements of parody are most

---

[118] Ferrari 1997.20–32. For other versions of Aesop's development in verbal skill and/or sage advising, see Jedrkiewicz 1989.108–11, 183–98; Finkelpearl 2003; Kamen 2004.

[119] See Hunter 2007 and chapters 2, 4, 5, 6, and 9 below.

[120] For critique of academic philosophers and rhetors, see Winkler 1985.282–91; Jedrkiewicz 1989.176–80; Holzberg 1992b.39n. 35, 74–75, 2002.83–84; Hägg 1997; Jouanno 2006.39–43; for exposure of the arbitrariness of the slave system, see Hopkins 1993, Fitzgerald 2000.33–34; for Cynic critique, see Jedrkiewicz 1989.116–27, Adrados 1999.659–83.

[121] Winkler 1985 is an exception: cf. his notion of a "grotesque tradition" going back to Thersites, Margites, and subsuming mime, etc.

visible late in the tradition, we can find them earlier, fragmented and dispersed, if we sift the evidence carefully.

A third element that several scholars have identified in the *Life of Aesop* is the prevalence of the theme of appearance versus reality, most commonly in the contrast between Aesop's abject status and hideously ugly body, on the one hand, and the excellence of his mind and counsel, on the other. As scholars have noted, this theme is closely connected with the element of satire or parody, since it functions to expose the falsehood and arbitrariness of conventional values and assumptions.[122] While all this is true, I would suggest that there is still more involved in this pervasive opposition as it attaches to Aesop in the *Life*. And here I would like to acknowledge as a significant precursor for my readings the brief and suggestive interpretation of the *Life of Aesop* offered by Annabel Patterson as a preface to her consideration of the political uses of fable in England from the late sixteenth to the early eighteenth century (the 150 years surrounding and containing the English civil wars).[123] Patterson, reading Francis Barlow's 1687 English translation of Rinuccio's Latin version of the Planudean *Life*, also notes the prominent "inside-outside dialectic" of the text, especially in its representation of "Aesop's uncouth body." Indeed, Patterson perceives in this opposition of appearance and reality "the hermeneutic key to the *Life*," whereby the entire narrative trajectory and the figure of Aesop serve to allegorize the power and workings of the literary form of fable. Thus for Patterson, the *Life* is itself a "metafable" that teaches us how to read the coded, indirect discourse of fable, which conceals a significant political message within the humble metaphors of the "irreducibly material"—the bodily and the animal. Aesop, the "father" of the genre, is thus "the philosopher of materialism and the body," the narrative of whose life and adventures offers a paradigm for the discursive resources available within conditions of oppression or unequal power relations. Or, in other terms, the *Life of Aesop* encodes an embodied political theory of fable.

Patterson's reading is mainly based on perceptions and representations of Aesop in the early modern period. But insofar as she is an attentive and astute reader of the implicit philosophy or literary theory of the (Planudean) *Life*, much of her interpretation is already applicable to the figure of Aesop and the traditions of his life circulating in the ancient world. And here again, it is a matter of a core signifying function of Aesop as "ideologeme" that we must track through the dialectic of text and tradition. Thus I will argue that the traditions about Aesop preserved in the ancient *Lives* offer us in narrative and embodied

---

[122] For the theme of appearance versus reality, see Jedrkiewicz 1989.77, 118; Holzberg 1992b.73–75, 2002.83–84, 92; Hopkins 1993.13; Ferrari 1997.11–12; Hägg 1997.186–87; Jouanno 2006.32–37; several of these scholars associate the theme with the text's satiric intent.

[123] Patterson 1991.13–43 on the *Life of Aesop*.

form a whole theory of the characteristic discursive weapons to be deployed by the weak against the powerful, that include (but are not limited to) fable. It is clear that the written *Lives* were understood in such terms at least late in the tradition, when they came to be prefaced to the fable collections (probably in the Byzantine era).[124] But long before that, we can find traces of similar models of characteristic Aesopic discourses informing early texts like Herodotus's *Histories* and Aristotle's *Rhetoric*, and even perhaps shaping the Platonic representation of Socratic *logoi*.

Based on this account of core signifying or semantic functions within the *langue* of the Aesop tradition and their relation to the *parole* of *Vita* G, I would suggest the following interconnections among *Vita* G, the Aesop tradition generally, and *Vita* W: I take *Vita* G to be a text written or rewritten in the first or second century CE, drawing on a large stock of popular oral tales about Aesop with a fairly stable sequence and narrative trajectory. On my reading, the G author/redactor is someone within the system of elite education who feels himself to be low-status or oppressed within that hierarchy—as Stefano Jedrkiewicz nicely puts it, "situated on the margin of the class of professionals of culture."[125] G appropriates and reuses traditional tales about Aesop's distinctive discursive weapons and his critique of *sophia* from below for his own purposes of playful parody of the institutions of education—academic philosophy and rhetoric. For this model, it is surely significant that the text of *Vita* G is in every respect the antitype to the Greek stylistic standards and values of the Second Sophistic: composed in *koinē* rather than Atticizing style and diction; almost entirely eschewing syntactic complexity, periodic style, and hypotaxis; and welcoming into the text a profusion of Latin loanwords, whereas Latinisms were generally banned from the purified archaizing Greek of the Second Sophistic.[126] I would suggest that we understand these stylistic features of our text as the product not of necessity—for example, Perry's theory that *Vita* G was written by an Egyptian nonnative speaker of Greek—but of deliberate choice. The G author/redactor is consciously flouting and overturning the ideologically loaded, fetishized Hellenism of high-style imperial Greek along with the educational system whose core values it represents. For this purpose, the low quasi-spoken idiom of popular stories about Aesop suits our Roman imperial redactor very well (and this is what allows for the preservation of many of these elements in his written text). In contrast, I find it much harder to say anything specific about the context of the two recensions of *Vita* W; like most commentators on the

---

[124] For different scholarly theories on the relation of the *Lives* to the fable collections, see section IIC below.

[125] Jedrkiewicz 1989.178.

[126] Holzberg 1992b.39n. 35 makes a similar point. For the thoroughgoing avoidance of Latinisms in Greek of the Second Sophistic, see Bowie 1974. For the point about avoidance of complex syntax, I am indebted to an unpublished seminar paper of Pavlos Avlamis (Avlamis 2006); cf. also Avlamis 2010a.

tradition, I take both of these to be early Byzantine redactions produced by scholars intent on preserving material inherited from antiquity in somewhat sanitized form. Thus *Vita* W generally smooths out the lowest stylistic elements of *Vita* G, just as it effaces its most ideologically aberrant and problematic narrative features (like the strand of Aesop-Apollo antagonism).[127]

IIC. Background on Fable and the Ancient Fable Collections

Finally, some brief background on ancient fable. It is important to bear in mind that in the ancient world, the definition and parameters of fable were broader and looser than our conventional modern conception of "beast fable." From early on in the tradition (fifth–fourth c. BCE), Aesop is associated with pithy stories of talking animals, but also with aetiological tales involving gods, personified abstractions, human beings, and (sometimes) animals.[128] Ben Edwin Perry acknowledges the breadth of the ancient category and its close affiliation with other forms like proverb, parable, *chreia*, and simile/metaphor. As a minimal definition intended to differentiate it from these kindred forms, Perry proposes three distinctive features for fable as narrative: (1) a fable "must be obviously and deliberately fictitious"; (2) "it must purport to be a particular action, series of actions, or an utterance that took place *once* in past time through the agency of particular characters"; and (3) "it must be told, at least ostensibly, not for its own sake as a story . . . but for the sake of a point that is moral, paraenetic, or personal."[129] Or, as Aelius Theon, the second-century CE author of *Progymnasmata*, succinctly defines fable, λόγος ψευδὴς εἰκονίζων ἀλήθειαν ("a fictitious story picturing a truth").[130] The oldest Greek term for a fable is αἶνος, which occurs in archaic Greek poetry (hexameter and iambic), but never appears with this meaning in classical Greek prose. By the fifth century BCE, the standard term for a fable in prose and poetry is λόγος, and by the fourth century the terms λόγος and μῦθος are both commonly used (with the latter predominating in Hellenistic and later usage).[131]

---

[127] For the various kinds of sanitizing (both of content and of style) engaged in by the two strands of *Vita* W and by the Planudean *Life*, see Jouanno 2006.48–54.

[128] Cf. (e.g.) Aristoph. *Birds* 471–75, Plato *Phd.* 60c, *Alc.* I.123a.

[129] Perry 1952.ix; cf. Perry 1959.17–25, 1965.xix–xxviii. For thorough review of modern and ancient definitions and theories of fable, see van Dijk 1997.3–73; van Dijk usefully adds one other criterion to Perry's definition: "fables are metaphorical" (van Dijk 1997.72).

[130] Theon II.72 Spengel (= Perry *Test*. 85); the same definition is repeated by the later authors of *Progymnasmata* Aphthonius and Nicolaus (II.21 Spengel [= Perry *Test*. 102] and III.453 Spengel, respectively). For discussion of Theon's definition, see Perry 1959.22–23 (whose translation I follow), 1965.xix–xx; van Dijk 1997.47–48.

[131] On the meanings, patterns of usage, and relative chronology of these three terms, see van Dijk 1997.79–111, Adrados 1999.3–17; on *ainos* in particular, see Meuli 1975b. As van Dijk 1997 notes, things are more complicated still, since all three of these terms are "polysemous" and can denote other verbal structures besides fable.

44   INTRODUCTION

The earliest written compilation of prose fables we know of in the Greek tradition is that of Demetrius of Phaleron at the end of the fourth century BCE; Diogenes Laertius informs us that Demetrius composed a single volume of Αἰσωπείων λόγων συναγωγαί (D.L. 5.80).[132] Demetrius's collection is lost, but is presumed to have formed the basis of later fable collections.[133] What we have preserved in medieval manuscripts are several different overlapping fable collections from antiquity. The oldest of these is generally thought to be the Augustana Collection (named for the best-known of the medieval manuscripts that contain it, a thirteenth- or fourteenth-century manuscript originally housed in Augsburg, now in Munich); the original collection is dated by B. E. Perry to the late first or second century CE.[134] The relation of all the different fable manuscripts preserved is very complicated, since it represents an open tradition in which different readers/redactors/copyists over centuries felt free to add or subtract material, as well as to rewrite or paraphrase existing fables. Indeed, we must assume abundant "contamination" among different written traditions as well as constant interaction with ambient orally transmitted fables and tales.[135] In addition to the prose fable collections, generally thought to be handbooks for writers and speakers looking for apposite exempla, we also possess versified fable collections by Phaedrus (Latin; first century CE); Babrius (Greek, probably second century CE); and Avianus (Latin; fourth–fifth century CE), which also presumably (at least in part) draw on earlier collections.[136]

In general, the later fable collections will not figure much in my discussion, except insofar as they can give us evidence for earlier fable traditions. Given the complex, layered, and permeable process of transmission I've described, it is in fact quite likely that the late fable collections preserve some fables that were known and circulated orally much earlier, but any attempt to date individual fables remains speculative. I will therefore use the evidence of the late fable collections in two circumscribed ways. First, where an earlier text provides a brief

[132] Some scholars contend that there was already a written collection of fables circulating in the fifth century, based on Aristophanes' use of the verb πεπάτηκας at *Birds* 471, but this is questionable (see discussion above). Thus (e.g.) Nøjgaard 1964.471–75.

[133] On Demetrius of Phaleron's collection, see esp. Perry 1959.32–35, 1962a. Perry suggests that the first-century CE *P.Rylands* 493 may actually represent a fragment of Demetrius's book, and also argues that it may have been an important source for Book 1 of Phaedrus's versified Latin fables in the first half of the first century CE.

[134] See Perry 1962a.288–89n. 8, 1965.xvi–xviii.

[135] For discussion of the mss containing fable collections and different analyses of the complex interactions among these, see Perry 1936.71–230, Adrados 1999.48–138 (somewhat wild and speculative). For helpful brief summary discussion (including charts of different scholars' theories of the mss interrelations), see Jedrkiewicz 1989.15–34.

[136] For the purpose of the prose collections: Perry 1940, 1959.29–36; contra (arguing that the prose collections are literary texts composed purely for entertainment and pleasure reading), Nøjgaard 1964.131–38, 464–513; Holzberg 2002.84–93. For a readily available text of Phaedrus and Babrius, see Perry 1965; for excellent recent discussion of literary, political, and ideological aspects of Phaedrus's verse fables, see Henderson 2001.

elliptical account or only an allusion to a particular fable, I will draw on the fuller version preserved in the late collections to supplement and fill out details.[137] Second, rather than insisting on the antiquity of specific individual fables, I will focus instead on continuities of story type and formulaic diction. Thus, for example, comparison with a whole set of fables from the fable collections about the allotment of various traits to mankind will help us contextualize the elaborate fable Plato puts in the mouth of Protagoras in the dialogue that bears his name. As for formulaic diction: scholarly work on fables has demonstrated that their language is highly formulaic, and that there are marked continuities of formula between early renditions of fables preserved in literary texts and those that figure in the *Life of Aesop* and the late fable collections. These continuities include introductory and closural formulae (much like our "once upon a time"), patterns of indirect discourse and direct quotation, and speech formulae. In addition, scholars have noted that the external "moral" or *epimuthion* attached to fables in the later collections corresponds to and continues the internal verbal quip or "punch line" frequently offered by one of the characters within the fable, which is properly termed the *epilogos* or "epilogue."[138] Such continuities of diction will help us track less obvious allusions to and echoes of fable in earlier written texts.

Finally, the *Lives* of Aesop and the fable collections stand in complex relation to each other. All the *Lives* we possess occur in manuscripts together with fable collections, as their preface and introduction. Scholars still debate whether the *Lives* were initially composed for this very purpose or only attached to the fable collections late in the process of transmission.[139] I concur with those scholars who see the development and circulation of the extended *Lives* like G and W and the fable collections as largely independent throughout the ancient world, because these two categories of texts seem very different in style, ideology, and presumed literary purpose (as I hope to have demonstrated).[140] I therefore imagine that the *Lives* came to be sutured to the fable collections only in the late

---

[137] Thus (e.g.) in chapter 3, section II below, I will use Babrius 95 to fill out an allusion to fable in Solon fr. 11 W. This procedure is analogous to what Burke 1978.81–85 describes as the "regressive method," used to "make ends meet" in the reconstruction of the popular culture of earlier periods.

[138] For various fable formulae and their continuity, see esp. Perry 1959.19n. 9, 29–30; Fraenkel 1964; Karadagli 1981.97–139; Adrados 1999.654–58; for the development from (internal) *epilogos* to (external) *epimuthion*, see Karadagli 1981.2, 53–71. For the prevalence of a verbal contest between two characters in traditional fables, see also Perry 1959.24–26, and for a similar project of identifying the formal features and "poetics" of the closely related popular prose genres of proverb, maxim, apophthegm, and anecdote, see Russo 1997.

[139] For the former theory, see Holzberg 2002.72–76; for the latter, Gasparov 1967; Adrados 1999.648–52, 682–83.

[140] For the general tendency of the fable collections to support the hegemonic ideology on such issues as slavery and status, see La Penna 1961, Gasparov 1967, Fitzgerald 2000.99–102, Zafiropoulos 2001, duBois 2003.170–88. For the misfit in ideology and purpose between the *Lives* and the fables, see especially Gasparov 1967.

46   INTRODUCTION

antique period, as a kind of bricolage by Byzantine scholars and monks making effective use of what they had at hand. Indeed, we might read the extensive revision and rewriting of the *Vita Accursiana* (whether or not we credit it to Maximus Planudes) as implicit acknowledgment by one such Byzantine scholar of the misfit or inappropriateness of much of the low, scurrilous, and obscene material in the traditional *Life* for this new purpose.

III. Synopsis of Method and Structure of Argument

Thus the goal of the readings I shall offer here is to respect and catch something of the dialectic of diachronic and synchronic; of popular oral tradition and elite written text in ongoing dialogue. This entails a two-pronged approach to Aesop and the traditions that surround him. On the one hand, I am attempting to reconstruct the ideological uses of a long-lived oral tradition behind our written texts that may go back in some cases to the fifth century BCE but continues for centuries thereafter. This diachronic approach acknowledges the aggregate or accretive structure of the written *Life*, in the first instance reading it piecemeal.[141] I will work backward from the end of the *Life*, the Delphic portion, since this is universally regarded as the oldest kernel of the tradition, and thence to the earlier sequences of Aesop as a political sage advising the Samian demos, Croesus, and Lycurgus, king of Babylon. These readings will suggest that Aesop is a focalizer for a civic critique of Delphic sacrificial and oracular practices, and limn his complex relations to a broadly diffused wisdom tradition. In each case, the diachronic analysis requires the careful reading against each other of all the versions of the *Life*, as well as the comparison with securely datable independent sources on Aesop and on the institutional, religious, and cultural systems he engages and critiques. I will thereby be trying to imagine an ongoing conversation of "great" and "little" traditions that spans hundreds of years.

But the other half of the dialectic is to put *Vita* G back together again and attempt to read it as a coherent text, tracing out several different patterns and leitmotifs that run through and unify this unique exemplar of the *Life*. Even here, our preliminary survey of ancient wisdom traditions will allow us to see some textual patterns as older and deeper, others as overlaid on those (perhaps by the *Vita* G author himself). Thus I will argue that the oldest elements of the *Life* are its representation of the characteristic trajectory or life cycle of an archaic sage, as well as its figuration of Aesop's distinctive positive and negative discursive tools. Superimposed on these patterns are the theme of a species-level anthropology of wisdom and frequent playful moments of philosophical parody. In order to disentangle these strands, even the approach to *Vita* G as a coherent text will be twofold. For the deeper patterns, *Vita* G is an essential

---

[141] For arguments in defense of such a methodology, see Hägg 1997.

resource simply because it is the fullest, best-preserved version of the *Life*, but we would expect to find older elements paralleled in the W recension, the papyri, and other scattered references to Aesop. On the other hand, where the G recension stands alone, offering specific features unparalleled in other parts of the tradition, we may be able to detect the distinctive imprint or shaping hand of the G author/redactor.

The argument of the book falls into two parts. The first half (consisting of five chapters) considers the figure of Aesop as he is implicated in or responds to various enduring religious institutions and cultural systems. I will begin with the end of the *Life* and what is generally acknowledged to be its oldest kernel—Aesop's adventures at Delphi. Chapter 1 will argue for Aesop as the bearer or vehicle for a popular critique of elitist practices that hedged round access to the Delphic oracle with a complex system of exclusions and sacrificial exactions. We will find recurrent motifs in the Aesop tradition of Aesop challenging Apollo's oracular monopoly and demystifying the peculiar sacrificial economy of Delphi. This critique of the Delphic god and his rapacious functionaries in fact provokes Aesop's death at the hands of the resentful Delphians in certain versions of the story, while elements of this same critique find parallels in several texts of the archaic and classical periods. Chapter 2 will turn from Delphic sacrificial and oracular practices to Greek wisdom traditions that were themselves in many cases intimately connected to Apollo and his Delphic shrine. There I will lay out in general terms the lineaments of a pre- or nonphilosophical system of competitive *sophia* that again has its roots in archaic and classical Greece, but (I will argue) endured as a widely diffused popular model for centuries, embracing poetic texts like those of Hesiod, Theognis, and Solon; traditions of the Seven Sages and pre-Socratic philosophers; and religious figures like Empedocles and Pythagoras. Chapters 3 and 4 then chart Aesop's complex implication in this system of *sophia*, as himself a sage with his own distinctive style of wisdom and discursive tools. Chapter 5 in turn will consider evidence for Aesop as a figure for critique or parody of the high wisdom tradition, and we will see that the oscillation of Aesop as sage and Aesop as parodist characterizes the tradition from its beginnings and is still visible in the late text of the *Life of Aesop*.

The second half of the book (consisting of six chapters) will then put the findings of the first half to work to excavate a significant Aesopic element at the beginning of Greek mimetic prose writing—both prose philosophy and prose history. Starting from the fact that, as I've already noted, both Herodotus and Plato explicitly identify Aesop with the making of narrative or mimetic prose and implicitly acknowledge the low fabulist as a precursor for their own projects, we must consider the possibility of an Aesopic strand in the "invention of Greek prose," a strand that implies its own problematic sociopolitics of literary form. Here again, at the moment of the emergence of written mimetic or narrative prose, Aesop and fable will turn out to be useful for multiple different appropriations, critiques, and cultural innovations. I will chart these first in the domains of technical rhetoric, Sophistic experimentation, and philosophy, since all of these emerge as new forms from the older tradition of *sophia* considered in chapters 2–5. In all these domains of a new technology of *logos* in the late fifth and fourth centuries, Aesop, playing at the margins of the wisdom tradition, is mobilized as a representational resource in ongoing heated contests of and over *sophia*. Thus we will find the Sophists recasting fable as an elegant form in artful prose, while Xenophon offers more traditional, humble renditions of fable to characterize Socrates' useful advice and teaching in certain circumscribed contexts. Plato, in turn, will exhibit the most radical appropriation of Aesop, borrowing his critical parodic edge and his distinctive discursive weapons for the literary representation of the "unique" Socrates. Finally, shifting to the beginnings of prose history, we will find Herodotus deploying Aesop for different purposes again, at times exploiting the disruptive power of the low fable-maker to explode the pretensions of Eastern potentates and Greek dynasts, while also taking advantage of a well-known Aesopic strategy for offering coded, indirect advice to a more powerful audience.

Especially in the cases of Herodotus and Plato, tracing out an Aesopic strand in their writings will help defamiliarize these texts and genres. We are too comfortable reading the texts of Herodotus and Plato teleologically as "history" and "philosophy," respectively, but in their original contexts, these categories did not yet exist as freestanding, autonomous disciplines or genres of writing, and these texts represented new—often startling—experiments and uneven generic mixtures. Attending to the Aesopic as itself a synecdoche for all kinds of low elements incorporated in these founding texts of Western literature will, I hope, restore something of the strangeness of the beginning of Greek prose writing— and of the cultural risks it entailed. For, as I noted at the outset, throughout the ancient world, Aesop and fable were consistently coded as both sociologically and generically low and abject (recall Philostratus's fable of the origin of fable). The welcoming of Aesop or the Aesopic within the boundaries of a "serious" text thus carried with it a potential status taint that could attach to the text and to the author himself. In each case, we must ask why Herodotus and Plato should take such risks.

To further this project of estrangement, I have followed a parallel practice in my discussions of Plato and Herodotus. In each case, I have started from ancient reception of these texts because ancient readers are often more alert than their modern counterparts to weird or anomalous generic and stylistic elements and to their problematic sociopolitics. Thus in chapter 6, I consider ancient as well as modern commentary on the Platonic dialogue and its literary and cultural sources, and in chapter 10, I examine something of the reception of Herodotus's *Histories*, focusing mainly on Plutarch's dyspeptic treatise *On the Malice of Herodotus*. But if we are to understand Plato's idiosyncratic appropriation of Aesop, it will turn out to be necessary to situate it in the context of competing deployments of prose fable by the Sophists and Xenophon (chapter 7), before considering Plato's parodic rewriting of Sophistic fable (chapter 8) and his own more adventurous uses of Aesop (chapter 9). The book will then conclude with an analogous reading of Aesopic elements in Herodotus in chapters 10 and 11. Finally, I have opted not to write a standard conclusion or epilogue, so as not to impose a single interpretive "moral" on these "fables of reading."

The two halves of the book thus mime the cultural dialogue or back-and-forth that is one of my central concerns. The chapters of part I will trace out a set of Aesopic responses to the Greek institutional culture of Delphic practices and wisdom traditions, whereas the analysis in part II will allow us to observe the ways in which high literary texts appropriate and respond to Aesop in turn. This dialogic structure means that the patterns of part I are difficult to date or pin down with any certainty, and we might best imagine them as cultural conversations that extend over centuries. But with the literary appropriations of and responses to Aesop in part II, the argument will be more localized to the fifth and fourth centuries BCE and what we might call the "battle over prose" initiated by the Sophists and their contemporaries. In any case, hearing both sides of the conversation must inevitably reorient our readings of ancient Greek texts *tout court*, insofar as it forces us to recognize the traces and strains of difference within.

And because the book covers such a wide range of topics, different readers may opt for different routes through the argument. To facilitate such selective reading, I have tried as far as possible to make each chapter a coherent, freestanding essay. Philosophical readers may want to focus on chapters 2, 4, 5, and 6–9, while historians and Herodotean scholars will find the most relevant material in chapters 1, 3, 10, and 11. As for nonclassicist readers, folklorists may target part I, while literary scholars interested in the beginnings of mimetic prose that led eventually to the novel may gravitate to part II.

But at the same time, it is my hope that the argument builds and gains persuasive force through the gradual accretion of evidence and connections across the individual chapters, so that it will repay sustained reading of the whole. Indeed, one thing I have learned in the process of writing this book is that, with ever greater professional specialization, different academic subfields (even within a small, relatively circumscribed discipline like classics) have become largely impermeable to each other. Thus, for example, Plato scholars rarely engage with Herodotus and the scholarly literature on Herodotus (and vice versa), while those who work on ancient fable seem to be generally ghettoized and ignored by almost everyone. To counter this kind of field myopia, I would advocate taking Aesop not just as our subject, but also as a model for a wayward, mobile practice that forces us to poach and to trespass—across the boundaries of different fields and subfields; across different texts, both literary and "sub-" or nonliterary, both canonical and marginal; and even across texts and images from wildly different periods, on the understanding that old material can be sedimented in late representations, and that later Greeks' own readings of their traditions have much to teach us.

PART I

COMPETITIVE WISDOM AND
POPULAR CULTURE

Chapter 1

AESOP AND THE CONTESTATION OF DELPHIC AUTHORITY

LET ME BEGIN WITH AESOP at Delphi. The strange, fissured, and uneven texts of the *Life of Aesop* and the open and permeable tradition that generated them necessitate the assumption of oral circulation of stories about Aesop, taking shape, traveling, and mutating over hundreds of years before the texts were set down in written form. At the same time, it is my contention that Aesop, like other folkloric trickster figures in other cultural traditions, enabled or gave voice to critiques of power and inequitable power relations from below. In these terms, Aesop was a mobile figure within the common or "little" cultural tradition in which nonelite and elite participated together, but a figure generally banned or excluded from elite high culture.[1] As such, stories about Aesop should give us unique access to the rifts and tensions within Greek culture—divergent views, counterideologies, and resistances to all kinds of hegemonic positions, encoded in narrative form.

Based on these assumptions, I'd like to try to reconstruct the elements of an ideological critique that may go back to the fifth century BCE, embedded in the story of Aesop at Delphi. For, as we know from Herodotus (2.134–35), traditions on the Life of Aesop were already current in the fifth century BCE—especially the story of his victimization and death at the hands of the Delphians. And Aristophanes (*Wasps* 1446–48) shows that certain fables already had a fixed place in the tradition of the *Life*, since he cites the fable of the "eagle and the dung beetle" in the context of Aesop's fatal adventures at Delphi (where it still appears in Perry's *Vita G*, dated to the first or second century CE). Thus, as scholars have long recognized, the Delphic episode that ends the *Life* has the oldest secure pedigree and must go back to oral traditions about Aesop already current in the fifth century BCE. I would therefore like to try the experiment of reading the Delphic portion of the *Life* as a coherent narrative, many of whose elements go back to the classical era. It is my contention that already by the fifth century, Aesop had become "good to think with"—a figure who gave voice to a common civic or popular critique of inequitable and exclusionary institutional practices at Delphi. This critique is not simply a form of "anticlericalism" (the anachronistic and ultimately unhelpful term often used to "explain" critiques of

---

[1] For the terms of these formulations, see Burke 1978 and Scott 1990 (as discussed in the introduction).

the Delphic priesthood); it is rather a symptom of ongoing tension between the egalitarian ideology that prevailed within most Greek cities and the exceptional privileges and practices exercised by the Delphians who controlled Apollo's Panhellenic oracle.[2] In order to clarify the terms of the critique of Delphi encoded in various Aesop traditions, I will first review the evidence we have for Delphi's distinctive status and practices going back to the archaic and classical periods but continuing for centuries.

I. Ideological Tensions at Delphi

As far back as the early archaic period, Delphi represented an anomalous site, and one that played a significant role in the development and autonomy of the Greek cities. As Catherine Morgan has argued for this period, the Delphic oracle was importantly instrumental in Greek state formation. In the eighth century, it appears that the oracle participated actively in the negotiation and adjudication of "community problems which . . . lay outside the collective experience of the elite of emerging states."[3] Delphi's marginal status, outside the boundaries of the consulting states, made it ideal for this role—as Morgan puts it, consulting the oracle represented "a step outside the spatial context of daily life to the fringes of the social world in order to obtain sanction for action on unusual problems."[4] Morgan concludes:

> Oracular divination at Delphi was instituted towards the end of the eighth century as a tool to help the authorities of emerging states to deal with unprecedented problems; divination thus served as a means of legitimising the gradual introduction of social change whilst apparently maintaining basic community values. . . . the real significance of an oracle at Delphi is that it constitutes the first move towards state domination of activity at a sanctuary which otherwise served the personal interests of the elite.[5]

---

[2] For the notion of "anticlericalism," cf. La Penna 1962.277–79; Delcourt 1965.39–40; Nagy 1979.126 (rejecting the term); Jedrkiewicz 1989.43–44, 83–88; and Ferrari 1997.13 (rejecting the term).

[3] Morgan 1990.159.

[4] Morgan 1990.183.

[5] Morgan 1990.184–85; cf. Morgan 1993.29. Note also Morgan's observation that "Almost all of the early consultor states were poleis, and moreover they were the poleis most likely to have been suffering from a conjunction of a crisis of authority and the appearance of new community problems" (Morgan 1990.185). Cf. Malkin 1989, esp. 131, 151–53: "Whereas Delphoi was evidently conservative in matters of religion and cult (and hence the 'conservative image'), the contrary was true in regard with its role in society and politics, where the oracle seems to have been rather consistent in its support of the leading forces of change and innovation. Moreover, it was precisely the openness and adaptability in its involvement in social and political changes which helps to explain the growing success, influence, and reputation of the Delphic oracle during the archaic period" (quotation from p. 131).

The intimate connection Morgan perceives between the rise of the Delphic oracle and Greek state formation is further borne out by the oracle's special prominence in the Greek colonization movement. For, as Carol Dougherty and others have well observed, the Delphic oracle was an essential element both in the reality and in the cultural representation of the colonial foundation of new poleis throughout the archaic and classical periods.[6]

But this same spatial marginality simultaneously made Delphi an ideal site for the expression of individual elite power and display that tended to be curtailed within the participants' home cities. Archaeologists have noted a significant shift in the use of scarce metal resources already in the second half of the eighth century, from lavish grave goods to dedication. Ian Morris has argued that this shift was the result of egalitarian pressure on burial practices; elites then turned to dedication outside polis boundaries as a new venue for conspicuous display and as a means of maintaining a monopoly on precious metal. Such highly visible dedications continued at Panhellenic sites like Olympia and Delphi throughout the archaic and classical periods.[7] In like manner, with the foundation of the Pythian Games in the early sixth century, Delphi became a Panhellenic center for elite athletic competition and display. Both these forms of elite display—dedications and athletics—were fraught with ideological tension in the archaic period, and we see a lot of cultural work being done to reconcile elite interests with civic ideology.[8] As a marginal site risen to Panhellenic prominence, Delphi is by no means unique in playing this role; Olympia shows very similar developments. But what is unique at Delphi is the pronounced tension between the important state functions of its oracle coexisting with its status as a highly visible venue for elite display. We might imagine these two tendencies straining against each other at the sanctuary.

Furthermore, it would be far too simplistic neatly to separate Delphi's oracular function (as serving state interests) from its sanctuary functions of athletics and dedication (as serving extrapolis elite interests). For individuals as well as states regularly consulted the Delphic oracle. More to the point, access to the oracle was itself inextricably implicated in what we might call an elite economy of dedication and sacrifice. In the first place, it was expensive to consult the oracle; hence the proverb, "Without bronze, Phoebus doesn't prophesy" (ἄνευ

---

[6] Forrest 1957; Malkin 1987, 1989.132–36; Dougherty 1993.

[7] See Snodgrass 1980; Morris 1986a, 1989, 2000.273–80; Morgan 1990.194–205. Thus Morgan 1990.204: "one finds that as cult institutions were established as expressions of civic identity within state boundaries, so the more personal dedications of local aristocracies began to spill over to sanctuaries further afield as a consequence of the increasingly intense competition for status and power which was developing *within* the new emerging states."

[8] For dedications, see Neer 2001, 2003. For athletics, we might see this as the whole ideological burden of epinician and other victor monuments; see Kurke 1991, 1998; Nicholson 2003, 2005. For an example of this tension preserved in a literary text, cf. Thucydides' account of the Spartan king Pausanias's dedication of an inscribed tripod at Delphi after the Battle of Plataea and the Spartan reaction thereto (Thuc. 1.132.2–3).

χαλκοῦ Φοῖβος οὐ μαντεύεται).[9] As we know from the text of two special "conventions" preserved between Delphi and individual consulting states, those who wished to consult first had to offer on the main altar a *pelanos*, or sacred cake, whose cost was fixed at a high price within the sanctuary (and at six to eleven times the price for states as for private individuals).[10] Then there were other special taxes or tariffs to be paid, to compensate the Delphians for the preliminary sacrifice of a goat and other preparatory rituals.[11] Finally, on entering the temple, the consultor was required to sacrifice sheep or goats, and from this sacrifice the Delphians exacted a special share for themselves. Thus in a Delphic convention with Sciathos, preserved in an inscription dating to the first half of the fourth century, this special share is referred to as an offering consecrated to the god "on the sacrificial table" (ἐπὶ τὰν τράπεζαν): scholars debate whether the Delphians appropriated some special cuts or the entire sacrificial victim "on the table."[12] In addition, later lexicographers, glossing the proverb "Delphic knife," explain that it derives from the Delphians' practice of "taking one share of the sacrificial victims, and [then] exacting another share 'for the knife'" (παρόσον οἱ Δελφοὶ τὸ μέν τι τῶν ἱερείων ἐλάμβανον, τὸ δέ τι ὑπὲρ τῆς μαχαίρας ἐπράττοντο, Leutsch-Schneidewin I.393, no. 94 = Macarius 179). Based on this ancient notice, Georges Roux speculates that "the subaltern personnel of sacrificers, the 'cooks' charged with killing and butchering the animal, claimed for themselves in the guise of a tip a portion 'for the knife.'"[13]

This unusual sacrificial procedure made the Delphians a byword in antiquity for greed and rapacity. Hence the Old Comic joke, "When you sacrifice at Delphi, you'll have to buy meat," as well as the proverbial expression, "Delphic knife," which we're told referred specifically to the greed of Delphic priests, or generally to "men who were lovers of profit and inclined to take [something] from everything" (ἐπὶ τῶν φιλοκερδῶν καὶ ἀπὸ παντὸς λαμβάνειν προαιρουμένων, Leutsch-Schneidewin I.393, no. 94).[14] Delphic sacrifice was notorious and, as

---

[9] This proverb is preserved in a fourteenth-century manuscript in Heidelberg, as part of a collection of Greek proverbs. For the text, see Treu 1889.199. The full text includes the gloss, τὴν ἰσχὺν τοῦτο σημαίνει τῶν δώρων ("this signifies the power of gifts").

[10] The *pelanos* later became simply a monetary tax or tariff, but at the time of Euripides' *Ion* was clearly still a real offering cake (cf. *Ion* 226–29 and discussion in Roux 1976.80–81). On the cost of the *pelanos*, see Parke and Wormell 1956.I.32, Roux 1976.80–81; for the text of the treaties with Phaselis and Sciathos, see Amandry 1939, 1944–45; *CID*, nos. 8 and 13 (pp. 23–26, 124–29).

[11] For these other taxes or tariffs for preliminary sacrifices (including the tax "for the pelt," the tax "for the two beans," and the preliminary sacrifice for Athena), see Roux 1976.82–86.

[12] For the text of the inscription, see Amandry 1939, 1944–45; *CID*, no. 13 (pp. 124–29). Cf. Eur. *Ion* 226–29. For extensive discussion of the sacrificial table (with the point that the god's share "on the table" almost certainly went to the officiating priest[s]), see Gill 1974; Jameson 1994.37, 40–41, 56–57; on the Delphic practice, see Roux 1976.86–89, Bruit 1984, Detienne 1998.74–76.

[13] Roux 1976.88: "Le personnel subalterne des sacrificateurs, les 'cuisiniers' chargés de tuer et de découper la bête, réclamaient en guise de pourboire une portion 'pour le coutelas.'"

[14] Comica Adespota fr. 460 Kock: Δελφοῖσι θύσας αὐτὸς ὀψωνεῖ κρέας; Leutsch–Schneidewin I.393, no. 94: Δελφικὴ μάχαιρα (= Zenobius 147). Cf. also the proverb Δελφοῖσι θύσας αὐτὸς οὐ

we shall see, much commented on throughout the archaic and classical periods. For, as Marcel Detienne has observed, this Delphic practice completely contravened the civic ideology of sacrifice, which constituted an egalitarian community of citizens through the direct and equal division of the sacrificial victim among all participants.[15]

Second, in addition to the expense, access to the oracle could be difficult and was not always equitably distributed. Oracular consultation regularly occurred only one day a month, although there is some evidence to suggest that extraordinary consultations could sometimes be scheduled for exceptional consultants.[16] On the regular twelve days per year, there could imaginably be quite a crush of visitors eager to consult the oracle.[17] On each day, the Delphians reserved for themselves the right of first consultation. Normally, the sequence of consultors thereafter was determined by a fixed order of precedence and by lot, but the Delphians could also award honorary grants of priority (called *promanteia*) to different individuals and states.[18] A remarkable sequence in Herodotus shows how this grant of *promanteia* might come about. According to Herodotus,

---

φαγῇ κρέας, which is glossed "for those who spend a great deal of money, but get no enjoyment from it. Since it used to happen that those sacrificing at Delphi, because of the number of people received at the hearth/participating in the feast, themselves got no taste [of the sacrifice]" (Leutsch-Schneidewin I.393, no. 95). On these various critiques of Delphic sacrifice, see Zeitz 1936.249 with n. 1, Wiechers 1961.16–18, La Penna 1962.277–79, Delcourt 1965.39–40, Nagy 1979.125–26, Burkert 1983.118–19, Detienne 1998.82.

[15] Detienne 1998.75–76, 177–80. On the civic ideology of sacrifice, whereby the distribution of sacrificial meat is coextensive with and constitutes the civic community, see Loraux 1981, Nagy 1985a, Detienne 1989.

[16] The ancient evidence on the schedule and frequency of consultation is very sketchy; the sole explicit discussion is Plut. *Greek Questions* 292e–f, which asserts only, "Formerly, the Pythia used to give out prophetic responses [only] once a year, on this day" (the seventh day of the month Bysios in the spring, which, according to Plutarch, "they consider the god's birthday"). Scholars therefore have taken very different positions based on complicated interpretations of a few casual references in other ancient sources. See Amandry 1950.83–85, Parke and Wormell 1956.1.30–32, Pouilloux 1974.162–65, Roux 1976.71–75. An older scholarly consensus held that regular oracular consultations occurred during only nine months each year, on the assumption that, during the three winter months when Apollo was believed to be visiting the Hyperboreans, no oracular consultations occurred (so Parke and Wormell 1956.1.30). This position is rejected by Roux 1976.72–73 (based on the wording of Pindar P.4.5–10); Roux (1976.74–75, following Amandry 1950.83–85) also argues that there must have been extraordinary sessions available in addition to the regular consultation days. Amandry's and Roux's arguments for extraordinary consultations are rejected, in turn, by Pouilloux 1974.162–65. It is worth noting that, even if we accept the argument for extraordinary sessions, the only two ancient examples of consultants who got such extraordinary sessions are Croesus (as implied by Hdt. 1.47–49) and Alexander the Great (according to Plut. *Alex.* 14); both powerful dynasts from the edges of the Greek world.

[17] Presumably, if one didn't get one's chance, one would have to wait at least a month, meanwhile paying for food and lodging at Delphi—thus incurring further expense and contributing to the local economy.

[18] On the order of precedence and use of lot, see Roux 1976.76–79; on the exact workings of *promanteia*, see Pouilloux 1952, Roux 1976.76–78.

when Croesus first ascertained that its oracle was a "true oracle," he dispatched lavish gifts to Delphi: three thousand of each kind of sacrificial animal; gilded and silver-plated furniture and purple garments immolated for the god; and huge numbers of gold and silver dedications (Hdt. 1.50–52). Then, on receiving two more oracular responses that pleased him, Croesus went even further; as Herodotus tells it:

> Sending again to Pytho, he presents the Delphians (having learned their number) with two staters of gold for each man. And the Delphians, in exchange for these things, gave to Croesus and the Lydians *promanteia* and *ateleia* and *prohedria*, and granted that it be permissible for any one of them who wanted to become a Delphian for all time. (Hdt. 1.54)

Here, Croesus and the Lydians are awarded *promanteia*, the right of priority in oracular consultation; *ateleia*, exemption from all taxes levied on those consulting; and *prohedria*, the right to front-row seats for the Pythian and other festivals at Delphi. Beyond that, Croesus and all his subjects in perpetuity can become Delphic citizens if they wish—that is, they are honorary Greeks. It is worth noting how, on both sides of this exchange, Apollo and his Delphic shrine are inseparably linked with the polis of Delphi and its citizens. Croesus combines gifts to the god (dedications) with the distribution of monetary gifts to each Delphic citizen, while his heroic-scale sacrifices clearly benefit both. The Delphians likewise reciprocate with an award of privileges that combine the oracular, the festive, and the properly civic. At Delphi, it appears, it is impossible to disengage the god of shrine and oracle from the citizens who are also his faithful servants.[19]

In practice, all these Delphic institutions give the lie to—or at least severely qualify—Pindar's ideologically loaded characterization of Apollo's shrine as a πάνδοκος ναός ("all-receiving temple," *Pythian* 8.61–62).[20] These practices might thus be said to produce a unique tension between individual cities' reliance on the Delphic oracle and the special access and status granted there to members of a Panhellenic (or even international) elite. Or—to put it in more

---

[19] Cf. Sourvinou-Inwood 1990.297–98: "At Delphi the *polis* schema articulated the operation of the oracle. The oracle's religious personnel consisted of Delphians, and the participation of non-Delphians was mediated by Delphians who acted as *proxenoi* and offered the preliminary sacrifice before consultation by non-Delphians . . . Within this basic articulation [of order of consultation] operated the *promanteia*, a privilege which the Delphic *polis* granted to individuals, *poleis*, or other collectivities. Here again, that is, the oracle is treated as a sanctuary of the Delphic *polis* in which the latter could grant special privileges to its benefactors." This intimate and thoroughgoing interconnection of the whole polis of the Delphians, the Delphic god, and his sanctuary reveals the term "anticlericalism" to be highly misleading, since almost all the early texts and inscriptions concerning the Delphic oracle and access to it through sacrifice designate the presiding authorities generically as "Delphians," not specifically as "priests." This applies to almost all the archaic and classical sources that critique Delphic practices, as also to the Aesop traditions.

[20] For discussion of Pindar's phrase and its ideological freight, see Neer 2003.136.

abstract terms—between the generally egalitarian ideology of the Greek cities and the Delphians' inequitable distribution of scarce symbolic resources (oracular access and sacrificial portions), over which they enjoyed a virtual monopoly.

II. THE AESOPIC CRITIQUE

I want to suggest that this tension generated a popular civic critique of such problematic Delphic practices through the figure of Aesop—a critique that dates back at least to the fifth century BCE but endures, as the Delphic practices themselves endure, for centuries. M. L. West has noted that there is a sudden explosion of references to Aesop starting in the mid-fifth century and continuing throughout the classical period.[21] It is at this point, I would contend, that Aesop becomes "good to think with" for a tradition of local, civic resistance to Delphi. Thus our earliest references to Aesop (in Herodotus and Aristophanes) suggest that stories about his ill-fated trip to Delphi circulated on Samos and in Athens (and we might imagine in other mainland and East Greek cities as well).[22] In these traditions of Aesop at Delphi, Aesop consistently challenges and demystifies the elitist practices and privileges I've just described, calling into question the delegated authority and autonomy of the Delphians and of the oracular god himself.[23]

These elements continue and survive in the traditions around Aesop because the Delphic institutions critiqued themselves continue for centuries. But this critique draws its point and animus from the organizing structure of the polis, and so (as we shall see) its elements begin to disaggregate and fade in a later period when the individual cities lose their primacy. This is a speculative claim, based as it is on the *Life of Aesop* and other traditions that were committed to writing many centuries later. In order to justify this claim for a critique that arises in the fifth century, I will attempt to demonstrate a coherent pattern in the *Life* and other traditions around Aesop, drawing on independent scholarly

[21] West 1984.116–20; see also Rothwell 1995. For the vase evidence, see Jahn 1847.434 and Tafel 12, 2; Wiechers 1961.32; Lissarrague 2000.137–39.

[22] Thus, by "local," I mean local to individual cities, not local to Delphi. My reading of the traditions of Aesop at Delphi thus bears some similarity to that of Nagy 1979.125–26, 279–316 in that I assume that there are important elements in the tradition that go back to the classical period at least, and that the stories of Aesop's death represent a significant cultural system of some sort. For more extended discussion and critique of Nagy 1979, see section III below.

[23] For an analogous argument for a critique of Delphi through the figure of Aesop that goes back to the archaic and classical periods, see Gluskina 1954. Gluskina draws on much of the same ancient evidence that I will use, but offers an analysis that is more relentlessly materialist, economistic, and Marxian than that offered here (thus, on Gluskina's reading, what is being critiqued via Aesop is the Delphic elite's control of trade and trade routes, as well as information). I am indebted to Boris Maslov for providing me with an English translation of Gluskina's original Russian article.

arguments that parts of the pattern at least seem to go back to the classical period. I will at the same time demonstrate that this pattern bears significant similarities to other, sixth- and fifth-century commentary on the problematic status and sanctity of Delphi. This is thus a structuralist approach, akin to the historian Peter Burke's "regressive method," that attempts to reconstruct a culturally distinctive signifying system from fragmentary details, some preserved in archaic and classical sources, others embedded in much later written accounts.[24]

In the first place, it is important to emphasize that the Aesopic critique is not limited to the human representatives of Apollo, but extends to the Delphic god himself and his claim to an "oracular monopoly." As the positive version is formulated, Apollo's Delphic oracle alone gives voice directly to the will or plan of his father Zeus. We find this claim made explicitly in the sixth-century Panhellenic and pro-Olympian discourse of the Homeric Hymns.[25] Thus, briefly, in the *Homeric Hymn to Apollo*, when the newborn god asserts his privileges (ll. 131–32): "Let the cithara and the curved bow be dear to me, and I shall prophesy to men the unerring plan of Zeus"; and much more elaborately in the *Homeric Hymn to Hermes*, in response to the younger god's importunate request for a share of Apollo's mantic power (ll. 528–40):

> But then I will give you the very beautiful staff of prosperity and wealth, golden, triple-leaved, which will guard you unharmed as it accomplishes all the settings of good words and deeds, however many things I claim to know from the divine voice of Zeus. But, as for the mantic power you ask for (O best of gods, Zeus-nurtured), it is

---

[24] See Burke 1978.79–87 and discussion in the introduction above. For a similar approach to ancient Greek cultural traditions, see Martin 1996 (excavating the archaic substrate of Anacharsis as a Cynic sage), 1998 (reconstructing an archaic model of the Seven Sages).

[25] On the date of the Homeric Hymns to Apollo and Hermes, see Allen, Halliday, and Sikes 1936.183–86, 275–76; Janko 1982.99–150. Scholarly disagreements on the dating of the major Homeric Hymns do not materially affect my argument, since my claim is that the Aesopic critique of Apollo's "oracular monopoly" dates back to the classical period but continues thereafter. All commentators on the Hymns would agree that the Hymns to Apollo and Hermes date back at least to the fifth century BCE, if not earlier.

On the consistently Panhellenic and Olympian ideology of the major Homeric Hymns, I follow Clay 1989.9–16, 267–70. Thus I do not accept the arguments of Brown 1947.66–132, that Hermes embodies the values and interests of a new class of Greek merchants in late sixth-century BCE Athens, and that the Hymn to Hermes is therefore genuinely subversive of older aristocratic values championed and embodied by Apollo. Brown's crude sociologizing, whereby each god represents the interests of a different class, does not seem to me to stand up to a close reading of the *Homeric Hymn to Hermes*, which, as Clay 1989.100–103, 149–51 points out, ultimately integrates and subordinates Hermes within the Olympian hierarchy. For similar simplistic sociological readings of the Hymn to Hermes, see Graefe 1963.523–26 (Hermes = Themistocles, Apollo = Cimon); Herter 1976.234–41, 1981.197–201 (Hermes worshipped by commoners at Delphi, while Apollo is the god of the aristocratic priests). For other, more nuanced structuralist analyses of Hermes and his complex character (which I find in general more persuasive), see Kahn 1978, Vernant 1983, Burkert 1984, Clay 1989.95–151.

ordained neither for you nor for any other of the immortals to know it; for the mind of Zeus knows it. But I, entrusted [with it], nodded and swore a mighty oath that no other of the ever-living gods apart from me would know the dense-thinking counsel of Zeus. And so, brother, bearer of the golden staff, do not bid me furnish the divine decrees, however many things broad-seeing Zeus plots and plans.[26]

Here Apollo's gift of the golden staff—one of Hermes' defining attributes— marks his younger brother's secure and unchangeable insertion into the Olympian hierarchy. A single line of delegation runs from the mind and divine voice of Zeus to the oracle of Apollo to the performative staff of Hermes, servant to both. When Apollo then addresses Hermes for the second time in this passage, using the epithet χρυσόρραπι ("he who wields the golden staff"), he thereby underscores the impossibility of Hermes' being allowed to share his mantic monopoly, behind which stands the absolute authority of Zeus. This insistence on Apollo's mantic monopoly is itself intriguing; that his status had to be asserted so vehemently suggests that there may have been serious competition. Indeed, Catherine Morgan observes that rivalry seems to have developed in the later archaic period between Delphi and Dodona, with Dodona allying itself more closely with the Zeus oracle at Ammon and contesting the primacy of Apollo's oracle.[27]

However that may be, we find Aesop critiquing Apollo's mantic monopoly in the first full-scale fable he tells in the course of the *Life* (a fable that occurs only in *Vita* G). When he is purchased by the Samian philosopher Xanthus and brought home, Xanthus's wife is enraged by the ugliness of the new-bought slave, especially since she had just dreamed that Xanthus had purchased a handsome male slave for her. Aesop consoles her with a fable about the origin of true and false dreams (*Vita* G, ch. 33):

> Don't be astonished, mistress, at your having been ensnared by the dream; for not all dreams are true. For, when the overseer of the Muses asked, Zeus gave him the mantic art, so that he even surpassed all others in prophecy (δεομένῳ γὰρ τῷ προστάτῃ τῶν Μουσῶν ὁ Ζεὺς ἐχαρίσατο τὴν μαντικήν, ὥστε καὶ πάντας τοὺς ἐν τῷ χρησμῷ ὑπερέχειν). But the overseer of the Muses, marveled at by all mortal men, becoming accustomed to looking down on all the rest, became too boastful and arrogant (ἀλαζονότερος) in all other respects as well. And so his boss (ὁ τούτου μείζων), angered and unwilling that this one have so much power among mortals, fashioned some true dreams, which told in sleep the things that were going to happen. And the boss of the Muses (ὁ μείζων τῶν Μουσῶν), realizing that no one had need of him for the mantic art, asked Zeus to be reconciled with him and not to deprive his mantic art of authority. And he reconciled with him and fashioned dreams of another sort among mortals, to show them false things in sleep, so that, deprived of any accurate

---

[26] For a fifth-century expression of the same idea, cf. Aesch. *Eumenides* 614–21.
[27] Morgan 1990.148–49, 222.

knowledge, they might revert to the original form of prophecy. On account of this cause, the dream that was fashioned first, when it appears, shows itself to be a true sleep-vision. So then, don't marvel that you've seen one thing in your sleep, but another thing has happened, since it was not the earlier sort you saw, but one of the false-speaking [dreams] appeared to you, deceiving you with false sleep-visions.

Because of its aetiological and mythological content, Ben Edwin Perry regarded this as the oldest type of Aesopic fable and suggested that it was very likely to date back to the fifth century BCE, and to have found a place in the earliest fable compilation of Demetrius of Phaleron.[28]

With this venerable fable, Aesop parodies and challenges Apollo's oracular authority. In the first place, here as in the rest of *Vita* G, Aesop never calls Apollo by name: he refers to him only as ὁ μείζων τῶν Μουσῶν ("the boss of the Muses") and as προστάτης τῶν Μουσῶν ("the overseer of the Muses"; cf. chs. 33, 142). While scholars have noted this pattern of designation (often taken to be a taboo periphrasis), they have no real explanation to offer for it.[29] In fact, my translation of *prostatēs* here as "overseer" is motivated by the internal evidence of the *Life*, for the term significantly appears in the first narrative sequence in *Vita* G.[30] As the story begins, the slave Aesop, hideously ugly and mute, is consigned to labor in the fields under the supervision of a slave overseer named Zenas (who is designated as τῶν ἀγρῶν προστάτης in ch. 9 of the *Life* [again, only in *Vita* G; cf. ch. 6]). Because of his pious assistance to a priestess of Isis, Aesop is miraculously cured of his muteness by Isis herself and endowed with exceptional powers of speech and the crafting of fables by the

---

[28] Perry 1962a.299–302, followed by Adrados 1999.194, 405, 481, 655. Thus I do not accept the argument of Ferrari 1997.13–20 (following Luzzatto 1988.437n. 46), who contends that all the anti-Apolline elements in *Vita* G (including the fable of ch. 33) are innovations in the tradition introduced by an anonymous redactor after the first or second century CE. For in fact what is striking about the critique of Apollo himself and his "mantic monopoly" in *Vita* G is how much it corresponds to the complete identification of Apollo and his Delphian "servants" throughout the positive, pro-Olympian representations preserved in archaic and classical texts, whereas the fact that Delphic "priests" are castigated in connection with Aesop for the first time in Libanius (fourth c. CE), as Luzzatto and Ferrari emphasize, suggests that in this late era, the intimate ideological connection between Apollo and the Delphian polis has broken down.

[29] The name of Apollo does occur in *Vita* G, but only in the narrative voice (at chs. 100 and 127). Wiechers 1961.14n. 21 regards the periphrastic designations of *Vita* G as an innovation; Nagy 1979.290–91 argues that the consistent periphrases are archaic and "amount to a clear acknowledgment by the narrative *that Aesop's essence as poet is defined not only by the Muses but also by their leader, Apollo himself*" (p. 290; italics in original). But the epithets of Apollo Nagy cites to prove his contention (*Mousarkhos, Mouseios,* and *Mousagetēs*) bear no resemblance to *prostatēs*, while Nagy ignores the internal evidence of *Vita* G on the denotation and connotations of *prostatēs* as "slave overseer." Cf. Compton 2006.28–31, 36, following Nagy's argument closely.

[30] I owe this important point about the use of *prostatēs* to Patricia Larash (an observation made in discussion in a graduate seminar I taught at Berkeley on the invention of Greek prose in fall 1999).

Muses, who become his particular patrons (*Vita* G, chs. 6–7).³¹ At that point, Aesop challenges the unjust authority of the slave overseer Zenas (who willfully and gratuitously beats the slaves under his supervision), threatening to denounce him to the master in the city. The cowardly Zenas, terrified by the threat of an articulate Aesop, rushes to town himself and cajoles the master into empowering him to sell or kill Aesop outright. Leading a slave merchant out to the farm, Zenas then dispatches another slave to fetch Aesop from the fields (*Vita* G, ch. 13):

> One of his fellow slaves, going and seeing Aesop digging, said to him, "Aesop, cast down your mattock and follow me—the master calls you." And he said, "What do you mean, 'master'? The one by nature, or the steward? (ποῖος δεσπότης, ὁ κατὰ φύσιν ἢ ‹ὁ› οἰκονόμος;) So, then, making a clear distinction, you should say, 'the steward,' and not 'the master.' For he himself also has been set under the yoke of slavery as a slave.... How evil a thing is slavery handed over to another slave—and, in addition to this, how hateful to the gods!"

This passage makes clear that Zenas, τῶν ἀγρῶν προστάτης, is himself a slave steward (οἰκονόμος). I am not thereby claiming that this use of the term *prostatēs* in the *Life of Aesop* itself goes back to the fifth century BCE, for in the fifth century, *prostatēs* is generally a positive or neutral term for a "leader" or "protector," as in the familiar expression προστάτης τοῦ δήμου.³² It is only by the second century BCE or later, in documentary sources, that it comes to develop the specialized meaning "administrator."³³ I am instead claiming that there is a coherent system of *content* in *Vita* G that may well be older than the particular diction of our written text.³⁴ For the whole internal complex of passages in *Vita* G serves

---

³¹ As with the antagonism with Apollo, Isis and the Muses figure only in *Vita* G; they are completely absent from the two recensions of *Vita* W (where it is the goddess Tuchē or Philoxenia who rewards Aesop for his piety). Many scholars assume that the Muses are an early element in the tradition, with Isis as a later (perhaps Egyptian) addition: thus Perry 1936.14–15, Nagy 1979. 289–90, Winkler 1985.286, Jedrkiewicz 1989.88–94, Compton 2006.22–23. More recently, scholars have recognized the cultural logic and appropriateness of Isis in this context: thus Dillery 1999.271–80, Finkelpearl 2003, Kamen 2005, Hunter 2007.

³² For προστάτης τοῦ δήμου, cf. Thuc. 3.75, 82, 4.46, 66; Aristoph. *Frogs* 569, *Knights* 1128; Plato *Rep.* 565d; [Arist.] *Ath. Pol.* 2.2, etc.; for other positive or neutral uses of *prostatēs* in the classical period, cf. Aesch. *Suppliants* 963; Hdt. 1.127, 5.23; Eur. *Heracl.* 964, *IA* 373; Xen. *HG* 3.1.3, 5.1.36; Isoc. 4.103; Dem. 9.23, 15.30, 22.78, etc.

³³ For *prostatēs* meaning "administrator" in Egyptian and Near Eastern documentary sources of the second century BCE through the third century CE, cf. *P.Teb.* 81.19, *OGI* 209.4, 531.3, *Ostr.* 412, and many more instances on papyri listed in Preisigke 1931, s.v. προστάτης. Likewise, ὁ μείζων occurs as a title ("headman" or "those in authority") in Egyptian documentary papyri of the third and fourth centuries CE: cf. *P.Oxy.* 1204.17, 1626.5, *P.Lond.* 2.214.22 and see LSJ s.v. μέγας, C.1., Preisigke 1931, s.v. μείζων.

³⁴ Cf. Nagy 1979.283, emphasizing in another context "that the *Life of Aesop* is deeply archaic in content if not in diction."

as a commentary on the nature of slavery and delegated authority, and all of it pertains to oracular Apollo as "overseer of the Muses." By this designation, Aesop implies that it is the Muses who do the real work, while they are abused and exploited by the corrupt overseer Apollo, who is himself merely the slave intermediary of the distant master Zeus. This is a very different—and, ultimately, subversive—version of Apollo's delegated oracular authority. And, as we shall see, the same issues of authority and autonomy that the designation *prostatēs* raises for Apollo will also be prominent in the Aesopic critique of the people of Delphi as the oracular god's servants and representatives.

Indeed, we can appreciate how radical Aesop's fabular critique of oracular Apollo is by comparison with a very different version of the tale narrated by the chorus of Euripides' *Iphigeneia in Tauris*. At the moment Iphigeneia, Orestes, and Pylades depart with the statue of Artemis to the seashore to make their escape from the barbarian land of Tauris and its horrific sacrificial practices, the chorus of Greek slave women give voice to a perfectly constructed hymn to Apollo, detailing his birth on Delos; Leto's transportation of him to Delphi; his killing of the fearsome serpent that guarded the chthonic oracle, and his own accession to the "unlying" oracular throne at the world's navel (*IT* 1234–58). The chorus continue in the song's antistrophe:[35]

> Θέμιν δ' ἐπεὶ Γαῖαν
> παῖδ' ἀπενάσσατο ‹   › ἀπὸ ζαθέων
> χρηστηρίων, νύχια
> Χθὼν ἐτεκνώσατο φάσματ' ὀ‹νείρων›,
> οἳ πόλεσιν μερόπων τά τε πρῶτα
> τά τ' ἔπειθ' ἅ τ' ἔμελλε τυχεῖν
> ὕπνῳ κατὰ δνοφερὰς χαμεύ-
> νας ἔφραζον· Γαῖα δὲ τὰν
> μαντεῖον ἀφείλετο τιμὰν
> Φοῖβον φθόνῳ θυγατρός.
> ταχύπους δ' ἐς Ὄλυμπον ὁρμαθεὶς ἄναξ
> χέρα παιδνὸν ἕλιξεν ἐκ Διὸς θρόνων,
> Πυθίων δόμων χθονίαν ἀφελεῖν μῆνιν θεᾶς.
> γέλασε δ' ὅτι τέκος ἄφαρ ἔβα
> πολύχρυσα θέλων λατρεύματα σχεῖν·
> ἐπὶ δὲ σείσας κόμαν παῦσεν νυχίους ἐνοπάς,
> ὑπὸ δ' ἀλαθοσύναν νυκτωπὸν ἐξεῖλεν βροτῶν,
> καὶ τιμὰς πάλιν θῆκε Λοξίᾳ
> πολυάνορι δ' ἐν ξενόεντι θρόνῳ θάρση βροτοῖς
> θεσφάτων ἀοιδαῖς.
> (Euripides, *IT* 1259–82)

[35] I print the text of Cropp 2000, rather than that of Diggle's (1981) Oxford Classical Text edition because Cropp's textual choices seem to me more cautious and judicious.

But when [Apollo] displaced Themis, child of Earth ... from the holy oracle, Earth bore nocturnal dream-apparitions, which were revealing to the communities of men the first things, and those that came after, and what was going to happen in the future as they slept on dark beds on the ground. And so Earth deprived Phoebus of his mantic honor, out of jealousy on behalf of her daughter. And having set out swiftly for Olympus, the lord wound his child's hand around the throne of Zeus, [supplicating him] to avert the chthonic wrath of the goddess from his Pythian home. And Zeus laughed at how quickly his child had come, eager to get offerings rich in gold (or, eager to get menial/slavish duties rich in gold). And shaking his hair [in assent], [Zeus] stopped the nocturnal declarations and surreptitiously took away the night-faced truth from mortals, and reestablished Loxias's honors and established confidence for mortals in the songs of oracular pronouncements at his throne thronged with many visiting strangers.

This mythological narrative offers striking similarities to Aesop's story—similarities that may thereby support Perry's contention that the fable version, too, was already current in the fifth century BCE.[36] Thus both tales describe a threat posed to Apollo's oracular monopoly from the divine crafting of prophetic dreams that come unmediated to mortals, and their eventual short-circuiting by Zeus himself.[37] But at the same time, the inflection and ideology of these two accounts could not be more different. In its general outlines, the Euripidean choral narrative conforms to a positive pro-Olympian version of a succession myth, whereby the newer male gods Zeus and his son Apollo oppose and ultimately defeat the primordial female power of Earth acting on behalf of her Titaness daughter Themis. In these terms, this mythic narrative resembles other such progressivist accounts of cosmic succession as Zeus's defeat of Typhoeus in Hesiod (*Th.* 820–80), Apollo's slaying of Pytho in the Homeric Hymn, and, of course, the triumph of male Olympians and civic justice over the relentless female Furies of Aeschylus's *Oresteia*.[38] Against this background of triumphalist succession myths, Aesop's fable looks very odd indeed. For here it is not some malevolent older female power who threatens the newborn Apollo's mantic prerogatives, but Zeus himself, intentionally to humble and undermine his arrogant intermediary to mortals. And where the Euripidean hymn emphasizes

---

[36] Thus Adrados 1999.194, 405, 481, 655 treats *Vita* G, ch. 33 as an ancient "fabulization" of Euripides' Delphic myth.

[37] It is not exactly clear how this is imagined to work in the *IT* chorus—whether by the simple suppression of dreams that offer prophetic truth (thus Platnauer 1938.167), or (as Cropp 2000.252 suggests) by the suppression of dreams' explicit "declarations" of prophecy (ἐνοπάς), so that they require interpretation and hence (like Iphigeneia's dream) are susceptible to misinterpretation. Although it makes no difference to my argument, I find Cropp's interpretation the most elegant and economical reading of the Euripidean story in context.

[38] For an excellent structuralist analysis of the *IT* myth read together with other Delphic succession myths, see Sourvinou-Inwood 1991.230–32; for the narrative trajectory of the succession myths in Hesiod's *Theogony* and Aeschylus's *Oresteia*, see also Arthur 1982, Zeitlin 1996.

Apollo's divine birth and genealogical connection to a sublimely Olympian, "Homeric" Zeus, the Aesopic fable version brings all its divine actors unceremoniously down to earth, connecting Zeus and Apollo only as "boss" (ὁ μείζων) and "overseer" (προστάτης) within a kind of cosmic bureaucracy.[39]

Finally, it is Aesop who proves himself the master of prophetic signs in the fable of *Vita* G, since he can differentiate the true and false dreams that appear identical to other mortals. This episode thus initiates a pattern that becomes more prominent later in the *Life*, whereby Aesop successfully interprets prophetic signs and enigmas of ever greater consequence (*Vita* G, chs. 77, 78–80, 81–91).[40] This sequence culminates in the scene in which Aesop wins his freedom from slavery as the precondition for accurately interpreting an ominous bird omen for the entire Samian demos, for which he later consecrates on the spot a shrine to the Muses, but not Apollo (*Vita* G, ch. 100).[41] In this activity, inspired by his patron Muses, Aesop competes directly with the oracular god of Delphi, undermining his claim to a mantic monopoly.

Indeed, in the last act of this oracular drama, Aesop seems, even after his death, to pose a threat to Apollo's mantic authority. For almost immediately after his narration of the fable of the eagle and the dung beetle, which ends with an appeal to Zeus Xenius and Olympius (*Vita* G, ch. 139), Aesop, unable to dissuade the Delphians from their brutal vengeance, curses them and hurls himself off a cliff. At that point (again, only according to *Vita* G), "The Delphians, oppressed by plague, got an oracle *from Zeus* to propitiate the doom of Aesop" (*Vita* G, ch. 142: λοιμῷ δὲ κατασχεθέντες οἱ Δέλφιοι χρησμὸν ἔλαβον παρὰ τοῦ

---

[39] For Apollo's divine birth and genealogical connection to Zeus in Euripides' choral hymn, note especially εὔπαις as the first word of the chorus and τέκος at the moment that Zeus accedes to the younger god's supplication (*IT* 1234, 1274). In spite of this emphasis on genealogy, we may find a quaver of a more negative representation of oracular Apollo in Euripides' phrase πολύχρυσα . . . λατρεύματα. The primary signification of this phrase is "offerings rich in gold," but all the words of the λατρ– family are also strongly associated with slavish or menial labor for pay (see, e.g., Soph. *Women of Trachis* 35, 357, Eur. *Trojan Women* 1106, *IT* 1115, *Ion* 4). Thus this phrase might carry as a secondary resonance Apollo's own "menial duties, rich in gold," referring obliquely to his oracular mediation of Zeus's will to mortals. Such a negative hint would conform well to the ambivalence toward Delphic Apollo that Cropp 2000.39, 248 notes in the chorus and the play generally. Indeed, we might even want to go further and suggest that Euripides' version offers us a mainly positive, pro-Olympian account (appropriately enough for its hymnic form), while slyly evoking something much more like the Aesopic fable of the *Life* by the deployment of the ambiguous and loaded term λατρεύματα (which on one interpretation comes very close to "menial servitude").

[40] I am indebted to an unpublished paper of Tamara Chin, "Aesop the Signifying Monkey" (Chin 1999), for underscoring the prevalence of scenes of signification and interpretation in the *Life*; for this strand in the *Life*, cf. also Ferrari 1997.20–32.

[41] There is a textual corruption here: Aesop either sets *Mnēmosunē* in the middle of the Muses (thus Perry 1952) or he sets up a "*mnēmosunon* of himself" (thus Papathomopoulos 1990/Ferrari 1997). I prefer the latter reading, but it should be acknowledged that both these readings are emendations of a garbled text; what is clear in any case is that Aesop specifically does not include Apollo (thereby provoking his wrath). For detailed discussion of this textual crux, see chapter 4, section I below.

Διὸς ἐξιλάσκεσθαι ‹τὸν› τοῦ Αἰσώπου μόρον). The fact that it is Zeus (perhaps through his shrine at Dodona) who intercedes here with a direct oracular command strikingly conforms to the competition between oracles of Zeus and of Apollo that Catherine Morgan observes for the Greek archaic period. And so it is noteworthy that the later *Vita* W, which consistently suppresses Aesop's hostile and competitive relation with Apollo, here elides also the high god's oracular intervention, indicating only, "The Delphians got an oracle to propitiate the doom of Aesop," without the specification παρὰ τοῦ Διός (*Vita* W, ch. 142).[42]

As with Apollo, so with his Delphic representatives: the many different accounts of Aesop's ill-fated trip to Delphi together constitute a comprehensive critique of the Delphians and their exclusionary, elitist religious practices. To see the positive Olympian version of Delphic ideology, we need only turn again to the *Homeric Hymn to Apollo*. The Hymn closely links Apollo's cult sites of Delos and Delphi and makes it a prominent part of the god's aretalogy that he can effortlessly transform rocky, barren places into rich and flourishing centers by guaranteeing a perennial supply of sacrificial victims. Thus, when Apollo waylays a shipload of Cretan traders to make them his Delphic servants and sacrificial officiants (ὀργιόνας, l. 389) in the second half of the Hymn, the Cretan captain asks with some consternation (ll. 528–30), "And how are we to live now? This we bid you show us. For this land, lovely as it is, is not fruit-bearing, nor broad-pastured, so that we can live well from it and at the same time serve men" (ἀνθρώποισιν ὀπηδεῖν). Apollo, smiling, offers his divine response (ll. 532–37):

νήπιοι ἄνθρωποι δυστλήμονες οἳ μελεδῶνας
βούλεσθ' ἀργαλέους τε πόνους καὶ στείνεα θυμῷ·
ῥηΐδιον ἔπος ὔμμ' ἐρέω καὶ ἐπὶ φρεσὶ θήσω.
δεξιτερῇ μάλ' ἕκαστος ἔχων ἐν χειρὶ μάχαιραν
σφάζειν αἰεὶ μῆλα· τὰ δ' ἄφθονα πάντα παρέσται,
ὅσσα ἐμοί κ' ἀγάγωσι περικλυτὰ φῦλ' ἀνθρώπων·

Foolish mortals, who desire cares difficult to endure, and terrible toils, and distresses for your heart! Easily I will tell you a word and I will put it in your wits. Let each one, holding a sacrificial knife in his right hand, perennially sacrifice sheep. And all these will be present in abundance, as many as the glorious tribes of men bring here for me.

---

[42] The omission of παρὰ τοῦ Διός can be said to encourage the assumption that Delphi is the source of the oracle; cf. Nagy 1979.302: "*Surely* the pestilence that descends upon the Delphians after Aesop's death is ordained by Apollo himself, *and it is his Oracle* that commands the Delphians to propitiate Aesop by worshiping him as a cult hero" (emphasis added). In this instance, Nagy reenacts *Vita* W's elision of Zeus's oracular intervention, in order to enlist Apollo as a partially beneficent force and thus support his model of mythic antagonism linked with ritual symbiosis. Still, it bears emphasizing that *Vita* G explicitly pits Zeus's oracular authority against Apollo's in this instance. For arguments supporting *Vita* G's version as older, see Perry 1936.16, Wiechers 1961.13–14, Jouanno 2006.49–50.

This vision of effortless prosperity from the relentless wielding of the sacrificial knife echoes the terms of Leto's offer to the skittish island of Delos in the first half of the Hymn (ll. 51–60):

> Δῆλ' εἰ γάρ κ' ἐθέλοις ἕδος ἔμμεναι υἷος ἐμοῖο
> Φοίβου Ἀπόλλωνος, θέσθαι τ' ἔνι πίονα νηόν·
> ἄλλος δ' οὔ τις σεῖό ποθ' ἅψεται, οὐδέ σε λήσει,
> οὐδ' εὔβων σέ γ' ἔσεσθαι ὀΐομαι οὔτ' εὔμηλον,
> οὐδὲ τρύγην οἴσεις, οὔτ' ἄρ φυτὰ μυρία φύσεις.
> αἰ δέ κ' Ἀπόλλωνος ἑκαέργου νηὸν ἔχῃσθα,
> ἄνθρωποί τοι πάντες ἀγινήσουσ' ἑκατόμβας
> ἐνθάδ' ἀγειρόμενοι, κνίση δέ τοι ἄσπετος αἰεὶ
> δημοῦ ἀναΐξει, βοσκήσεις θ' οἵ κέ σ' ἔχωσι
> χειρὸς ἀπ' ἀλλοτρίης, ἐπεὶ οὔ τοι πῖαρ ὑπ' οὔδας.

Perhaps, O Delos, you would be willing to be the seat of my son Phoebus Apollo, and he would establish his rich temple here? But no other [god] will ever fasten on to you nor will it escape your notice, since I do not think that you will be good for oxen or for sheep, nor will you bear grain, nor will you ever grow innumerable plants. But if you hold a temple of the far-worker Apollo, all men will lead hecatombs for you, gathering here, and the unquenchable savor of fat will always leap up for you, and you will feed whoever holds you from another's hand, since you do not have rich soil.

Within the normative Olympian discourse of the Hymn, to feed "from another's hand" (χειρὸς ἀπ' ἀλλοτρίης) is the ultimate affirmation of Apollo's power and the magical abundance he bestows.

But in the topsy-turvy world of Aesop, "to feed from another's hand"—in parasitic dependence on sacrificial offerings—represents an indictment of the authority and autonomy of the Delphians as Apollo's representatives. Over and over again, the Aesopic critique demystifies the august status of the Delphians by reimagining the Cretan captain's ἀνθρώποισιν ὀπηδεῖν and Leto's χειρὸς ἀπ' ἀλλοτρίης in the most coarsely bodily and literal terms possible. Intriguingly, the two halves of this critique (corresponding to ἀνθρώποισιν ὀπηδεῖν and χειρὸς ἀπ' ἀλλοτρίης, respectively) occur in complementary distribution within the Aesop tradition. In the later full-scale *Lives* of Aesop, the emphasis falls on the Delphians as "slaves of all the Greeks," whereas fragments of what seems to be an older tradition highlight the Delphians' savage and self-serving sacrificial practices.[43] And yet, I would contend, these two aspects together

---

[43] This pattern of complementary distribution is noticed by Zeitz 1936.249–50, who observes that none of the full-scale versions of the *Life* contains any explicit reference to unusual Delphic sacrificial practices, but that those references are preserved only in a tradition that goes back to the Hellenistic period (as preserved in Call. *Iambi*, Schol. *ad* Aristoph. *Wasps*, P.Oxy. 1800); cf. Ferrari 1997.8–11. Based on this observation, Zeitz assumes that Aesop's sacrificial critique is a later "scholarly" accretion, while the version of the story in the *Life* preserves the "original" popular tradition.

limn a coherent critique of Delphic greed, servile dependence on pilgrims, and inequitable sacrificial exactions—a cluster that may date back to the classical period.

Let me consider each of these in turn. In *Vitae* G and W, as scholars have noted, Aesop plays the role of a traveling rhetor or sophist of the Roman imperial period, touring the Greek cities "giving displays of his wisdom and education" (περιερχόμενος δὲ τὰς λοιπὰς πόλεις ἐπεδείκνυτο τὴν ἑαυτοῦ σοφίαν καὶ παιδείαν, *Vita* G, ch. 124).[44] In that capacity, he comes to Delphi and offers performances of his verbal skills there as well. But here, we're told, the mob of Delphians "enjoyed listening to him, but offered him nothing" (*Vita* G, ch. 124; cf. *Vita* W, "gave him no honor"). Aesop, apparently annoyed at their stinginess, jokingly compares the pale-faced Delphians to vegetables by quoting the famous line from *Iliad* 6, οἵη περ φύλλων γενεή, τοίη δὲ καὶ ἀνδρῶν (only in *Vita* G, ch. 124). Then, still annoyed at the Delphians, Aesop scathingly compares them to driftwood, which looks like something from a distance, but turns out to be worthless when you get closer to it (*Vitae* G + W, ch. 125).

Thus far, Aesop's actions and reactions are perfectly comprehensible within the milieu of the Roman imperial education and rhetorical system I've proposed as a plausible context for the composition of *Vita* G (whose author/redactor can't resist showing off the witty use he can make of a learned Homeric quotation).[45] In these terms, the *Life* offers us a comic or parodic narrative based on what must have been a frequent occurrence in the period—a new sophist comes to town, offers performances, but receives no material remuneration or patronage. And thus far, the setting could be any Greek-speaking city of the Roman imperial period. But, of course, tradition going all the way back to the fifth century BCE requires that Aesop meet his end at Delphi, and as the story progresses, there is a strange surcharge or surplus to Aesop's abuse of the Delphians that goes far beyond what would be necessary to critique their nonreciprocation of a traveling sophist. And it is here that I would locate the

---

Zeitz's argument here is based on his belief in a sixth- or fifth-century written *Volksbuch* of the *Life of Aesop* whose lineaments are still preserved in *Vita* W and the Planudean *Life*. Since more recent scholarship has thoroughly debunked the theory of the *Volksbuch* (see Introduction, pp. 19–20), I would precisely invert Zeitz's account of what is early and what is late in the tradition. Thus Zeitz's "scholarly" or "learned tradition" dating back at least to the Hellenistic period could be seen to preserve the lineaments of an older critique of distinctive Delphic sacrificial practices (as Callimachus and other Hellenistic scholars often did record and preserve local, civic traditions, practices, and myths), while it is not at all surprising that the full-scale *Lives*, circulating for centuries through a wide geographic area, would over time come to mute or adapt the critique of these same distinctive practices. (For an analysis of the complementary distribution of the sources similar to that offered here, see Ferrari 1997.10–11.)

[44] For Aesop as a typical Roman imperial sophist or rhetor on a grand tour, see Ferrari 1997.7, Holzberg 2002.77, Avlamis 2010b.

[45] For this as a plausible milieu for the composition of *Vita* G, see Jedrkiewicz 1989.177–82, Hopkins 1993.11, Jouanno 2006.14, and introduction pp. 12, 38, 42.

residue of an older tradition whereby Aesop gives voice to a popular civic critique of Delphi and Delphic religious practices.

For Aesop's most often reiterated abuse of the Delphians in the *Life* is that they are "the slaves of all the Greeks" (*Vitae* G + W, chs. 126, 140). He first offers this abuse immediately after the driftwood image, provocatively concluding that the Delphians "do nothing unworthy of their ancestors" (*Vitae* G + W, ch. 125).[46] Predictably enough, the Delphians take the bait, asking, "Who were our ancestors?" and Aesop responds (*Vita* G, ch. 126):

> "Slaves—if you don't know it, learn. The Greeks had an ancient custom that, whenever they take a city, they send a tenth share of the spoils to Apollo, for example, ten from a hundred oxen, from goats the same, and from the rest the same—from money, from men, from women. Sprung from these, you are stingy/illiberal/unfree (ἀνελεύθεροι), like men in bondage. For being from that source, you are established as the slaves of all the Greeks." And, saying these things, he prepared for departure.

Aesop's "ancient custom" in fact refers to a practice known—and threatened—in fifth- and fourth-century Greece: the consecration and destruction of a city with the dedication of a tithe to Pythian Apollo. H. W. Parke, who collects all ancient references to the practice, observes that the only known historical instance of its being enacted was against the city of Crisa in the First Sacred War (ca. 590 BCE), but he notes that the threat of Apolline tithing was included in the oath sworn by the Greek allies before the Battle of Plataea (against states that Medized) and may also have figured in the debate of Sparta and her allies about the fate of Athens in 404 BCE. Parke demonstrates that the Plataea Oath's pledge to consecrate and tithe Medizing states was a very prominent theme in fourth-century Athenian public rhetoric, when Athens found herself again allied with Sparta against a newly powerful Thebes, but notes that the religious concept of tithing pretty much disappeared after Alexander's conquest.[47]

Anton Wiechers has taken Aesop's reference here as a dim historical memory of the actual events of the First Sacred War, but such an interpretation seems overly specific in light of Parke's discussion.[48] For Parke's survey establishes that the concept of Apolline tithing (even if not the reality) figured prominently in several cities throughout the fifth and fourth centuries but not later—thus he establishes that the kernel of this Aesopic tradition is ancient, without its necessarily being narrowly connected with the First Sacred War. Wiechers's account also seems historically naive insofar as it in no way motivates the centuries-long preservation of this historical memory in the Aesop tradition. In contrast to Wiechers, I suggest that this element in the Aesopic story serves not to memo-

---

[46] Even this line plays on the standard formulae for epideictic eulogy of a community as it would have been purveyed by traveling rhetors and sophists; cf. the topics recommended by Menander Rhetor for praise of cities, including praise of their origins, foundations, founders, etc. (Treatise I.353–59 in Russell and Wilson 1981).

[47] Parke 1948.

[48] Wiechers 1961.7–30.

rialize the Delphians' real *origin* in some dim past, but to comment critically on their slavish or stingy *behavior* in the present. Thus, from a first- or second-century CE perspective, the "punch line" of this little display of erudition about an "ancient custom" inheres in the multiple meanings of the single word ἀνελεύθεροι, which signifies "illiberal," "niggardly," or "stingy" in money matters, but is here literalized to mean "servile."[49] This adjective implies that the Delphians' own behavior—their refusal to give Aesop anything for his displays of verbal prowess—is immanent proof of their degraded descent. But this implication is, in a sense, the creative reuse by the G author/redactor of older traditional material that carries with it the resonance of an additional pointed critique of the Delphians as "slaves of all the Greeks." For, after all, a negative or parodic version of the Delphians' special claim to authority over the temple of Apollo and its oracle is that they act as servants of all the Greeks, engage in menial labor, and take pay for doing so. At the same time, starting from a line that promises conventional praise of noble ancestry ("You do nothing unworthy of your ancestors"), Aesop reduces the Delphians to war-captives of all the Greeks, while he pointedly puts them on the same level as the sacrificial animals from which they make their living.

Thus Aesop's abuse in the *Life* highlights the Delphians' dependency as "servants" to visiting pilgrims. Other older traditions preserve a more explicit and specific critique of Delphic sacrificial practices. In these other traditions, Aesop savagely demystifies the sacrificial code to expose the Delphians as mere beggars and scavengers. We find the elaboration of this latter critique preserved in the Scholia to Aristophanes (*ad Wasps* 1446 = Perry *Test.* 21):

ὅν [sc. Αἴσωπον] φασιν ἐλθόντα ποτὲ εἰς τοὺς Δελφοὺς ἀποσκῶψαι αὐτοὺς ὅτι μὴ ἔχοιεν γῆν ἀφ' ἧς ἐργαζόμενοι διατρέφοιντο, ἀλλὰ περιμένοιεν ἀπὸ τῶν θεοῦ θυμάτων διαζῆν. οἱ δὲ Δελφοὶ χαλεπήναντες φιάλην ἱερὰν τοῖς Αἰσώπου σκεύεσιν ὑπέβαλον. ὁ μὲν δὴ οὐκ εἰδὼς τὴν ἐς Φωκίδα φέρουσαν ὥρμησεν ὁδόν. οἱ δὲ ἐπιδραμόντες καὶ φωράσαντες ἱεροσυλίας αὐτοῦ κατηγόρουν.

They say that Aesop, when he came once to Delphi, jeered at the Delphians because they did not have land from which they could support themselves by agricultural labor, but instead they waited around to make their living from the sacrifices of the god. And the Delphians, annoyed, secreted a sacred phiale in Aesop's luggage. And he—of course not knowing—set out on the road leading to Phocis, but [the Delphians] ran after him and, catching him red-handed, accused him of *hierosulia*.

Precisely the terms valorized by the Homeric Hymn—miraculous prosperity from sacrifice even in the most barren setting—are here viciously lampooned. The Delphians, instead of being noble autonomous farmers (the Greek ideal),

---

[49] For ἀνελεύθερος meaning "cheap, niggardly," see Aristoph. *Wealth* 591, Arist. *NE* 1107b13, 1122a5; for the meaning "mean" or "slavish," see Lysias 10.2, Plato *Tht.* 182c, Arist. *NE* 1121b33, *Pol.* 1336a29. ἀνελεύθεροι here is Perry's emendation for *Vita* G's ἀπελεύθεροι ("freedmen"), based on the text of *Vita* W.

are reduced in Aesop's rendering to beggars or scavengers living off scraps of sacrificial meat.[50]

Yet another version of the Delphians' sacrificial greed is preserved in a second-century CE papyrus that contains a brief *Life of Aesop* (*P.Oxy*. 1800 = Perry *Test.* 25):

ἐπὰν [εἰσέ]λθῃ τ[ις] τῷ θεῷ θυσιάσ[ων ο]ἱ Δελφ[ο]ὶ περ[ι]εστήκασι τὸν βωμ[ὸ]ν ὑφ' ἑαυτοῖς μαχαίρας κ[ο]μίζοντες, σφαγιασαμένου δὲ τοῦ ἱερείου [sic, l. ἱερέως] καὶ δείραντος τὸ ἱερεῖον καὶ τὰ σπλάγχνα περιεξελομένου, οἱ περιεστῶτες ἕκαστος ἣν ἂν ἰσχύσῃ μοῖραν ἀποτεμνόμενος ἄπεισιν, ὡς πολλάκις τὸν θυσιάσαντα αὐτὸν ἄμοιρ[ο]ν ἀπι[έ]ναι. τοῦτο οὖν Αἴ[σ]ωπ[ο]ς Δελφοὺς ὀνιδ[ί]ζων ἐπέσκωψεν, ἐφ' οἷς διοργισθέντες οἱ πολλοὶ λίθοις αὐτὸν βάλλοντες κατὰ κρημνοῦ ἔωσαν. μετ' οὐ πολὺ δὲ λοιμικὸν πάθος ἐπέσκηψε τῇ πόλει, χρηστηριαζομένοις δ' αὐτοῖς ὁ θεὸς ἀνεῖπεν οὐ πρότερον [λήξ]ειν τὴν νόσ[ον μέ]χρις [ἂν Α]ἴσωπον ἐξι[λάσκωντ]αι. οἱ δὲ περιτει[χίσ]αντες τὸν τόπον [ἐν ᾧ κ]ατέπεσεν βωμὸ[ν θ' ἱ]δ[ρυσά]μενοι λυτήρ[ι]-ο[ν] τῆς νόσου, ὡς ἥρῳ θ[υσίας] προ[σ]ήνεγκαν.

Whenever someone comes to sacrifice to the god, the Delphians stand around the altar, each one carrying a sacrificial knife concealed on his person. And when the priest has slain the victim and skinned it and removed [and apportioned] the innards, each of those standing around hacks off whatever share he can and departs, so that, on many occasions, the sacrificer himself departs without any share at all. Censuring this custom, Aesop mocked the Delphians, and the masses, enraged on account of this, stoned him and thrust him off a cliff. And not much later, the experience of plague swept down on the city, and to them, consulting the oracle, the god declared that the disease would not cease until they propitiated Aesop. So, having walled round the place at which he fell and having established an altar to deliver them from disease, they brought sacrifices to him as a hero.[51]

---

[50] As Ferrari 1997.11 points out, even though Aesop's abuse of the Delphians in the *Life* nowhere explicitly articulates this critique of their sacrificial livelihood, it is implicit in Aesop's mocking citation of *Il.* 6.146. For Aesop's sneer that the Delphians are the "same color as vegetables" implies that they are pale and pasty because they do not earn their living by agricultural labor. For a similar critique of the Delphians dating to the second century CE, see Lucian *Phalaris* II.8. In this hilarious, slyly parodic rhetorical set piece, Lucian imagines a speech delivered by an unnamed citizen to the whole Delphian demos, arguing that the Delphians should accept the tyrant Phalaris's offer of his notorious bronze bull as a dedication to Delphic Apollo. Along the way, the speaker urges the Delphians to be honest and realistic about their own means of livelihood: "That we live on crags and cultivate rocks is something we need not wait for Homer to tell us—anyone can see it for himself. As far as the land is concerned, we should always be cheek by jowl with starvation: the temple, the god, the oracle, the sacrificers and the worshippers—these are the grain-lands of Delphi, these are our revenue, these are the sources of our prosperity and of our subsistence. We should speak the truth among ourselves, at any rate!" (trans. Harmon 1961).

[51] I translate Perry's supplement λυτήρ[ι]ο[ν] instead of Grenfell and Hunt's λυτηρ[ί]ο[υς] (*P.Oxy* vol. XV, p. 140) in the last sentence (thus "an altar to deliver them from disease" instead of "sacrifices to deliver them from disease"). For the oldest preserved version of this story, cf. Call. *Iambi* fr. 191 Pfeiffer, ll. 26–28 with Schol. *ad loc.* (*PSI* 1094 = Perry *Test.* 26). For an argument that *P.Oxy*.

In place of the sacred regulations of the Delphic convention with Sciathos, decorously allotting the Delphians extra shares "on the sacrificial table," the Aesopic critique represents the orderly process of sacrifice degenerating into a free-for-all because of the literal (and violent) self-serving of the Delphians present. In this limit vision, sacrifice, the ultimate model of civic order, descends into savage chaos, as the Delphians themselves metamorphose from participants in a sacrificial community into ravenous and solitary beasts or brigands.[52]

In fact, we find striking parallels for many of the terms of these two different traditions of Aesopic critique (Delphic greed, slavish behavior, and problematic sacrifice) combined in texts of the archaic and classical periods. Even the *Homeric Hymn to Hermes* may reflect a twinge of ambivalence toward the Delphic god himself, since it repeatedly (if comically) refers to Apollo's greed for booty as a familiar feature of his character. Thus, when Apollo first arrives on Olympus clutching the infant Hermes, Zeus jokingly refers to Hermes as Apollo's "plentiful booty" (μενοεικέα ληῖδ', l. 330), and Apollo responds (a bit defensively), "Though you abuse me that I alone am fond of booty..." (φιλολήϊος, l. 335).[53] Later, when the two gods get down to negotiating the actual division of *timai* (Apollo at this point mollified by Hermes' gift of the lyre), Hermes tells Apollo he will take the other god's herds and increase them. As he observes wryly to his older brother in this context, "Nor is it fitting for you to be violently angry, though you are always out for gain" (κερδαλέον περ ἐόντα, ll. 494–95). Finally, the *Homeric Hymn to Hermes* puts in the mouth of Apollo himself the fundamental rule of the Delphic economy; describing the workings of his oracle, Apollo explains that some inquirers will get the illumination they seek, while "another, trusting to vain bird omens ... will go a fruitless road, but I would still receive his gifts" (ἐγὼ δέ κε δῶρα δεχοίμην, ll. 543–49).[54]

1800 represents a learned anthology of brief *Bioi* that probably dates back to the Hellenistic period, see Lamedica 1985, esp. 57–58 on the Aesop entry.

[52] Nagy 1979.126 offers a similar reading of this narrative: "the *jest* may represent the ritual practice as if it really were greedy behavior," although Nagy then backs down from this reading by qualifying, "but even the jesting itself may have had a formalized ritual basis."

[53] Cf. Bielohlawek 1930.209.

[54] Again, this is not to agree with Brown 1947.66–132, who sees in the *Homeric Hymn to Hermes* a genuinely subversive document that challenges aristocratic, Apolline values. Brown can finesse such a reading only by athetizing the Hymn's last seventy lines (Brown 1947.141–47). I would instead follow Clay 1989.95–151 on the Hymn's unity and participation in a coherent Panhellenic, pro-Olympian ideology that allows references to Delphic Apollo's problematic greed but ultimately subsumes them in its final reconciliation.

We might also note Apollo's choice of Cretan traders to be his Delphic functionaries in the *Homeric Hymn to Apollo* (ll. 388–99). Modern scholarly discussion tends to focus on the religious or political significance of their being Cretans (thus, for example, Allen, Halliday, and Sikes 1936.253; Morgan 1990.144–46). But we should perhaps also ask why it is felt to be appropriate for them to be *traders* (l. 397)—and especially why Apollo himself, at the moment of waylaying them, should ask if they are ληϊστῆρες, "pirates" out for booty (ll. 453–55). This may represent an implicit

Again, the classical critique extends from Apollo to the entire demos of Delphians as his representatives, most prominently in the public, civic genres of Old Comedy and satyr play. Thus, in a fragment of Aristophanes preserved by Athenaeus, Apollo himself is invoked as "you who sharpen the most sacrificial knives of the Delphians, O Phoebus, and teach your servants first of all . . ." (ἀλλ᾿ ὦ Δελφῶν πλείστας ἀκονῶν Φοῖβε μαχαίρας καὶ προδιδάσκων τοὺς σοὺς προπόλους, Aristophanes fr. 705 KA *ap.* Athen. 4.173d).[55] Other passages of abuse preserved by Athenaeus in the same context tend to link together Apollo's cult centers of Delphi and Delos (much as the *Homeric Hymn to Apollo* itself does, but with a very different inflection). Athenaeus tells us, "When Polycraton, the son of Crithon of Rhenea, brought suit against the Delians, he did not call them that, but brought charges against 'the commonality of Table Dodgers'" (τὸ κοινὸν τῶν Ἐλεοδυτῶν, Athen. 4.173b). Both Aristophanes' fragment and Polycraton's forensic abuse exploit the same style of demystifying critique we have already seen in the *Life of Aesop* traditions. For both transform the mystified practices of sacrifice into the debased and banausic labor of butchers and table-attendants; as Athenaeus glosses the term *Eleodutai*: "A law of the Amphictyons bids '*Eleodutai*' to furnish water, signifying table-makers and other such servants" (καὶ ὁ τῶν Ἀμφικτυόνων δὲ νόμος κελεύει ὕδωρ παρέχειν ἐλεοδύτας, τοὺς τραπεζοποιοὺς καὶ τοὺς τοιούτους διακόνους σημαίνων; Athen. 4.173b). In like manner, Athenaeus tells us that the fifth-century BCE playwright Achaeus of Eretria, in his satyr play *Alcmeon*, "calls the Delphians spiced-gravy-makers" (καρυκκοποιούς) and has his chorus of satyrs "abuse the Delphians for their assiduous cultivation of sacrifices and feasts" (ἐπισκώπτουσι γὰρ οἱ σάτυροι τοὺς Δελφοὺς ὡς περὶ τὰς θυσίας καὶ τὰς θοίνας διατρίβοντας; Athen. 4. 173c–e). The fact that these lampoons of Delphic and Delian sacrificial greed occur in Old Comedy, satyr play, and law-court speeches may confirm my contention that they participate in a popular, polis-based critique of elitist practices at Apollo's interstate sanctuaries. At the same time, these ironic commentaries on the sacrificial greed of Apollo and his human representatives make only fleeting appearances in the "public transcript" (as far as we can tell). It is as if a full-throated critique of Delphic practices requires the free-floating and anonymous tradition of stories about Aesop, in which the low fabulist provides a perfect mask or alibi for tellers of tales throughout the Greek cities who want to voice their resistance to Delphi.

---

acknowledgment—even within the high tradition—that the activities of the Delphians are somehow akin to those of brigands or pirates.

[55] "Teach your servants first of all . . ." what? Note προδιδάσκων. The humor of this fragment works by the excessive embodiment and banausic activity of the god himself, as the one who whets or sharpens (ἀκονῶν) the knives of the Delphian sacrificers/butchers.

III. Neoptolemus and Aesop: Sacrifice, Hero Cult, and Competitive Scapegoating

It is my claim, then, that the various different traditions of Aesop's misadventures at Delphi preserve a historically specific, popular or civic critique of a unique constellation of practices at Apollo's sanctuary. But any attempt to offer a coherent reading of Aesop's Delphic adventures must also account for the striking similarities that exist between legends of Aesop and traditions of the death of Neoptolemus at Delphi. Such an argument, in turn, requires a critical reevaluation of the theories of Anton Wiechers and Gregory Nagy. Wiechers in 1961 was the first scholar to offer sustained arguments for a connection between the story of Aesop at Delphi and that of Neoptolemus, noting the structural similarities of the two narratives.[56] Wiechers argued that, besides preserving dim historical reminiscences of the First Sacred War, the *Life of Aesop* offered a mythological aetiology for a Delphic *pharmakos* ritual (otherwise entirely unattested for Delphi in the historical period), while the similarities between Aesop's story and Neoptolemus's prove that the latter's misadventures at Delphi also provide a mythological aetiology for the same (unattested) *pharmakos* ritual at Delphi. Gregory Nagy in turn accepted Wiechers's arguments for deeply archaic reminiscences of the First Sacred War and of *pharmakos* ritual in the two narrative traditions, and added the notion that both Neoptolemus and Aesop were also recipients of hero cult (the former as a warrior, the latter as a "poet"), locked in the same relationship of "ritual antagonism" with the god of Delphi. As Nagy explains, "antagonism between hero and god in myth corresponds to the ritual requirements of symbiosis between hero and god in cult."[57]

Both Wiechers's and Nagy's theories remain influential in the scholarship.[58] Indeed, Nagy's treatment of Aesop is probably the most ambitious and significant modern attempt to offer a coherent reading of Aesop at Delphi, and as such I am much indebted to it. At the same time, I have significant methodological disagreements with both Wiechers and Nagy, which I would sum up by saying that their method sees only similarities; this style of reading does not distinguish—and therefore cannot account for—differences of various sorts:

---

[56] Wiechers 1961.31–49; Perry in his review of Wiechers's monograph (1962b.621) emphasizes the originality and significance of the connection Wiechers makes between the two traditions.

[57] Nagy 1979.118–41, 279–97 (quotation taken from 121). Cf. Jedrkiewicz 1989.94–104, who argues for a similar model without reference to Nagy.

[58] Thus versions of these arguments are accepted (or at least unquestioned) by Adrados 1979, 1999.277, 280–81; West 1984.117, 124; Winkler 1985.286–88; Ogden 1997.38–40; duBois 2003.174; Finkelpearl 2003; Compton 2006.19–40; for an explicit challenge to these theories, see Rosen 2007.98–104.

1. Ritual differences between *pharmakos* and hero cult. It bears emphasizing that *pharmakos* ritual and hero cult are two completely different phenomena in Greek religion, which Wiechers's analysis collapses. As Walter Burkert has noted, critiquing Wiechers and others, it is a misnomer to call every ritual killing a *pharmakos* rite. Burkert particularly objects to the application of the *pharmakos* pattern to the death of Neoptolemus at Delphi (since there is plenty of ancient evidence that Neoptolemus became a cult hero at Delphi).[59] Indeed, I would go a step further and suggest that we might think of *pharmakos* and hero cult as two ends of a spectrum available to the Greeks for representing the possible outcome of a conflict involving a problematic figure. Thus I have argued that we find in the poetry of Alcaeus an attempt to transform his political enemy Pittacus into a *pharmakos*—an attempt that rebounds on the poet himself, while the demos of Mytilene chooses to honor Pittacus as a cult hero instead.[60]

2. Differences of genre, level of style, and literary decorum. It is symptomatic in this respect that Nagy (1979) consistently refers to Aesop as a "poet" or "blame poet," even though it seems that Aesop's defining characteristic (at least in the fifth century; cf. Hdt. 2.134.4) is that he is a maker of *prose* fables (*logopoios*).[61] In contrast, I would contend that it is significant that the traditions of the death of Neoptolemus mainly occur in high poetic genres (epinician, paean, tragedy), while traditions about Aesop mainly occur in low poetic genres (Old Comedy, Callimachus's *Iambi*) and prose.[62]

3. Political/historical difference. If we think of religion as a "cultural system," in any period that system is being used and adapted for the particular needs of

---

[59] Burkert 1966.439n. 2. This criticism applies a fortiori to Compton 2006, who consistently conflates or collapses the categories of *pharmakos* and cult hero by assimilating a whole set of mythological figures (e.g., Androgeos, Codrus, the Aglaurids) to *pharmakoi* although they are never designated as such in their respective myths. It might be more productive to follow Jedrkiewicz's (1989.105–7) line of argument: Jedrkiewicz thinks in terms of elements drawn at will from different ritual scenarios and combined in the *Life of Aesop* traditions (this is related to difference no. 3, discussed in text). Cf. Rothwell 1995.234n. 5: "the ancient accounts of the murder of Aesop have been assimilated to (or fabricated from) myths of atonement in which a *pharmakos* was killed," and Suárez de la Torre 1997.163.

[60] See Kurke 1994, based partly on Burnett 1983.159–63 for the suggestion that Alcaeus attempts to transform Pittacus into a monstrous outcast by the conjuring power of his own poetry. Cf. the analogous binary of king and *pharmakos* proposed by Vernant 1988.128–35; Vernant argues that the narrative trajectory of the *Oedipus Tyrannus* depends on a preexistent cultural pattern that opposes the king at the top of the social hierarchy to the *pharmakos* at the bottom (with Oedipus moving from one status to the other in the course of the play). For the mythic binary king-*pharmakos*, see also Bremmer 1983.303–7.

[61] Nagy 1979.281–83. In contrast, Nagy 1990b does not insist on Aesop as a "poet" but instead links the figure of Aesop closely with Herodotus, since both are "makers of prose" (*logopoioi* or *logioi*). For extensive discussion and critique of Nagy 1990b, see chapters 10 and 11 below.

[62] Pherecydes *FGrH* 3 F 64a, telling a version of the Neoptolemus story, is an exception, but it could be argued that, as a mythographer, he aims to achieve the prestige of poetry for his prose accounts. On the prevalence of Aesop traditions and fables in low genres, see Lasserre 1984, Rothwell 1995.

the culture at that point. And in general, I would contend, such well-known cultural systems as hero cult or *pharmakos* ritual are available for different competing or contested appropriations by different groups or ideological positions within the culture. Nagy's model of a myth-ritual complex does not allow for either diachronic or synchronic change, development, or contestation. That is to say, did everyone believe in god-hero antagonism in just the same way in every period? Or should we instead conceptualize the stories of the interaction of different figures with Apollo at Delphi as available for competing appropriations at the same time and at different times?[63]

I would like to offer an alternative account of Neoptolemus and Aesop that acknowledges and combines differences (1), (2), and (3), and that is predicated on the relation of parody or pastiche to a parodied "original." Since parody and pastiche are inherently parasitic forms, simply cataloging similar elements will never reveal the relation of "original" to parodic "imitation" or "replay." (It's as if an anthropological observer studying the twenty-first century were to take a real news broadcast and *Saturday Night Live*'s "Weekend Update" together as an analytical set from which to deduce the proper content of American news programs.) I would suggest that this is precisely the relation between the Neoptolemus tradition and the Aesop tradition.

Thus we might think of the Neoptolemus tradition as the official Delphic (or Amphictyonic) line: Neoptolemus's death serves as the aetiology for peculiar Delphic sacrificial practices, while the Aesop tradition offers a popular parodic critique thereof.[64] Given the possibility of this relation, it is essential not to merge the two traditions together, using elements of the Aesop tradition to supplement and flesh out the story of Neoptolemus, especially in the domain of sacrificial practice. Yet scholars routinely use the text of *P.Oxy.* 1800, with its vivid depiction of sacrifice descending into bestial violence, to gloss much earlier, high poetic accounts of the death of Neoptolemus.[65] I would contend that this merging of traditions is misleading, and we must first consider the two separately. If we focus solely on the earliest preserved accounts of the death of Neoptolemus in Pindar's Sixth *Paean* and Seventh *Nemean*, we may be able to develop a clearer account of what needs and interests this particular narrative served.

Neither Pindaric poem is securely dated, though many scholars place both in Pindar's mature period on the basis of style.[66] What we have preserved of the

---

[63] Thus, in contrast to Nagy, see Kowalzig 2007.197–201 for an exemplary reading of complex political negotiations transacted through shifting mythological and ritual relations between Apollo and Neoptolemus at Delphi.

[64] On the Neoptolemus tradition as an aetiology for Delphic sacrificial practice, see Burkert 1983.118–20, followed by Nagy 1979.126. Cf. Currie 2005.301–3, 330; Kowalzig 2007.192–200.

[65] See, e.g., Burkert 1966.439–40, 1983.118–19; Nagy 1979.123–26; Currie 2005.301n. 27.

[66] Thus Radt 1958.90–93, Rutherford 2001.331. There is of course an immense scholarly literature on *Paean* 6, *Nemean* 7, and their relation to each other. Since Pindar's poetry is not the main

myth of *Paean* 6 tells first of Achilles slain by Apollo in the "mortal form/body of Paris" (*Paean* 6.79–86), then of Neoptolemus:[67]

σχεδὸν δ[ὲ Το]μάρου Μολοσσίδα γαῖαν
ἐξίκετ᾽ οὐδ᾽ [ἀ]νέμους ἔ[λ]α[θ]εν
οὐδὲ τὸν [ε]ὐρυφαρέτραν ἑκαβόλον·
   ὤ[μο]σε [γὰρ θ]εός,
γέ[ρον]θ᾽ ὅ[τι] Πρίαμον
π[ρ]ὸς ἑρκεῖον ἤναρε βωμὸν ἐ[π-
   εν]θορόντα, μή νιν εὔφρον᾽ ἐς οἶ[κ]ον
μ]ήτ᾽ ἐπὶ γῆρας ἱξέ-
   μεν βίου· ἀμφιπόλοις δὲ
   κ]υριᾶν περὶ τιμᾶν
δηρι]αζόμενον κτάνεν
‹ἐν› τεμέ]νεϊ φίλῳ γᾶς παρ᾽ ὀμφαλὸν εὐρύν.
   ‹ἰὴ› ἰῆτε νῦν, μέτρα παιηό-
   ν]ων ἰῆτε, νέοι.
(*Paean* 6.109–22)

And he reached the Molossian land near Tomarus, but he did not escape the winds nor the broad-quivered far-darter. For the god swore, because he had slain the old man Priam as he leapt up on his household altar, that he would not reach his kindly house nor come to old age. But as he was fighting with servants over legitimate (or abundant) honors in the god's own sacred precinct beside the broad navel of the earth, he killed him. Now sound the *iē*-cry, young men, the measures of paeans.

This version clearly represents Delphic orthodoxy, with the god's killing of Neoptolemus closing the epode and initiating the "*iē Paean*" cry, as if Neoptolemus himself were an allomorph of Apollo's ancient foe, the primordial dragon Pytho.[68]

In this context, it is worth attending to Pindar's precise language in narrating the sacrificial quarrel: Apollo killed Neoptolemus, he says, as he was "fighting with his servants over legitimate (or abundant) honors."[69] As often, Pindar's

---

focus of this discussion, I will not encumber the argument with full citation of that scholarly literature; for exhaustive treatment of *Paean* 6, with some glances at *Nemean* 7 and full bibliography, see Kurke 2005. For more recent discussions, see Burnett 2005.179–202, Currie 2005.296–343, Kowalzig 2007.181–223.

[67] For the text of *Paean* 6, I follow Rutherford 2001.298–302 (except where otherwise noted), and I print a simplified text that does not register all the gaps and uncertainties of the papyrus where these do not materially affect my argument.

[68] Cf. Nagy 1979.121; and specifically on the refrain assimilating Neoptolemus to Pytho, see Rutherford 1991.7–8, 2001.319–20.

[69] Although it makes no substantial difference to my argument, I prefer κυριᾶν (Housman's emendation, accepted by Snell–Maehler), to Rutherford's μυριᾶν; for discussion, see Kurke 2005.100n. 58.

language is as vague and abstract as it could possibly be.[70] No mention of meat or sacrificial knives; instead, the act of sacrifice is immediately and unproblematically sublimated into that which it symbolizes—the proper allotment of honors or prerogatives between gods and men.

Indeed, this extremely general, abstract language exposes the larger issue between Neoptolemus and Apollo as one of boundaries: the proper respect for divine space, altars, divine prerogatives, the very boundary between divine and mortal, which Neoptolemus consistently threatens and Apollo consistently defends. Thus Neoptolemus had ruthlessly slain the old man Priam, though he had taken refuge at his own household altar (ἑρκεῖον ... βωμόν), and so (in Pindar's language) in perfect retribution, Apollo did not allow Neoptolemus to reach his own home or old age.[71] Other traditions preserved in later sources told of Neoptolemus's attempt to sack the Delphic shrine, or to demand recompense from Pythian Apollo for the killing of his father Achilles.[72] Both stories imply rampant aggression combined with a refusal to accept the boundaries and prerogatives appropriate to god and mortal.[73] And so, in response, Apollo punishes Neoptolemus by killing him at his own altar, in a savage rearticulation of divine space and divine prerogatives.

Furthermore, we make a mistake if we regard this as a simple narrative of sin and righteous divine punishment. Though Apollo serves as the enforcer of boundaries here, that does not make him a moral force. As Marcel Detienne has recently emphasized, rejecting a whole school of older, idealizing conceptions of Apollo, the god's cults identify him as a butcher and ruthless killer, so that Apollo and Neoptolemus are more like uncanny doubles of each other. Neoptolemus seeks to loot Delphi, while Apollo is the god "who loves booty" (φιλολήϊος, *Homeric Hymn to Hermes* l. 335). Both are violent and bloodthirsty

---

[70] Cf. Rose 1974.154–55 on the ideological functions of Pindar's pervasively generalizing, abstract language.

[71] Notice the striking zeugma here that collapses the categories of space and time (ἐς οἶκον and ἐπὶ γῆρας both depend on ἱξέμεν); Apollo, the "broad-quivered far-darter" (111), effortlessly controls the boundaries of both. For other ancient sources on Neoptolemus's killing of Priam, see Arctinus *Iliou Persis* arg. 13–14 Bernabé; Eur. *Hecuba* 23–24, *Trojan Women* 15–17, 481–83; Paus. 4.17.4, 10.27.1; Apollodorus *Epitome* 5.21; Vergil *Aeneid* 2.469–558, Heliodorus *Aethiopica* 2.34.

[72] Neoptolemus's attempt to sack Delphi: Schol. *ad* Pindar N.7.58, 150a; Paus. 2.5.5, 10.7.1; Strabo 9.3.9/C421; Apollodorus *Epitome* 6.14; Eur. *Andr.* 1092–95 (Orestes' lying tale to provoke the Delphians); Neoptolemus demanding recompense from Apollo for Achilles' slaying: Eur. *Andr.* 51–53, 1002–3, 1107–8, *Or.* 1656–57; Schol. *ad* Pindar N.7.58; the two stories combined: Strabo 9.3.9/C421. On these two versions, see Fontenrose 1960.212–18, Rutherford 2001.322–23, Burnett 2005.192, Kowalzig 2007.198–99. As Rutherford (2001.323) notes, the story of Neoptolemus's demand for recompense for Achilles' slaying first occurs in Euripides, and his threat to sack the Delphic shrine only much later. But I would argue that at least the latter tradition, and probably also the former, are part of the mythological background Pindar is polemically revising in *Nemean* 7.

[73] In particular, in demanding recompense from Apollo for his father's slaying, Neoptolemus seems to be following in the footsteps of Achilles himself; cf. the remarkable exchange between Achilles and Apollo at *Il.* 22.8–20.

in their vengeance; both sacrilegious in killing within the sacred space of altar and temenos.[74]

Still, Neoptolemus's death and burial within Apollo's sacred precinct, as they are represented in Pindar's *Paean*, found and support for all time the sacrificial order of Delphi. Moral or not, Apollo, by killing Neoptolemus, definitively establishes the boundaries of his own "legitimate (or abundant) *timai*" at the Panhellenic shrine, no matter how these may diverge from "normal" civic sacrificial practice.

The version of the myth told in *Nemean* 7, while it diverges radically in the motivations of the principal actors, ultimately endorses the same sacrificial order.[75] Composed for the Aeginetan victor Sogenes, Pindar's ode offers what looks like a positive revision of the entire Neoptolemus tradition.[76] Instead of coming to loot the Delphic shrine and/or to demand blood money from the god for his father's killing, the pious Neoptolemus of *Nemean* 7 comes to Delphi in order to offer the god the first fruits of the captured city of Troy. While on this holy mission, Neoptolemus—apparently accidentally—becomes embroiled in a quarrel over sacrificial meat:

ᾤχετο δὲ πρὸς θεόν,
κτέατ' ἄγων Τροΐαθεν ἀκροθινίων·
ἵνα κρεῶν νιν ὕπερ μάχας
ἔλασεν ἀντιτυχόντ' ἀνὴρ μαχαίρᾳ.
βαρύνθεν δὲ περισσὰ Δελφοὶ ξεναγέται.
(N.7.40–43)

---

[74] For Apollo as butcher and ruthless killer, see Detienne 1998. In a sense, Pindar registers the uncanny likeness of Neoptolemus and Apollo in *Paean* 6 by his repeated use of εὐρυ- compounds: when he is first introduced, Neoptolemus is εὐρυβίαν (103), while Apollo, at the moment of preventing Neoptolemus's return home, is εὐρυφαρέτραν (111). Finally, in the very last word of the narrative of Neoptolemus's death, Apollo kills him παρ' ὀμφαλὸν εὐρύν (120). In addition, Pindar is explicit about Apollo's violent, murderous nature: thus the god is said to kill Achilles, "having shackled him with bold slaughter" (θρασεῖ φόνῳ πεδάσαις; *Paean* 6.86; for the harshness of this phrase, see Radt 1958.143–44).

[75] Cf. Burkert 1983.119–20: "Thus, in sacrificing, [Neoptolemus] himself became the victim in this specifically Delphic ritual.... Just as Zeus was united with Pelops, so Delphic Apollo is associated with his chosen victim, whom the poets made the son of Achilles. His death occurs in the sacred precinct in a violent ritual which the Delphians regularly repeat." Thus also Nagy 1979.126: "we may see in the death of Pyrrhos the official Delphic myth that integrates the ideology of the ritual."

[76] Thus I am skeptical about the theory first propounded by Aristarchus and reported by the ancient scholiasts (*ad* N.7.70), that *Nemean* 7 represents Pindar's specific palinode or apology for the version of the Neoptolemus story told in *Paean* 6, in response to objections by the Aeginetans; see full discussion in Kurke 2005 passim (and on the "apology hypothesis" specifically, 93–94n. 37). More recently, the "apology hypothesis" has been rejected by Burnett 2005.185–86, 201–2; Currie 2005.321–31; Kowalzig 2007.193. Instead of the "apology hypothesis," I would read *Nemean* 7 as Pindar's self-conscious positive revision of the entire Neoptolemus tradition; for similar readings of the revisionism of *Nemean* 7, see Rutherford 2001.322–23, Kowalzig 2007.221–22.

And he went to the god, bringing possessions consisting of the first fruits from Troy. And there, as he happened into a fight over cuts of meat, a man killed him with a sacrificial knife. And the Delphians who guide strangers were exceedingly grieved.

Though in some ways more specific than the account of *Paean* 6 (there is at least mention of "meat" and a "sacrificial knife"), this narrative is still strikingly vague and spare of detail. In an account that exculpates simultaneously the Aeginetan hero Neoptolemus, the Delphic god, and the Delphians, Pindar tells us only that Neoptolemus was killed by an anonymous "man with a knife." Scholars ancient and modern have been quick to fill out this account from other sources on Delphic sacrifice, assuming that it is Neoptolemus's own sacrifice and that the ἀνήρ must be a Delphian, helping himself to a portion of Neoptolemus's sacrificial offering, when the hero objects and so provokes the fatal attack.[77] But none of this detail is offered by Pindar, whose account is as vague as it could possibly be. Indeed, I would suggest that the strongly contrastive juxtaposition of the anonymous "man" with the "Delphians who guide strangers" grieved by his action (42–43) encourages us to believe that the offending "man" is not himself even a Delphian, by a typically Pindaric sleight of hand.[78]

However that may be, Pindar immediately recuperates the accidental killing of Neoptolemus at the Delphic shrine as a kind of *felix culpa*:[79]

ἀλλὰ τὸ μόρσιμον ἀπέδω-
κεν· ἐχρῆν δέ τιν' ἔνδον ἄλσει παλαιτάτῳ
Αἰακιδᾶν κρεόντων τὸ λοιπὸν ἔμμεναι
θεοῦ παρ' εὐτειχέα δόμον, ἡροΐαις δὲ πομπαῖς
θεμισκόπον οἰκεῖν ἐόντα πολυθύτοις.
(N.7.44–47)

But he paid the fated allotment; for it had to happen that one of the ruling Aeacids be for all time within the most ancient grove beside the well-walled house of the god, and dwell there as overseer of right for heroic processions rich in sacrifice.

---

[77] Thus Schol. *ad* Pindar N.7.62a: "they say that when Neoptolemus was sacrificing, the Delphians snatched the sacrificial offerings, as is their custom. But that Neoptolemus, taking it ill, tried to prevent them, and they did him in, having swords." The scholia go on to cite the assertion of Asclepiades that "nearly all the poets agree concerning his death, that he died at the hands of Machaireus, and was first buried under the threshold of the temple, but that, after these things, Menelaus came and took him up and made his tomb in the precinct. And they say that Machaireus is the son of Daitas" (Schol. *ad* N.7.62b). Notice that, although "nearly all the poets agree" on this, it is not what Pindar says. In like manner, Nagy 1979.123–25 and Burkert 1983.118–20 immediately fill in all the scholiast's details.

[78] For the spareness of Pindar's account, cf. Burnett 2005.192. I don't mean to suggest that Pindar thinks the nameless "man" *isn't* a Delphian, merely that he cultivates a particular kind of ambiguity that allows everyone to look good in this account. Cf. Cole 1987 for other examples of Pindar's finely calibrated, optimizing ambiguity.

[79] Cf. Stevens 1971.2, Kowalzig 2007.221–22.

It is here again (though in a very different sense from *Paean* 6) an issue of boundaries and fated allotments. Neoptolemus, though he has not transgressed, "rendered" or "paid" the "fated allotment" (τὸ μόρσιμον ἀπέδωκεν); it "had to happen" (ἐχρῆν). Behind the seemingly random and anonymous human violence, a fateful and orderly divine plan plays itself out. And that plan is precisely that Neoptolemus should reside forever in the god's precinct as the "overseer" (θεμισκόπον) of proper sacrificial allotments "for heroic processions rich in sacrifice." Neoptolemus, himself cut down in a violent quarrel over sacrificial allotments, will guarantee in perpetuity the fair and orderly distribution of offerings within Apollo's precinct. In this context, it is no accident that Pindar uses the clan name, "one of the ruling Aeacids," for he thereby assimilates Neoptolemus to his founding ancestor Aeacus, who figures elsewhere in the epinicia as a just and impartial arbiter for men and gods alike (cf. N.8.8–12, I.8.22–24).[80]

As in *Paean* 6, the myth of *Nemean* 7 thus confirms and supports the absolute propriety of sacrificial practice in Apollo's precinct. And as this is accomplished in Pindar's poems through the myth, it is accomplished in ritual practice through the hero-cult honors offered to Neoptolemus in intimate connection with Apollo's divine worship at Delphi.[81] But we may be able to go even further on the aetiological and legitimating function of the myth of Neoptolemus's end at Delphi. For it may be that both Pindaric poems narrate the hero's death in the context of the same festival—the Delphic Theoxeny. *Paean* 6 tells us explicitly that the Theoxeny is the context for its performance: the poet's *ego* speaks of "going down to the broad assembly of Loxias at the hosting of the gods" (ἐν θεῶν ξενίᾳ, *Paean* 6.60-61).[82] As for *Nemean* 7, the scholia to that ode gloss Pindar's phrase ἡροΐαις δὲ πομπαῖς θεμισκόπον . . . πολυθύτοις (N.7.47–48) thus: "there occurs in Delphi *xenia* for the heroes, at which the god seems to invite the heroes for hospitality" (γίνεται ἐν Δελφοῖς ἥρωσι ξένια, ἐν οἷς δοκεῖ

---

[80] Differently Nagy 1979.120, taking this phrase to mean it could just as well have been Achilles, and Currie 2005.297–301, offering a different interpretation of ἡροΐαις δὲ πομπαῖς θεμισκόπον. If the Heroxenia of *Nemean* 7 is the same festival as the Theoxenia of *Paean* 6, it may be that the mention of Aeacus here has an important ritual resonance as well: Radt 1958.132–34 tentatively suggested that the Delphic Theoxeny was somehow linked to an Aeginetan festival in which Aeacus was supplicated to intercede with Zeus Panhellenius on behalf of all Greece. For extended discussion of this ritual connection, see Kurke 2005, citing earlier scholarship, and Kowalzig 2007.181–223.

[81] Although Pausanias (1.4.4, 10.24.6) tells us that the Delphians instituted yearly offerings (*enagismata*) at the tomb of Pyrrhus/Neoptolemus only after the defeat of the Gauls in 279/8 BCE, there is evidence, both literary and archaeological, to suggest that Neoptolemus enjoyed hero-cult honor at Delphi already in the classical period. In addition to the evidence of *Nemean* 7 itself, cf. Schol. *ad* N.7.62c, Heliodorus *Aethiopica* 2.34–3.6, 3.10; for archaeological evidence of what may have been Neoptolemus's tomb at Delphi (dating back to the fourth or third c. BCE at least), see Pouilloux 1960.49–60. On the antiquity of Neoptolemus's cult at Delphi, see Fontenrose 1960.191–98, Burkert 1983, Suárez de la Torre 1997.174–76, Currie 2005.296–307.

[82] For extended discussion of who the *ego* is here, see Kurke 2005, citing earlier scholarship.

ὁ θεὸς ἐπὶ ξένια καλεῖν τοὺς ἥρωας, Schol. *ad* N.7.68a Drachmann). Many scholars have assumed that the scholiast's "Heroxeny" is simply an alternative designation for the Delphic Theoxeny.[83] Unfortunately, we simply do not have enough information about the Delphic Theoxeny to know for sure. But I would like to try the thought experiment of assuming for a moment that it *is* the same festival: what would the implications be of that common ritual context?

The Theoxeny took place every year in the Delphic month of Theoxenios (March–April) and appears to have been a major Panhellenic festival.[84] In this context, Apollo seems to have "hosted" other gods and perhaps heroes, though we do not know exactly who all the immortal "guests" were. According to *Paean* 6 (our earliest source for the festival), "sacrifice was made on behalf of all flourishing Greece" (θύεται γὰρ ἀγλαᾶς ὑπὲρ Πανελλάδος, *Paean* 6.62); the scholia to this line inform us that prayers were offered for εὐετηρία, "a good agricultural season." Finally, the Paean of Philodamus (dated 339 BCE) suggests that all the Greek cities sent representatives to the festival to supplicate on behalf of their local populations (σὺν Ἑλλάδος ... πανδήμοις ἱκετείαις, ll. 113–14). It is at least possible that these representatives also provided the sacrificial animals on the occasion of the Theoxeny festival.[85]

As for the distribution of sacrificial meat at the Delphic Theoxeny, we are as much in the dark about it as about most other aspects of this festival, simply because of the spottiness of our evidence. What evidence we have seems to suggest that there was no general distribution of sacrificial meat among the participants in the festival (or at least not the non-Delphian participants). Instead, it seems it was very much the prerogative of the Delphians to allot sacrificial portions (*moirai*) selectively as a mark of honor.[86] And if it was indeed the emissaries from other Greek states who provided some or all of the victims for the Theoxeny, this represents a remarkable act of sacrificial legerdemain on the part of the locals officiating: as the god's representatives, they claim for themselves

---

[83] For the assumption that Heroxeny = Theoxeny (and that therefore Neoptolemus had a special link to Delphic Theoxeny in particular), see Wilamowitz-Moellendorff 1922.129–30, Bruit 1984.365–66, Detienne 1998.193; more tentatively, Amandry 1944–45.415; Rutherford 2001.314–15; Currie 2005.307, 330. Contra: Nilsson 1906.161n. 2, Fontenrose 1960.197. I should also record here the doubts of the late Michael Jameson, who expressed to me (*per litteras*) "a certain unease over the Pindaric scholia [to *Nemean* 7]. How much, I wondered, was simply elaborated from the poet's text?"

[84] For the timing of the festival, see Radt 1958.83; for its Panhellenic scope, see Amandry 1944–45.413, Rutherford 2001.310.

[85] For the text of the Paean of Philodamus, see Powell 1925.165–71, Käppel 1992.375–80 (Paean no. 39). For the possibility that the visiting representatives provided the sacrificial victims, see Rutherford 2003.722–23.

[86] For a collection of ancient evidence and detailed analysis thereof to justify this claim, see Kurke 2005.98–99. Kowalzig 2007.181–201 also emphasizes the exclusivity of access at the Theoxenia, through the Delphians' control of the allotment of sacrificial shares, which she brilliantly connects with the participants' claims to Hellenicity.

sole authority to adjudicate the distribution of meat, even to those who have furnished the victims.

We might say that the Theoxeny both intensifies and legitimates the structure of everyday Delphic sacrifice—that this festival in fact founds the entire Delphic sacrificial order. For it is full-scale Theoxeny and its ideology that justify the everyday Delphic practice of deposition on the table—a practice that assumes Apollo's proprietary rights in sacrificial offerings.[87] Indeed, it seems that the whole system depends on a kind of paradox or religious fiction, that Apollo takes all year round in order to give once a year; in order to be the generous host of the Theoxeny.[88] And the central issue the Delphic Theoxeny makes most clear and most clearly legitimates is that of delegation, in at least two senses: (1) the god is the host, but the Delphians (acting on his behalf) decide who gets meat, and (2) the Theoxeny is a festival on behalf of all Greece, but the Delphians control it. These same two levels of delegation are operative in everyday Delphic sacrificial practice, whereby the Delphians control access to Apollo's Panhellenic oracle and claim as their share the sacrificial offerings deposited on the god's table.[89]

Thus it is significant if both of Pindar's poems (*Paean* 6 and *Nemean* 7) link the myth of Neoptolemus's death to the institution of the Delphic Theoxeny and its specific practices of distribution of sacrificial meat. For the myth then functions as an aetiology that founds and legitimates the whole Delphic sacrificial system. In favor of such an interpretation of the two poems together (speculative as it is), we might note that the slippage about who actually kills Neoptolemus in Pindar's two versions of the myth is exactly analogous to the process of delegation in Delphic cult. Was Neoptolemus killed by Apollo himself, by a nameless "man with a knife" (or, as Asclepiades has it, by a Delphic priest named Machaireus son of Daitas)? In a sense, it doesn't matter; this double agency is precisely the point. For in its mythic origins as in its ongoing ritual practice, Delphic sacrifice is predicated on Apollo's working through the Delphians as his instruments and intermediaries.[90]

---

[87] Jameson 1994.52n. 60 notes the interesting observation of Dow and Healey 1965.28, that the use of a *trapeza* was specifically associated with the cult of Apollo Pythius and often mandated by his oracle. As Jameson observes, if this was a general rule, "one might suppose the practice was promoted by Delphi." Jameson himself is skeptical, however, since only in the case of the cult of Plouton at Eleusis do we have firm evidence that the use of a table was prescribed explicitly by the Delphic oracle.

[88] For this reciprocal relation between everyday Delphic sacrificial exactions and the god's hospitality at the Theoxeny, cf. Bruit 1984.359–67, Detienne 1998.191–94.

[89] Bruit 1984.353–55, 361–67 emphasizes the pervasive collapse or identification between the god and his officiating priests in the practices of Delphic sacrifice in general and Theoxeny in particular.

[90] For Neoptolemus's aetiological connection to the Theoxeny ritual, see Rutherford 2001.314–15, Kowalzig 2007.192–201, and, for a similar point about double agency, Rutherford 2001.314. In fact, the myth of *Paean* 6 seems almost compulsively to repeat this theme of double agency in

In contrast, we might think of the Aesop tradition as a low or popular parodic replay of the Neoptolemus stories. Like Neoptolemus, Aesop comes to Delphi, engages in a conflict with the Delphians, and meets his death there. But unlike the Neoptolemus traditions, the accounts of Aesop's death (especially *P.Oxy.* 1800) are all too explicit in exposing the material conditions of Delphic sacrifice and thereby undermining its legitimacy. In the Aesop tradition, there is no talk of abstract *timai*, but only the graphic vision of the Delphians greedily hacking off hunks of meat and scuttling away. And while Neoptolemus by his death achieves heroic cult status, the Delphians, according to the Aesop story, do everything in their power to transform Aesop into a *pharmakos* (what we might think of as the nadir of a spectrum of religious identities that has the cult hero as its apex). Thus, as Wiechers observes, Aesop already conforms to the type of the *pharmakos* in that he is grotesquely ugly and of low social status. Furthermore, the Delphians plant a golden phiale belonging to the god in his luggage before he departs, so that they can then condemn him for *hierosulia*. When he is caught and convicted, Aesop is, like a scapegoat, led through the town for execution and ultimately condemned to a death enacted by the whole people, either by stoning or by being thrown off a cliff.[91]

While Wiechers is right that all these elements in the Aesop story identify him with the figure of the *pharmakos*, what he and most other scholars have failed to note is that the making of a *pharmakos* is a *competitive* activity in the story of the death of Aesop.[92] That is to say, because of Aesop's demystification of Delphic sacrificial practices (according to the story), Apollo and the Delphians attempt to turn him into a *pharmakos*; but Aesop contests that attempt, endowing the Delphians themselves (through his jibes and fables) with all the characteristics of *pharmakoi*. In reading the narrative of Aesop at Delphi as a contest of scapegoating, I follow the lead of Carles Miralles and Jaume Pòrtulas, who have argued that the generic character of the archaic iambic poet is that of the ugly, marginalized, scapegoated one who paradoxically has the power to scapegoat others through his iambic invective. Miralles and Pòrtulas develop this model through a study of Archilochus and extend it through a careful and comprehensive reading of the fragments of Hipponax.[93] In applying Miralles and Pòrtulas's model of competitive scapegoating, however, I do not intend to

---

the account of the death of Achilles at Apollo's hands. The language preserved (Πάριος ἑ[καβόλος βροτησίῳ δέμαϊ θεός, ll. 79–80) seems deliberately ambiguous: does it mean, "the god far–darter in the mortal form of Paris" or "the god far–darter by means of the mortal body of Paris"?

[91] Wiechers 1961.31–42. Cf. *Vitae* G + W, chs. 127–42, Perry *Test.* 21–32; and for parallels, Hipponax frr. 5–10 W, Istrus *FGrH* 344 F 50, Bremmer 1983, Vernant 1988, Compton 2006. Technically, of course, in *Vita* G Aesop preempts the latter style of execution by throwing himself off the cliff.

[92] An important exception is Steiner 2008, discussing Aesop's fable of the eagle and the dung beetle.

[93] Miralles and Portulàs 1983, 1988.

assimilate Aesop unproblematically to the figure of the blame *poet* (as Gregory Nagy does). For it is my contention that it is still a significant fact that Aesop was for the ancients a *logopoios* and not an iambic poet. Nonetheless, according to the strict hierarchy of ancient Greek generic forms, iambic poetry with its characteristic abuse is the lowest of poetic forms and therefore most nearly akin to the prose fable at the very bottom of the generic spectrum.[94]

In any case, we can read the sequence of Aesop's adventures at Delphi as a set of dueling narrative performances, each side aiming to constitute the other as debased social outcasts.[95] Thus the Delphians try to impose their narrative on Aesop, transforming him into a temple-robber by planting a golden phiale in his luggage and then killing him as a scapegoat. But Aesop is simultaneously trying to impose the same narrative on the Delphians.

According to Tzetzes, who quotes several fragments of Hipponax to support his account (Tzetzes *Chil.* 5.728–761, citing Hipponax frr. 5–10 W), the *pharmakos* was "a purification of old" (κάθαρμα ... τὸ πάλαι) for the city suffering from divine wrath (θεομηνίᾳ) in the form of famine or plague or other harm. In this instance, they would "lead the one who was the ugliest of all (τὸν πάντων ἀμορφότερον) as for sacrifice." Other ancient sources indicate that the one chosen for scapegoating was not only ugly, but socially low and marginalized as well.[96] Finally, from other fragments of Hipponax (the ancient author with the most references to *pharmakos* ritual), Miralles and Pòrtulas deduce further characteristics that seem to align with or invite scapegoating. These include excessive greed and gluttony, even to the point of sacrilegious theft of offerings to the gods (cf. Hipponax frr. 118, 128 W) and sexual incontinence, including incest (cf. Hipponax fr. 12, 70 W).[97]

If we turn back to the *Life of Aesop* with these characteristics of the *pharmakos* in mind, we notice that the whole sequence of quips and fables Aesop levels against the Delphians systematically assimilates them to the scapegoat. In the first place, as I've already noted, when Aesop arrives and offers his performance of wisdom but the Delphians give him nothing in return, he parodically quotes the Homeric line οἵη περ φύλλων γενεή, τοίη δὲ καὶ ἀνδρῶν as a commentary on the Delphians' pasty complexions (*Vita* G, ch. 124). Aesop then proceeds to tell the fable of the driftwood, which from a great distance looks like something, but turns out to be nothing (*Vitae* G + W, ch. 125), and informs the

---

[94] Cf. Arist. *Poet.* 4.18–19, 1449a23–28, *Rhet.* 3.1.9, 1404a28–35 on the similarity of iambic meter to ordinary speech; and Phil. *Apoll.* 5.15 (= Perry *Test.* 62; quoted at beginning of the introduction) on the ranked hierarchy of Greek genres. For modern discussions of the hierarchy of genres, see West 1974.22–34 (on iambic); Rothwell 1995.233–39 (on fable); Kurke 1999, 2000.

[95] For similar readings of the Delphic episode as a competition in abuse or scapegoating, see Ogden 1997.39–40, Steiner 2008.

[96] Cf. Bremmer 1983.303, citing Schol. *ad* Aristoph. *Knights* 1136, Schol. *ad* Aristoph. *Frogs* 733; Vernant 1988.128–29; Compton 2006.4–5, 14–15.

[97] Miralles and Pòrtulas 1988.9–36, 45–69, 133–59; cf. Steiner 2008.

Delphians that they are "the slaves of all the Greeks" (*Vitae* G + W, ch. 126). Thus, with his very first utterances, Aesop constructs the Delphians as ugly, worthless, and socially debased, and the Delphians respond immediately with the decision to frame and kill him (*Vitae* G + W, ch. 127).[98]

Then, starting from the time of his imprisonment in Delphi awaiting execution, Aesop tells a series of fables about and to the Delphians.[99] First, to a friend who visits him in prison and reproaches him, "Why did it seem good to you to insult them in their own homeland and city, especially when you were under their authority? Where is your education? Where is your learning? You have given advice to cities and peoples, and have you become a fool toward yourself?" (*Vitae* G + W, ch. 130). Aesop responds with a fable about a woman who had a foolish daughter, for whom she used to pray constantly (in the daughter's presence) that she "get some sense" (νοῦν λαβεῖν). One day the girl encounters a man violently screwing an ass and asks him what he's doing. The man replies, "I'm putting some sense in her" (νοῦν ἐντίθημι αὐτῇ). The girl responds, "Please put some in me too," persuades the man, and returns triumphantly to her mother, announcing, "I have sense, mother." The mother, once she's gotten the whole story, laments, "O child, you've lost even the sense you originally had." Aesop draws the moral: "It's happened in the same way to me also, friend; for I lost even the sense I originally had when I came to Delphi" (*Vitae* G + W, ch. 131). Here we might note that, in the analogical relation Aesop constructs between the fable and his own situation, the friend and Aesop play the roles of mother and daughter, respectively, while the Delphians are cast in the role of the man raping an ass. Thus this fable aligns them with sexual transgression (in this case, bestiality), one of the traits Miralles and Pòrtulas identify with the scapegoat.[100]

When the Delphians themselves arrive and announce that they have voted to cast Aesop off a cliff, on the grounds that he is "an evil-speaker and imposter and temple-robber" (ὡς βλάσφημον καὶ ἀλαζόνα καὶ ἱερόσυλον, *Vita* W,

---

[98] Note that, according to *Vita* G, Apollo also colludes in the effort to make Aesop into a scapegoat: καὶ τοῦ Ἀπόλλωνος μηνίοντος διὰ τὴν ἐν Σάμῳ ἀτιμίαν . . . (*Vita* G, ch. 127; cf. P.Ross.Georg. I.18, l. 22, [Ἀπόλλω]νος συνεργοῦντος αὐτοῖς διὰ τὴν ἀτ[ιμίαν]). Furthermore, there may be some ritual significance to the "driftwood" of Aesop's first fable to the Delphians, since ancient evidence from Hipponax and elsewhere strongly connects the *pharmakos* and *pharmakos* rituals to the use of barren or "wild" wood like squills and wild fig branches (cf. Hipponax frr. 6, 9, 10, 152, 153 W; Tzetzes *Chil.* 5.736–37; Bremmer 1983.308–13). This context may be relevant for Hipponax fr. 41 W, where the word usually glossed as "good-for-nothing" means literally "made of wild fig wood" (and see the discussion of Miralles and Pòrtulas 1988.84–85 on this fragment).

[99] The first fable Aesop tells in prison at ch. 129 (which is often compared to Petronius's story of the Widow of Ephesus) does not seem to bear any significance for the pattern of competitive scapegoating I am tracing here. Nor is this surprising, since this fable is entirely concerned with the relationship between Aesop and his friend, and Aesop's mourning (that is to say, this fable is neither about the Delphians nor addressed to them).

[100] For a reading of the other details of this fable, see chapter 5 below.

ch. 132),[101] Aesop tells them the fable of the mouse and the frog.[102] The mouse invites the frog for a generous dinner; the frog then reciprocates, leading the mouse back to his "house" in a pond. When the mouse objects that he doesn't know how to dive and swim, the frog binds them leg-to-leg and dives in himself, drowning the mouse. As he suffocates, the mouse predicts, "Though a corpse, I shall punish you who are alive" (νεκρὸς ὢν ζῶντά σε ἐκδικήσω, Vitae G + W, ch. 133). And, sure enough, a hawk seizes the body of the mouse as it floats on the surface of the pond, carrying off with it the frog still bound leg-to-leg. Aesop again spells out the moral: "In the same way, I too, O men, shall be a doom for you; for the Lydians, the Babylonians, and nearly the whole of Greece will reap the fruits of my death" (ὁμοίως κἀγώ, ἄνδρες, ἀποθανὼν ὑμῖν μόρος ἔσομαι· καὶ γὰρ Λύδιοι, Βαβυλώνιοι, καὶ σχεδὸν ἡ Ἑλλὰς ὅλη τὸν ἐμὸν καρπίσονται θάνατον, Vita G, ch. 133).

This verbal exchange represents a contest of dueling performative utterances. By invoking the vote of the demos, the Delphians assert the absolute authority of their communal voice, while they denigrate and reject any verbal power Aesop might have by labeling him simultaneously "an evil-speaker and an imposter."[103] Aesop responds with a fable that constitutes the Delphians as violators of *xenia*, even as he appropriates for himself the verbal authority to prophesy and to curse that characterizes the dying Homeric hero.[104]

Next, as he's led to the cliff, Aesop flees to a shrine of the Muses. The Delphians, ignoring his supplication there, drag him off, provoking Aesop to tell the fable of the eagle and the dung beetle, whose hostile relations are caused by the eagle's refusal to respect the dung beetle's supplication on behalf of a poor rabbit the eagle is pursuing.[105] In revenge, the dung beetle repeatedly finds and

---

[101] There appears to be a lacuna at this point in *Vita* G, which Perry supplements based on *P.Ross. Georg.* I.18 as <ὡς ἱερόσυλον> καὶ βλάσφημον.

[102] For extended discussion of this fable and comparison with other versions, see Merkle 1992.

[103] Notice that, at least in *Vita* W, both of these terms take pride of place before ἱερόσυλον, the actual crime of which Aesop is accused. Notice also that we cannot translate βλάσφημον as "blasphemer," since Aesop has said nothing irreverent or hostile to Apollo himself: instead, βλάσφημον seems to refer to his invective against the Delphians, which threatens to transform them into scapegoats.

[104] Cf. *Il.* 16.851–4, 22.356–60 and especially the *Batrachomyomachia* (itself an elaborate Homeric parody): in this text, the war of the mice and the frogs starts from an identical cause, when the noble mouse Psicharpax is drowned by the king of the frogs, Physignathus, who offers him *xenia* and then dives into the pond with the hapless mouse on his back (*Batr.* ll. 9–121). Note in particular the verbal parallels with the *Life of Aesop*: (1) at the moment of his death by drowning, the mouse "is not able to fend off his doom" (μόρον δ' οὐκ ἦν ὑπαλύξαι, *Batr.* l. 90); (2) his last words prophesy vengeance (ἔχει θεὸς ἔκδικον ὄμμα, *Batr.* l. 97). Cf. Wiechers 1961.10 on the significance of μόρος as a poetic and archaic Ionic word that occurs only in *Vita* G.

[105] For a subtle literary analysis of this fable, see Steiner 2008. Steiner suggestively connects the Aesopic fable with Hesiod's fable of the hawk and the nightingale and Archilochus's fable of the failed alliance of fox and eagle, reading the unequal power dynamics between two antagonists as they are encoded in all three fables.

destroys the eagle's eggs, until the eagle, in desperation, deposits them on the very lap of Zeus. The dung beetle responds by "smearing himself with much shit" and flying around Zeus's face. Zeus, in alarm at the unclean thing, leaps up, entirely forgetting the eagle's eggs deposited in his lap, which are destroyed. From this, Zeus comes to understand that the dung beetle has been wronged by the eagle and informs the latter that he has "justly lost his children." The fable ends with the dung beetle's assertion to Zeus, "Not only did [the eagle] wrong me, but he was greatly irreverent toward you as well, since adjured in your name he did not fear, but killed my suppliant" (*Vitae* G + W, ch. 138). Aesop's parallel appeal to the Delphians conjures them "not to dishonor this shrine to which I fled, even if it be little . . . and to respect Zeus Xenius and Olympius" (*Vita* G, ch. 139).[106] Thus the two animal fables Aesop tells in quick succession represent the Delphians as violators of divine law—first of *xenia* and then of supplication, both under the aegis and protection of Zeus.

Finally, with his last two fables, told on the cliff-edge itself, Aesop gives up even the pretense of trying to persuade the Delphians, resorting to pure blame.[107] Thus he tells the story of the old farmer who wanted to see the city, so his children send him off in an ass-cart. In a storm, the asses wander off the road and wind up on the edge of a cliff. The old man, perceiving his danger, cries out, "O Zeus, what wrong have I done you that I perish thus, and not even at the hands of horses, but of despicable little asses?" (καὶ ταῦτα οὐχ ὑφ᾽ ἵππων, ἀλλ᾽ ὑπὸ καταπτύστων ὀναρίων). Aesop immediately spells out the analogy, "Thus also I take it hard that I perish not at the hands of worthy men, but at the hands of despicable little slaves" (ὅτι οὐχ ὑπὸ ἀξιολόγων ἀνδρῶν ἀλλ᾽ ὑπὸ καταπτύστων δουλαρίων ἀπόλλυμαι, *Vita* G, ch. 140).[108] With this fable, Aesop echoes the analogy he had drawn originally between the Delphians and "worthless" driftwood, as well as his earlier abuse of them as "slaves of all the Greeks." Then, as he is about to be cast from the cliff, Aesop tells one last fable:

> A certain man once conceived a passion for his daughter and, wounded by love, he sent his wife to the country and raped the daughter. And she said, "Father, you do

[106] In one of its most interesting moves to mute or suppress the narrative strand of conflict between Aesop and Apollo, *Vita* W transforms the little shrine of the Muses into the temple of Apollo himself, to whom Aesop then appeals to endorse his supplication (*Vita* W, chs. 135, 139). As Perry (1936.16, 1952.11–14) notes, this change makes nonsense of Aesop's emphasis on the "littleness" of the shrine (which, of course, conditions the choice of the dung beetle in the fable); and on this basis, Perry regards it as almost certain that the version in *Vita* G is the original. I do not find the counterarguments of Ferrari 1997.17–18 persuasive on this point; see introduction pp. 35–37.

[107] Cf. van Dijk 1995.141–49 for the different rhetorical function of these two fables.

[108] *Vita* W at this point enthusiastically expands the fable's punch line, adding adjectives, inserting mules as a third term to the old man's lament ("I perish not at the hands of honored horses or noble mules, but at the hands of the lowest little asses"), and heightening the contrast between "honored or distinguished men" and the Delphians as "basest and useless slaves" (οὐχ ὑπὸ ἐντίμων ἢ ἐλλογίμων ἀνδρῶν ἀλλ᾽ ὑπὸ κακίστων καὶ ἀχρείων δούλων, *Vita* W, ch. 140).

unholy things (πάτερ, ἀνόσια πράσσεις). I would have preferred to furnish myself to a hundred men rather than to you." (*Vita* W, ch. 141).[109]

With this, his final fable, Aesop identifies the Delphians with the "unholy" sexual transgression of a father's incestuous rape of his daughter.[110]

Thus, taken as a set, all the fables Aesop tells in the Delphic portion of the *Life* construct the Delphians as ugly, low slaves, violators of the divine ordinances that protect strangers and suppliants, who engage in the sexual transgressions of bestiality and incest—in short, as perfect candidates for scapegoating.

Furthermore, we can apply this same reading to the traditions preserved in other sources in which Aesop abuses the Delphians for their irregular sacrificial practices. We have already considered these traditions as a popular, civic critique of Delphic sacrifice: here, we need only add that that critique takes the specific form of representing Delphic sacrificial practice as itself *bōmolochia* and *hierosulia*. *Bōmolochia*, which comes to mean the coarse, ribald jesting characteristic, for example, of Old Comedy, refers literally to "lurking around altars to steal scraps of sacrificial meat" (from βωμός, "altar" and λοχάω, "to wait or lurk in ambush"). Similarly, a gloss in Hesychius indicates that ἱερόσυλος can mean not just one who steals precious objects from a temple, but also "one who steals sacrifices" (ἱερόσυλος· τὰ ἱερὰ κλέπτων, Hesychius *Lexicon*. ι 324 Latte). Finally, there is evidence in the fragments of Hipponax to suggest that such *bōmolochia* or *hierosulia* could provoke the punishment of scapegoating.[111]

If we look again at the specific language used in the tradition to characterize Aesop's abuse of the Delphians, we find that in both the Scholia to Aristophanes and *P.Oxy*. 1800, Aesop's censure reads as an exact calque or gloss on the term

---

[109] Most of this fable is lost because of a lacuna in *Vita* G, but it survives in *Vita* W. Perry 1952.19–20 expresses certain reservations about whether this was the original fable at this point, based on what he perceives as a misfit or illogicality between the exact terms of this fable and what follows; but in defense of this fable in this context, see van Dijk 1995.

[110] Miralles and Pòrtulas 1988.59–60 almost get this; they note that Aesop's death is that of a *pharmakos*, and that his very last fable is about incest. But, because they do not connect Aesop's story with their own model of *competitive* scapegoating, this is for them simply a suggestive juxtaposition. I would contend that it is more than that, as Aesop struggles desperately to make the Delphians into scapegoats by identifying them with the incestuous father of the fable.

[111] Thus we may have preserved among the fragments of Hipponax a specific link between such *bōmolochia* or *hierosulia* and scapegoating. In a poetic fragment with extensive commentary preserved on papyrus, Hipponax abuses one Sannos (Hipponax fr. 118 W). Miralles and Pòrtulas, following Degani, interpret the ῥῖνα θεό[συλιν of the poem's first line as "a sacrilegious nose that smells the sacrificial smoke, since the owner of the nose intends to steal the offerings" (Miralles and Pòrtulas 1988.62; cf. Steiner 2008). That is, as Degani observes, Sannos is represented by the poet as a literal *bōmolochos* (Degani 1980.514; cf. the commentary's paraphrase ἱερόσυλιν ῥῖνα, fr. 118A W, l. 14). After these opening lines, the poem becomes much more fragmentary and difficult to interpret. I follow Miralles and Pòrtulas (1988.63–68), who suggest that the preserved commentary represents the poet urging Sannos in mock-friendly fashion to take poison and die a scapegoat's death (I find this interpretation much more plausible than that of Masson 1962.163–64 and West 1974.147–48, who see in the poem's continuation Hipponax's advice to Sannos to begin a diet-and-exercise regime).

bōmolochia. In the Scholia to Aristophanes' *Wasps*, Aesop "jeered at the Delphians because they did not have land from which they could support themselves by agricultural labor, but instead they waited around to make their living from the sacrifices of the god" (ἀλλὰ περιμένοιεν ἀπὸ τῶν θεοῦ θυμάτων διαζῆν, Schol. *ad* Aristoph. *Wasps* 1446 = Perry *Test.* 21). Here, περιμένοιεν ("they waited around") glosses λοχάω, the verbal element in the compound, while ἀπὸ τῶν θεοῦ θυμάτων stands in place of βωμός. In like manner, *P.Oxy.* 1800 emphasizes how the Delphians "stand around the altar" (περιεστήκασι τὸν βωμόν, οἱ περιστῶτες), each ready to hack off a piece of someone else's sacrifice. Thus in both these accounts, Aesop deauthorizes or delegitimates official Delphic sacrificial practice by transforming it into its opposite—criminal *bōmolochia*. It is no wonder, then, given what's at stake in this representation, that in these accounts the Delphians immediately transform Aesop himself into a *hierosulos* (Schol. *ad* Aristoph. *Wasps*) or simply kill him outright as a *pharmakos* (*P.Oxy.* 1800). For in both cases, the Delphians are precisely reciprocating what Aesop has tried to do to them.

Thus, as with the critique of Delphic practices considered in section II, the older, fragmentary Aesop traditions and the Delphic narrative of the *Life* in fact mutually support and reinforce each other in their representations of this pattern of competitive scapegoating. For the older traditions that focus on the Delphians' aberrant sacrificial practices articulate more explicitly Aesop's accusation of *bōmolochia*, while the proliferation of abusive fables Aesop tells to and about the Delphians in the later *Life* implicitly encode the typical characteristics of the scapegoat in other terms.[112] The two traditions thereby conform to each other like the two halves of an ancient *sumbolon*.

The same could be said for the different conclusions of the Aesop story in the various traditions. In all the different accounts, the Delphians actually kill Aesop (or force him to kill himself), so they may be construed to have won this contest of scapegoating. But this is by no means the end of the story.[113] In the oldest preserved and apparently mildest version (in Herodotus), the Delphians are forced "from an oracle" to announce on many occasions that they will pay "recompense for the life of Aesop" (ποινὴν τῆς Αἰσώπου ψυχῆς) to whoever wishes to take it (Hdt. 2.134.4). Herodotus's use of ποινή here is striking and

[112] This reading of the fables clustered at the end of the *Life* refutes the interpretation of Holzberg 1992b.41–42, 69–75, 1993, 1996, 2002.82–84, that Aesop's fabular eloquence fails him in Delphi (as a kind of divine punishment for his hubris). Holzberg's reading fails to acknowledge (1) that the fables in the Delphic portion of the *Life* generally have a different function from those told earlier—not pleasure and persuasion, but abuse (cf. van Dijk 1995.141–49, Ogden 1997.39–40, Rosen 2007.98–104, Steiner 2008); and (2) that insofar as the goal of these fables is to transform the Delphians into scapegoats, they actually *succeed* (see discussion in text, below). For further argument against Holzberg's style of moralizing reading of the end of the *Life*, see chapter 4 below.

[113] Hence the inadequacy also of Hopkins's (1993.25) reading of this part of the *Life*: "From the masters' point of view, Aesop is too clever by half and finally, like the villain in a western, gets what he richly deserves; the hostility of the god Apollo helps legitimate his execution."

unusual. This word, which is rare in prose, occurs only three more times in the *Histories*, in two separate contexts where it designates the punishment exacted for the bestial, sacrilegious killing of sacred heralds (Hdt. 3.14.5, 7.134.2, 7.136.2). Indeed, in the latter episode (7.133–37), Herodotus tells us that the killing of Persian heralds by the Spartans evoked divine wrath (μῆνις ... Ταλθυβίου, emphatically referred to four times in the text: 7.134.1, 7.137.1, and twice in 7.137.2).[114] The use of ποινή in the context of Aesop, then, suggests that behind Herodotus's brief aside lurks a more complex story of divine wrath and punishment. After all, Herodotus does not say what provoked the Delphians to consult an oracle in this instance, but he may know a tradition like that preserved in Plutarch and the *Life*. Plutarch, who otherwise follows Herodotus's account quite closely, reports, "from [the killing of Aesop] it is said that the divine, in anger (μηνῖσαν τὸ θεῖον), afflicted them with barrenness of the land and every form of unusual disease, so that going around, they had to announce at all the festal assemblies of the Greeks and always to invite the one who wished to take recompense from them on behalf of Aesop" (Plut. *Div.Veng.* 557a = Perry *Test*. 24). Or, as *Vita* G tells it, "Oppressed by plague, the Delphians got an oracle from Zeus to propitiate the doom of Aesop" (ch. 142).[115]

It is worth noting that these factors together—barrenness of land, plague, and divine wrath—precisely correspond to Tzetzes' conditions for initiating *pharmakos* rite "in the old days." That is to say, rather than curing themselves of these problems by the killing of Aesop, the Delphians thereby provoke them.[116] And this pattern may also account for a strange overdetermination at the end of the *Life of Aesop*. In both G and W, the Delphians are oppressed by plague until they "propitiate the doom of Aesop," but both versions also tell of a great military force that descends on the Delphians and punishes them for the killing. It is hard to see why the latter (military expedition) is necessary, given the ritual resolution attached to the former (divine punishment). But perhaps the violence suffered by the Delphians in war fills the slot of literal scapegoating at the end of their story, or—to put it in other terms—military defeat figures the scapegoating of an entire community.

However that may be, the Delphians can be said to suffer all the blights and indignities of scapegoating; but what of Aesop? Some strands in the Aesop tradition assert that the Delphians had to recompense Aesop with cult-hero hon-

---

[114] According to LSJ, ποινή is "rare in prose, δίκη being the usual word." This is certainly borne out by Herodotus's usage: ποινή occurs only at 2.134.4, 3.14.5, 7.134.2, and 7.136.2, while τίσις, ζημίη, and δίκη occur a total of twenty-six times.

[115] As already noted, *Vita* W omits the phrase παρὰ τοῦ Διός from this sentence, leaving open the possibility that it is the Delphic oracle. In light of this omission, it is interesting to note the (deliberate?) vagueness of Herodotus (which oracle?) and of Plutarch (which god is angry?).

[116] Cf. Rosen 2007.100–107 who makes the same point to refute the convoluted *hysteron proteron* argument of Wiechers 1961.38–52 for the story of Aesop's death as a mythological aetiology of *pharmakos* ritual.

ors (although this is suppressed in *Vita* G).[117] Thus *Vita* W tells us, "having built a temple, they set up a stele for him" (ch. 142), while *P.Oxy.* 1800 is even more explicit: "having walled round the place where he fell, and established an altar as release from disease, they sacrificed [to him] as a hero" (οἱ δὲ περιτει[χίσ]-αντες τὸν τόπον [ἐν ᾧ κ]ατέπεσεν βωμὸ[ν θ᾽ ἱ]δ[ρυσά]μενοι λυτήρ[ι]ο[ν] τῆς νόσου, ὡς ἥρῳ θ[υσίας] προ[σ]ήνεγκαν).[118] If, as I have suggested, the status of *pharmakos* represents the lowest and most degraded identity in the discursive system of ancient Greek religion, hero cult forms its apex. Thus Aesop definitively triumphs over the Delphians in this contest of scapegoating authority.

Modern scholars have occasionally taken these traditions at face value and assumed that Aesop did, in fact, receive hero cult worship at Delphi. But it is worth emphasizing that, in contrast to the wealth of evidence for the cult of Neoptolemus at Delphi, there is no independent literary or archaeological evidence outside the *Life of Aesop* traditions to confirm the existence of such a cult.[119] Here again, I suggest, we detect the lineaments of parody. The popular imagination parodies even as it appropriates the lofty narrative of Neoptolemus's cult honors for the scurrilous, low hero Aesop.

Nor is this the only version of Aesop's triumph preserved in the tradition: in an alternative story that goes back at least to Plato Comicus (late fifth century BCE), Aesop comes to life again. As the late paroemiographer Zenobius tells it (glossing the proverb Αἰσώπειον αἷμα, "Aesopic blood"), "for Aesop was so beloved of the god(s) that it is told that he came to life again, like Tyndareus and Heracles and Glaucus" (οὕτω γὰρ θεοφιλὴς ἐγένετο ὁ Αἴσωπος ὡς μυθεύεται αὐτὸν ἀναβιῶναι, ὡς Τυνδάρεων καὶ Ἡρακλῆν καὶ Γλαῦκον).[120] Here we see with particular clarity how popular fantasy riffs on high mythological traditions, assimilating its hero's fate to Heracles' apotheosis on Oeta or Glaucus's transformation into a sea-god. In contrast to the Delphians, ground down by plague, blight of the land, and war, Aesop's success is the most extreme imaginable within the semiotic systems of Greek mythology and religion.

Thus I hope to have shown how the story of Aesop at Delphi programmatically contests and undermines such high discourses and hegemonic ideologies as

---

[117] For discussion of the suppression of cult-hero honors in *Vita* G, cf. Jouanno 2006.48 and 212n. 134, and see chapter 4, section III below.

[118] Text after Perry 1952 (*Test.* 25), reading Perry's suggested λυτήρ[ι]ο[ν] instead of λυτηρ[ί]ο[υς].

[119] For the evidence for Neoptolemus's hero cult at Delphi, see the thorough discussion of Currie 2005.296–307, and see n. 81 above; for scholars who accept at face value Aesop's hero cult at Delphi, see Nagy 1979.285–90, 302–3, 307–8, 316; Clay 2004.127–28; Compton 2006.30–31, 36. It is perhaps this lack of any other evidence for Aesop's hero cult that explains Parke and Wormell's bemused comment on *P.Oxy.* 1800: "Is there a confusion with Neoptolemus?" (Parke and Wormell 1956.II.27)

[120] Sources: Plato Comicus fr. 70 KA preserved in the Schol. *ad* Aristoph. *Birds* 471 (= Perry *Test.* 45); Zenobius Athos *Proverbia*, vol. 5, no. 107 ed. Bühler (= Perry *Test.* 27); Suda s.vv. Αἰσώπειον αἷμα, ἀναβιῶναι I.161, II.182–83 Adler (= Perry *Test.* 45).

Apollo's oracular monopoly; the god's delegation of oracle and sacrifice to his Delphic "servants"; the practices of Delphic Theoxeny; and the collusion of Olympian religion and hero cult. In producing such a reading, I have suggested that we must be attentive to different factions and interests as they play through our sources. We cannot necessarily accept at face value ancient traditions about (for example) the mode of Delphic sacrifice, or the reality of scapegoat ritual or hero-cult honors, without interrogating whose traditions they were and whose interests they served. The formation of the Aesop traditions suggests it is perhaps better to view Greek religion and mythology not as monolithic, coherent, and static constructs but as complex and mobile signifying systems available for multiple, competing improvisations and inspired bricolage.

Chapter 2
~

SOPHIA BEFORE/BEYOND PHILOSOPHY

BY THE EXPERIMENTAL READING offered in chapter 1, I hope to have demonstrated that it is possible to extract from the Aesopica elements of long-lived ideological commentary and critique of enduring Greek cultural formations. In this and the following chapters, I will attempt to do the same for aspects of the Aesop tradition (especially the *Life of Aesop*) in dialogue with the complex traditions of Greek "wisdom" (and this analysis will ultimately offer us additional insight into the story of Aesop's adventures at Delphi). As a precondition for tracing such dialogue, I must first specify what I mean by "wisdom traditions"—their participants, their associations and contexts, and their claims to cultural authority. I will argue that there was a native Greek conceptualization of Hesiod, Theognis, Pythagoras, and the Seven Sages (among others) as a coherent tradition, designated as *sophia,* and its practitioners as *sophoi* or *sophistai.* The concept of *sophia* embraces poetic skill, practical political wisdom, and religious expertise—especially in the domains of sacrifice and seercraft/mantic art. This complex I will refer to as the "high wisdom tradition." When I have laid out in some detail what I mean by the wisdom tradition, I will turn in the next three chapters to consider Aesop's relation to it, which seems, throughout the Aesop tradition and still in our preserved *Life of Aesop*, oddly double. For the figure of Aesop seems to circulate in popular tradition as a participant—or competitor—in this field of *sophia* and simultaneously as a vehicle for parody and criticism thereof. Thus chapters 3 and 4 will be devoted to considering representations of Aesop as a sage, purveying his own distinctive brand of practical, situational wisdom, while chapter 5 will focus on elements of the Aesopica that seem to function as parodies of high wisdom or of its philosophical appropriation.

I. The Tradition of *Sophia*

> *Sophia* then was so called, as being some sort of 'clearness' (σάφεια), as making all things clear (ὡς σαφηνίζουσα πάντα). And clarity is called this, being a certain brightness in relation to light, on account of bringing the hidden things to light. Since, then, the objects of intellection and divine things, even if (as Aristotle says) they are most perspicuous according to their own being, seem to us shadowy and dim because of the mist of the body that is overlaid, the skill/knowledge [ἐπιστήμη] that brings these

things to light for us they suitably named *sophia*.... For [*sophia* and *sophos*] have been conceived by the ancients in five ways, which also Aristocles says in the ten books *On Philosophy*. For one ought to recognize that human beings perish in different ways: for in fact [they perish] from plagues and famines and earthquakes and wars and complicated diseases and other causes, but most of all from thronging floods, what sort is said to have happened at the time of Deucalion—great, but not so great as to have overcome all [men]. For the herdsmen and those who spend their time in the mountains or in the foothills, they are saved, but the plains and those inhabiting them are overwhelmed by floods.... These then, the survivors, having no source of nourishment, under the pressure of necessity were thinking up (ἐπενόουν) the things [that addressed] their need—grinding grain with handmills or sowing or any other such thing, and they called such thinking, which found out what was advantageous for the necessities of life, *sophia* and the one who had thought it up [they called] *sophos*. Again, they thought up arts (τέχνας), as the poet says, "by the teachings of Athena," established not to the sole end of necessity for livelihood, but advancing even as far as the noble and the urbane. And this again they called *sophia* and the one who invented it *sophos*, as in "the wise craftsman fitted"—"knowing well by the teachings of Athena."[1] (For on account of the exceptional quality of the inventions they used to attribute the ideas for these things to a god.) Again they concerned themselves with political affairs and invented laws and all the things that hold cities together. And this conception (ἐπίνοιαν) again they called *sophia*; for such were the Seven Sages, men who had invented certain forms of political excellence. And then, advancing further along the road, they came to their own bodies and nature as their maker (τὴν δημιουργὸν αὐτῶν ... φύσιν), and this study of nature, rather peculiarly, they called *theōria*, and we [still] call such men wise (σοφούς) with respect to the things concerning nature. The fifth thing left after these things, they were taking note of the things that were entirely divine and beyond the cosmos and unchangeable (τὰ θεῖα καὶ ὑπερκόσμια καὶ ἀμετάβλητα παντελῶς), and knowledge of these they named *sophia* in its most proper signification (κυριωτάτην σοφίαν ὠνόμασαν). (Philoponus, *Commentary on Aristotle's Nicomachean Ethics* 1.1 = Aristotle *On Philosophy* fr. 8 Ross)

This account of the five progressive stages of human *sophia* (attributed to the second-century CE Peripatetic Aristocles, and perhaps deriving ultimately from Aristotle)[2] conformed only too well to nineteenth- and early twentieth-

---

[1] These represent two different quotations from Homer ("the poet"): *Il.* 23.712 (reading σοφὸς ἤραρε τέκτων instead of the generally accepted reading κλυτὸς ἤραρε τέκτων) and *Il.* 15.412 (on which more below).

[2] Untersteiner (1963.14–15, 121–23, following Bywater 1877 and Festugière 1949.II.2.222 with n. 1, 587–91) accepted this lengthy passage as a fragment of Aristotle's lost work *On Philosophy* and placed it at the beginning of the text; cf. Vernant 1982.69–70. Bywater's identification of this whole passage as a fragment of a lost work of Aristotle was rejected in turn by Jaeger 1948.137n. 1, Cherniss 1959.38–39, and Tarán 1966.467–68. Thus, although this passage of Philoponus is included by Ross 1958 under his fr. 8 of Aristotle *On Philosophy*, it does not appear in Gigon's (1987) edition of the fragments of Aristotle. As we shall see, the five historical stages of *sophia* here posited in fact con-

century scholarly assumptions about the ways in which languages and cultures develop. As a result, something quite similar to this Peripatetic developmental schema still dominates the handbooks and lexica of classical scholarship. According to this modern account, the meaning of *sophia* developed from concrete to abstract and from specific to general (as Greek culture itself developed): first, designating the skill of craftsmen (as in Homer); then the specific expertise of poetic craft; then practical, political wisdom or know-how; and, finally, abstract theoretical speculation.[3] But such an evolutionary model of *sophia* was roundly critiqued and debunked already in 1976 by G. B. Kerferd, who argued that this schema was itself the product of fifth-century Sophistic speculation on the development of culture and the progressive ascent of *bioi* (several examples of which Kerferd reviews). As he suggests, this Greek sophistic model came to be codified and enshrined in all the ancient lexica and commentaries that then formed the basis in turn of modern classical scholarship's "scientific" philology. Kerferd also notes that this evolutionary schema made sense and appealed to nineteenth- and early twentieth-century scholars because it conformed to several different "modern expectations"—which Kerferd succinctly catalogs:

> 1. that as we go back in time there is likely to be a single primitive or original meaning for a term or set of terms from which later meanings were derived by various kinds of logical development; 2. that this univocal primitive meaning will be simpler, more concrete and probably more limited in range than later derivatives. Both these expectations have had a deep influence on the approach to the identification of meanings in the Indo-European language, and to a considerable degree, also in Homeric Greek. But they are now seriously questioned and should probably be dismissed as myths. In the particular case with which we are concerned, however, they have coincided all too neatly with 3. the Marxist tendency to relate the origins and development of philosophy to technology, and the basically contrary view that the history of Greek thought can be understood as involving the progressive emergence of *Geist* (Mind or the Spiritual) from humbler, lower, more primitive levels of thought.[4]

Kerferd's analysis allows us to see the Peripatetic five-stage narrative not as historical truth, but as a founding myth for philosophy, tendentiously appropriating an older Greek wisdom tradition and inserting it into a teleology that leads inevitably to the crowning achievement of theoretical speculation ("*sophia* in

---

form pretty closely to Aristotle's typology of intellectual faculties in *NE* Book 6 (although Aristotle's typology is somewhat less elaborate). Ultimately, though, the usefulness of this quotation for Greek conceptions of *sophia* (and my argument thereon) does not at all depend on or require the attribution of these views to Aristotle himself.

[3] Cf. LSJ s.v. *sophia*, *sophistēs*; Snell 1924.1–20; Gauthier and Jolif 1959. II.2.478–89; Gladigow 1965; Chantraine 1968–80.IV.1030–31; Guthrie 1969.27–34; Maier 1970; Nestle 1975.14–17. Note that this modern four–stage sequence is similar but not identical to Aristocles' five–stage model of the development of *sophia*.

[4] Kerferd 1976.18–19.

its most proper signification"). Kerferd's discussion thus strongly suggests that we need to be wary of such developmental or evolutionary schemata, and that we must start over in our attempt to understand the native Greek (pre- or non-philosophical) conceptualization of *sophia*.

The noun *sophia* is derived from the adjective *sophos*, which itself denotes supreme skill in some domain. The noun is extremely rare in Attic prose, apparently originally a poetic word, which Kerferd speculates may have been popularized in Athens from Ionian prose and the Sophists.[5] In any case, Kerferd notes that in its sole occurrence in Homer, σοφίη characterizes the "wisdom" or "skill" of a shipwright as the special gift of Athena (ὅς ῥά τε πάσης/ εὖ εἰδῇ σοφίης ὑποθημοσύνῃσιν Ἀθήνης, *Il.* 15.411–12):

> It is thus linked with, not set aside from or contrasted with, the highest form of human wisdom. The particular knowledge of the ship-wright is here linked with 'all wisdom' and we are not justified in concluding that the reference to 'all wisdom', still less the *meaning* of 'wisdom' is to be restricted to skill in the crafts, although this is certainly included in the reference.[6]

Likewise, Kerferd rejects earlier scholarly attempts to limit the meaning of *sophia* in the domain of poetry to technical musical skill, noting that more often in archaic poetry it designates the *content* of the poet's song as the special gift of the Muses: "It is the poet, the seer and the sage in early Greece who reveal visions not granted otherwise to mortals."[7]

Following Kerferd, I would contend that *sophia* (especially in its early poetic occurrences) not only is bestowed by the gods, but also often pertains to divine things or religious expertise. And, precisely because of its divine sources and fields of application, we might say simply that *sophia* is always a superlative.[8] As such, it is also always a domain of contest among competing claims, because the possession of *sophia* endows its possessor with enormous cultural authority.

---

[5] As Kerferd 1976.22 notes, *sophia* does not occur in Thucydides (who has σοφός, σοφιστής, σόφισμα, and φιλοσοφοῦμεν each once), nor at all in Antiphon, Andocides, or Aeschines. It occurs only once in Demosthenes (5.11); in contrast, σοφίη occurs 20 times in Herodotus, together with 4 occurrences of σοφίζομαι, 3 of σόφισμα, 3 of σοφιστής, and 29 of forms of σοφός (for all of which, see Powell 1938 s.vv.). Kerferd also notes, "When we realise that there are 30 examples of the word and its derivatives in Aristophanes' *Clouds* it begins to be likely, even bearing in mind the subject matter of the play, that the term was a newish term in Athens in 423 B.C., and it may well have been made familiar there by the sophists" (Kerferd 1976.22).

[6] Kerferd 1976.24.

[7] Kerferd 1976.26. For passages where *sophia* designates specifically the content of the poet's song, Kerferd cites *Homeric Hymn to Hermes* 511; Hes. fr. 306 MW; Xenophanes B 2 DK, ll. 12, 14. One might add: Solon fr. 13 W, l. 52; Thgn. 770; Pindar O.9.38, P.6.49. Cf. Havelock 1963.162n. 27, 287; Griffith 1990.188–90.

[8] Cf. Snell 1924.7 (allowing for his Hegelian, developmental bias): "Insofern sind die oben zitierten Grammatiker-Bemerkungen, σοφία sei ursprünglich gleich τέχνη gewesen, zu berichtigen. Sehr viel feiner nannte Aristoteles die σοφία die ἀρετή τέχνης" (quotation from Arist. *NE* 6.7, 1141a12). See also Havelock 1963.163n. 28, 287–88.

Such an account of prephilosophical *sophia* in fact conforms strikingly well to Mary Helms's anthropological model of the power and prestige of "skilled crafting" within traditional cultures. Based on a wide-ranging survey of many cultures (including ancient Greece), Helms defines a category of activities of "skilled crafting" that act to create or transform objects or energies in the world; to impose order from chaos; and to mediate between "civilization" and some realm "outside" (whether this is conceived as the otherworld of the divine, the realm of wild nature, or that of distant peoples and places as themselves endowed with magical energies).[9] An important point for Helms's argument is the assimilation or identification of the vertical and horizontal axes of distance, such that distant people "out there" are analogous to the representing culture's gods and ancestors.[10] Thus for Helms, "skilled crafting" embraces not only carpentry, metallurgy, and weaving, but also medicine, hunting, seercraft, shamanic power, navigation, song making and dance, political oratory, and the arts of judge, mediator, and ambassador, for all of these tap into and deploy for intrasocietal benefit the powers and energies of an other world not readily available to normal human consciousness.

Helms also observes that in many traditional cultures, all these domains of "skilled crafting" are intimately associated with long-distance travel to places "outside" and the acquisition there of precious goods (including information and skills, but also exotic objects) to be brought back to the realm of "civilization" (i.e., the home culture).[11] In Helms's analysis, long-distance travel is itself a form of "skilled crafting," as are its products of esoteric knowledge and highly valued objects from elsewhere.

Finally, Helms emphasizes that cross-culturally such forms of skilled crafting, because of their special access to other realms and their power to impose order from chaos, tend to endow their possessors (whether the craftsmen themselves or their elite patrons) with political authority and ideological legitimacy. This obviously applies to those superlatively skilled in political oratory, advising, and arbitration, but in many traditional cultures, skilled artisans, musicians, religious experts, and navigators also wield significant political power, or those in power actively cultivate these arts to legitimate their authority. In such contexts, every act of skilled crafting re-creates or conjures up the time of

---

[9] Helms 1993; for ancient Greek material, Helms draws on Brown 1947 (qualities of Hermes as trickster and thief); Havelock 1963 (on the functions and powers of poetry in preliterate Greece); Austin and Vidal-Naquet 1977; Detienne and Vernant 1978 (on *mētis*).

[10] On this identification, see in particular Helms 1993.173–209.

[11] Helms 1993.91–170; cf. Helms 1988. Helms uses the concept of acquisition to differentiate her model from preexisting anthropological models of "trade" and "exchange": in contrast to those, Helms's emphasis is on one-way acquisition (vs two-way exchange); on the symbolic and ideological value attached to objects within the home culture (vs the material, economic emphasis of much work on trade); and on the potency of such objects intrasocietally (rather than the ways in which exchange forges bonds between persons from different cultures).

origins, reactivating the energies of the first creation by gods and ancestors, themselves conceived as craftsmen and culture heroes.[12] By the same token, as Helms notes, successful crafting can itself bring new social groups into being:

> With respect to tangible objects, to the Eskimo skilled crafting is a "ritual of discovery" by which hidden patterns of nature are revealed.... Thus, the carver "examines [a piece of unworked ivory] to find its hidden form and, if that is not immediately apparent, carves aimlessly until he sees it, humming or chanting as he works. Then he brings it out: Seal, hidden, emerges. It was always there: he didn't create it; he released it; he helped it step forth" (Carpenter 1971: 163).
>
> New social groups can be released or aided in their "stepping forth" from chaotic or formless conditions in much the same way. Among the Yoruba ordered towns may be shaped and civilized living achieved in clearings perceived as crafted from the all-enveloping natural forest.... In comparable fashion, creation of a new motif or new patternings of traditional motifs by master carvers and painters among the Ilahita Arapesh signals the creation of a new spirit entity. If political conditions warrant it, the new spirit entity can become a sacred patron supporting the emergence of a new descent group as an autonomous political entity.[13]

Thus Helms's model also suggests ways in which skilled crafting can serve as the domain or ground for social and political contest within culture.[14]

I would contend that *sophia* is the single Greek term that, in its prephilosophical usage, best embraces the cluster of elements and powers Helms identifies with skilled crafting.[15] Helms's model essentially allows us to reconceive the

---

[12] Helms 1993.69–87 and cf. 1993.17–18: "By extension, skilled artisans and/or the elite patrons for whom they may work also become vehicles or spokespersons not only for technical knowledge but especially for moral qualities and for the supernaturally or ancestrally sanctioned ethics, political-ideology, and myth-history of the polity. Moreover, by their own acts of skilled crafting, artisans and their patrons also actively maintain the vital links believed to connect the polity and its people with the supernatural energetics of the outside world that sustain them. Skilled crafters become present-day transformers and culture hero creators. Their acts of crafting compress the original creations and transformations recorded in myth and legend into still existing actions, maintaining a direct, living connection between the temporal/spatial here-and-now of the cultural setting and the there-and-then of outside dimensions that relate the present to the past by the metaphor of distance."

[13] Helms 1993.26.

[14] Cf. especially Helms's notes 8 and 9 on p. 222: [8] "Alternatively, if the community rejects the new art as aesthetically unacceptable, the dissident group has failed in its political attempt"; [9] "Greene reminds us, however, that the socially constructive powers of speech in the hands of a skilled and supernaturally influenced artisan can be transmuted into destructive powers when the poet or seer expresses or releases the damaging power of words by satirizing."

[15] Although Helms 1993 on occasion seems to identify skilled crafting with *mētis* (drawing on Detienne and Vernant 1978), I would contend that *mētis* is part of the armory of *sophia*, but not the whole. We might say that *mētis* is the trickier subcategory of *sophia*, while Zeus's first two mates together from the end of the *Theogony* (Mētis and Themis) constitute the full semantic and symbolic field of *sophia*. It is also worth noting that Detienne and Vernant 1978 often indiscriminately cite passages where the term *sophia* is used to develop their argument about *mētis*; see, e.g., pp. 39, 308, 310, 313–18.

developmental schema with which we began as a synchronic nexus: as skilled crafting, *sophia* is at once the otherworldly perspicuity of the skillful agriculturalist; the superlative skill of the *tektōn*; the special access to invisible realms of the poet, seer, and sacrificial expert; the political order-imposing faculty of lawgivers and judges; and the contemplation of otherworldly and divine things of the early *physikoi*. Thus, to take again the example of *Iliad* 15.411–12 (the only occurrence of *sophiē* in all of Homer): it is significant not only that the shipwright's skilled craft is a divine gift that endows him with all *sophiē* (as Kerferd notes), but also that his *sophiē* is highlighted here in a simile precisely at the moment that he is laying out or "straightening by rule" a ship's timber. For, as Helms observes, in many cultures shipbuilding is itself a magical art, which in turn enables the skilled crafting deployed in and further enhanced by long-distance travel.[16] Indeed, in light of Helms's rich array of ethnographic data, we can lend more credence to the folk etymology of *sophia* that leads off the Peripatetic anthropology cited above—not for its value as etymology (which is nil), but for its articulation of the native Greek conceptualization of "wisdom." *Sophia* is simply the "bringing to light" (σάφεια) of that which is normally hidden or invisible to human senses in any of a number of different domains.[17]

Such a model of *sophia* is further supported by G. B. Kerferd's exhaustive collection of occurrences of the term σοφιστής applied to various classes of people who preexisted the "Sophistic Movement" of the late fifth century. As Kerferd observes, there is a fairly broad and diverse prephilosophical application of the term attested in our extant texts. Once we look beyond Plato and Xenophon, who apply the term *sophistēs* almost exclusively to the late fifth-century "Sophists" and thereby make it a derogatory term, there is abundant evidence for an older, broader usage. It designates poets (including Homer and Hesiod), musicians and rhapsodes, diviners and seers, religious experts like Pythagoras, political leaders and lawgivers including the Seven Sages, other early wise men, Presocratic philosophers, and "contriver[s], often with the suggestion of mysterious power."[18] Kerferd concludes:

---

[16] Cf. Helms 1993.21, on the special skill required to craft canoes for the Gawa of Papua New Guinea. We might also note that the Iliadic simile marks a crucial, fateful moment in the narrative—a *kairos*; for at this moment, the battle line is drawn straight, as Hector is about to set fire to the Achaean ships and Patroclus is about to enter the battle in the guise of Achilles to assist the beleaguered Greeks. For more on the connections of *sophia* and *kairos*, see below, chapter 3, section II.

[17] In fact, the word family *sophos/sophia* has no known etymology in Greek; see Chantraine 1968–80.IV.1031. For the idea of (poetic) *sophia* as bringing to light what is normally invisible, cf. Carson 1988.149–50, 1999, esp. 45–62.

[18] Kerferd 1950.8, based on a full list of relevant ancient passages. Cf. Morrison 1949, Lloyd 1987.92–99, Hartog 1988.88, Nightingale 1995.10. Guthrie 1969.32–34 contends that the negative connotations attached to the term *sophistēs* are part of a more general Greek anti-intellectualism in the second half of the fifth century, as evidenced by the usage of Aristophanes as well as that of Plato and Xenophon.

It should be clear from this list what the earlier meaning of σοφιστής was. Whereas σοφός and σοφία can be used of all sorts of skills, the term σοφιστής is confined to those who in one way or another function as the Sages, the exponents of knowledge in early communities. Moreover, it is not the skill of such persons which is in question, but simply the functions which they perform as a class.[19]

That is, in Helms's terms, *sophistai* are skilled craftsmen who mediate between this and an other world—functionaries or professional practitioners of *sophia*.[20]

II. Sophists and (as) Sages

We can connect the parameters of this tradition with Richard Martin's argument about the Seven Sages in the archaic and classical period. Martin argues that already in the archaic period, one way in which the Greeks represented wisdom to themselves was through the legends of a corporate group of Seven Sages, whose members all exhibited a set of common features: poetic composition, political skill, competitive public performance, and involvement in religious activity.[21] In all these respects, Martin's composite rendering of the typical Sage resonates with Helms's cross-cultural model of skilled crafting. And, although Martin does not specifically discuss the term *sophistēs*, its pattern of distribution seems to conform precisely to the parameters of archaic "wisdom" Martin outlines. Thus the semantic sphere of *sophistēs* suggests a couple of extensions of Martin's model of archaic "wisdom" (since the term seems to integrate the Sages into a larger system), while Martin's discussion allows us to nuance in turn Kerferd's model of *sophistēs* as a function. First, Martin's analysis allows us to recognize an important religious component in the term (a component that corresponds to Helms's notion that skilled craftsmen crucially serve as mediators between this and some magical, invisible other realm).[22] Consider in this

---

[19] Kerferd 1950.8–9.

[20] This account of *sophistēs* as "professional practitioner of wisdom" / "Sage" conforms to its etymology, for *sophistēs* is an agent noun derived from the verb σοφίζομαι ("to be skilled in speech or action; to practice wisdom"). Hence *sophistēs* = "practitioner of wisdom." The verb σοφίζομαι, in turn, is a denominative verb derived from σοφός. Thus σοφίζω (active) means "to make skilled" or "instruct"; σοφίζομαι (medio-passive) "to be skilled." On the etymological relations of all these terms, see Chantraine 1933.316–17, 1968–80, s.v. σοφός (= IV.1030–31); for the semantics of the agent noun, see Chantraine 1933.310–20.

[21] Martin 1998, refuting the argument of Fehling 1985 that the notion of a corporate group of the Seven Sages did not preexist Plato, who invented the group in his *Protagoras*.

[22] Guthrie 1969.29, 33 (unusually among scholars) considers the term *sophistēs* on its own and suggests that the closest English equivalent might be "teacher" or "professor." It is true that the term very often occurs in contexts of teaching or instruction, but Guthrie's account fails to note: (1) that the instructional context is often religious; and (2) that there is usually emphasis on competition of wisdom (which may indeed be an inevitable concomitant of the instructional situation in ancient Greece; cf. Lloyd 1987.50–108; Tell 2010).

respect Herodotus's uses of the term *sophistēs*: in 2.49, he applies it to the followers of Melampus in the context of their introduction of Dionysiac rites from Egypt to Greece; in 4.95, he characterizes Pythagoras as "not the weakest *sophistēs* among the Greeks" in the context of his supposedly tutoring his Thracian slave Salmoxis in the "practices of immortality."[23] Consider also the context of Pindar's single use of *sophistai* instead of his more usual *sophoi* to designate poets:

> μελέταν δὲ σοφισταῖς
> Διὸς ἕκατι πρόσβαλον σεβιζόμενοι·
> ἐν μὲν Αἰτωλῶν θυσίαισι φαενναῖς
> Οἰνεῖδαι κρατεροί,
> ἐν δὲ Θήβαις ἱπποσόας Ἰόλαος
> γέρας ἔχει, Περσεὺς δ' ἐν Ἄργει, Κάστορος δ' αἰχ-
>   μᾷ Πολυδεύκεός τ' ἐπ' Εὐρώτα ῥεέθροις.
> ἀλλ' ἐν Οἰνώνᾳ μεγαλήτορες ὀργαί
> Αἰακοῦ παίδων τε·
> (I.5.28–35)

And they [sc. ἥρωες], being reverenced, have provided matter for thought for *sophistai* [= poets] thanks to Zeus: amidst the shining sacrifices of the Aetolians the Oeneidae are mighty, and in Thebes, horse-saving Iolaus has honor, and Perseus in Argos, and the spear of Castor and of Polydeuces upon the streams of Eurotas. But in Oenone, great-hearted are the tempers of Aeacus and his sons.

It is noteworthy that Pindar links the activity of *sophistai* closely with acts of reverence implied by the participle σεβιζόμενοι and then spelled out in the following lines in terms of specific local hero-cult practices and offerings.

Second (and perhaps more importantly) Martin's analysis allows us to see a significant element of competition built into the term *sophistēs*. This aspect, I would contend, is very marked in a couple of Herodotus's uses of the term. Thus in 4.95, Herodotus's use of a superlative adjective to modify *sophistēs* (Pythagoras was "not the weakest *sophistēs* among the Greeks") already suggests competition within a group, while his particular point is in fact a competition in religious wisdom between Pythagoras and Salmoxis. For Herodotus here rejects the claim of the Greeks of the Hellespont and Pontus that the Thracian Salmoxis learned his doctrine as a slave from the Greek sage Pythagoras; contending in his own voice that Salmoxis "lived many years earlier than Pythagoras," Herodotus awards the palm of religious *sophia* to him (Hdt. 4.96). At 1.29, Herodotus tells us that,

---

[23] For this translation of ἀθανίζοντες/ἀθανίζουσι (Hdt. 4.93, 94, 5.4), see Hartog 1988.89–91. For general discussion of the prominence of religious and ritual elements in the oldest layers of Pythagorean lore (the Pythagoras biography and the *acusmata*), see Burkert 1972.97–192.

κατεστραμμένων δὲ τούτων καὶ προσεπικτωμένου Κροίσου Λυδοῖσι, ἀπικνέονται ἐς Σάρδις ἀκμαζούσας πλούτῳ ἄλλοι τε οἱ πάντες ἐκ τῆς Ἑλλάδος σοφισταί, οἳ τοῦτον τὸν χρόνον ἐτύγχανον ἐόντες, ὡς ἕκαστος αὐτῶν ἀπικνέοιτο, καὶ δὴ καὶ Σόλων ἀνὴρ Ἀθηναῖος, ὃς Ἀθηναίοισι νόμους κελεύσασι ποιήσας ἀπεδήμησε ἔτεα δέκα. . . .

And when these [the Greeks of Asia Minor] had been subdued and Croesus had added them to the possession of the Lydians, there came to Sardis, then being at its height in wealth, the others, all the Wise Men of Greece, who happened to be living at this time, as each of them would come, and especially Solon the Athenian, who left town for ten years when he had made laws at the behest of the Athenians. . . .

Richard Martin has already noticed that Herodotus's diction here implies that all the Sages lived at the same time as contemporaries of Croesus.[24] More than that: Herodotus's narrative at this point seems to suggest a serial contest of Sages, since Solon on his arrival (and so presumably the other Sages in their turn) is asked who he's seen who is most blessed or fortunate. Solon's answer, of course, does not please the Lydian king, so he sends him away, judging him "of no account and extremely ignorant" (κάρτα . . . ἀμαθέα, Hdt. 1.33).[25] Thus, here, Herodotus seems to designate the Sages as *sophistai* precisely in the context of a competition of wisdom.[26]

This aspect of competition is perhaps something we could identify as distinctively Greek in relation to Helms's cross-cultural model.[27] For, though I have noted above occasional instances in Helms's discussion that would allow a space for competition or contestation over what constitutes skilled crafting

---

[24] Martin 1998.125n. 16: "the syntax of Hdt. 1.29.1, 'the wise men (*sophistai*) who happened to exist (*etunkhanon eontes*) at that time,' with an imperfect indicative verb (rather than indefinite relative construction, 'whichever . . . existed') implies that Herodotus thought the sages were actually all living at the same time." Cf. Momigliano 1971.35: "The meeting of the Seven Wise Men at Croesus' court is implied in Herodotus 1.29." Notice that Plutarch (*Mal.Hdt.* 857f) understands Herodotus's *sophistai* here to be a designation of the Seven Sages as a group.

[25] Notice that Croesus's question takes the form τί μάλιστα;, a form specifically associated with the wisdom of the Seven Sages by Aristotle (as preserved in Iambl. *VP* 83; see Burkert 1972.166–70 for the attribution). For other examples of Seven Sages wisdom in this form, cf. Plut. *Banq.* 153c, 154d, 155c; D.L. 1.35–36, 77, 86–87; Stobaeus 1.34, 72, 102, 157, 4.28.7, 25.1, 27.16, 15.5, and see Konstantakos 2004.97, 126–27, 2005.20–21. Compare also the accounts preserved in Diodorus Siculus (9.26–28) and the Paroemiographers, which imagine the Seven Sages and Aesop all together at Croesus's court, offering different answers to his question about who is most fortunate (cf. Perry *Test.* 37; material collected in Snell 1971.90–95); I will consider this material in more detail in chapter 3, section I below. Martin 1998.126n. 29 makes the same point about the implicit agonistic context of Hdt. 1.30 (crediting it to the volume's anonymous reader).

[26] At Hdt. 2.49 (the one other occurrence of *sophistai* in the *Histories*), the element of competition seems to be implicitly with the *histor* himself; thus the narrator competes with the *sophistai* who are the "successors of Melampus" in his knowledge of the Egyptian source of Greek Dionysiac worship and of the "sacred story" that motivates the particulars of the rite.

[27] Alternatively, we may suppose that contestation is likely to exist in all the cultures whose ethnographies she draws on, but that her approach (and that of many of her anthropological sources) is limited by functionalist assumptions.

within culture, Helms's account is in fact overwhelmingly one of traditional cultures as stable, homeostatic systems. That is to say, hers is generally a functionalist model in which everything in culture serves to support and maintain a system already formed and closed.[28] And yet, as several scholars have noted, competition over claims to wisdom seems to be pervasive in our Greek sources as far back as we can trace them—certainly throughout the archaic and classical periods. Martin, who clearly articulates the prominence of competition in wisdom in the archaic period, attributes it at least partly to the jockeying between local and Panhellenic versions of Sage traditions.[29] G.E.R. Lloyd also notes the importance of competitive claims to superlative skill among *sophistai* (including the early medical writers), which he links to developing professionalization within the framework of free and open debate provided by the Greek polis.[30] I would add to these accounts a more basic motivation that both scholars in fact presuppose. Greece of the archaic and classical periods saw the emergence and establishment of the polis as the hegemonic order; this development, I would contend, continued to be hotly contested throughout the sixth and fifth centuries.[31] And precisely because *sophia* as skilled crafting endowed its possessors with real political status and authority within the city, what *sophia* was and who had it were objects of intense competition—long before the appearance of the Sophists of the late fifth century as professional purveyors of wisdom.[32]

Third (and finally), I would add to Martin's argument that the Sages seem to emerge from an older poetic tradition in which *sophia* can designate poetic skill (e.g., Solon fr. 13 W, ll. 51–52; Pindar O.1.116, O.9.38, P.1.12, P.4.248,

---

[28] While Helms's model allows for constant ongoing change and adjustment, it does not much acknowledge the possibilities of intracultural competition and contestation. Thus, for example, Helms 1993.214: "Constant repetition of transformative acts that either expose or impose order allows a sufficient degree (or sense) of shifting order in the face of constant flux so that under normal circumstances society achieves the necessary adjustments, large or small, to its ecological, demographic, even ideological world by frequent, flexible, manageable processes of change rather than by more abrupt jolts that could threaten social dissolution. In the process the cosmology and the actuality of political structure and operation are matched to achieve a reasonably functioning fit between action and legitimation." For critique of functionalism from a historical perspective, see Morris 1993, 1996.19; for cultural change and contestation within culture, see Scott 1990, Bell 1992, Sewell 1999.

[29] Martin 1998.123. For another account of the centrality of competition to Greek (poetic) *sophia*, see Griffith 1990.

[30] Lloyd 1987; cf. also Thomas 2000.

[31] For extended argument for this contention, see Kurke 1999, Morris 2000.

[32] In support of this political motivation, we might look again at the fifth-century passages I've quoted where forms of *sophistēs* appear significantly linked to competition. For both Hdt. 1.29 and 4.95 deploy *sophia* as a diacritic that differentiates and hierarchizes Greeks and non-Greeks, while 4.95 introduces another axis of differentiation—slave and free. (On the complex politics of Herodotus's self-positioning in his account of Pythagoras and Salmoxis, see Hartog 1988.102–9.) We might also note that Pindar's context for characterizing poets as *sophistai* (I.5.28–35) is closely linked to hero cult as a practice that constitutes and unites different civic communities. For the link between traditions of the Seven Sages and the archaic "crisis of the city," cf. Vernant 1982.69–81.

P.6.49, N.7.23, I.7.18, *Pae.* 7B.20), but also political wisdom (as in Xenophanes B 2 DK, ll. 12, 14). For just where the derived agent noun *sophistēs* comes to predominate in later prose sources, participles formed from the verb σοφίζομαι seem to function in earlier poetry, appearing especially in contexts of overt competition in *sophia*.[33] Thus Hesiod in the *Works & Days* promises his brother:

δείξω δή τοι μέτρα πολυφλοίσβοιο θαλάσσης,
οὔτε τι ναυτιλίης σεσοφισμένος οὔτε τι νηῶν·
(*WD* 648–49)

I will show you the measures of the much-sounding sea, though I am not at all versed in the art of sailing or ships.

In Helms's terms, it is particularly appropriate that the practice of *sophia* is here linked to knowledge of ships, seafaring, and long-distance travel. At the same time, by a cunning *recusatio*, Hesiod's lines imply that he is not "versed in" sailing or ships, but rather in poetry—hence he knows the "the measures (μέτρα) of the much-sounding sea."[34] In support of this interpretation of σεσοφισμένος, we should note that these lines lead immediately into Hesiod's poetic competition with Homeric epic and his boast that he won a tripod in a contest of song at the funeral games of Amphidamas—a tripod he has dedicated to the Heliconian Muses (*WD* 648–59).[35]

Theognis also uses a participial form of σοφίζομαι at a significant moment:

Κύρνε, σοφιζομένῳ μὲν ἐμοὶ σφρηγὶς ἐπικείσθω
τοῖσδ᾽ ἔπεσιν—λήσει δ᾽ οὔποτε κλεπτόμενα,
οὐδέ τις ἀλλάξει κάκιον τοὐσθλοῦ παρεόντος,
ὧδε δὲ πᾶς τις ἐρεῖ· Θεύγνιδός ἐστιν ἔπη

---

[33] Cf. *Et. Magn.* 722.16 (Gaisford) s.v. σοφιστής· κυρίως ὁ σοφιζόμενος. The prior occurrence of participial forms of σοφίζομαι in older poetic sources, replaced in later prose by σοφιστής, conforms to the etymological relation of these two words: as noted above (note 20), the verb σοφίζομαι is derived from the adjective σοφός; the agent noun σοφιστής is then a secondary derivative from the verb. On this latter derivation as "recent" within the history of Greek, see Chantraine 1933.317. For the integration of the Seven Sages with an older poetic tradition of *sophia*, see Havelock 1963.162n. 27, 287–88.

[34] Thus Griffith 1983b.62, Rosen 1990.101–3. For a reading of the entire Nautilia as poetic *recusatio* and metapoetic program, see Rosen 1990; Dougherty 2001.20–27, 39–40; Steiner 2005.349–50.

[35] West 1978.320 notes that Hesiod here reverses the standard Homeric epithets for Greece and Troy in line 653, but concludes nothing from this; Graziosi 2001.61 sees in this inversion of epithets "a competitive stance in relation to the epic tradition" (cf. Graziosi 2002.169–71). It is also significant that Hesiod's starting point here is Aulis; cf. Griffith 1983b.62, Nagy 1990a.77–79, Rosen 1990.99–103. Hesiod's statement that, in a context of overt poetic competition, he dedicated his victory tripod to the *Heliconian* Muses becomes an important signifier within the tradition for competition in *sophia* (as we shall see in Ibycus and the *Life of Aesop*; for the former, see below, n. 37; for the latter, chapter 4, section I below).

τοῦ Μεγαρέως· πάντας δὲ κατ' ἀνθρώπους ὀνομαστός·
ἀστοῖσιν δ' οὔπω πᾶσιν ἁδεῖν δύναμαι.
(Theognis, ll. 19–24)

> Cyrnus, let a seal be laid upon these verses for me as I am practicing my *sophia*—and they will never escape notice being stolen, nor will anyone substitute a worse one when a noble one is present. And thus everyone will say, "These are the verses of Theognis of Megara, and his name is known among all mankind"—but not yet am I able to please all the citizens.

Whatever we take to be the "seal" of Theognis, σοφιζομένῳ here characterizes the poet at a moment of overt competition in the quality of wisdom.[36] Thus Theognis asserts in the context of offering advice to Cyrnus that his precious *sophia* will not escape notice being stolen or replaced with a lower-quality product. It is noteworthy that these early occurrences of participial forms of the verb *sophizomai* figure in texts of didactic poetry or *hypothēkai*, whose goal is the practical education and indoctrination of the addressee.[37]

Thus the dictional cues *sophia, sophizomai, sophos,* and *sophistēs* seem to articulate a unified tradition, spanning poetry and prose, characterized by verbal skill (poetic and rhetorical) aimed at practical political effects, combined with religious expertise and (very often) an element of competition. In support of this model, we should perhaps take seriously the characterization of precursors Plato puts into the mouth of the Sophist Protagoras in the dialogue that bears his name:

> I say that the sophistic art (σοφιστικὴν τέχνην) is ancient, but that the men of old who had a hand in it, fearing the hatred it caused, made a screen and veiled it, some as poetry, like Homer, Hesiod, and Simonides, others as initiatory rites and the singing of oracles (those around Orpheus and Musaeus). Still others I perceive disguised it also as the gymnastic art—like Iccus of Tarentum and Herodicus the Selymbrian, who, still living now, is a sophist inferior to no one. And your Agathocles has made the musical art his disguise (being a great sophist) and Pythocleides the Cean and many others. (*Prot.* 316d3–e4)

---

[36] The nature and meaning of Theognis's "seal" have been much debated: see (e.g.) West 1974.40–43, 149–150; Griffith 1983b.42–44; Ford 1985; Edmunds 1997. I find most persuasive the interpretations of Griffith 1983b and Edmunds 1997. We should note in addition Edmunds's point that Theognis's use of ἁδεῖν at line 24 specifically evokes a political, deliberative context in which the speaker's competition in *sophia* takes place (1997.33–34).

[37] On the tradition of *hypothēkai*, see Friedländer 1913, Griffith 1983b, Martin 1984, Kurke 1990, Edmunds 1997. Cf. also the phrase Μοῖσαι σεσοφισμέναι εὐ Ἑλικωνίδες in Ibycus fr. 282a *PMG*, ll. 23–24, in a context shot through with allusions to the Hesiodic *Nautilia* and therefore also presumably a scene of poetic competition. On Ibycus's poem as an elaborate *recusatio* that trumps the Homeric Muses with Hesiodic Heliconian Muses, cf. Bowra 1961.255, Woodbury 1985, Steiner 2005. For one more occurrence of a participial form of σοφίζομαι in a context of competition or ranking and a claim to superlative skill, cf. Ps.-Phocylides, *Sententiae* 122–31.

While Protagoras's extended list of poets, religious teachers, and specialists in gymnastic training and musical art, all "masking" or "disguising" *sophistikē technē* under other forms, seems partly tongue-in-cheek (on Protagoras's part or Plato's), we may still take it as a genuine indicator of the breadth and complexity of a long-standing tradition of *sophia*. Particularly significant in this genealogy is the close association of poets with experts in initiatory rites and oracles, and the revealing conclusion (which subsumes the entire list) that these men attempted to disguise their *sophia* in order to escape the notice of those who were "powerful in the cities."[38] For by this latter motivation, Protagoras implies that those who were superlatively skilled in these various domains might somehow challenge or threaten the city's constituted political authority.

This is not to claim that everything within this tradition was identical—that there were no differences among Hesiod, Solon, Xenophanes, Musaeus, Pythagoras, Protagoras, and Hippias (among others). It is rather to suggest that all of these were conventionally conceived as a common tradition of prephilosophical *sophia*—a tradition that was, in turn, annexed and appropriated by Plato, Isocrates, and Aristotle, when they came to invent their different versions of "philosophy."[39] And for all its variety and complexity, a couple of elements seem to unify this common tradition of high *sophia*. One is the frequently claimed affiliation and special association with Apollo, especially as god of Delos, Delphi, or Didyma.[40] There is an element of this already in the poetic tradition. Thus Hesiod not only acknowledges briefly that "singers are from the Muses and far-casting Apollo" in the *Theogony* proem (*Th.* 94–95), but also, perhaps more tellingly, begins his almanac of significant days in the *Works & Days* with those sacred to Apollo—"the first, fourth, and seventh [are] holy days, for on it Leto bore gold–sworded Apollo" (*WD* 770–71).[41] The Theog-

---

[38] Kerferd 1976.27–28 likewise advocates taking Protagoras's remarks here seriously as representative of a genuine older conception of *sophia*. See also Morrison 1949, Kerferd 1950, Griffith 1990.187 with n. 7. It is striking that in this context, Protagoras specifically doesn't mention the Seven Sages: I would read this as part of a concerted effort on Plato's part to disengage the Sages from practical political activity. For more on this, see below, pp. 119–20 on Thales.

[39] For extended discussion of Plato's and Isocrates' competing "inventions of philosophy," see Nehamas 1990, Nightingale 1995.10–59; for the philosophical appropriation of older traditions, see further below, this chapter, section III, and chapters 6–9.

[40] We might think of these—the site of Apollo's birth and his important oracular centers—as places where Helms's horizontal and vertical axes converge; where spatially distant locations are conceived as points of special access to or communication with gods and ancestors. On the special status of Delphi as a mediating site, see also Dougherty and Kurke 2003.9–11, 14.

[41] On the religious associations of first, fourth, and seventh, see West 1978.351–353. As the odd syntax of these lines makes clear (and as West 1978.353 notes *ad loc.*), all three days, first, fourth, and seventh, are assimilated to Apollo here, though in fact only the first and seventh are really his (the first associated with the new-moon festival of Apollo; the seventh his birthday). The fourth was the birthday of Hermes, but notice that Hermes is here entirely elided in favor of Apollo. Perhaps because of their association with Apollo, all the firsts, fourths, and sevenths in the catalog of days are propitious days for various activities (*WD* 794–800, 809, 819–20).

nidea also begins significantly with two poems invoking Apollo (Thgn. 1–10), which follow conventional hymnic format—the second even includes a narrative of the god's sacred birth on Delos.[42]

Within the later tradition, Pythagoras, too, was closely identified with Apollo: Aristotle recorded that the Crotoniates called him "Hyperborean Apollo" (the saying also occurs among the *acusmata*), while Aristoxenus claimed that Pythagoras got his doctrines from the Delphic oracle.[43] Most of all, the Seven Sages were closely associated with Apollo at Delphi and (sometimes) at Didyma. Thus Socrates in the *Protagoras*, in the earliest explicit reference to the Sages as a group of Seven, describes how

> These men also having come together in common dedicated the first fruits of their wisdom (ἀπαρχὴν τῆς σοφίας ἀνέθεσαν) to Apollo at his temple in Delphi, having written these things which everyone hymns, "Know thyself" and "Nothing in excess." (*Prot.* 343a8–b3)

Plato refers here to the two most familiar sayings of the Seven Sages—"Know thyself" and "Nothing in excess"—as inscribed conspicuously at Delphi.[44] On occasion, these wise sayings were instead attributed directly to Delphic Apollo, the gift of his oracle to one of the Seven.[45] In addition to the famous sayings, inscriptional finds throughout the Greek world make it clear that a much longer list of "Sayings of the Seven Sages," consisting of 147 pithy maxims also preserved in Stobaeus, was inscribed at Delphi, at least by the fourth century

---

[42] Reitzenstein 1893.74 suggests that the opening prayers to Apollo are explicable because Apollo is the city god of Megara; but notice that, in contrast to the brief prayer to Artemis that immediately follows (Thgn. 11–14), neither poem addressed to Apollo mentions any particular local cult features. Reitzenstein also contends that the four invocations and prayers that open the collection of Theognidea still reflect the performance context of the sylloge in the symposium (comparing the first four Attic scolia as quoted by Athenaeus 694c–95f; Reitzenstein is followed in this interpretation by Kroll 1936.45, West 1974.42). I would agree with this and suggest that beginning the collection with invocations of Apollo may also preserve a reflex of the custom of articulating symposium from banquet by the singing of a paean (on which see Rutherford 2001.50–52). For intimations of a special connection between Apollo and the poet in the Theognidea, see ll. 757–60, 1119–22.

[43] Aristotle cited by Aelian *VH* 2.26; Aristoxenus cited by D.L. 8.8, 21; cf. D.L. 8.11; Iambl. *VP* 30, 140; Lucian *Dialogues of the Dead* 20.3. On Pythagoras's identification with Apollo as an early part of the Pythagorean tradition, see Burkert 1972.91, 141–43, 178. Cf. also the tradition, preserved by Herodotus (1.65.4) that the Spartan lawgiver Lycurgus got his law code directly from the Delphic oracle.

[44] Cf. [Plato] *Hipparch.* 228e1–3. According to Pausanias (10.24.1), *gnōthi sauton* and *mēden agan* were inscribed "in the pronaos of the temple of Apollo at Delphi." Note that Pausanias's account does not in fact preclude the possibility that the sayings were inscribed on a stele set up in the pronaos of the temple.

[45] Thus Clement of Alexandria tells us, "Some attribute the γνῶθι σαυτόν to Chilon; Chamaeleon [attributes it] to Thales in his [treatise] *On the Gods*; Aristotle [attributes it] to the Pythia" (*Strom.* 1.14.60.3 = Aristotle fr. 29 Gigon). Jaeger 1948.130 contends that this attribution to the Pythia must be Aristotle's own invention, but it is equally imaginable that he was drawing on a preexisting tradition.

BCE. For in 1966, French archaeologists excavating a Hellenistic Greek settlement on the site of Ai Khanoum in Afghanistan unearthed a stele base bearing the following verse inscription:

ἀνδρῶν τοι σοφὰ ταῦτα παλαιοτέρων ἀνάκει[τα]ι
  ῥήματα ἀριγνώτων Πυθοῖ ἐν ἠγαθέαι·
ἔνθεν ταῦτ[α] Κλέαρχος ἐπιφραδέως ἀναγράψας
  εἵσατο τηλαυγῆ Κινέου ἐν τεμένει.

> These wise sayings of older men, far-famed, are dedicated in holy Pytho; from where Clearchus assiduously copied these things and set them up in the temenos of Cineas to shine out far and wide.

Louis Robert, who published the inscription, dated it to ca. 300 BCE on the basis of its letter forms and identified the dedicant Clearchus with the Peripatetic philosopher, student of Aristotle, Clearchus of Soli.[46] In addition to the epigram, the base contained five sayings, which are identical to the last five sayings of Stobaeus's text of "Sayings of the Seven Sages." Robert explained these appended maxims as spillover from the stele itself: the stonecutter had miscalculated the spacing of 147 maxims in three columns and, rather than omit the last five, had inscribed them on the stele base. The stonecutter's miscalculation thus guarantees that the "wise words of men of old, far conspicuous" referred to in the dedicatory epigram are indeed the "Sayings of the Seven Sages" as preserved in Stobaeus's text and in other fourth- and third-century inscriptions from around the Greek world.[47] More than that: as Robert observed, the second couplet of the epigram makes it certain that the full list of Sayings of the Seven Sages was inscribed at Delphi, available for Clearchus's "assiduous copying."[48]

Another tradition that strongly links the Sages with oracular Apollo is that of the tripod. This story exists in many different versions preserved in late sources, but seems to contain elements of high antiquity. Thus, according to various different traditions, a tripod magically emerges from some other world (e.g., the sea) and causes strife among its discoverers until an oracle of Apollo (at Delphi or at Didyma) is consulted. Apollo's oracle commands that it be given "to the wisest" (σοφωτάτῳ); it then makes a full circuit of the Seven Sages, each ceding it to the next until it comes back around to the first recipient, who removes it from circulation by dedicating it to Apollo (at Delphi or at Didyma). In other versions of the story, the numinous tripod is replaced by a precious cup or phiale offered by a wealthy man (Bathycles) or an Eastern potentate (Croesus) "to the wisest," which then makes the rounds of the Sages before being dedicated at

---

[46] Robert 1968 = *IK Estremo oriente* no. 382.

[47] Other inscriptions: Thera (fourth c.); Miletoupolis in Asia Minor (ca. 300 BCE); for texts, see *SIG*³ no. 1268, *Inscriptiones Graecae* XII.3, no. 1020 and discussion in Robert 1968.438–41; Oikonomides 1980, 1987.

[48] Robert 1968.438–42.

an oracular shrine of Apollo.[49] The circulation of the tripod in this tradition makes manifest the element of competition among a group of Sages all imagined to be contemporaries. But the tripod itself is a polyvalent signifier within the tale: it is an archaic prize for competition, but also an essential utensil for sacrifice, perhaps underscoring the Sages' constitution as a sacrificial *collegium*.[50] Finally, as a dedication to Apollo at Delphi or Didyma, it participates in a system of top-rank Panhellenic gift exchange, a circuit that doubles and makes material the Sage's "dedication" of wise sayings.[51]

All these links with Apollo strongly evoke an older, prephilosophical model of *sophia*, not yet entirely shorn of its religious affiliations. Within this system, the god's otherworldly authority supports and legitimates that of the Sages' teachings, while the cults of Delphi and Didyma themselves draw enhanced status and prestige from their association with archaic *sophoi*. Indeed, we find reflexes or echoes of this affiliation of Apollo with the highest forms of human wisdom still lingering in the Greek philosophical tradition (suggesting its emergence from and continuity with older forms of *sophia*). As scholars have noted, Heraclitus's famous dictum, "the lord whose oracle is at Delphi neither speaks nor hides, but signifies" (ὁ ἄναξ, οὗ τὸ μαντεῖόν ἐστι τὸ ἐν Δελφοῖς, οὔτε λέγει οὔτε κρύπτει ἀλλὰ σημαίνει, B 93 DK), in its indirect and riddling style seems to characterize Heraclitus's own writing, thus assimilating his philosophical treatise to the pronouncements of the mantic god.[52] Socrates also, in Plato's rendering, reports that his friend Chaerephon "dared to ask the Delphic oracle if there was anyone wiser than Socrates," and got the response that "no one was wiser than he" (*Apol.* 21a4–7).[53] Socrates goes on to wonder, "What in the world is the god saying, and what in the world is he riddling?" (τί ποτε αἰνίττεται;, *Apol.* 21b3–4), since he is himself convinced that he cannot be the wisest. Thus in Plato's *Apology*, it is precisely Apollo's oracle that motivates

---

[49] The main sources for these traditions are Call. *Iambi* 1 (fr. 191 Pfeiffer, ll. 32–77); D.S. 9.13.2; Plut. *Sol.* 4.1–4; Schol. *ad* Aristoph. *Wealth* 9; D.L. 1.28–33, 82. For a survey of the different versions, see Wiersma 1933–34; for the relevant texts, Snell 1971.116–19. For arguments for the antiquity of elements in these traditions, see Snell 1971.114–15, Wehrli 1973.195, Gernet 1981a.116–19 (tripod as an *agalma* shuttling from another world), Martin 1998.120 (tripod as prize for an *agōn* is archaic).

[50] On the Seven Sages as a sacrificial *collegium*, see Martin 1998.121–23.

[51] Or, in the alternative tradition of the sayings as Apollo's oracular gift, the dedication of the tripod reciprocates that gift. On the complexities of this story, see Gernet 1981a.116–19, Martin 1998.120–23, Tell 2003.168–75; for the polyvalent significance of the tripod at Delphi, see also Neer 2001.295–97.

[52] Thus (e.g.) Hölscher 1968.136–41, Kahn 1979.123–24. We might also note here the tradition that he dedicated his book in the temple of Artemis (in Ephesus? D.L. 9.6)—like the wise sayings of the Seven Sages dedicated at Delphi.

[53] Notice that a similar oracular query is attributed to Chilon and Anacharsis among the Seven Sages ("Who is wiser than I?" D.L. 1.30, 106). In both cases, the Pythia's response (quoted in hexameters) is that Myson of Chen is wiser. On the traditional nature of this oracle to Socrates within stories told about him, see Compton 1990, 2006.154–55; Stokes 1992.60–68.

Socrates' characteristic activity—his relentless questioning of those thought to be wise in different domains.[54]

A second element that connects many of the figures in this common tradition of high *sophia* is extensive travel to distant places. This aspect has been noted independently by several scholars for different categories of *sophoi*; I would connect all these discussions with Helms's model of skilled crafting as intrinsicate with long-distance travel for the acquisition of otherworldly knowledge and precious goods. Thus Carol Dougherty has convincingly shown that a special connection between superlative craft and long-distance travel is deeply entrenched in the Greek tradition, already informing the *Odyssey*, while Richard Martin has argued for a link between archaic poetic *sophia* and the status of *metanastēs*, the wanderer or exile who comes from "outside" endowed with special knowledge and skills.[55] Entirely independently of these poetic traditions, Andrew Szegedy-Maszak, focusing on the legends of early Greek lawgivers, noted that these legendary figures tend to travel at two different points in their careers—early, before they engage in politics and legislative activity, to acquire wisdom; and again, after the law code has been established, to ensure the stability of the code by its maker's absence.[56] Szegedy-Maszak's first stage of travel in fact applies to many early Sages as well as lawgivers; thus in addition to the lawgivers Lycurgus, Solon, and Charondas, we are told that Thales, Cleobulus, Anacharsis, and Pythagoras all traveled extensively—often to Egypt, the ultimate exotic locale—in pursuit of arcane wisdom.[57]

As for the lawgiver's second phase of travel, James Ker has recently refined Szegedy-Maszak's observations and brilliantly characterized this later phase as *theōria*, drawing on the traditions of Solon's *theōria* preserved in Herodotus, the pseudo-Aristotelian *Constitution of the Athenians* (*Ath. Pol.*), and later sources.[58] In Ker's analysis, the lawgiver's *theōria* at the end of his career combines political self-imposed exile and religious pilgrimage. By casting himself in the role of *theōros* (a sacred ambassador sent to consult an oracle), Solon

---

[54] Indeed, Socrates concludes his account of his questioning of supposed *sophoi* by referring to this activity as his "servitude to the god" (τὴν τοῦ θεοῦ λατρείαν, *Apol.* 23c1). We might connect this with his self-description as a slave consecrated to Apollo at *Phd.* 85b5 (thus Burnet 1911.80).

[55] Dougherty 2001, Martin 1992; cf. Helms 1988.

[56] Szegedy-Maszak 1978.202, 207–8.

[57] Sources for Lycurgus, Solon, and Charondas: Ephorus *ap.* Strabo 10.14.9 (*FGrH* 70 F 149); Hecataeus of Abdera *ap.* D.S. 1.96.2–3 (*FGrH* 264 F 25); Plut. *Mor.* 345e, *Lyc.* 4, *Sol.* 2.1; D.S. 12.11.1. Sources for travel of the early sages: Hdt. 4.76; D.L. 1.24, 27, 89, 101; for Pythagoras: Isoc. *Busiris* 28, D. L. 8.2–3, Iambl. *VP* 11–19. For other recent discussions of the prevalence of travel among Greek sages and wise men (including philosophers and sophists), cf. Lloyd 1987; Montiglio 2000, 2005; Nightingale 2001, 2004; Tell 2003.107–47, 2010; Konstantakos 2004.95, 2005.13. In this regard, we might note Socrates' reference to his systematic questioning of those thought wise in Plato's *Apology* as τὴν ἐμὴν πλάνην (*Apol.* 22a6); I would suggest that this is a conscious acknowledgment of the tradition of the sage's wandering, here transposed into metaphor.

[58] Ker 2000, citing Hdt. 1.29–30; [Arist.] *Ath. Pol.* 11.1; Plut. *Sol.* 2.1, 25.5; D.L. 1.50.

retrospectively refashions his law code as itself an oracular pronouncement that must remain sacrosanct from all addition, subtraction, or interpretation by the intermediary who delivers it back to the civic community. At the same time, Solon's *theōria* firmly establishes and purifies the city by his absence, replacing the lawgiver's physical body with the henceforth immutable body of his law code at the center of the city.[59] As a parallel for Solon's *theōria*, Ker cites the example of the legendary Spartan lawgiver Lycurgus, whose code, according to one ancient tradition, came directly from the Delphic oracle (Hdt. 1.65.4; cf. Plut. *Lyc.* 6.1), and who ensured the permanence and immutability of the code by his departure at the end of his life on a *theōria* to Delphi from which he never returned.[60] Again, we might note that the pattern of significant political activity followed by *theōria* extends beyond the lawgivers to other archaic sages. Thus Diogenes Laertius recounts that, after several consequential political interventions, Thales died while "watching an athletic contest" (ἀγῶνα θεώμενος, D.L. 1.39); the participle here evokes a *theōria* at the end of the sage's life. Likewise, we are told of the Spartan sage and ephor Chilon that he died in Pisa, having just congratulated his son on an Olympic boxing victory—thus also on a *theōria* (D.L. 1.72, citing Hermippus). Intriguingly, the shadowy sage Pherecydes is also credited with two different "theoric" deaths. In Diogenes Laertius's account, immediately after Pherecydes offers significant political advice to the Lacedaemonians (that they should honor neither gold nor silver), we are told that "some say that he went to Delphi and threw himself off Mt. Corycus"; alternatively, Aristoxenus claimed that "he died of disease and was buried by Pythagoras on Delos" (D.L. 1.117–18).[61] Finally, we might add to this collection the persona of Theognis as it is constructed by the corpus of Theognidea. For, as Gregory Nagy has argued, different poems within the corpus characterize the speaker as lawgiver, civic mediator or judge, and *theōros* sent to consult the Delphic oracle, while several other elegies in the collection allude bitterly to the speaker's exile from his homeland.[62]

I find Ker's analysis particularly useful for two reasons. First (in general), Ker's exploration of all the cultural resonances in Solon's *theōria* allows us to recognize in *theōria* the sacralization of travel in its intimate linkage with the acquisition of otherworldly wisdom. That is to say, *theōria* makes manifest for the Greeks what Helms claims is true for traditional cultures in general: space is never a neutral category. Instead, certain outside places are conceptualized from the center as the meeting point of a spatial axis of distance with the vertical axis

---

[59] Ker 2000.317–22.

[60] Ker 2000.322–26, citing Plut. *Lyc.* 29. As Ker notes, Plutarch does not use the precise term *theōria*, but his account of Lycurgus's going to Delphi to consult the oracle falls clearly within this category of sacred travel.

[61] These are only two of four different accounts of his death preserved by D.L. (1.118).

[62] Nagy 1985b.22–74, 1990b.165–66. For the poet as *theōros*, see Thgn. 805–10; for the poet in exile, see Thgn. 783–88, 1197–1202, 1209–16.

of gods and ancestors. *Theōria* for the Greeks is precisely marked travel to such potent points of convergence.[63]

Second (specifically), Ker's discussion suggests that already by the fifth century BCE, political activity followed by *theōria* could be conceived as the climactic sequence in the life cycle of a typical sage. In light of this traditional pattern, we can see the Peripatetic developmental schema with which we began as a philosophical appropriation that preserves this climactic sequence (political activity and lawgiving; *theōria* as the study of nature; and finally contemplation of the divine and ὑπερκόσμια), even while projecting it from a single lifetime across the ages of human development writ large.

Indeed, the last stage in this Peripatetic sequence (contemplation of "things divine, beyond the cosmos, and unchangeable") points to one more common feature in older traditions of the life cycle of the sage. On the basis of preserved story patterns, we might say that there are two characteristic supernatural outcomes for the prephilosophical master of *sophia*: (1) after a lifetime of mediating between this and the invisible world of the divine, he is finally subsumed into the latter, often while on a *theōria*. He then receives hero-cult or even divine honors attached to his tomb; or (2) he descends to the land of the dead as his ultimate voyage to an other place and returns, bearing the esoteric wisdom he's acquired back to the world of the living. For an example of the first of these—which we might call the "Elijah model"—let us consider again the Spartan lawgiver Lycurgus. For not only does Lycurgus end his life on a *theōria* from which he never returns (thus binding the Spartans permanently to his law code), but also, as we know already from Herodotus, he receives cult worship after death (Hdt. 1.66). In like manner, according to Pausanias, the Spartan Sage Chilon had a heroon within the territory of Laconia (Paus. 3.16.4). Finally, Pherecydes, together with his proliferation of "theoric deaths," is also credited with hero-cult honors in the territory of Magnesia (D.L. 1.118).

As for the second otherworldly end of the archaic Sage—descent to the underworld and return with esoteric knowledge: figures who participate in this story pattern include Pythagoras, Epimenides, Empedocles, and perhaps also Hesiod by the fifth century BCE. Ruth Scodel, in her collection of the abundant ancient evidence for this story pattern, observes,

> Nothing is greater proof of wisdom or a more impressive sign of power than successful *catabasis* or remembered metempsychosis, where the latter is not yet a universal, but an indication of special status. In Aristophanes' [*Frogs*], the nether powers are remarkably helpful about sending back to this world the adjudged victor in poetic

---

[63] This sacralization of travel is particularly clear in the Greeks' own double etymology of the first element of the word—as both from *thea* ("sight, spectacle") and from *theos* ("god"). On these etymologies, see Ker 2000.308–11. I would thus disagree with the assumption of Nightingale 2004.63–70, that a firm and clear distinction can be drawn between *theōria* as "sacred embassy" or "pilgrimage" and as secular "sightseeing" or "tourism" in Greek texts.

σοφία; in *Gerytades*, a delegation of poets was sent to confer with the poets below (fr. 150 Kock). The intermingled types of poet and 'wise man' link the two worlds.[64]

Insofar as the underworld is the ultimate "other" place, we might conceive of Scodel's pattern of individual *catabasis* and return with esoteric knowledge as itself a kind of *theōria* reserved for the superlatively "wise" in the Greek imagination.[65]

In the literal translation from "human nature" to the "divine and supernatural" (τὰ θεῖα καὶ ὑπερκόσμια) that both these story patterns enact, we may detect the origins of the very last stage of the Peripatetic schema—the ascent to "*sophia* in its most proper signification." Here again, the life cycle of a single prephilosophical sage has been mapped onto the successive ages of the world in such a way that the highest numinous prestige of the sage's end has been utterly co-opted for the ongoing practice of philosophy. And, lest all this be rejected as merely a late scholastic fantasy, we should note that Aristotle's account of the intellectual faculties in Book 6 of the *Nicomachean Ethics* itself reproduces much the same sequence. Indeed, Aristotle's discussion makes a fitting conclusion to this survey—as simultaneously one last participant in the heated competition over *sophia* and also the text that marks an epochal divide between prephilosophical models of high wisdom and the philosophical tradition that inherits—or, better, appropriates—them.

III. Aristotle and the Transformation of *Sophia*

In *Nicomachean Ethics* Book 6, Aristotle turns from the moral to the intellectual excellences, which he differentiates as five separate faculties corresponding to different objects of intellection: τέχνη, ἐπιστήμη, φρόνησις, σοφία, νοῦς ("technical skill, systematic knowledge, practical intelligence, wisdom, intelligence," *NE* 6.3, 1139b15–17).[66] Aristotle first makes a distinction between things

---

[64] Scodel 1980, arguing for knowledge of Hesiod's return to life and double youth informing the second stasimon of Euripides' *Heracles*, thereby establishing a firm fifth-century terminus ante quem for this tradition (quotation taken from p. 317). We might add to Scodel's collection of reborn or resurrected sages the speaker of Thgn. 341–50, if we accept the argument of Murray 1965 and Nagy 1985b.68–74 that these lines represent the speaker as an avenging revenant.

[65] For this equivalence of "other" places—the underworld, the sea—and their connection with precious, numinous objects, see already Gernet 1981a. We might extend Scodel's argument to note that the descent to the underworld in Aristophanes' *Frogs* is figured as a *theōria*; as is also the otherworldly journey of Er in the myth that concludes Plato's *Republic* (as noted by Nightingale 2004.76–77).

[66] Here and throughout this discussion of *NE*, I rely heavily on the translation of Rowe in Broadie and Rowe 2002 (as well as on Broadie's extremely clear and useful philosophical introduction and commentary). Nevertheless, I have modified Rowe's translation where it diverges significantly from the way I have been using terms thus far in this chapter—most importantly, in his choice to translate *phronēsis* as "wisdom" rather than "practical intelligence," and *sophia* as "intellectual ability."

that are necessarily so and things that can be otherwise. Within the former sphere, the philosopher locates ἐπιστήμη (systematic knowledge), which he defines as "a disposition that is active in demonstration" from first principles (*NE* 6.3, 1139b32–35). Second, Aristotle introduces within the sphere of things that can be otherwise a second distinction between "things within the realm of production and things that belong within that of action"; τέχνη (technical expertise) he then defines as "a disposition in the domain of production accompanied by true rational prescription" (ἕξις μετὰ λόγου ἀληθοῦς ποιητική, *NE* 6.4, 1140a11). *Phronēsis* is then defined in opposition to *technē* as a disposition concerned not with production but with action, an ability to "deliberate well about things that are good and advantageous to oneself," "whenever they [those we call *phronimoi*] calculate well toward some serious end on matters where no exact technique applies" (*NE* 6.5, 1140a25–31). This bouleutic faculty, Aristotle observes, is associated with the good management of households and cities (1140b11) and with figures like "Pericles and such men, because they are capable of forming a clear view [θεωρεῖν!] of what is good for themselves and for men in general" in the domain of becoming and of things that could be otherwise (*NE* 6.5, 1140b7–10).

At this point, Aristotle oddly doubles back to "systematic knowledge" (ἐπιστήμη), in order to argue that the capacity by which we know the starting points from which systematic knowledge develops its demonstrations cannot itself be "systematic knowledge," "technical expertise," "practical intelligence," or "wisdom" (*epistēmē, technē, phronēsis,* or *sophia*); it must therefore be "intelligence" (*nous*). The result of this backtracking in argument is that Aristotle defers to the very last place in the sequence the discussion and definition of *sophia* (thereby inverting the order of the list in which he had originally introduced the five faculties).

This deferral is itself symptomatic, for here the philosopher seems to be struggling with common conceptions that confound his neat grid of faculties and objects of intellection. He begins by saying, "*sophia* we ascribe, in the case of the various kinds of technical expertise, to those experts in them who are most precise, e.g. Pheidias is a wise worker in stone (λιθουργὸν σοφόν), Polycleitus in bronze, here at any rate meaning no more by '*sophia*' than excellence in technical expertise" (ἀρετὴ τέχνης, *NE* 6.7; 1141a9–12).[67] Then, in order to move beyond *technē*, Aristotle introduces the distinction between "those who

---

rather than "wisdom." As I will argue below, this shift in meaning is itself symptomatic of what I take to be a highly polemical and tendentious argumentative move on Aristotle's part. Other discussions of *NE* 6 I have found particularly useful are Broadie 1991.179–265 and Nightingale 2004.187–253. Although Nightingale's discussion is focused specifically on Aristotle's treatments of *theōria* as a philosophical concept, her account has many points in common with the brief discussion of *sophia* offered here.

[67] Broadie (in Broadie and Rowe 2002.371) calls this characterization of *sophoi* "a commonplace."

are wise in some domain" (κατὰ μέρος or ἄλλο τι σοφούς) and "those who are wise in general or without qualification" (σοφούς... ὅλως). This latter category allows him to define *sophia* as "the most precise of systematic knowledges" (ἀκριβεστάτη... τῶν ἐπιστημῶν), to which he then adds that, since the *sophos* has a true grasp not only of "things from first principles, but of first principles themselves," *sophia* must in fact be "a combination of intelligence and systematic knowledge—systematic knowledge, as it were with its head now in place, of the highest objects" (ὥστ᾽ εἴη ἂν ἡ σοφία νοῦς καὶ ἐπιστήμη, ὥσπερ κεφαλὴν ἔχουσα ἐπιστήμη τῶν τιμιωτάτων, *NE* 6.7, 1141a18–20). Clearly, throughout this passage, Aristotle wants to retain the conventional notion that *sophia* is a superlative in some domain, but at the same time he is having trouble subduing the multifariousness of traditional *sophia* to his system. How can *sophia* be both a *technē* (a disposition related to production within the realm of things that could be otherwise) *and* an *epistēmē* (a disposition within the realm of things that are necessarily so)? This Aristotle finesses by a tendentiously curtailed quotation of the *Margites*, from which he derives the distinction "wise in something" and "wise in general."[68]

But even so, the philosopher has not yet entirely fought through the thickets and brambles of traditional *sophia*. He proceeds with an air of feigned incredulity:

> For it is a strange thing (ἄτοπον) to think—if anyone does—that political expertise, or *phronēsis*, is what is to be taken most seriously; unless, that is, man is the best thing there is in the universe. (Now if healthy and good are different for human beings and for fish, while white and straight are always the same, everyone will agree that *to sophon* too is always the same thing, whereas *phronimon* differs; for each kind of creature asserts that *phronimon* is what successfully considers the things relating to itself; and will hand over decisions to that.... It is also evident that *sophia* and political expertise will not be the same, for if people say expertise about what is beneficial to themselves is *sophia*, there will be many *sophiai*; there will not be one, dealing with the good of all kinds of creatures, but a different one for each—unless there is also a single form of medical expertise appropriate to every kind of being.) (*NE* 6.7, 1141a20–34; trans. Rowe 2002, slightly modified)

Aristotle's claim here is that *sophia*, as the superlative faculty, must deal with the best things in the cosmos; with universals rather than particulars; and must be singular and unchanging.

---

[68] On Aristotle's misleading quotation of the *Margites*, cf. Bollack 1968.551, Kerferd 1976.24–25: "Aristotle quotes these lines in order to contrast being wise in general (overall) and being wise in some particular field or in any other limited respect, apparently supposing that the *Margites* passage established the overall wisdom of Margites by contrasting this wisdom with various kinds of particular wisdom which Margites did *not* possess. But the completion of the quotation by Clement ... makes it clear that the passage refers to the overall stupidity of Margites.... Aristotle's interpretation is in fact completely unhistorical and also linguistically absurd."

There are several things to notice about this argument in terms of the traditional conception of *sophia* we have been considering. First, like the Peripatetic schema of five stages of *sophia* with which we began, Aristotle's definition of *sophia* works successively through the superlative skill of the *tektōn* (Pheidias and Polycleitus), political expertise, and finally contemplation of divine things. Second, it is clear that Aristotle urgently needs to disentangle *sophia* from political expertise (in spite of the disingenuous ἄτοπον with which he introduces the topic), from the fact that in the discussion, *sophia* has already subsumed *technē*, *epistēmē*, and *nous*. That is to say, the only term left of Aristotle's original list of five is *phronēsis*, so that the *real* opposition here is between *sophia* and *phronēsis*.[69] And indeed, scholars have identified the rigorous discrimination of these two terms as Aristotle's polemic against his precursors Plato and Isocrates. For Plato did not yet make a rigorous distinction between *sophia* and *phronēsis*, while he also seemed to allow the faculty of wisdom to remain embedded in the sphere of political activity.[70] Though different from Plato's position, Isocrates in the *Panegyricus* claimed that man was the best thing in the cosmos and that political activity was man's highest end.[71] Thus on this reading, in Book 6 of the *Nicomachean Ethics*, Aristotle corrects and improves Platonic and Isocratean doctrine by methodically disentangling *sophia* from *phronēsis*.

While all this may be true, it is worth noting that the Aristotelian polemic is directed not just at these philosophical precursors, but at a much more broadly held cultural conception of *sophia* as "skilled crafting" in many domains, including (perhaps preeminently) politics. And in relation to this common conception, Aristotle goes a long way toward achieving his goal even before he engages in any argumentation, by a crucial shift in vocabulary: for he displaces onto *phronēsis* all the elements of political deliberation and lawgiving traditionally associated with *sophia*. We can see this displacement clearly in Aristotle's constant analogizing between *phronēsis* and medicine as "stochastic" arts concerned with particulars in the realm of becoming (twice, for example, in the passage just quoted).[72] For, like the poet, the seer, and the steersman, the man

---

[69] Cf. Broadie 1991.187–260, who sees this as a three-way opposition between "practical wisdom" (*phronēsis*), "theoretical wisdom" (*sophia*), and "craft" (*technē*), whereby each term is progressively defined and clarified against the others.

[70] On Aristotle's argument here as a polemic against Plato, see Broadie 1991; Broadie in Broadie and Rowe 2002.46–47, 369, 375; Nightingale 2004.189–206; on Plato's conception of *sophia* and *theōria* as still politically embedded, see Nightingale 2004.72–138 and, somewhat differently, Ferrari in Ferrari and Griffith 2000.xviii–xxxi, Ferrari 2005. For the complexity of Plato's position, see also Mann 2009. Mann argues that although, in many instances, Plato uses the terms *sophia* and *phronēsis* interchangeably, in the famous "digression" of *Tht.* 172c–77b he constitutes a category of completely detached, theoretical wisdom akin to Aristotle's *sophia*, although he does not use that term.

[71] On this section of the *NE* as engaging in a polemic with Isocrates' position, see Broadie in Broadie and Rowe 2002.52–54, 372.

[72] On the characteristics of this "stochastic" realm in Greek thought, see Detienne and Vernant 1978; for the endurance of the opposition, see Ginzburg 1989. For the tensions in Aristotle's deploy-

of medical expertise is *sophos* or *sophistēs* in traditional Greek parlance.[73] Even more revealing for this semantic displacement are Aristotle's cited exemplars of *sophoi*:

> Anaxagoras and Thales and such men they say are *sophoi*, but not *phronimoi*, whenever they see them being ignorant of the things that are advantageous for themselves, and they say that they know things that are exceptional and marvelous and difficult and divine, but useless, because [such men] do not seek human goods (καὶ περιττὰ μὲν καὶ θαυμαστὰ καὶ χαλεπὰ καὶ δαιμόνια εἰδέναι αὐτούς φασιν, ἄχρηστα δ', ὅτι οὐ τὰ ἀνθρώπινα ἀγαθὰ ζητοῦσιν). (*NE* 6.7, 1141b3–8)

Striking here is Aristotle's co-option of a generic plural "they" ("they say... they see... they say")—conjuring a common (we might even say "choral") Greek voice to underwrite an oddly skewed and partial representation of Thales as Sage.[74] Of course, Plato had already tendentiously represented Thales as the unworldly astronomer who fell down the well: the theoretical scientist with no interest in practical political affairs (*Tht.* 174a; *Hipp. Mai.* 281c2–7). But as we know from Herodotus, Thales was already in the fifth century associated with the forethought to predict eclipses (Hdt. 1.74), the practical know-how of the engineer (Hdt. 1.75), and the superlative bouleutic skill of the political adviser (Hdt. 1.170), while Aristotle himself in the *Politics* recounts the story of his effortless moneymaking coup of renting in advance all the olive presses for a low price, in anticipation of a good olive harvest (*Pol.* 1.11, 1259a6–19).[75] Thus in the common conception, Thales, perhaps more fully than any other archaic Sage, embodied the whole complex cluster of practical, political skills and activities denominated by *sophia* in prephilosophical usage.

By laying claim to Thales (through the anonymous "they say"), Aristotle effectively disembeds him from the practical, political activities commonly associated with the Seven Sages, making him different from (and better than) Pericles; at the same time, Aristotle thereby constitutes a hierarchy of practical

---

ment of "the craft analogy" (including medicine) in *NE* 6, see Broadie 1991.185–212. And while I accept much of Broadie's philosophical analysis, I would contend that Aristotle relies so heavily on the "craft analogy" not merely because it was an argumentative staple for Socrates and Plato, but because it derives from a much deeper and broader traditional cultural association of superlative wisdom (*sophia*) with "skilled crafting."

[73] Cf. Lloyd 1987.83–108, Thomas 2000.156–61.

[74] Cf. Nightingale 2004.204.

[75] Jaeger 1948.426–27, 452–61 notes the complex equivocations surrounding Thales as a Sage already in Herodotus, Plato, and Aristotle, though he is inclined to make Thales' and the other Sages' pragmatic side the product of Dicaearchus's polemicizing for the supremacy of the *bios praktikos*. Against this position, see Martin 1998.126n. 22: "Jaeger... believes Dikaiarchos stressed in the tradition the stories about sages that emphasized their political and legal expertise—but this is not to say he made the stories up." For an insightful account of Aristotle's tendentious deployment of Thales here in *NE* 6 in contrast to an older model of Thales as practical Sage, see Nightingale 2004.22–26, 31–32, 204–5.

phronēsis and theoretical *sophia*. So much is obvious; what is worth noting in addition is that Aristotle actually appropriates the traditional narrative trajectory of the individual sage's life in order to construct his philosophical hierarchy of faculties and objects of intellection. For Aristotle's sequence *phronēsis*, then *sophia* precisely corresponds to (indeed, I would argue, derives from) the sage's traditional progression from consequential political activity to *theōria* (religious pilgrimage). (We might recall that, according to Diogenes Laertius, Thales appears to be one of the sages who meets his end on a *theōria*, expiring as he's "watching an athletic contest," ἀγῶνα θεώμενος, D.L. 1.39.) But Aristotle simultaneously abstracts this older pattern, decisively transforming *theōria* from "pilgrimage" or "sacred travel" to the disembodied "contemplation of the divine" and thereby laying the groundwork for the privileging of metaphysics and theory in Western philosophy.[76] Even so, Aristotle's list of the objects of knowledge of the *sophoi* has not entirely shed the numinous resonances of that older *theōria*: "they say," says the philosopher, "that such men know things extraordinary, marvelous, difficult, and divine" (καὶ περιττὰ μὲν καὶ θαυμαστὰ καὶ χαλεπὰ καὶ δαιμόνια). περιττά suggests things that are outside of or beyond the normal range of human experience, while θαυμαστά echoes the common expressions of wonder linked to the sacral viewing of *theōria*.[77] Most of all, the climactic term δαιμόνια reveals the religious ground from which Aristotle's abstract, philosophical *theōria* springs, and suggests the otherworldly divine to which the traditional sage returns.

We might finally ask why Aristotle goes to so much trouble to appropriate *sophia* and transform it into the consummate philosophical faculty—an effort that requires the displacement onto *phronēsis* of many of *sophia*'s traditional practical associations and the abstraction of *theōria* from its cultural surround. I would contend that what motivates this is power: that even Aristotle's seemingly disinterested philosophical treatises are engaged in a deadly serious contestation for what is perceived to be one of the culture's highest goods. *Sophia* is still in this period and later the bearer of tremendous cultural and political prestige and authority—a form of "symbolic capital" to which all participants in the cultural field want to be able to lay claim.[78] Indeed, Aristotle himself ac-

---

[76] See Nightingale 2004 passim, arguing that this model of philosophical *theōria* is a new invention of Plato, Aristotle, and others in the fourth century BCE.

[77] For wonder in travel/*theōria* contexts, see (e.g.) Pindar P.1.26, P.10.30; Hdt. 1.59, 68. Of course, at the beginning of the *Metaphysics*, Aristotle lays claim to precisely this quality of "wonder" as the beginning of philosophy (*Met.* 1.2, 982b; cf. Plato *Tht.* 155d25), but this, too, I would contend, is a philosophical appropriation of an older association of performances of *sophia* with wonder. Cf. Albert 1983 and, for the older semantic field of "wonder" (*thauma*), see Neer 2010.

[78] Cf. Havelock 1963.163n. 28 (referring mainly to the Sophists, but also applicable to Aristotle in the fourth century): "I conclude that the words *sophos*, *sophia* at the end of the fifth century represented a set of prestige claims staked out in the culture. When a new variety of verbal skill began to emerge, its practitioners did not coin a new word for it. They preferred the old one, as offering a field-site already prepared, but one from which they had to eject the previous tenant."

knowledges this (tipping his hand, as it were) in another account of the progression of objects of human knowledge or scientific study at the beginning of the *Metaphysics*. Here, after cross-referencing his discussion of intellectual faculties in the *Nicomachean Ethics* in order to ground his definition of *sophia* as "a science of certain first principles and causes," Aristotle proposes that we can best understand what these first principles and causes are by considering "what [views] we hold concerning the wise man" (περὶ τοῦ σοφοῦ, *Met*. 1.2, 982a7). There follows a quick summary of the different aspects of *sophia* as defined in the *Nicomachean Ethics*, which Aristotle then concludes:

> Again among the sciences we consider that that science which is desirable in itself and for the sake of knowledge is more nearly wisdom (σοφίαν) than that which is desirable for its results, and that the superior is more nearly wisdom than the subsidiary (καὶ τὴν ἀρχικωτέραν τῆς ὑπηρετούσης μᾶλλον σοφίαν); for the wise man should give orders, not receive them; nor should he obey others, but the less wise should obey him. (*Met*. 1.2, 982a14–19, trans. Tredennick 1980)

It would be easy to treat this as a mere analogy, a manner of speaking, but I think that would be a mistake.[79] That the issue of authority here is a real one is suggested by the fact that the image of differential human power relations recurs in more extreme form as the cap of the next stage of Aristotle's argument—that theoretical *epistēmē* is superior to practical, and that the inquiry into first causes is the best of all:

> Clearly then it is for no extrinsic advantage that we seek this knowledge; for just as we call a man free (ἐλεύθερος) who exists for himself and not for another, so we call this the only free science (ὡς μόνην οὖσαν ἐλευθέραν τῶν ἐπιστημῶν), since it alone exists for itself. For this reason its acquisition might justly be supposed to be beyond human power, since in many respects human nature is servile (πολλαχῇ γὰρ ἡ φύσις δούλη τῶν ἀνθρώπων ἐστίν); in which case, as Simonides says, "God alone can have this privilege," and man should only seek the knowledge which is within his reach. Indeed if the poets are right and the Deity is by nature jealous, it is probable that in this case He would be particularly jealous, and all those who excel in knowledge unfortunate. But it is impossible for the Deity to be jealous (ἀλλ᾽ οὔτε τὸ θεῖον φθονερὸν

---

[79] Indeed, that Aristotle's assertion—*sophia* "should give orders"—is something of a philosophical embarrassment is clear from W. D. Ross's commentary on this passage: "The description of 'wisdom' as the ruling or most authoritative science is difficult. It is easy to see how πολιτική can be described by Aristotle as exercising authority over such sciences as strategy.... But σοφία is not a practical but a purely theoretical science; in what sense then does it issue commands?" (Ross 1924.I.121). Ross must then engage in half a page of fancy logical footwork to justify Aristotle's assertion within his own philosophical system. Cf. Nightingale 2004.229–30, who also acknowledges the incoherence of this claim within Aristotle's own system. Nightingale's solution is that "this inconsistency can be explained by the fact that the aristocratic rhetoric which Aristotle uses here is pulling him in different directions," since "the aristocratically 'good' man is defined both by his freedom from work and by his possession of power."

ἐνδέχεται εἶναι)—indeed, as the proverb says, "poets tell many a lie," nor must we suppose that any other form of knowledge is more precious (τιμιωτέραν) than this; for what is most divine is most precious. Now there are two ways only in which it can be divine. A science is divine if it is peculiarly the possession of God, or if it is concerned with divine matters. And this science alone fulfils both these conditions; for (a) all believe that God is one of the causes and a kind of principle, and (b) God is the sole or chief possessor of this sort of knowledge. Accordingly, although all other sciences are more necessary than this, none is more excellent. (*Met.* 1.2, 982b24–983a11, trans. Tredennick 1980)

Here, the giving or taking of orders from the earlier passage has come to be reified as the difference between slave and free, with the conclusion that metaphysics alone is a "free science" because it aims at no end beyond itself and because it alone assimilates man to "the divine."[80] It is furthermore striking that, precisely in the course of making this argument for the absolute primacy of his own version of *sophia*, Aristotle feels the need to engage and refute two different literary stagings of competition in wisdom. First, he cites the poem in which Simonides in his turn had contested the *sophia* of Pittacus (fr. 542 *PMG*, quoted in Plato's *Protagoras*). Indeed, not only does Aristotle quote Simonides—he *misquotes* him. For Simonides is talking not about the possession of *sophia* when he says, "a god alone could have this honor," but instead about the possession of perfect "nobility" or "goodness," unscathed by negative fortune. The fact that the quotation of Simonides is not actually apt suggests that what motivates its inclusion is the competition in wisdom that Simonides' poem itself stages. Second, Aristotle's formulation τὸ θεῖον φθονερόν derives not from a poet (as he represents it), but from Herodotus—precisely from the speech of Solon to Croesus early in Book 1 (Ὦ Κροῖσε, ἐπιστάμενόν με τὸ θεῖον πᾶν ἐὸν φθονερόν τε καὶ ταραχῶδες ἐπειρωτᾷς ἀνθρωπηίων πρηγμάτων πέρι, Hdt. 1.32.1).[81] Thus again, by refuting this position, Aristotle is engaging in a competition of *sophia* with Solon in one of his most famous representations as traditional sage. And it is worth noting that—in what we might consider a final turn on the competition in *sophia*—Aristotle here uses Solon to refute (Herodotus's) "Solon." For already in antiquity, the proverbial quip "singers tell many lies" was attributed to Solon himself.[82]

---

[80] On Aristotle's deployment of aristocratic discourses of slavery, freedom, leisure, and power to valorize his new model of theoretical philosophy, see Nightingale 2004.195, 227–35.

[81] While the concept of divine envy occurs not infrequently in fifth-century poetry (e.g., Pindar P.10.20, I.7.39; Aesch. *Ag.* 468–71, 946–47, *Persians* 362, *Prom.* 859; Eur. *Alcestis* 1135, *IA* 1097, *Or.* 974, *Suppl.* 348), the only pre-Aristotelian author who uses the abstract form τὸ θεῖον in collocation with φθονερόν is Herodotus (twice at 1.32.1 and 3.40.2; for different language, cf. 7.10ε, 7.46.4). And, as we know from Plut. *Mal.Hdt.* 857f, Herodotus's version of Solon's statement to Croesus was very well known in the later philosophical tradition—presumably because it was regarded as scandalous.

[82] See Ross 1924.I.123 ad loc. and Solon fr. 29 W.

As it had always been, *sophia* is here the ground of competition, and Aristotle's dismissal of the poets (itself achieved through the proverbial wisdom that "singers tell many lies") effectively clears the field for his new version of philosophical, theoretical wisdom. At the same time, of course, in its identification with "the divine," Aristotle's *sophia* comes trailing clouds of glory: precisely because it still carries the otherworldly, numinous aura of traditional skilled crafting, *sophia* remains the "most precious"—and therefore most contested—cultural good.

I have tarried over Aristotle's discussions of *sophia* in the *Nicomachean Ethics* and the beginning of the *Metaphysics* because they offer us in concentrated form many of the bundle of features already associated with *sophia* in archaic and classical Greek texts, both poetry and prose. And yet Aristotle has effectively transposed or sublimated all these features into a philosophical framework that has irrevocably colored the interpretation of *sophia* in a high tradition extending from the ancient Peripatos to modern philosophical scholarship. We need to understand this watershed moment and its effects in order to see clearly what the *Life of Aesop* is—and what it is not. For, as I shall argue in chapter 4, we could conceive of the *Life of Aesop* as a whole as participating in a philosophical debate on the relative value of the *bios praktikos* and the *bios theōretikos* (a debate that we know exercised prominent figures in the early Peripatos).[83] But I think such a reading would represent the too-hasty assimilation to the domain of philosophy of something that may in fact lie outside or beyond its boundaries. To shift metaphors: beneath the obvious echoes of various philosophical schools in the *Life*, we may be able to catch the deeper rumblings of something else.[84] That is to say, I suspect we might better conceive of the *Life* as continuing a popular nonphilosophical tradition of the sage's career that builds progressively to a climax in political activity followed by *theōria* and/or ascent to the divine. I say "nonphilosophical" rather than "prephilosophical" here deliberately, in order to avoid the implication that the existence of this pattern in the *Life of Aesop* provides us any kind of terminus ante quem for dating the tradition. For I would contend that, in spite of the critical interventions of Isocrates, Plato, and Aristotle (and their schools) in the meaning and value of *sophia*, significant portions of the population throughout the ancient world continued happily on conceiving of *sophia* as skilled crafting and the *sophos* or *sophistēs* as the culture hero of its magical, transformative arts. It

---

[83] For this as a lively topic of debate in the fourth century BCE, see Jaeger 1948; Nightingale 2004.

[84] On philosophical elements in the *Life*, see Jedrkiewicz 1989.108–56, 189–94, 205–12; Adrados 1999.665–83; Hägg 1997. Notice especially Hägg's observations about the parodies of philosophical material in *Vita* G: "the caricature of the philosophical life it provides is not distinct enough, as far as I can judge, to allow us to identify what particular philosophical sect the author is ridiculing. It is not the kind of refined satire that would have appealed to people with a more intimate knowledge of the different schools of Hellenistic philosophy, and which has survived in other anecdotal material" (Hägg 1997.196–97).

is within this broader nonphilosophical tradition that the Seven Sages continued to enjoy enormous popularity as "performers of wisdom," and within this tradition that Aesop, too, participated as competitor and debunker of high *sophia*.[85]

---

[85] I borrow the phrase "performers of wisdom" from Martin 1998. We might cite as evidence for the continuing popularity of the Seven Sages Diogenes Laertius's collection of material dating from the second or third century CE (D.L. 1.13, 22–108); the second-century CE wall paintings of the Seven Sages preserved in a tavern in Ostia (for more extended discussion of which, see chapter 5, section II); and several late-antique floor mosaics of the Seven Sages from all over the Mediterranean (on which, see Studemund 1890). For the continuing popularity of Aesop in the first and second centuries CE, cf. Jouanno 2006.13–14.

Chapter 3

AESOP AS SAGE: POLITICAL COUNSEL
AND DISCURSIVE PRACTICE

IN THIS CHAPTER, we will consider evidence for Aesop as a sage, set against the lineaments of the pre- or nonphilosophical tradition of wisdom I outlined in chapter 2. This will necessitate drawing together scattered fragments of a tradition that constituted Aesop as a wise man in competition with other sages, purveying his own distinctive brand of low or bodily *sophia*. The very fact that traces of this version of Aesop are so fragmented, muted, or occluded in our preserved texts suggests that this was in some way a popular tradition whose value was contested and challenged throughout antiquity.

I will begin from dictional traces in Herodotus that allow us to see Aesop as a participant or competitor with the group of Seven Sages already in the fifth century, in oral traditions that lay behind and informed Herodotus's narrative. At the same time, the occluded presence of Aesop in a Herodotean scene of sage advising will help us tease out what is distinctive about Aesop's style of *sophia* in relation to the other traditional sages. Finally, the Herodotean background will enable us to see fable as a genre whose discursive authority was contested within the wisdom tradition. From Herodotus, I will turn in the second section of the chapter to a reading of the extended sequence in the *Life* in which Aesop emerges as a full-fledged political adviser to the Samian demos (*Vitae* G + W, chs. 87–97). For the material collected in the first section of the chapter will make clear the extent to which this sequence is informed by a pre- or nonphilosophical paradigm of the sage's intervention in political affairs. And I will elaborate on this model by comparison of this sequence in the *Life* with a whole set of passages from different authors where we find beast fable deployed in scenes of political advising.

I. Aesop among the Sages

Scholars have recognized that a tradition of the meeting (perhaps banquet) of the Sages including Aesop at the court of Periander or that of Croesus goes back to the fourth century, but it has often been argued that Herodotus's silence on the matter proves that this tradition could not have existed in the fifth century.[1]

---

[1] Fourth-century evidence: Ephorus *FGrH* 70 F 181 (this tradition attributed to Ephorus by D.L. 1.40); Alexis fr. 9 KA = Perry *Test.* 33 (probably a dialogue of Solon and Aesop from a comedy

I would contend that this argument *ex silentio* is highly dubious, and that, in fact, careful attention to Herodotus's language in a couple of passages will suggest just the opposite. Although Herodotus has written Aesop out of a particular scenario of sage advice, he has left several verbal cues—the dictional fingerprints of Aesop, as it were—to mark the elision.

As I have already noted, Herodotus's diction when he first brings Solon to the court of Croesus (Hdt. 1.29) seems to imply that he already conceives of the Sages as a corporate body, all living at the same time, all contemporary with Croesus—and, we might add, all traveling to his court to perform their wisdom.[2] I would like to introduce into evidence a second Herodotean passage, which, I think, strongly suggests that (in some versions at least) Aesop figured in this corporate group of Sages at the court of Croesus already in the fifth century. At 1.27, Herodotus tells the story of Croesus's encounter with a Greek Sage (although he is somewhat vague about which Sage it is):

ὡς δὲ ἄρα οἱ ἐν τῇ Ἀσίῃ Ἕλληνες κατεστράφατο ἐς φόρου ἀπαγωγήν, τὸ ἐνθεῦτεν ἐπενόεε νέας ποιησάμενος ἐπιχειρέειν τοῖσι νησιώτῃσι. ἐόντων δέ οἱ πάντων ἑτοίμων ἐς τὴν ναυπηγίην, οἱ μὲν Βίαντα λέγουσι τὸν Πριηνέα ἀπικόμενον ἐς Σάρδις, οἱ δὲ Πιττακὸν τὸν Μυτιληναῖον, εἰρομένου Κροίσου εἴ τι εἴη νεώτερον περὶ τὴν Ἑλλάδα, εἰπόντα τάδε καταπαῦσαι τὴν ναυπηγίην· Ὦ βασιλεῦ, νησιῶται ἵππον συνωνέονται μυρίην, ἐς Σάρδις τε καὶ ἐπὶ σὲ ἐν νόῳ ἔχοντες στρατεύεσθαι. Κροῖσον δὲ ἐλπίσαντα λέγειν ἐκεῖνον ἀληθέα εἰπεῖν· αἲ γὰρ τοῦτο θεοὶ ποιήσειαν ἐπὶ νόον νησιώτῃσι, ἐλθεῖν ἐπὶ Λυδῶν παῖδας σὺν ἵπποισι. τὸν δὲ ὑπολαβόντα φάναι· Ὦ βασιλεῦ, προθύμως μοι φαίνεαι εὔξασθαι νησιώτας ἱππευομένους λαβεῖν ἐν ἠπείρῳ, οἰκότα ἐλπίζων· νησιώτας δὲ τί δοκέεις εὔχεσθαι ἄλλο ἤ, ἐπείτε τάχιστα ἐπύθοντό σε μέλλοντα ἐπὶ σφίσι ναυπηγέεσθαι νέας, λαβεῖν ἀρώμενοι Λυδοὺς ἐν θαλάσσῃ, ἵνα ὑπὲρ τῶν ἐν τῇ ἠπείρῳ οἰκημένων Ἑλλήνων τείσωνταί σε, τοὺς σὺ δουλώσας ἔχεις; κάρτα τε ἡσθῆναι Κροῖσον τῷ ἐπιλόγῳ καί οἱ, προσφυέως γὰρ δόξαι λέγειν, πειθόμενον παύσασθαι τῆς ναυπηγίης. καὶ οὕτω τοῖσι τὰς νήσους οἰκημένοισι Ἴωσι ξεινίην συνεθήκατο. (Hdt. 1.27)

When the Greeks in Asia had been subdued to the paying of tribute, [Croesus] next set his mind to building a navy and making an attempt on the islanders. And when all things were ready for the shipbuilding, some say Bias of Priene came to Sardis—others Pittacus of Mytilene. And when Croesus asked if there was any news concern-

---

entitled *Aesop*; see Arnott 1996.75–79). Wilamowitz-Moellendorff 1890.218; Zeitz 1936; La Penna 1962.295; Perry 1962a.313n. 27, 333–34; Jedrkiewicz 1989.136–38; Hägg 1997.183; Adrados 1999.273–74, 652–54 all trace the tradition back to the fourth century, while La Penna, Perry, and Jedrkiewicz (1989.136n. 103) explicitly make the argument *ex silentio* for Hdt. Differently: Snell 1966b argues for a fifth-century "Banquet of the Seven Sages" in hexameter verse; Momigliano 1971.27–38 follows Snell and assumes fifth-century written versions of a meeting of the Seven Sages at the court of Croesus and of the "popular wisdom of Aesop." Cf. Edmunds 1997.44–45, envisioning competitive traditions of wisdom (including Aesop's) already circulating in the classical era. Jedrkiewicz 1989.110 also seems to imagine an early sympotic circulation of oral traditions, although he denies a fifth-century link between Aesop and the Seven Sages.

[2] See Martin 1998.125n. 16, quoted above, chapter 2, n. 24; cf. Momigliano 1971.35.

ing Greece, [the sage] saying these following things stopped him from his shipbuilding: "O King, the islanders are buying up ten thousand horse, intending to make an expedition against you in Sardis." And Croesus, believing that that man spoke the truth, said, "Would that the gods would put this in mind for the islanders, to come against the sons of the Lydians with horses!" And the other took it up and said, "O King, eagerly you appear to me to pray to catch the islanders on horseback on the mainland, expecting the likely outcome. But what else do you imagine the islanders pray for, as soon as they learned that you were going to build a navy against them? Praying [what other thing] than to catch the Lydians at sea, in order to punish you on behalf of the Greeks living on the mainland whom you have enslaved?" And [they say that] Croesus was overjoyed at the concluding sentence and persuaded by him, since he seemed to speak appositely, he ceased his shipbuilding. And so it was that he made a pact of guest-friendship with the Ionians inhabiting the islands.

There are several noteworthy things about this anecdote. First, the *Life of Aesop*, probably written down in the first or second century CE, preserves the story of a similar encounter, where it is *Aesop* who persuades Croesus not to attack the islanders by telling him a fable (*Vitae* G + W, chs. 98–100). Second, the geography of this anecdote doesn't quite make sense; the two sages credited are from the wrong places. Bias is from Priene on the mainland; Pittacus is from Mytilene on Lesbos—a bit too far north to be the spokesman of the Ionian islanders at Sardis.[3] Triangulating between Lesbos and Priene would land us on Samos—the island whose freedom Aesop in fact secures in the *Life*.

These are external arguments for the possibility that Aesop is lurking behind Herodotus's anecdote; but there are also several internal arguments based on the text of the *Histories*. In the first place, this little episode exhibits unique or anomalous features when it is considered against Herodotus's normal narrative practice. Thus this is the only occasion in the text of the *Histories* in which Herodotus expresses uncertainty about the identity of a speaker of sage advice.[4] In addition, this is the only place in the narrative in which a sage is credited with a statement acknowledged by the narrator to be untrue. Finally, this anecdote is filled with rare and unusual dictional features that seem to me to point to Aesop and Aesopic fable:

---

[3] It is worth noting that, where we have parallels for this kind of story elsewhere in the tradition, the sage involved usually represents or advises *his own* civic community: cf. Plut. *Greek Questions* 296a–b; D.L. 1.25 (quoted below in text), 1.83–84. For the connection between Hdt. 1.27 and Aesop's political activity on Samos in the *Life*, cf. Zeitz 1936.241–43. Zeitz contends that Aesop's political activity is an old element in the tradition, and even suggests that we might imagine a native Samian oral tradition that credits Aesop with securing the island's freedom from Croesus as an allomorph to the tradition represented by Hdt. 1.27. Other scholars by contrast assume that the *Life of Aesop* tradition draws on and adapts Hdt. 1.27: thus La Penna 1962.294–96, Konstantakos 2004.102–3, Jouanno 2006.19–20.

[4] Of course, there are moments when Herodotus cannot put a name to a sage adviser (e.g., Hdt. 4.3, 5.80), but nowhere else does he hesitate between two possible named speakers.

1. There is, first, the formula Herodotus uses for the Sage's response to Croesus's overjoyed exclamation: ὑπολαβόντα φάναι. Herodotus's most common verb for "answering" or "responding" is the Homeric ἀμείβομαι, which he uses seventy times; another thirty-four times he uses forms of ὑποκρίνομαι and (perhaps) ἀποκρίνομαι.[5] Just seven times, he uses the expression ὑπολαβὼν ἔφη or ὑπολαβὼν εἶπε. LSJ gloss ὑπολαμβάνω, especially in the form of aorist participle plus a verb of speaking, as "rejoin, retort, [he] said in answer."[6] But what distinguishes these different verbs for answering or responding? Why does one appear rather than another in a particular context (especially in the case of the relatively rare expression ὑπολαβὼν ἔφη/ εἶπε)? Based on a survey of all classical occurrences of ὑπολαμβάνω in speech formulae, I would contend that ὑπολαμβάνω (either by itself or as a participle with a verb of speaking) is a more lively, colloquial expression that originates in contexts of aggressive or competitive verbal dueling between two interlocutors. In these contexts, it signifies rapid-fire dialogue or exchange, but more specifically, this formula frequently marks the moment at which one speaker makes a clever observation or offers a witty quip that turns his interlocutor's thought or language against him and thereby ends discussion. That is to say, ὑπολαβὼν ἔφη/ εἶπε introduces an utterance that caps or trumps the interlocutor's words and thus "wins" the argument.[7]

And while we find this expression used occasionally in literary prose[8] (Herodotus, Thucydides, Xenophon, most frequently Plato), it seems to be in origin a low or nonliterary expression most at home in popular oral narrative, especially

---

[5] These figures are based on Powell 1938, s.vv. ἀμείβω II, ὑποκρίνομαι. On the etymological development of ὑποκρίνομαι meaning "answer, respond," and its restriction to Ionic, see Koller 1957; Thucydides' usage confirms that ὑποκρίνομαι is the Ionic dialect form, while ἀποκρίνομαι is the favored form in Attic. Thus ὑποκρίνομαι occurs only once in the text of Thucydides in a quotation from the *Homeric Hymn to Apollo* (3.104.5), while ἀποκρίνομαι occurs thirty-three times. In addition, ἀμείβομαι meaning "answer" never occurs in Thucydides or Plato, confirming that it is poetic and/or Ionic.

[6] LSJ s.v. ὑπολαμβάνω I.3.

[7] This use to mark a capping utterance in rapid-fire dialogue of two speakers accounts for all seven of Herodotus's uses; three of four occurrences in Thucydides; the majority of Xenophon's uses, and the single occurrences in Demosthenes and Hypereides. Only in Xenophon and Plato does ὑπολαβὼν ἔφη/ εἶπε develop a broader semantic range, marking the moment at which a new speaker claims the discursive floor and (especially in Plato) makes a significant intervention to the style or content of argument. I would contend that this diachronic pattern is revealing for the origins of the formula in popular colloquial narrative, especially given that the fifth-century occurrences (in Hdt. and Thuc.) conform most closely in context and meaning to the fable formulae. Thus, to some extent, I agree with the analysis of ὑπολαμβάνω as a term for competitive turn taking offered in Nagy 2002.9–22, with the reservation that this is a broader phenomenon than just the rhapsodic performance of Homer (which is how Nagy would limit the term, based on the occurrence of the phrase ἐξ ὑπολήψεως at [Plato] *Hipparch.* 228b9). For a fuller discussion of ὑπολαβὼν ἔφη/ εἶπε within a Greek "ethnography of speaking," see Kurke 2010.

[8] ὑπολαμβάνω in this meaning almost never occurs in poetry; thus far, I have found only a single exception (which more or less proves the rule)—in the low, scurrilous *Chreiai* of Machon (Gow 1965, l. 216).

Aesopic fable. For in the later collections of Aesop's fables, the phrase ὑποτυχὼν εἶπε (or ἔφη) occurs at least thirty-six times in exactly the same contexts; thus Triantaphyllia Karadagli lists ὑποτυχών, -οῦσα among her characteristic fable formulae, noting that it marks one character's trumping another with a witty concluding speech.[9] The verb ὑποτυγχάνω is entirely postclassical, but I would suggest that it represents a kind of lexical replacement for an earlier ὑπολαμβάνω in this same formula.[10] The precise equivalence of the two verbs in this colloquial quotative formula is confirmed by the fact that in eighteen of the thirty-six occurrences of ὑποτυχών/ -οῦσα in this phrase in the fable collections, ὑπολαβών/ -οῦσα shows up instead in some manuscript traditions of the relevant fables. In addition, I have found four more occurrences of ὑπολαβών/ -οῦσα in other fables where ὑποτυχών/ -οῦσα does not occur. Thus altogether, some version of this formula occurs at least *forty times* in the late fable collections (twenty-two times ὑπολαβών/ -οῦσα; partially overlapping with thirty-six occurrences of ὑποτυχών/ -οῦσα).[11] I am not thereby claiming that every occurrence of ὑπολαβὼν ἔφη/ εἶπε signifies fable; this is not even true of all seven occurrences of this formula in Herodotus. Still, I would contend that, where this formula occurs in the context of a whole cluster of distinctive dictional or thematic

---

[9] For the phrase as a fable "formula," see Karadagli 1981.127–28. Karadagli's count of this expression depends on Hausrath's edition of the fables. Based on my own count, the formula ὑποτυχὼν εἶπε (or ἔφη) occurs thirty-six times in Perry's fables 4, 7, 12, 17, 19, 20, 29, 33, 62, 64, 89, 93, 114, 122, 125, 134, 137, 145, 154, 156, 160, 175, 200, 205, 215, 222, 223, 227, 229, 236, 237, 238, 239, 242, 243, 252.

[10] ὑποτυγχάνω is itself fairly rare, and so perhaps also colloquial or subliterary: cf. Hippocrates *Epistolae* 17; Dionysius of Halicarnassus *Roman Antiquities* 6.87, 7.16; Josephus *Jewish Antiquities* 6.11.9; Plut. *Mor.* 113b. It is striking that the two occurrences in Dionysius of Halicarnassus's *Roman Antiquities* show up in the vicinity of Menenius's telling of the fable of the belly and the limbs to the Roman plebs, while Plutarch's use of τινες ὑποτυχόντες for an anonymous, hypothetical hectoring response or question precisely corresponds to the use of ὑπολαμβάνω at Plato *Apol.* 20c4, *Meno* 74c6, *Phd.* 87c7, *Gorg.* 450e6–7, *Laws* 875d8; Xen. *HG* 6.1.7; ps.-Xenophon *Athenaiōn Politeia* 3.12.

[11] For the substitution of ὑπολαβών/ -οῦσα for ὑποτυχών/ -οῦσα, see Karadagli 1981.128: "Manchmal findet sich auch das Partizip ὑπολαβών, -οῦσα mit derselben Bedeutung wie ὑποτυχών, -οῦσα: so in den Fabeln 288, 185, 214, 283, 216, und 235 [Hausrath]." Although Karadagli lists only six such occurrences, I have counted eighteen in Perry's edition of the fables: Perry nos. 20, 29, 62, 64, 93, 114, 134, 156, 175, 200, 215, 222, 223, 227, 229, 237, 239, 252 (in all these cases, ὑπολαβών appears in Perry's *apparatus criticus*). In addition to these eighteen, one must add Hausrath nos. 283 and 288; these prose texts do not appear in Perry because they paraphrase choliambic versions by Babrius that Perry prints instead. Finally, the formula ὑπολαβὼν ἔφη occurs twice more in the fables attributed to Syntipas (Syntipas fables 50 and 61 in Perry's numeration). Thus altogether, I count twenty-two occurrences of ὑπολαβών/ -οῦσα in speech formulae in Perry's edition of the fables. For the purpose of both counts, I have used Perry's edition of the fables as the most readily accessible; a count based on Chambry 1925–26, with Chambry's fuller collation of mss and *apparatus*, yields slightly higher numbers for both speech formulae. (On the different editorial practices of Chambry, Hausrath, and Perry, and their respective strengths and weaknesses, see Holzberg 2002.5–6.)

elements that seem to point to Aesop and/or fable, we should then hear in ὑπολαβὼν ἔφη/ εἶπε a resonance of this particular "speech genre."[12]

2. And this notion of a cluster of distinctive features brings me to my second point. We should notice the Herodotean *hapax* that designates the sage's clever punch line here: ὁ ἐπίλογος. LSJ quite unsatisfactorily translate this word as "*reasoning, inference*" in this passage. J. Enoch Powell's rendering "*concluding sentence, 'the point*,'" is closer to the mark.[13] In fact, I would contend that ἐπίλογος here is a technical term that designates the "punch line" or "moral" of a fable. This "tag" later came to be called τὸ ἐπιμύθιον, when μῦθος had replaced λόγος as the standard term for a fable.[14] But, of course, Herodotus still regularly calls the fable a λόγος,[15] so that ἐπίλογος would be the appropriate word for the fable's punch line.

3. The third and final dictional cue for Aesop's occluded presence lurking behind this anecdote is Croesus's response to the "punch line": we are told he was "very delighted" (κάρτα ... ἡσθῆναι) by the sage's conclusion. Stewart Flory long ago observed that when Eastern despots in Herodotus respond with joy or laughter, they are usually badly misinterpreting a message; their excessive pleasure, according to Flory, signals their imminent destruction.[16] Interestingly, Hdt. 1.27 does not conform to Flory's pattern: here apparently, Croesus's joy at the message leads him to the right conclusion and course of action. I would suggest that Flory's historiographic pattern does not apply here because

---

[12] All seven occurrences in Herodotus: 1.11.5, 1.27.4, 6.129.4, 6.139.4, 7.101.3, 7.147.3, 9.94.3; for discussion of these, see chapter 11 below and Kurke 2010. Particular contexts in which ὑπολαμβάνω or ὑπολαβὼν ἔφη seems to co-occur with other dictional or thematic markers for fable: Hdt. 1.27.4, 6.129.4, 7.101.3; Xen. *Mem.* 2.1.29, *Cyr.* 2.2; Plato *Prot.* 320c5, *Phd.* 60c8–9, *Sym.* 193b6. Most of these passages will be discussed in more detail in later chapters.

[13] LSJ and Powell 1938, s.v. ἐπίλογος.

[14] For the development of the terminology for fable, see van Dijk 1997.79–90, Adrados 1999.3–17. Perry 1940 regards the *epimuthion* as a late, extrinsic development within the rhetorical tradition; contra Perry, Karadagli 1981.2, 53–71 argues, based on close dictional parallels, that the later rhetorical *epimuthion* external to the fable develops out of the earlier *epilogos*, a tag or moral internal to the fable spoken by one of the fable characters. For this usage of *epilogos*, cf. Arist. *Rhet.* 2.21, 1394b8–34. Karadagli 1981.127–28 also notes that the speech formula ὑποτυχών/ ὑπολαβών generally introduces the fable character's formulation of the *epilogos*, and that, very commonly, the fable shifts at this point from indirect discourse to direct quotation.

[15] Thus Hdt. 1.141.1, 1.141.3; also notice that Herodotus calls Aesop a λογοποιός at 2.134.

[16] Flory 1978.150–53 (quotation from p. 150): "Because Herodotus so often portrays joy as foolish or misplaced, the reader begins to see that when the author describes any character experiencing joy or pleasure, he simultaneously criticizes that character for ignorance. Joy is almost always ominous and foreshadows the unhappy end of the character who feels it. Herodotus regularly uses the verb ἥδομαι in association with characters of whom he is in some sense critical. The ominous quality of men's joy is even more apparent in Herodotus' use of the adjective περιχαρής and of the verb ὑπερήδομαι." Cf. Lateiner 1977 on the ominous quality and ignorance of Herodotean laughter. In like manner, note that Hdt. 1.27 is also aberrant within Lattimore's system of "tragic warners" vs "practical advisers" (Lattimore 1939). Thus, as Lattimore acknowledges, Hdt. 1.27 properly belongs with the "tragic warners" who attempt "to halt headstrong action in a chief"—but in this case (highly unusually), the sage's advice actually succeeds (Lattimore 1939, esp. 24–29).

there is, in fact, another discursive pattern informing this anecdote—and again, it is that of Aesopic fable in performance. In this instance, this discursive characterization will also illuminate what is distinctive about Aesop's style of *sophia* in relation to that of the other Sages.

Several late sources recount a moment of Aesopic advice to the Seven Sages or to Solon in particular. Thus the fragments of Diodorus Siculus's Ninth Book preserve the notice "that Aesop flourished at the same time as the Seven Sages, and said that these men had no idea how to keep company with a dynast. For in fact, one must live with such men either as little as possible or as sweetly as possible" (ὅτι Αἴσωπος κατὰ τοὺς αὐτοὺς χρόνους συνήκμαζε τοῖς ἑπτὰ σοφοῖς καὶ εἶπεν ὡς οὐκ οἴδασιν οὗτοι ὁμιλεῖν δυνάστῃ· καὶ γὰρ ὡς ἥκιστα δεῖν ἢ ὡς ἥδιστα συμβιοῦν τοῖς τοιούτοις, D.S. 9.28).[17] Plutarch gives us a more elaborated version that (naturally) allows Solon to have the last word (*Life of Solon* 28):

> ὁ δὲ λογοποιὸς Αἴσωπος, ἐτύγχανε γὰρ εἰς Σάρδεις μετάπεμπτος γεγονὼς ὑπὸ Κροίσου καὶ τιμώμενος, ἠχθέσθη τῷ Σόλωνι μηδεμιᾶς τυχόντι φιλανθρωπίας, καὶ προτρέπων αὐτὸν "ὦ Σόλων" ἔφη, "τοῖς βασιλεῦσι δεῖ ὡς ἥκιστα ἢ ὡς ἥδιστα ὁμιλεῖν." καὶ ὁ Σόλων "μὰ Δί'," εἶπεν, "ἀλλ' ὡς ἥκιστα ἢ ὡς ἄριστα."

> The fable-maker Aesop, for he happened to have been summoned to Sardis by Croesus and honored, was grieved at Solon's happening upon no generosity. And advising him, he said, "O Solon, one must keep company with kings either as little as possible or as sweetly as possible." And Solon said, "No, by Zeus, but as little as possible or as virtuously as possible."

It might appear that Aesop is here advocating simple rank flattery with no paraenetic content, but I think that's not quite right. Instead, I suggest, this admonition refers to "pleasure" as the characteristic audience reaction to the "sweetness" of implicit advice via fable—in contrast to the explicit, blunt, and unadorned advice offered by the Sages (perhaps especially Solon). This is at least the generic contrast posited by an epigram of Agathias (sixth century CE), ostensibly composed for a Lysippan statue group of Aesop and the Seven Sages (*Palatine Anthology* 16.332):

> Εὖγε ποιῶν, Λύσιππε γέρων, Σικυώνιε πλάστα,
>   δείκελον Αἰσώπου στήσαο τοῦ Σαμίου
> ἑπτὰ σοφῶν ἔμπροσθεν· ἐπεὶ κεῖνοι μὲν ἀνάγκην
>   ἔμβαλον, οὐ πειθώ, φθέγμασι τοῖς σφετέροις,
> ὃς δὲ σοφοῖς μύθοις καὶ πλάσμασι καίρια λέξας,
>   παίζων ἐν σπουδῇ πείθει ἐχεφρονέειν.
> φευκτὸν δ' ἡ τρηχεῖα παραίνεσις· ἡ Σαμίου δὲ
>   τὸ γλυκὺ τοῦ μύθου καλὸν ἔχει δέλεαρ.

---

[17] Jacoby (commentary to *FGrH* 70 F 58–62) and Snell 1971.95 assume Ephorus as Diodorus Siculus's source here (perhaps based on D.L. 1.40).

> You did well, old man Lysippus, Sicyonian sculptor, when you set up a representation of Samian Aesop in front of the Seven Sages; since those men cast necessity, not persuasion, on their words. But Aesop, by speaking opportunely with wise fables and fabrications, playing in seriousness persuades to be sensible. And harsh advice is a thing to be avoided; but the Samian has the sweetness of fable as lovely bait.

Thus Agathias makes explicit that "sweetness" (τὸ γλυκύ) inheres in Aesop's fabular medium, which playfully conveys a serious message and so persuades (in contrast to the "harsh necessity" of the Sages' sayings).[18]

It is finally worth noting that on one occasion Aesop himself in the *Life of Aesop* offers a similar justification for his indirect advice through fable. And, strikingly, this generic motivation occurs precisely in the context of his offering advice to the Samian islanders on their best course of action in response to Croesus's demand for tribute (*Vita* G, ch. 93):

> The magistrates were advising the masses to promise to pay, so as not to acquire so great a king as their enemy. But [the people] honored Aesop as a true seer of the outcome of the sign and they were calling him forth to advise them whether to send [the tribute] or to refuse. And Aesop says to them, "Men of Samos, when your leading citizens give you the advice (γνώμην) to pay tribute to the king, you inquire of me whether you ought to give it or not? If I say, "Don't give [it], I expose myself as an enemy to king Croesus." And the crowd shouted, "Give your advice." And Aesop said, "Advice I will not give, but I will speak to you with a fable ..." (οἱ δὲ ὄχλοι ἀνεκραύγασαν "γνώμην δός." ὁ δὲ Αἴσωπος ἔφη "γνώμην μὲν οὐ δώσω, λόγῳ δέ τινι λέξω ὑμῖν ...").

Aesop makes manifest here the distinction between explicit political advice (γνώμη) and implicit fable (λόγος), deploying the latter to avoid the wrath of the Lydian king. Later in the same episode, in a direct encounter with Croesus, Aesop amazes and delights the king with his distinctive style of speaking (*Vita* G, ch. 99; ὁ δὲ βασιλεὺς θαυμάσας αὐτὸν καὶ μειδιάσας ἔφη ... [this clause only in *Vita* G]).

But how exactly does Aesop speak to the Lydian king? In fact, he makes two separate speeches of advice: the first an analogy, the second a fable, both designed to magnify the power and authority of Croesus while gently nudging him toward a different course of action. Croesus had demanded Aesop from the Samians as a hostage on the advice of one of his ministers, who warned the king that he would never be able to dominate Samos as long as Aesop was giving the Samians advice (*Vitae* G + W, chs. 95–96). Aesop returns voluntarily with the minister to the Lydian court, where Croesus, on first sight of him, is appalled and annoyed that he has been prevented from exacting tribute from

---

[18] Perry 1962a.308 cites Agathias's epigram as evidence for a distinction between *Peithō* and *Bia*. This, I think, misunderstands the generic contrast Agathias is making, since the Sages' ἀνάγκη is not the same as *Bia*.

Samos "not by a man, but by an enigma and monstrosity among men" (*Vita* G, ch. 98). At this point, Aesop must first persuade Croesus, as he had initially the Samian demos (*Vitae* G + W, chs. 87–88), that in spite of his appearance, his *logos* has value and efficacy:

> "Lord King, not by force have I been led to you, but I am present voluntarily at your feet. And you are suffering something like those who are suddenly wounded, shouting out at the sharpness of the thing suddenly occurring. And wounds are the particular skill of doctors, but my speech will heal your anger (τὰ μὲν τραύματα ἰατρῶν ἐπιστήμη, τὴν δὲ σὴν ὀργὴν ὁ ἐμὸς λόγος θεραπεύσει). I, if I die at your feet, will shame your kingship, for you will [then] always have your friends giving you advice opposed to your best interest. For conjecturing that those who advise you well meet their end at your hands, they will say things that are entirely opposed to your kingship." (*Vita* G, ch. 98)

With the analogy to medicine and the subsequent claim about the effect of his death on the quality of advice Croesus will receive in future, Aesop makes his own survival all about the king's best interest, just as "Bias" or "Pittacus" in Herodotus's anecdote had guided the king by analogy to recognize the self-destructive folly of his naval aspirations. It is at this point that Croesus responds with amazement and pleasure (θαυμάσας αὐτὸν καὶ μειδιάσας), saying "Can you do me another favor and speak words/tell tales about fortune for men?" (καὶ πρὸς τὴν εἰς τοὺς ἀνθρώπους τύχην λόγους εἰπεῖν; *Vita* G, ch. 99). Aesop responds to this odd request with a beast fable, whose point is again the value of his humble *logoi* as a plea for his survival:

> And Aesop says, "At a time when beasts shared the same language as men, I say indeed that a poor man, being at a loss for his means of nourishment, used to catch those locusts that are called 'whistlers' and pickled them and sold them for a certain price. And, having seized a locust, he was about to kill her, but she, seeing what was going to happen, said to the man, 'Don't kill me in vain, since I wrong neither your crop, nor branches, nor growing things, nor have I harmed the boughs. Instead, by the synchronization of my wings and the harmony of my feet, I make useful sound (lit. I utter useful things, χρηστὰ φθέγγομαι). I am a [source of] relaxation for wayfarers.' The man, sympathetic to her words, released her into her maternal wilderness. Likewise, I also fall at your knees. Pity me: for I am not so strong as to harm any army, nor so attractive as to bear false witness against someone and be believed unjustly on account of the beauty of my appearance. But in a cheap little body, I speak sensible things, benefiting the life of mortals." (ἐν εὐτελεῖ δὲ σωματίῳ φρενήρη φθέγγομαι βίον τῶν μερόπων ὠφελῶν, *Vita* G, ch. 99)

The king, taking his cue from the man in the fable, feels sympathy for Aesop (συμπαθήσας αὐτῷ τοῖς λόγοις) and so grants him his life and whatever he asks for; Aesop, in turn, requests that Croesus be reconciled with the Samians, and so he is.

Several things are noteworthy about this exchange. First, elements in the diction of the fable seem quite old—indeed, it is a fable Perry identified as going back at least to the fable compilation of Demetrius of Phaleron.[19] Thus the fable introduction, "at a time when beasts shared the same language as men" (which occurs here for only the second time in the *Life*), finds an almost exact parallel in a beast fable Xenophon puts into the mouth of Socrates (*Mem.* 2.7.13). And Aesop's concluding line, "In a cheap little body, I speak sensible things, benefiting the life of mortals," resonates with rare and archaic vocabulary: φρενήρη, a word rarely used after the fifth century (and a particular favorite of Herodotus); and, most strikingly, μερόπων as a substantive, a usage otherwise entirely confined to poetic texts and already satirized as bombastic and archaic by the comic playwright Straton at the end of the fourth century BCE.[20]

Second, in this archaic context, Croesus's leading question, "Can you tell tales about fortune (τύχην) for men?" seems strikingly to echo Herodotus's narrative of the encounter of Solon and Croesus (for what else constitutes Solon's lecture to Croesus but the variability of human fortune?).[21] Aesop, however, responds very differently, foregrounding not the dynast's vulnerability to fortune and outside powers, but his own. In so doing, his fable response flatters Croesus by portraying him as the one with all the power, but simultaneously cajoles from him precisely what Aesop wants—his life spared and Samos saved from Croesus's domination.

It is easy to imagine Aesop's dialogue with Croesus told and retold as a fantasized response to Herodotus's famous narrative of the meeting of Greek sage and Lydian dynast, but I would suggest that the story may be older still (perhaps part of the rich oral tradition Herodotus himself inherited). For this whole tradition of the persuasive pleasure of indirect fable advice offered to dynasts may lurk behind Croesus's κάρτα ... ἡσθῆναι at Hdt. 1.27. That is to say, in this anecdote, one or the other of the Seven Sages is credited with the implicit, analogical style of advice through fable that belongs properly to Aesop, and that produces the fable's characteristic pleasure and persuasion.[22] Again the objection could be made that all our sources for this way of formulating the generic impact of fable are very late, so that there is no justification for retrojecting this system onto Herodotus's text. In response to that objection, I would point to

[19] Perry 1962a.332.

[20] For φρενήρη, cf. Hdt. 3.25, 30, 35; Eur. *Heracl.* 150; Philodemus *On Death* 39; Plut. *Mor.* 323c; Lucian *Slander* 3; for μέροψ as a rare, poetic word, see Karla 2001.53. Notice that *Vita* W, while it retains μερόπων, replaces φρενήρη with the more common χρηστά.

[21] It is interesting that *Vita* W omits Croesus's question, seguing instead directly into Aesop's fable narrative.

[22] Only after I had constructed this entire argument based on specific dictional elements did I discover a similar intuition about Hdt. 1.27 in Griffin 1990.65: "Solche Anekdoten werden nicht nur von Äsop erzählt, obwohl sie ganz besonders typisch für ihn sind.... [Summary of Hdt. 1.27] Das entspricht ganz Äsops Manier: der *ainos*, der uns nebensächlich erscheint, der aber eine verheerende Wirkung hat." (Thanks to Robert Parker for calling my attention to Griffin's essay.)

another telltale dictional trace in a much more familiar episode of Herodotus—Solon's encounter with Croesus. At the moment Solon launches into his response to Croesus's question, "Who of mortals have you seen who is the most blessed?", Herodotus characterizes his style of answering thus: Σόλων δὲ οὐδὲν ὑποθωπεύσας, ἀλλὰ τῷ ἐόντι χρησάμενος λέγει· ("But Solon, not at all responding with flattery, but using only the unadorned truth, says . . . ," Hdt. 1.30.3). Implicit in Herodotus's language here, I suggest, is a traditional contrast between Aesop and Solon in their styles of interaction with Croesus. Thus Herodotus's τῷ ἐόντι corresponds to Agathias's ἀνάγκην, while the contemptuous participle ὑποθωπεύσας negatively characterizes the "sugared pill" of Aesopic fable advice from a Solonian perspective. We should also note that Herodotus's characterization of Solon's "using only the unadorned truth" corresponds to what is implicitly negated in Croesus's response to the generic sage's "news report" in 1.27: Κροῖσον δὲ ἐλπίσαντα λέγειν ἐκεῖνον ἀληθέα εἰπεῖν ("But Croesus, since he expected that that man was speaking the truth, said . . .").[23]

Thus it is my contention that Hdt. 1.27 draws on a tradition of Aesop offering fabular advice to Croesus, and (bizarrely) frames that scene of advising as itself a fable (for this is what is implied by Herodotus's use of the fabular formula ὑπολαβόντα φάναι and the technical term ἐπίλογος). At the same time, Herodotus displaces Aesop in favor of one of the canonical Seven Sages as purveyor of the advice.[24] The question then arises—why should Herodotus's text enact this erasure of Aesop from the scene of sage advising? I would suggest that Herodotus's problem with Aesop resides in the fable-maker's double relation to the wisdom tradition. On the one hand, I suspect that the constitution of the corporate body of the Seven Sages was much more fluid and contested throughout the fifth century than has been recognized, and that Aesop was a popular contender for inclusion in the group. But at the same time, Aesop was a figure who deployed his own very distinctive style of *sophia* through indirect fable advice (as we've already seen, and as we'll see further in section II). Within this competitive tradition, Aesop's special brand of *sophia* then also entailed a

---

[23] Notice also the specific reference to "fictions" (πλάσμασι) as well as "wise fables" in Agathias's characterization of Aesop's distinctive style of advising in contrast to that of the Seven Sages in the epigram quoted above; we find the same emphasis on the useful fictionality of fable in the terse definition offered by Aelius Theon in his second-century CE *Progymnasmata* (II.72 Spengel = Perry *Test*. 85): λόγος ψευδὴς εἰκονίζων ἀλήθειαν. This linkage of "fables and fictions" may also be implied in *Vita G*, ch. 7 (the gift of the Muses to Aesop): αἱ δὲ ἐχαρίσαντο λόγων εὕρεμα καὶ μύθων Ἑλληνικῶν πλοκὴν καὶ ποιήσεις. In addition, note that προσφυέως . . . λέγειν in Hdt. 1.27 (with προσφυέως as another Herodotean *hapax*, meaning "suitably" or "appositely") precisely corresponds to Agathias's καίρια λέξας.

[24] Indeed, Herodotus's text at 1.27 could even be read to imply a meeting of all the Sages—including Aesop—at Croesus's court; such an assembly might explain the uncertainty over *which* Sage it was who gave the implicit advice via fictive analogy. Note also that Herodotus makes Solon and Aesop exact contemporaries, since he links both of them with the reign of Amasis in Egypt (Hdt. 1.30—Solon; 2.134–35—Rhodopis/Aesop).

popular demystification of the Seven Sages' wisdom. Thus the figure of Aesop simultaneously served as a focalizer for a popular critique of the high wisdom tradition—a critique that often mobilized coarse, bodily, and obscene representations to undermine the high tradition from below.[25]

More specifically, I suspect that Herodotus's repression is motivated by a tradition that preexisted the historian, of pitting Solon and Aesop against each other in a competition of high and low wisdom adjudicated by Croesus. For at this point in his text, Herodotus is just about to launch into his narrative of the meeting of Solon and Croesus (Hdt. 1, chs. 29–33). This is, of course, in Herodotus's staging a momentous encounter—a confrontation of Greek sage and Eastern dynast (and their different conceptions of the "good life") that will turn out to be programmatic for the whole of the *Histories*. In this setting, I would suggest, Herodotus does not want Aesop distracting from, and perhaps undermining in advance, Solon's sage authority—particularly since it seems that, in the tradition, Aesop actually succeeds where Solon fails, modifying Croesus's megalomaniacal schemes by his fictive analogy. It may also be a factor in Herodotus's repression of Aesop that Aesop is traditionally conceived as non-Greek (either Phrygian or Thracian)—an element that would complicate Herodotus's neat (and extremely important) opposition of Greek and Eastern, modest polis wisdom and tyrannic Lydian luxury.

And yet, as we have seen, Herodotus has not effaced Aesop entirely from the scene of sage advising at 1.27. Why is this? Why leave clues or dictional traces of Aesop at all in this context? This is a question I shall have to hold in suspension and return to in chapter 11, where we shall take the full measure of Herodotus's complex use of Aesop. In the meantime, I would contend that, fragmentary and elusive as this evidence is, it is enough to reconstruct oral traditions dating back to the fifth century BCE of Aesop as a participant (or perhaps, better, competitor) with the other Sages at the court of Croesus (traditions known to Herodotus, but displaced by him for his own purposes). To use Mary Helms's terms, we might think of Aesop as a particular kind of "ancestral culture hero" in popular traditions of the classical era: he is imagined to be the "inventor" of the genre of fable as a distinctive form of skilled crafting. Thus the *Life* endows the genre of fable with otherworldly authority (it is the special gift of the Muses to Aesop; *Vita* G, ch. 7),[26] and shows the efficacy of fable in speech contexts (as we'll see in more detail in the next section). But the *Life* also represents fable or Aesopic discourse as a genre whose status is contested—as a low form trying to

---

[25] For Herodotus himself in competition with the Sages, see Fowler.1996.86–87, Thomas 2000. For the fluidity of the tradition and competition to get into the group continuing into the fifth century, consider Simonides' various poetic attacks on individual members of the Seven Sages: frr. 542, 581 *PMG*. For Aesop's parodic critique of Seven Sages wisdom, see chapter 5 below.

[26] Notice that in *Vita* G, Isis is involved in this process only insofar as she removes the shackle from Aesop's tongue, thereby restoring his voice; the Muses alone endow him with the skill to craft Greek fables. On this sequence as analogous to a poetic initiation, see Dillery 1999, Compton 2006.22.

establish its authority. This we can recognize not just in its explicit statements about fable (as in chs. 93 and 99, cited above), but also in the obsessive imagery throughout the *Life* of Aesop as an animal, an inanimate object, or a prodigy itself requiring interpretation (*Vita* G, chs. 10, 11, 14, 16, 30, 32, 87, 88). For Aesop's homely or repulsive aspect here serves as a figure for fable itself—precious wisdom clothed in low or base forms.[27]

Indeed, I would suggest that we find scattered hints of the contested status of fable as a speech genre *specifically in relation to the wisdom of the Seven Sages*. I have already noted that Herodotus's characterization of Solon's blunt protreptic to Croesus (οὐδὲν ὑποθωπεύσας, Hdt. 1.30.3) can be read as an implicit sneer at the flattery of *Aesop's* style of intercourse with the Eastern dynast. Precisely the same critique of Aesop's rank flattery of Croesus recurs in the proverb collections of the paroemiographers. Thus, in Zenobius's version:

> "Rather the Phrygian": When Croesus had led together (as they say) the Sages (τοὺς σοφούς), he asked who they had seen who was most blessed. And with different [Sages] saying different things, Aesop the Phrygian fable-maker (ὁ μυθοποιός) said that Croesus surpassed all the rest as much as the sea surpassed the rivers. And Croesus when he heard [this] said, "Rather the Phrygian" (μᾶλλον ὁ Φρύξ; Zenobius 5.16, Leutsch-Schneidewin I.122 = Perry *Test.* 37)

This gloss reveals that the paroemiographers, too, know a tradition of the meeting of the Seven Sages (including Aesop) at the court of Croesus.[28] And in this context, they preserve the story of a competition in wisdom in which each Sage answers a question that takes the form τί μάλιστα;[29] But from the perspective of

---

[27] For a similar reading of the *Life of Aesop* as a metafable for Aesop's peculiarly animal or bodily wisdom, see Patterson 1991.13–43. This, I would suggest, is the reason for the repeated emphasis on the misfit between Aesop's appearance and his mind or intelligence (noted by Jedrkiewicz 1989.77, 118; Holzberg 1992b.73–75, 2002.83–84, 92; Ferrari 1997.11–12; Hägg 1997.186–87; Jouanno 2006.32–37); cf. *Vita* G, chs. 19, 26, 37, 88, 88a. We might read this as a formulation of the inherent doubleness of fable—true wisdom conveyed through the humblest, most common language and characters.

[28] There is a great deal of other, scattered evidence associating Aesop with the Seven Sages and/or with Croesus: (1) Alexis fr. 9 KA (= Perry *Test.* 33), probably a dialogue of Solon and Aesop, in a comedy entitled *Aesop*; (2) Plut. *Sol.* 5–6, which has Aesop pop up oddly—reincarnated as Pataecus ("Shorty")—at the end of two chapters full of anecdotes about Solon's interaction in private with other Sages; Plutarch attributes the otherwise unknown Pataecus's claim to be the reincarnated Aesop to Hermippus; perhaps (3) Call. *Iambi* 2 (*P.Oxy.* 1011, ll. 171–73 = Perry *Test.* 23) and Plut. *Div.Veng.* 556 suggest that Callimachus and Plutarch might have known a version where Aesop goes straight from Croesus's court to Delphi (this could explain why Callimachus calls Aesop "Sardian"); (4) D.L. 1.69 reports a conversation between Chilon and Aesop.

[29] Photius, the Suda, and Apostolius also cite the proverb with similar explanations. It should be noted, however, that Herondas (*Mimiambi* 5.14) seems to use it in a different sense—referring to eunuchs; cf. Headlam 1922.237. On τί μάλιστα; as a form of wisdom particularly connected with the Seven Sages, see Iambl. *VP* 83, a passage that Burkert 1972.166–70 traces back to Aristotle's treatise on the Pythagoreans; cf. Konstantakos 2004.97, 126–27, 2005.20–21. On τί μάλιστα; as a traditional sympotic form, cf. Burnett 1983.281; for a parallel, cf. Plut. *Banq.* chs. 8–9, 152f–153d.

138   CHAPTER 3

the Sages' wisdom, as represented in this tradition, Aesop's response constitutes (non-Greek) flattery and nothing more.

More tentatively, I would suggest that there may be dim traces of a proverbial opposition between Aesop and the Seven Sages in their discursive styles preserved in Aristotle and the Aristotelian commentary tradition. In *Metaphysics* Book 14, in the course of refuting Plato's position that the Forms can be represented by numbers, Aristotle observes disdainfully,

πάντα δὴ ταῦτα ἄλογα, καὶ μάχεται καὶ αὐτὰ ἑαυτοῖς καὶ τοῖς εὐλόγοις, καὶ ἔοικεν ἐν αὐτοῖς εἶναι ὁ Σιμωνίδου μακρὸς λόγος. γίγνεται γὰρ ὁ μακρὸς λόγος ὥσπερ ὁ τῶν δούλων ὅταν μηθὲν ὑγιὲς λέγωσιν. (Arist. *Met.* 14.3, 1091a5–9)

To be sure, all these views are irrational, and they conflict both with themselves and with good reasoning, and in them we are likely to have the "long story" of Simonides. For the "long story" occurs, just as of slaves, whenever they have nothing sound to say.

Alexander of Aphrodisias, in his commentary on this passage, expatiates on Aristotle's glancing reference to the "long story" of Simonides:

It will be clear from the foregoing things what the "*logos* of Simonides" is. Simonides in the *logoi* he entitles *Ataktoi* ("Disordered Accounts" or "Miscellaneous Tales"[?]) imitates and says the words that slaves are likely to say when they've tripped up to their masters cross-examining them on why they made these mistakes. And he makes them, in the course of their self-defense (ἀπολογουμένους), speak many long speeches, but nothing sound or persuasive, but everything that comes later the opposite of what was said before. For such (as is likely) is the barbarous and that which is without a share of education (τοιοῦτον γὰρ ὡς εἰκὸς τὸ βάρβαρον καὶ παιδείας ἄμοιρον, Alex. Aphrodis. *Comment. in Ar. Graec.* 1.818.3 Hayduck = Simonides fr. 653 *PMG*)

Much here is in doubt. First, we might suppose that Alexander is simply fabricating a fuller account based on Aristotle's terse explanation[30]—but notice that Alexander's gloss preserves the specific title *Ataktoi logoi* (which may suggest that he had access to the text itself or a summary thereof). Second, even those scholars who regard Alexander's fuller account as reliable disagree on *which* Simonides Aristotle is citing: is this Simonides of Ceos, the lyric poet; Semonides of Amorgos, the iambic poet; or yet a third Simonides, a writer of genealogies?[31]

---

[30] This was suggested to me by Christian Wildberg (to whom I am grateful for illuminating discussion on the relation of Alexander's commentary to Aristotle's text).

[31] Schmid and Stählin (1929.149n. 4) take this to refer either to Semonides of Amorgos or to a Simonides who wrote genealogies; Wilamowitz-Moellendorff (1913.149–50n. 4) and Page (*PMG* p. 323, Simonides fr. 653) attribute the *Ataktoi logoi* instead to Simonides of Ceos. Note that the inclusion of *logoi* in the title means that this text was almost certainly prose, not poetry, which would

In fact, this latter problem of attribution makes no difference to my argument: what is significant for my purposes is that Aristotle can cite an early source which identifies the *makros logos* with slaves who "say nothing sound" in their own defense (ἀπολογουμένους) when caught by their masters doing wrong.[32] For intriguingly, the *Life of Aesop* preserves a very similar reproach of Aesop, put into the mouth of his master, the philosopher Xanthus. Xanthus has sent Aesop to the public baths to see "if there are many people at the baths" (*Vitae* G + W, ch. 65). On arrival, Aesop notices a stone at the entrance, which everyone trips over as they go in, but nobody moves. Finally, as Aesop watches, one man trips over the stone, curses the one who put it there, and moves it. Aesop returns home and announces, "Master, I found one man at the baths," whereupon Xanthus decides that it's an opportune moment to bathe. But when the philosopher finds a great crowd at the baths, he challenges Aesop, "Didn't you tell me, 'I found one man at the baths'?" Aesop responds with a narrative of the whole drama of the stone he'd witnessed—that nobody else had the "human sense" (ἀνθρωπίνας φρένας) to move the stone, except one man—and he concludes, "Having approved that one [alone] as a man in contrast to the other people, I revealed the truth to you." In response, Xanthus quips, "There's nothing idle from Aesop when it comes to self-defense of what things he's done wrong" (οὐδὲν παρὰ Αἰσώπου ἀργὸν πρὸς ἀπολογίαν ὧν ἁμαρτάνει, *Vita* G, ch. 66).

We might note, first, that there is nothing particularly silly—or slavish—about Aesop's account here. Indeed, a similar anecdote is attributed to Diogenes the Cynic in Diogenes Laertius's *Life* (D.L. 6.40), so that Xanthus's reproach looks more like a power play between philosophical schools—a put-down by high philosophy of Cynic diatribe.[33] Second, Xanthus's wry response—especially in the shorter version of *Vita* W, "Nothing idle from Aesop when it comes to self-defense" (οὐδὲν παρὰ τῷ Αἰσώπῳ ἀργὸν πρὸς ἀπολογίαν)—has the pithiness and point of a proverb that we might imagine circulating independently of this particular narrative. However that may be, it is tempting to imagine that the *makros logos* of Simonides and Aristotle, which characterizes slave speech in general, might apply a fortiori to the tradition of Aesop, that quintessential

---

seem to militate against Simonides of Ceos. On the opposition between Aesop and the Seven Sages mapped between prose and poetry, see below, p. 141.

[32] We find a close parallel for the thought here (without specific reference to Simonides or the *makros logos*) in Arist. *Rhet.* 3.14.10–11, 1415b22–24 (apropos of the contexts in which a long prooemium is appropriate): "This is what those also do who have, or seem to have, a bad case; for it is better to lay stress upon anything rather than the case itself. That is why slaves never answer questions directly but go all round them, and indulge in preambles" (trans. Freese 1982). In fact, a reference in Eur. *IA* 313 strongly suggests that the *makroi logoi* of slaves defending themselves for wrongdoing was already proverbial in the fifth century BCE.

[33] For the same anecdotes attributed to Aesop and Diogenes the Cynic, see Zeitz 1936.230–33, Jedrkiewicz 1989.116–27.

slave speaker.³⁴ If we may posit a privileged connection between Aesop and the *makros logos*, this would again contrast Aesop's style of speaking with that of the Seven Sages, whom tradition strongly identified with βραχυλογία.³⁵ This is, of course, Socrates' account of what distinguishes the Seven Sages' wisdom in *Protagoras*: τοῦ δὴ ἕνεκα ταῦτα λέγω; ὅτι οὗτος ὁ τρόπος ἦν τῶν παλαιῶν τῆς φιλοσοφίας, βραχυλογία τις Λακωνική ("Why do I mention these things? Because this was the style of the philosophy of the ancients—a certain Laconic terseness . . ." *Prot.* 343b3–5). And while Socrates' claim that all Seven derived this style from Sparta may be Plato's (tongue-in-cheek?) invention, a fragment of a lost work of Aristotle may indicate that this was a more widespread conception of the Sages' peculiar form of *sophia*. Thus Synesius of Cyrene glosses the conditional statement, "If indeed proverb also is a [form of] wisdom" (εἰ δὲ καὶ ἡ παροιμία σοφόν):

πῶς δ᾽ οὐχὶ σοφὸν περὶ ὧν Ἀριστοτέλης φησὶν ὅτι παλαιᾶς εἰσι φιλοσοφίας ἐν ταῖς μεγίσταις ἀνθρώπων φθοραῖς ἀπολομένης ἐγκαταλείμματα περισωθέντα διὰ συντομίαν καὶ δεξιότητα. (Synesius *Praise of Baldness* 22.85c = Aristotle *On Philosophy* fr. 8 Ross = *Proverbs* fr. 463 Gigon)

But how could it not be a [form of] wisdom concerning those things about which Aristotle says that when ancient philosophy was destroyed in the greatest cataclysms of men, the things left behind were preserved because of their conciseness and cleverness.

Although Synesius does not specifically mention the Seven Sages in his citation of Aristotle (so that we might assume that the philosopher is making a more general point about proverbial lore), the context of proverb (παροιμία) linked with the notion of "ancient philosophy" (παλαιᾶς . . . φιλοσοφίας) resonates strongly with Plato's discussion in the *Protagoras*, while Plato's βραχυλογία corresponds neatly to Aristotle's συντομία καὶ δεξιότης.³⁶ Indeed, such a character-

---

³⁴ As Deborah Kamen reminds me, Aesop is identified with garrulity and with lengthy, idle speeches made in his own defense twice more in the *Life of Aesop* and twice in the preserved Aesopic proverb collections (*Vita G*, chs. 26, 50; *Aesopi Proverbia* no. 107 Perry). Thus in *Vita G*, ch. 26 (in the slave market), Xanthus asks Aesop, "Why are you such a chatterbox?" (τί οὖν πολύλαλος εἶ;); Aesop responds (according to Perry's supplement), "Sparrows that talk a lot (τὰ πολύλαλα στρουθία) fetch a great price." *Vita G*, ch. 50 offers an even closer parallel for the anecdote of the baths, for here, after another clever Aesopic speech of self-defense, Xanthus denounces Aesop's βαττολογία to his wife (Hesychius glosses βαττολογία as ἀργολογία or ἀκαιρολογία).

³⁵ I am indebted to Andrew Ford for the idea that we should see a contrast between the slavish *makros logos* and the *brachylogia* of the Sages (private conversation).

³⁶ We should also note that Ross 1958 pairs Synesius's citation with the long passage from Philoponus quoted at the beginning of chapter 2. There, in the context of a discussion of the periodic cataclysms that wipe out large portions of the human race and the slow stages by which *sophia* develops thereafter, Aristocles (perhaps citing Aristotle) explicitly identifies only one group out of the five stages—the Seven Sages. The association of these two quotations by Ross suggests that he at least thinks that the "ancient philosophy" referred to in Synesius's citation of Aristotle should be

ization makes perfect sense given the popularity of the Sayings of the Seven Sages—those succinct, explicit maxims that often consisted of a single imperative verb and its nominal object. But if I am right to see the figure of Aesop strongly associated with something like Aristotle's *makros logos*, we might interpret the opposition of *makros logos* and *brachylogia* as yet another negative valuation of the circuitousness and indirection of Aesopic fable within an ongoing contestation of modes of *sophia*.

And here we might consider yet one more possible sense of *brachylogia* or *suntomia* (Aristotle's term). Perhaps, in addition to the famous Sayings of the Sages, these designations positively acknowledge the specific *poetic* skills of the Seven. Recall that, in Richard Martin's analysis, one significant common characteristic of the Sages was their poetic composition.[37] This is an element to which I have paid scant attention, but we might think of it in Helms's terms as a magical or otherworldly ability to impose order on chaos. Against this background, it is significant that Aesop's special purview or domain of excellence is the *prose* fable, especially when we recall Jan Vansina's remarks on the differences between poetry and nonpoetic tale traditions in oral cultures:

> From the point of view of the historian the form is important, as some categories such as poetry require a composition by a single author. Quite clearly one person brought a new message into being. Even so, compositions can be significantly altered by the successors of the creators who perform these pieces....
>
> Improvisation on an existing stock of images and forms is the hallmark of fictional narrative of all sorts. Such tales develop during performance. They never are invented from scratch, but develop as various bits of older tales are combined, sequences altered or improvised, descriptions of characters shifted, and settings placed in other locales. Unlike poetry and its sisters there is no moment at which a tale is composed. Innovation is only incremental from performance to performance.[38]

That is to say, there may be a clear hierarchy of power and prestige involved, since poetic composition requires special skills, while nonpoetic tale-telling

---

aligned with the wisdom of the Seven. We should also note that Synesius's quotation does not necessarily imply on this reading that the Seven Sages existed before the flood or some other cataclysm—since Synesius's point is precisely that proverbs *survived* the cataclysms because of their "conciseness and cleverness," we might imagine the Sages inheriting older proverbs and making them their own.

[37] Martin 1998.113–15, discussed above, chapter 2, section II. Cf. Pellizer, Tedeschi, et al. 1981; their edition with commentary of scolia attributed to the Seven Sages suggests that poetic form and pithy cleverness are not so easy to separate. Apropos of these brief poetic forms (which they date to the fifth c. BCE, following Wilamowitz-Moellendorff 1925.300–301 and Momigliano 1971.27), the editors observe, "Le massime contenute in queste canzoni appaiono enunciate in forma breve ed efficace, non priva di una certa *deinotēs*, e i metri appaiono agili e coerenti" (quotation from Pellizer, Tedeschi, et al. 1981.7).

[38] Vansina 1985.11–12 (partially quoted in introduction, p. 28n. 85).

may be much more broadly diffused among members of the culture.[39] Thus, if Aesopic fable be acknowledged as a form of *sophia*, many more within society would have access to forms of verbal efficacy and cultural authority. In these terms, Aesop as the "culture hero" who invents fable might be said thereby to empower—in Helms's terms, even "bring into being"—new social groups.[40]

II. Political Animals: Fable and the Scene of Advising

In light of the evidence from Herodotus and elsewhere that suggests an early tradition of Aesop as wise man, I would like to consider in more detail a section of the *Life of Aesop* I have thus far only glanced at—the extended episode in which Aesop becomes a full-fledged political adviser (*Vitae* G + W, chs. 87–97). For in this sequence, as in his successful encounter with the Lydian king, Aesop plays the role of archaic sage, intervening with a public performance of wisdom to avert civic disaster.[41] In order to identify archaic elements this sequence may preserve, I will read it against several other moments in classical texts where a sage offers political counsel, interprets a divine sign, or deploys beast fable in the context of advising the demos on freedom and slavery.

The stage is set for Aesop's performance when, with the entire Samian people gathered for an assembly in the theater,[42] an eagle swoops down and carries off the public seal. With the priests and bird diviners unable to interpret this ominous portent and the assembly about to dissolve, the eagle returns and drops the seal in the lap of the public slave (*Vitae* G + W, chs. 81–82). At this point, the crowd appeals for interpretation to the philosopher Xanthus, who, as usual, fails utterly to solve the intellectual puzzle posed him. Xanthus eventually persuades the apparently reluctant Aesop to interpret the sign at a full assembly held the next day, but when the crowd catches sight of Aesop, they are so amused and appalled by his appearance that they refuse to believe him capable of sign interpretation. Aesop's first speech, therefore, like his first speech to

---

[39] This is not to deny that prose storytelling also requires particular narrative and compositional skills, so that there will be better and worse prose storytellers; I am simply suggesting that prose storytelling is a skill imaginably more broadly diffused (and less specifically linked to elite education) than the composition of poetry.

[40] Cf. Helms 1993.26 (quoted above, Chapter 2, p. 100).

[41] For examples of this story pattern, cf. Szegedy-Maszak 1978; Martin 1998.115–19. We might cite as parallels the story of Solon feigning madness to incite the Athenians to renew their war with Salamis (Plut. *Sol.* 8.1–3; D. L. 1.46; cf. Dem. 19.252) and the tradition that Thales persuaded the Milesians not to ally with Croesus (D. L. 1.25; cited in text). Zeitz 1936.237–43 regards this sequence of Aesop's political advice to the Samians as a very old element in the *Life*: "Denn Aesop ist ursprünglich ein σοφός, so wie er auch am Ende des Volksbuches erscheint."

[42] According to *Vita* G, ch. 81, the people are assembled for public elections; according to *Vita* W, ch. 81, it is the occasion of a public festival, including theatrical performances.

Croesus (ch. 98), is an argument for not judging the quality of his words and intellect on the basis of his external appearance:

> "Men of Samos, why do you mock, looking intently at me? You must not view the appearance, but consider the intelligence (φρόνησιν σκοπεῖν). For it is strange to censure a man's mind because of the form of his imprint. For many, having the worst form, have a sensible mind (νοῦν ... σώφρονα). Let no man, then, seeing the small size of a man, blame the things he does not see—the mind. For a doctor doesn't give up hope by [just] looking at a sick man, but by feeling his pulse, he comes to know his strength. And if you disdain the jar without ever taking a taste from it, when will you know [the quality of the wine]? The Muse is judged in theaters, Cypris in bed; thus also intelligence in words.... For just as I know how to speak, thus also I know how to be silent again. For the boundary of wisdom is to know the opportune moment." (*Vita G*, ch. 88)

The Samians, impressed by his verbal agility, encourage Aesop to take heart and speak (ch. 88). Whereupon, Aesop first argues that he should interpret the sign as a free man before the demos, for only thus can he enjoy full *parrhēsia* (ch. 89). After some wrangling with Xanthus, his liberation is accomplished (chs. 90–91), and Aesop, "going into the middle" (εἰσελθὼν εἰς τὸ μέσον), begins to speak:

> "Men of Samos, come to your own aid and deliberate on behalf of your own freedom. For this is a sign of the siege of the city and an omen that leads into slavery."

Aesop proceeds to explain to them that, since the eagle is king of birds, the omen portends the imminent threat of a king who will nullify their city laws and attempt to enslave them (ch. 91). Immediately after Aesop has finished speaking, an emissary appears with a letter from Croesus, demanding that the Samians submit to him and pay tribute (ch. 92). At this point, the civic leaders urge the people to submit and pay, but, in a sequence I've already quoted, the people appeal for advice to Aesop; in ch. 93, Aesop refuses to give them explicit political advice (γνώμη), but instead tells them a fable:

> When Zeus once commanded it, Prometheus showed to mortals two roads, one of freedom and one of slavery. And the road of freedom he made at the beginning harsh and difficult of access and steep and waterless, and crammed with burrs, entirely risky, but at the end a level plain, having space to stroll around on, in a grove crammed with fruit, well-watered, where it comes to a pause which holds the end of the experience of evils. But the road of slavery he made at the beginning a level plain, full of flowers and having a sweet prospect and much luxury, but in the end difficult of access, entirely hard and precipitous. And the Samians, recognizing what was useful from Aesop's words [fables], all together cried out to [Croesus's] letter-bearer, saying "the harsh road." (*Vita G*, chs. 94–95)

Croesus's emissary returns to Sardis and reports these events to the king. A sage kinsman of Croesus at that point warns him that he'll never subject the Samians as long as Aesop is giving them advice—so Croesus sends the kinsman himself on a second embassy, demanding Aesop as a hostage if they want to maintain friendly relations with the Lydian king. The Samian demos is then perfectly willing to surrender Aesop, who "goes into the middle" for one last speech (*Vita G*, chs. 96–97):

> [96] "Men of Samos, I pray to perish at the feet of the king. But I wish to tell you one fable, so that after my death, you can inscribe it on my tomb:
>
> [97] At the time when beasts spoke the same language as men, I say indeed that the wolves and the sheep had a war against each other. And the wolves, having the upper hand, were badly mangling the sheep, but then the dogs, having forged an alliance with the sheep, drove away the wolves. And the wolves, pursued by the dogs, sent one [of their number] as ambassador to the sheep. And the wolf, having gone and having taken his stand in the middle like a public speaker, said to the sheep, 'If you wish neither to make war nor to be warred on, give us the dogs as hostages and sleep with no fear, having no suspicion of war.' And the sheep, being idiots and persuaded, were furnishing the dogs as hostages. And the wolves ripped them apart. And later, the wolves subjected the sheep. So then, according to the fable, you ought not to hand over useful men at random." [98] And the Samians, understanding that these words were addressed to them, held Aesop back.

Thus the Samians take to heart the message of Aesop's second fable, and refuse to hand him over. Nonetheless, Aesop volunteers to accompany the kinsman back to Croesus, with the happy sequel that we've already seen.

Altogether, this is a remarkable sequence. Aesop first proves his eloquence and intellectual worth; exacts his freedom; correctly interprets the fearful omen; and finally advises the Samians on the proper course of action by narrating two fables—the first about the nature of freedom and slavery, the second about the constitution of political community and the proper valuation of advisers and allies. Many elements in this sequence seem to resonate with traditions of the Seven Sages as political advisers, some of which were already current in the fifth century BCE. Thus it is worth noting that the last words of Aesop's first speech, "the boundary of wisdom is to consider the opportune moment" (ὅρος γὰρ σοφίας ἐστὶν τὸ καιρὸν σκοπεῖν) represent the very first occurrence of the term *sophia* in the text of *Vita G*, while the sentiment has the ring of the archaic sayings of the Sages.[43] We might compare Aesop's tag with the gnome attributed

---

[43] Perry brackets the last two sentences of ch. 88 (οὐ γὰρ παρέστη . . . τὸ καιρὸν σκοπεῖν) as the intrusion of an alien marginal gloss, but as I will attempt to demonstrate here and in the next chapter, the reference to *sophia* and Aesop's veiled threat to stop speaking are perfectly appropriate in this context. Papathomopoulos 1990.129 retains these sentences in his text, but heavily rewrites them, changing the first-person verbs in the last sentence to third-person (with the personified

to Pittacus, "Know the opportunity" (καιρὸν γνῶθι; D.L. 1.79; Stobaeus, *Anth.* 3.1.173 Wachsmuth-Hense). And, in its implication that *kairos* consists precisely of knowing when to speak and when to keep silent, Aesop's words parallel even more closely Solon's remark that "speech is sealed with silence, and silence with the opportune moment" (ἔφασκέ τε σφραγίζεσθαι τὸν μὲν λόγον σιγῇ, τὴν δὲ σιγὴν καιρῷ, D.L. 1.58).[44]

In this context, under the sign of *sophia* and *kairos*, Aesop combines the reading of divine signs with political advising on freedom and slavery—a combination that conforms closely to a prephilosophical model of the characteristic wisdom performances of the Seven Sages. First, with Aesop's consequential political activity here we might compare the brief report of Diogenes Laertius:

> Thales is also credited with having given excellent advice on political matters. For instance, when Croesus sent to Miletus offering terms of alliance, he prevented it. The very thing that saved the city when Cyrus defeated [Croesus]. (D.L. 1.25)

Just as Aesop advises the Samian islanders against submission to Croesus and the paying of tribute, so Thales here critically intervenes to save his own city of Miletus.[45]

Other accounts of the Seven Sages preserved in the text of Herodotus bear an even closer family resemblance to Aesop's scene of political activity, insofar as Herodotus's Sages combine sign reading or the forecasting of an uncertain

---

Phronēsis as their subject). In my opinion, neither scholar has found an adequate solution for the textual corruption of the first sentence (to be fair, Perry has not even attempted one, since he regards this passage as an intrusive gloss): οὐ γὰρ παρέστη μοι ὡς πολλάκις συνχρομένη, ἀλλὰ τὸν λόγον ἀκοῦσαι τὸν πείθοντα ἡμᾶς. This sentence is therefore gapped in the translation offered in the text, while I follow the ms reading for the second sentence (that is, I retain the first-person verbs). For further discussion of the different terms used for mental abilities and intellectual faculties in *Vita G*, see chapter 4 below.

[44] In fact, the closest parallel for Aesop's gnome here (to my knowledge) is an exchange of dueling hexameters between "Hesiod" and "Homer" in the *Contest of Homer and Hesiod* (Allen 1974, p. 232 ll. 170–171):

τῆς σοφίης δὲ τί τέκμαρ ἐπ᾽ ἀνθρώποισι πέφυκεν;
γιγνώσκειν τὰ παρόντ᾽ ὀρθῶς, καιρῷ δ᾽ ἅμ᾽ ἕπεσθαι.

The *Contest* as we have it is a composition of Hadrianic date, but papyrus evidence suggests that it may go back to the fourth-century *Museum* of Alcidamas (see West 1967, 1984.123; Renehan 1971; Collins 2004.177–78, 185–91). Richardson 1981 has argued that this version was in turn based on an archaic *Contest of Homer and Hesiod*; cf. Steiner 2005.355 for Ibycus's possible knowledge of such an archaic *Contest*.

[45] Although Herodotus does not tell this story, he knows a tradition that Miletus alone of the Ionian cities and islands swore an oath with Cyrus—an oath that saved the Milesians after the fall of Croesus (Hdt. 1.141). It is intriguing that precisely in this context, Cyrus communicates with the other Ionian cities via a fable, "The Aulos-Player and the Fish" (which also shows up in the Augustana Collection of Aesop's fables; = fable no. 11 Perry). On this fable in context, see Meuli 1975a.728 no. 3, 1975b.744; Karadagli 1981.23, 65; Cecarelli 1993; van Dijk 1997.270–74; and see below, chapter 11.

future with advice on freedom and slavery. At the same time, these episodes clarify by contrast what is distinctive about Aesop's form of *sophia*. Consider first the anecdote Herodotus tells about the Lacedaemonian Sage Chilon in his early history of Athens:

> Croesus learned that Pisistratus the son of Hippocrates was tyrant of Athens at this time. Since for [this] Hippocrates, being a private citizen and on a pilgrimage to the Olympic games (καὶ θεωρέοντι τὰ Ὀλύμπια), a great marvel (τέρας) had occurred. For when he had sacrificed victims, the vessels that were standing by, full of meat and water, began to boil without fire and began to overflow. And Chilon the Lacedaemonian, who happened to be present and saw the marvel, advised Hippocrates (συνεβούλευε Ἱπποκράτεϊ), in the first place, not to lead a wife into his house for childbearing; but if he happened to have one [already], in the second place, to send the woman away, and if he happened to have a child, to disown him. And although Chilon advised these things (ταῦτα παραινέσαντος Χίλωνος), [they say that] Hippocrates was not willing to obey; afterwards, this Pisistratus was born to him. . . (Hdt. 1.59.1–3)

Admittedly, this is a scene of private one-on-one advising, rather than of public performance before an assembled demos. Nonetheless, there are striking parallels: thus Chilon combines the skillful impromptu reading of a divine sign (τέρας) with the offering of advice that is essentially political. For the Sage intuits from the boiling-over of the sacrificial cauldron the looming threat of tyranny from Hippocrates' unborn son and attempts to intervene to save the Athenians' freedom. But, in contrast to Aesop's successful advising via fable, Herodotus here tells us pointedly that the Sage's explicit unadorned advice fails to persuade its recipient (οὐκ ὦν ταῦτα παραινέσαντος Χίλωνος πείθεσθαι θέλειν τὸν Ἱπποκράτεα), so that the fateful child is ultimately born.

In another sequence, Herodotus remarkably doubles the scene of Sages offering consequential political advice:

> But when Harpagus [Cyrus's general] had overcome the Ionians on the mainland, those Ionians who held the islands, in terror, turned themselves over to Cyrus. But even though the Ionians had fallen on evil times, they were nonetheless still assembling at the Panionion, and it was then, as I learn, that Bias of Priene displayed the most useful advice (γνώμην) to the Ionians, which, if they had obeyed, would have made them the most fortunate of the Greeks. He was urging the Ionians to raise a fleet in common and sail to Sardinia (ἐκέλευε κοινῷ στόλῳ Ἴωνας ἀερθέντας πλέειν ἐς Σαρδώ), and then to found a single city of all the Ionians [there]. That way, he said, released from slavery, they would be fortunate, inhabiting the greatest of all islands and ruling over others. But as long as they remained in Ionia, he said that he couldn't foresee freedom still existing for them (καὶ οὕτω ἀπαλλαχθέντας σφέας δουλοσύνης εὐδαιμονήσειν, νήσων τε ἁπασέων μεγίστην νεμομένους καὶ ἄρχοντας ἄλλων· μένουσι δέ σφι ἐν τῇ Ἰωνίῃ οὐκ ἔφη ἐνορᾶν ἐλευθερίην ἔτι ἐσομένην). This was the

advice (γνώμη) of Bias of Priene, offered to the Ionians when they were already ruined; but excellent also was [the advice] that Thales of Miletus offered them before the destruction of Ionia.... he was urging the Ionians to hold [in common] a single Bouleuterion [council house], and for it to be on Teos (for Teos is the middle of Ionia), but to regard the other inhabited cities as nothing less than districts [of a single polis]. (Hdt. 1.169.2–170)

Notice the parallels here with the story of Aesop and the Samians, focusing for the moment just on the account of Bias (which is more fully narrated). Thus, in the context of the subduing of the Ionians to the rule of an Eastern potentate, Bias offers political advice to the people assembled at the Panionion. His advice speaks crucially to the issue of freedom or slavery, like Aesop's first fable (οὕτω ἀπαλλαχθέντας σφέας δουλοσύνης εὐδαιμονήσειν), while it enjoins unified, coordinated action on the part of all the Ionians, much like Aesop's second fable of sheep, dogs, and wolves (notice especially κοινῷ στόλῳ). Finally, as narrated by Herodotus, Bias's political advice here is actually based on an element of prophecy, in the Sage's unique ability to "see into" and predict an uncertain future: this is the implication of Herodotus's phrase "otherwise he said he couldn't foresee freedom still existing for them" (οὐκ ἔφη ἐνορᾶν ἐλευθερίην ἔτι ἐσομένην).[46]

But we should also note the significant contrasts between Aesop's performance and these wisdom traditions: first, where Thales and Bias perform γνώμη (explicit political advice), Aesop tells fables. (I will consider in greater detail in a moment the use of fables in scenes of political advising, as well as the particular fables Aesop tells in this context.) The second salient difference in Aesop's performance is related to the first: in Herodotus's account, these two Sages utterly fail to persuade their audiences, although their advice is flagged as "excellent" by the narrator himself. Just like Solon to Croesus (1.30–33) and Chilon to Hippocrates (1.59), the Sages' simple blunt advising fails, whereas with both fables, Aesop succeeds.[47] And this is the result of the particular way fables work: as in the subsequent colloquy with Croesus, Aesop's λόγοι empower his auditors by giving them the agency to interpret and apply them for themselves.

Let us now turn to consider in more detail the specific fables that Aesop tells in this scene of political advising. Both fables appear to be quite old. The first, the fable of the two roads, picks up a motif already known from Hesiod, Simonides,

---

[46] See Powell 1938, s.v. ἐνορῶ, 2. Indeed, in all six occurrences Powell lists with the meaning "foresee," the verb ἐνορᾶν figures at significant moments of political advising, where a sage—or aspiring sage—asserts his ability to "see into" an uncertain and volatile future (Hdt. 1.89.1, 1.120, 1.123, 1.170, 5.36.2, 8.140β2).

[47] Note that, like Hdt. 1.27, Hdt. 1.169–70 is aberrant in terms of Lattimore's opposition of "tragic warners" vs "practical advisers." Here, highly unusually for Hdt., two sages offering positive, practical advice fail to persuade their advisees (cf. Lattimore 1939.24–28). I would conclude from this not that Lattimore's categories are inadequate, but that Hdt. 1.27 and 1.169–70 participate in a *different* pattern or system (of Aesop vs the Seven Sages) that crosscuts his.

and Prodicus, and transposes it from "virtue and vice" to "freedom and slavery."[48] The second, the fable of sheep, dogs, and wolves (which Aesop wants carved on his tomb), is in fact the first full-fledged beast fable narrated in the *Life*, introduced by the archaic formula, "at the time when beasts spoke the same language as men. . . ."[49] In relation to Aesop's second fable, we should note that Plutarch's *Life of Demosthenes* preserves a scene of the orator using exactly the same fable in speaking to the Athenian demos—a vignette that suggests that the story of Aesop's advice to the Samians may already have been well known in the fourth century BCE.[50]

Immediately after the murder of Philip of Macedon, Demosthenes incites the Greek cities to band together, and Thebes to rebel against its Macedonian occupying force. Alexander reacts swiftly, crushing Thebes and demanding of the Athenians that they surrender to him their popular leaders, including Demosthenes. Plutarch continues,

> This was when Demosthenes, having narrated also the [well-known] fable of the sheep who surrendered their dogs to the wolves (ὅτε καὶ τὸν περὶ τῶν προβάτων λόγον ὁ Δημοσθένης ἃ τοῖς λύκοις τοὺς κύνας ἐξέδωκε διηγησάμενος), likened himself and those with him to dogs fighting on behalf of the demos, while he called Alexander the Macedonian lone wolf (τὸν Μακεδόνα μονόλυκον). And in addition, he said, "Just as we see grain-merchants, whenever they carry about a sample in a bowl, selling the rest of the crop through a few grains of wheat, thus you unwittingly surrender also yourselves, all of you, in [surrendering] us." These things Aristobulus of Cassandreia has recorded. (Plut. *Dem.* 23.5–6)

Plutarch cites as his source for this anecdote Aristobulus of Cassandreia, a historian contemporary with Alexander who accompanied him on campaign. Thus, whether or not Demosthenes *really* told this fable to the Athenian assembly, we have a contemporary fourth-century source recounting the tradition.[51]

Even so, at first glance, we might be inclined to assume that Demosthenes' use of the fable has priority, and that the Aesop tradition has borrowed it from

---

[48] Cf. Hes. *WD* 287–92; Simonides fr. 579 *PMG*; Prodicus as described in Xen. *Mem.* 2.1.21–34. On the antiquity of this fable, cf. Perry 1962a.331, Adrados 1999.655. For more discussion of the fable of the two roads, see chapter 7 below.

[49] On the antiquity of this fable, cf. Adrados 1999.655. For the formulaic opening, cf. Xen. *Mem.* 2.7.13 (also a fable about sheep, dogs, and wolves, narrated by Socrates) and discussion above, p. 134. Hunter 2007.55 also notes that Aesop tells his first full-fledged beast fable (complete with *epimuthion*) here, as a free man in a context of political advising; cf. Kamen 2004.

[50] Jedrkiewicz 1989.401 notes the parallel. Thanks to Boris Maslov for calling my attention to this passage.

[51] Karadagli 1981.28–29 and Jedrkiewicz 1989.401 assume the historical authenticity of the tale, but it was challenged by Meuli 1975b.756. Van Dijk 1997.293–94 cautiously leans toward historicity. Isidore *Etymologies* 1.40 and Melanchthon *On the Usefulness of Fables* offer slightly different versions of the same story involving Demosthenes; for thorough discussion of all the variants, see van Dijk 1997.291–96.

the tale of the Athenian orator's performance.⁵² But I would contend that it is equally likely that the borrowing went in the other direction, with Demosthenes (or whoever made up the tale) consciously citing a well-known story about Aesop. I say this, first, because the Aesopic resonance gives added bite to Demosthenes' use of the fable, insofar as it refigures the Macedonian king as a barbarian Eastern despot oppressing the Greek cities. But, more significantly, I would see Aesop lurking behind Demosthenes' use of fable because of the low, fabular elements that permeate this whole chapter of Plutarch's biography. Thus even before the assembly scene, Plutarch tells us that Demosthenes wrote letters to the Great King's generals in Asia inciting them to make war on Alexander, "whom he derisively called 'boy' and 'Margites'" (παῖδα καὶ Μαργίτην ἀποκαλῶν αὐτόν, Plut. *Dem.* 23.2). As a low, foolish character (and protagonist of his own burlesque epic), Margites has much in common with the slavish, hideous Aesop.⁵³ Then again, immediately after the assembly scene, Plutarch notes that the orator Demades volunteered to go on a mission to Alexander, to appeal on behalf of those popular leaders demanded, "whether trusting to his friendship [with the king], or expecting that he would find him crammed full, just like a lion glutted with slaughter" (ὥσπερ λέοντα φόνου κεκορεσμένον, Plut. *Dem.* 23.6). Here, intriguingly, the Aesopic beast-fable element seems to leak from Demosthenes' usage into Plutarch's own narrative, even as the chapter as a whole charts the dubious ascent of Alexander from "Margites" to "Macedonian lone wolf" to royal "lion."⁵⁴ Thus Plutarch himself at least seems to sense and echo an Aesopic resonance in Demosthenes' fable.⁵⁵

⁵² Thus Jedrkiewicz 1989.401, followed by van Dijk 1995.139–40, 1997.293n. 44. Notice that at one point in the *Life*, Aesop is described as "a veritable Demosthenes" (ch. 32, only in *Vita G*).

⁵³ On Aesop and Margites, cf. Winkler 1985.288–89: "The *Life of Aesop* can thus be interpreted as a witness to a submerged, largely unwritten and unlettered cultural tradition in which the Deformed Man speaks both comically and seriously against the tyranny of conventional wisdom. If Aesop tends more to the serious, his non-identical twin, Margites, tends to represent the merely comic formulation of the same elements." For the Aesopic element in Plutarch, we might also note Demosthenes' derisive use of παῖς. Although its primary reference is clearly to Alexander's youth (he is a mere "boy" or "child"), it may also carry a secondary resonance of "slave."

⁵⁴ De Falco 1932.94 (fr. 51, followed by van Dijk 1997.295–96) attributes the lion image to Demades himself. I am less confident that the image that shows up here and again (in the same context) in Plut. *Alex.* 13 should be attributed to the Athenian orator, since in both contexts the image is contained within an εἴτε . . . εἴτε construction that expresses Plutarch's own hesitation between two different options. Still, even if the image of the "sated lion" *is* drawn from Demades, the construction of this chapter of the *Life of Demosthenes*, with its three ascending Aesopic references, is due to Plutarch.

⁵⁵ This familiar Aesopic resonance may also explain Plutarch's use of the definite article in the phrase τὸν περὶ τῶν προβάτων λόγον. That is, τόν here perhaps indicates "the [well-known] fable of the sheep"; in contrast, the Aesop tradition designates this merely as "one" or "a fable" (ἕνα λόγον, *Vita G*, ch. 96). Van Dijk 1997.291 makes the same point about the allusive function of the definite article for each of the animals within the fable, although he assumes simply an allusion to a well-known fable, but not to Aesop.

150 CHAPTER 3

Beyond Demosthenes' (or "Demosthenes'") possible restaging of a specific scene of Aesopic political advice through fable, there are several moments in archaic and classical texts that bear a family resemblance to the political use of fable in this sequence of the *Life of Aesop*. Thus, among the examples offered by Aristotle in the *Rhetoric* for "fable" as a subspecies of invented example, we find a fable told by the poet Stesichorus to the people of Himera.[56] When they had already chosen Phalaris as dictator and were about to give him a bodyguard, as Aristotle sets the scene,

> Stesichorus . . . after many arguments related a fable to them (τἆλλα διαλεχθεὶς εἶπεν αὐτοῖς λόγον): "A horse was in sole occupation of a meadow. A stag having come and done much damage to the pasture, the horse, wishing to avenge himself on the stag, asked the man whether he could help him to punish the stag. The man consented, on condition that the horse submitted to the bit and allowed him to mount him javelins in hand. The horse agreed to the terms and the man mounted him, but instead of obtaining vengeance on the stag, the horse from that time became the man's slave. "So then," said he, "do you take care lest, in your desire to avenge yourself on the enemy, you be treated like the horse. You already have the bit, since you have chosen a dictator; if you give him a bodyguard and allow him to mount you, you will at once be the slaves of Phalaris." (Arist. *Rhet.* 2.20.5, 1393b10–22, trans. Freese 1982)

As in the sequence in the *Life of Aesop*, the poet Stesichorus is here credited with a fable of cross-species alliances whose message is the imminent enslavement of the people of Himera to the tyrannical Phalaris.[57] And, strikingly, Aristotle introduces Stesichorus's fable with the idea of a contrast between logical argumentation and beast fable (τἆλλα διαλεχθεὶς εἶπεν αὐτοῖς λόγον)—a contrast that exactly corresponds to Aesop's assertion to the people of Samos, "I will not give you advice, but I'll tell you a fable" (γνώμην μὲν οὐ δώσω, λόγῳ δέ τινι λέξω ὑμῖν, *Vita* G, ch. 93). The same opposition is perhaps implied in Plutarch's use of καί to introduce the [well-known] fable of sheep, dogs, and wolves in the *Life of Demosthenes* ch. 23.5 quoted above (καὶ τόν . . . λόγον). That is: "Demosthenes [having offered many arguments,] narrated in addition a fable. . . ." If indeed this is the sense of καί τόν . . . λόγον, it is noteworthy that both "Stesichorus" and "Demosthenes" control both modes of speaking, and deploy fable only as a supplement to reasoned argument—or when reasoned argument has failed.[58]

---

[56] This fable is immediately followed by the fable Aesop told to the Samians while defending a Samian demagogue in court (the fox and its dog-fleas; *Rhet.* 2.20.6, 1393b22–94a1), but, for our purposes, the fable attributed to Stesichorus offers a closer contextual parallel.

[57] The first-century BCE historian Conon connected this same fable with Gelon, not Phalaris (*FGrH* 26 F 1, l. 42). For discussion of the variants, see Cope and Sandys 1877.II.199–200; van Dijk 1997.155–58.

[58] Note that the performances of "Stesichorus" and "Demosthenes" thus correspond to Aristotle's recommendations in the *Rhetoric* on the proper relations, frequency, and order of reasoned argu-

But the association of beast fable with public debate on issues of slavery, freedom, and threatened tyranny is much older than Aristotle, for we find it already in the preserved fragments of Solon. In an iambic trimeter fragment quoted in the *Ath. Pol.* as evidence for Solon's cancellation of debts, the poet-lawgiver boasts that he has freed the Attic earth, "formerly enslaved" (πρόσθεν δὲ δουλεύουσα, fr. 36 W, l. 7), by pulling out the boundary stones. He goes on to speak of those sold into slavery abroad for debt bondage, whom he has repatriated and freed (fr. 36 W, ll. 9–15). The fragment as quoted then concludes:

> κέντρον δ᾽ ἄλλος ὡς ἐγὼ λαβών,
> κακοφραδής τε καὶ φιλοκτήμων ἀνήρ,
> οὐκ ἂν κατέσχε δῆμον· εἰ γὰρ ἤθελον
> ἃ τοῖς ἐναντίοισιν ἤνδανεν τότε,
> αὖτις δ᾽ ἃ τοῖσιν οὕτεροι φρασαίατο,
> πολλῶν ἂν ἀνδρῶν ἥδ᾽ ἐχηρώθη πόλις.
> τῶν οὕνεκ᾽ ἀλκὴν πάντοθεν ποιεόμενος
> ὡς ἐν κυσὶν πολλῇσιν ἐστράφην λύκος.
> (Solon fr. 36 W, ll, 20–27)

If another had taken the goad as I did, a man who was evil-plotting and property-loving, he would not have restrained the demos. For if I had been willing [to do] the things that were then pleasing to the opposite side, or the things in turn that the other party plotted for these,[59] the city would have been bereft of many men. On account of these things, I turned, making defense from all sides, like a wolf among many dogs.

At first glance, it seems surprising that Solon casts himself not as the loyal dog defending the sheep flocks, but as the wolf. Attempting to make sense of Solon's final image, commentators have often compared it to a Homeric simile, but, as Emily Anhalt has noted, there is an odd misfit in this comparison as well. For in the Homeric simile most often adduced as a parallel, the embattled Hector is compared to a boar or a lion turning to defend itself against attacking dogs (*Il.* 12.41–42). In fact, individual warriors in epic are never compared to wolves, for

---

ments (enthymemes) and examples (*paradeigmata*): "If we have no enthymemes, we must employ examples as demonstrative proofs, for conviction is produced by these (ἡ γὰρ πίστις διὰ τούτων); but if we have them, examples are to be used as evidence and as a kind of epilogue (ἐπιλόγῳ) to the enthymemes. For if they stand first, they resemble induction, and induction is not suitable to rhetorical speeches except in very few cases; if they stand last, they resemble evidence, and a witness is in every case likely to induce belief (ὁ δὲ μάρτυς πανταχοῦ πιθανός). Wherefore also it is necessary to quote a number of examples if they are put first, but one alone is sufficient if they are put last; for even a single worthy witness is of use (μάρτυς γὰρ χρηστὸς καὶ εἷς χρήσιμος)." (*Rhet.* 2.20, 1394a9–16, trans. Freese 1982, slightly modified). Cf. Jedrkiewicz 1989.397–401 for the parallels between Aristotelian theory and rhetorical practice.

[59] I agree with Anhalt 1993.134n. 34 that Solon is intentionally vague about who the two sides are here; I have therefore avoided a translation that would pin down these vague characterizations. For deliberate ambiguity here, cf. Irwin 2005.243n. 108; contra: Mülke 2002.392.

Homeric wolves always travel in packs.[60] On Anhalt's reading, Solon's audience expects a Homeric image, only to have their expectations contravened by λύκος, the very last word in the line (and perhaps the poem). At the same time, Solon's image exploits the traditional associations of the lone wolf as "outcast or antithesis of civilized relations," a kind of scapegoat who unifies the community left behind by his exclusion.[61] This resonance Anhalt connects with the problematic status of the legendary lawgiver:

> Solon's effort to create social unity and his alienation from the community are consistent with the traditional relationship between the generic lawgiver and his community. Legend recognizes that the lawgiver's exclusive power to change the code he himself instituted makes him a potential threat to its stability. The solution to this problem is either the lawgiver's death or self-imposed exile.[62]

I agree with Anhalt's analysis; I would add to it that Solon here displaces Homeric imagery in favor of an evocation of Aesopic fable.[63] In the Greek bestiary, as Marcel Detienne and Jesper Svenbro have demonstrated, the wolf is characterized as a political animal, insofar as wolves hunt in packs and divide up their kill with mouths that function like the *machaira*, the sacrificial knife. But at the same time, wolves in the Greek imaginary expose the limits (or precariousness) of civic order and the isonomic sacrificial division that represents it by their individual greed (*pleonexia*) and their willingness to engage in cannibalism.[64] In

---

[60] For the Homeric comparandum, see Campbell 1967.253, Gerber 1970.143, Mainoldi 1984.128, Mülke 2002.394–5, Irwin 2005.245–60. Mainoldi 1984.128 and Anhalt 1993.125–30 note the misfit; Mülke 2002.395 and Irwin 2005.247, 260 also note that λέων would scan in this position, so that the choice of λύκος, so surprising in Homeric terms, must be deliberate; cf. also Loraux 1984.207, Detienne and Svenbro 1989.149.

[61] Anhalt 1993.130–35, quotation from p. 131; cf. Loraux 1984.207. Buxton 1986.63–64 also notes the associations of the "lone wolf" with exile or outsider status. Other scholars offer different interpretations of the surprising "wolf" instead of the expected Homeric "lion": thus Mainoldi 1984.128 suggests that Solon intends a deliberate contrast with the lion as "le symbole de l'aristocratie guerrière"; Mülke 2002.394–97 emphasizes the wolf's association with cunning and reads the final image as "more a threat than a self-curse" ("eher eine Drohung als eine Selbstbeschimpfung," p. 397). Most recently, Irwin 2005.245–61 has usefully emphasized the dark side and ambiguities of Solon's choice of the wolf, which imagistically assimilates the lawgiver and the tyrant.

[62] Anhalt 1993.135. On the lawgiver's "self-imposed exile," cf. Ker 2000.

[63] Irwin 2005.252–60 also notes the importance of Aesopic fable to Solon's image here.

[64] Detienne and Svenbro 1989.148–58. As they observe, "A proverbial phrase says it all: 'wolf's friendship' means disunity, the negation of all common interest, as if in this animal—otherwise such a remarkable butcher-cook and so clever at dividing up the portions—there were a fault, a secret vice that prevents him from working with his fellows in a common enterprise. This ambiguity about the wolf can be seen in another proverb that tells of meat and distribution: 'The wolf distributes the meat. (This is said) of someone who wants more than his fair share (*pleonektein*) and (who wants to) give.' . . . Thus it seems that the wolves' spontaneous isonomy is undermined by a congenital 'pleonexia.' The city that the wolves create each time they begin to move their jaws is doomed from the outset to tyranny and cannibalism" (quotation from pp. 157–58).

particular, Detienne and Svenbro focus on an Aesopic fable that draws together all these lupine characteristics:[65]

> λύκος τῶν λοιπῶν λύκων στρατηγήσας νόμους ἔταξε πᾶσιν ἵνα, εἴ τι ἂν ἕκαστος κυνηγήσῃ, πάντα εἰς μέσον ἄξῃ καὶ μερίδα ἴσην ἑκάστῳ δώσῃ, ὅπως μὴ οἱ λοιποὶ ἐνδεεῖς ὄντες ἀλλήλους κατεσθίωσιν. ὄνος δὲ παρελθὼν τὴν χαίτην σείσας ἔφη, "ἐκ φρενὸς λύκου καλὴ γνώμη· ἀλλὰ πῶς σὺ τὴν χθεσινὴν ἄγραν τῇ κοίτῃ ἐναπέθου; ἄγε ταύτην εἰς μέσον ἀπομερίσας." ὁ δὲ ἐλεγχθεὶς τοὺς νόμους ἀνέλυσεν.

> A wolf, having been made commander of the rest of the wolves, ordained laws for all so that, if any one of them catch anything, he bring everything into the middle and give an equal portion to each, in order that the rest, being in need, not eat each other. And an ass happened by and, shaking his mane, said, "A noble plan from the mind of a wolf. But how is it that you have put away for yourself yesterday's catch in your lair? Bring this out into the middle and divide it up." And the wolf, [thus] convicted, dissolved the laws. (Fable no. 348 Perry = 228 Chambry³)

Here the attempted lawgiving of the wolf commander, devised to prevent cannibalism within the wolf pack, is undermined by the lawgiver's pleonectic sequestering of his own booty from the hunt.

I would suggest that Solon's iambics allude to this fable—or something very like it. This is not necessarily apparent as the poem progresses, but the incongruity of the final image—Solon as wolf where we expect a Homeric lion or boar beset by dogs—sends us back to the earlier lines. There we notice that Solon's hypothetical "other man" who could have "taken the goad" posesses the characteristics of the nomothetic wolf in the fable: he is "evil-planning" (κακοφραδής) and "property-loving" (φιλοκτήμων), and under his leadership each faction would have been allowed to indulge its plots against the other. The result, in Solon's rendering, would be *stasis*—a kind of civic "cannibalism": "this city would have been bereft of many men."[66] We might say that, in the final image, Solon opts for the role of the outcast—the lone wolf—so as not to become the pleonectic lupine lawgiver of the fable.

Another fragment of Solon also seems to allude to beast fable in the context of political advising. In a poem in elegiac couplets quoted by Diodorus Siculus, Diogenes Laertius, and in part also by Plutarch, Solon is said to chastise the Athenians after the establishment of Pisistratus's tyranny (against which he had earlier warned them in vain):

---

[65] Detienne and Svenbro 1989.150–53.

[66] For the thought, cf. Solon fr. 33 W, where another hypothetical man mocks Solon's simple-mindedness and asserts that, given the same opportunity, he would have "seized abundant wealth and made himself tyrant of Athens [even if] only for a day, then been flayed for a wine-skin and his generation utterly extirpated." For the identification of the tyrant with the wolf (in the context of civic cannibalism, promises of "cancellation of debts," and redistribution of land), see Plato *Rep.* 8.565d4–566a4 and extended discussion in Irwin 2005.248–61.

εἰ δὲ πεπόνθατε λυγρὰ δι' ὑμετέρην κακότητα,
    μὴ θεοῖσιν τούτων μοῖραν ἐπαμφέρετε·
αὐτοὶ γὰρ τούτους ηὐξήσατε ῥύματα δόντες,
    καὶ διὰ ταῦτα κακὴν ἔσχετε δουλοσύνην.
ὑμέων δ' εἷς μὲν ἕκαστος ἀλώπεκος ἴχνεσιν βαίνει,
    σύμπασιν δ' ὑμῖν χαῦνος ἔνεστι νόος·
ἐς γὰρ γλῶσσαν ὁρᾶτε καὶ εἰς ἔπη αἱμύλου ἀνδρός,
    εἰς ἔργον δ' οὐδὲν γιγνόμενον βλέπετε.
(Solon fr. 11 W)

If you have suffered grievous things because of your own baseness, do not attribute the allotment of these things to the gods. For you yourselves exalted these men by giving them defenses, and because of these things you got evil slavery. And each of you individually goes in the tracks of a fox, but for you all together, the mind is vain and empty. For you look to the tongue and the words of a wheedling man, but you don't at all consider the action happening [right in front of you].

The poet's reproach that the Athenians "have exalted these men by giving them protections" (ῥύματα) resonates oddly with the political context of "Stesichorus'" fable of interspecies exploitation in Aristotle's *Rhetoric* (where the poet warns the demos against giving "Phalaris" a bodyguard). But I suspect that another fable of interspecies manipulation and betrayal lies behind Solon's fragment. For the expression χαῦνος . . . νόος in line 6, Douglas E. Gerber notes an intriguing parallel from a choliambic fable of Babrius (second century CE?): a deer, "his mind puffed up by the false words" of a fox, is lured into the den of an ailing lion (τῆς δ' ὁ νοῦς ἐχαυνώθη/ λόγοισι ποιητοῖσιν, Babr. 95.36–37). Gerber cites this as a local parallel, but does not note that Solon's entire elegiac fragment seems to play off the ancestor of Babrius's fable.[67]

In Babrius's versified narrative, the ailing lion recruits the crafty fox to lure a deer into his den "with honied words" (λόγοισι . . . μελιγλώσσοις, Babr. 95.9). This the fox does by telling the deer that the lion on his deathbed has chosen the deer to succeed him as ruler of the wild beasts (θηρίων τυραννήσει, Babr. 95.16; τυραννεῖν, Babr. 95.20). The deer, gulled by this promise of power, follows the fox into the lion's den, where the lion, too eager for the prey, leaps up precipitously and just scratches the deer's ear. The deer bolts in terror, and the lion sends his minion, the fox, to find him and coax him back. The fox, on finding the deer, reproaches him for his cowardice and recasts the scene in the lion's den as an attempt at kingly advising:

"Are you so ignoble and full of fear? So suspicious of your friends? The lion, intending to give you useful advice and rouse you from your former sloth, [just] touched your

---

[67] Gerber 1970.136. D. L. Page *apud* Cook 1954–55.3 had already argued that "Solon was referring to the fable Babrius 95." Based on the chronology of the written texts, Mülke 2002.225 denies the influence of the fable on Solon's verses.

ear, like a dying father. For he was going to give you every precept, by which to take and hold so great a rule. But you couldn't [even] endure the scratch of his enfeebled hand, but by pulling violently away, you exacerbated your injury. And now that one is angrier than you are, having found you by testing too untrusting and light-minded, and he says he'll set up the wolf as king. O woe for a wicked master! What shall I do? You are to blame for evils for all of us. But come and be noble in future, and do not flutter in fear like a sheep from the flock. For I swear to you by all the leaves and springs, as I hope to be enslaved to you alone, that the lion is not at all your enemy, but out of goodwill he makes you master of all the animals." With such wheedling words (τοιαῦτα κωτίλλουσα) she persuaded the young stag to go twice into the same house of death. (Babr. 95.67–88)

After this moment of high rhetorical elaboration, Babrius wraps the narrative up quickly. The lion rapidly consumes every bit of the stag, except its heart, which had fallen apart from the rest as the lion rent the stag to pieces. The fox surreptitiously grabs the heart and eats it, and when the lion, enumerating his victim's innards, wonders at the missing organ, the fox "cunningly covering up the truth" (ἀπαιολῶσα τῆς ἀληθείης) quips, "Don't bother looking—he simply didn't have one. For what kind of heart could he have, who came twice into the lion's den?" (Babr. 95.99–103).[68]

We should note first that Babrius's fable is itself preoccupied with issues of tyranny and enslavement, which the fox wittily figures in her "fable within a fable" as the fantasized supremacy of the wolf over the stag as cowardly "sheep." But more significantly for Solon's fragment, the dim-witted deer in Babrius's fable is doomed because he trusts the cunning words of the fox more than his own immediate experience of danger (the lion leaping out to grab him). This precisely corresponds to the last four lines of Solon's elegy, and the parallel allows us to fill out the fable background of Solon's allusive version. Thus we might tendentiously paraphrase, "Each of you Athenians individually has the cunning of a fox, but all together you have the empty mind [of the stag]. For you look to the tongue and the words of a wheedling man, but you don't at all consider the [dangerous] action occurring right in front of you."[69] It might be objected that an allusion to this fable in Solon's version requires the tyrant Pisistratus to do double duty, since he is cast both as the cunning fox (as speaker of words) and as the voracious lion (as source of the "present action"). And yet

---

[68] As Perry explains in his Loeb edition, "Here, as often, the heart is spoken of as synonymous with mind or intelligence" (Perry 1965.123).

[69] Thus I do not agree with Gerber's gloss on ἴχνεσι βαίνει: "'follows in the tracks', i.e. 'follows blindly'" (Gerber 1970.136); cf. Page apud Cook 1954–55.3, who understands ἴχνεσι βαίνει to mean "follow where the fox leads." This interpretation makes meaningless the pointed contrast εἰς μὲν ἕκαστος —σύμπασιν δ' ὑμῖν in ll. 5–6, since both lines then simply describe the stupidity of the demos. On these two lines as pointing a strong antithesis, see Cook 1954–55.3, Mülke 2002.224–25 (who notes, contra Page, that ἴχνος is never used in Greek poetry of literal "following in the footsteps of").

Solon has already told us that the characters in his civic fable play double parts by his double identification of the demos as foxes (individually) but deer (collectively).

But if we can indeed connect Aesop with all these scenes of political advising via fable, is this not a contradiction of the claim made in section I, that Aesop, while he participates in the Sages tradition, does so by purveying his own distinctive style of low, fabular wisdom? I think not. What saves these two arguments from contradiction is the striking fact that all the other adviser figures considered in this section say either *more* or *less* than Aesop. That is, those figures engaged in political oratory ("Stesichorus" and "Demosthenes"), as we have seen, are represented as marshaling rational arguments and only then adding beast fable as a supplement thereto (even if the fables alone endure in the anecdotal tradition as the most memorable part of those speeches). Conversely, where these figures of political oratory say more, Solon in his poetry of political advice says less. On the reading offered here, Solon's evocation of fable is so allusive and elliptical as often to escape notice altogether (indeed, many readers on that account may reject my interpretation of Solon's fragments). I would contend that this pattern of more and less is no accident: that Aesop represents (even embodies) fable in its purest form, but that that low genre must be handled with care—diluted or abstracted—when it enters more respectable genres of speaking.

Thus the pattern noticed here exactly conforms to Kenneth Rothwell's observation about the distribution of fable in classical poetic genres; Rothwell notes that (with a single exception) high genres like lyric and tragedy only allude to fables, but never narrate them straight through, while fables proliferate in a low genre like Old Comedy.[70] Solon's elegies (and even his iambics) fit perfectly into Rothwell's model of fable distribution—since here, fables are only alluded to, not told straight through.[71] In addition, Rothwell notes the same pattern of avoidance in the prose form of Attic oratory. For it is an intriguing paradox that, although Aristotle in the *Rhetoric* specifically recommends the use of fable (as a subspecies of fictional exemplum) in public oratory (*Rhet.* 2.20, 1394a2–5), there is not a single full fable to be found in the entire corpus of Athenian speeches—neither private nor public, dicastic nor bouleutic.[72] At the same time,

---

[70] Rothwell 1995; the exception (which Rothwell discusses) is Soph. *Ajax* 1142–62. Indeed, Rothwell also notes that even in comedy, it is only characters of low socioeconomic status who narrate fables straight through (1995.236–44).

[71] Cf. Lasserre 1984 for a survey of the distribution of fable and allusions to fable in different genres of archaic Greek poetry, and West 1974.32–34 on the generally higher stylistic register of Solonian iambics as compared to those of the archaic Ionian tradition (Archilochus and Hipponax): "Serious politics in the iambic metres is found a little later in Solon. Solon's tetrameter and trimeter discourses cannot be separated from his elegies. We cannot regard them as true iambi" (quotation from p. 32).

[72] On a couple of occasions, we find what may be allusions to fable in preserved speeches: [Dem.] 25.40; [Dem.] 26.22. On these allusive references, see van Dijk 1997.294 with n. 48.

biographical and anecdotal traditions preserve stories of rhetors telling fables in the courts and in the assembly.[73] How to account for this perfect complementary distribution? My guess is that rhetors told fables all the time, but that these low, entertaining forms punctuating speeches did not survive the passage from oral performance to written text. When the orators themselves or later editors redacted their speeches for circulation in written form, the disreputable fable elements were ruthlessly excised (much like speakers' tearful appeals and parading of their young children before the jury).[74] And yet oral tradition remembered—or fabricated—a few of these moments as rhetorical high points or particularly effective bons mots.

Indeed, on one occasion at least, the anecdotal tradition preserves an account of the oratorical use of fable that itself thematizes the unworthiness of fable as an object of the audience's attention within a deliberative setting.[75] In the *Lives of the Ten Orators* preserved among the *Moralia* of Plutarch, we find the following story about Demosthenes:

> And once when he was being prevented by the Athenians from speaking in the assembly, he said that he only wished to speak briefly to them, and when they became silent he said, "A young man in the summer time hired an ass to go from the city to Megara. When noon came and the sun was blazing fiercely, both he and the owner of the ass wished to lie down in its shadow. Each tried to prevent the other from so doing, the owner maintaining that he had rented him the ass, not its shadow, and the one who had hired the ass that he had complete rights in him." When he had said this, he began to go away; and when the Athenians stopped him and asked him to tell the rest of the tale (πέρας ἐπιθεῖναι τῷ λόγῳ), he said, "You are willing to listen when I

---

[73] For the contradiction between Aristotle's recommendations in the *Rhetoric* and the preserved evidence of the Attic orators, see Meuli 1975b.756, Rothwell 1995.245–47, Adrados 1999.379. As Meuli and Rothwell note, Aristoph. *Wasps* 566 provides further evidence that fables were indeed a common feature in the actual performance of law-court speeches: here Philocleon mentions as one of the pleasures of perennially serving on juries that some of those on trial "tell us stories, others some laughable thing of Aesop."

In addition to the anecdotes in Aristotle and Plutarch considered in this section, cf. all the passages listed and discussed in van Dijk 1997.287–310. Van Dijk 1997.309 himself notes that all of these instances of fables in political oratory are "preserved only by other writers," but draws no conclusions about the decorum of fable narration from this complementary distribution—mainly, I suspect, because he follows a nineteenth-century scholarly practice of treating every anecdote of an orator telling a fable as a fragment of a lost written oration.

[74] For the process of editing orations for written "publication" or dissemination, see Worthington 1991; for a similar explanation of the nonoccurrence of fables in the texts of the Attic orators, see Rothwell 1995.246.

[75] This anecdote about Demosthenes is frequently cited together with an anecdote about Demades using an interrupted fable to get the audience's attention: thus Meuli 1975b.756, Jedrkiewicz 1989.401–2, Rothwell 1995.247, van Dijk 1997.291–305, Adrados 1999.379–80. Both these interrupted fables correspond to the folkloric category of the "catch tale" (on which, see in general Uther 2004.II.531–34; in particular Hansen 2002.75–79); I consider here only the "Demosthenes" fable, since it alone (unlike the "Demades" fable) thematizes the unworthiness of fable.

speak about the shadow of an ass, but when I speak about serious matters (ὑπὲρ σπουδαίων πραγμάτων), you refuse." ([Plut.] *Mor.* 848a–b, trans. Fowler 1991)

There are several different versions of this tale (which van Dijk classifies as a fable) preserved among the scholiasts, paroemiographers, and lexicographers, who also know "the shadow of an ass" as a proverb for things that are utterly trivial or of no account.[76] Van Dijk treats this as a rare example of a deliberately unfinished fable, but in a sense, Demosthenes does supply the moral—that is, the condemnation of fable as low and trivial in contrast to the "serious matters" on which the assembly should be deliberating.[77] This is fable as a self-consuming deliberative artifact, in an anecdote that perfectly captures the ambivalence of high deliberative oratory toward this low form. But the final paradox, of course, is that this anecdote was wildly popular in antiquity; whether the fable was ever really spoken by Demosthenes or some other orator or simply made up, it floats free of the texts of the written orations, endures, and proliferates as a satisfying bon mot in the popular memory of oral tradition.

[76] There are several accounts of the story without the oratorical frame: cf. Leutsch-Schneidewin I.287 (Diogenianus), I.439–40 (Appendix), II.566 (Apostolius); Schol. *ad* Plato *Phdr.* 260c; Schol. *ad* Lucian *Hermotimus* 71; Photius *Bibl.* 265 (495a15–44). The Suda preserves both the story itself and the Demosthenic frame (with some variations from the Ps.-Plutarchan version): s.vv. ὄνου σκιά (III.543 Adler), ὑπὲρ ὄνου σκιᾶς (IV.657–58 Adler). In addition, Macarius simply glosses the proverb: ἐπὶ τῶν μηδενὸς ἀξίων (Leutsch-Schneidewin II.193).

[77] Thus van Dijk 1997.298. The Suda's version actually fills out the implicit contrast between "serious" deliberation and frivolous or pleasurable fable: thus, in one narrative iteration, Demosthenes gets the attention of jurymen by promising them a "sweet narrative" (διηγήματος τερπνοῦ, IV.657 Adler), while in the other, Demosthenes breaks off the tale to rebuke the jurymen "when he sees them very attentive and taking pleasure and longing to hear the rest" (προσέχοντας σφόδρα καὶ ἡδομένους καὶ ποθοῦντας τὰ ἑξῆς ἀκοῦσαι, III.543 Adler).

Chapter 4

READING THE *LIFE*: THE PROGRESS OF A SAGE AND THE ANTHROPOLOGY OF *SOPHIA*

THE PROJECT OF THIS CHAPTER is to offer a sustained reading of the whole of the *Life of Aesop* in terms of the themes of *sophia* I have traced out in the last two chapters. In the latter of these, we reviewed the evidence for Aesop as a sage interacting with the Seven Sages in traditions that may antedate Herodotus's writing, and we considered (in reverse order) the scenes in the *Life* in which he offers advice, first to the Samian demos, then to the Lydian king (*Vitae* G + W, chs. 87–100). At this point, I would like to widen the focus to reinsert these scenes of the sage's bouleutic activity into the development of the *Life* as a whole and its narrative trajectory. Thus I will attempt to read the arc of the *Life* as a coherent narrative that culminates in significant political activity and then *theōria* to Delphi (a sequence I identified in chapter 2 as characteristic of the life cycle or progress of a typical archaic sage). In this chapter, we will find that that pattern interacts with another in the development of the *Life*—an anthropology of *sophia* that has been traced back to the Sophists and perhaps beyond them to the first half of the fifth century. Both the progress of a sage and the anthropology of *sophia* seem to have figured in the common tradition that stands behind the texts of G and W, for the episodes that make up these patterns occur in both (although the elements are clearer in the fuller *Vita* G).[1] At the same time, as we shall see, G has muted certain elements that properly belong to the life story of an archaic sage (and that show up elsewhere in the tradition for Aesop)—specifically, his assimilation to the divine at the end of his life.

In order to do such a reading, I will work through in sequence chapters 1–100 of the *Life* and the Ahiqar section (chs. 101–23), and I will then revisit the Delphi episode (chs. 124–42), in each instance attempting to tease out the layers of the wisdom tradition and its renovation as an anthropology of *sophia*. The sequential reading of the first one hundred chapters of the *Life* will help us understand in turn the logic of the assimilation of Aesop and Ahiqar (even if we cannot date this process) and the folding into the *Life* of the Ahiqar segment in

---

[1] Thus we might imagine these two strands or layers as a phenomenon of the dialectic of oral tradition and written text. Oral tradition represents the story of Aesop's life as that of an archaic sage with his own distinctive style of *sophia*, while the first textual fixation of the *Life* (the written ancestor of G and W), perhaps composed within a rhetorical/sophistic/educational milieu, adapts or refashions that trajectory as an anthropology of human *sophia* in miniature.

the particular place it occupies, while it will also shed new light on the Delphi section as an allomorph of the theoric death of the sage. Finally, in the last section of the chapter, we will see that Aesop's fable telling is just one aspect of his distinctive style of *sophia* as characterized throughout the *Life* (and here Helms's model and categories of analysis will assist us in refining our conception of what is peculiar—and peculiarly challenging—about Aesopic wisdom).

I. An Aesopic Anthropology of Wisdom

There are at the outset two reasons to think that the first one hundred chapters of the *Life* should be read as a unified narrative constructed to culminate in the sequence of political advising. First, there is the intriguing formulation that begins the narrative proper (after an introductory chapter devoted to a detailed description of Aesop's hideous appearance): "His master, finding this one in all respects mute and not equipped for work in the city, sent him to the country [to dig . . .]" (τοῦτον ὁ δεσπότης κατὰ πάντα σιγηλὸν ἔχων καὶ ἀποίητον τῇ πολιτικῇ ἐργασίᾳ, ἔπεμψεν εἰς τὸν ἀγρόν . . . , *Vita* G, ch. 2).[2] In context, since we have just been told that Aesop is a slave, the primary meaning of πολιτικὴ ἐργασία must be "work in the city." But it is difficult to resist endowing this phrase with the secondary meaning "political activity"—a meaning that points forward and receives its triumphant fulfillment in the scenes of political advising considered in the previous chapter.[3] Together with this pointed reference to "political activity" at the beginning of the narrative, there is the fact (noted briefly in the previous chapter) that the word *sophia* appears for the very first time in the text of *Vita* G in this scene of sage advising, at the end of Aesop's first speech to the Samian demos (*Vita* G, ch. 88). Nor do I think this pattern of occurrence a mere accident, since the text of the *Life* teems with words for intelligence, cleverness, and resourcefulness from beginning to end. Before ch. 88, we find a whole host of different terms (nouns, adjectives, and verbs of intellection): πολυπειρία, ἐνθύμημα, νοῦς, εὕρεμα, λόγος, πολύνους, φρένες, ἐπίνοια, εὐεπινόητος, φιλόσοφος, φιλοσοφία, τὸ ἕτοιμον τῶν λόγων, εὐτράπελος, λόγιος, τὸ φρόνιμον, εὑρεσίλογος, ἀγχινοία, φρόνημα, συνετός, φρόνησις.[4] Then again, after Aesop

---

[2] Some words have been lost from the text of *Vita* G after ἀγρόν; σκάπτειν supplied from *Vita* W.

[3] Note that the version of *Vita* W (ὡς ἄχρηστον τῆς πολιτικῆς ὑπηρεσίας) preserves the ambiguity of πολιτική, while ὑπηρεσία perhaps gives more weight to Aesop's lowly, slave status at the outset. Contrast the political emphasis of both G and W with the Accursiana version of the *Life*: ὁ κεκτημένος τοίνυν αὐτόν, ἅτε πρὸς οὐδὲν τῶν ἐντὸς οἰκίας ἔργων οἰκείως ἔχοντα, σκάπτειν εἰς ἀγρὸν ἐξαπέστειλεν (Eberhard 1872.228 = Perry *Test.* 2). The Accursiana's substitution of household for polis as the proper ambit of a slave's activity represents a Byzantine normalization that reveals by contrast what is distinctive in G and W.

[4] It must be acknowledged that the adjective σοφός and the adverb σοφῶς each occur once in *Vita* G before ch. 88: (1) Aesop ironically characterizes Xanthus's wife as σοφή in his first encounter

has become a full-fledged political adviser, *sophia* occurs several more times in the text of *Vita* G, especially in the Ahiqar sequence in which Aesop engages in his duel of wits with the Egyptian king Nectanebo.[5] This pattern perfectly conforms to what I noted in chapter 2 about pre- or nonphilosophical *sophia*, for it is here a superlative term within a contest of wisdom, reserved for the sage and efficacious interpretation of divine signs or riddles in a political context. Thus the opening reference to πολιτικὴ ἐργασία and the long-deferred mention of *sophia* in *Vita* G together mark out the scene of political advising as a kind of climax to which the *Life* up to that point has been building.

In contrast, *Vita* W uses forms of σοφός and σοφία much more freely and abundantly throughout.[6] Thus these terms seem to be much more generic and much less marked in *Vita* W. How are we to account for this? Is this an older pattern that *Vita* G preserves, but that has become meaningless by the time of *Vita* W's loose paraphrase and epitome of the common ancestor of G and W? Or is the G author/redactor thereby showing off a pedantic and archaizing knowledge of an older, marked use of *sophia*? Because of the co-occurrence of this careful patterning of mention of *sophia* with the opening reference to "political activity" (which occurs in *both* G and W), I incline to the former explanation, although there is no way to be sure.

In any case, what does the narrative of the *Life* offer on the way to this significant political climax? In the progression leading up to this scene of political advising, Aesop goes through his own ascent of wisdom or "skilled crafting."[7] The stages of that ascent in many cases bear striking similarities to what has been reconstructed as a Sophistic anthropology (whose remnants we find preserved in *Antigone*'s "Ode to man," *Prometheus Bound*, Euripides' *Suppliants*, Protagoras' great speech in Plato's dialogue, the pseudo-Platonic *Epinomis*, and various moments in Aristotle).[8] In brief, this Sophistic anthropology posits the slow and gradual emergence of human civilization, through such stages as the invention of language and naming, agriculture, hunting, religious practices,

---

with her (ch. 32); (2) Xanthus praises the astuteness of Aesop in locating a man who is truly ἀπερίεργος by saying, σοφῶς, νὴ τὰς Μούσας (ch. 62). Note that this pattern of occurrence actually conforms to Kerferd's (1976.22) observation (about classical texts) that "σοφία itself is hardly a regular Attic prose word," while forms of the adjective *sophos* occur more commonly.

[5] On the occurrences of *sophia* in the Ahiqar section, see section II below.

[6] Thus (besides their occurrences in the equivalent chapters of *Vita* G) the noun, adjective, and/or adverb occur in *Vita* W, chs. 36, 41, 67, 77b (three times), 85, 101, 109 (twice), 119, 130.

[7] For a similar reading of the progression of *Vita* G, see Ferrari 1997.20–32 (who conceives it in terms of the progression of Aesop's particular verbal skills).

[8] For these texts as providing the elements of a Sophistic anthropology, see Havelock 1957.57–154, Dodds 1973, Kerferd 1976, Cole 1990. In general, I find more persuasive the reconstructions of Havelock 1957, Dodds 1973, and Kerferd 1976 than that of Cole 1990. While I have learned a great deal from Cole's careful collection and analysis of ancient evidence, I am not comfortable tracing everything in this tradition back to Democritus, as he does.

house building, and ultimately cooperative life in cities and the laws that enable it. In this respect, the *Life of Aesop* seems oddly to participate in a long-lasting tradition of philosophical speculation on the species-level stages and nature of human *sophia*. Thus Aesop starts on the margins, at the most primitive level as a radically "unaccommodated man"; he acquires skills, moves eventually to the center, and ultimately performs his wisdom as the highest "political activity."

At the same time, I would contend, this Sophistic model itself represents the elaboration and systematization of some aspects of an older pattern of prephilosophical *sophia*. This, in a sense, was the lesson of Aristocles' account (cited by Philoponus) of the five stages in the ascent of human wisdom quoted at the beginning of chapter 2. For our consideration of the pre- or nonphilosophical model of *sophia* allowed us to see Aristocles' sequence as the projection across generations of what had traditionally been elements in the life cycle of a single sage. In the *Life of Aesop*, we find this whole sequence restored to an individual, who thereby rehearses in a single life the anthropology of *sophia*. But at the same time, we can on occasion detect in the *Life of Aesop* remnants of a still older paradigm of Aesop as a sage more akin to the Seven Sages, on which this Sophistic anthropology is overlaid. This is perhaps clearest in the concluding movements of the *Life*, wherein Aesop follows the pattern of an archaic sage, progressing to consequential political activity followed by *theōria*.

I want to go through and trace out both these levels or layers at once. In tracking these patterns, we will be assisted by prominent appearances of the Muses, since in fact each of the stages of Aesop's ascent of wisdom is flagged or articulated in *Vita* G by significant mention of the divine daughters of Mnemosyne or their Hesiodic home on Helicon. *Vita* W, by contrast, has entirely effaced all mention of the Muses from Aesop's story (together with excising every trace of Aesop's feud with Apollo).[9]

As the story begins, Aesop is mute, and that is the reason given for his exclusion from the civic sphere. But as a reward for his pious treatment of a priestess

---

[9] Cf. Perry 1936.14: "The association of Isis with the Muses is an interesting bit of Hellenistic syncretism. . . . More important for us, since it concerns the *Leitmotif* of the entire biography, is the fact that the Muses, to which there is not a single reference in the Westermann recension, are frequently alluded to in the Morgan text." As Perry himself acknowledges, μοῦσαι does occur once in *Vita* W as a common noun meaning "arts" (*Vita* W, ch. 53). But this complete exclusion of the Muses (capital "M") even extends to the use of the oath "by the Muses," which occurs twelve times in *Vita* G but never in *Vita* W. Different scholars disagree on whether the Muses have been excised from the tradition by the author/redactor of *Vita* W (thus Perry 1936) or carefully added to *Vita* G (thus Ferrari 1997.13–20, Braginskaia 2005). As discussed in the introduction, I would argue for a compromise position—seeing the prominent mentions of the Muses throughout the *Life* as old elements (since they flag significant moments of ascent of wisdom or contests of *sophia* that are common to G and W), while I would treat the very common oath "by the Muses" as a distinctive verbal tic of the G author/redactor.

of Isis, the goddess restores his voice and prevails upon the Muses to supplement her gift with "the best speech":

> "ἐγὼ μὲν οὖν τὴν φωνὴν ἀποκαθίστημι, ὑμεῖς δὲ τῇ φωνῇ τὸν ἄριστον χαρίσασθε λόγον." εἰποῦσα δὲ ταῦτα καὶ τὸ τραχὺ τῆς γλώττης ἀποτεμοῦσα, τὸ κωλῦον αὐτὸν λαλεῖν, αὐτὴ δὴ ἡ Ἶσις ἐχαρίσατο ‹τὴν φωνήν›, ἔπεισεν δὲ καὶ τὰς λοιπὰς Μούσας ἑκάστη‹ν› τι τῆς ἰδίας δωρεᾶς χαρίσασθαι. αἱ δὲ ἐχαρίσαντο λόγων εὕρεμα καὶ μύθων Ἑλληνικῶν πλοκὴν καὶ ποιήσεις. κατευξαμένη δὲ ἡ θεὸς ὅπως ἔνδοξος γένηται, εἰς ἑαυτὴν ἐχώρησεν. καὶ αἱ Μοῦσαι δέ, ἑκάστη τὸ ἴδιον χαρισάμεναι, εἰς τὸ Ἑλικῶνα ἀνέβησαν ὄρος. (*Vita* G, ch. 7)

> "I then restore his voice, but you add the gift of the best speech to his voice." And when she had said these things and cut the shackle on his tongue that prevented his speaking, Isis endowed him with voice, and she persuaded all the rest of the Muses each to endow [him] with something of her own individual gift. And so they gave him the invention of words and the weaving and crafting of Greek fables. And the goddess, having prayed that he become famous, went off to her own [place]. And the Muses, each having bestowed her own particular gift, went up to Mt. Helicon.

After this elaborate scene of divine investiture with the powers of voice, speech, and fable making, Aesop's first social speech is a denunciation of the overseer's injustice:[10]

> The overseer of the fields, coming up to the workers, savagely beat one of Aesop's fellow workers. And Aesop, no longer able to control himself, says, "Man, why do you thus bitterly torment and unsparingly beat the one who has done you no wrong (τὸν μηδὲν ἀδικήσαντα)—you who each hour [of the day] do the most wrongs (πλεῖστα ἀδικήματα ποιῶν) and are beaten by no one?" (*Vita* G, ch. 9)

This whole sequence (with its careful articulation of the graded gifts of φωνή, then λόγος) strikingly echoes a familiar passage from the beginning of Aristotle's *Politics*:

> From these things it is evident, then, that the city belongs among the things that exist by nature, and that man is by nature a political animal. He who is without a city through nature rather than chance is either a mean sort or superior to man. . . . That man is much more a political animal than any kind of bee or any herd animal is clear. For, as we assert, nature does nothing in vain; and man alone among the animals has speech. The voice indeed indicates the painful or pleasant, and hence is present in other animals as well; for their nature has come this far, that they have a perception of the painful and pleasant and indicate these things to each other. But speech serves to reveal the advantageous and the harmful, and hence also the just and the unjust. For it is peculiar to man as compared to the other animals that he alone has a perception of

---

[10] I say "social speech" because Aesop first has a brief monologue when he wakes from his siesta and realizes that he's regained the power of speech (*Vitae* G + W, ch. 8)—more on this passage below.

good and bad and just and unjust and other things [of this sort]; and partnership in these things is what makes a household and a city. (λόγον δὲ μόνον ἄνθρωπος ἔχει τῶν ζῴων. ἡ μὲν οὖν φωνὴ τοῦ λυπηροῦ καὶ ἡδέος ἐστὶ σημεῖον, διὸ καὶ τοῖς ἄλλοις ὑπάρχει ζῴοις . . . , ὁ δὲ λόγος ἐπὶ τῷ δηλοῦν ἐστὶ τὸ συμφέρον καὶ τὸ βλαβερόν, ὥστε καὶ τὸ δίκαιον καὶ τὸ ἄδικον. τοῦτο γὰρ πρὸς τἆλλα ζῷα τοῖς ἀνθρώποις ἴδιον, τὸ μόνον ἀγαθοῦ καὶ κακοῦ καὶ δικαίου καὶ ἀδίκου καὶ τῶν ἄλλων αἴσθησιν ἔχειν, ἡ δὲ τούτων κοινωνία ποιεῖ οἰκίαν καὶ πόλιν.) (Arist. *Pol.* 1.2.9–11, 1253a1–18; trans. Lord 1984)

Precisely because he has just been endowed not only with φωνή, but also with λόγος, Aesop has the ability to perceive injustice—as well as the language to articulate it.[11] And while this speech in its immediate context first puts Aesop's life in danger (for the slave overseer Zenas panics at the prospect of his newfound articulateness, denounces him to the master in the city, and gets the master's permission to sell or to kill him outright), within the broader narrative, this diatribe on injustice is what actually propels Aesop from digging in the fields to the slave market of Samos, to the household of Xanthus, and ultimately to the assembly at the center of the city.

It is not, however, my claim that the *Life of Aesop* as we have it transcribed in *Vita* G preserves a textual allusion to this specific passage in Aristotle. Instead I

---

[11] Indeed, the echo of the Aristotelian passage is even stronger if we take into account Aesop's very first speech on awakening from his siesta: "Wow, I slept sweetly" (οὐᾶ, ἡδέως ὕπνωσα, *Vita* G, ch. 8). Thus Aesop's first two speeches correspond precisely to Aristotle's categories of φωνή and λόγος; the first simply registers pleasure, while the second (what I have termed his first "social speech") ascends to the level of "the advantageous and the harmful, and thus also the just and the unjust." It is interesting to note that *Vita* W diverges in two significant respects in this sequence, which together mute the Aristotelian echo: (1) the distinction between the two divine gifts of φωνή and λόγος is much less clear in ch. 7, and (2) in his second speech in ch. 9, Aesop is much less concerned with the overseer's injustice than with the fact that he wastes time and does no work himself.

Dillery 1999.271–80 connects this story of the restoration of Aesop's speech with the cult of Isis in Roman Egypt: "Plutarch, in the *De Iside et Osiride* ch. 3 (352b), observes that Isis was connected to Hermes, 'the discoverer of writing and of music and of poetry'; and that in Hermopolis in Egypt the one who was 'the leader of the Muses' (Μουσῶν τὴν προτέραν, trans. Griffiths) was called at one and the same time Isis and Justice" (quotation from Dillery 1999.275; cf. Finkelpearl 2003, Hunter 2007.41–46). While the associations among Isis, the Muses, and Dikaiosyne are intriguing, it should be noted that Dillery's cult connection accounts less well for the details of this passage than does the Aristotelian parallel, since none of the Isis-Muses passages he cites makes the salient distinction φωνή-λόγος. In addition, Dillery's association of the Muses with the cult of Isis cannot account for the repeated appearances of the Muses within the Aesop narrative, and on one point, Dillery's treatment is actually misleading. He concludes: "Inasmuch as the Life does not really feature Isis and the Muses consistently throughout the narrative, but chiefly at the beginning and the end, I do not think that we can see in it a treatment of the initiate's life in the Mysteries" (Dillery 1999.280). In fact, the Muses *do* feature throughout the *Life*, whereas Isis makes only one appearance after the investiture sequence in an oath (*Vita* G, ch. 15) and certainly plays no part at the end of the narrative. Hunter 2007.48–56 also reads *Vita* G, chs. 6–8 in light of Greek developmental accounts of the origins of human language. Hunter's discussion is very compatible with the interpretation offered here, while he usefully emphasizes the connections to bucolic/pastoral literature of such scenes (thereby helping to explain the striking *ekphrasis* of *Vita* G, ch. 6).

READING THE *LIFE* 165

would contend that the opening chapters of Aristotle's *Politics* draw on and synthesize several commonplaces of Sophistic anthropology, among them the intimate link between humankind's unique possession of *logos* (both speech and reason) and the constitution of household and civic communities.[12] We might furthermore imagine that, after Aristotle, such commonplaces were familiar and broadly diffused in debates and speculation that continued within the philosophical, rhetorical, and educational milieus I have posited as a plausible context for the textual fixation of the *Life*.[13]

We can see another stage in this ascent of *sophia*—the development of agricultural know-how—in the story of Aesop's encounter with the market-gardener, his first foray out into the world after he has come to Samos and entered the household of Xanthus the philosopher (*Vitae* G + W, chs. 34–37).[14] It may seem paradoxical to locate the beginnings of agricultural τέχνη here, since we saw Aesop already at the beginning of the *Life* "digging in the country" (*Vita* W, ch. 2; *Vitae* G + W, ch. 4). And yet we are never told what Aesop is digging or why. More to the point, when he gives what he can as hospitality to the priestess of Isis, in addition to the bread and olives he takes from his pack, all he has to offer her as his own production are "wild vegetables" (ἄγρια λάχανα ἀποκείρας ἐκόμισεν, *Vita* G, ch. 4).[15] Given that he possesses bread and olives,

[12] Cf. Dodds 1973.16: "[Aristotle's] account of the growth of society from the individual household through the clan to the city state follows the lines of fifth-century anthropology." For other reflexes of a similar linkage between speech, the perception of justice, and civic order, cf. Soph. *Ant.* 354–56, 365–70; Plato *Prot.* 322a3–323a4. Protagoras's speech in Plato's dialogue offers a slightly different sequence of development: once Prometheus has stolen ἔντεχνος σοφία σὺν πυρί from the common workshop of Athena and Hephaestus and transmitted it to men, men develop (1) religious worship/practices; (2) φωνή and ὀνόματα; (3) other skills—building houses, making clothing and shoes, working the earth for nourishment. Still, even at this point in Protagoras's schema, men lack (4) πολιτικὴ τέχνη, so that when they cluster together in cities to defend themselves against wild animals, they wrong each other until Zeus sends Hermes to give all men a share of πολιτικὴ τέχνη. Developments (1) and (2) in "Protagoras'" speech also find a very close echo in the *Life of Aesop*, since it is specifically Aesop's piety that earns the reward of voice and speech, while the first thing Aesop does when he realizes he's regained his voice is to name all the common objects around him (καὶ τὰ βλεπόμενα ὀνομάζων, *Vitae* G + W, ch. 8). Cf. Dillery 1999.270 and Hunter 2007.49–50, connecting this scene of Aesop naming the objects with Herodotus's famous *bekos* story (Hdt. 2.2; another reflex of fifth-century anthropological speculation). It is this correspondence to several different fifth-/fourth-century anthropologies that suggests that the *Life* is participating in a more broadly diffused discourse or debate, rather than narrowly alluding to Aristotle's *Politics*.

[13] Evidence for this diffusion in fifth-century and later tragedy: Aesch. *Prom.* 442–506, Soph. *Ant.* 332–75, Eur. *Suppl.* 198–213, Moschion fr. 814 N². Indeed, we find a reflex of the same association of ideas in a comic sequence later in the *Life* where Aesop defends himself for serving only tongues for a meal on the grounds that the tongue is the best and most useful thing in life: ἀλλὰ διὰ γλώσσης πόλεις ἀνορθοῦνται, δόγματα καὶ νόμοι ὁρίζονται ("But through the tongue, cities are set upright, beliefs and laws are defined," *Vita* G, ch. 53; similar—if briefer—version in W).

[14] For the development of agriculture as a stage in Sophistic anthropologies, cf. Aesch. *Prom.* 454–56, 462–65; Soph. *Ant.* 337–41; Eur. *Suppl.* 205–7; Plato *Prot.* 322a7–8.

[15] Note also that in both G and W, Aesop offers the priestess springwater to drink—i.e., he has no wine.

those products of civilized cultivation, why add the apparently gratuitous touch (preserved only in *Vita* G) of "wild vegetables"? This detail seems to locate Aesop in a quasi-wild or savage position in the opening chapters of the *Life*, somehow not yet fully integrated into civilized agricultural production.

From this strange limbo state Aesop emerges only after his acquisition of language and his integration into the household of the philosopher Xanthus. At that point, Xanthus orders the new slave to attend him to the market-gardener's, to purchase "vegetables for boiling" (*Vitae* G + W, ch. 34). Having provided a neat bouquet of vegetables, the market-gardener then refuses payment, hoping instead that the philosopher can resolve for him "a problem" (ζήτημα) that has been worrying him:

> The market-gardener says, . . . "Only deem me worthy of a single word/explanation" (ἑνὸς λόγου). Xanthus said, "By the Muses, I will take neither the coin nor the vegetables, unless you tell me first in what way my reason (ὁ ἐμὸς λόγος) can benefit you being a market-gardener. For I am neither a craftsman nor a smith, so as to make a hoe or a leek-slicer, but I am a philosopher." The market-gardener says, "Master, you will do me a great benefit, for I lie awake nights grieving over a certain problem, reckoning and seeking why it is that the plants I cast into the earth—plants that I hoe and water and lavish much attention on—why it is that the wild plants from the earth grow more quickly than the ones I've put in. Xanthus, having heard the problem of a philosopher (φιλοσόφου μὲν ζήτημα), but not finding a solution for it right away, says, "All things are ordered by divine forethought." Aesop, standing behind Xanthus, laughed out loud. Xanthus says, "Aesop, are you laughing, or are you laughing at me?" Aesop said, "No, not at you." Xanthus said, "But at whom?" Aesop said, "At the master who taught you." Xanthus says, "Accursed one, you speak blaspheming the common [treasure] of Greece, since I studied in Athens among the philosophers, rhetors, and *grammatikoi*. Is it then permissible for you to approach Helicon of the Muses? (ἔξεστιν οὖν σοὶ εἰς τὸν Ἑλικῶνα τῶν Μουσῶν εἰσελθεῖν;)" Aesop said, "If you speak nonsense (lit. say nothing), it's necessary to mock you." Xanthus says, "Does the problem have another solution? For the things ordered by divine nature cannot be sought out by philosophers. You then—can you solve it for him?" Aesop said, "Promise and I will solve it." Xanthus, turning back [to the market-gardener], says, "Most clever fellow, it is inappropriate for me who discourse in such great auditoria to engage in philosophical discussion in orchards, but follow me." And as they're going, Xanthus says to the market-gardener, "I have a slave of much experience (παῖς πολύπειρος), the one walking with us—put it to him and he will solve the problem." The market-gardener says, "What! This repulsive fellow knows his letters?" Aesop, laughing, says to the market-gardener, "And do you, wretch?" The market-gardener says, "Am I a wretch?" Aesop says, "Well, you're a market-gardener, aren't you?" The market-gardener says, "Yes." Aesop says, "Are you annoyed being called 'wretch,' when you're a market-gardener? You seek to know why the plants that you cast in the earth—that you hoe and water and lavish much attention on—why, you say, the wild plants

[sprung] automatically from the earth grow more quickly than the ones you've put in.[16] Listen and understand. In the way a woman coming to a second marriage, having children from her former husband, has found her current husband also having children from his former wife. She is mother to the children she brings with her, but stepmother to those she finds. And the difference between these things is great, since she lovingly nurtures the children born from herself, but the ones born from another's birth pangs she hates and treats grudgingly, and intercepting their nourishment as much as she can, she gives it to her own children. For by nature she loves her own, but she hates those of her husband as strangers. In just the same way then, also the earth is mother to the weeds, but stepmother to the plants that you've put in, and preferring to nurture her own, she causes them to flourish more than the ones planted by you, [which she treats] as bastards." (*Vitae* G [+ W], chs. 35–37)

In his analogy of the earth as mother or stepmother to different categories of plants, Aesop reveals a precise understanding of the processes of human intervention in nature that constitute civilized agriculture. At the same time, the different responses of Xanthus and Aesop can be read as enacting a debate over the relative value of the *bios praktikos* and the *bios theōretikos*. This is certainly a prominent element in the tale: thus Xanthus insists that as a philosopher he has no practical skills to help a market-gardener, but he also fails utterly to resolve the gardener's "philosophical" problem, while Aesop's practical know-how effortlessly trumps his master's lame invocation of "divine forethought" and "lightens [the gardener's] grief."[17]

But in this context, I would suggest, Xanthus's mention of Helicon and the Muses adds another element. In the first place, this divine constellation (which figures only in *Vita* G) recalls the scene of Aesop's investiture (*Vita* G, ch. 7), where we were specifically told that the Muses, after bestowing each her special gift on Aesop, "ascended Mt. Helicon." Thus here, the mention of Helicon and the Muses prepares us for a dazzling display of divinely inspired verbal wit on Aesop's part. But more generally, we should perhaps read the references to the Hesiodic home of the Muses in the *Life* as flagging significant moments in Aesop's ascent of *sophia* and his success in competitions of wisdom. As we saw in chapter 2, the Heliconian Muses figure prominently in contexts of competition in poetic *sophia* already in the archaic wisdom tradition (as for example in Hesiod's *Works & Days* and in Ibycus fr. 282a *PMG*).[18] But this tradition seems to have been playfully elaborated in the philosophical schools and education system in which the text of the *Life* may have taken shape. Thus here perhaps, behind or beneath the philosophical clash of *bioi*, we have preserved

---

[16] At this point, it appears, a single folio is missing from the ms of *Vita* G, but the text can be supplemented from *Vita* W.

[17] Contrast La Penna 1962.302–3, who sees in this episode the triumph of something approaching "science" over Xanthus's "philosophico-religious explanation"; cf. Hägg 1997.192.

[18] See above, chapter 2, pp. 106–7 with nn. 35 and 37; cf. Steiner 2005.

a remnant of an older system of competitive performances of wisdom as "skilled crafting." We might also recall in this context the tradition about Thales, preserved by Aristotle (*Pol.* 1.11, 1259a6–19), that he deployed his practical know-how to predict the weather and thus make a financial killing by hiring in advance all the olive presses in anticipation of an abundant harvest. As I suggested in chapter 2, this tradition, which so clearly contradicts the later philosophical appropriation of Thales as paragon of the *bios theōretikos*, must represent an older conception of him as Sage pragmatically engaged with the world around him.[19]

Another stage in Aesop's ascent of *sophia* is his sudden access to prophetic or divinatory power—a skill that again partakes of an older, pre- or nonphilosophical model of wisdom, but also figures in some of the Sophistic anthropologies.[20] We might see Aesop exhibiting mantic expertise already in the very first fable he tells in *Vita* G, on the origin of false dreams (*Vita* G, ch. 33, quoted and discussed in chapter 1 above).[21] For his account (however tongue-in-cheek) reveals privileged knowledge of the inner workings of the pantheon, while it also constitutes his unique authority to differentiate false from true dreams. But Aesop's prophetic skill is more vividly displayed in a kind of accidental contest with his master Xanthus later in the *Life*:

> Xanthus says to Aesop, "Since I'm a reader of bird-signs (οἰωνιστής), go outside and see if there's any troublesome bird in front of the gateway. If you see a pair of crows sitting before the gate, call me; for this sign reveals festivity for the one who sees it." Aesop then going out front by chance observes a pair of crows sitting in front of the gateway and he goes in and tells Xanthus, "Master, the moment is right for you to go out; for a pair of crows sits [there]." The Master: "Let's go." But as [Aesop] went away, one of the crows flew off, and the master approaching observes [only] one [crow] and says, "Accursed wretch, didn't I say to you, 'If you see a pair of crows, call me'? But you've called me when you saw a single crow." Aesop: "One flew away, master." The master: "Now you've really made a mistake. Strip him. Bring the leather straps." He was assiduously flogged. And while he was still being beaten, there came a slave belonging to friends of Xanthus, inviting him to dinner. Aesop: "Master, you flay me unjustly." Xanthus: "Why unjustly?" Aesop: "Because you said that a pair of crows is a good and festive [omen]. I saw a pair of crows and while I was approaching and making it known to you, one of them flew off. But you, going out and seeing a single crow, got an invitation to dinner. And I, who saw a pair of crows, have gotten a beating. Surely then bird omens and signs are all in vain (εἰς μάτην)." And amazed at this too,

---

[19] See chapter 2, section III and cf. Nightingale 2004.22–26, 204–5.

[20] Cf. Aesch. *Prom.* 484–99, with notes of Griffith 1983a.173–76; Eur. *Suppl.* 211–13; [Plato] *Epinomis* 975c6; Democritus A 138 DK; and see Cole 1990.105n. 19.

[21] This fable occurs only in *Vita* G. Perry 1962a.299–302 regards it as a fable that may well date back to the fifth century BCE; cf. Adrados 1999.655–56 and the parallel version narrated in Eur. *IT* 1259–82.

Xanthus says, "Let him go, don't beat him anymore," saying that he will come to dinner. (*Vita* G, ch. 77)

This is an episode I will consider in more detail in the next chapter for the ways in which it parodies traditional forms of bird lore. For now, I would simply note that this sequence is anomalous in the *Life* as the only point at which the normally rational Xanthus lays claim to mantic expertise; indeed, his utter inability a bit later to interpret a bird omen for the entire Samian demos is what finally gives Aesop the opportunity to win his freedom and emerge as a sage adviser (*Vitae* G + W, chs. 81–90). Here, I suspect, the narrative has Xanthus claim this skill simply in order to stage a contest of sign reading between master and slave. For even though Aesop at the end of the episode dismisses the validity of bird omens altogether, he nonetheless proffers a better interpretation of the omen than his foolish master does. At the same time, his debunking of bird lore seems itself a mere local effect, since the bird omen that appears to the demos a little later is treated by Aesop (as by the narrative) as a true prognosticator of the threat of domination by a foreign king.

Significantly, this scene of competitive sign reading is immediately juxtaposed in the text of *Vita* G with another, as Xanthus and Aesop are enjoying themselves strolling through a graveyard and reading the inscriptions on the tombstones:[22]

> [78] And Aesop seeing inscribed on a gravestone unconnected letters A B Δ O E Θ X, <showing them to Xanthus, says, "What are these then?">[23] And when Xanthus was seeking what the inscription was and what it reveals, when he didn't find it, he was suffering terribly. And he says, "Aesop, what does it mean?" And Aesop, seeing him on the rack, himself having gotten a share of divine grace and <having been allotted> understanding from the Muses (θείας αὐτὸς μεταλαβὼν χάριτος καὶ ἀπὸ Μουσῶν τὸ φρόνημα ‹λαχών›[24]), says, "Master, if, through this stele, I find you a treasure of gold, what will you give me?" And his master, when he heard, says, "Half the treasure and your freedom."
>
> [79] And Aesop, when he heard, immediately picked up a large potsherd and, having paced off four steps and having dug the earth, brought up a treasure of gold and gives it to his master. And he says, "Master, give what you promised." Xanthus: "No, by the gods, I will not give it, unless you tell me by what understanding (ποίᾳ ἐπινοίᾳ) you found the treasure. For it's much more important for me to learn [that] than the dis-

---

[22] *Vita* W inserts two other, unrelated stories between the episode of the crows and the scene in the graveyard, and thereby mutes G's pattern of a clear ascent in Aesop's competitive sign-reading skills, building up to the climactic Assembly sequence.

[23] The bracketed words are supplied by Perry (1952.60) from the text of *Vita* W.

[24] I follow Ferrari 1997.186 in adding λαχών as a supplement to explain the shift from the genitive to the accusative in the nouns conjoined by καί. Papathomopoulos 1990.119 offers a similar solution, reading καὶ ἀπὸ Μουσῶν σχὼν τὸ φρόνημα, "and having gotten understanding from the Muses."

covery [itself]." Aesop says, "Master, the one who deposited the treasure here, being a philosopher (ἀνὴρ ὢν φιλόσοφος), took care and hid it under the number of the signs. For you see how he has inscribed the first letters of the words: for he says, A 'pace off'; B 'steps'; Δ 'four'; O 'dig'; E 'you will find'; Θ 'treasure'; X 'of gold.'" Xanthus: "Well, by the gods, since you're so reliable (?) [or enterprising (?)][25] and clever (συνετός), you won't get what I promised." Aesop, understanding that he's deprived of the promise, says, "Master, at this point then I exhort you to return the gold to its owner." Xanthus says, "And who is the owner of the treasure?" Aesop said, "Dionysius, king of Byzantium." Xanthus: "And from where did you figure this out?" Aesop: "From the letters—for they themselves reveal it." Xanthus: "How?" Aesop: "Hear what they say: A 'give back'; B 'to the king'; Δ 'Dionysius': O 'what you've found'; E 'here'; Θ 'treasure'; X 'of gold.'"

[80] Xanthus, seeing that he speaks well, says, "Aesop, take half the treasure and keep quiet." Aesop: "Don't give it to me as a favor, but as the gift of the one who deposited it." Xanthus: "How?" Aesop: "The letters make it clear; for they say, A 'take up'; B 'go'; Δ 'divide'; O 'what you've found'; E 'here'; Θ 'treasure'; X 'of gold.'" Xanthus: "You're a great marvel (σὺ μέγα δαιμόνιον εἶ). [Come] here to the house, so we can divide the gold and you get your freedom." But [Xanthus] being in the house and fearing lest [Aesop] reveal to the king from where he had gotten the treasure, ordered him to be bound and locked up. And Aesop says, "Give me my freedom and keep the gold." Xanthus: "Well done—that way, according to the justice of freedom, you're in a stronger position to demand back the gold and more believable in your slander to the king; but you will not persuade me." And Aesop: "Look here, Master: If you will not free me by your own free choice, you will be compelled to do it by force." Xanthus said, "Since you've been utterly negated (ἐξουθενηθείς), keep quiet." (*Vita* G, chs. 78–80)

Jack Winkler finds in this episode "the elementary letter-play" that forms one component of the "world of popular narrative": "This primitive 'Gold Bug' story illustrates the delight that popular narrative takes in codes and riddles, especially ones that are misunderstood."[26] While at one level I agree with Winkler's characterization of this episode in terms of a popular fascination with codes, I would contend that he does not adequately acknowledge the uncanniness and heft of the story in context. That Xanthus and Aesop discover the cryptic inscription *in a graveyard* strongly associates both the riddling acronym and the treasure to which it leads with the otherworld of the dead. In this setting, Aesop displays a special or uncanny ability to bring to light what is hidden from the world of men (precisely Helms's definition of "skilled crafting" and Kerferd's of

---

[25] The reading of G is the otherwise unattested ἑδράστερος; Perry (1952.60 [ad loc.]) suggests that the adjective is related to the verb ἑδράζω and glosses it "stabilis?" W reads πανοῦργος in this same slot; Papathomopoulos 1990.120 reads ἐμοῦ πανουργέστερος; Ferrari 1997.188 reads δραστήριος ("intraprendente").
[26] Winkler 1985.285.

the *sophia* of poet, seer, and sage in early Greece):[27] the buried treasure *and* the identity of its original owner. And in spite of Winkler's implication that the code is "misunderstood" here, the narrative gives us every encouragement to believe that all three of Aesop's decipherments of the acronym correspond to reality.[28]

Finally, Winkler's account of popular playfulness ignores the explicit recollection at the beginning of this interpretative sequence of Aesop's divine gift from the Muses:[29] "And Aesop, seeing his master on the rack, himself having gotten a share of divine grace and <having been allotted> understanding from the Muses, says ..." (θείας αὐτὸς μεταλαβὼν χάριτος καὶ ἀπὸ Μουσῶν τὸ φρόνημα ‹λαχών›, λέγει . . . , *Vita* G, ch. 78). This strong reminder of Aesop's investiture finds its complement in Xanthus's response to Aesop's third decoding at the end of the episode: "You are a great marvel" (σὺ μέγα δαιμόνιον εἶ, *Vita* G, ch. 80).[30] It is my contention that we should take seriously these articulations of Aesop's divine or uncanny interpretative power bookending this episode.

On this interpretation, these two sign-reading competitions between master and slave (the interpretation of bird omens in ch. 77 and the fraught decoding in the graveyard in chs. 78–80) prepare us for and appropriately build up to the Assembly sequence that immediately follows (chs. 81–97). For, of course, in the Assembly sequence as well, Aesop must interpret a portentous bird omen in a competitive context. When the entire Samian demos is assembled in the theater to elect magistrates, an eagle swoops down and carries off the public seal ring, which the guard of the laws has just "placed in the middle." The people, in agony over what they regard as a great sign, immediately consult the professional "seers and priests" (μάντεις καὶ ἱερεῖς), who are utterly at a loss to explain it. At that point, an old man rises from the crowd and proposes consulting the eminent philosopher Xanthus, who will surely be able to interpret the omen (*Vita* G, ch. 81). But the philosopher, just like the professional sign-readers, is at a loss: "Xanthus stood in the middle and, finding nothing to say according to his understanding, got a postponement in order to interpret the omen." But then, as the Assembly is dissolving, the eagle returns, swoops down, and drops the seal ring in the lap of the public slave. Again Xanthus is asked what the sign means, and again, unable to answer, he promises

---

[27] See Helms 1993, esp. 13–27; Kerferd 1976.26; and discussion above, chapter 2, sections I and II.

[28] For multiple different interpretations of an acronym (all correct) as a theme in popular humor, see Hansen 1998.108, citing Cicero *de Oratore* 2.69.280.

[29] At the same time, the fact that Winkler cites this Aesopic episode as a comparandum for the all-purpose oracular response devised by the Syrian priests in Apuleius's *Golden Ass* implicitly supports the connection of this sign reading with divinatory practices.

[30] It is noteworthy that *Vita* W omits both these moments in the narrative. As these omissions make clear, neither is necessary for the simple completion of the story; yet *Vita* G lays great emphasis on the divine source of Aesop's deciphering skills here.

a solution the next day (*Vita* G, ch. 82). He returns home, hoping to mollify Aesop (whom he has kept bound in the house to prevent him from reporting the finding of the treasure) and win his help (*Vita* G, ch. 83). But Aesop, "wishing to grieve him, says, 'If it is some problem concerning speech/reason (περὶ λόγου ζητήματος), I am ready to answer. But concerning what you have narrated, it is impossible, for I am not a seer'" (οὔτε γάρ εἰμι μάντις, *Vita* G, ch. 84). Xanthus, now in despair over his anticipated public humiliation, sneaks out in the middle of the night to hang himself; Aesop follows, chides him on his utter failure to live by his own philosophy and "dogma of self-control," and coaxes him out of the noose by promising that he himself will solve the riddling omen if Xanthus puts him in front of the Assembly crowd the next day (*Vita* G, ch. 85).

All the emphasis on Xanthus as a philosopher here might tempt us again (as in the episode of the market-gardener) to read the *Life* as staging a contest in which the *bios praktikos* trounces the *bios theōretikos*. And yet the combined skills of divination and political advising Aesop displays in this sequence do not fit comfortably within the ambit of the *bios praktikos*. Instead, the combination of mantic skill and bouleutic activity conforms more closely to the lineaments of pre- or nonphilosophical *sophia*. Thus recall the Herodotean scenes of the Spartan Sage Chilon interpreting a τέρας and advising the father of Pisistratus to avoid producing a son (Hdt. 1.59), or Bias's political advice to the Ionians predicated on his ability to "see into" an uncertain future (Hdt. 1.170).[31] In fact, yet another passage in Herodotus offers an even closer parallel for Aesop's competitive sign reading before the assembled demos: Themistocles' famous interpretation of the oracle of the "wooden wall" (Hdt. 7.141–43). There, too, the reading of the professional oracle interpreters (οἱ χρησμολόγοι) is opposed and refuted by the amateur Themistocles, an ordinary citizen who "is no *mantis*" (to borrow Aesop's self-description).

The parallel with Themistocles is intriguing, since at least one ancient report strongly identifies him with a tradition of prephilosophical, practical *sophia* through the shadowy figure of Mnesiphilus of Phrearrion. At the beginning of his *Life of Themistocles*, Plutarch rejects on chronological grounds the claim of Stesimbrotus that Themistocles was a student of Anaxagoras and Melissus. Instead, Plutarch asserts,

> μᾶλλον οὖν ἄν τις προσέχοι τοῖς Μνησιφίλου τὸν Θεμιστοκλέα τοῦ Φρεαρρίου ζηλωτὴν γενέσθαι λέγουσιν, οὔτε ῥήτορος ὄντος οὔτε τῶν φυσικῶν κληθέντων φιλοσόφων, ἀλλὰ τὴν τότε καλουμένην σοφίαν, οὖσαν δὲ δεινότητα πολιτικὴν καὶ δραστήριον σύνεσιν, ἐπιτήδευμα πεποιημένου καὶ διασῴζοντος ὥσπερ αἵρεσιν ἐκ διαδοχῆς ἀπὸ Σόλωνος· ἣν οἱ μετὰ ταῦτα δικανικαῖς μείξαντες τέχναις καὶ μεταγαγόντες ἀπὸ τῶν πράξεων τὴν ἄσκησιν ἐπὶ τοὺς λόγους, σοφισταὶ προσηγορεύθησαν. τούτῳ μὲν οὖν ἤδη πολιτευόμενος ἐπλησίαζεν. (Plut. *Them*. ch. 2.6)

---

[31] See chapter 3, section II above.

Rather, then, might one side with those who say that Themistocles was a disciple of Mnesiphilus the Phrearrhian, a man who was neither a rhetorician nor one of the so-called physical philosophers, but a cultivator of what was then called "*sophia*" or wisdom, although it was really nothing more than cleverness in politics and practical sagacity. Mnesiphilus received this "*sophia*," and handed it down, as though it were the doctrine of a sect, in unbroken tradition from Solon. His successors blended it with forensic arts, and shifted its application from public affairs to language, and were dubbed "sophists." It was this man, then, to whom Themistocles resorted at the very beginning of his public life. (Trans. Perrin 1914, slightly modified)

This characterization of Mnesiphilus as a follower of Solon, a practitioner of "what was then called *sophia*—political shrewdness and practical sagacity," has been identified by G. B. Kerferd as an authentic old tradition of prephilosophical and pre-Sophistic practical wisdom.[32] Indeed, we might even detect a polemical rejection of the Mnesiphilus genealogy in Thucydides' famous assessment of Themistocles (Thuc. 1.138.3):

ἦν γὰρ ὁ Θεμιστοκλῆς βεβαιότατα δὴ φύσεως ἰσχὺν δηλώσας καὶ διαφερόντως τι ἐς αὐτὸ μᾶλλον ἑτέρου ἄξιος θαυμάσαι· οἰκείᾳ γὰρ ξυνέσει καὶ οὔτε προμαθὼν ἐς αὐτὴν οὐδὲν οὔτ' ἐπιμαθών, τῶν τε παραχρῆμα δι' ἐλαχίστης βουλῆς κράτιστος γνώμων καὶ τῶν μελλόντων ἐπὶ πλεῖστον τοῦ γενησομένου ἄριστος εἰκαστής· καὶ ἃ μὲν μετὰ χεῖρας ἔχοι, καὶ ἐξηγήσασθαι οἷός τε, ὧν δ' ἄπειρος εἴη, κρῖναι ἱκανῶς οὐκ ἀπήλλακτο· τό τε ἄμεινον ἢ χεῖρον ἐν τῷ ἀφανεῖ ἔτι προεώρα μάλιστα. καὶ τὸ ξύμπαν εἰπεῖν φύσεως μὲν δυνάμει, μελέτης δὲ βραχύτητι κράτιστος δὴ οὗτος αὐτοσχεδιάζειν τὰ δέοντα ἐγένετο.

Indeed, Themistocles was a man who showed an unmistakable natural genius; in this respect he was quite exceptional, and beyond all others deserves our admiration. Without studying a subject in advance or later, but using simply the intelligence that was his by nature, he had the power to reach the right conclusion in matters that have to be settled on the spur of the moment and do not admit of long discussions, and in estimating what was likely to happen, his forecasts of the future were always more reliable than those of others. He could perfectly well explain any subject with which he was familiar, and even outside his own department he was still capable of giving an excellent opinion. He was particularly remarkable at looking into the future and seeing there the hidden possibilities for good or evil. To sum him up in a few words, it may be said that through force of genius and by rapidity of action this man was supreme at doing precisely the right thing at precisely the right moment. (Trans. Warner 1972, slightly modified)

Kerferd sees in Thucydides' οὔτ' ἐπιμαθών an implicit polemic against those who associated Themistocles with Anaxagoras and Melissus, while he locates in the historian's οὔτε προμαθών a rejection of the tradition that he was a student

---

[32] Kerferd 1950.9–10, 1976.21; cf. Morrison 1949.59–60.

of Mnesiphilus.[33] But perhaps more significant than Thucydides' specific rejection of various accounts of Themistocles' teachers is the broader participation in the same tradition of practical, stochastic, or improvisatory *sophia* his encomium of Themistocles bespeaks. Thus notice especially the historian's assertion that Themistocles' swift understanding allowed him to the greatest extent "to look into the future and see there the hidden possibilities for good or evil." In this respect, even the normally rationalizing Thucydides suggests an intimate link between successful political advising and a kind of uncanny mantic skill, while his imagery (of seeing into what is invisible to other men) resonates with Helms' model of magical skilled crafting.[34] Together, Plutarch's characterization of Mnesiphilus and Thucydides' of Themistocles constitute a composite portrait of a politically efficacious sage that, in connection with Herodotus's account of Themistocles' decisive intervention in the deliberation over the "wooden wall" oracle, provides a striking parallel for Aesop's activity as combined sign-reader and political guide.

Finally, we should note that, as with every other stage in Aesop's ascent of *sophia* in *Vita* G, his consequential political activity on Samos is marked or flagged by prominent mention of the Muses. Thus Aesop concludes his first speech to the Samian demos (explaining why they should listen to him at all): "The Muse is judged in theaters, Cypris in bed; thus also *phronēsis* in words" (*Vita* G, ch. 88). Taken at face value, the reference to "the Muse" evokes dramatic performances as her proper sphere of activity (analogous to Aphrodite's in bed). But recall that we have just been told that the Samian demos has assembled *in the theater* (εἰς τὸ θέατρον, *Vita* G, chs. 81, 85); Aesop's gnome thus wittily refers to his own theatrical performance of political advising as the combined province of "the Muse" and *phronēsis*. This metarhetorical reading finds its confirmation in Aesop's dedicatory activity at the end of the whole Samian sequence. Here Aesop returns to Samos from the court of Croesus, summons an Assembly, and reads letters from the king announcing his reconciliation with the Samians:

> οἱ δὲ Σάμιοι γνῶντες αὐτοῖς τὸν Κροῖσον διηλλάχθαι διὰ τοῦ Αἰσώπου τιμὰς αὐτῷ ἐψηφίσαντο, καὶ ἐκάλεσαν τὸν τόπον ἐκεῖνον Αἰσώπειον, ὅπου ἦν ἐνηλλαγμένος. ὁ δὲ Αἴσωπος θύσας ταῖς Μούσαις ἱερὸν κατεσκεύασεν αὐταῖς, στήσας μέσον ἑαυτοῦ μνημόσυνον, οὐκ Ἀπόλλωνος. ⟨δι'⟩ ὃ Ἀπόλλων ὀργισθεὶς αὐτῷ ὡς τῷ Μαρσύᾳ. (*Vita* G, ch. 100)

> And the Samians, since they understood that Croesus had been reconciled with them through the agency of Aesop, voted honors for him and called that place the *Aisōpeion*

---

[33] Kerferd 1950.9; cf. Ferrara 1964.56n. 1. As Kerferd notes, Xen. *Mem.* 4.2.2 suggests that "the question of the teachers of Themistocles was early a much discussed topic," against which Thucydides seems to be reacting.

[34] Thus compare Thucydides' προεώρα here with Herodotus's use of ἐνορᾶν of Bias at Hdt. 1.170.

where his status was changed.³⁵ And Aesop, having sacrificed to the Muses, established a shrine to them and set in the middle a memorial of himself, not Apollo.³⁶ On account of this, Apollo became angry with him as with Marsyas.³⁷

The place "where [Aesop's] status was changed" (ὅπου ἦν ἐνηλλαγμένος) is of course the Samian theater, and it is there, we might imagine, that he consecrates his shrine to the Muses in thanks for their divine gift of efficacious *logoi*. Significantly, *Vita* W omits all mention of the Muses here—Aesop neither sacrifices to the Muses nor erects statues of them—just as Aesop makes no reference to "the Muse" in his first assembly speech in *Vita* W. Instead, what is much more strongly suggested at the end of the whole Samian sequence in W is that Aesop receives cult-hero honors from the grateful demos; thus, we're told, "The Samians, having enjoyed this benefaction, voted honors and a sacred precinct for him, calling that place the *Aisōpeion*" (οἱ δὲ Σάμιοι εὐεργετηθέντες τιμὰς καὶ τέμενος αὐτῷ ἐψηφίσαντο, καλέσαντες τὸν τόπον Αἰσώπειον, *Vita* W, ch. 100). The mention of a temenos as well as "honors" in *Vita* W makes clearer that the *Aisōpeion* constitutes a holy or cult site, while the bestowal of cult-hero honors conforms to an older pre- or nonphilosophical pattern of the sage's heroization as a reward for extraordinary civic service.³⁸ G, in contrast to W, seems much less interested in this otherworldly end of the sage, which we may take to be an older tradition associated with Aesop.

---

³⁵ I diverge here from Lloyd Daly's translation (in Hansen 1998.151); he understands ὅπου ἦν ἐνηλλαγμένος as "where [Aesop] had been turned over." But technically, Aesop is not "turned over"—he goes voluntarily. More to the point, it seems more appropriate for the Samian assembly and Aesop himself to celebrate and commemorate his change of status (slave to free) and his successful political advising, rather than his surrender by a craven demos. On the appropriateness of the theater as a location for the commemoration of Aesop's manumission, see Kamen 2005. Thus better the translation of Bonelli and Sandrolini in Ferrari 1997.14: "il luogo in cui egli aveva acquistato la libertà." In fact, the interpretation of this phrase makes no difference to the argument here presented, since both Aesop's change of status and his "handing over" presumably occurred in the theater.

³⁶ In reading μέσον ἑαυτοῦ μνημόσυνον, οὐκ Ἀπόλλωνος, I am accepting the emendations suggested by Ferrari 1995.257 (building on and improving Papathomopoulos 1990.139) rather than those of Perry 1952, who reads μέσον αὐτῶν Μνημοσύνην, οὐκ Ἀπόλλωνα. It should be emphasized that both the text of Perry and that of Papathomopoulos/Ferrari represent emendations of a corrupt ms; I prefer the latter text because it suggests that the *Aisōpeion* and Aesop's dedicated shrine to the Muses are one and the same (whereas Perry's text makes them different sites). In addition, while Aesop and the Muses are constantly linked in *Vita* G, Mnemosyne shows up nowhere else in the text.

³⁷ I follow Papathomopoulos 1990.139 in reading ‹δι'› ὅ for the ms's ὁ.

³⁸ For examples of this pattern, see chapter 2, section II above—and for a specific connection with political service, we might note the parallels of Lycurgus and Chilon in Sparta, Pittacus in Mytilene, and Themistocles in Athens/Piraeus (Sources: Hdt. 1.66, Paus. 3.16.4, D.L. 1.75, Plut. *Them*. 32). We might also note in connection with *Vita* W, ch. 100 the suggestion of Zeitz 1936.253 that ch. 100 might represent the end of an old, specifically Samian version of the *Life*, which culminates in the conferral of local, cult honors on the political sage Aesop; cf. Nagy 1979.285–86§8n. 1.

176   CHAPTER 4

But what are we to make of this elaborate progression in the *Life*—of Aesop's ascent of *sophia*? Is it meant to be taken seriously or is it parodic? It seems oddly to be both at once. I would suggest that the Aesop tradition that is the common source for G and W offers us the life story of Aesop as an archaic sage, while it also represents Aesop as parodying the high wisdom tradition and the philosophical appropriation thereof through his escalating competitions in *sophia* with his self-important but incompetent master Xanthus. (And we'll see more of this parodic strand in the next chapter.) From this common background, the G author/redactor seems to have chosen to highlight the more parodic elements in the tradition, while muting the more serious or somber representation of Aesop's heroic end.[39]

II. Aesop and Ahiqar

One element that supports a "serious" reading of Aesop as sage in the pre- or nonphilosophical tradition is his assimilation to the Near Eastern vizier and wise man Ahiqar. The *Story of Ahiqar* was an enormously popular tale throughout the Near Eastern Mediterranean and beyond.[40] Around 1900, versions of it were known in manuscripts ranging from the twelfth to the eighteenth century CE in Syriac, Arabic, Armenian, Karshuni, and Old Church Slavic, with fragments in Ethiopic. The tale was also eventually translated into Georgian, Old Turkish, Romanian, Russian, Serbian, and neo-Syriac.[41] At the same time, references to Ahiqar in the apocryphal Book of Tobit suggested a tradition of high antiquity, and this was confirmed in 1908 when an Aramaic version of the story was discovered on a late fifth-century BCE papyrus excavated from a Jewish military colony at Elephantine in Egypt.[42] When it was first discovered, this Aramaic version was thought to be a translation of an original Akkadian (i.e., Assyrian) text, but closer analysis of the language of the Elephantine version

---

[39] Thus this reading shares significant elements with that of Winkler 1985.282, who sees the entire Aesop tradition as a popular parody of "the claims of the educated elite to have proprietary rights over wisdom and shrewdness." While I agree that this is an element in a long-lived oral tradition of Aesop stories, I read the text of *Vita G* as an appropriation of that tradition by a marginalized or disaffected participant within the institutional structure of elite education (for which, cf. Jedrkiewicz 1989.177–82, Hopkins 1993.11, Jouanno 2006.13–14, and see discussion in introduction).

[40] For the material in this paragraph, I rely heavily on Conybeare, Harris, and Lewis 1913a and especially on Lindenberger 1983.3–34, 1985.479–92; cf. also Greenfield 1995, Konstantakos 2008.

[41] On this diffusion, see Conybeare, Harris, and Lewis 1913a.719–22, 1913b; Lindenberger 1983.4, 1985.480; Greenfield 1995. For parallel translations of the Syriac, Arabic, and Armenian versions, see Conybeare, Harris, and Lewis 1913a.724–76.

[42] *Editio princeps* by Sachau 1911; see also Cowley 1923.204–48. The proverbs of the Aramaic version were reedited by Lindenberger 1983; for English translation of the Aramaic version, see Lindenberger 1985.494–507.

eventually convinced most scholars that Aramaic must have been the original language of composition. In fact, it appears that different stages in the development of Aramaic are preserved in the proverb (as opposed to the narrative) portions of the text, suggesting an older independent collection of proverbs (perhaps dating back to the beginning of the seventh century BCE), which was eventually given a narrative frame in the *Story of Ahiqar*, wise adviser to the kings of Assyria.[43]

Indirect evidence suggests Greek knowledge of the *Story of Ahiqar* already by the fifth or fourth century BCE. Thus Clement of Alexandria denounces Democritus (among other pagan philosophers) as a student of barbarians: "For it is said that he put into his own treatises a translation of the stele of Akikar" (λέγεται γὰρ τὴν Ἀκικάρου στήλην ἑρμηνευθεῖσαν τοῖς ἰδίοις συντάξαι συγγράμμασι).[44] And Diogenes Laertius lists among the many works of Theophrastus one volume entitled "Akikaros" (D.L. 5.50).[45] Other scholars have recently argued for echoes of elements of the Ahiqar story in the plays of Aristophanes and in Herodotus, but these are more controversial.[46] Slight as this

---

[43] On the language of the text and development of the story as preserved in the Aramaic version, see Lindenberger 1983.16–23, 1985.480–84; Greenfield 1995.47–50. Lindenberger 1985.483 goes so far as to call it "a historical novel," since there is some evidence for the real existence of Ahiqar from an Akkadian cuneiform tablet of the Seleucid period discovered and published in the early 1960s.

[44] Clem. *Strom.* 1.15.69 = Democritus B 299 DK. Diels-Kranz catalog Clement's report among the *unechte Fragmente* of Democritus, and their skepticism is followed by most scholars: e.g., Conybeare, Harris, and Lewis 1913b.xlvi, Nöldeke 1913.21–23, M. L. West 1969, S. West 2003.426n. 45, Konstantakos 2008.II.17–81. On the other hand, Clement's report is accepted at face value by Meyer 1912.123–26, Wilsdorf 1991, Luzzatto 1992.17–30 (who contends that Democritus literally copied a cuneiform version of the *Story of Ahiqar* from a stele in Babylon). It is nonetheless worth noting, as Lindenberger points out, that "the Arab philosopher Shahrastānī [1085–1153 CE] attributes to the same 'Democrates' (*sic*) several proverbs known from the later versions of Ahiqar, including one which can be traced back to the Elephantine version" (Lindenberger 1985.491; cf. Nöldeke 1913.22, Luzzatto 1992.28, Konstantakos 2008.II.67–81). Thus, even if the Ahiqar material is only "pseudo-Democritean," it was a plausible attribution by the time of Clement (or his sources; note λέγεται) and the proverbs were independently known and cited in both Greek and Arabic traditions.

[45] Strabo, too, may be referring to the same Ahiqar in a passage devoted to a catalog of divinely inspired *manteis* among the barbarians (Strabo 16.2.39/C762), but the identification of Strabo's seer Ἀχαίκαρος with Ahiqar, based on a proposed emendation of his locale, has been strongly challenged by Daniel 1996.34 with n. 13, following Nöldeke 1913.23–24.

[46] For Aristophanes: Luzzatto 1992.30–42 (partly following Cataudella 1942) argues for substantial explicit echoes of Ahiqar, meant to be caught by the elite members of Aristophanes' audience, in particular proverbs and the trial of the dog in Aristophanes' *Wasps* and in the descriptions of the building of *Nephelokokkugia* in the *Birds*. The first of these I find implausible, since it depends on Luzzatto's assuming an Akkadian original and an original structure of the tale with two speeches of advice (both of which assumptions seem now to have been discredited by Near Eastern scholars working on Ahiqar). On the other hand, the echoes of something like Ahiqar's building of towers in the sky at *Birds* 837–45, 1125–51 seem to me to be compelling. But this in itself is problematic, given that the Egyptian episode does not appear at all in the fragmentary Elephantine papyrus;

evidence is, it is clear that at some point in the Greek tradition, the figure of Ahiqar was assimilated to that of Aesop and the story of the Babylonian vizier folded into the *Life of Aesop*, where the whole narrative was preserved (*Vitae* G + W, chs. 101–23). Comparison of the narrative in the different versions shows the Greek version to be remarkably faithful to the later (especially Syriac and Armenian) traditions of Ahiqar.

In the Aramaic version of the story, Ahiqar, scribe and adviser to Assyrian kings, is childless and so adopts his sister's son Nadin (or Nadan) and teaches him all his wisdom. In spite of Ahiqar's benevolence, Nadin falsely accuses him of treason and persuades the king of Babylon, who orders him put to death. The officer sent to kill him, however, turns out to be an old friend whose life he had once saved. In return, the friend spares Ahiqar's life and hides him; a slave eunuch is killed in his stead to provide a body. At this point, the narrative in the oldest Aramaic text of the story breaks off; when the papyrus resumes, the narrative frame has disappeared and what we have preserved are nine fragmentary columns of proverbs. James M. Lindenberger, a recent editor and translator of the Aramaic text, supplements this version from the later traditions as follows:

> According to the later versions, when the king of Egypt hears that Ahiqar is dead, he writes the Assyrian monarch challenging him to send a wise man who can answer a series of riddles and supervise the construction of a palace between heaven and earth. Nadin declares that not even the gods themselves could meet the challenge. The Assyrian is at his wits' end, and laments his lost sage, offering a rich reward if only Ahiqar could be returned to him alive. The officer, seeing the time is ripe, brings the old scribe out of hiding to receive the king's profuse apologies and reinstatement at the court. After a series of adventures in Egypt, Ahiqar returns to Assyria and asks permission to discipline Nadin. The young man is put in chains and beaten, after which Ahiqar addresses him with a long series of reproaches. The speech concluded, Nadin swells up and dies.
>
> It cannot be ascertained how much of this was included in the Elephantine version. No doubt it was much shorter. The surviving fragments of the Aramaic text have no trace of the Egyptian episode, and there may have originally been only a rather

---

Konstantakos 2008.II.83–122 therefore argues that the similarities between the later Ahiqar tradition and the *Birds* depend on a common Near Eastern source or story pattern. For arguments against Luzzatto's reconstruction, see Fales 1993, 1994 (with response by Luzzatto 1994); Konstantakos 2008 (esp. vol. 2) seems to me to offer decisive arguments against Luzzatto. For Herodotus: S. West 2003.418–28 (following Aly 1921.21, 87; Perry 1960.20n. 45) argues that the episode of Croesus saved from execution and hidden from Cambyses (Hdt. 3.36) depends on the motif of the *Scheintod* and rehabilitation of the wise minister Ahiqar in the *Story of Ahiqar*. Note, however, that West does not therefore assume Greek/Herodotean knowledge of the story in the fifth century BCE; instead, she assumes the migration of this Near Eastern story pattern informing an account offered to Herodotus by a local (Persian or other Near Eastern) informant; cf. Konstantakos 2008. II.167–224.

brief statement of Ahiqar's rehabilitation and the disgrace and punishment of his adopted son.[47]

As the story continues in the Syriac and Armenian versions—which, according to Lindenberger, are closest to the Aramaic—the Egyptian episode is much elaborated, with Ahiqar solving all the problems and riddles that figure in the Aesop version and more besides.[48] But in all the extant versions, Ahiqar returns in triumph from Egypt, and asks as a special boon from the king of Assyria the handing over of his perfidious adopted son. The narrative ends with Ahiqar's lengthy speech to the adopted son, filled with proverbs, beast fables, parables, and similitudes that often have little or no connection to the narrative setting. When the speech ends, the adoptive son "swelled up like a bag and died."[49]

It is impossible to know when the assimilation of Ahiqar to Aesop took place in the Greek tradition: according to different theories, this convergence might already have happened in the fifth century BCE or in the Hellenistic period.[50] It is perhaps easier to understand *why* the assimilation took place and why the Ahiqar section occupies the particular place it does within the *Life*. For the former: I would suggest (partially following Adrados) that the salient points of similarity that motivate the assimilation are (1) Aesop's status as political adviser, first to the Samian demos, then to an Eastern king; and (2) Aesop's unjust accusation and execution at the hands of the Delphians.[51]

---

[47] Lindenberger 1985.498; cf. Greenfield 1995.48, Konstantakos 2008.I.143–83.

[48] On the close affinity of Syriac and Armenian versions to the Aramaic, see Lindenberger 1985.480 (where it is also noted that the Armenian version derives ultimately from the Syriac); see also Greenfield 1995.50, who notes that the (third/second c. BCE) Book of Tobit seems to presuppose "both the story line and the sayings of the Syriac" rather than the Aramaic version of Ahiqar. It is possible that the more elaborated Egyptian episode in the Syriac, Armenian, and Arabic versions is ultimately derived from the Greek version; this seems to be the view of Fales 1994.57n. 88, 59–60, because he finds the cunning and cleverness Aesop/Ahiqar exhibits in the Egyptian episode uncharacteristic of the honest and loyal minister of the Aramaic version. But if this really is the direction of influence (from Aesop to Ahiqar), it strengthens my argument that the Greek narrative is primarily interested in Aesop's political, international activities, rather than in the domestic story of betrayal by the adopted son. In addition, it is then distinctively *Aesop* who achieves political success through his characteristic practical intelligence and cunning.

[49] Thus the Syriac version, as translated by Rendel Harris in Conybeare, Harris, and Lewis 1913a.776.

[50] Most scholars favor the Hellenistic period: thus S. West 2003.426, Konstantakos 2008.II.225–70; for the possibility that the assimilation of Aesop and Ahiqar might have occurred already in the fifth century, see Adrados 1979.98–100, 1999.274–85. Grottanelli 1982a does not commit himself on the dating.

[51] Cf. Adrados 1979, 1999.274–85, 653, 662–65. I would thus disagree with Holzberg 1992b.63–69, 2002.78–81, who contends that it was the Ahiqar tradition (once assimilated in the Roman imperial period) that inspired the story of Aesop's activity as a political adviser in the *Life*, chs. 92–100. Holzberg's argument is predicated on his contention that "none of the events reported in [chs. 92–100] are mentioned in older narrative material on the life of Aesop" (Holzberg 2002.81), but, as I hope to have demonstrated in chapter 3 above, there is indirect evidence for knowledge of these episodes in the Greek tradition already in the classical era.

As for the placement of the Ahiqar section, this is an issue to which I will return. But first I would like to consider the points of significant divergence between the Greek version and the other extant Ahiqar traditions to which the *Life of Aesop* is otherwise so faithful. For these moments of difference will reveal to us what is distinctive about the Greek Aesop, and will help us in turn to understand the logic of the Ahiqar section within the narrative trajectory of the *Life* as a whole. First we should note the almost complete replacement of the wisdom or proverb sections of the text. Even within the Ahiqar tradition, there is a significant split between the oldest Aramaic version and all the later instantiations of the story: it appears that the Aramaic version circumscribed the teaching of Ahiqar within a single long speech of chastisement of the adoptive son loosely attached at the end of the narrative.[52] In contrast, all the later versions (excluding the Greek) divide up Ahiqar's wisdom into two speeches—an initial instruction of Nadin when he has just been adopted and a lengthy speech of chastisement at the end of the narrative proper. As Lindenberger notes, "The version which lies behind the Life of Aesop represents an intermediate stage in the integration of the sayings and the narrative," since in the Greek version, there is only a single block of advice (corresponding to the Aramaic text), but it is structurally more fully integrated into the narrative (in this respect closer to the later traditions).[53]

But leaving aside issues of formal structure (to which I'll return in a moment), I would like to focus first on content. It is striking that, with only two exceptions, there is no overlap between the content of Ahiqar's wisdom and that attributed to Aesop.[54] Reconstruction of the Greek version is complicated

---

[52] Lindenberger (1983.17–19, 1985.480–81) argues that this was the original structure: "Thus the farther back we go in the tradition, the more distant is the formal relationship between the two parts of the work" (1983.18). Cf. Fales 1993, 1994; Greenfield 1995.47–50; Konstantakos 2008.II.143–66.

[53] Quotation from Lindenberger 1985.480; cf. Lindenberger 1983.18. Perry 1952.5–10, 1966.290 (followed by Haslam 1986.151), contrariwise, assumes that the later versions of Ahiqar more accurately preserve an original text with two separate speeches (thus also Luzzatto 1992), while the *Life of Aesop* borrows from a "defective" or "aberrant" Aramaic version that circulated in Egypt. Although it makes no substantial difference to my argument, I prefer Lindenberger's reconstruction to that of Perry, for two reasons: (1) Perry 1959, 1966 is still operating on the assumption that the Aramaic version is a translation of an Assyrian original (an assumption that Lindenberger demonstrates is false, on the basis of the language of both the narrative and proverb portions of the Aramaic text); (2) Perry's reconstruction does not adequately account for the fact, noted by Lindenberger, that "even in the late versions there is a certain artificiality about the position of the sayings. A number of the reproaches at the end are quite inappropriate to the literary context in which they are placed, and some sayings found in the first collection in one version appear in the second collection in another" (Lindenberger 1985.481). This fluidity of content between the two speeches suggests that they are differently divvied up in the different traditions from an original single block of instructional material.

[54] Cf. Haslam 1986.153–54, noting the two exceptions: (1) Not to reveal what you hear in the king's chamber; (2) "Be affable to those you meet, knowing that the dog's tail wins bread, but its mouth blows" (in the version of *P.Oxy.* 3720, ll. 82–84).

by the fact that at this point in the narrative (Aesop's speech of instruction to his adoptive son; *Vitae* G + W, chs. 109–10), both manuscript traditions are terribly corrupt. As Michael Haslam puts it, "the text of *G* is horribly mutilated, and *W* has been invaded by gnomic monostichoi."[55] Fortunately, we have other witnesses for Aesop's paraenesis: it is excerpted in the fourteenth-century manuscript Cod. Vindobonensis theol. gr. 128; it is partially preserved on a single loose parchment leaf dated to the tenth or eleventh century CE, currently in the Library of the University of Thessaloniki (which Perry 1966 designates *Th*); and it is now also represented by a third-century CE papyrus edited by Michael Haslam in 1986 (*P.Oxy.* 3720).[56] Without getting into all the complexities of the relations of these different textual witnesses to each other, I would simply like to emphasize that the Near Eastern wisdom of Ahiqar has been almost entirely evacuated from the speech of Aesop and replaced by native Greek wisdom material, much of which overlaps with the Sayings of the Seven Sages as preserved by Stobaeus and the inscriptional record.[57] Thus, for example, Aesop's first substantive admonition to his adoptive son is "honor the god" (καὶ πρῶτον μὲν θεὸν σέβου), the same injunction that figures prominently in the list of Sayings of the Seven Sages attributed to Sosiades by Stobaeus.[58] Other parallels include the warning not to reveal things that are forbidden, and the injunctions to "control anger" (θυμοῦ κράτει) and to "be affable" (εὐπροσήγορος ἔσο, *Vita* W, ch. 110).[59] It is perhaps not surprising that narrative crosses cultural boundaries

[55] Haslam 1986.152.

[56] The different textual witnesses and their relations are concisely summarized by Haslam 1986.151–53. Because of the extreme textual corruption at this point, Perry 1952.69 actually substitutes the Cod. Vind. text of chs. 109–10 for that of *Vita* G, which he relegates to footnote 556 ad loc. For *Th*, see Perry 1966.285–90; for *P.Oxy.* 3720, see Haslam 1986. Führer 1986 adds another partial witness to this run of advice, cod. Paris. 1166, f. 308b–312a.

[57] For this process of cultural adaptation through the evacuation and renewal of a loose and amorphous collection of proverbs, see Cowley 1923.210, Grottanelli 1982a.561–65. Haslam 1986.154–55 notes the overlap between Aesop's speech of advice and the precepts of the Seven Sages. It is worth noting that Ahiqar's sayings in the Aramaic version are permeated with fables, parables, and proverbs about animals and plants—exactly what we would expect as "Aesopic" wisdom. But paradoxically, these elements have all but disappeared from the Aesop versions, to be replaced by much more generic Seven Sages wisdom. On all this material, see chapter 2, section II with bibliography cited there.

[58] The third and fourth sayings in Stobaeus's collection: θεοὺς σέβου, γονεῖς αἰδοῦ (Stobaeus *Anth.* 3.1.173 Wachsmuth-Hense). Note that the *Vita* G text (reproduced by Perry 1952.69 in n. 556) also includes "love your parents" (στέργε τοὺς γονεῖς). The combination "Honor the god(s) and your parents" is a very old one in the Greek wisdom tradition: for a collection of its occurrences, see Kurke 1990.89–90 with n. 20; cf. Haslam 1986.166. Appropriately enough, the Aesop version (Cod. Vind.) replaces the second member of the pair with "honor the king," and adds, as a third, "honor your teacher"—or, as *P.Oxy.* 3720, ll. 39–42 has it, "honor your adoptive father"— since your parents are under the necessity of nature to treat you well, while your teacher (or adoptive father) does so by choice.

[59] For the first parallel, cf. Haslam 1986.168. Among the Sayings of the Seven Sages, it occurs in the form ἀπόρρητα κρύπτε in *SIG*[3] no. 1268, col. 2, l. 16; in *P.Oxy.* 3720, ll. 75–76 as [τ]ῇ γ[υναικὶ

more easily than paraenesis; that wisdom traditions tend to be more culturally specific.[60] Still, the point is that within the Greek tradition, what fills the structural slot of Ahiqar's teaching is the wisdom of the Seven Sages, with Aesop felt to be an appropriate avatar thereof. Thus both his original assimilation to Ahiqar and the wise advice with which he is credited confirm Aesop's status as a sage within Greek popular imagination.[61]

But perhaps more interesting than this evacuation and replacement of wisdom traditions is the structural divergence of the Aesop story from the Ahiqar traditions: the Greek version inverts the narrative order of the Egyptian episode and the chastisement of the faithless adopted son. In all the extant versions of Ahiqar, the climax of the tale is the Sage's disciplining and lengthy wisdom speech to Nadin, once he has returned from his Egyptian adventures.[62] Given

---

σου]/κρυπτῶν καὶ ἀπορρήτων μη[δὲν δῆλον τίθει· (with Haslam's supplements based on the version in Cod. Vind.). For "control anger" (θυμοῦ κράτει) and "be affable" (εὐπροσήγορος γίνου), cf. Stobaeus *Anth.* 3.1.173 Wachsmuth-Hense, *SIG*³ no. 1268, col. 2, l. 5. Note that the latter bit of advice is linked in the Aesop versions with one of the two sayings that overlaps with one of the Aramaic proverbs, "knowing that the dog's tail wins him bread, his mouth blows."

[60] This split also conforms to the linguistic, stylistic, and generic differences that scholars of the Near Eastern material have noted between the narrative and proverb sections of Ahiqar; thus S. West 2003.424n. 34 cites Meyer 1912.111 for "the stylistic differences between the simple popular narrative and the more intellectually demanding manner of expression employed in Ahiqar's maxims."

[61] In this regard, it is intriguing that Clement speaks of a "*stele* of Akikar" when he reports Democritus's incorporation of Babylonian wisdom, while *Vita* W concludes with the Delphians setting up "a *stele* to [Aesop]" to propitiate his doom (*Vita* W, ch. 142). Is it possible that these are both reflexes of a tradition that the stele containing the Sayings of the Seven Sages, which was set up at Delphi, properly belonged to Aesop? Konstantakos 2008.II.43–55 also connects the "stele of Akikaros" in Clement's account with the stelai on which the Sayings of the Seven Sages were inscribed and the stele set up by the Delphians for Aesop in *Vita* W, ch. 142.

[62] There is no evidence for the Egyptian episode in the Aramaic papyrus (the narrative portion breaks off at the point where Ahiqar is hidden by his friend), so that many Near Eastern scholars doubt whether it figured in the narrative at all. But for defense of the Egyptian interlude in the Aramaic version, see Greenfield 1995.48–49; if there was a challenge by the Egyptian king, it must have been handled very cursorily in the narrative (see Lindenberger 1985.480–81, 498, quoted above; cf. Konstantakos 2008.I.143–57, suggesting a much briefer "riddle contest," perhaps by letter without a trip to Egypt). Taking a different tack, Haslam (1986.150) suggests that Ahiqar's long wisdom speech would have preceded his trip to Egypt in the Elephantine version: "The rest of the Elephantine fragments . . . , of unfixed order and location, are all taken up with the sayings of Ahiqar. Their place (or places) in the narrative is unclear, except in so far as they do not occupy the position occupied by the proverbs in the Syriac etc.; most probably, I think, they will have constituted a single speech and have preceded the Egyptian episode (of which there is no trace in the Elephantine fragments: but it is an integral part of the tale)." While I agree with Haslam that the Egyptian episode is "an integral part of the tale," I do not find his reconstruction plausible, given the unanimity of structure of all the later versions of Ahiqar and the apparent relative independence of the narrative and proverb portions in the Aramaic version—that is to say, it seems much more likely that a very brief version of the Egyptian episode preceded the lengthy, and somewhat separate, rendition of the Sayings of Ahiqar in the Aramaic version.

this narrative order and emphasis, Ahiqar is a story about trust and familial relations betrayed, and the righteous punishment of that betrayal in the end.[63] Thus the relationship of Ahiqar and Nadin is clearly the narrative focus, whether there were originally two speeches of advice to the adopted son (bracketing the false accusation and the Egyptian episode) or only one at the end. In contrast, the Aesop version treats the adopted son plot as much less important: the narrative efficiently (we might even say cursorily) gets it out of the way *before* Aesop's Egyptian adventure (*Vita* G, chs. 103–4, 108–10).[64] By this inversion, the Aesop narrative progresses from the familial to the political, building to a climax in the contest of wisdom between two kings mediated by the sage Aesop. That is to say, Aesop as sage serving his king is here the real narrative focus, rather than Aesop as a father-figure teaching and disciplining a wayward son. The narrative arc of the Aesopic Ahiqar section thus repeats in miniature the pattern of development we have already traced for the first hundred chapters of the *Life*, moving from the household as the ambit of Aesop's wisdom performances to the realm of politics and international affairs (in this respect, Aesop's confrontation with Nectanebo doubles and repeats his confrontation with Croesus).

In fact, this narrative trajectory within the Ahiqar section is confirmed by the artful deferral in the text of *Vita* G of mention of *sophia*. Just as in the first hundred chapters (as we have seen) the word *sophia* is deferred until the moment of Aesop's first political performance of wisdom on Samos, so also within the Ahiqar section, we find a similar pattern plotted in miniature. When Aesop, now vizier of Babylon, first adopts his son, we are told that he "set him beside the king as successor of his *sophia*. And he made every effort over his *paideia*" (τῷ βασιλεῖ παρέστησεν ὡς διάδοχον αὐτοῦ τῆς σοφίας. πᾶσαν δὲ αὐτοῦ ἐποιήσατο ἐπιμέλειαν τῆς παιδείας, *Vita* G, ch. 103).[65] But after this initial occurrence of

---

[63] Cf. Greenfield 1995.47, who notes that it is this theme that seems to motivate the mention of Ahiqar and his treacherous adopted son in the apocryphal Book of Tobit, where their relationship serves as negative foil for the extremely positive father-son relationship of Tobit and Tobias.

[64] Even if we cannot be absolutely certain about the narrative order in the oldest version of Ahiqar, there is a clear contrast between the Greek and all the other Ahiqar versions in relative length of different parts of the story. Thus the fragmentary remains of the Elephantine papyrus devote five columns to narrative and nine to proverbs, while the later, full versions of Ahiqar (Syriac, Arabic, Armenian), by my rough calculation based on the translations of Conybeare, Harris, and Lewis 1913a, devote almost twice as much space to Ahiqar's two speeches to Nadin as to the preparations and encounters in Egypt (seventeen columns vs nine columns). *Vita* G inverts that ratio, devoting nearly twice as much space to Aesop's Egyptian adventures as it does to his false accusation by his adopted son and eventual punishment of him (four pp. vs two pp. in Perry's edition). It is also symptomatic of this difference in emphasis that no one in the Greek story seems to expect the adopted son to take Aesop's place in solving Nectanebo's riddles (in contrast to the later Ahiqar versions)—for in the Ahiqar versions, this is part of the drama of the adopted son's total inadequacy and failure to live up to the standard of Ahiqar, whereas in the Greek version, Aesop's wisdom is assumed to be unique and irreplaceable.

[65] The ms actually reads τῷ βασιλεῖ παρέστησεν ὡς διάδοχον αὐτοῦ τῆς παιδείας. πᾶσαν δὲ αὐτοῦ ἐποιήσατο ἐπιμέλειαν τῆς σοφίας at this point, but Perry transposes the two terms

sophia to alert us to the familial transmission of political wisdom, the term seems deliberately to be avoided in the long sequence of Aesop's confrontations with the Egyptian king until his final, definitive triumph.[66] Thus, after their first duel of wits, Nectanebo recognizes Aesop's "skill at hitting the mark and good use of his tongue" (‹τὴν› εὐστοχίαν . . . καὶ τὸ εὔθετον τῆς γλώττης, *Vita* G, ch. 116), while after their second, the pharaoh "becomes frightened that he will have to pay the tribute seeing [Aesop's] intelligence" (τὸν νοῦν, *Vita* G, ch. 118). Only for their final encounter do the friends of the king suggest, "Let us ask him this problem, saying, 'what is it that we have never seen or heard?' And whatever he contrives (σοφίσηται), we will tell him that we have seen and heard it, and at a loss over these things, he will be defeated" (*Vita* G, ch. 121). Aesop, of course, contrives a ruse to entrap his opponents (in a sequence we will consider in more detail in section IV below); but it is only when he has triumphantly solved this last problem that the Egyptian king and the narrative itself bestow on Aesop the superlative designation *sophia*:

> And Nectanebo said, "Fortunate [is] Lycurgus in his kingship, since he possesses such wisdom (σοφίαν)! And giving him three years' worth of tribute he sent him [back] with letters of peace. And Aesop, when he got back to Babylon, narrated to Lycurgus all the things done in Egypt, and handed over to him the money. Lycurgus then ordered a golden statue to be set up for Aesop together with the Muses, and the king made a great festival celebration over the wisdom of Aesop (ἐπὶ τῇ τοῦ Αἰσώπου σοφίᾳ). (*Vita* G, ch. 123)

Thus this concluding chapter of the Ahiqar section in *Vita* G frames Aesop between two occurrences of *sophia*—first in the Egyptian king's *makarismos* of his fellow ruler; then in Lycurgus's lavish honors for Aesop's superlative skill. And this final occurrence (which forms the very last word of the Ahiqar section) figures together with mention of the Muses, whose narrative appearance here signals yet another Aesopic victory in a contest of wisdom.

σοφίας—παιδείας (which improves the logic; Perry's transposition is accepted by both Papathomopoulos and Ferrari in their editions). But even this transposition is not crucial to my argument, which would work just as well retaining the ms reading. In fact, notice that, on the ms reading, the occurrence of the word *sophia* stands in for Ahiqar's first speech of instruction. This perhaps suggests that there were in fact two speeches in the version adapted for Aesop; that the author of *Vita* G simply uses *sophia* as shorthand for a whole speech of advice.

[66] Admittedly, κατασοφιζόμενος occurs once in Aesop's speech to his adopted son (Cod. Vind. ch. 109 in Perry; σοφιζόμενος occurs in the same spot in *P.Oxy.* 3720, l. 67). This seems to parallel the occurrences of σοφή and σοφῶς earlier in the *Life*, once each before the climactic appearance of *sophia* in ch. 88. And, as in chs. 1–100, *Vita* W does not maintain the careful patterning and sparing usage of *sophia* and *sophos* observable in *Vita* G; thus, in addition to all the places where forms of *soph-* words occur in chs. 101–23 of *Vita* G, *Vita* W adds mention of *sophia* in chs. 101 and 109, and of *sophoi* in chs. 109 and 119. In addition, *Vita* W removes *Vita* G's emphatic, doubled mention of *sophia* in ch. 123, omitting one occurrence and replacing the other with *philosophia*.

We are now (finally) ready to consider the precise placement of the Ahiqar section within the *Life*. In the logic of the narrative, it reenacts the ascent of wisdom of chapters 1–100 and reinforces the stage of the Wise Man's consequential political activity. It is thus appropriately inserted here between the emergence of Aesop as political adviser (to the Samian demos and to Croesus) and his final, fateful *theōria* to Delphi.

III. Delphic *Theōria* and the Death of a Sage

But, precisely insofar as we take seriously the narrative's claim for Aesop's special *sophia*, the last section of the *Life*, its Delphic denouement, represents a problem. For here Aesop's *logoi* fail over and over again. Niklas Holzberg, observing the narrative's threefold repetition of Aesop's wrongful accusation for theft, proposes a moralizing reading for the end of his story:

> The opening and closing sections of the book thus form a contrast that is deliberate and is clearly meant to tell us something; as slave and mute Aesop is able to keep his enemies at bay, but as a rich and famous itinerant speaker he seeks in vain to save his skin with his λόγοι. This is so blatantly paradoxical that it must surely be the narrator's way of expressing his view of the behavior displayed by Aesop after the gods have endowed him with λογοποιία.
>
> The explanation for this radical inversion of the fabulist's earlier experiences lies in the three-stage development of the plot in the central part of the novel.... There Aesop appears first as a 'troubleshooter' for Xanthus, next for the Samians, and then for King Lycorus, the recipients of his help coming in each instance from progressively higher rungs of the social ladder. This three-stage sequence is combined with a development in Aesop's character from piousness—by which he distinguishes himself particularly in the exposition—to increasingly manifest hubris, with which he eventually brings the wrath of Apollo upon himself.... Aesop's rise and fall is very reminiscent of the fate suffered by many a tragic hero, such as Oedipus, for example: he helps the people of Thebes by solving a riddle and is made king, but he fails to interpret correctly the Delphian oracle regarding his own person and so comes to grief. The author of the *Aesop Romance* clearly wanted to present his hero as the type of sage who is first superior to all his surroundings, but ends up blinded by this very superiority.[67]

Holzberg's reading is predicated on a moralizing (even Christianizing) notion that as a divinity, Apollo can do no wrong.[68] In addition, it seems to me, his

---

[67] Holzberg 2002.83; cf. Holzberg 1992b.69–75, 1996.635–38. For a similar reading of the Delphic section as tragic punishment for Aesop's hubris, see Jedrkiewicz 1989.157–82.

[68] The same assumption, I would contend, vitiates Keith Hopkins's conclusions about the end of the *Life*: "The murder of the scapegoat is not just a convenient end to the story. It also reflects, I

model of a shift from Aesopic piety to Aesopic hubris fails to do justice to much of the narrative of the *Life* and the reader's experience thereof.[69] But even if we reject Holzberg's moralizing interpretation, a nonmoralizing alternative might still insist that the Delphi section represents the failure of Aesop's (divinely inspired) wisdom and *logoi*, formally so efficacious. Both these readings, I would contend, rely too heavily on a pair of chapters in the Delphi section: the former (Holzberg's) puts too much weight on the nameless friend's question, "Why did it seem best to you to insult them in their own country and city?" (ὑβρίζειν, *Vita* G, ch. 130); the latter puts too much weight on Aesop's answer, that, like the "idiot girl," he's "lost even the sense he had before" (*Vita* G, ch. 131).[70] This dialogue in prison is a complex sequence I will consider in more detail in the next chapter.

In the meantime, I would argue that the Delphi section is complicated insofar as it maintains the double parodic and serious strands that have run through the *Life* as a whole (though perhaps tipping the balance of emphasis more toward the parodic), while also continuing the confluence of what I have identified as Sophistic anthropology and archaic sage traditions. In relation to all that has come before, the Delphic denouement can be seen to represent (while it also parodies) the traditional sage's *theōria* at the end of his life. As I suggested in chapter 2, for the archaic sage, such a religious pilgrimage to a divine site from which he never returns figures the wise man's final assimilation to an other world that he has made ever more fully manifest to the human community through his skilled crafting. On this model, the activities of the sage's life represent his ongoing mediation between human and divine realms, carrying across the products of his skilled crafting to benefit his community, until he is finally subsumed within the divine sphere to which his *sophia* had given him special access.[71]

---

think, the endemic hostility to the clever slave in Roman society. From the masters' point of view, Aesop is too clever by half and finally, like the villain in a western, gets what he richly deserves; the hostility of the god Apollo helps legitimate his execution." This reading fails to acknowledge that at the end of the *Vitae* the Delphians are severely punished by both divine and human forces for their unjust engineering of Aesop's death (*Vitae* G + W, ch. 142); given the end of the narrative, I would strongly resist reading Aesop as akin to "the villain in a western." Cf. discussion in chapter 1 above.

[69] This is the weakness of a reading entirely predicated on formal patterns of the threefold repetition of themes or motifs: it ignores a great deal of text and texture not caught in the hermeneutic net of repetition. Thus I am more in agreement with West 1984.133, who challenges the moralizing reading of the *Life of Aesop* as a narrative of piety rewarded.

[70] Holzberg (1996.635) following Nøjgaard (1964.159–60) reads this statement of Aesop as equivalent to many fable characters' sudden realization (too late) that they have caused their own destruction—usually by going against their fundamental nature in some way. While this is an interesting parallel, this statement is of course not Aesop's last word in the Delphi section (as this self-realization always is in the fables). In addition, as I will argue in the next chapter, Aesop's assertion that he's lost the sense he originally had is at least partly motivated here by a parody of Theognidean didactic (see chapter 5, Section IB below).

[71] See discussion above, chapter 2, section II.

In contrast to this pattern, Aesop's death at Delphi represents not assimilation to the divine, but a scathing critique of the Delphians and of the Delphic god himself. We have considered the elements of this critique already in chapter 1 as a form of resistance to Delphic sacrificial practices and to Apollo's claimed "mantic monopoly." Here we might add that, in terms of the patterns we have been tracing in this chapter, Aesop's confrontation with the Delphians and the Delphic god also enacts a contest over claims to *sophia*. Thus, by emphasizing the greed and low, servile status of the Delphians, Aesop denies their claim to otherworldly authority and the power to mediate the god's prophetic message to mortals. At the same time, the Delphi sequence represents the culmination of Aesop's competition with Apollo, not just as mantic god, but also as the god who oversees and aligns himself with the tradition of high *sophia*. And if, in the previous narrative, the parodic strand required the success of Aesop's distinctive *logoi* (versus the inept philosopher Xanthus), the parodic critique of the Delphians requires just the opposite—their utter failure to be persuaded by Aesop's fabular wisdom. Or, to formulate this in other terms: Aesop may lose his life, but he wins the contest of *sophia*.

This contest plays itself out in several ways. First, we should note that the Delphians are consistently represented (by Aesop and by the narrative) as themselves a reversion to a brutish state of nature, unconstrained by law and without any social contract to constitute a community. Thus (as noted in chapter 1), Aesop's fable narratives cast them in the roles of men committing bestiality and incest, plotting against guests and violating sanctuary. Indeed, the first two images Aesop offers on encountering them make them not even human—they are the color of vegetables and like driftwood afloat in the sea (*Vita* G, ch. 124; *Vitae* G + W, ch. 125). We might also note how many of the fables Aesop tells in the Delphi section are set in the country or the wilds: this is true of the plowman who seduces the grieving widow (ch. 129), as of the idiot girl and her mother (ch. 131). Most emphatically, Aesop's penultimate fable, delivered at the cliff-edge from which he will cast himself to his death, tells the story of an old farmer whose desire is to see the city once before he dies. His children send him off in a cart drawn by asses, but driven off the road by a terrible storm, they wander in the wilderness to a cliff-edge where the farmer confronts a bitter death "not even from horses, but from accursed asses" (*Vitae* G + W, ch. 140). In the perfect coincidence of setting (poised on a cliff-edge), Aesop's fable transforms Delphi itself from a polis to a place of wild and savage nature—the negation of polis order. This, we might say, is the always available negative figuration of Delphi as an other place set apart from the world of the cities: the flip side of its status as a numinous center to which the sage makes his pilgrimage. Given this figuration of Delphi as wilderness and the Delphians as unscrupulous savages who reject all the norms of community, it is unsurprising that Aesop's repeated *logoi* about justice and injustice have no effect on them. But, I would contend, this pattern serves as an indictment of the *Delphians* and their claims to otherworldly authority, rather than as a condemnation of *Aesop's* supposed hubris.⁷²

In contrast to the unconstrained savagery of the Delphians, Aesop is represented in this closing episode as a true sage and seer. In the first place, we might note that Aesop's repeated message to the Delphians is a paradoxical appropriation of Delphic wisdom par excellence, for he tells them over and over again that they do not "know themselves"—that they are ignorant of their ancestry and their status as "slaves of all the Greeks." At the same time, Aesop in this section twice speaks true prophecies through fable. First, the fable of the mouse and the frog tells how the frog maliciously reciprocates the hospitality of the mouse by inviting him to dinner in his pond, binding their legs together, and drowning the hapless mouse when he dives. The mouse, as he's drowning, prophesies, "Being a corpse, I will punish you living" (*Vita* G, ch. 133). The mouse's prophecy is fulfilled when a crow seizes his rodent corpse floating on the surface of the pond and carries off with it the frog still bound leg to leg. At this point, Aesop explicitly draws the analogy to the present situation: "Likewise I also, having died, will be a doom for you. For the Lydians, the Babylonians, and nearly the whole of Greece will avenge (literally, make fruitful [καρπίσονται]) my death" (*Vita* G, ch. 133). Second, Aesop's fable of the eagle and the dung beetle ends with Zeus's intervention to validate the claims of the humble dung beetle, at which point Aesop draws the apposite moral: "Likewise also you, men of Delphi, do not dishonor this shrine [of the Muses] to which I have fled, even if it is little, but bear in mind the [tale] of the dung beetle and show respect for Zeus Xenius and Olympius" (*Vita* G, ch. 139).

The prophecies of these two fables (explicit and implicit) are in fact fulfilled in chiastic order in the very last chapter of the *Life*: first, the Delphians, "oppressed by plague, get an oracle *from Zeus* to propitiate the doom of Aesop" (corresponding to Zeus's intervention in the fable); second, a combined force of "men from Greece and Babylon and the Samians" make war on Delphi, thereby "avenging the death of Aesop" (as predicted in the fable of the mouse and the frog; *Vita* G, ch. 142). Thus, against Holzberg's reading of the Delphi episode, we should note that, insofar as the Delphians do not know themselves and their ancestry and commit a murder that precipitates a plague upon the land, *they*

---

⁷² For this failure of rational *logoi*, notice the language used in ch. 127 of the Delphians (only in *Vita* G): μὴ ἔχοντες εὔλογον αἰτίαν ἐμηχανήσαντό τι πανοῦργον, ἵνα μὴ οἱ παραδημοῦντες δυνήσωνται αὐτῷ βοηθῆσαι ("and, having no rational cause [to kill Aesop], they contrived some unscrupulous thing in order to prevent visitors [to the shrine] from being able to come to his aid . . ."). Thus the Delphians' activity opposes "good reason" with an unscrupulous willingness to do anything to subvert the basic protections of men in society coming spontaneously to each other's aid. The Delphians in this characterization have much in common with Aristotle's description of the man who is "without a city through nature rather than chance": "he is 'without clan, without law, without hearth,' like the person reproved by Homer; for the one who is such by nature has by this fact a desire for war . . ." (Arist. *Pol.* 1.2.9–10, 1253a3–6, trans. Lord 1984).

(not Aesop) play the role of Oedipus, while Aesop here acts the part of Tiresias, the divinely inspired sage and seer whose warnings go unheeded.[73]

And of course, with his access to true prophetic power, Aesop is here in competition not just with the Delphians but with the Delphic god himself. In this respect, his privileging of the shrine of the Muses over the temple of Apollo as the site where he seeks sanctuary completes the pattern we have been tracing of the Muses' appearance at significant moments of competition in *sophia*.[74] Here, since the Muses' authority is ultimately endorsed by Zeus himself (*Vita* G, ch. 142), Aesop would seem to be the winner also in this competition with Apollo. Still, it is worth noting that the judgment of Aesop as the winner in these Delphic competitions of *sophia* is outside the narrative frame. Here it falls to the reader or listener to make that final judgment, based on the narrative's cues and patterns—in contrast to earlier scenes in which the narrative itself clearly affirmed Aesop's victory (e.g., over Xanthus or Nectanebo). In this respect, the end of *Vita* G functions as I have argued fable itself does, offering its audience implicit connections that require their own interpretative activity to draw the moral.

As for Aesop's end, *Vita* G seems to mute the elements that would complete Aesop's trajectory as an archaic sage—specifically, his assimilation to the divine in some form at the end of his life.[75] Recall that we noted two characteristic supernatural outcomes for the archaic sage or *theios anēr*: (1) death while on a *theōria*, often coupled with hero-cult honors; or (2) descent to the underworld (itself the ultimate *theōria*) and return with esoteric knowledge.[76] It is striking that, in spite of the reticence of *Vita* G, different traditions about Aesop attribute to him *both* these otherworldly ends (as we have already seen in chapter 1). For the first: *Vita* W and *P.Oxy.* 1800 tell of a stele or an altar dedicated to Aesop and the offering of cult honors.[77] For the second: in other traditions, we find scattered references to Aesop's resurrection or metempsychosis. The Scholia to Aristophanes and the Suda preserve a few lines by Plato the comic poet (late fifth century BCE) that presuppose a well-known tradition of the return of Aesop's

---

[73] It is entirely consonant with the pattern of competitive scapegoating I noted in chapter 1 that the Delphians are simultaneously cast as brutish savages *and* as Oedipus (himself the ultimate scapegoat figure). On Oedipus as scapegoat, see Vernant 1988.

[74] For the shrine of the Muses as an old element, see Perry 1936.14–16, Dillery 1999.279–80, and see discussion in the introduction. Contra: Ferrari 1997.17–18.

[75] Cf. Compton 2006.31n. 54: "The ending of G seems somewhat abrupt."

[76] See chapter 2, section II above.

[77] *Vita* W, ch. 142 speaks of the Delphians "building a temple and setting up a stele for him," while *P.Oxy.* 1800 explicitly specifies the establishment of an altar and the offering of "sacrifices, as to a hero." For hero cult as an essential element of Aesop's Delphic end, see Nagy 1979.284–90, Compton 2006.19–40, Jouanno 2006.48, and discussion above, chapter 1, section III. In fact, even in *Vita* G, the oracle the Delphians receive from Zeus to "propitiate the doom of Aesop" in the context of plague may itself imply hero-cult honors, for how else are they going to "propitiate" Aesop for his "violent death" (τοῦ Αἰσώπου μόρον, *Vita* G, ch. 142)?

soul to life, while Hermippus reported that an otherwise unknown Pataecus ("Shorty") "claimed to have the soul of Aesop."[78]

Finally, both these traditions seem to be conflated in the paroemiographer Zenobius's gloss on the phrase Αἰσώπειον αἷμα:

ἐπὶ τῶν δυσαπονίπτοις ὀνείδεσι καὶ κακοῖς συνεχομένων· ἐπειδὴ τοῖς ⟨Δελφοῖς⟩ ἀδίκως τὸν Αἴσωπον ἀνελοῦσιν ὠργίσθη τὸ δαιμόνιον· καὶ διὰ τοῦτο τὴν Πυθίαν φασὶν ἀνῃρηκέναι αὐτοῖς ἱλάσκεσθαι τὸ ἐπὶ Αἰσώπῳ μύσος. οὕτω γὰρ θεοφιλὴς ἐγένετο ὁ Αἴσωπος ὡς μυθεύεται αὐτὸν ἀναβιῶναι, ὡς Τυνδάρεων καὶ Ἡρακλῆν καὶ Γλαῦκον. (Zenobius I.47; Leutsch-Schneidewin I.18 = Perry *Test.* 27)

Aesopic blood: For those afflicted by reproaches and evils that are difficult to wash away; since the divine became angry with the Delphians because they killed Aesop unjustly. And on account of this they say that the Pythia prophesied to them to propitiate the pollution over Aesop. For Aesop was so dear to the gods that the story is told that he came back to life again, like Tyndareus and Heracles and Glaucus.[79]

In the report that the "Pythia prophesied to [the Delphians] to propitiate the pollution over Aesop," we seem to have an echo of the version that Aesop ultimately enjoyed hero-cult worship at Delphi. But then this account is oddly sutured, via the specious logic of οὕτω γάρ, to another tradition that Aesop "came back to life again" (ἀναβιῶναι) just like the distinguished mythological heroes Tyndareus, Heracles, and Glaucus. This latter account seems to credit Aesop with a personal descent to the underworld and return of the kind we find associated with Pythagoras, Epimenides, Empedocles, and perhaps even Hesiod by the fifth century BCE.[80] These references, scattered and confused as they are, suggest the status Aesop enjoyed in the popular imagination; I would contend that the accounts of hero-cult honor, or of resurrection and rebirth, like many other elements of his life story, confirm Aesop's popular identification as sage in this archaic tradition.

---

[78] Schol. *ad* Aristoph. *Birds* 471; Suda s.v. ἀναβιῶναι, I.161 Adler (= Plato Com. fr. 70 KA); Hermippus *ap.* Plut. *Sol.* 6. Cf. also Ptolemaeus son of Hephaestion *ap.* Photius, who claimed that "Aesop, having been killed by the Delphians, came back to life and fought with the Greeks at Thermopylae" (Photius *Bibl.* cod. 252). For the relevant Greek texts, see Perry *Test.* 45–47.

[79] Another version of this proverb attributes the saying and explanation to Aristotle in his *Constitution of the Delphians* (fr. 487 Rose = frr. 494, 1, 2, 3 Gigon).

[80] For all these figures associated with personal *catabasis* and return by virtue of their exceptional *sophia*, see Scodel 1980; the pivot-figure here is perhaps Heracles, who descended to the underworld while alive, but also enjoyed hero-cult and divine honors (see Scodel 1980.308–11). Scodel (1980.316–17) in fact considers the traditions about Aesop's resurrection in this context, but she is reluctant to add him to the august company of sages and shamans, suggesting instead that "in the case of Aesop, whose legend is a reflection of *pharmakos* ritual, the motive for a story of rebirth can be guessed" (p. 317). I must confess that I cannot guess the link Scodel implies between *pharmakos* ritual and rebirth. I suspect that, in fact, Scodel has no clear connection in mind—she simply feels that it is impossible to include Aesop in her distinguished group of resurrected sages.

IV. The Bricoleur as Culture Hero, or the Art of Extorting Self-Incrimination

In the last three sections, we've considered elements in the *Life* that align the Aesop tradition with patterns of prephilosophical *sophia* and Sophistic anthropology. In this section, I would like to highlight other patterns that run through and unify the *Life* as a whole—patterns that seem to belong uniquely to Aesop and endow him with a distinctive form of *sophia* all his own. In every case, the episodes that form these patterns are common to G and W, and so must go back at least to their common source. Indeed, I would contend that these distinctive features of Aesop's *sophia* are quite old in the tradition. Given this pattern of occurrence, I will be privileging the evidence of *Vita* G in this section, as in the earlier sections of this chapter, simply because G preserves a fuller text.

At one point in her discussion of the sociopolitical authority often associated with "skilled crafting" in traditional cultures, Mary Helms concisely formulates her thesis: "Power over Things as Power over People." In context, this refers to special artisanal products that reveal "the artisan's ability for exposition and especially imposition of form as manifestation of the fundamental crafting capacity for outside-inside transformation and creation by which the invisible is given tangible credence and the potentially chaotic is controlled."[81] Several times throughout the *Life*, Aesop exhibits a special "power over things," but with a distinctive twist: he is the master of humble or everyday objects (not the precious artifacts of skilled crafting), especially adept at making use of what is readily available in the environment. Still, this power over ordinary things does endow him with a special, unexpected "power over people." Thus, in the very first episode in the *Life*, two of Aesop's fellow slaves plot to eat the master's figs and pin the crime on Aesop, since he is mute and therefore (they imagine) unable to defend himself (*Vitae* G + W, chs. 2–3).[82] As he is about to be beaten for the theft, Aesop falls at the master's feet and signals for him to hold off a little:

> And as he was holding off, [Aesop] seeing a pitcher ready to hand (ἰδὼν παρακείμενον ξέστην), took it and through gestures asked for warm water, and placing a basin beside himself in the middle (εἰς τὸ μέσον) and drinking, cast his fingers into his mouth and gagging himself, vomited up [only] the warm water he had drunk: for he hadn't eaten anything. And giving a demonstration thanks to his extensive experience (διὰ δὲ τῆς πολυπειρίας δοὺς ἀπόδειξιν), he asked that his fellow slaves also do this, in order that it be known who is the one who ate the figs. And the master, amazed at his invention (θαυμάσας δὲ ὁ δεσπότης τὸ ἐνθύμημα αὐτοῦ), bid the others also to drink and throw up. (*Vita* G, ch. 3)

---

[81] Helms 1993 (both quotations from p. 75).
[82] There is a lacuna at the beginning of this episode in G, which can be supplemented from W.

In this way, of course, the real thieves are exposed, as his fellow slaves are forced to vomit up the figs they had illicitly consumed.

This episode is permeated with the language of the public performance of skilled crafting and the wonder its products inspire: πολυπειρία, ἀπόδειξις, τὸ ἐνθύμημα, θαυμάσας. Indeed, through the resonant phrase εἰς τὸ μέσον, this sequence of Aesop's clever dumb show even foreshadows his triumphant bouleutic activity before the assembled Samian demos (where this properly political formula occurs five times; *Vita* G, chs. 81, 82, 91, 96, 97). But strikingly, Aesop's self-defense here develops as a brilliant improvisation from the accidental presence of an ordinary water-jug "ready to hand" (παρακείμενον).[83] It is noteworthy that Aesop evinces this special skill over humble objects even before Isis and the Muses endow him with voice and the "invention of *logoi* and the weaving and crafting of Greek fables" (*Vita* G, ch. 7).[84] He is already a skilled craftsman of the ordinary and adventitious—an appropriate sphere, given his utterly abjected status as mute slave.

One more example will suffice. After he has changed hands and is now in the possession of a slave merchant, Aesop again displays his special power over everyday objects. The slave merchant announces to his assembled slaves that they are crossing to Asia and, since he has been unable to acquire pack-animals, the slaves themselves must bear all the equipment. In this context, Aesop first begs his fellow slaves to allow him to bear a light burden, on the grounds that he is newly bought and weak of body. They respond, "Carry nothing at all then." But Aesop claims to fear shaming himself and appearing useless to his new master (*Vitae* G + W, ch. 17). In the end, Aesop inspects the equipment, and "seeing a circular basket crammed with bread lying there" (κείμενον), which four slaves were going to bear together, he volunteers to carry it all by himself. The other slaves respond with incredulity and contempt: "We see no one more foolish than this little mannikin. He asked to bear something lighter than all, and he's chosen something heavier than all." Seeing Aesop laboring under his enormous burden, his new master is impressed by his eagerness for toil (*Vitae* G + W, ch. 18). Next we are told that Aesop "going out to the road, taught the bread basket to walk (ἐξελθὼν γὰρ εἰς τὴν ὁδὸν περιπατεῖν τὸν γούργαθον ἐδίδασκεν). For coming to a rise, he tipped the bread basket over and was dragging it up with his teeth as long as he was ascending. But for the descent, he went down without effort; for he rolled the bread basket down and he himself was riding on it" (*Vita* G, ch. 19; *Vita* W is similar). Finally, periodically on their trip, all the slaves pause and get their ration of bread. The result: Aesop runs out in front, easily carrying on his shoulder the bread basket, now almost empty.

---

[83] *Vita* W omits παρακείμενον and the setting of the basin "in the middle," but preserves the main lines of this episode, so this skillful, improvisatory use of humble objects is common to both G and W.

[84] Cf. Winkler 1985.286 (citing the episode of the figs): "Aesop before the miracle is already extraordinarily clever."

The other slaves finally get the trick: "One [says], 'You fail to recognize how clever (πολύνουν) the little man is.' Another [says], 'These mannikins short on looks are long on brains.[85] For he asked to carry the bread which is consumed under his hand, while we bear firewood and bedding and bronze, the things that can't be consumed'" (*Vitae* G + W, ch. 19).

Again, Aesop's unique ability is to make brilliant and unexpected use of the ordinary objects he finds "lying around" (κείμενον).[86] And, true to Helms's formulation, this use of everyday objects does indeed give him "power over people." His *sophia* is thus a superlative version of bricolage, as Claude Lévi-Strauss defines it:

> The 'bricoleur' is adept at performing a large number of diverse tasks; but, unlike the engineer, he does not subordinate each of them to the availability of raw materials and tools conceived and procured for the purposes of the project. His universe of instruments is closed and the rules of this game are always to make do with 'whatever is at hand', that is to say with a set of tools and materials which is always finite and is also heterogeneous because what it contains bears no relation to the current project, or indeed to any particular project, but is the contingent result of all the occasions there have been to renew or enrich the stock or to maintain it with the remains of previous constructions or destructions.[87]

---

[85] I borrow this snappy formulation from Lloyd Daly's translation (in Hansen 1998.118); the Greek at this point reads: ταῦτα τὰ ἀνθρωπάρια τὰ λειπόμενα τῇ μορφῇ φρένας ἔχει.

[86] Again (as in ch. 3), *Vita* W omits κείμενον, but preserves the general lines of the story. For the age of this episode, cf. Perry 1966.286n. 2, who notes an echo of this bread basket story in Horace *Satires* I.1.47–49. Perry assumes that Horace must be alluding to Demetrius of Phaleron's *Aesopia*, but (as Hägg 1997.182 with n. 19 points out) this could be an allusion to something like G—or perhaps to an oral tradition about Aesop. Two other examples of this same pattern from later in the *Life*: (1) In the Samian section, Xanthus, looking for an excuse to beat Aesop, filches one of four pig's trotters boiling for guests. Aesop notices that one trotter is missing and immediately understands that Xanthus has done it in order to be able to punish him. Noticing in the courtyard the special piglet that is being raised for the mistress's birthday celebration, he gags it and cuts off one of its feet. In the meantime, Xanthus, fearing that Aesop will notice the theft and try to run away, returns the original trotter to the pot. When Aesop pours the pot of trotters into a basin in the presence of the guests, both he and Xanthus are surprised to find five trotters. Xanthus blanches and asks Aesop "How many feet does one pig have?" Aesop, without missing a beat, responds, "Yes, it comes out right—this one had five and the piglet outside grazes three-footed" (*Vitae* G + W, chs. 42–43). (2) In light of this pattern, we can read the shrine of the Muses in the Delphi section (*Vita* G, chs. 134, 139) as also a small or humble object, but ready to hand as Aesop is being led to his death.

[87] Lévi-Strauss 1966.16. Bricolage is, famously, Lévi-Strauss's analogy for the logic of mythic thought (vs scientific thought). The analogy is elaborated in the introductory chapter of *The Savage Mind* (*La Pensée sauvage*), entitled "The Science of the Concrete." That chapter title, in turn, suggests the affinity of Lévi-Strauss's notion with Bourdieu's concept of "practical logic"; cf. Bourdieu 1977, 1990. Aesop's mastery of "bricolage" or the "Science of the Concrete" throughout the *Life* encourages us to see this not just as a stage in the diachronic development of human thought (as Lévi-Strauss would have it), but also synchronically as a sociopolitical diacritic. That is to say, perhaps disinterested, abstract thought is a luxury beyond the exigencies and resources of society's disempowered.

Indeed, we might say, using Helms's terms, that Aesop represents the bricoleur as culture hero. And this is, in a sense, analogous to Aesop's distinctive skill in the "weaving and crafting of fables," since fables, too, deploy low animal characters and ordinary situations in unexpected combinations to achieve their witty and persuasive effects. That this pattern, which figures in both G and W but is preserved with more nuance and detail in *Vita* G, is in fact intended to represent a significant analogy or allegory for the crafting of fables is suggested by the motto appended at the end of the text of *Vita* G in the Morgan manuscript. After a tagline that summarizes the contents of the *Life* (Αἰσώπου γέννα, ἀνατροφή, προκοπή, καὶ ἀποβίωσις), marked off in its own decorative frame we read, τὰ μετ᾽ εὐκολίας εὑρισκόμενα καὶ εὐκαταφρόνητα πολλοῖς εἶναι δοκεῖ ("The things discovered with ease also seem to be despicable to many"; fig. 4.1). Perry regarded this tag, which occurs only in the Morgan manuscript of the *Life*, as an intrusive "philosophical comment" on the fictive narrative of the *Life* by a late reader/copyist.[88] But, whether this tag is original to *Vita* G or a later addition, it is strikingly apposite to the pattern I have noted, of Aesop's skillful bricolage with what he finds ready to hand. And while this tag thus forms a fitting reflection on the narrative of the *Life* that precedes it, it simultaneously points forward to the text of the fable collection that follows immediately, starting on the same folio of the Morgan manuscript (see fig. 4.1).

For humble beast fables are also "things discovered (or invented) with ease" that the many regard as "despicable" or "easily disdained," but that are in fact "useful" (ὠφέλιμοι).[89]

Indeed, this notion of the easy (rhetorical) invention of fables is already articulated by Aristotle, in a passage whose ambivalence seems simultaneously to confirm the defensive εὐκαταφρόνητα of the motto. In Book 2 of the *Rhetoric*, in a discussion devoted to different forms of παράδειγμα ("example") used as proof, Aristotle weighs the relative merits of Aesopic fable (λόγοι) and historical examples (πράγματα . . . γεγενημένα):

> εἰσὶ δ᾽ οἱ λόγοι δημηγορικοί, καὶ ἔχουσιν ἀγαθὸν τοῦτο, ὅτι πράγματα μὲν εὑρεῖν ὅμοια γεγενημένα χαλεπόν, λόγους δὲ ῥᾷον· . . . . ῥᾴω μὲν οὖν πορίσασθαι τὰ διὰ τῶν λόγων, χρησιμώτερα δὲ πρὸς τὸ βουλεύσασθαι τὰ διὰ τῶν πραγμάτων· ὅμοια γὰρ ὡς ἐπὶ τὸ πολὺ τὰ μέλλοντα τοῖς γεγονόσιν. (*Rhet.* 2.20, 1394a2–8)

---

[88] Thus Perry 1936.167; his judgment of this tag as an intrusive gloss is followed by Ferrari 1997.258, who omits this line altogether. I'm not quite sure what Perry means by "philosophical comment": it would be possible to understand εὐκολία here as endorsing an (Aesop-like) life that is "easygoing, content with little," but I prefer to understand it to mean tricks or fables that are "easy to invent" for two reasons: (1) Aesop is not particularly "easygoing" or "content with little" as the *Life* progresses; (2) εὑρισκόμενα doesn't quite fit this metaphysical reading; it seems rather to conform to the rhetorical concept of *inventio*.

[89] Thus the line that introduces the actual fable collection in the Morgan ms: Αἰσώπου μῦθοι κατὰ στοιχεῖον ὠφέλιμοι· μῦθος ἇ. Cf. Perry 1936.167.

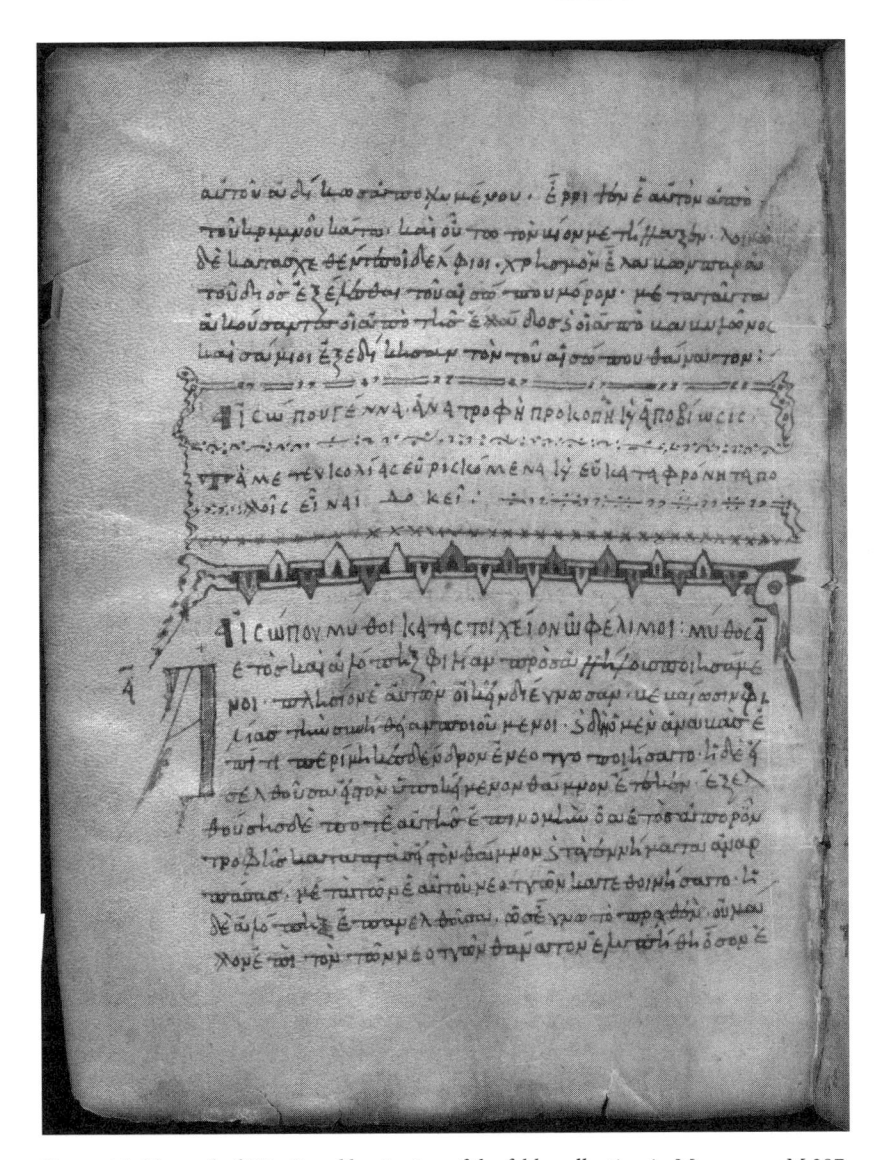

Figure 4.1. The end of *Vita* G and beginning of the fable collection in Morgan ms M.397, folio 67ᵛ (late tenth or early eleventh century CE). Photo: Schecter Lee, 2009; courtesy of The Pierpont Morgan Library.

And fables are suitable for public speaking and they have this virtue, that it is hard to find past events that are similar, but easier to invent fables.... Examples via fables are thus easier to provide, but examples via historical events are more useful for deliberation, since things that are going to happen are for the most part like things that have happened.

Aristotle starts with what looks like praise of Aesopic fables: they are easier to discover/invent than apposite historical examples. But almost immediately, this praise is qualified: yes, proof via fables is "easier to provide," but historical examples are "more useful" in deliberative contexts, since "things that are going to happen are for the most part like things that have happened." With this immediate qualification, Aristotle pries apart δημηγορικοί from τὸ βουλεύσασθαι, and implies a clear hierarchy of serious historical examples and frivolous Aesopic fable.[90] This hierarchy, in turn, retrospectively transforms δημηγορικοί from the neutral "suitable for public speaking" to the judgmental "claptrap of popular oratory."

Thus, based on this parallel from Aristotle's *Rhetoric*, I would suggest that the Morgan manuscript's tag is intentionally Janus-faced, pointing backward to Aesop's skillful improvisations with everyday objects throughout the *Life* and forward to the rhetorical "found objects" of the fable collection that follows, neatly suturing the two together.[91]

In addition, there seems to be a second distinctive form of Aesopic *sophia* that functions as a leitmotif throughout the text of the *Life*: Aesop exhibits an uncanny ability to force his (usually more powerful) opponents to incriminate or bear witness against themselves. We see this ability in action, even before Aesop regains his voice, in the episode we've already considered—Aesop's framing for eating the figs by his two fellow slaves. Appropriately enough given Aesop's muteness and the bodiliness generally attributed to slaves, his oppo-

---

[90] In fact, the ambivalences and equivocations of this Aristotelian passage are still more complex, since, in the lines I have omitted, it also inserts [Socratic] παραβολή into its ranked hierarchy of kinds of example. See fuller discussion of this bit of Aristotle's *Rhetoric* in chapter 6, section II below.

[91] I assume that the extended *Life* represented by G and W and the fable collections were joined together only in the late antique/Byzantine period; see discussion in the introduction, section II C. Given that assumption, we might imagine this Janus-faced tag as the editorializing addition of a Byzantine monk/scholar (perhaps the same person who put the *Life* and fables together in the first place?). Still, I would contend that the association of Aesopic fable with this kind of bricolage of things ready to hand is much older in the tradition and in fact helps us account for the strange language Plato's Socrates uses to explain why and how he chose Aesopic fables to versify in the *Phaedo*: οὓς προχείρους εἶχον μύθους καὶ ἠπιστάμην τοὺς Αἰσώπου, τούτων ἐποίησα οἷς πρώτοις ἐνέτυχον ("The fables of Aesop that I had ready to hand and knew by heart, of these I composed the first ones that occurred to me [lit. the first ones I happened upon]," *Phd.* 61b5–7). Notice that Socrates' account here oddly doubles the adventitious or easily found nature of fable (προχείρους, ἐνέτυχον) in what we might call a suitably Aesopic homage. For more on Aesop in the *Phaedo*, see Kurke 2006.13–19, 35–38, and chapter 6 below.

nents' self-incrimination occurs here entirely in the bodily register.[92] Thus, even though the two slaves plan not to stick their fingers down their throats, but only in their cheeks (*Vita* G, ch. 3), their bodies betray them; merely drinking warm water causes them to regurgitate the figs and so expose their crime.

We see the same pattern of leveraging an opponent's self-incrimination in much more complex form at the beginning of the Assembly sequence. Having first tormented Xanthus by his assertion, "I am no *mantis*" (*Vita* G, ch. 84), Aesop then interrupts his master on the verge of suicide and promises that he will interpret the portents if Xanthus will put him in front of the popular assembly the next day: "Lead me back to the theater with you and make up a plausible excuse for the masses from the sign based on the dignity of philosophy, and cast me forth as your pupil. I will solve [the omen] and I will be called forth to speak at the opportune moment" (εὐκαίρως, *Vita* G, ch. 85). Xanthus does exactly what Aesop has suggested, claiming to the Assembly that his commitment to philosophy prevents him from sign reading, but offering them Aesop instead as "a slave whom I have philosophically instructed in such things, who will interpret your sign" (*Vita* G, ch. 86).

The initial reaction of the Samian demos on catching sight of Aesop is that he is himself a τέρας in need of a sign-interpreter, so that Aesop must first persuade them not to judge the inner qualities of mind from the outer appearance (*Vita* G, ch. 88, quoted in chapter 3). As we've seen, Aesop concludes this speech with the first mention of *sophia* in *Vita* G: "For just as I know how to speak, thus also I know how to be silent again; for the boundary of *sophia* is to consider the *kairos*" (*Vita* G, ch. 88). At this point the assembled people, impressed by his intelligence and speaking skill, shout out their encouragement, and Aesop, "recognizing himself praised, took the opportunity of freedom of speech and began to speak" (παρρησίας λαβὼν καιρὸν ἤρξατο λέγειν, *Vita* G, ch. 88). After this elaborate setup, Aesop does not, as expected, interpret the omen, but instead exploits this very public opportunity (καιρός) by asking for his freedom:

> "Men of Samos, it's not rational (εὔλογον) for a slave to solve this omen for a free people; wherefore, bestow on me freedom of speech of the things said, so that, if I succeed, as a free man I get in return appropriate honors, and if I fail, I be chastised not as a slave but as a free man. If then you bestow on me the freedom of speech that belongs to free status, I will begin to speak free of all fear." (*Vita* G, ch. 89; similar in W)

The Samian demos accordingly appeals to Xanthus to free Aesop and, when he refuses, offers instead to buy him from the philosopher for his original price. Xanthus, ashamed to admit the absurdly low price he had originally paid for Aesop, lest he be thought to be holding out "on account of avarice" (διὰ φιλαργυρίαν), is forced by the public setting simply to free Aesop outright (*Vita* G, ch. 90). And at this point, Aesop finally interprets the omen (*Vita* G, ch. 91).

---

[92] For the significant bodiliness of this episode, cf. Patterson 1991.25–26.

In retrospect, we realize that there was no altruism in Aesop's intervention to prevent Xanthus from hanging himself; instead everything Aesop has done from the moment he's released from his bonds (ch. 83) has been an elaborate manipulation to get himself, Xanthus, and the Samian demos to this point.[93] With unerring skill, Aesop plays on and exploits his master's vanity and philosophical self-importance to maneuver both of them into a very public setting where Xanthus must either incriminate himself before the assembled populace or free Aesop (as he had promised in private to do earlier in the *Life*; *Vita* G, ch. 78). Aesop's skillful manipulation of Xanthus and of the Samian demos makes his assertion "I know how to be silent again" into an implicit but effective threat: just as he had initially denied his sign-reading abilities to Xanthus, so also he raises the possibility of withholding from the Assembly the verbal skill he has just so ably demonstrated. These threats together animate and make irresistible his request for freedom as a condition of true *parrhēsia*. This in turn gives a secondary resonance to the gnomic conclusion of his first speech: "The boundary of *sophia* is to consider the *kairos*" refers not just to the bouleutic skills of the archaic sage in general, but specifically to Aesop's uncanny knack for turning an opponent's will and power against himself. This is Aesop's special brand of *sophia*, as is signaled by the repeated occurrence of forms of *kairos* in the narrative sequence (εὐκαίρως in *Vita* G, ch. 85; καιρός twice in *Vita* G, ch. 88).[94]

We find the same pattern repeated even within the Ahiqar section, in Aesop's duel of wits with Nectanebo, pharaoh of Egypt. First, briefly, the pharaoh asks Aesop to answer a question for him: he claims that he has "sent for pregnant mares from Greece, but whenever they hear the horses neighing in Babylon, they miscarry." Aesop promises to answer the next day and returns to his lodging, where he catches and publicly beats a large cat. The Egyptians, appalled by this act of impiety against one of their sacred animals, complain to Nectanebo, who reproaches Aesop for his bad behavior (*Vitae* G + W, ch. 117). Aesop responds that the cat has wronged Lycurgus, king of Babylon, by killing his new fighting cock. At this point, Nectanebo bursts out in exasperation, "Aren't you ashamed of such a baldfaced lie? For how could a cat in a single night make it to Babylon from Egypt?" Unperturbed, Aesop responds, "How are mares [in Egypt] able to hear horses neighing in my land and miscarry?" (*Vitae* G + W, ch. 118). Thus the pharaoh is forced to acknowledge himself defeated by his own exclamation.

---

[93] In this case, while W preserves the main lines of this whole sequence, the epitomated version seems to have missed—or to be deliberately domesticating—the more self-interested and cunning maneuvers of Aesop as preserved in G. Thus notice that *Vita* W, chs. 83–85 explains that Aesop saves his master from hanging himself simply because he is φιλοδέσποτος, while *Vita* W, ch. 90 removes all mention of Xanthus's anxiety that he will be exposed as greedy or stingy before the entire demos. For W's "social censorship" of this as one of *Vita* G's "more subversive elements," cf. Jouanno 2006.50–51.

[94] This reading, I hope, provides another argument against Perry's bracketing of the end of Aesop's first speech in *Vita* G as an irrelevant intrusion from a marginal comment.

Again, more elaborately, Nectanebo's last attempt to stump Aesop consists of a challenge to name something the pharaoh and his courtiers "have neither seen nor heard." Aesop, well aware that, whatever he says, they will claim to have seen and heard it, forges the record of a loan of a thousand talents of gold from Lycurgus to Nectanebo, including in the document a date to indicate that the loan is now past due. When he arrives with the document at Nectanebo's court, the friends of the king immediately say, "We have seen and heard this many times." Aesop responds, " 'I'm delighted at [your] bearing witness (χαίρω μαρτυρούντων). Let the money be paid back immediately, since the appointed date for repayment has passed.' But king Nectanebo upon hearing [this] said, 'Why do you bear witness (μαρτυρεῖτε) concerning things I do not owe?' And they said, 'We've never seen or heard it.'" (*Vitae* G + W, ch. 122).[95] Here Aesop cleverly catches the friends of the king in a double bind of self-incrimination: if they bear false witness that they've seen the document before, the pharaoh is liable for a huge debt; if they bear true witness that they've never seen or heard about the debt, the pharaoh loses the contest of wisdom and must pay three years' tribute to the king of Babylon.[96]

Strikingly, Aesop deploys the same technique against Apollo himself at the very end of the *Life*. After telling his final fable poised on the Delphic cliff-edge,

Αἴσωπος καταρασάμενος αὐτούς, καὶ τὸν προστάτην τῶν Μουσῶν μάρτυρα προσκαλούμενος, ὅπως ἐπακούσῃ αὐτοῦ ἀδίκως ἀπολλυμένου, ἔρριψεν ἑαυτὸν ἀπὸ τοῦ κρημνοῦ κάτω. καὶ οὕτω τὸν βίον μετήλλαξεν. λοιμῷ δὲ κατασχεθέντες οἱ Δέλφιοι χρησμὸν ἔλαβον παρὰ τοῦ Διὸς ἐξιλάσκεσθαι ‹τὸν› τοῦ Αἰσώπου μόρον. (*Vita* G, ch. 142)

Aesop, having cursed [the Delphians] and called to witness the overseer of the Muses, to heed him as he's perishing unjustly, cast himself down from the cliff. And so he ended his life. But the Delphians, oppressed by plague, got an oracle from Zeus to propitiate the doom of Aesop.

---

[95] For the motif "never heard before" as a cross-cultural story type, see Uther 2004.I, no. 921E.

[96] Both these episodes appear in the Syriac, Arabic, and Armenian versions of the *Story of Ahiqar* in mss dating from the twelfth to the eighteenth century CE (cf. the translations of Conybeare, Harris, and Lewis 1913a.762–64). It is impossible to know whether these stories—or, indeed, the whole Egyptian episode—figured in the oldest versions of Ahiqar, since the late fifth–century BCE Aramaic papyrus from Elephantine breaks off before this point in the narrative. There are thus two possibilities, given the marked similarity of the Aesop version of both these stories with the later Ahiqar tradition: (1) The Egyptian adventure of Ahiqar predates the assimilation with Aesop (in which case, these episodes of the Babylonian vizier's forcing his opponents to bear witness against themselves perhaps encouraged the identification with Aesop), or (2) Traditions about Aesop shaped these episodes of the Ahiqar story, which perhaps passed back from the Greek version into Syriac, Arabic, and Armenian. Either way, it is interesting to note that none of these three versions bears any trace of the language of witnessing that is so prominent in the Greek account. This seems to be a distinctive feature of the *Life of Aesop* (both G and W), which is picked up again at the very end of the *Life*.

Here, Aesop's calling Apollo himself to witness the injustice of his death extorts from his divine antagonist assistance and support against the Delphians, Apollo's own servants. And the narrative sequence, with its emphatic λοιμῷ δέ almost immediately after Aesop's public summons of Apollo, suggests that his conjuring of the god is in fact efficacious, for Apollo as far back as the *Iliad* is the god who sends plague in punishment for human wrongdoing. Thus we may suppose (though this is not explicitly stated) that the plague comes from Apollo, even if the oracular command comes from Zeus. In effect, Aesop calls Apollo to witness against himself[97] and forces him into the role of dutiful slave overseer (προστάτης), mediating between the Muses (whose shrine has been violated by the Delphians) and the true master Zeus.[98]

In all these instances, Aesop displays a unique ability to leverage a hegemonic opponent's will and power in a kind of martial art of the abjected that cunningly turns the social "weight" of the powerful against themselves. Or, to use another image: Aesop has an uncanny knack for finding the Archimedean point that allows him to tip the world of the powerful on its head.[99] And just as his skilled use of what is available at hand makes him a Rube Goldberg culture hero for those who feel themselves disempowered, so his ability to extort the self-incrimination of the powerful functions as a wish-fulfillment fantasy (or

---

[97] This is particularly true in the version preserved in *P.Ross.Georg.* I 18, which reads ⟨Ἀπόλλω⟩νος συνεργοῦντος in place of G's Ἀπόλλωνος μηνίοντος in ch. 127. *Vita W* mutes the pattern of Aesop's forcing his opponents to bear witness against themselves in this case by replacing Aesop's adjuration of Apollo to witness with a bland invocation of the gods in general (θεοὺς μαρτύρομαι, *Vita W*, ch. 142)—so, notice, *Vita W* preserves the theme of "witnessing" but not Aesop's special skill of leveraging an opponent's cooperation.

[98] While Holzberg (1992b.46–47, 2002.82–83) notices the repeated pattern of Aesop's false accusations for theft, he does not note that, in both instances of this pattern at the beginning and end of the *Life*, Aesop in response forces his opponents to bear witness against themselves. The occurrence of this latter repeated pattern vitiates Holzberg's claim that (paradoxically) the mute Aesop triumphs at the beginning, while the sage Aesop fails at the end—and with it, undermines his moralizing reading of the end of the *Life*. The same critique applies to Dillery 1999.280. In addition, this pattern of Aesop's ability to force his opponents to bear witness against themselves or their own interests makes unnecessary the argument of Nagy 1979.279–90, 301–8, that Apollo is simultaneously maleficent and beneficent in his relation to Aesop in the *Life*.

[99] Cf. de Certeau 1984.xviii–xx, 34–39 on the difference between the "strategies" of the dominant order and "tactics": "The space of a tactic is the space of the other. Thus it must play on and with a terrain imposed on it and organized by the law of a foreign power.... It does not, therefore, have the options of planning general strategy and viewing the adversary as a whole within a district, visible, and objectifiable space. It operates in isolated actions, blow by blow. It takes advantage of 'opportunities' and depends on them, being without any base where it could stockpile its winnings, build up its own position, and plan raids. What it wins it cannot keep. This nowhere gives a tactic mobility, to be sure, but a mobility that must accept the chance offerings of the moment, and seize on the wing the possibilities that offer themselves at any given moment. It must vigilantly make use of the cracks that particular conjunctions open in the surveillance of the proprietary powers. It poaches in them. It creates surprises in them. It can be where it is least expected. It is a guileful ruse" (quotation from p. 37).

how-to guide) for the marginal or weaker members of society. And just as we saw an analogy between the former skill and the ordinary events and humble animal characters of fable, so we might see this latter ability as akin to the peculiar way fables achieve their effect in context. For as I suggested in the previous chapter, Aesop's indirect and fabular style of speaking persuades by allowing its (more powerful) audience itself to deduce the fable's relevance and point. Where fable works positively, Aesop's coercion of assent or self-incrimination works negatively, but still locates the decisive moment of pivot—of acquiescence—with the interlocutor rather than with Aesop himself. Thus these patterns, already characteristic of the mute Aesop at the beginning of the *Life*, perhaps help explain why at a certain point Aesop became *the* fable-maker (ὁ λογοποιός), the narrative of whose life figures both the humble form and the peculiar efficacy of this modest popular genre.

Chapter 5

THE AESOPIC PARODY OF HIGH WISDOM

IN THE TWO PREVIOUS CHAPTERS, we have marshaled the dispersed and fragmentary evidence for Aesop as a sage, participating in a pre- or nonphilosophical tradition of *sophia*. We have seen Aesop hobnobbing with the Seven Sages at the court of kings and tyrants; Aesop saving his city from crisis with wise counsel; Aesop engaged in a sage's pilgrimage at the end of his life; and even Aesop assimilated to the Near Eastern sage Ahiqar in what seems like a pan-Mediterranean confluence of wisdom traditions.

This popular representation of Aesop as a contender or participant in the sphere of *sophia* accounts, in turn, for his occasional appearances within a philosophical tradition that inherits (or, perhaps better, appropriates) elements of this prephilosophical system of high wisdom. Thus, for example, Aristotle in the *Rhetoric* refers to Aesop defending a Samian demagogue in court by the use of an apposite fable (*Rhet.* 2.20, 1393b22–33).[1] Or again, consider Lysippus's statue group of the Seven Sages together with Aesop—the monument that ostensibly inspired Agathias's sixth-century CE epigram (quoted in chapter 3). There is also Socrates' choice to versify the fables of Aesop while in prison awaiting his execution (as mentioned in *Phd.* 60d–61b) and the intriguing fact that Demetrius of Phaleron wrote a book about the Seven Sages, and also produced the earliest known prose compilation of Aesop's fables.[2] All this is evidence for a high philosophical tradition that refers glancingly to Aesop, but also, in a sense, domesticates him.[3] Indeed, a fit emblem for this tradition (which

---

[1] Cf. Aristotle fr. 573 Rose (= fr. 591, 1 Gigon)—a report in the Scholia to Aristophanes' *Birds* that "Aristotle in his *Constitution of the Samians* says that [Aesop] became famous by telling a fable" (καὶ Ἀριστοτέλης ἐν τῇ Σαμίων πολιτείᾳ εἰπόντα φησὶν αὐτὸν μῦθον ηὐδοκιμηκέναι). It is not clear whether this refers to the same anecdote as that in the *Rhetoric*, or to a different occasion of public speaking on Samos.

[2] For Demetrius of Phaleron as a scholarly collector of archaic wisdom traditions, see Acosta-Hughes 2002.173, Konstantakos 2005.40. For extended discussion of Aesop in the *Phaedo*, see Kurke 2006.13–19, 35–38, and chapter 6 below.

[3] It is Aesop's participation in the philosophical tradition that is the main focus of Jedrkiewicz 1997, Adrados 1999.659–83. Jedrkiewicz 1997 sees Aesop as a vehicle for a tradition of *spoudogeloion*—comic representation with an ultimately serious philosophical purpose, while Adrados 1999 regards the final form of the *Life* and fables as the products of Cynic philosophy. While there is much useful material in both these discussions, I think that their conceptualization of Aesop as entirely contained within the philosophical tradition is too limited; see chapter 4 above. Compare Martin 1996 on Anacharsis as a Cynic sage; for Martin, this tradition predates its Cynic appropriation.

effectively puts Aesop in his place) is Plutarch's representation in his *Banquet of the Seven Sages*; there we are told that the fabulist was "seated on a low chair next to Solon, who reclined above him" (καὶ παρῆν ἐπὶ δίφρου τινὸς χαμαιζήλου παρὰ τὸν Σόλωνα καθήμενος ἄνω κατακείμενον, Plut. *Banq.* ch. 4, 150a).[4]

At the same time, I have suggested that Aesop's relation to the system of *sophia* is oddly double; throughout his tradition and still in the preserved *Life*, Aesop seems to participate in the field of high wisdom and also to critique or parody it from below. Other scholars have noted elements of critique or parody in the *Life of Aesop*: thus Holzberg, Hägg, and especially Winkler have argued for Aesop's comic subversion of the pretensions of Hellenistic or Roman imperial philosophers and academicians.[5] While I agree with these scholarly assessments, I would extend the scope of Aesop's parody behind or beyond philosophy to a more broadly diffused cultural system of *sophia*. And while I have tried to suggest that the low Aesopic parody of high wisdom may in fact have antedated Herodotus (and may partly account for the historian's displacement of Aesop from a scene of sage advising), it bears emphasizing that we have no way of fixing this tradition in time. Beyond the narrow circles of academic philosophy, the age-old patterns of *sophia* endure—for much of the population, the stochastic or improvisatory skills of political sagacity, verbal agility, and mantic or sacrificial expertise continue to be venerated as "wisdom."[6] Within this broader sphere of popular conceptualizations of *sophia*, Aesop plays at the margins, a vehicle or focalizer for parodic commentary and critique.

Having now also considered what is distinctive about Aesop's *sophia* in the previous chapter, we are in a better position to understand what I have characterized as his odd double relation to the wisdom tradition. For insofar as Aesop embodies a distinctive *sophia* of the abjected and disempowered, the Aesop tradition contests the established forms of high wisdom; thus we might say that it has as its necessary concomitant parodic demystification of those forms. Such Aesopic parody often mobilizes coarse, bodily, and obscene representations to undermine the high tradition from below. Thus we see the violent or indecorous eruption of the bodily deployed to challenge the tradition of *sophia* and to

---

[4] For extended discussion of the symbolism of Plutarch's placement of Aesop and a reading of the *Banquet* as a whole, see Jedrkiewicz 1997; on the symbolism of the "low chair," see also Nagy 1990b.326n. 64, 335; Jouanno 2006.12.

[5] Winkler 1985.279–91; cf. Hausrath 1913; Perry 1936.14–15; Goins 1989.30; Jedrkiewicz 1989.136, 164–81; Holzberg 1992b.39n. 35, 74–75, 1993, 1996, 2002.83–84; Hägg 1997; Adrados 1999.659, 677–80; Jouanno 2005, 2006.39–43.

[6] For the popularity of the Seven Sages traditions starting in the Hellenistic period, see Konstantakos 2005.40–1; for later periods, cf. Diogenes Laertius's collection of material dating from the second or third century CE (D.L. 1.13, 22–108); the second-century CE wall paintings of the Seven Sages preserved in a tavern in Ostia (for more extended discussion of which, see section II below); and several late-antique floor mosaics of the Seven Sages from all over the Mediterranean (on which, see Studemund 1890). For the continuing popularity of Aesop in the first and second centuries CE, cf. Jouanno 2006.13–14.

deny its practitioners' claims to otherworldly sources of authority (whether divine or ancestral).[7] From their claimed status as mediators between this and another world, the practitioners of *sophia* are reduced and located in the realm of brute meat. At the same time, the Aesopic parody often works by exposing how such claims to high wisdom endorse and enable inequitable power relations and the oppression of the weak by the strong.

I. Demystifying *Sophia*: Hesiod, Theognis, and the Seven Sages

Thus I will consider here what I have termed parody of the high wisdom tradition, which is mainly to be found in the prose *Life of Aesop* and popular accounts connected with it. This complementary distribution is itself significant: reputable texts give us only the sage Aesop (and that only in somewhat muted form), while the anonymous, open tradition of the *Life* contains both, but emphasizes the Aesop who parodies, critiques, and demystifies high *sophia*. Indeed, since all the episodes I will consider in this chapter occur in both G and W, and on occasion also in the late papyri, we must assume that they belong to the common tradition from which all these textual instantiations derive. In this section I will consider in turn the dialogue between the Aesop legend and three different avatars of the tradition of high wisdom I described in chapter 2: Hesiod, Theognis, and the Seven Sages. Taken together, these episodes will reveal the lineaments of an Aesopic critique of ritual prohibitions, bird lore, the symposium and its didactic traditions, and (perhaps most prominently) the mystified exchanges of sacrifice.

IA. Hesiod

The relevant Hesiodic text is the *Works & Days*, and more specifically the detailed religious and ritual prescriptions of the last forty or so lines of the *Works*, before the poem turns to the *Days* (*WD* 724–64). The great German philologist Ulrich von Wilamowitz-Moellendorff long ago proposed athetizing most of this section as popular superstition unworthy of our poet, while M. L. West defended it in his edition, observing that "superstition is instilled by upbringing."[8] In a touching personal testimonial, West asserts,

> I have read the rest of [Hesiod's] work and am unable to find in it anything that might suggest he was a man who would pee at the sun, copulate after a funeral, cut his nails at a feast, or wash in a woman's bath-water with equanimity.[9]

---

[7] For Aesop's potent bodily critique, cf. Winkler 1985, esp. 280–82; Patterson 1991.22–26.

[8] Wilamowitz-Moellendorff 1928.124–30, 132–33 (Wilamowitz would retain *W&D* 695–705, 707–23, 760–64, while rejecting 706 and 724–59); see the counterarguments of West 1978.329–30, 333–34 (quotation from p. 333).

[9] West 1978.333.

Preferable to the biographical approach of both these commentators, in my opinion, is the comparative, genre-based reading of Gregory Nagy:

> As the *Works and Days* proceeds, the advice becomes more and more meticulous: for example, one must not cut one's nails at a "feast of the gods" (742–743). Or again, a man must not urinate while standing up and facing the sun (727), or in a road (729), or into rivers or springs (757–758). We may compare the parallel advice in the Indic *Law Code of Manu*. . . . The legal traditions of the Indic peoples are clearly cognate with those of the Greeks, and in this connection it is especially interesting to observe the uses of *memnêménos* 'being mindful' at *Works and Days* 728, in the specific context of the injunctions now being considered. . . . The [Indo-European] root *men-/ *mneh$_2$- of *memnêménos* recurs in the Indic name *Mánu-*, meaning 'the mindful one': this ancestor of the human race gets his name (which is cognate with English *man*) by virtue of being 'mindful' at a sacrifice. Manu is the prototypical sacrificer, whose sheer virtuosity in what Sylvain Lévi has called "the delicate art of sacrifice" confers upon him an incontestable authority in matters of ritual.[10]

Following Nagy, I would suggest that part of the importance of this section is the way in which it brings to the forefront the religious dimension of *sophia* as ritual expertise. Thus it is significant that the designation θεῖος ἀνήρ for one who meticulously practices ritual correctness occurs only here in Hesiod, and that many of the rules and prescriptions we find in this section show up also in the Pythagorean *acusmata*.[11] But I would add to Nagy's genre-based justification the issue of power: mastery of specific ritual prescriptions endows the θεῖος ἀνήρ or one who knows with special authority and status within his community (think of the Brahman or Pythagorean adept). Thus paradoxically, I would turn Wilamowitz's formulation on its head: this is not popular superstition, too low and debased for our classy, literate poet; it is rather part of the weaponry of the elite, enabling them to exert and maintain social control through privileged religious knowledge and practice.[12] And this is precisely why, I suggest, such religious prescriptions and ritual practices would come in for parody from below.

But I focus on this section of the *Works & Days* for the simple reason that the Aesop tradition seems to contain three extensive parodies of prescriptions that occur in these forty lines. (This is partly an accident of preservation: if we still had texts like the Hesiodic *Ornithomanteia*, *Melampodeia*, or *Cheirōnos Hypothēkai*, we might well find specific parodies of their elements as well.) I

---

[10] Nagy 1990a.70.

[11] See Bieler 1967 on the concept of the *theios anēr*; and Currie 2005.172–200 for its currency in the fifth century BCE and earlier. See Burkert 1972.166–90 on the Pythagorean *acusmata* as the oldest strand in the Pythagoras tradition and their frequent overlap with age-old ritual prescriptions.

[12] Thus the issue is not authenticity, but the cultural/ideological work this section of the poem can be understood to do. On the power issues, see Burkert 1972.118–20, 132–33 and Detienne 1996.

would emphasize that I am not claiming a narrow literary intertextuality between Hesiod's ritual injunctions and their Aesopic parody. I am instead envisioning an ongoing dialogue of two more or less fluid traditions. Thus I assume that this forty-line segment of the *Works & Days* is the tip of the iceberg, as it were—representative of a vast store of specific ritual rules and prohibitions that circulated as authoritative *sophia* within ancient Greek culture. On this model, it is somewhat accidental which specific prescriptions are preserved, though we might imagine it is those of particular importance. And, of course, whether or not they are authentically "Hesiodic" becomes entirely irrelevant, except insofar as Hesiod's putative authorship gives them added cultural authority.

First, let us consider the set of injunctions that contains the phrase θεῖος ἀνήρ (*WD* 727–32):

μηδ' ἄντ' ἠελίου τετραμμένος ὀρθὸς ὀμείχειν·
αὐτὰρ ἐπεί κε δύῃ, μεμνημένος, ἔς τ' ἀνιόντα,
μηδ' ἀπογυμνωθείς· μακάρων τοι νύκτες ἔασιν·   730
μήτ' ἐν ὁδῷ μήτ' ἐκτὸς ὁδοῦ προβάδην οὐρήσεις   729
ἑζόμενος δ' ὅ γε θεῖος ἀνήρ, πεπνυμένα εἰδώς,
ἠ' ὅ γε πρὸς τοῖχον πελάσας ἐυερκέος αὐλῆς.

> Do not urinate standing upright, turned toward the sun; and when it has set, being mindful, till its rising, do not do it uncovered at all—for the nights belong to the blessed ones. And do not urinate in the road, nor off the road while walking. But a godly man at any rate, one who knows sensible things, [does it] squatting or when he has approached the wall of the well-fenced courtyard.

Here I follow the suggestion of M. L. West in transposing lines 729 and 730; this gives a better construction for αὐτάρ and a more logical sequence for the clause μακάρων τοι νύκτες ἔασιν. A by-product of the transposition is that the prohibition against urinating in the road or right off the road as you're walking becomes an absolute prohibition rather than just something you shouldn't do at night. And this seems appropriate given the parallel from the Indic *Laws of Manu* cited by West (4.45–50), "Let him not void urine on a road . . . nor while he walks or stands, nor on reaching the bank of a river. . . . Let him never void faeces or urine facing the wind or fire, or looking towards a Brahman, the sun, water or cows. He may ease himself . . . wrapping up his body and covering his head." Of particular interest is the prohibition against urinating in the road, which from the parallels looks to be very old. As West observes, the rule presumably exists to prevent the pollution of others; for the same reason, many cultures ban menstruating women from the common paths.[13]

---

[13] For full discussion of textual issues and parallel prohibitions, see West 1978.334–36.

I would like to juxtapose Hesiod's prohibition with an episode in the *Life of Aesop*. The pompous philosopher Xanthus has just purchased Aesop at a slave market in town and is hurrying home to present the new-bought slave to his wife (*Vita* G, ch. 28; shortened version in W):

> And Aesop followed him. And when it was the hottest hour and the sun was at its zenith and the road was deserted because of the heat, Xanthus girt up his garments and began to urinate as he walked. And Aesop seeing it was annoyed. Then having laid hold of him from the part of his cloak thrown over his shoulder, he tugged at him and he says, "Sell me [now], since you certainly won't put up with my running away." And Xanthus [says], "Aesop, what's happened to you?" Aesop says, "Sell me—I can't be your slave." Xanthus: "Some one of those men accustomed to overturn well-established households has entirely carried you off; someone has approached you and slandered me to you, abusing me as bad to my slaves or a drunkard or a [slave]-beater or dyspeptic or irascible. Don't pay attention to slanders; slander that's sweet to hear provokes a man in vain. For such are the significant signs about me." Aesop: "Your own outpouring has slandered you, Xanthus; for when you yourself, the master, not out of fear of anyone, lest going into the house you get trial of blows or you have to submit to the punishment of bonds or more terrible necessity, but though you have complete authority over yourself, you haven't allowed [even] a half-hour's pause for the constraints of nature, but you urinate as you go—what then must I, the slave, do when I've been sent for an answer—short of shitting entirely on the fly?" Xanthus: "Because of this you're troubled?" Aesop: "Very much so." Xanthus: "Wishing to escape three base things I urinated while walking." Aesop: "What are these?" Xanthus: "The boiling of the earth, the bitterness of the urine, and the scorching beam of the sun." Aesop: "How's that?" Xanthus: "You see that the sun stands in mid-heaven and has burned the earth with its heat; whenever I stand still and urinate, the ground seething burns my feet, and the bitterness of the urine runs up to my nostrils, and the sun scorches my head. Wishing to escape these three things I urinated as I walked." Aesop: "OK, you've persuaded me, you've clearly explained your purpose. Just keep walking then." Xanthus: "I hadn't realized I'd bought a master for myself."

The rueful observation that ends this episode—Xanthus's "I hadn't realized I'd bought a master for myself"—recalls several anecdotes told about Diogenes the Cynic sage when he is sold into slavery.[14] But here, oddly, it is *Xanthus* rather than *Aesop* who plays the role of Diogenes, insofar as he rejects ossified convention in favor of the rationality of natural law. (As a parallel for Xanthus's eminently reasonable justification for urinating while walking, we might recall

---

[14] Cf. D.L. 6.29: "Menippus in his *Sale of Diogenes* tells how, when he was captured and put up for sale, he was asked what he could do. He replied, 'Govern men.' And he told the crier to give notice in case anybody wanted to purchase a master for himself" (trans. Hicks 1959); cf. also D. L. 6.30, 6.36.

Diogenes' response when reproached for masturbating in the agora: "I only wish I could satisfy my hunger by rubbing my belly," D. L. 6.45).[15]

But it is an earlier moment in this episode that interests me here—a kind of anecdotal *para prosdokian*.[16] When we first hear that Aesop becomes annoyed at Xanthus's urinating while he walks, we are, I suggest, supposed to think of the religious prohibition. That is, we are meant to think that Aesop, who has only recently had his speech restored because of his pious treatment of a priestess of Isis, is himself a *theios anēr*, prevented by religious scruple from serving a man who unthinkingly violates this age-old taboo. But as we soon realize from Aesop's response, his annoyance has nothing to do with religious scruple; it is instead all about the unequal power relations of master and slave. When even the master, who "has complete authority over himself," won't take the time to turn off the road, that bodes ill for the slave. In Aesop's vivid formulation, the slave then will have to "shit while flying."[17]

The structure of the anecdote thus pulls us up short, first encouraging us to think of the religious prohibition and then offering a completely different motivation for Aesop's dismay. By doing so, it forces us to reflect on the religious taboo and effectively demystifies it; it is only an issue of labor and leisure, not of pollution and religious feeling. *Not* urinating while walking is simply the privilege of those who enjoy freedom and self-possession, while society's powerless and abjected cannot afford the luxury of such ritual punctiliousness.

In another moment of specific advice from the same section of the *Works & Days*, Hesiod warns (*WD* 746–47),

μηδὲ δόμον ποιῶν ἀνεπίξεστον καταλείπειν,
μή τοι ἐφεζομένη κρώξῃ λακέρυζα κορώνη.

When building a house, don't leave it unfinished, lest a screaming crow sit upon [the roof] for you and caw.

As West notes, authors of the classical period generally consider the cawing of crows an omen of bad weather, while Aelian reports that "the voice of a single

---

[15] For Diogenes' consistent valorization of the rationality of nature in preference to mere convention, see Long 1996. For parallels between Diogenes the Cynic and Aesop, see Zeitz 1936.230–33; Jedrkiewicz 1989.116–27; Adrados 1999.664–65, 673–81; on this anecdote and Xanthus's punch line in particular, Jedrkiewicz 1989.117–18, Jouanno 2006.21 (Jedrkiewicz and Jouanno note but offer no explanation for the fact that Xanthus is here playing the usual Diogenes role).

[16] *Vita* W actually omits Xanthus's Diogenes punch line, demonstrating that it is not really necessary for the effectiveness of the joke.

[17] I do not regard it as a compelling counterargument (as one audience member once objected to me) that Hesiod's prescriptions are already very bodily. For the Hesiodic prescriptions are precisely intended to contain and put the body in its place (hence they are very often about *not* doing things: *not* cutting one's nails at a feast of the gods; *not* having sex after a funeral; *not* bathing in a woman's bath water). The Aesopic episodes, by contrast, deploy the body very differently, for here the bodily erupts or intrudes indecorously, where it does not belong.

crow is a bad omen for a wedding, crows being on the whole remarkably faithful to their mates."[18]

Against the backdrop of this kind of bird lore, I would like to read another episode from the *Life of Aesop* that I considered briefly in the previous chapter (*Vita* G, ch. 77; slightly shorter version in W):

> Xanthus says to Aesop, "Since I'm a reader of bird-signs (οἰωνιστής), go outside and see if there's any troublesome bird in front of the gateway. If you see a pair of crows (δικόρωνον) sitting before the gate, call me; for this sign reveals festivity (εὐφροσύνην) for the one who sees it." Aesop then going out front by chance observes a pair of crows sitting in front of the gateway and he goes in and tells Xanthus, "Master, the moment is right for you to go out; for a pair of crows sits [there]." The Master: "Let's go." But as [Aesop] went away, one of the crows flew off, and the master approaching observes [only] one [crow] and says, "Accursed wretch, didn't I say to you, 'If you see a pair of crows, call me'? But you've called me when you saw a single crow (μονοκόρωνον)." Aesop: "One flew away, master." The master: "Now you've really made a mistake. Strip him. Bring the leather straps." He was assiduously flogged. And while he was still being beaten, there came a slave belonging to friends of Xanthus, inviting him to dinner. Aesop: "Master, you flay me unjustly." Xanthus: "Why unjustly?" Aesop: "Because you said that a pair of crows is a good and festive [omen]. I saw a pair of crows and while I was approaching and making it known to you, one of them flew off. But you, going out and seeing a single crow, got an invitation to dinner. And I, who saw a pair of crows, have gotten a beating. Surely then bird omens and signs are all in vain (εἰς μάτην)." And amazed at this too, Xanthus says, "Let him go, don't beat him anymore," saying that he will come to dinner.

On the one hand, this story follows a common pattern in the *Life*—of Aesop showing up his master, repeatedly exposing the hollowness of Xanthus's pretensions to rhetorical and philosophical "wisdom." On the other hand, this passage uniquely in the *Life* has Xanthus claim the special religious expertise of reading bird omens. Aesop then challenges that expertise, not only proving himself a better sign-reader, but ultimately debunking the validity of such interpretive activity *tout court* with his final dismissive observation.[19]

In the inversion of meaning of one and two crows and in the final dismissal of the whole enterprise, I suggest, we see the popular tradition of Aesop in dialogue with the kind of bird lore preserved in Hesiod's poem. And it is significant for the nature of this dialogue that the Aesop episode, like the story about urinating

---

[18] Quotation from West 1978.341. For the cawing of crows as an omen of bad weather, West cites Theophr. *Signs of the Seasons* 39; Aratus 949, 1022; Euphorion 89; for a single crow as a bad omen at weddings, Aelian *On the Nature of Animals* 3.9.

[19] Notice that the text here seems to endorse Aesop's position in saying that he saw the original pair of crows "by chance" (κατὰ τύχην). But it is also worth noting that the *Life* as a whole makes no effort to maintain consistency—either about Xanthus's claim to be able to interpret bird omens, or about the validity of bird omens overall (see discussion in chapter 4, section I above).

in the road, is ultimately all about the unequal power relations of master and slave. Who has the power to say what a bird omen properly means—the slave who reads it or the master who wields the whip? The slave may read the signs, but the master has the power to constitute the slave's future as he will. Thus notice that there is nothing seriously at stake here for Xanthus (in the end, he gets a dinner invitation), while the master's investment in a certain reading of bird omens can have life-or-death consequences for the slave. Those with power, we might say, constitute meaning, even if they do not constitute it just as they will.

Finally, there is a third prescription in this section of the *Works & Days* that seems to resonate with a whole tradition of Aesopic commentary, though the *Works & Days* passage is itself problematic and somewhat obscure. Very close to the end of this sequence of specific ritual injunctions, we find the lines (*WD* 755–56)

> μηδ' ἱεροῖσιν ἐπ' αἰθομένοισι κυρήσας
> μωμεύειν ἀΐδηλα· θεός νύ τε καὶ τὰ νεμεσσᾷ.

> And do not, when you come upon a burning sacrifice, balefully find fault with it: the god resents that too. (Trans. West 1988.59)

I follow M. L. West's text and translation of this passage; West explains the point of the prohibition as avoiding "criticiz[ing] the sacrificers for meanness."[20]

The phrase μωμεύειν ἀΐδηλα is in fact unparalleled, and West cites, but dissents from, an article by Noel Robertson arguing that we must understand ἀΐδηλα here in relation to its most common epic formula, πῦρ ἀΐδηλον. Robertson contends that the primary meaning of this phrase is "fire that makes invisible or consumes," and that the other epic uses of this obscure adjective (as an epithet modifying ἀνήρ or ἔργα) derive from this primary sense.[21] In Hesiod's line, Robertson notes, ἀΐδηλα occupies the same metrical *sedes* that it almost invariably has in the formula πῦρ ἀΐδηλον, and he suggests that we understand it as a *nomen actionis*, "'the consuming,' that is, the action of the fire" (as direct object of μωμεύειν). On this interpretation, Hesiod's admonition means, "If you are present when offerings are ablaze on the altar, do not carp at what is consumed; this too the god rather resents."[22] Even though he prefers to take ἀΐδηλα adverbially ("carp balefully"), West still endorses Robertson's argument that what is being criticized is the sacrificial allotment—what is offered to the gods on the fire and what is consumed by the sacrificial participants themselves:

> This is indeed the likeliest object of criticism at a sacrifice, whether on the ground that too much of the meat was being given to the gods (as Robertson assumes) or too

---

[20] West 1978.343–44, 1988.59, note p. 79.
[21] Robertson 1969.166–67.
[22] Quotations and translation from Robertson 1969.168 (reading mss' τι, rather than West's τε in l. 756).

little.... The latter suits a casual spectator (ἐπὶ ... κυρήσας), and those presiding were as likely to threaten the god's νέμεσις to avert such criticism as in the other case.²³

Thus, on either interpretation of μωμεύειν ἄϊδηλα, Hesiod's admonition functions as a warning against criticizing diverse local sacrificial practices. As we know from inscriptional evidence, different Greek communities allotted different parts and proportions of the sacrificial animal to the gods, the officiating priests, and the sacrificial "congregation" at large.²⁴ Here we find a general Panhellenic admonition to respect the diversity of epichoric practice, endorsed by the threat of the god's *nemesis*.

I suggested in chapter 1 that criticizing the idiosyncratic sacrificial practices and allotments of a particular community is precisely what Aesop does at Delphi—and the reason he is finally framed and killed as a scapegoat by the irate Delphians. In this instance, this particular aspect of Aesopic critique does not figure prominently in the *Life* (where Aesop ridicules the *greed* of the Delphians in general terms, but not their sacrificial practices). It does, however, surface in other remnants of the Aesop tradition (as we have seen); thus a scholiast to Aristophanes' *Wasps* reports:

> They say that Aesop, when he came once to Delphi, jeered at the Delphians because they did not have land from which they could support themselves by agricultural labor, but instead they waited around to make their living from the sacrifices of the god. And the Delphians, annoyed, secreted a sacred phiale in Aesop's luggage. And he—of course not knowing—set out on the road leading to Phocis, but [the Delphians] ran after him and, catching him red-handed, accused him of *hierosulia*.

And again, we have a second-century CE papyrus that preserves a brief account of the death of Aesop (*P.Oxy*. 1800):

> Whenever someone comes to sacrifice to the god, the Delphians stand around the altar, each one carrying a sacrificial knife concealed on his person. And when the priest has slain the victim and skinned it and removed [and apportioned] the innards, each of those standing around hacks off whatever share he can and departs, so that, on many occasions, the sacrificer himself departs without any share at all. Censuring this custom, Aesop mocked the Delphians, and the masses, enraged on account of this, stoned him and thrust him off a cliff.²⁵

Scholars (including Walter Burkert and Gregory Nagy) have been too quick, I think, to accept this latter narrative at face value as an objective account of

---

²³ West 1978.343–44.
²⁴ For local differences in sacrificial allotments as represented by inscriptional evidence, see Puttkammer 1912; Gill 1974; Ekroth 2008.
²⁵ Translation follows Perry's text; see discussion in chapter 1, section II.

Delphic sacrificial practice. I have suggested that it is, in fact, a deliberate parodic misrepresentation of Delphic sacrifice as antisacrifice—the dissolution of the sacrificial community into a group of solitary ravening beasts or brigands; not lawful sacrificial practice, but marauding *bōmolochia*. Indeed, this critique of Delphic sacrificial practice is not unique to the Aesop tradition—we find elements of it already in fragments of Old Comedy and proverbial sayings like "Delphic knife."[26]

Finally, I would contend that the critique of Delphic sacrifice we find in the Aesop tales, Old Comedy, and proverb is not merely the grumbling of hungry peasants who begrudge the amount of sacrificial meat dedicated to the god or claimed by his priests (as Robertson and West imagine the background to the Hesiodic injunction). It is also a political critique of inequitable power relations through their manifestation in the sacrificial code. At Delphi in particular (as we have seen), access to the god's oracle was controlled and regulated by Delphians and hedged round with sacrificial exactions. And the division of the sacrificial animals required for oracular consultation and Theoxeny gave a lion's share to the officiating Delphians—in marked contrast to the ideology of egalitarian sacrificial distribution that characterized the norm of civic sacrifice. In the stories told about him, Aesop skewers these sacrificial exactions and their inequitable distribution, parodically resignifying them as vandalism and *bōmolochia* and thereby provoking the Delphians to scapegoat him in turn.

I would note a structural similarity in the three instances where the Aesop tradition seems to interact with or comment on the kinds of ritual prescriptions we find in the *Works & Days*. In each case, the Aesop narrative works to expose the power inequity that lurks behind and often subtends a religious injunction. Thus, for the Aesop tradition, not urinating in the road and correctly reading bird omens are simply the prerogatives of the master, one "who has complete authority over himself," rather than the special religious expertise of the *theios anēr*. In like manner, "the god's *nemesis*" that prevents criticism of local sacrificial practice is exposed as mere cover, cloaking and justifying the greed and gluttony of the officiating authorities.

IB. Theognis

At this point, I would like to turn from the *Works & Days* to Theognidean sympotic poetry. Although they may seem to engage very different issues, both poetic corpora, I would contend, participate in a common tradition of *sophia* (as outlined in chapter 2 above). And while the Hesiodic tradition grounds its ritual prescriptions in divine authority, the Theognidea (as we shall see) prominently invokes the authority of ancestors—the unbroken chain of "good men"— to legitimate its teachings. Aesop in the *Life* challenges and undermines both

---

[26] For extended discussion and presentation of ancient evidence, see chapter 1, sections I and II.

these claims to authority by parodically transposing these wisdom traditions to the obscene realm of the body. We can see this clearly in one example of what I take to be an Aesopic parody of Theognidean didactic. With this example, we will move beyond the narrowly religious expertise of the Hesiodic prescriptions to the tradition of aristocratic, sympotic *hypothēkai* and their appropriation, in turn, by a Socratic philosophical tradition.

Toward the end of the *Life of Aesop*, when Aesop has already been framed and incarcerated by the irate Delphians, he is visited in his Delphic prison by a friend who reproaches him for his foolish behavior. The friend remonstrates (*Vita* G, ch. 130):

> Why did it seem best to you to insult them (ὑβρίζειν αὐτούς) in their own homeland and city—especially when you were in their power? Where's your education (ἡ παιδεία)? Where's your learning (τὸ φιλόλογον)? You have given advice (γνώμας) to cities and peoples—and have you become witless (ἄφρων) when it comes to yourself?[27]

Aesop responds with a fable (designated in both *Vitae* G and W as a λόγος; *Vita* G, ch. 131; this fable also occurs in *P.Ross.Georg.* I.18):

> A woman had a daughter who was an idiot. And she used to pray to all the gods that her daughter get some sense (νοῦν λαβεῖν), and on many occasions, the girl heard her as she was praying. And one time they went to the country. And the girl, leaving her mother behind, outside of the steading, saw an ass being violated by a man (ὄνον βιαζομένην ὑπὸ ἀνθρώπου), and asked the man, "What are you doing?" And he [said], "I'm putting some sense into her (νοῦν ἐντίθημι αὐτῇ)." And the idiot girl, remembering the prayer, said, "Put some sense in me too." But he, in his current luxurious state, refused, saying, "There is nothing more ungrateful than a woman." But she: "Don't give it a thought, sir, and my mother will thank you, giving you as much as you want as payment—since she's [always] praying that I have sense." And so he deflowered her. And overjoyed, she ran to her mother and said, "I have sense, mother." And her mother [said]: "How'd you get sense, child?" And the idiot girl told her, "A long red sinewy thing running in and out cast it into me."[28] And when her mother heard her daughter's account, she said, "O child, you've lost even the sense you had originally (ὦ τέκνον, ἀπώλεσας καὶ ὃν πρῶτον εἶχες νοῦν)." Likewise it's happened for me also, friend; for I lost even the sense I had originally when I came to Delphi." And weeping many tears, the friend left him.

What strikes us most forcefully on reading this fable (I think) is the incongruity of the obscene ancedote with the seriousness of its surround—the direness of

---

[27] It is worth noting that the shorter version of the friend's rebuke in *Vita* W effectively subsumes all three terms—ἡ παιδεία, τὸ φιλόλογον, and γνώμας—under the single rubric of σοφία.

[28] I retain the ms text of *Vita* G here (with Ferrari), rather than Perry's supplemented text (which Papathomopoulos 1990 follows); thanks to Mark Griffith for pointing out to me that the ms text is comprehensible without Perry's supplement.

Aesop's plight as he waits in his Delphic prison for execution. And indeed, scholars have been taken aback by the apparent gratuitousness of this anecdote in particular.[29]

I would suggest that one thing this episode enacts is a parody of aristocratic *hypothēkai* traditions like that of Theognis (a tradition that may perhaps be flagged by the friend's mention immediately before of Aesop's wise γνῶμαι).[30] Thus I would like to juxtapose Aesop's obscene fable with Theognis lines 31–38. These lines occur in our corpus of Theognis almost immediately after Theognis's "seal" and the programmatic couplet in lines 27–28:[31]

σοὶ δ' ἐγὼ εὖ φρονέων ὑποθήσομαι, οἷάπερ αὐτός
Κύρν' ἀπὸ τῶν ἀγαθῶν παῖς ἔτ' ἐὼν ἔμαθον.

But kindly disposed, I shall give you the advice, what sorts of things I myself, Cyrnus, learned from good men when I was still a child.

To judge from their prominent placement in the collection, lines 31–38 constitute some of the speaker's most significant advice to the boy Cyrnus:

ταῦτα μὲν οὕτως ἴσθι· κακοῖσι δὲ μὴ προσομίλει
ἀνδράσιν, ἀλλ' αἰεὶ τῶν ἀγαθῶν ἔχεο·
καὶ μετὰ τοῖσιν πῖνε καὶ ἔσθιε, καὶ μετὰ τοῖσιν
ἵζε, καὶ ἅνδανε τοῖς, ὧν μεγάλη δύναμις.
ἐσθλῶν μὲν γὰρ ἄπ' ἐσθλὰ μαθήσεαι· ἢν δὲ κακοῖσι
συμμίσγῃς, ἀπολεῖς καὶ τὸν ἐόντα νόον.
ταῦτα μαθὼν ἀγαθοῖσιν ὁμίλει, καί ποτε φήσεις
εὖ συμβουλεύειν τοῖσι φίλοισιν ἐμέ.

Know these things thus: and do not keep company with base men, but always stick to the good. And with them drink and eat, and with these sit, and be pleasing to these, whose power is great. For from noble men you will learn noble things. But if you mix with base men, you will destroy even the sense you have. Having learned these things, keep company with the good, and at some point you will affirm that I give good advice to my friends.

I would suggest that Aesop's fable here constitutes a deliberate parody of this kind of elite didactic poetry. Thus we might note that Aesop's explanation for

---

[29] Cf. (e.g.) Wiechers 1961.9n. 5, who finds the version in *Vita G* "ohne jeden Witz." Wiechers's argument is elaborated by Nagy 1979.283§6n. 1: "The point of the whole story depends on a misunderstanding by way of metathesis: **ónos** instead of **nóos**, the Ionic equivalent of **noûs**. The form **noûs**, which is what we read in the Koine of our attested *Vitae*, conceals the play on words and in effect renders the story unintelligible." Hansen 2002.251–55 regards Wiechers's theory as "unnecessary" for an understanding of the tale, pointing to cross-cultural parallels for the story, but also acknowledges that "the employment of the tale in the *Aesop Romance* is unusual for an Aesopic fable" (quotations taken from p. 254).

[30] For γνῶμαι as a generic marker for this tradition, see Kurke 1989.542n. 23.

[31] On the programmatic status of this couplet and the importance of the verb *hupothēsomai*, see Friedländer 1913.577–78.

how he got into his current mess exactly parallels Theognis's warning: *because* he's been associating with the Delphians (who are base), he's lost even the sense he originally had. Within the fable, the mother's words to the daughter, ὦ τέκνον, ἀπώλεσας καὶ ὃν πρῶτον εἶχες νοῦν, almost exactly parallel the Theognidean speaker's admonition to the boy (ἀπολεῖς καὶ τὸν ἐόντα νόον), while the fable obscenely literalizes Theognis's συμμίσγῃς.[32]

And that literalization illuminates the ways in which this is not simply an appropriation of the wisdom tradition but a parody thereof. By transposing advice originally offered by a man to a boy to a mother-daughter dyad, the fable makes it bodily and obscene since, of course, what the girl has lost is not her "mind" or "intellect," but the chastity and integrity of her body—her *sōphrosunē*, which for a woman inevitably inheres in her flesh.[33] By transposing the genders involved, Aesop's fable comically transmutes "mind" into body and thereby mocks the aristocratic obsession with purity of association.

As often with good parody, the savagely witty lampoon of the *Life* sends us back to the original with new eyes. For the Aesopic parody, with its foregrounding of the body, forces us to see the bodiliness implicit in but generally occluded from the Theognidean original. Thus the gender inversion and graphic depiction of sex in the Aesopic fable color our reading not just of Theognis's συμμίσγῃς but also (in retrospect) of καὶ ἄνδανε τοῖς. How, after all, is the boy going to "please good men"? And is there really then that much difference between the company of good men and base, if, in both cases, the boy gets his "wisdom" from a "long, red, sinewy thing running in and out"? That is to say, the Aesopic fable exposes an issue about the boy's bodily integrity and challenges from below the pederastic foundation of Theognidean didactic.

Indeed, the same obscene bodily deconstruction applies also to the poet's claim to represent in unbroken sequence the wisdom of the ancestors, for his claim to authority here retrojects the same pederastic relationship backward in time ("what sorts of things I myself, when I was still a boy, learned from good men," Thgn. 27–28). We might even be tempted to read this whole sequence along the lines of the analyses I've offered of the Hesiodic parodies, as again a demystification of inequitable power relations—here, the relations between man and boy in elite pedagogy. I think, though, that this would be to succumb to a modern impulse, since I do not find any sympathy for the idiot girl in the fable (who on this reading stands in for the elite boy in pederastic didactic). Instead, the only figure in the story who seems to receive any sympathy from

---

[32] The fable here, I think, also parodies Thgn. 429–38 (on the possibility of "putting in" noble wits). In addition, the man's assertion that "there is nothing more ungrateful than a woman" sounds very like a sentiment of the wisdom tradition: cf. Hes. *WD* 702–3, Semonides fr. 6 W (also for the positive version, cf. Thgn. 1225). But notice that this sentiment is used here to justify screwing an ass, which we might read as an obscene bodily parody of the ideal of χάρις/reciprocity in the high wisdom tradition.

[33] Cf. North 1966.1, Carson 1990.142–43: "feminine *sôphrosynê* always includes, and is frequently no more than, chastity" (quotation from p. 142).

the narrative is the poor ass, whose victimization is injected with pathos by the participle βιαζομένην. That is to say, the Aesopic narrator invites audience identification (if he invites it anywhere) with the absolute bodily and bestial entirely outside the pederastic circuit.

Finally, we might read the context and point of this parody more broadly, once we notice that Theognis's sympotic didactic was readily appropriated by a whole lofty discourse of elite philosophical education, figuring in the debate on the teachability of virtue. For these specific verses were much quoted in antiquity—they show up in Plato's *Meno*, twice in Xenophon, twice in Aristotle's *Nicomachean Ethics*, as well as much later in Clement and other authors.[34] One very revealing citation is Xenophon's use of these lines early in the *Memorabilia*, in the context of exculpating Socrates for the wrongdoing of his "disciples" Critias and Alcibiades. As part of his defense of Socrates, Xenophon anticipates a philosophical objection:

> But many self-styled lovers of wisdom may reply: A just man can never become unjust; a prudent man can never become wanton (ὁ σώφρων ὑβριστής); in fact no one having learned any kind of wisdom can become ignorant of it. I do not hold with this view. I notice that as those who do not train the body cannot perform the functions proper to the body, so those who do not train the soul cannot perform the functions of the soul: for they cannot do what they ought to do nor avoid what they ought not to do. For this cause fathers try to keep their sons, even if they are prudent lads, out of bad company: for the society of honest men is a training in virtue, but the society of the bad is virtue's undoing. As one of the poets says: "From the good shalt thou learn good things: but if thou minglest with the bad thou shalt lose even what thou hast of wisdom." ... To me indeed it seems that whatever is honorable, whatever is good in conduct (τὰ καλὰ καὶ τἀγαθά) is the result of training, and that this is especially true of prudence (οὐχ ἥκιστα δὲ σωφροσύνη). For in the same body along with the soul are planted the pleasures which call to her: "Abandon prudence, and make haste to gratify us and the body." (Xen. *Mem*. 1.2.19–20, 23, trans. Marchant 1979)

Several things here resonate with the Aesopic passage: first, Xenophon frames the quotation within a hypothetical father-son relationship;[35] second, the issue is specifically the boy's *sōphrosunē*; and third, Xenophon takes a lot of trouble

---

[34] Plato *Meno* 95d6; Xen. *Mem*. 1.2.20, *Sym*. 2.4; Arist. *NE* 1170a11–13, 1172a12–14; Clem. *Strom*. 5, p. 572 (I have drawn these citations from Bluck 1964.392).

[35] Cf. Xenophon's other citation of these Theognidean lines, which again occurs in a father-son context at *Symposium* 2.4 (Lycon and his son Autolycus). For Xenophon's use of Theognis, it is worth noting that Stobaeus (4.29.53) actually preserves a short text entitled Ξενοφῶντος ἐκ τοῦ περὶ Θεόγνιδος, which would seem to imply that Xenophon wrote a treatise on Theognis. Many scholars are reluctant to accept this possibility, since Stobaeus is our only witness: for arguments for and against authenticity, see Immisch 1888 and Persson 1915, respectively. West 1974.56 cautiously accepts the authorship of Xenophon or some other writer of the first half of the fourth century BCE and prints an excerpt from the Stobaeus passage at the beginning of his text of Theognis.

sharply to distinguish body and soul. The Aesopic parody, I have suggested, by flipping the genders effectively deconstructs this body-soul opposition, since the girl's *sōphrosunē* so patently *is* her bodily integrity.

But beyond the narrow correspondences here, I would suggest that the broader context is also significant and relevant for the Aesopic parody. What Xenophon is concerned with, after all, is the accusation, trial, and execution of Socrates by the Athenian demos. In light of this context, it is difficult not to read Aesop's exchange with his friend as he awaits execution in Delphi as a parody of the ultimate philosopher Socrates' last exchanges as he's in prison waiting to die (as depicted in such texts as Plato's *Crito* and *Phaedo*).[36] The *Phaedo*, in particular, represents Socrates propounding at great length the separability of body and soul, while it also gives us a glimpse of Socrates versifying Aesop's fables at the behest of a dream vision (*Phd.* 60c9–61b7). In the next several chapters, we will consider in detail the complex relation of the *Sōkratikoi logoi* of Plato and Xenophon to the Aesop tradition. In the meantime, we might read ch. 131 of the *Vitae* as Aesop's revenge within an ongoing dialogue of traditions. For here, Aesop deconstructs the Socratic body-soul opposition; violently reasserts the recalcitrant crudeness and bodiliness of the *prose* fable; and finally suggests by parodic reenactment that Socrates got just what he deserved. In Aesopic terms: as a philosopher, Socrates screwed his disciples; the Athenian demos responded by screwing him in turn. My mother always used to say, "Once a philosopher, twice a pervert." This was a saying that, as a child, I never understood, puzzled over, and ultimately collapsed for myself into a simpler message: A philosopher *is* a pervert. This is, I think, in essence Aesop's parodic riposte to the philosophical tradition and its appropriation of an older cultural system of *sophia*.

IC. The Seven Sages

Finally, I would like to consider one example of what I take to be Aesopic parody of the wisdom of the Seven Sages—a tradition that combines the religious element of the Hesiodic prescriptions with the sympotic setting of the Theognidea, while it remains extremely popular from classical Greece to late antiquity. It is often noted—and I have noted above in chapter 4—that there is a great deal of overlap between Sayings of the Seven Sages and those credited to Aesop.[37] In addition, in one case we find exactly the same ζήτημα solved by Aesop and one of the Sages. This is the challenge to "drink the sea," which in Plutarch's *Banquet of the Seven Sages* the Ethiopian king sends to Amasis, pharaoh of Egypt, as a "contest of wisdom" whose prize is "many villages and cities" in the

---

[36] Cf. Jouanno 2006.45–46 for a similar reading of this episode in the *Life* as a parody of Socrates' death scene.

[37] Cf. Zeitz 1936.234–39, 242–45; Kindstrand 1981.59n. 34, 60n. 35, 76, 136, 142, 154; Haslam 1986.154–55; Jedrkiewicz 1989.135–43, 1997; Holzberg 1992a.XIII, 1992b.62–69, 2002.79.

disputed territory between the two kingdoms (σοφίας ἅμιλλαν, Plut. *Banq.* ch. 6, 151b).[38] Amasis immediately dispatches a letter to Bias to solve the challenge, which the Sage readily does; he instructs the pharaoh to "declare to the Ethiopian to hold back the rivers that cast [their water] into the sea while he himself is drinking up the sea as it is now. For the order concerns this, not the sea as it will be later" (Plut. *Banq.* ch. 6, 151d). In the *Life*, Aesop resolves precisely the same challenge for Xanthus, who has foolishly gotten drunk at a symposium and, in response to a student's leading question ("Are all things possible for a man?"), has claimed that he himself can drink the sea dry. In his drunken befuddlement, Xanthus is tricked by the student into wagering all his property (including Aesop!) on the challenge (*Vitae* G + W, chs. 68–69). The next day, Aesop saves his (now hungover and repentant) master by instructing him to challenge his opponent "to close off all the mouths of all the rivers that flow into the sea, so that [he] will drink up the sea alone." As Aesop forecasts, these competing impossibilities cancel each other out, and the bet is dissolved (*Vitae* G + W, chs. 70–73).[39] Though the context of the challenge has descended here from the wisdom competition of kings to the antics of drunken philosophers, it is noteworthy that in both cases, the ζήτημα is posed at a symposium and that in both, a great deal of real property is at stake.[40]

But in addition to Aesop's participation as a sage in the lore of the Seven Sages, there is at least one instance in the *Life* where the particulars of an Aesopic wisdom performance transmute it from a mere allomorph of sage activity into a parodic reenactment. The saying that "the best and worst thing is the tongue" was often quoted in antiquity as the wisdom of one of the Seven Sages; we find it variously attributed to Thales, Bias, Pittacus, and Anacharsis in different sources. In particular, the story of this sage observation seems to be a special favorite of Plutarch's, for he tells it four times in almost identical language, though twice he attributes it to Pittacus of Mytilene and twice to Bias of Priene.[41]

---

[38] Notice how similar this contest of kings and its prize are to the Ahiqar tradition; Konstantakos 2004 argues for a common set of stories of Eastern kings engaging in contests of wisdom, and specifically traces Plutarch's story of Amasis's "riddle contest" with the king of the Ethiopians back to an Egyptian original that entered the Greek tradition much earlier.

[39] Notice the prominence of the theme of witnessing here, which is not in Plutarch's version: thus Aesop instructs Xanthus to set up a chair and table on the beach, draw a large crowd, and then "call [all the spectators] to witness" the exact terms of the wager (μαρτυρούμενος, *Vita* G, ch. 71). This mention of witnessing participates in the pattern we have noticed throughout the *Life*, of Aesop's skill at extorting witnessing or assent from the more powerful in public contexts (see discussion above, chapter 4, section IV).

[40] For the parallel between these anecdotes, cf. Zeitz 1936.236–37, Jedrkiewicz 1989.143, Konstanakos 2004.102–3, Jouanno 2006.20–21. Note that this challenge is immediately preceded at the symposium by Aesop's advice on the proprieties of drinking—advice that is nearly identical with that elsewhere attributed to Anacharsis (D.L. 1.103, Stobaeus 3.18.25; cf. Kindstrand 1981.114–15; *Apophthegmata* A26A–B, A27A–H).

[41] For the strong association of the saying that the tongue is "best and worst" with the Seven Sages, see Konstantakos 2004.98–100, Jouanno 2006.20–21. The saying is attributed to Anacharsis

One of these renditions occurs at the beginning of Plutarch's *Banquet of the Seven Sages*, where we are told as background to the challenge to "drink the sea" that Amasis had earlier posed a first trial of wisdom for Bias:

> "ἱερεῖον," εἶπεν, "ἔπεμψεν αὐτῷ, κελεύσας τὸ πονηρότατον ἐξελόντα καὶ χρηστότατον ἀποπέμψαι κρέας. ὁ δ' ἡμέτερος εὖ καὶ καλῶς τὴν γλῶτταν ἐξελὼν ἔπεμψεν· ὅθεν εὐδοκιμῶν δῆλός ἐστι καὶ θαυμαζόμενος."

> "The king," said he, "sent to Bias an animal for sacrifice, with instructions to take out and send back to him the worst and best portion of the meat. And our friend's neat and clever solution was, to take out the tongue and send it to him, with the result that he is now manifestly in high repute and esteem." (Plut. *Banq.* ch. 2, 146f, trans. Babbit 1956)

The *Life of Aesop* stages a very similar sequence, though with much comic elaboration:

> [51] The next day, Xanthus, having invited to dinner the students who had previously invited him, says, "Aesop, since I have invited friends to dinner, go away and cook whatever is good, whatever is useful in life." Aesop says to himself, "I'll show him not to give foolish orders." So he went to the butcher's shop and bought the tongues of sacrificed pigs (τῶν τεθυμένων χοιριδίων τὰς γλώσσας) and going home, he prepared them all—some boiled, some roasted, some seasoned. And at the appointed hour the guests are present. Xanthus says, "Aesop, give us something to eat." Aesop brings for each a boiled tongue, and put beside it vinegar. The students said, "Wow, Xanthus, even your dinner is crammed with philosophy—for nothing with you lacks loving attention to detail. For immediately, from the beginning of the meal, tongues are placed beside us."

> [52] And after they had drunk two or three cups, Xanthus says, "Aesop, give us something to eat." Aesop again set beside each of them a tongue, roasted with salt and pepper. The students said, "Divinely [and] beautifully [done], master, by the Muses! Since every tongue is sharpened by fire, and even more strongly through salt and pepper—for the salt mixes together with the bitterness of the tongue to reveal eloquence and bite." Xanthus again after they had drunk [some more] says for the third time, "Bring us to eat." Aesop brings for each a seasoned tongue. The students were saying one to another, "Democritus! I have gotten a tongue-ache from gnawing on tongues!" Another student said, "Is there nothing else to eat? Where Aesop toils, there's nothing good there." The students eating the seasoned tongues were overcome

---

at D.L. 1.105; cf. Kindstrand 1981.111 (*Apophthegmata* A20A–G). Plutarch cites the same, slightly longer version in *Mor.* 38b ("On Listening to Lectures"), *Mor.* 146f ("Banquet of the Seven Sages"), *Mor.* 506c ("Concerning Talkativeness"), and *Comm. on Hesiod's Works & Days, ad* l. 719; the former two citations attribute the wisdom to Bias, the latter two to Pittacus. Plutarch's oscillation between Bias and Pittacus is interesting, given that these are the two Sages who occur together at Hdt. 1.27 (for discussion of this passage, see chapter 3, section I).

with nausea. Xanthus says, "Aesop, give each of us a soup dish." Aesop set beside them a broth of tongues. The students were no longer stretching out their hands [for the food], saying, "This catastrophe is from Aesop. We are vanquished by tongues." Xanthus says, "Aesop, do we have anything else?" Aesop said, "We have nothing else."

[53] "Nothing else, accursed one? Didn't I say to you, 'If there is anything useful in life, if there is anything sweet, buy this'?" Aesop says, "I'm grateful to you for blaming me when there are learned men present. You said to me, 'If there is anything useful in life, if there is anything sweeter or greater, buy [it].' What then is more useful in life or greater than the tongue? Understand that through the tongue all philosophy and all education have been constituted. Apart from the tongue there is nothing—neither giving, nor taking, nor sale. But through the tongue, cities are set upright, beliefs and laws defined. If then all life is constituted through the tongue, nothing is stronger than tongue." The students said, "By the Muses, he speaks well. You were wrong, master." The students departed. All night long, they were suffering, seized by diarrhea.

[54] The next day, the students blamed Xanthus. Xanthus says, "Learned men, the fault was not mine, but that of my useless slave Aesop. But today I will render you a proper dinner and in your presence I will give him the order." And indeed, having summoned Aesop, he says to him, "Since it seems best to you to turn everything on its head [literally, to babble topsy-turvy], go to the market and if there is anything rotten, if there is anything bad, buy it." Aesop, having heard him and not at all perturbed, went to the butcher's shop and again bought the tongues of all the sacrificed pigs (τῶν τεθυμένων χοίρων). And he went home and prepared them for dinner. Xanthus, arriving at his house with the students, reclined with them. And after a toast, he says, "Aesop, give us something to eat." Aesop set beside each of them a pickled tongue and vinegar. The students said, "What is this—tongues again?" Xanthus turns pale. The students said, "Perhaps he wants our stomach[s] to recover from yesterday's diarrhea through the vinegar." And after they had drunk a couple [rounds], Xanthus says, "Give us something to eat." Aesop put beside each of them a roasted tongue." The students said, "Ugh, what is this? Is that idiot from yesterday again preparing weakness for us through tongues?"

[55] Xanthus says, "What is this again, you scum? Why have you bought these? Didn't I say to you, 'Go away to the market and if you find anything bad, anything rotten, buy this'?" Aesop said, "And what bad thing is there that is not through the tongue? Through the tongue enmities, through the tongue plots, ambushes, battles, animosities, quarrels, wars. Surely there is nothing worse than that most polluted tongue." (*Vita* G, chs. 51–55)

Beyond Aesop's baroque expansion of the Sage's terse message that the tongue is "best and worst" (an example of Aesopic *makrologia*?), I would like to focus on two peculiarities of the Aesopic version that expose and demystify the power inequities that here subtend the wisdom performance. The narrative makes clear that this exposure is, in some sense, the point of the whole episode by having Aesop say to himself at the outset, "I'll show him not to give foolish orders" (ἐγὼ αὐτῷ δείξω μωρὰ μὴ διατάττεσθαι, *Vita* G, ch. 51). In the first place, it is worth noting that in all four of Plutarch's renditions of the story, a king sends a sacrificial animal to the Sage *as a gift*; the Sage himself performs the sacrifice and sends the tongue back to the king as part of the division of sacrificial meat. I would contend that the sacrificial context is significant here, for it forms the basis for a gift-exchange relationship between Sage and king, wherein the latter's power is matched and reciprocated by the former's sacrificial expertise. Thus sacrifice is a mystified code, linked to gift exchange in a system that naturalizes the community and equality of the two "interlocutors" through the body of the sacrificed animal.[42]

Strikingly, the Aesopic version demystifies that sacrificial exchange: instead of the sacrificial allotment of meat, we have the butcher's shop; instead of gift, we have purchase. Nor do I think this is simply an unwitting reflection in the Aesop narrative of an inevitable diachronic process of commodification that took place in the "real world," since the narrative goes to some trouble to tell us (twice) that Aesop bought not just pigs' tongues at the butcher's, but *sacrificed* pigs' tongues (τῶν τεθυμένων χοιριδίων, *Vita* G, ch. 51; cf. ch. 54). This detail, so apparently gratuitous in the narrative, preserves the memory of the sacrificial context even as it exposes the "dirty secret" of sacrifice—that sacrificial meat is sold at all. We know from occasional references in inscriptions and other nonliterary sources that sacrificial meat was sold, but this is a fact that is almost never acknowledged in literary texts: high literature almost universally maintains the fiction that sacrificial meat is divided among the participating community rather than sold.[43] I would go so far as to suggest that the selling of

---

[42] For gift exchange and reciprocity as essential elements of the sacrificial system, see Davidson 1997.17–18, Parker 1998.

[43] For nonliterary evidence for the sale of sacrificial meat, see Drexhage 1997, Ekroth 2008.271; for the extreme paucity of literary references to the practice, cf. Davidson 1997.18: "Meat did find its way occasionally from the altar to the market but it is only represented there on very rare occasions." To my knowledge, the only references in Greek literary texts to the sale of sacrificial meat essentially prove the rule that this is a shameful or unsavory practice not normally mentionable within the decorum of high texts: thus, Theophr. *Char.* 22.4 characterizes the "illiberal man" (ἀνελεύθερος) as someone who will sell the meat from his daughter's wedding feast. Even more remarkable for its negative associations with the practice of selling sacrificial meat is Artemidorus *Oneirocritica* 5.3: "Someone dreamt that he brought forward his own wife as a sacrificial victim, that he offered her up, cut her flesh into pieces, sold them, and made a very large profit from them. In addition to this, he dreamt that he enjoyed what he had done and attempted to conceal the money he had collected [from the butcher's shop] in order to avoid the envy of the bystanders. This man prostituted his own wife and earned his living from her indecent activities. While her occupation was a profitable source of income for him, it deserved to be hidden" (trans. White 1975).

Indeed, the entire contribution of Isenberg 1975 is simply to point out that mention of the sale of sacrificial meat occurs in the *Life of Aesop*. Besides the *Life*, Isenberg knows of only three other passages in literary texts of the Roman period that mention the sale of sacrificial meat: Pliny *Epistles* 10.96.10; St. Paul I Corinthians 10:25 and 28 (all three referring to the refusal of Christians to buy

222 CHAPTER 5

sacrificial meat is a taboo topic in reputable Greek literature, because sacrificial participation and the distribution of meat therein so strongly symbolize the forging of community.[44] Against this background, Aesop's repeated purchases of sacrificial meat not only demonstrate that the tongue is the "best and worst"; they also explode the naturalized fiction of a sacrificial community of equals.

The second peculiarity in the Aesop version is related to the first: there is a relentless bodiliness to this narrative that prevents the unproblematic metaphorization of "tongue." Thus we have the proliferation of tongues (in contrast to the single tongue of Plutarch's narrative), as well as the comic specificity of all the different modes of preparation—boiled tongues, roasted tongues, tongues seasoned with salt and pepper. Most strikingly, there is the narrative report that the consumption of so many tongues gave the students diarrhea all night long (an extreme literalization, we might say, of tongues as "worst"). All these intrusions of the grotesque body keep forcing us back to the level of brute meat, and thereby disrupt the metaphorical message about the good and bad features of tongue (= language) in human life.[45] This disruption of the circuit of metaphor, I would contend, is related to the function of sacrifice, for sacrifice itself, to be efficacious, depends on a crucial metaphorization. By that, I mean a couple of different things. First, in general, the sacrificial victim functions as a *substitute*— in the place of—the sacrificer himself, as various theories of sacrifice argue.[46] But second, specifically for the Greek context, insofar as the body of the sacrificial victim *symbolizes* the whole sacrificial community, its corporeality is sublimated into *moirai* ("shares," "allotments") for the community and *timai* ("honors") for the divine recipients.[47] Thus, through the bodiliness of "tongues," the code of sacrifice is itself demystified and exploded in this anecdote, its component signs (the sacrificial animal and the human participants) reduced to the physicality of meat, eating, and shitting.

---

meat from sacrificed animals). Isenberg himself offers an entirely pragmatic explanation for why the *Life of Aesop* (*Vita* G) preserves this detail: a lavish public sacrifice would account for the large number of pigs' tongues available for Aesop to buy. But Isenberg's explanation does not take into consideration the close parallel with a Sage's wisdom performance, which must surely be relevant to this sequence in the *Life*.

[44] On sacrificial division symbolizing the civic community in the classical era, see Loraux 1981; Nagy 1985a; Detienne 1989, 1998; Davidson 1997.12–15, 290–92. We might also note as the flip side of this the argument of Davidson 1997.12–20, that fish can become the ultimate luxury items and commodities in Greek culture because they are *not* sacrificial animals. That is to say, sacrificial meat and commodities are conceived by Greek culture as mutually exclusive categories. Note that in Plutarch, the civic community has been replaced by the community of autocrat and Sage, but the relation of community members is still mystified as gift exchange.

[45] For the disruptive literalization of metaphor in this anecdote, see Patterson 1991.26.

[46] See Bloch 1992, building on (among others) Hubert and Mauss 1964 and Detienne and Vernant 1989; cf. Girard 1977.

[47] Cf. Pindar *Paean* 6, ll. 117–18 (as discussed in chapter 1, section III above).

In this context, we should recall Richard Martin's argument that the Seven Sages may originally have constituted a sacrificial *collegium*, as well as the intimate association we found in chapter 2 between *sophia* and religious—especially sacrificial—expertise.[48] As Martin observes:

> The "sympotic" strain in the stories of the Seven Sages (as in the tale of their banqueting together) would not, then, be a recent invention, but a relic of a much older context. This is to say, the setting of Plutarch's *Banquet of the Seven Sages* may be an expression of a continuing tradition, not just Plutarch's innovation. We can imagine that these learned specialists not only ate and drank but performed the sacrifice that began the meal. A communal, public form of the all-important sacrificial meal could, in turn, have been the original stage for the sages' "performance" of wisdom.[49]

Archaic or not, the performance of wisdom in a sacrificial context is precisely what we find in Plutarch's account of Bias, which thus entails another level of community or communion beyond that of Sage and king. Insofar as they are sacrificial experts, the Sages play a special role in mediating and enabling communication between human and divine. This claim to special otherworldly access and authority is also disrupted by the relentless bodiliness of the Aesopic version. For here, although Aesop's wisdom performance takes place at a symposium, the scene of sacrifice is explicitly *somewhere else*, so that there is no participation by Xanthus and his students in that ritual activity. Instead, the circuits of sacrifice, meant to forge both human community and human-divine communion, have been entirely displaced by the narrow focus on food preparation, consumption, and excretion.

Indeed, we may find traces of Aesop's parodic challenge to the sacrificial expertise of the Seven Sages in yet another anecdote in the *Life*. Again in the context of a symposium, the philosopher and his students are playing at ζητήματα ποικίλα ("complicated problems" to be solved, *Vita* G, ch. 47):

> One of the students says to the others, "Why is it that the sheep doesn't bawl when it's led to sacrifice, but the pig makes a great noise?" When no one could find a solution to the question, Aesop says, "Because the sheep has milk that is useful and hair to make it attractive, and because it is periodically shorn of the hair that weighs it down and again lightened by being milked, so when it is led away to sacrifice, not suspecting that it will suffer anything bad, it follows gladly and does not flee the iron when it is proffered. But the pig makes a great noise because of this—because it has neither useful hair nor milk. Appropriately then it bawls, since it knows that it's being led away for the use of its meat. The students said, "Clearly, by the Muses." (*Vita* G, ch. 48; similar version in W and cf. fable no. 85 Perry)

---

[48] See Martin 1998.121–24 (discussed above, chapter 2, section I).

[49] Martin 1998.123, and cf. Snell 1966b (arguing for a fifth-century poetic version of the Banquet of the Seven Sages).

Aesop here demonstrates a kind of sacrificial expertise, but it is somehow oddly askew to what we might expect from an archaic sage. Thus Epimenides, for example, knows and prescribes the correct sacrifices to purify the Athenians from the *miasma* of blood guilt after the debacle of the Cylonian conspiracy.[50] And while Aesop, too, is concerned with sacrifice and the different sacrificial animals, his focus here is entirely on the physical level of wool, milk, and meat. There is no space in Aesop's world for the metaphorical or symbolic value of different sacrificial animals as appropriate to different divinities or different communal crises. More peculiarly still, Aesop's solution (acknowledged by the students as "clearly" correct) focalizes from the point of view of the sacrificial animal, its fears and self-knowledge. This, I would contend, is an impossible position for the norm of efficacious sacrifice, which must treat the sacrificial victim as radically other to achieve its metaphorical sublimation.[51] And yet there is a certain consistency to the Aesopic position: just as we saw Aesop sympathizing with the ass in the fable of the idiot girl (*Vita* G, ch. 131), so here he identifies with the absolute bodiliness of the sacrificial animal. In both cases, of course, this is to speak from the position of society's utterly abjected—slaves and others who are by a common social fiction conceived as entirely bodily and therefore made the invisible ground on which the "higher" forms of culture can be erected.[52] Or in other terms: the traditional sage's sacrificial wisdom communicates "upward" with the divine by means of metaphorization, while Aesop's *sophia* communicates "downward" with the sacrificial animal through its insistence on the literal and bodily.

II. Aesopic Parody in the Visual Tradition?

I would like to conclude this chapter with two (Aesopic?) parodies of *sophia* in the visual tradition that seem to function analogously to the "literary" parodies I've already considered. As with the parodies embedded in our texts, the material remains span many centuries—from the mid-fifth century BCE to the era

---

[50] For Epimenides' prescription of purifying sacrifices, see Plato *Laws* 642d, D.L. 1.110, and cf. Plato *Sym.* 201d3–5, where Socrates claims that Diotima (characterized as *sophē*) delayed the plague by ten years by prescribing certain sacrifices for the Athenians.

[51] Cf. Bloch 1992 on the dynamics of sacrificial violence. I am indebted to Boris Maslov for calling my attention to this peculiarity of point of view (private conversation).

[52] Cf. Aesop's responses to Xanthus's questions in the slave market (*Vita* G, ch. 25): " 'Of what sort are you?' Aesop: 'Of flesh' (σάρκινος). Xanthus: 'I don't mean this, but where were you born?' Aesop: 'In the belly of my mother.' " Again, Aesop's responses explode the cultural fiction of ethnicity in favor of the local and the absolute bodily—the flesh of mother and son (on the absolute bodiliness of this exchange, see Patterson 1991.22–25). It is worth noting also that Aelian (*VH* 10.5) introduces this same ζήτημα and solution (responses of sheep vs pig as they're led away to sacrifice) as Φρύγιος οὗτος ὁ λόγος· ἔστι γὰρ Αἰσώπου τοῦ Φρυγός. It is as if the identification with the sacrificial animal can come only from a non-Greek, other position.

THE AESOPIC PARODY OF HIGH WISDOM   225

of Trajan or Hadrian (98–138 CE). (Indeed, if we accept the red-figure cup I will discuss as visual parody, it provides our single best piece of evidence for a parodic strand in the Aesop tradition dating all the way back to the fifth century BCE.) And in spite of the extreme chronological range represented by these two examples, I would like to juxtapose them here because they evince many similarities in theme and method of parody with each other and with the textual traditions.

The first is the tondo of an Attic red-figure cup found in Vulci, dated to the mid-fifth century, now in the Museo Gregoriano of the Vatican (fig. 5.1).[53] The interior of the cup shows a fox in animated conversation with a man who is drawn in the grotesquely disproportionate style of caricature. Both sit on outcroppings of rock and both have their mouths open, while the fox, seated on the right, gestures emphatically with his right front paw. The man, seated on the left, has an absurdly large head for his tiny body (whose form is masked by the cloak wrapped tightly around him) and holds an (oddly phallic) walking stick jutting forward. Neither figure is labeled, but Otto Jahn in 1847 suggested that this was a representation of Aesop in colloquy with one of his fable characters, the fox. This identification has generally been accepted by archaeologists and art historians, most recently by François Lissarrague.[54] Page duBois aptly characterizes the humor of this caricatured image:

> The humor of the cup arises from the contrast between the great size of the deformed human being, especially his enormous head, typical of caricatures, and the tiny body of his interlocutor, as well as from the dumb intensity of the human being, who attentively listens, seemingly recording the discourse of Mr. Fox as he helpfully, generously holds forth about something he knows well, carrying on like an experienced, skilled *rhetor* or storyteller.[55]

While I entirely agree with duBois that the image requires no further outside referent to achieve its comic effect, I would suggest that it can also be understood as parody of another very familiar representation—Oedipus's confrontation with the sphinx.[56] This scene has a fixed iconography, appearing more than twenty times in fifth-century Attic red-figure, with a characteristic form in

---

[53] Vatican, Museo Gregoriano Etrusco inv. 16552; Beazley attributes it to the Painter of Bologna 417 (*ARV*[2] 916, 183, *Para.*[2] 430, *Add.*[2] 304).

[54] See Jahn 1847.433–34, Schefold et al. 1997.86–87 fig. 21, Lissarrague 2000.137–38. On the caricature elements of the image, see also Swindler 1929.178; Herrmann 1949.435–37.

[55] DuBois 2003.171; cf. Lissarrague 2000.138: "The image of Aesop and of the fox is presented, in this context, not as an honorific portrait of the classical type, but as the depiction of a speech situation, an amusing allusion not only to the fabulist himself, but to the game of the fable, of the animal endowed with speech."

[56] Herrmann 1949.435 had already suggested that the caricatured figure in conversation with a fox on the Vulci cup represented a parody of the familiar scene of Oedipus and the sphinx. Herrmann, however, denied that the caricatured figure should be identified as Aesop, arguing instead that it represents a Cynic philosopher, specifically Phaedrus, the first-century CE composer of

Figure 5.1. Aesop(?) in conversation with a fox. Vatican, Museo Etrusco Gregoriano inv. no. 16552. Interior of Attic red-figure cup, attributed to the Painter of Bologna 417, ca. 450 BCE. Photo courtesy of the Vatican Museums.

which Oedipus is seated, specifically adapted for the tondi of cups.[57] Perhaps the most famous version is the name piece of the Oedipus Painter, a cup dated ca. 470 BCE, now in the Vatican (fig. 5.2).[58] Here Oedipus sits pensively on the left, legs crossed, with the paraphernalia of a traveler—short cloak, traveling hat

---

Latin fables in iambics. This identification is clearly chronologically impossible; Herrmann apparently assumed, because the cup was found in an Etruscan context, that it was a Roman artifact.

[57] According to Moret (1984.I.1), the type scene of Oedipus and the sphinx appears around 490/480 in Attic vase painting and entirely replaces two older type scenes (one of the sphinx carrying off a single male figure; the other of the sphinx with multiple Thebans). For a list of fifth-century Attic red-figure representations of the scene, see Moret 1984.I.49: Moret lists nineteen examples of the sphinx confronting a standing Oedipus (all on the exterior of containers of various shapes) and four examples of the sphinx with a seated Oedipus (two in the tondi of cups; two on the neck of containers). Moret (1984.I.55) specifically notes that "le type assis . . . a été créé pour la form du tondo."

[58] Vatican, Museo Gregoriano Etrusco inv. 16541; ARV^2 451, 1, 1654, $Para.^2$ 376, $Add.^2$ 242.

THE AESOPIC PARODY OF HIGH WISDOM   227

Figure 5.2. Oedipus in conversation with the Sphinx. Vatican, Museo Etrusco Gregoriano inv. no. 16541. Interior of Attic red-figure cup, attributed to the Oedipus Painter, ca. 470 BCE. Photo courtesy of the Vatican Museums.

(*petasos*), and staff. The sphinx sits above him on the right, perched on an Ionic column. The name ΟΙΔΙΠΟΔΕΣ (oddly plural) curves above the heads of the two figures, and the letters ΑΙΤΡΙ run in retrograde between them. Albin Lesky took the latter inscription to represent the last words of the sphinx's riddle: "Warum gerade diese Worte gewählt sind, ist klar: die drei Füsse sind das letzte Stadium des Rätselwesens, die Sphinx hat damit ihre Frage beendet, nun hat Oidipus das Wort."[59] Consonant with this interpretation, the sphinx's mouth is closed, Oedipus's lips just parted, as if he is about to formulate his response.[60]

---

[59] Lesky 1966.322n. 12. François Lissarrague informs me (private conversation) that a recent cleaning and examination of the cup reveal the letters ΚΑΙΤΡΙ (= καὶ τρι[) for the inscription running in retrograde between the two figures—a supplement that further supports Lesky's theory.

[60] On the image's representation of this crucial moment, poised between the posing of the riddle and its answer, see Moret 1984.I.50–51.

228   CHAPTER 5

Figure 5.3. Oedipus in conversation with the Sphinx. Museum für Regionalgeschichte und Volkskunde, Schloss Friedenstein Gotha, no. 80. Interior of Attic red-figure cup, attributed to the Veii Painter, 470–460 BCE. Photo: Lutz Ebhardt Photograf, courtesy of the Stiftung Schloss Friedenstein Gotha.

Other versions of the Oedipus-sphinx scene offer even closer parallels of detail for the image of Aesop in colloquy with a fox. Thus in another red-figure tondo, dated 470–60 BCE (now in Gotha; fig. 5.3), both Oedipus and the sphinx sit on outcroppings of rock, and much of Oedipus's body is covered by his cloak wrapped tightly around him.[61]

In these images, Oedipus functions as the human emblem of *sophia*, engaged in a contest of wisdom with the otherworldly, uncanny figure of the sphinx.[62]

---

[61] Schloss Friedenstein Gotha, no. 80; Beazley attributes it to the Veii Painter (*ARV*² 902, 36, *Para.*² 429).

[62] It is worth noting (as Moret 1984.I.2–3, 50–61 observes) that this scene of Oedipus's confrontation with the riddling sphinx is much more popular in the visual tradition than the later, tragic episodes of the saga. Cf. Keuls 1997.284: "The pictorial tradition, on the other hand, knows little of the killing of the father and the incestuous marriage of Oedipus and Jocasta, but concentrates on the confrontation of Oedipus and the sphinx; this theme is transformed, both earnestly and comically, into an emblem of man's eternal preoccupation with and awe of the female, and of the *powers of wisdom* and destruction both that she was thought to hold over men" (my italics). Cf. also the

And, especially in the name vase of the Oedipus Painter, his triumphant wisdom is figured and matched by his bodily perfection—he is the very paradigm of the mature Greek male, the "classical body" par excellence. In this respect, it is significant that, although the sphinx's last words hover in the air between them, she sits with mouth closed, while Oedipus's lips are just slightly, discreetly parted; thus both maintain a certain serenity and composure of form. It is further striking that, in most versions of the scene, the sphinx occupies a higher register, so that Oedipus must gaze upward at the daemonic creature.[63]

In radical contrast to this ideal figuration of human *sophia*, Aesop's form is misshapen and grotesque. It is perhaps appropriate for the clever craftsman of fables that his head is out of scale to his body, but the image also clearly represents his ugliness. His hair is receding, his forehead lined with wrinkles, his nose overlarge and protuberant, his beard scraggly. And perhaps in a gesture toward Aesopic *makrologia* or garrulity, both figures have their mouths wide open, in contrast to the largely closed forms of Oedipus and the sphinx.[64] Again, there is a witty appropriateness in the artist's replacement of sphinx with fox, that Aesopic embodiment of *mētis*. But where Oedipus gazes upward toward the daemonic, Aesop's animal interlocutor draws his gaze downward. Thus even as the Aesop "portrait" reenacts the Oedipus scene in its form, both the content and the style of the image mark it as parody.[65]

There is a second parodic representation I would like to read as "Aesopic," although it does not actually include the figure of Aesop. Still, in many other respects, it conforms to the lineaments of what we have seen of the Aesopic parody of high wisdom. This is a Roman wall painting of the Seven Sages in a tavern in Ostia, dated to the Trajanic or Hadrianic era (Terme dei Sette Sapienti, Ostia III x 2, Room 5).[66] The Seven Sages were originally disposed on three

---

second-century CE funerary frieze from Hermoupolis, in which Oedipus is attended by a figure labeled ZHTHMA as he confronts the sphinx (Moret 1984.I.120; Cat. 157).

[63] Cf. Moret 1984.I.52: "Mais contrairement aux autres dragons ou serpents, la Sphinx n' est jamais localisée dans une caverne ou quelque autre anfractuosité. Elle réside sur les hauteurs, colonne ou rocher, montagne ou Acropole."

[64] Cf. Stallybrass and White 1986.22 on the closed perfection of the "classical body": "The classical statue has no openings or orifices whereas grotesque costume and masks emphasize the gaping mouth, the protuberant belly and buttocks, the feet and the genitals.... The grotesque body is emphasized as a mobile, split, multiple self, a subject of pleasure in processes of exchange; and it is never closed off from either its social or ecosystemic context. The classical body on the other hand keeps its distance. In a sense it is disembodied, for it appears indifferent to a body which is 'beautiful', but which is taken for granted."

[65] We should also note that the Oedipus-sphinx type scene seems to have inspired several different forms of parodic reimagining: for discussion, see Moret 1984.I.139–50 with his catalog figs. 188–96; cf. Keuls 1997.285–86 with her figs. 55–58.

[66] For description of the room and wall paintings in this and the following paragraphs, I rely heavily on Calza 1939; for excellent recent discussions, see Clarke 2003.170–80, 2007.125–31. Calza 1939, Picard 1947, and Schefold et al. 1997.380 date the wall paintings to the Hadrianic era; Meiggs

sides of the corner room of a large complex, which was open on its fourth side through an unusually broad aperture to the via della Calcara to the east.[67] Thus there were two figures of Sages on each of the side walls and three along the back wall of the original chamber. But at some later point, the whole complex was converted into baths, and the tavern into a changing room. This renovation entailed serious alterations to the structure, including a door put into the back wall, entirely obliterating one of the figures; whitewashing over the others; and a bench or shelf installed around the walls that largely destroyed a lower register of wall painting below the figures of the Sages.[68]

The wall paintings were discovered and published in the 1930s.[69] Under the whitewash three seated figures were found—each about ninety centimeters tall, painted in a largely monochromatic chestnut brown, each floating in space with a thick green line to articulate the ground level. Their chairs, clothes, and beards are recognizably Greek and Hellenistic, which has led scholars to think that the artist copied some earlier image (perhaps another wall painting or a pattern book).[70] Each of the three figures is labeled in a large and even Greek cursive hand (in black), with the name on the left of the figure and the ethnic on the right: in order from the leftmost figure, ΣΟΛΩΝ ΑΘΗΝΑΙΟΣ; ΘΑΛΗΣ ΜΕΙΛΗΣΙΟΣ; ΧΕΙΛΩΝ ΛΑΚΕΔΑΙΜΟΝΙΟΣ. Then, after the figure entirely obliterated by the added doorway, there are remains of one more figure on the right with the preserved ethnic tag ΠΡΙΗΝΕΥΣ (figs. 5.4–6).

Thus far, we could take these as standard representations of the Seven Sages—even as a poor man's version of the sculpted herms with busts of Greek thinkers, poets, and artists that were so popular in Roman decorative art of the period.[71] But what frames the figures transforms these respectable representations into parody and makes this decorative program unique. Above each of the Sages is a tag in Latin iambic *senarii*, also written in a black, cursive hand (slightly smaller than the Greek labels): above Solon, *ut bene cacaret ventrem palpavit Solon* ("in order to shit well, Solon rubbed his belly"); above Thales,

---

1973.134, 429 contends that the whole complex was originally constructed under Trajan and that the wall paintings are original; Clarke 2003.170 dates the decorative program to around 100 CE.

[67] According to Heres 1992–93.110n. 26, the original aperture from the corner room to the via della Calcara to the east was quite large, measuring 3.34 meters (i.e., most of the length of the original chamber). This opening was eventually narrowed and ultimately closed off entirely in the later conversion of the complex into baths.

[68] Calza 1939.99–100, 103.

[69] Original publication by Calza 1939.

[70] Calza 1939.106–8; von Salis 1947.22–24. Von Salis suggests M. Terentius Varro's book of *illustrium imagines* as a source for the Ostia images.

[71] Clarke 2003.171–74 points out that the figures of the Sages are set on plinths above the eye level of the viewer to suggest "sculptural types." Thus, according to Clarke: "They are images from elite culture: of statues adorning gardens, lecture halls, libraries, and the villas of the rich. Our taverngoers would have known them from grand public spaces at Ostia, Rome, or any large city" (Clarke 2003.174; cf. Clarke 2007.125).

THE AESOPIC PARODY OF HIGH WISDOM 231

Figure 5.4. Wall paintings of the Seven Sages, Terme dei Sette Sapienti, Ostia III x 2, Room 5, ca. 100–120 CE. Detail of Chilon, showing barrel vault, all three registers of the wall painting, and doorway. Photo Michael Larvey.

durum cacantes monuit ut nitant Thales ("Thales advised the constipated to press hard");[72] above Chilon, *vissire tacite Chilon docuit subdolus* ("crafty Chilon taught to fart silently").[73] Below the imposing images of the Sages, a lower

---

[72] On the strange active form *nitant* instead of *nitantur*, see Clarke 2003.311n. 46: "*Nitor*, a deponent verb meaning 'to strain with physical exertion,' is used actively, as often happens to deponent forms in colloquial speech."

[73] Calza 1939.100–102. The last words of the Latin tag above the figure of Bias of Priene have been read variously as *invenib Bias* (thus Solin 1972.198—with external sandhi for *invenit Bias*) or as *enis Bias* (thus Mols 1999). There are also additional Latin words inscribed below Solon and Thales, but scholars have not been able to make sense of these: below Solon, IVDICI (?)VERGILIVM LEGIS(SE) PVERIS (?)/ OR(di) NA (?); below Thales, VERBOSE TIBI/ NEMO/ DICIT DUM PRISCIANU(S)/ (?) (U)TARIS XYLOSPHONGIO NOS/ (?A) QUAS (Calza 1939.100–101). For the latter inscription, Neudecker 1994.36 suggests that "use the *xylosphongium*" refers to the Roman

Figure 5.5. Wall paintings of the Seven Sages, Terme dei Sette Sapienti, Ostia III x 2, Room 5, ca. 100–120 CE. Detail of Thales and sitting man below. Photo Michael Larvey.

Figure 5.6. Wall paintings of the Seven Sages, Terme dei Sette Sapienti, Ostia III x 2, Room 5, ca. 100–120 CE. Detail of Chilon and sitting men below. Photo Michael Larvey.

register of the frieze is fragmentarily preserved, representing in the same monochromatic chestnut brown a continuous series of smaller figures (two-thirds life size). Although this frieze was badly damaged by the later addition of a bench or shelf running around the walls of the room (so that it is impossible to tell whether these figures were standing or seated), enough remains to suggest that these were originally a series of users of a communal latrine. For each of these figures is also accompanied by a Latin tag: on either side of the leftmost, *mulione sedes* ("you're sitting on a mule-driver," to the left of the figure) and *propero* ("I'm hurrying," to the right of the figure); above the second left-hand figure,

---

practice of using a sponge on a stick to wipe oneself in the latrine, thus suggesting the use of the Sage's staff for that purpose (cf. Clarke 2007.127). In the images, both Solon and Thales are represented holding the staff characteristic of a sage.

agita te celerius pervenies ("bestir yourself—you'll get there quicker"); above the rightmost figure, *amice fugit te proverbium bene caca et irrima medicos* ("friend, the proverb escapes you, 'shit well and screw the doctors'"). Guido Calza, in the original publication of the wall paintings, aptly characterizes the relation of the two registers of the frieze. The lower register, which Calza characterizes as "a 'physiognomic gallery' of latrine users," shows "how they have realized in practice the mottoes ascribed to the philosophers."[74] Finally, the decorative scheme is completed by four amphorae painted on the ceiling, one of them labeled *falernum*—helpfully confirming that the room originally functioned as a tavern or public house.

In their interpretation of this decorative program, scholars are divided: is this parody or just the kind of advice conducive to good health we would expect from the Seven Sages?[75] Those who advocate the latter interpretation cite as a parallel a conversation that occurs in Plutarch's *Banquet of the Seven Sages* between the doctor Cleodorus and Solon, on the merits of different diets (sparked by Epimenides' odd regime of almost complete abstinence; Plut. *Banq.* chs. 15–16, 158c–160c).[76] But this is entirely to miss the point of Solon's tirade here against food consumption, which transforms him into a mouthpiece for Plutarch's own denunciation of the body, its needs and desires, in favor of the final liberation of the soul from its prison of flesh.[77] And while this appropriation of the Seven Sages is clearly a phenomenon of Plutarch's Platonism,[78] it is by no means unique or unusual. We might note that much of what circulated as wisdom of the Seven Sages is about controlling—even renouncing—the bodily.

---

[74] Calza 1939.103: "Man hätte so eine 'physiognomische Galerie' von Latrinenbenutzern, die wiedergegeben waren, wie sie die Philosophen zugeschriebenen Leitsätze in die Praxis umsetzten." For the comic effect of the visual and verbal echoes between the two registers, see Clarke 2003.172–74, 178, 2007.125–31.

[75] Meiggs 1973.429; Clarke 2003.170–80, 2007.125–31 read the images as comic parody; Picard 1947.75, Snell 1971.141, and Neudecker 1994.35–38 take them as offering serious advice for good health; Calza 1939 advocates both positions simultaneously.

[76] Thus Calza 1939.112, Picard 1947.75, Neudecker 1994.35. I would contend that a more apposite literary parallel for this decorative program would be the *Life of Aesop*; for the association of these parodic images of the Seven Sages with scatological episodes in the *Life*, cf. Jedrkiewicz 1989.211–12, Jouanno 2005.413, and see below.

[77] See especially Solon's remarks at *Banq.* 159c–d: "Would it not, then, be right and fair, my friend, in order to cut out injustice, to cut out also bowels and stomach and liver, which afford us no perception or craving for anything noble, but are like cooking utensils, such as choppers and kettles, and, in another respect, like a baker's outfit, ovens and dough-containers and kneading-bowls? Indeed, in the case of most people, one can see that their soul is absolutely confined in the darkness of the body as in a mill, making its endless rounds in its concern over its need of food; just as we ourselves, only a few moments ago, as a matter of course, neither saw nor listened to one another, but each one was bending down, enslaved to his need of food" (trans. Babbitt 1956). Cf. also *Banq.* 160b–c, where Solon analogizes the human foraging for food to the incessant, pointless labor of the Danaids in the Underworld. Clarke 2003.174–75 also points out the very different tone of the Sages' remarks about eating and digestion in Plutarch's *Banquet*.

[78] On Plutarch's Platonism, see Lamberton 2001.

Thus, for example, Diogenes Laertius tells us that statues of Anacharsis were inscribed, "Rule tongue, belly, genitals" (γλώσσης, γαστρός, αἰδοίων κρατεῖν, D.L. 1.104), while negative comments about bodily pleasure and the need to control it are also attributed to several of the other Sages.[79] Given this common association of the Seven Sages with the valorization of soul over body and with bodily ascesis, the Latin tags on the wall paintings in Ostia are surely meant to be read as parody. Indeed, in their extreme emphasis on the body and lower bodily functions, they represent just the kind of humorous explosion of the high wisdom tradition we have seen associated with Aesop. For the message of the Latin tags above the Sages and the smaller latrine users below is that even Sages and philosophers have to shit—and that, if they were to give us advice in that domain, those precepts would be genuinely useful life lessons. We might compare Aesop's version of the tongue as "best and worst," which converts the Sages' moralizing, metaphorical message into a recipe for diarrhea.[80]

The other element of the wall-painting program that seems reminiscent of the Aesopic parodies we have been considering (although it is almost never remarked upon by scholars) is the juxtaposition of Greek and Latin inscriptions within a single image. For it is in fact extremely unusual for Latin to be incorporated into elite visual images at all in this period: the representation of Greek thinkers, poets, and artists (often labeled in Greek and accompanied by Greek quotations from their works) is part of a visual culture whose goal is to conjure up *Greekness*—Greek urbanity and Greek learning.[81] That style of representation

---

[79] Cf. D.L. 1.92, 97, 103, and note among the sayings preserved in Stobaeus "Control coupling" (γάμους κράτει), "Control the eye" (ὀφθαλμοῦ κράτει), and the adjuration to young men in particular to practice self-control (ἡβῶν ἐγκρατής, all in Stobaeus *Anth.* 3.1.173 Wachsmuth-Hense). Though we might regard this as a later development in the Sages tradition, it could be argued that insofar as they are associated with Apollo as far back as we can trace them in the tradition (e.g., in Plato's *Protagoras*), the Sages are always aligned with voice and *pneuma* and opposed to the body (as the god himself is).

[80] As another Aesopic parallel for this message, we might cite also ch. 67 the *Life* (in the version of *Vita* G): "[At a symposium] when the drinking had advanced, his cup spurred Xanthus to withdraw for the call of nature. And Aesop also went out and stood beside him holding a towel and a pitcher of water. And Xanthus [says] to him, 'Can you tell me why, whenever we shit, we carefully study our own excretion?' Aesop: 'Because in the old days there was the son of a king who, because of his self-indulgence and luxury used to sit a long time shitting—so much time in fact until he unwittingly shat his own brains out. From that time men, when they take a shit, bend over it in fear lest they've shit their brains out. But you—have no anxiety about this—you'll never shit your brains out, since you don't have any.'" Calza 1939.113 and Snell 1971.141 both also cite the evidence of Petronius *Satyricon* ch. 47 (in which Trimalchio quite unapologetically and unself-consciously discusses his constipation) as evidence that this was normal and appropriate dinnertime conversation. Again, this misses the point that Petronius is specifically mocking the uncouth and inappropriate behavior of *freedmen*. For a better treatment of the Petronius parallel as an elite parody of the low-class "mixing [of] eating and shitting," see Clarke 2003.177. In the close identification of the socially low with the bodily obscene we see something very similar to the Aesop stories considered in this chapter.

[81] As Chris Hallett observes to me, "In the Roman period where one finds inscriptions added to Greek sculptures, or captions added to Greek paintings, these are almost always written in the

is echoed in the Ostia wall paintings by the figures of the Sages with their Greek names and ethnics (all of which may well derive from a Hellenistic model).[82] But the juxtaposition of these emphatically Greek figures with obscene Latin tags above and with the unexpurgated Latin conversations of the humble latrine users below maps out an antagonistic politics of language that accompanies and animates the parody. In this light, the Latin inscriptions read as the aggressive self-assertion of nonelite native culture against the body-hating traditions of Greek wisdom. And here, too, we have seen something very similar with Aesop, who often focalizes not just the socially low and bodily, but also the non-Greek as an other position.[83]

It is for these reasons that I would like to see in the Ostia tavern paintings an Aesopic parody without Aesop. We might say that the Aesopic position is here outside the frame, for by this decorative program, the artist enables every viewer to play the role of Aesop, crudely and unceremoniously debunking the lofty Greek wisdom of the Sages. And the large opening to the street in the fourth wall—the very thing that made the chamber literally a "public house"— rendered the Aesopic position available to every passerby in the busy port city of Ostia.[84]

I began this chapter with Plutarch's image of Aesop sitting on a low chair at the feet of Solon—a perfect emblem, I suggested, of the domestication of Aesop

---

Greek language. In the case of sculpture one most commonly finds sculptors' signatures, or the identifying names carved on herm portraits of famous Greek poets, orators or philosophers (sometimes even including a short quotation from one of their works). Such inscriptions are virtually never written in Latin. In the case of paintings, one thinks of the captions added to figures—as in the *Odyssey* landscape paintings from the Esquiline, or in the long frieze of scenes from the Trojan war found in the 'House of the Cryptoporticus' at Pompeii. In painting there exist, it is true, one or two exceptions to this rule: the scenes from the *Iliad* with Latin captions in the triclinium of the House of C. Octavius Quartio at Pompeii, for example. But such exceptions are very rare. For the most part, the art produced for Roman elite villas, and even the houses and gardens of ordinary prosperous families—what has been called 'Roman art of the private sphere'—is consistently marked as Greek by the use of the Greek language in connection with it" (private communication).

[82] Cf. von Salis 1947.22–23: "Dass die Figuren in Ostia nicht etwa von dem römischen Dekorationsmaler erfunden sind, sondern nach älterem Vorbild kopiert sein müssen, sieht man auf den ersten Blick; sie sind, nach Erscheinung, Tracht und Gehaben, so unrömisch wie möglich, sind echt griechisches Gewächs." Cf. Clarke 2003.178.

[83] Cf. for example the implied opposition between Aesop and the Seven Sages figured as ethnic difference in the proverb "Rather the Phrygian" (discussed above, chapter 3, section I). And we might recall, as analogous to the language politics of the Ostia wall paintings, the large number of Latinisms and Latin borrowings in *Vita* G (which I have suggested represents a deliberate rejection of the decorum of pure, Atticizing Greek of the Second Sophistic; see introduction, section IIB).

[84] For the original 3.34-meter aperture opening onto the via della Calcara to the east, see Heres 1992–93.80, 110n. 26. For discussion of the nonelite clientele of the tavern, see Clarke 2003.176–80, rejecting the proposal of Calza (1939.104), based entirely on the decorative program, that this must have been an exclusive private club for the "Bohemians of the time."

within the Greek philosophical tradition. I would like to end with another image that evokes by contrast the shiftiness, mobility, and ambiguity of Aesop's relation to the wisdom tradition. We might recall that (as mentioned in chapter 2) an alternative version of the story of the tripod of the Seven Sages replaces that numinous object with a golden phiale to be given to "the wisest," which makes the rounds of the Seven Sages and winds up dedicated at Delphi.[85] We might imagine that it is this phiale that the Delphians plant in Aesop's luggage in order to frame and kill him. If we may be permitted to indulge this fantasy, the message of this odd narrative conjuncture seems two-sided (at the very least). On the one hand, the Delphian institutional authorities thereby constitute Aesop's relation to the Seven Sages tradition as one of theft or poaching—the illicit commandeering of cultural capital that, in Michel de Certeau's formulation, characterizes the constant and largely unnoticed rebellions and appropriations of the common man.[86] On the other hand, the Delphians are also unwittingly—in spite of themselves, as it were—awarding to Aesop the prize in a contest of wisdom, acknowledging his triumph not only over the Seven Sages, but over the Delphic god himself. And while the golden phiale presumably returns to the Delphic shrine (this is never mentioned in the stories), we might hold in suspension the moment at which it travels away from Delphi and from the closed circuit of the Sages, in the paradoxical possession of Aesop.

---

[85] Thus Plut. *Sol.* 4 notes that some versions of the story replace the tripod with a phiale sent by Croesus, or "a cup (ποτήριον) left behind by Bathycles." Cf. D.L. 1.28–32, which recounts the version of the "cup of Bathycles" left to the "one who had done most good by his wisdom," and ultimately dedicated to Apollo at Didyma, derived from Callimachus's First *Iamb* (fr. 191 Pfeiffer, ll. 32–77).

[86] De Certeau 1984; cf. Scott 1990.187–92 on theft, poaching, and pilfering. (I would note that Page duBois makes a similar connection between Aesop's fable narratives and Scott's idea of theft or pilfering; see duBois 2003.187–88.)

PART II

AESOP AND THE INVENTION
OF GREEK PROSE

Chapter 6

AESOP AT THE INVENTION OF PHILOSOPHY

"Im Sklaven fängt die Prosa an"
—G.W.F. Hegel

PRELUDE TO PART II: THE PROBLEMATIC
SOCIOPOLITICS OF MIMETIC PROSE

IN PART I, I CONSIDERED Aesop as a voice of resistance in relation to religious institutions, and as a simultaneous participant in and subversive challenger to the high wisdom tradition. In this part, I want to excavate Aesopic elements in the beginnings of Greek mimetic or narrative prose—by which I mean both prose philosophy and prose history. This represents a shift in perspective that will importantly refine our vision of the Aesopic conversations of high and low traditions. For much of the previous five chapters, I have tracked the movement *from* institutionally authorized systems of cult, ritual, and *sophia to* the Aesop tradition. As a result, these cultural transactions were difficult to date or pin down with much specificity. With no firm terminus ante quem, we might imagine them as ongoing cultural conversations that span centuries. On the other hand, in the domains of philosophy and history, as I will argue in this and the following five chapters, there is evidence for impact in the other direction: here we can see Aesop traditions contributing to Sophistic epideictic, the *Sōkratikoi logoi* of Plato and Xenophon, and the historical narrative of Herodotus. Movement in this direction thus gives us a better purchase on the lineaments of Aesop traditions as they existed in the fifth and fourth centuries BCE, while also (perhaps more importantly) demonstrating the ways in which a "little" or popular tradition could influence and leave its imprint on the rarefied products of high culture.

In charting the affiliations of "Socratic" philosophy and Herodotean history with Aesop and Aesopic fable, we will have to confront directly issues of form and style as well as those of content. That is to say, this and the following chapters will argue for an occluded Aesopic strand in the genealogy of Greek prose writing. This narrative is usually constituted within literary history as the inevitable, triumphal march from "*muthos* to *logos*," from the ritually embedded and inspired utterances of the poet-seer to the rational writing of prose.[1]

---

[1] For versions of this traditional account, see (e.g.) Havelock 1963, Cole 1991, Detienne 1996, Goldhill 2002.

The presence of the Aesopic lurking behind and within the *Sōkratikoi logoi* of Plato and Xenophon and Herodotean history necessarily complicates this narrative, for from his earliest appearance in Greek literature, Aesop is associated with the "making of prose," while also identified with the lowest rung of a generic hierarchy that is simultaneously (at least notionally) a sociopolitical one.

In his *Lectures on Fine Art*, Hegel pronounced apophthegmatically "im Sklaven fängt die Prosa an" ("In the slave, prose begins"; which provides the epigraph to this chapter). By this he meant precisely to distinguish the quotidian, trivial matter of Aesopic fable from the lofty forms of "poetry and philosophy."[2] Paradoxically, I think that Hegel's apophthegm is exactly right as a characterization of one strand in the Greeks' own conception of mimetic prose, but to appreciate its implications, we must disengage this lapidary formulation from its Hegelian narrative of the transcendental in art. What is repressed in the Hegelian account that still dominates many versions of Greek literary history is that this low-class or abject figuration of mimetic or narrative prose would also have applied, to some extent, to prose philosophy and prose history. Indeed, in passages I will consider in detail in this chapter and chapter 10, both Herodotus and Plato themselves explicitly identify Aesop with prose and implicitly acknowledge their own affiliation with him (Hdt. 2.134, Plato *Phd.* 60c9–61b7). From these references it is clear that, at least by the fifth and fourth centuries BCE, the fables attached to the figure of Aesop were indisputably thought of as prose.[3] And both Herodotus and Plato, the earliest writers of fully extant texts in their two traditions, thereby affiliate their own mimetic prose with that of the lowly fabulist Aesop.

But what evidence do I have for the generic and sociopolitical abjection I've claimed for prose fable? Here we have to do with two axes of differentiation: poetry versus prose, and then within each of those forms, a strict hierarchy of style and content that was perceived to correspond to a sociopolitical hierarchy.

---

[2] Cited by de Man 1983.101 and Patterson 1991.13. In English translation: Hegel 1975.387: "In this situation Aesop does not regard animals and nature in general, as the Indians and Egyptians do, as something lofty and divine on their own account; he treats them, on the contrary, with prosaic eyes as something where circumstances serve only to picture human action and suffering. But yet his notions are only witty, without any energy of spirit or depth of insight and substantive vision, without poetry and philosophy. His views and doctrines prove indeed to be ingenious and clever, but there remains only, as it were, a subtle investigation of trifles. Instead of creating free shapes out of a free spirit, this investigation only sees some other applicable side in purely given and available materials, the specific instincts and impulses of animals, petty daily events; this is because Aesop does not dare to recite his doctrines openly but can only make them understood hidden as it were in a riddle which at the same time is always being solved. In the slave, prose begins, and so this entire species is prosaic too."

[3] I insist on this to disagree with Nagy 1979.281–83, who consistently refers to Aesop as a "poet" or "blame poet"; instead I would contend that the diacritic of poetry vs prose is significant, both generically and sociopolitically. For Aesop's association with prose, cf. M. L. West 1985.94, critiquing Parker 1983.284 and see above, chapter 3, section I.

As in many other traditions, poetry long preceded prose as an artistic form in ancient Greece. Among the forms of poetry, there existed a clear hierarchy of elaboration of performance, style, and level of decorum that descended from Homeric epic and choral lyric at the top to monodic lyric, elegy, and finally iambic poetry.[4] It is clear where fable fit within this combined generic-sociopolitical system: at the bottom. Thus we find beast fables (for which the archaic, Ionic term is *ainos*) in Hesiod's middling didactic poem, the *Works & Days*, in the remains of archaic iambic, but never in Homer's elitist epic.[5] In this respect, Old Comedy strongly continues the iambographic tradition: thus Aristophanes mentions Aesop by name eight times, and his comedies and plots are filled with Aesopic fable elements. Kenneth Rothwell has developed this point about the sociopolitics of Aesopic fable, noting that high literary genres may allude to Aesopic fables but almost never narrate them straight through, as this is felt to be too déclassé, while even Aristophanes can mark the sociopolitical status of his various characters by whether or not they tell beast fables.[6] As Rothwell observes:

> Although one might think that fables would be a useful tool for any poet, or that upper-class characters would resort to them as an indirect and sophisticated way of communicating, the fable remains strikingly rare in archaic or classical literature. In the more serious genres no Greek of the respectable classes tells a complete animal fable; instead, fables were relegated more to comedy and iambos than to epic and tragedy.[7]

---

[4] See West 1974, Bowie 1986, and summary in Kurke 2000. Auerbach 1953 develops a similar model for a much later period; cf. his discussion of the "strict separation of styles" in the writing of classical literature (esp. 24–49).

[5] Crusius 1920.IX noted the complete absence of beast fables in Homer in contrast to Hesiod; Meuli 1975b.739–43 pointed out that there is in fact an *ainos*—a coded, indirect tale with a specific purpose narrated by a weaker speaker to a stronger—at *Ody*. 14.457–522 (the disguised Odysseus's fictive tale to Eumaeus about Odysseus and himself at Troy, told to gain a cloak). As Rothwell 1995.237 notes, the humble setting of the swineherd's hut, with Odysseus in disguise as a beggar, is "precisely the social context that might allow for [fable narration]," while it is also significant that this *ainos* involves a traditional form but autobiographical content (in the elegant formulation of one of the anonymous readers). On Odysseus's *ainos*, see also Perry 1959.23, Cole 1991.49. For the general pattern of distribution of fable in archaic and classical Greek poetry, see also Lasserre 1984; West 1984; Adrados 1999.240–85, 367–83. For a significant distinction between Homeric and Hesiodic hexameter poetry as our earliest extant representatives of "elitist" and "middling" traditions, respectively, see Morris 1996, 2000.163–76; for specific discussion of beast fable as a low generic element within Hesiod's *Works & Days*, see Martin 1992.21–22.

[6] Rothwell 1995. Rothwell notes as the exception that proves the rule the remarkable exchange of fables between Menelaus and Teucer in Sophocles' *Ajax* (1142–62): in this context, the low-class fabular sniping of the characters vividly illustrates how mean and sordid the world has become after the death of the play's heroic protagonist; for this point, cf. Fraenkel 1977. We also find two beast fables (told straight through or alluded to) in Aeschylus: *Ag*. 717–36 and *Myrmidons* fr. 139 Radt; for these as examples of Aeschylus's willingness to descend to popular forms and language, see Fraenkel 1964, West in discussion in Lasserre 1984.100, and Rothwell 1995.237 with n. 17.

[7] Rothwell 1995.237. Note also Rothwell's general conclusions about fable as a genre (many of which will be relevant for discussion of fable elements in Plato, Xenophon, and Herodotus): "The

As we saw in chapter 3, Rothwell's pattern of distribution seems also to apply to the comparatively decorous political poetry of Solon in the sixth century and to the preserved speeches of the Attic orators in the fifth and fourth. For in the former, Solon seems occasionally to conjure beast fable scenarios through cryptic allusion, but never to narrate them explicitly and fully. In the case of the latter, we noted the paradox that although Aristotle in his *Rhetoric* recommends the use of fables in contexts of public deliberative and forensic oratory, and although the anecdotal tradition preserves many instances of orators telling apposite fables, there is not a single fable narrated in the almost 150 Attic orations we have preserved from the fifth and fourth centuries in textual form.[8] These complex patterns of reference and avoidance within a strict hierarchy of genre and decorum suggest that meaning and politics inhere in form, and that this is as true of prose genres as of poetry. Simply put: Aesop and fable are identified with lowly prose storytelling, and therefore storytelling in prose is a problem. And yet, to my knowledge, the problematic sociopolitics of narrative or mimetic prose has never been confronted in discussions of the beginnings of prose history or prose philosophy.

The goal here is also partly to estrange and defamiliarize the prose writings of Plato and Herodotus: to recover what is deeply odd or anomalous in them when they are viewed from the perspective of the strict system of Greek literary decorum. For we have become too comfortable with these texts—we take them for granted as simply our earliest fully preserved monuments of Western philosophy and Western history. Yet situated in their contemporary Greek contexts, both Herodotus's *Histories* and Plato's Socratic dialogues emerge as bizarre and aberrant generic mixtures, in which the choice of prose is by no means necessary or inevitable. More than that: prose in these texts is linked to mimesis and to complex moments of the rupture of literary decorum; and these phenomena, which make the texts of Herodotus and Plato so deeply strange, I will argue, are characteristically Aesopic.

I. Mimēsis and the Invention of Philosophy

Let me start with Plato, the invention of philosophy, and the problem of *mimēsis*. I am thus proceeding in reverse chronological order in this and the following

---

fable genre is fundamentally concerned with relationships between individuals or groups of unequal power and thus is frequently associated with the lower classes. Even where not an absolute indicator of class or status, a fable can be a relative measure in a relationship between a person with more money, prestige, or power and a person with less; it could therefore be spoken by or addressed to the aggrieved or disadvantaged party in any given context" (Rothwell 1995.238).

[8] For the contradiction between Aristotle's recommendations in the *Rhetoric* and the preserved evidence of the Attic orators, see Meuli 1975b.756, Rothwell 1995.245–47, Adrados 1999.379, and discussion above, chapter 3, section II.

chapters: here and in the next three chapters, I will focus on Plato in the context of Sophistic rhetoric and Xenophon's *Memorabilia*; only in chapters 10 and 11 will I turn to Herodotus. I do this, first, because the Sophists, Plato, and Xenophon emerge from and (to a great extent) still participate in the wisdom traditions considered in the previous four chapters, so that close analysis of this fifth-/fourth-century milieu forms the logical conclusion of our treatment of ancient Greek wisdom traditions. Second, many of the lessons learned as we tease out the bizarre generic motley and Aesopic strands in Platonic dialogue will enable us to see these same elements more readily and to see what they are doing in the text of Herodotus. I should also note here at the outset that I make no attempt to offer a comprehensive account of the Aesopic in Plato, for such a project would fill several volumes (and occupy several lifetimes). I will attempt instead in this and chapters 8 and 9 to offer exemplary readings of some Platonic texts where we can make out with particular clarity Plato's strategic deployment of Aesop.

At the beginning of the Western tradition of theorizing *mimēsis* stands Plato's philosophical indictment of poetry and banishment of the poets from his ideal city. This founding, hostile gesture of literary criticism has been impossible to ignore: literary criticism (if not literature itself) still labors under the weight of Plato's opprobrium.[9] For Platonic authority has constituted a critique of poetry that seems to stand outside of time—stark, monolithic, based on an idealist metaphysics and a complex modeling of audience psychology. It has thus served for millennia as a basis for attacks on the ethical status of fiction and drama, or as a provocation for defenses of poetry. More recently, a different approach has been not to acquiesce in the ahistorical prestige of Plato's account, but instead to historicize and contextualize his attack on the poets, locating it in the fraught cultural shift from orality to literacy; the beginnings of the professionalization of education; and the complex performance culture of the ancient Greek city.[10] Indeed, several scholars have insisted that we must understand Plato's banishment of the poets as philosophy's constituting gesture. For Plato invents a very particular version of "philosophy" in the fourth century BCE, which needs to define itself in opposition to poetry and other forms of traditional "wisdom" (*sophia*) within Greek culture. As Andrea Nightingale formulates it:

> In order to create the specialized discipline of philosophy, Plato had to distinguish what he was doing from all other discursive practices that laid claim to wisdom. It is for this reason that, in dialogue after dialogue, Plato deliberately sets out to define and defend a new and quite peculiar mode of living and of thinking. This alone, he claimed, deserved the title of "philosophy." It should be emphasized that gestures of

---

[9] Among many recent responses, see (e.g.) the essays collected in Cascardi 1987, and see Naddaff 2002.

[10] For all three contexts, see especially Havelock 1952, 1963; for Plato in the context of ancient performance culture, see Ferrari 1989, Nightingale 1995, Naddaff 2002.

246   CHAPTER 6

opposition and exclusion play a crucial role in Plato's many attempts to mark the boundaries of "philosophy." Indeed, it is precisely by designating certain modes of discourse and spheres of activity as "anti-philosophical" that Plato was able to create a separate identity for "philosophy." This was a bold and difficult enterprise whose success was by no means guaranteed: because history has conferred upon the discipline of philosophy the legitimacy and the high status that Plato claimed for it, we moderns tend to overlook the effort it took to bring this about.[11]

In this context, the *Republic*'s apparently casual reference to the well-known "ancient quarrel between philosophy and poetry" (*Rep.* 10.607b) is in fact "one of Plato's more powerful fictions":

> the notion that "poetry"—as a mode of discourse that promulgates a certain set of values—is fundamentally opposed to "philosophy" (and vice versa) was not articulated before Plato. It is Plato's private quarrel, then, which is retrojected back onto the ancients in *Republic* 10 and thereby made to escape the contingency and specificity of Plato's own historical moment.[12]

And, as Nightingale and others have demonstrated in great detail, even as Plato has Socrates banish poetry from the ideal city, the Platonic dialogues teem with appropriations, assimilations, and parodies of diverse poetic forms—Plato's intertextual dialogues, as Nightingale has it.[13]

I wish here to carry this historicizing project yet further. For what tends to get missed even in these more recent scholarly accounts is why Plato chooses to write *prose*—and *mimetic prose* at that.[14] For this was a relatively new form in his time. Earlier prose in what we would call the philosophical tradition, insofar as we can reconstruct it, had no dialogue or mimetic frame, but consisted simply of bare assertions or propositions articulated as a series of impersonal third-person statements. In addition, even in the "philosophical" tradition before Plato, the use of prose was relatively new and not universally adopted: thus

---

[11] Nightingale 1995.10–11. Cf. Nehamas 1990.5: "in the fourth century B.C. terms like 'philosophy' and 'sophistry' do not seem to have had a widely agreed-upon application. On the contrary, different authors seem to have fought with one another with the purpose of appropriating the term 'philosophy,' each for his own practice and educational scheme. In the long run, of course, Plato (followed in this respect, and despite their many differences, by Aristotle) emerged victorious. He thereby established what philosophy is by contrasting it not only with sophistry but also with rhetoric, poetry, traditional religion, and the specialized sciences. This was a grandiose project." Naddaff 2002 also argues for the *Republic*'s censorship of the poets as philosophy's founding, self-constituting gesture, which on her reading Plato problematizes and subverts as the dialogue proceeds.

[12] Nightingale 1995.65; cf. Most 1999.359–60.

[13] Nightingale 1995 passim; cf. Morgan 2000, Naddaff 2002.

[14] Thus scholars have asked repeatedly, why does Plato *write*? And why does he write *dialogues*?— but almost never, why does he write *prose*? For scholars engaged with the two former questions (writing and dialogue), see (e.g.) Derrida 1981; Ferrari 1987; Frede 1992; Clay 1994, 2000; Nightingale 1995; Kahn 1996; Nussbaum 2001.122–35; Blondell 2002.37–52.

Xenophanes, Parmenides, and Empedocles chose to compose in verse (dactylic hexameter) and in the first person even after Anaximander, Heraclitus, and Anaxagoras had begun to compose prose treatises.[15] So Plato's choice of mimetic prose was radical within his own tradition and, according to some scholars (including Bakhtin), served as an important precursor for the modern novel.[16] But then what are the sources or precursors for Plato's mimetic prose? I will suggest that we need to supplement earlier historicizing, intertextual readings of Plato by acknowledging Aesop and the traditions around the figure of Aesop as significant precursors for Platonic dialogue in general and the characterization of Socrates in particular.

Why Aesop? Within the ancient Greek tradition, Aesop was supposedly a non-Greek (Thracian or Phrygian), hideously ugly, who started out as a slave on the island of Samos in the sixth century BCE, but who eventually won his freedom through his own wit and interpretative skills. Whether or not such a figure actually existed, by the fifth century BCE, we begin to see legends of an unusual life and death crystallizing around Aesop, while the lowly genre of fable comes to be attached to him as maker and founding father. As we have seen in part I, throughout this tradition, Aesop's relation to the system of prephilosophical *sophia* is strangely double, for he seems both to participate in the field of high wisdom (as a popular contender, closely associated with the Seven Sages) and also to critique or parody it from below. And since the invention of philosophy itself stands in complex relation to these older wisdom traditions, simultaneously working to appropriate and to differentiate itself therefrom, the figure of Aesop in his own double relation to the wisdom tradition turns out to be very serviceable to philosophy.

One reason, I would suggest, that so little scholarly attention has been paid to Plato's choice to write mimetic prose goes back to the *Republic* itself. For here Plato artfully engineers a conceptual blind spot or occlusion of prose *mimēsis* in his detailed discussion of *mimēsis* in *Republic* Books 3 and 10. Initially, already

---

[15] On all this see Most 1999.335, 350–60.

[16] It must also be acknowledged that Plato was writing as part of a whole emergent genre of prose, mimetic *Sōkratikoi logoi* ("Socratic Discourses" or "Conversations with Socrates") whose composition may have dated back to the late fifth century, but in any event proliferated in the fourth—the work of many different philosophical followers of Socrates. Among all these writers of *Sōkratikoi logoi*, Plato and Xenophon appear to be relative latecomers, though only their works now survive as complete texts. Still, it is worth noting in this context the argument of Clay 1994.41–47, that Plato's innovation within this genre was the specific grounding of the dialogues in time and place. That is to say, on Clay's argument, it was *Plato* who made the Socratic dialogue more mimetic or "novelistic" in our terms. Cf. Nussbaum 2001.122–25 on Platonic dialogue as "a new kind of writing."

For the purposes of my argument, I will not consider the fragmentary remains of the other Socratics, but focus entirely on the Sophists, Plato, and Xenophon. For the preserved remains of other Socratics and testimonia, see Giannantoni 1990; for illuminating discussion of Plato and Xenophon in the context of these other writers of *Sōkratikoi logoi*, see Clay 1994 and the other essays collected in Vander Waerdt 1994.

in Book 2, Adeimantus had complained that "everyday speech" (ἰδίᾳ τε λεγόμενον) agrees with poetry about the nature of justice and injustice (363e6–4a1) and that no one has ever yet "in poetry or in everyday speech produced a sufficient account of how justice is in itself the greatest good" (366e7–9). Socrates then picks up and transforms Adeimantus's distinction of poetry and everyday speech within his fantasy account of the education of the guardians, for here (throughout Books 2 and 3) he refers repeatedly to poetry and (prose) storytelling or poets and (prose) storytellers as equally in need of regulation and supervision.[17] And yet the genus of "prose storytelling" keeps getting folded into that of poetry—until it seems finally to disappear altogether as a separate category.[18] Thus, for example, Socrates insists on the need to oversee and regulate the first stories "nurses and mothers" tell to children (377b5–c3). And while we might construe this as covering a very broad range of stories in prose as well as verse, Socrates immediately focuses on the "greater false tales" purveyed by "Hesiod, Homer, and the other poets," offering the example of Hesiod's account of the sky god Uranus's violence against his own children and his son Cronus's castration of him in retribution, as narrated in the *Theogony* (377d4–78a6).[19] This is the first, but by no means the last, assimilation or appropriation of all "tales" or "stories" into the category of "poetry."[20]

Significantly, this assimilation or strange eclipsing of the category of prose storytelling by poetry occurs most densely in the force field of Socrates' definitions and discussions of *mimēsis*. Thus in Book 3, when Socrates first introduces the concept of narration (*diēgēsis*) as the essence of all storytelling, he still maintains the two terms:

"Here's a way of looking at it which may give you a better idea. Aren't all stories told by storytellers and poets (μυθολόγων ἢ ποιητῶν) really a narrative—of what has hap-

---

[17] Throughout Books 2 and 3, Socrates uses several different terms for the pair "poetry and prose storytelling" or "poets and prose storytellers": μήτ' ἐν μέτρῳ μήτε ἄνευ μέτρου μυθολογοῦντα (2.380c1–3), τούς τε λέγοντας λέγειν καὶ τοὺς ποιοῦντας ποιεῖν (2.380c6–9), λεκτέον τε καὶ ποιητέον (3.387c9), ἐν λόγῳ ἢ ἐν ποιήσει (3.390a1–2), ποιηταὶ καὶ λογοποιοί (3.392a13), ᾄδειν τε καὶ μυθολογεῖν (3.392b5–6).

[18] Thus I cannot agree with Annas 1982.1, when she asserts that "Plato is uninterested in prose.... and shows no serious concern with written works of prose fiction"; for a similar assertion, cf. Blondell 2002.30n. 87. Such bland assertion does not sufficiently attend to the rhetorical feints and slippages of Socrates' discourse in the *Republic*. We might also wonder what exactly "prose fiction" would have looked like at Plato's time.

[19] Cf. Annas 1982.24n. 2 (though Annas herself does not pursue the point): "When he talks in book 3 about harmful stories and tales, Plato has in mind chiefly fables about the gods and what we would call fairytales."

[20] In fact, what helps this assimilation along is that Socrates is using *logos* and *legein* in two different senses throughout this discussion: (1) the telling of prose tales (as opposed to the composition of poetry) and (2) "true stories" (as opposed to *muthoi*, "false stories"). The deliberate collapse of these two different meanings allows Socrates eventually to subsume "prose tales" as simply the content of "poetry."

pened in the past, of what is happening now, or of what is going to happen in the future?" (392d1–3, trans. Griffith in Ferrari and Griffith 2000)[21]

But when he proceeds to posit the distinction between "simple narrative, narrative expressed through imitation, or the combination of the two" (392d5–6), his interlocutor Adeimantus demurs in confusion. Socrates responds with apparent self-deprecation that he's likely to be a "laughable and unclear teacher," and therefore, just like those who are not skilled speakers, he will avoid generalizations and instead offer a particular example to clarify what he means (392d8–e2). The particular example proffered is the beginning of the *Iliad*, where Homer shifts from simple narration in his own voice to the direct speech of the priest Chryses. With this focus on the particular example of *Iliad* 1, Socrates deftly causes prose storytelling to disappear entirely from his account, for he resumes the argument, "In passages like this, apparently, Homer *and the rest of the poets* use imitation to construct their narrative" (393c8–9, trans. Griffith in Ferrari and Griffith 2000, my italics). Even when it appears that (prose) storytelling makes its return a little later, the context and examples with which Socrates surrounds it effectively shut down any possibility of thinking *mimēsis* and prose together:

> "Now I think I can make clear to you what I couldn't make clear before, that one type of poetry and storytelling (τῆς ποιήσεώς τε καὶ μυθολογίας) is purely imitative—this is tragedy and comedy, as you say. In another type, the poet tells his own story. I imagine you'd find this mainly in dithyramb. The third type, using both imitation and narrative, can be found in epic poetry, and in many other places as well." (394b8–c5, trans. Griffith in Ferrari and Griffith 2000)

Here, pure *mimēsis* is characterized by—but also circumscribed to—the poetic genres of comedy and tragedy; we are thus prevented from thinking of the low, prose form of mime (for example).[22] And even when Socrates appears to offer the final catchall of "many other places as well" for mixed narration, given his example set of tragedy, comedy, dithyramb, and epic, it is highly unlikely that we will look for those "other places" beyond the boundaries of poetry.[23] At this

---

[21] Here and elsewhere, I cite the translation of Tom Griffith from Ferrari and Griffith 2000, because it makes particularly clear the common pairing of "poetry and prose storytelling" throughout *Rep.* Books 2 and 3.

[22] We have almost no preserved remains of "mime," but from the remains we have and references to the genre in other ancient texts, we can be pretty certain that mime was a lowly form of "skit comedy" with stock characters, written in prose and publicly performed, whose existence predated Plato's writing. On mime in general and the fifth-century mime-writer Sophron in particular, see Hordern 2004.

[23] A measure of the effectiveness of Plato's rhetorical prestidigitation here is the response even of modern commentators to the phrase "many other places as well." Thus, for example, G.R.F. Ferrari in his note on this passage (Ferrari and Griffith 2000.82–83n. 38): "The 'other places' in which both imitation and narrative are found would include the victory odes of Pindar and much other lyric

point, and in all that follows, "storytelling" has come to be subsumed as simply the *content* of poetry, while all the issues around the fraught category of *mimēsis* (the *how*, not the *what*, as Socrates puts it) attach themselves to poetry.

This erasure of prose storytelling is even more extreme in Book 10. For here, Socrates begins immediately talking only about poetry (περὶ ποιήσεως) in order to condemn more thoroughly "however much of it is imitative" (ὅση μιμητική, 595a5). I will not rehearse here the well-known arguments Plato deploys in Book 10 to indict poetry *tout court* and banish it entirely from his ideal city. The traditional scholarly problem concerning Platonic *mimēsis* has been how to reconcile the two accounts of *mimēsis* Plato offers in the *Republic*. In Book 3, the opposition of *mimēsis* and *diēgēsis* as narrative modes focuses on *mimēsis* as "impersonation," while Book 10 seems to broaden the scope of the term to include all poetry as "image making"—the representation or imitation of reality.[24] And while ongoing scholarly discussion of this crux has produced much fruitful analysis within the domains of philosophy, aesthetics, and literary criticism, close attention to the rhetorical moves of the *Republic* suggests that Plato's indictment of poetry and banishment of the poets through the argument about *mimēsis* is, at least to some extent, a feint or alibi. Plato thereby offloads onto poetry all that is problematic about *mimēsis*, while simultaneously distracting our attention from a different set of generic affiliations for his own writing (with attendant sociopolitical associations) that are perhaps even more problematic. Or, to put it differently: by so strongly identifying *mimēsis* with poetry, Plato conjures the illusion that his own prose is nonmimetic.

So, for Andrea Nightingale, Plato's claim that "there is an ancient quarrel between philosophy and poetry" is a tendentious fiction that conjures the illusion that "philosophy" (newly constituted by Plato) has always existed as such. That is to say, Nightingale focuses her critique on the "ancient." What I want to suggest is another kind of tendentious misdirection in Plato's formulation: by setting it up as a quarrel of only two terms (philosophy versus mimetic poetry), Plato occludes the mimetic dimension of philosophical prose and, with it, the complex generic and sociopolitical ground of his own writing—the low forms of mimetic prose.

Indeed, Platonic prose is "mimetic" in several senses: it is a fictive imitation or representation of a whole social world (and as such, as already noted, it was

---

poetry." But there are many examples of mixed narrative *in prose* (both oral and written) that would have been familiar to Plato's readers—perhaps mime, certainly the *Life* and fables of Aesop (which constantly combine simple narration and direct speech), and, of course, the Socratic dialogues of Xenophon and Plato, including the *Republic* itself.

[24] For important discussions of the two accounts of *mimēsis* in the *Republic*, attempts to reconcile them, or arguments that they are ultimately not entirely reconcilable, see Nehamas 1982, Woodruff 1982b, Belfiore 1984a, Ferrari 1989.108–41, Asmis 1992, Naddaff 2002. Of these, I have found Ferrari (building on Belfiore) the most detailed and compelling argument for the logical coherence of the two treatments of *mimēsis* in *Rep.* Books 3 and 10.

a relatively new form when Plato wrote); at the same time, the Platonic dialogues teem with direct speech or "impersonation" of individual characters. But I have in mind yet another kind of *mimēsis*, which is the deliberate imitation or impersonation of the figure of Aesop in the modeling and characterization of Socrates throughout the Platonic corpus. It is this third form of *mimēsis* that will be my subject, for it will allow us to tackle directly the problem of Platonic prose and to restore to the discourse of *mimēsis* the complex sociopolitics of form Plato's account simultaneously acknowledges and struggles to disavow.

II. The Generic Affiliations of *Sōkratikoi logoi*

Thus the *Republic*'s feints and occlusions encourage us to focus on the category of mimetic prose; but why bring in Aesop? In fact, Plato himself, in the *Phaedo*, invites us to see Aesop as a precursor and model for Socrates. Early in this dialogue, Socrates, who has just had his leg-shackles removed in prison, is inspired thereby to tell a "tale" (μῦθον) of the inevitable linkage of pleasure and pain:

> Socrates sat up on the bed, bent his leg and rubbed it with his hand, and as he rubbed he said: "What a strange thing that which men call pleasure seems to be, and how astonishing the relation it has with what is thought to be its opposite, namely pain! A man cannot have both at the same time. Yet if he pursues and catches the one, he is almost always bound to catch the other also, like two creatures with one head. I think that if Aesop had noted this he would have composed a fable (μῦθον) that a god wished to reconcile their opposition but could not do so, so he joined their two heads together, and therefore when a man has the one, the other follows later. This seems to be happening to me. My bonds caused pain in my leg, and now pleasure seems to be following." (*Phd.* 60b1–c7, trans. Grube 1997)

Socrates' mention of Aesop here provokes Cebes, one of his visitors, to "take it up and say (ὑπολαβών... ἔφη), 'O Socrates, you did well to remind me.'" Cebes proceeds to ask about the "poems [Socrates] has composed putting the fables of Aesop into verse and composing the hymn to Apollo" (τῶν ποιημάτων ὧν πεποίηκας ἐντείνας τοὺς τοῦ Αἰσώπου λόγους καὶ τὸ εἰς τὸν Ἀπόλλω προοίμιον, *Phd.* 60c9–d2).[25] Socrates explains that he was trying to obey the urgings of a dream vision, which had come to him frequently in his earlier life and bidden

---

[25] Translation from Grube 1997. Somewhat different is Burnet's interpretation of ἐντείνας; he notes on προοίμιον, "This instance shows that ἐντείνας is 'setting to music', not merely 'versifying'; for no προοίμιον could have been in prose" (Burnet 1911.16 ad 60d2). While I agree with the point about *prooimion*, I am positing instead a slight zeugma in the meaning of ἐντείνας that would then correspond exactly to the double imperative "compose and perform *mousikē*" (μουσικὴν ποίει καὶ ἐργάζου, *Phd.* 60e6–7). For ἐντείνας used for "versifying," cf. [Plato] *Hipparch.* 228d5–6 (where the object is specified as "elegiac couplets," which were generally not sung but recited). Cf. Rowe 1993.120, who opts for the translation "putting into verse" for reasons slightly different from those offered here.

him, "O Socrates, compose and practice *mousikē*" (μουσικὴν ποίει καὶ ἐργάζου, *Phd.* 60e6–7). In the past, he had always understood this to be encouragement to do what he was already doing, practicing philosophy "as being the greatest [form of] *mousikē*" (*Phd.* 61a3–4). But now, after his trial and the postponement of his execution because of the festival of Apollo:

> I thought that, in case my dream was bidding me to practice this popular art (ταύτην τὴν δημώδη μουσικήν), I should not disobey it but compose poetry. I thought it safer not to leave here until I had satisfied my conscience by writing poems in obedience to the dream. So I first wrote in honor of the god of the present festival. After that I realized that a poet, if he is to be a poet, must compose *muthoi* rather than *logoi* ["fictional tales" or "fables" rather than "rational arguments"].[26] Being no teller of fables myself (καὶ αὐτὸς οὐκ ἦ μυθολογικός), I took the stories I knew and had at hand, the fables of Aesop, and I versified the first ones I came across (οὓς προχείρους εἶχον μύθους καὶ ἠπιστάμην τοὺς Αἰσώπου, τούτων ἐποίησα οἷς πρώτοις ἐνέτυχον). (*Phd.* 61a5–b7, trans. Grube 1997, slightly modified)

Let us start with the question, why *fable*? Why should Socrates be devoting his time to the fables of Aesop at the end of his life? Scholars have had surprisingly little to say about this moment in the *Phaedo*, apparently assuming that this is an instance of Plato's accurate reportage of his beloved master's last days.[27] In contrast to this style of reading the Platonic dialogues, I do not believe we can draw any conclusions about the historical Socrates from the texts of Plato or Xenophon. Instead, I concur with those scholars who understand the genre of *Sōkratikoi logoi* as a fabricated literary form, and Socrates himself as a fictional character in the writings of Plato and Xenophon.[28] Thus the "real" Socrates is

---

[26] Thus Burnet 1911.18, commenting on *Phd.* 61b4 (citing several Platonic parallels): "The distinction is almost the same as ours between 'fiction' and 'fact.'" Cf. Rowe 1993.122: "i.e., the sphere of the poet is fiction rather than (true) accounts of things (or 'rational arguments')."

[27] Thus (in general, for the *Phaedo* as an accurate representation of Socrates' last day), see Burnet 1911. intro.; for acceptance of Socrates' having composed "a hymn to Apollo and versified the fables of Aesop," see Guthrie 1969.326n. 1, West 1984.109 with n. 9, Vander Waerdt 1994a.4–5; and see the entry for Socrates in West 1992. 138–39. Partly perhaps also scholars have been taken in by Socrates' emphatic statement of the casual or adventitious nature of his stumbling upon Aesop's fables as his raw material at *Phd.* 61b5–7. But, as a general methodological principle, I think we should see Platonic design most at work where he insists most vehemently on accident. In chapter 4, section IV (n. 91), above, I have suggested that Socrates' claim that the fables were simply "ready to hand" in fact represents a suitably Aesopic homage, playing on the fable-maker's well-known ability skillfully to exploit humble or everyday objects that happen to be available in his environment.

[28] Or, perhaps better: with Momigliano, we might see the *Sōkratikoi logoi* as a complex mixture of history and fiction, but a mixture that is impossible for us to disentangle: "We shall not understand what biography was in the fourth century if we do not recognize that it came to occupy an ambiguous position between fact and imagination. Let us be in no doubt. With a man like Plato, and even with a smaller but by no means simpler man like Xenophon, this is a consciously chosen ambiguity. The Socratics experimented in biography, and the experiments were directed towards capturing the potentialities rather than the realities of individual lives. Socrates, the main subject

no more accessible to us than the "real" Aesop; we have instead to deal with two imaginary figures and the traditions that proliferated around them.

But even if it be insisted that Plato represents Socrates engaged in his Aesopic compositions here simply because *that's how it really happened*, we must still explain why Plato chose to include this detail within the artful literary structure of the *Phaedo*; why he described it in this precise form; and what functions this vignette serves within the text as a whole.[29] As a preliminary answer to these questions, I would suggest that this is a programmatic passage in which Plato goes to some trouble to affiliate his prose dialogues with Aesopic fable and Socrates himself with Aesop. Thus we should note that Socrates' exposition presupposes a familiar structural opposition of ordinary speech or prose versus *mousikē*, even if his goal is ultimately to deconstruct that opposition by the claim that philosophy itself represents the "greatest [form of] *mousikē*." That is to say, this Platonic text clearly knows the distinction of poetry/song and prose and unequivocally locates Aesopic fables (in their normal form) in the latter category. Since Plato's text is itself prose, philosophy would seem to align with Aesopic fable even as it claims to be the "greatest [form of] *mousikē*."

Other features of the *Phaedo* passage, in fact, support the implied genre affiliation of *Sōkratikoi logoi* with Aesopic fable. Thus notice the phrase ὑπολαβὼν ἔφη that marks Cebes' inquiry about the condemned prisoner's activity of "versifying Aesop's fables." As I suggested in chapter 3, ὑπολαβὼν ἔφη is a colloquial speech formula that often occurs in contexts of aggressive verbal dueling, when one speaker imagines that his statement will cleverly trump his interlocutor's words and end discussion. Clearly the phrase carries none of that force here; but, as I also noted in chapter 3, ὑπολαβὼν ἔφη is a veritable formula of Aesopic fable, easily recognizable as such in a context that contains other marked Aesopic elements. Here, of course, Socrates has just narrated the fable Aesop "would have composed had he thought of it," and it is this that provokes Cebes' question about Socrates' "versifying the fables of Aesop." In this context, per-

---

of their considerations . . . was not so much the real Socrates as the potential Socrates. He was not a dead man whose life could be recounted. He was the guide to territories as yet unexplored" (Momigliano 1971.46–62, quotation taken from p. 46). For other scholars who argue for the basic fictionality of the representations of Socrates by Plato and Xenophon, see (e.g.), Wilamowitz-Moellendorff 1879; Kahn 1981, 1996; Woodruff 1982a.xii; Havelock 1983; Clay 1994; Vander Waerdt 1994a; Blondell 2002.

[29] Cf. Rowe 1993.120 (*ad* 60d1): "Whether such a work existed, or represents an invention of P.'s, is impossible to say . . . ; it clearly has a dramatic function in emphasising S.'s piety and devotion to his calling." Still, note that Rowe's thematic explanation does not at all address the question of why Socrates should be versifying *Aesop's fables* as a show of piety. Otherwise, Compton 1990.341, 2006.159–60 explains this vignette of Socrates' versifying Aesopic fables in the *Phaedo* as Plato's way of calling attention to the parallels between Aesop's unjust execution and Socrates'. This reading, I would contend, is too limited an approach to this scene in the *Phaedo*, since it entirely ignores its complex generic and metanarrative functions.

meated with references to Aesop and fable, the fabular resonance of the phrase ὑπολαβὼν ἔφη is unmistakable.

In addition, consider the specific terms used for "fable" here. While Socrates consistently designates Aesopic fables as *muthoi*, his interlocutor Cebes—apparently comfortably and unself-consciously—refers to them as *logoi*. At the level of *langue*, these two designations are just what we would expect within the diachronic development of Greek linguistic usage: for Aristophanes and Herodotus in the fifth century mainly designate fable as *logos*, while Aristotle uses the terms *muthos* and *logos*, apparently interchangeably.[30] But at the level of *parole* (of Plato's own word choice), these two terms are suggestive for the affiliation or kinship of Plato's own writing with Aesopic fable. Cebes' designation *logoi* resonates with the label Aristotle gives to the entire genre at the beginning of the *Poetics* (perhaps a term of art?)—*Sōkratikoi logoi*, "Socratic discourses" or "Conversations with Socrates."[31] Socrates' own strict preference for *muthos* is itself perhaps even more suggestive, since it raises the possibility that Platonic *muthos*, universally and unproblematically understood as "myth" in the reading of Plato's dialogues, may—at least on occasion—denote Aesopic fable.[32]

But we still have not exhausted this complex programmatic scene; why, after all, is Socrates shown *versifying* the humble prose fables of Aesop? This transposition from prose to poetry, and from low to high forms, I suggest, is a measure of the ambivalence of Plato's text toward Aesop as a precursor to Socrates. For if this passage implies the affiliation of Plato's prose *Sōkratikoi logoi* with those of Aesop, it simultaneously distances itself or disavows that kinship. This it does by the complex interplay of four terms: high poetry/hymn, low prose fable, "common *mousikē*," and philosophy as the "greatest [form of] *mousikē*." Even within the umbrella of *dēmōdēs mousikē*, Socrates' activity (and exposition thereof) articulate a graded hierarchy of high poetry/hymn aligned with Apollo and low prose fable aligned with Aesop. For (as we have seen) there was a pervasive ancient tradition—best represented by the *Life of Aesop* (Vita G), but I would contend much older—of antagonism between Aesop and Apollo as leader of the Muses and lord of the oracular shrine at Delphi.[33] Insofar as So-

---

[30] For *logos* meaning "fable," see Hdt. 1.141.1, 3; Aristoph. *Peace* 129–30, *Wasps* 1258–59, 1393–94, 1399–1400; Arist. *Rhet.* 2.20, 1393a–94a; for *muthos* meaning "fable," Aristoph. *Peace* 131, Arist. *Meteorologica* 356b11. On the terminology for fable, see van Dijk 1997.79–90 (although I do not agree with all the distinctions of meaning van Dijk proposes), Adrados 1999.5–17.

[31] Arist. *Poet.* 1447b2–4 (quoted below, p. 257). I take these translations of *Sōkratikoi logoi* from Kahn 1996.1.

[32] Thus I shall consider the implications of reading Protagoras's *muthos* in the *Protagoras* and Aristophanes' speech in Plato's *Symposium* as fables in chapters 7 and 8 below.

[33] See especially chapters 1 and 4 above. On the strand of Apollo-Aesop antagonism in *Vita G* and its antiquity, see Perry 1936.15–16, Nagy 1979.279–97, Hansen 1998.109–11; differently, Ferrari 1997.5–39 argues for this strand of Apollo-Aesop antagonism as a late, idiosyncratic imposition on the legend by the anonymous author of *Vita G*. But against Ferrari's position, see discussion in the introduction, section IIB and chapter 7, n. 98 below.

crates in the *Phaedo* and elsewhere strongly affiliates himself with the god Apollo, this complicates or disrupts his unproblematic kinship with Aesop. Furthermore, the ranked hierarchy of forms of *mousikē* itself registers simultaneous similarity and difference: Socratic *logoi* ("rational arguments") are to "true" *mousikē* what Aesopic *muthoi* ("fictional tales") are to *dēmōdēs mousikē* ("the common signification of *mousikē*," but also "common or popular *mousikē*").

Aristotle, too, registers a kinship between Socratic and Aesopic genres of speaking, while his treatment also exposes a rift between these two forms that corresponds to Plato's ambivalence (and so helps us understand its causes). In the *Rhetoric* (2.20, 1393a23–94a18), cataloging the universal forms of proof (πίστεις), Aristotle first distinguishes example (παράδειγμα) from enthymeme, then subdivides the former category into historical examples and those that are invented. Finally, the two subcategories or species of invented example, according to Aristotle, are "analogy" (ἓν μὲν παραβολή) and "fables, like the Aesopic or the Libyan" (ἓν δὲ λόγοι, οἷον οἱ Αἰσώπειοι καὶ Λιβυκοί). Within this typology, Aristotle's sole example of *parabolē* is τὰ Σωκρατικά ("the sayings of Socrates"):

> For example, if one should say that magistrates should not be chosen by lot. For it's just as if someone should choose athletes by lot, not by their ability to compete, or [as if] one would choose by lot any one of the sailors to be the steersman, as if it were necessary that it be the one chosen by lot, rather than the one who knew his business. (*Rhet.* 2.20.4, 1393b4–8)

Aristotle then proceeds to offer two examples of the use of Aesopic fable in contexts of public speaking, each narrated with great gusto and plenty of circumstantial detail. The first, the poet Stesichorus advising the people of Himera against giving Phalaris a bodyguard, we have considered already in chapter 3. The second features Aesop himself, "defending a Samian demagogue being tried on a capital charge" by telling the fable of a fox trapped for a long time in a ravine and afflicted with throngs of dog-fleas (κυνοραιστάς). When a kindhearted hedgehog passing by offers to remove the fleas, the fox declines, explaining

> that these [fleas] are already full of me and draw little blood. But if you take these away, others will come that are hungry and will utterly drain what's left of my blood. But to you in like manner, O men of Samos, this one will do no further harm (since he's wealthy). But if you kill this one, others will come who are poor, who will steal and squander your common [funds]. (*Rhet.* 2.20.6, 1393b28–94a1)

Thus, in formal terms, within Aristotle's schema, Socratic *parabolē* and Aesopic *logos* are very intimately related—first cousins, we might say, within the family of "invented examples."[34]

---

[34] Cf. Gigon 1959.176–77, Jedrkiewicz 1989.114.

But even within Aristotle's apparently matter-of-fact account, there are a couple of odd features that suggest a tension or problematic misfit between these kindred forms. First, notice the *content* of Aristotle's specific examples, which hints at an opposition in the characteristic politics of Socratic *parabolē* and Aesopic fable. The former, challenging by analogy the appointment of magistrates by lot, is clearly antidemocratic, while the two fables, so expansively narrated, can both be read as prodemocratic.[35] Stesichorus's fable warns against the incipient tyranny of Phalaris and, as we saw in chapter 3, resonates with Solon's advice to the Athenian demos, warning them against Pisistratus. Aesop's fable offers a cold-blooded defense of a demagogue—that is to say, from a conservative perspective, it cynically legitimates one of the worst abuses characteristic of the democratic system.[36]

Aristotle's concluding remarks on *paradeigmata* offer further anomalies that reinforce the tension or misfit implied by the content of his examples. Aristotle concludes:

> εἰσὶ δ' οἱ λόγοι δημηγορικοί, καὶ ἔχουσιν ἀγαθὸν τοῦτο, ὅτι πράγματα μὲν εὑρεῖν ὅμοια γεγενημένα χαλεπόν, λόγους δὲ ῥᾷον· ποιῆσαι γὰρ δεῖ ὥσπερ καὶ παραβολάς, ἄν τις δύνηται τὸ ὅμοιον ὁρᾶν, ὅπερ ῥᾷόν ἐστιν ἐκ φιλοσοφίας. ῥᾷω μὲν οὖν πορίσασθαι τὰ διὰ τῶν λόγων, χρησιμώτερα δὲ πρὸς τὸ βουλεύσασθαι τὰ διὰ τῶν πραγμάτων· ὅμοια γὰρ ὡς ἐπὶ τὸ πολὺ τὰ μέλλοντα τοῖς γεγονόσιν. (*Rhet.* 2.20.7–8, 1394a2–8)

> And fables are suitable for public speaking and they have this virtue, that it is hard to find past events that are similar, but easier to invent fables. For it is necessary to fashion them, just as also analogies, if someone is able to see the likeness, the very thing which is easier from a literary/philosophical education. Examples via fables are thus easier to provide, but examples via historical events are more useful for bouleutic oratory, since things that are going to happen are for the most part like things that have happened.

Aristotle's phrasing here is ambiguous, but the passage can be read to confer only on *parabolē*, not *logos*, an essential connection with a "literary" or "philosophical" education.[37] Then, having first asserted that *logoi* are "suitable for

---

[35] Socrates' use of analogies to argue against the selection of magistrates by lot is, in fact, explicitly interpreted as antidemocratic by the anonymous "accuser" in Xenophon's *Memorabilia* (1.2.9).

[36] Thus notice that even between "Stesichorus" and "Aesop," there is a graded hierarchy of the nobility and morality of the advice via fable. We might also note the ways in which the "punch line" of Aesop's fable here reads like a parody of Socrates' final prophecy to those jurors who voted for his execution in Plato's *Apology*. Recall that Socrates, who had described himself as a "gadfly" (μύωψ, *Apol.* 30e5) to the demos, predicts that they will suffer a "harsher punishment" after his death: "There will be more [men] cross-examining you, whom I was now restraining but you didn't perceive it. And they will be harsher insofar as they are younger, and they will annoy you more" (*Apol.* 39c8–d3).

[37] Depending how technically φιλοσοφία is meant; see the remarks of Cope and Sandys 1877.2.202 *ad loc.*: "Philosophy is used here in a vague and popular sense, for intellectual study, and mental exercise in general."

public speaking" (δημηγορικοί), Aristotle concludes that historical examples are, in fact, "more useful for bouleutic oratory" (χρησιμώτερα δὲ πρὸς τὸ βουλεύσασθαι), although harder to come up with. Thus he demotes fable to a rank below historical examples (somewhat paradoxically, since he has just devoted the most space and enthusiasm to the recounting of at least one fable explicitly set in a bouleutic context). Finally, by a kind of rhetorical sleight of hand, *parabolē* disappears entirely from any context of public speaking (and this conforms to the implied antidemocratic politics of the examples offered). Thus *logoi* (fables) are δημηγορικοί while, at the end, the options for bouleutic oratory are reduced to two terms in opposition—historical example versus fables. In all of this, *parabolē* is first narrowly identified with *philosophia* and implicitly opposed to *dēmēgorikos*. This suggests the hierarchy: (1) *parabolē* linked to private elite philosophical or literary education; (2) historical examples for public bouleutic speaking; (3) fable as the poor relation to both.

There are also scattered throughout the doxographic tradition intriguing suggestions of the low-class affiliations of *Sōkratikoi logoi* in general and Platonic dialogue in particular. First, consider Aristotle's offhand affiliation of *Sōkratikoi logoi* with "the mimes of Sophron and Xenarchus" at the beginning of the *Poetics*:

> There is further an art that imitates by bare language alone (λόγοις ψιλοῖς), or by meters [sc. without music] ... and these [forms of *mimēsis*] are nameless to this day. For we would have no common name for the mimes of Sophron and Xenarchus and the *Sōkratikoi logoi*, nor if someone should compose the *mimēsis* through trimeters or elegies or some other such [spoken meters]. (*Poet.* 1, 1447a28–b13)

By this conjunction, is Aristotle implying a significant generic affiliation between the *Sōkratikoi logoi* of Plato and Xenophon and the generically and sociologically low form of mime? Is he indeed "outing" Plato as a closeted writer of mimes? Scholars have been reluctant to think so, since, at this point in his discussion, Aristotle is considering only *medium* and not yet *objects* of *mimēsis* (i.e., people "better" or "worse" or "the same" as we are). That is to say, we could understand Aristotle's (very compressed) point here to imply an analogy: the *Sōkratikoi logoi* of Plato and Xenophon are to the mimes of Sophron and Xenarchus as tragedy is to comedy. Thus, just as tragedy and comedy use the same *medium* to represent characters and situations that are *spoudaioi* and *phauloi*, respectively, as Aristotle will go on to observe (*Poet.* 5, 1449a32–b24), Socratic dialogue shares its medium with low mime, but uses it to represent "worthy" or "serious" objects. At the very least, then, we must understand the nameless common form here to be mimetic prose.[38]

---

[38] For the argument that all Aristotle means here is the common form of mimetic prose, see Lucas 1968.58–60; Haslam 1972; Clay 1994.23–24, 33–37; Hordern 2004.16, 26–27. For helpful discussion and elucidation of what distinctions Aristotle is making in this typically compressed and elliptical passage, I am much indebted to Mark Griffith.

Still, there was an enduring tradition that Plato was a great admirer and imitator of the (low, sometimes obscene) Sicilian mimes of Sophron, which, according to Diogenes Laertius, were found under his pillow.[39] The fact that these stories get told and retold suggests that there was felt to be a kinship between Plato's dialogues and the mimes of Sophron that extended beyond the commonality of mimetic prose medium. Diogenes Laertius also preserves a tradition that Plato borrowed extensively from Epicharmus, the Sicilian comic poet (D.L. 3.9–17). And whether or not the fragments of Epicharmus quoted by Diogenes Laertius to make the case are genuine, the claim itself bespeaks a felt connection between Plato's writing and the low form of comedy.[40] There is in addition the intriguing notice, again preserved by Diogenes Laertius, that the first to write down Socratic conversations in dialogue form was Simon the cobbler (D.L. 2.123). Thus we are told that Socrates used to frequent his shop and that Simon took notes on the conversations he conducted there, ultimately publishing thirty-three in a single volume. "And this is why," Diogenes Laertius concludes, "they call his dialogues 'cobbler's'" (ὅθεν σκυτικοὺς αὐτοῦ τοὺς διαλόγους καλοῦσιν, D.L. 2.122). Again, it is impossible to know if these "cobbler's tales" were genuine or a later fabrication, but either way, they attest to the (real or imagined) humble, banausic origins of prose *Sōkratikoi logoi*, while the figure of thirty-three in a single volume (i.e., a papyrus roll of 1,000–1,200 lines) suggests compositions on the scale of mimes.[41]

We also find preserved in Athenaeus's *Deipnosophistae* a long riff on Plato's malice (κακοήθεια), envy, vanity, and ambition, gleaned from various hostile sources (Athen. 11.504e–509e). Much of this material turns out to be a com-

---

[39] This tradition of Plato's admiration and imitation of Sophron was very robust in antiquity: see Riginos 1976.174–76 and Hordern 2004.26–27 for exhaustive collections of ancient testimonia. Clay 1994.34–35 and Hordern 2004.26–27 suggest that these anecdotes had their origin in a tradition hostile to Plato, though both also acknowledge their enduring mainstream popularity. On Plato's relation to mime, see also R. B. Rutherford 1995.12; Blondell 2002.14; Worman 2008.154, 159, 162.

[40] Notice especially the last fragment quoted by Diogenes Laertius (3.17) in which "Epicharmus" predicts that some later writer will memorialize his *logoi*, "stripping them of the meter that now holds them and clothing them in a purple garment, elaborating them with fine phrases." The mantic content here strongly suggests that all these fragments of "Ephicharmus" are later fabrications, while the imagery of the fragment also inverts the usual ranked hierarchy of poetry vs prose to suggest the (quasi-poetic) grandeur of Platonic prose writing.

[41] Different scholars are more or less optimistic about the reality of a historical Simon and his "Socratic Conversations." Thus Clay 1994.32–33 with n. 19 is more optimistic (even citing archaeologists' claims to have found Simon's workshop in the Athenian Agora); Kahn 1996.10 (following Wilamowitz-Moellendorff 1879.187–89 and Zeller 1889.243n), on the contrary, assumes that "Simon" was the fictional creation of the Socratic Phaedo, which then spawned a whole "literature of shoe-maker dialogues." I am inclined to agree with Kahn, especially given D.L.'s notice in his *Life of Phaedo* (2.105) that the "Cobbler's Tales" (σκυτικοὺς λόγους) were variously attributed in the tradition to Phaedo and to the Socratic Aeschines. For a recent discussion of the figure of Simon and his significance for a post-Socratic Cynic tradition, see Sellars 2003.

mentary not so much on Plato's character as on the low, parodic elements of his writing; that is to say, this is genre criticism transformed into biography. Thus, for example, the report of the interaction of Plato and Gorgias:

> It is reported that Gorgias, himself reading the dialogue named after him, remarked to his intimates, "What nice satire Plato knows how to write!" (ὡς καλῶς οἶδε Πλάτων ἰαμβίζειν). And Hermippus in his work *On Gorgias* says: "When Gorgias arrived in Athens after dedicating the gold statue of himself at Delphi, Plato seeing him said: 'Here comes our noble and golden Gorgias!'; to which Gorgias replied: 'Noble indeed and new is this Archilochus that Athens has produced.'" (ἦ καλόν γε αἱ Ἀθῆναι καὶ νέον τοῦτον Ἀρχίλοχον ἐνηνόχασιν). (Athen. 11.505de, trans. Gulick 1980)

The picture of Gorgias reading the Platonic dialogue named after him is presumably a chronological impossibility—a doxographic fantasy—but one that bespeaks a perception of generically low, scurrilous elements in Plato's mimetic prose writing.[42] For "Gorgias" here characterizes Plato's genre as iambic blame poetry and identifies Plato himself with Archilochus, the preeminent archaic practitioner of this low form.

And yet, in spite of the description of Socrates' literary activity in the *Phaedo*, Aristotle's close association of Socratic analogy and Aesopic fable in the *Rhetoric*, and the hints of low generic affiliations for the *Sōkratikoi logoi* in the doxographic tradition, there is almost no discussion in the scholarly literature on Plato of Aesop as a precursor for Socrates or Aesopic fable as a speech genre that might have contributed to Socratic dialogue.[43] Why is this? Literary treatments of the origins and generic affiliations of Socratic dialogue have tended to focus on poetic forms, especially on tragedy and comedy. Thus Diskin Clay, in an essay entitled "The Origins of the Socratic Dialogue," acknowledges but downplays the possible influence of the lowly mimes of Sophron and the beginnings of biography, in order to emphasize the impact of Attic comedy and tragedy.[44] Likewise Andrea Nightingale, in her insightful treatment of the many

---

[42] For this anecdote as a representation of genre criticism within Platonic reception, cf. Blondell 2002.32, Worman 2008.162. I'll consider some of these low, parodic elements in Plato's *Gorgias* in chapter 9 below.

[43] Admittedly, there are a few treatments of the relevance of specific fables to the dialogues/texts in which they occur: e.g., Dover 1966; Desclos 1997, 2000 for Plato. There are also occasional brief acknowledgments that Aesop might be a significant precursor or model for Socrates: thus Gigon 1959.177, 180; Winkler 1985.289n. 23; Jedrkiewicz 1989.114–15. But, to my knowledge, there has been no extended treatment of the influence of Aesopic fable on *Sōkratikoi logoi* as a general phenomenon.

[44] Clay 1994; see especially his summary statement on pp. 45–46: "if the comic poets of Athens offered models for the literary Socratics while Socrates was alive, the tragic poets of Athens offered models for the dramatic representation of Socrates once he was dead. In dealing with history, the literary Socratics who wrote after Socrates' death could exploit a resource available to both the tragedian and the historian; the actors in the events they narrate or dramatize were unaware of the full implications of their words and actions." Notice how in this account (prose) history gets slipped

genres and discourses subsumed into Platonic dialogue for Plato's own philosophical purposes, focuses mainly on Plato's complex engagement with comic and tragic drama.[45] In this respect, these scholars, like many others, draw their inspiration from a remarkable passage at the end of Plato's *Symposium*:

> Aristodemus said . . . that he woke up toward daybreak when the cocks were already singing, and, when he awoke, he saw that the rest were asleep or gone, but that Agathon and Aristophanes and Socrates alone were still awake and were drinking from a large phiale passed left to right. And [he said that] Socrates was engaged in conversation with them. And the rest of what was said Aristodemus said he didn't remember—for he wasn't present from the beginning and he was getting a bit drowsy—still, he said, the main point was Socrates was compelling them to agree that it was characteristic of the same man to have the skill to compose comedy and tragedy, and that the one who was a tragic poet by art would also be a comic poet (καὶ τὸν τέχνῃ τραγῳδοποιὸν ὄντα ‹καὶ› κωμῳδοποιὸν εἶναι). And these men, as they were being compelled in these things and not following very well, were falling asleep—and first Aristophanes dropped off, and then, as it became day, Agathon. (*Sym.* 223c2–d8)

Scholars have found it irresistible to read Socrates' argument here as a veiled programmatic statement for Plato's own artistry, which masterfully weaves together high and low forms to produce the unique generic hybrid of Socratic dialogue.[46] And yet, I would contend, the beginning of the *Phaedo* offers us an equally provocative programmatic scene for the complex generic affiliations of Socratic dialogue—but a scene that has been studiously ignored by most Plato scholars.[47]

At the same time, paradoxically, other scholars working on the beginnings of rhetoric or on ancient fable traditions are well aware of the prevalence of Ae-

---

in, but not really acknowledged. Cf. Nussbaum 2001.122–35, characterizing Platonic dialogue as "Plato's anti-tragic theater."

[45] Nightingale 1995.4–12, 60–92, 172–92, with abundant references to earlier scholars who connect Plato's writing with tragedy and/or comedy. See also Clay 1972, 2000 and Loraux 1989, aligning Plato's portrayal of Socrates with that of Homeric heroes. For the connections of Platonic dialogue with all three forms of Greek poetry (epic, tragedy, and comedy), see also Blondell 2002.

[46] Thus Bacon 1959; Clay 1975, 1994.46; Nightingale 1995.2, 68; R. B. Rutherford 1995.204–5; Nussbaum 2001.194–99. Nightingale 1995.1–8 is particularly good on drawing out the paradoxical relation of Plato's own generic hybridity to his strong opposition to the mixing of poetic genres in the *Laws*.

[47] Or perhaps one should say, often mentioned, but never really explained: thus (e.g.) Nightingale (1995.2) cites this passage together with *Sym.* 223d and *Phdr.* 241e as evidence for Plato's self-conscious genre mixing and hybridity; but she never pursues the implications of the precise genres specified in the *Phaedo* (in contrast to *Symposium* and *Phaedrus*). Cf. Martin 1998.124 (quoted in chapter 9 below). This is partly, as I shall note below, an issue of preservation and fragmentary evidence: in contrast to tragedy and Old Comedy, the remains of Sophron are pitifully meager and fragmentary, those of the Aesop tradition almost invisible, whereas preserved Aesopic texts like the *Life* and the fables are assumed to be late and therefore not relevant to the writing of Plato and Xenophon.

sopic or fabular elements in *Sōkratikoi logoi*, but they have been content in general simply to list or catalog examples of fables embedded in the texts of Plato and Xenophon.[48] There has been almost no consideration of such deployments of fable within the dynamic and evolving literary system of late- fifth-/fourth-century prose writing, in which genre, content, and level of style were all inextricably bound up with issues of sociopolitical power and prestige. But why this unevenness of scholarly recognition of Aesopic elements within different subfields? And why the pervasive reluctance to follow out the implications (stylistic *and* political) of the Aesopic lurking behind and within *Sōkratikoi logoi*? This is partly an inevitable problem of the modern proliferation of scholarship and the attendant necessity for individual scholars to focus and specialize within the field of classics (as in every other discipline).[49] Thus the voluminous works of Plato have spawned an immense amount of scholarly literature in the modern era, dominated mainly by philosophers and some literary critics. And, while there has been a recent boom in the field of Aesop/fable studies, this material and its scholarship still remain largely segregated within classics (for reasons noted in the introduction).[50] Finally—since Sophistic writing and teaching will figure prominently in our story—we must acknowledge that the importance and influence of the Sophists is still downplayed or underestimated within much scholarly discourse.

To some extent, of course, the heft and prominence of these respective bounded scholarly fields depend on and correlate with the accidents of preservation; we possess everything Plato ever wrote (and apparently much he didn't), while for the Sophists and Aesop/fable we have only miserable fragments, embedded in (often hostile or tendentious) sources or much later paraphrase or summary. I say "accidents of preservation," but of course the survival—or disappearance—of certain texts and kinds of texts is itself politically motivated. In the case of Plato and the Sophists, the brute facts of survival signify Plato's ultimate victory in a hotly contested battle over the forms of education, the nature of *philosophia*, and (I would contend) the conventions and norms of prose writing in the Greek tradition. And if this is true for the survival of ancient texts, we must also acknowledge the extent to which a politicized hierarchy of value still informs the particular formation of scholarly subdisciplines with boundaries

---

[48] Thus Karadagli 1981.165, 167–88; Cole 1991.58–62; Desclos 1997, 2000; van Dijk 1997.311–50 (324–40 on Plato and Xenophon); Adrados 1999.402; these approaches will be considered in more detail at the beginning of the next chapter.

[49] Cf. the astute observations of O'Sullivan 1992.151–52 on blind spots produced by field specialization.

[50] For a boom in Aesop/fable scholarship starting in the late 1980s and1990s, see (e.g.) Jedrkiewicz 1987, 1989, 1997; Holzberg 1992, 1993, 1996, 2002; Hopkins 1993; van Dijk 1997; Adrados 1999, 2000, 2003 (English translations), as well as new editions of the Greek texts of the *Life* (Papathomopoulos 1990, 1999; Ferrari 1997; Karla 2001; Jouanno 2006) and readily available English translations of the *Life* and fables (Hansen 1998, Temple and Temple 1998, Gibbs 2002). See above, introduction, section IIB.

often impermeable to each other. That is to say, it is disturbing (but perhaps not surprising) how much the relative ranking of scholarly subfields and the allowable questions within each still conform to the lineaments of Hegel's aesthetic hierarchy of poetry, philosophy, and Aesopic fable, quoted at the beginning of this chapter. Nor is this an accident, for Hegel's account of the transcendent in art in fact reproduces many elements of a powerful Platonic model—what we might call "the Platonic mirage," whereby all Socrates' intellectual competitors are first parodied and vilified and then finally eclipsed by a philosophical project that represents itself as monolithic, timeless, and transcendent.

Thus modern Plato scholars are responding to something genuinely Platonic in their reluctance to see the affiliations of the philosopher's art with the low-class forms of mime and Aesopic fable. Our narratives of Greek literary history—consciously or unconsciously—still succumb to the Hegelian privileging of philosophy and Plato's art as transcendent; Plato's Socrates therefore simply cannot be thought together with Aesop and the representatives of other scurrilous low forms. The corollary or side effect of this Hegelian repression is that modern scholars, much like many ancient critics, desperately want to transform Plato's writing into poetry. For what these literary-historical accounts gap or occlude is the crucial fact that Plato chose the medium of mimetic prose.[51]

We should perhaps instead follow (the more heretical, anti-Hegelian) lead of Nietzsche and Bakhtin, who offer more complex, variegated models of generic mixture in the *Sōkratikoi logoi*. The former, hostile to Socrates as the embodiment of the rational Apollinian energies that destroyed tragedy, observes at one point with characteristic bite and vividness:

> If tragedy had absorbed into itself all the earlier types of art, the same might also be said in an eccentric sense of the Platonic dialogue which, a mixture of all extant styles and forms, hovers midway between narrative, lyric, and drama, between prose and poetry, and so has also broken the strict old law of the unity of linguistic form. This tendency was carried still further by the *Cynic* writers, who in the greatest stylistic medley, oscillating between prose and metrical forms, realized also the literary image of the "raving Socrates" whom they represented in real life.
>
> The Platonic dialogue was, as it were, the barge on which the shipwrecked ancient poetry saved herself with all her children: crowded into a narrow space and timidly submitting to the single pilot, Socrates, they now sailed into a new world, which never

---

[51] For one ancient example of the transformation of Plato into poetry, see Longinus *On the Sublime* ch. 13.3 (trans. Roberts 1935): "Was Herodotus alone a devoted imitator of Homer? No, Stesichorus even before his time, and Archilochus, and above all Plato, who from the great Homeric source drew to himself innumerable tributary streams." Hegel, in his close alignment of "poetry and philosophy" as transcendent forms opposed to the lowly, quotidian Aesopic fable (in the passage quoted above, n. 2), participates in this same mystification of Platonic writing. Among modern scholars, Nightingale 1995.91 and Nussbaum 2001.129–33 are rare exceptions, insofar as they explicitly acknowledge that Plato's choice of prose and common language significantly differentiate his texts from tragedy.

tired of looking at the fantastic spectacle of this procession. Indeed, Plato has given to all posterity the model of a new art form, the model of the *novel*—which may be described as an infinitely enhanced Aesopian fable, in which poetry holds the same rank in relation to dialectical philosophy as this same philosophy held for many centuries in relation to theology: namely, the rank of *ancilla*. This was the new position into which Plato, under the pressure of the demonic Socrates, forced poetry.[52]

The value of Nietzsche's clear-sighted assessment is that he sees the essential combination of poetry and prose in Platonic dialogue. Thus, though he is mainly interested in characterizing Platonic philosophy's piratical waylaying of poetry in the second paragraph quoted, Nietzsche embeds in the middle of his account the provocative phrase (which finds no elaboration in his text), "an infinitely enhanced Aesopian fable."

Bakhtin, in turn, celebrates the very generic hybridity and dialogic appropriation of older literary forms that Nietzsche so reviles, seeing in the Socratic dialogue an important precursor to the "carnivalized genre" of Menippean satire. According to Bakhtin, the common genre of Socratic dialogue and Menippean satire is the seriocomic (σπουδογέλοιον), characterized by its contemporary setting and concerns (in contrast to "epic or tragic distance"); its free invention and critical relationship to myth and legend; and its deliberate rejection of stylistic unity in favor of "hetero-voiced" hybridity.[53] This last feature, in particular, aptly captures the generic motley of Socratic dialogue:

> Characteristic of these genres are a multi-toned narration, the mixing of high and low, serious and comic; they make wide use of inserted genres—letters, found manuscripts, retold dialogues, parodies on the high genres, parodically reinterpreted citations; in some of them we observe a mixing of prosaic and poetic speech, living dialects and jargons ... are introduced, and various authorial masks make their appearance.[54]

This model of the complex generic polyphony of the Socratic dialogue invites us to read the programmatic end of the *Symposium* allegorically or synecdochically, rather than literally. That is, perhaps the genres of tragedy and comedy spotlighted there stand in for or represent not just themselves, but the entire spectrum of genre, ranging from the highest forms to the lowest. That spectrum

---

[52] Nietzsche 1967.90–91.

[53] Bakhtin 1984a.106–22; on the Socratic dialogue specifically, 109–12. Cf. Bakhtin 1981.21–26.

[54] Bakhtin 1984a.108. And while Bakhtin was apparently unacquainted with the *Life of Aesop* (which is never mentioned in his writings), many of the features of *spoudogeloion* he identifies in the Socratic dialogue resonate strongly with characteristic elements of the Aesop tradition. (For helpful conversation and confirmation that Bakhtin never in fact refers to Aesop, I am indebted to Boris Maslov and Nancy Ruttenburg). Cf. Nightingale 1995.191–92 with n. 53, who makes the same point about Bakhtin in relation to the comedies of Aristophanes (as significantly standing behind Socratic *spoudogeloion*). Finally, for a reading of the whole Aesop tradition in terms of a long-lived philosophical genre of *spoudogeloion*, see Jedrkiewicz 1989.157–64, 1997.

is figured differently in the *Phaedo*, where high poetic hymn to Apollo and low prose Aesopic fable substitute for tragedy and comedy, respectively, and differently again in the doxographical tradition, which makes Plato an aspiring tragic playwright who slept with the texts of Sophron under his pillow (D.L. 3.5, 3.18).[55] At the same time, we cannot understand Plato's own programmatic statements or the affiliations asserted in the ancient tradition for *Sōkratikoi logoi* until we recognize that Plato, Xenophon, and the Sophists were all engaged in a deadly serious struggle over the field of intellectual activity—a struggle that was also, necessarily, a battle over style and the shape of prose writing. I would contend that the Sophists, in different ways from Plato, engaged in generic and stylistic experimentation that might (in an alternate universe) have put their stamp on the tradition of Western prose writing. As we shall see in the next three chapters, both sides mobilized Aesop, the Aesopic, and the fabular in this competition over prose; that Plato eventually won is due in part to his more radical deployment of Aesop combined with a more thoroughgoing disavowal. The former helps account for the extreme generic motley of the Socratic dialogue, while the latter has spawned and authorized a still-robust tradition of reading Plato's texts as works of philosophical genius that transcend time and history. Thus it is not my intention to deny the many generic influences and appropriated forms earlier scholars have detected in the *Sōkratikoi logoi*—simply to supplement them at the lowest end of the generic spectrum with a consideration of Aesopic elements and thereby also to draw out more explicitly the situatedness of Platonic writing and its paradoxical politics of form.

[55] Plato's inclusion of the entire generic spectrum may also explain a tantalizing fragment of Aristotle preserved by Diogenes Laertius, "And Aristotle says that the form of his [sc. Plato's] words is between poetry and prose" (φησὶ δ' Ἀριστοτέλης τὴν τῶν λόγων ἰδέαν αὐτοῦ μεταξὺ ποιήματος εἶναι καὶ πεζοῦ λόγου, D.L. 3.37 = Arist. ΠΕΡΙ ΠΟΙΗΤΩΝ fr. 862 Gigon). On the meaning of this fragment, cf. R. B. Rutherford 1995.15.

Chapter 7

THE BATTLE OVER PROSE: FABLE IN SOPHISTIC EDUCATION AND XENOPHON'S *MEMORABILIA*

STILL, BEFORE WE CAN FULLY unpack the complex relation of Plato's Socrates to Aesop and Aesopic fable, we need to set the stage by considering the broader fifth-/fourth-century context of what we might call "the battle over prose." For this purpose, we must at least dip into the "Sophistic movement" as the milieu in reaction to which Plato produced much of his written work. Having long suffered under the burden of Plato's tendentious misrepresentation and opprobrium, the Sophists have recently enjoyed something of a renaissance, receiving more respectful scholarly treatment that acknowledges their far-reaching influence, complexity of goals and interests, and diversity as a group.[1] Yet in spite of this ongoing recuperation of the Sophists, scholarly field specialization and the idealist developmental narratives still prevalent in classics and ancient philosophy have often consigned the Sophists entirely to the realm of "rhetoric," while Socrates and Plato, by contrast, enjoy the mantle of "philosophy." This is, of course, artificially to split the domain of *logos* or the literary field into "mere" form or style versus content, relegating the Sophists to the former, while Plato and his master Socrates are credited with all that has weight and substance.[2] And yet, as older generations of scholars well understood, the strict ancient hierarchy of genre and decorum made it impossible to sunder style and content: in the traditional system, elevation of content dictated level of style, while stylistic choices that cut athwart this hierarchy always carried semantic and political significance as well.[3] Such an artificial division, then, inevitably reduces the Sophists to the trivial and the superficial, while all credit for innovation, originality, and profundity accrues to Plato as a solitary genius (the "Platonic mirage" I referred to at the end of the previous chapter).

In fact, the fragmentary evidence we have suggests that the Sophists were (among other things) engaged in fairly wild generic and stylistic experimenta-

---

[1] Precursors for a more positive evaluation of the Sophists: Grote 1851.VIII. 477–550, Sidgwick 1872, Havelock 1957. More recently: Guthrie 1969; de Romilly 1975, 1992; Kerferd 1981; Cole 1991; O'Sullivan 1992, 1996; Ford 1993, 2002; Gagarin 2002; Tell 2003, 2010.

[2] Cf. Gagarin 2002.4–6; Gagarin prefers to designate the area of the Sophists as "logos" (discourse) rather than "rhetoric."

[3] For examples of this older understanding, see Norden 1915.1–12 and passim; Nietzsche 1967.90: "the strict old law of the unity of linguistic form" (quoted in chapter 6, section II above); Auerbach 1953.

tion at the boundaries between poetry and prose, in a period when the nature and norms of the latter were still very much up for grabs. Gorgias's elaborate art prose is perhaps only the most familiar example of such stylistic/generic experimentation. For, as Jacqueline de Romilly argued long ago, Gorgias sought to capture for prose the prestige and power—even magical qualities—traditionally associated by the Greeks with poetry through rhythmical effects, homoioteleuton and *parisōsis*, high poetic diction, and bold metaphor.[4] Other Sophists transposed to prose genres and content traditionally cast in verse: for example, Plato tells us that Hippias composed and performed an artful *logos*, in which he described Nestor advising the young Neoptolemus at the sack of Troy "on what behavior would make a young man most reputable" (*Hipp. Mai.* 286a3–b6). From Plato's characterization, this appears to be a recasting in prose of the genre of mythological *hypothēkai*, a traditional poetic form known from the archaic period.[5] In addition, we know of at least a few Sophists who seem to have composed poetry as well as prose: Hippias (again), according to *Hippias Minor* 368c8–d2, came to Olympia once "having epics and tragedies and dithyrambs," as well as "many diverse, carefully composed *logoi* in prose"—presumably all of his own composition.[6] There is also Evenus of Paros, whom Plato in the *Apology* clearly considers a Sophist, since he has Socrates mention him together with Gorgias, Prodicus, and Hippias as one of those "wise" and "blessed" men who can teach virtue to the young—for a stiff fee (*Apol.* 19e1–20c1). This same Evenus pops up in the *Phaedrus*, credited by Socrates with the invention of several mixed generic or discursive forms, among them "indirect censures in verse as an aid to memory" (παραψόγους ... ἐν μέτρῳ ... μνήμης χάριν, *Phdr.* 267a2–5).[7] And, of course, if we are willing to count the Athenian Critias in the ranks of the Sophists, his literary production clearly spanned many genres, both prose and verse: hexameters, elegiacs, tragic drama, *politeiai* in both poetry and prose, and many other compositions.[8]

[4] De Romilly 1975.3–22; cf. the classic treatment of Norden 1915.63–71 and recent discussion in O'Sullivan 1992.23–62, 106–29; Ford 2002.172–87.

[5] On *hypothēkai*, see Friedländer 1913; on the specific tradition of mythological *hypothēkai*, see Kurke 1990 (esp. 104–7); on Hippias's "Trojan *logos*" in the didactic tradition, see also Gray 1998.165.

[6] In order to argue for the Sophists' "overwhelming preference for prose," O'Sullivan (1996.116 with n. 7) insists that the poems Hippias is said to have brought to Olympia need not be his own compositions: "these poems (unlike the items of clothing mentioned before) are not specifically said to be Hippias' own work, ... an equally valid interpretation of the passage would be that Hippias has come to expound other people's poetry." I find this a forced and artificial interpretation of Plato's Greek, especially given the connective πρὸς δὲ τούτοις at *Hipp. Min.* 368c8.

[7] For preserved elegiac fragments attributed to Evenus, see West 1992.63–67; the references to Evenus at *Phd.* 60–61 also imply that he is a poet as well as a philosopher—hence his (slightly anxious, territorial) interest in Socrates' activity of "versifying" in prison.

[8] See fragments in DK 88; for Critias's literary experimentation between prose and verse, see also Cole 1991.165n. 8. Most scholars accept Critias as part of the Sophistic movement, but see doubts expressed by Guthrie 1969.301, Kerferd 1981.52–53. O'Sullivan 1996.116–17 questions the validity

THE BATTLE OVER PROSE 267

Still other kinds of stylistic/generic experimentation have left their traces in the fragmentary remains of the Sophists: we find the mixture of different (even antithetical) genres of discourse within a single composition, as well as the transposition of traditionally low content to high style. For the former, we might cite again Evenus's invention of strange hybrid forms—*parepainos* and *parapsogos* ("indirect praise" and "indirect blame" or mixtures of praise and blame?)—in prose and poetry, as mentioned in the *Phaedrus* (267a4–5). In addition, we should consider the generic and stylistic weirdness represented by Hippias's *Sunagōgē*, which (by his own statement) seems to have incorporated "the best" of earlier poetry and prose writing in order to construct "this new and multiform *logos*" (ἐγὼ δὲ ἐκ πάντων τούτων τὰ μέγιστα καὶ ὁμόφυλα συνθεὶς τοῦτον καινὸν καὶ πολυειδῆ τὸν λόγον ποιήσομαι, Hippias, 86 B 6 DK).[9] For the latter, we might recall Eryximachus's quotation of Phaedrus's bemused commentary on "paradoxical encomia" in Plato's *Symposium*:

> But if you wish to consider in turn the worthy Sophists, [isn't it strange] that they compose praises in prose of Heracles and of others, just like the excellent Prodicus—and this is less to be marveled at, but I have already [even] happened upon some book by a wise man in which salt got marvelous praise for its usefulness, and you would see many other such things celebrated. (*Sym.* 177b1–4)

Artful literary encomia composed for such lowly objects as salt represent (among other things) a conscious breach by their composers of the strict traditional correlation between level of content and level of style and genre that subtended the entire ancient literary system. It is therefore intriguing to find mention of Prodicus's "Choice of Heracles"—a work I will consider at length below—in this context. For while Phaedrus is willing to grant that Heracles is a fit subject for encomium, the other topics and prevailing tone of this passage suggest that some kind of generic or stylistic anomaly lurks in Prodicus's composition as well (as we shall see).

After all this, we should understand Aristotle's account in Book 3 of the *Rhetoric* of the different styles and features appropriate for prose as opposed to

---

of this categorization more strenuously (partly to buttress his assertion that the Sophists as a group were interested only in prose). It would perhaps be better to abandon the label "Sophist" entirely (as Tell 2010, ch.1 suggests) and instead talk about "practitioners of wisdom" who composed or performed in many different forms and genres, poetry and prose. This category would certainly include Protagoras, Gorgias, Hippias, Prodicus, but also Critias and Socrates among its members.

[9] Thanks to Håkan Tell for calling my attention to Hippias's *Sunagōgē* and the philosophical discussions thereof by Snell 1966a, Mansfield 1990, and Frede 2004. Snell, Mansfield, Frede, and Tell 2010 offer fascinating arguments for the importance of Hippias's *Sunagōgē* for the "invention of philosophy." Less attention has been paid to the issue of generic/stylistic experimentation in this text, though this is the feature Hippias himself emphasizes in what appears to be the rhetorical climax of his prologue (τοῦτον καινὸν καὶ πολυειδῆ τὸν λόγον). For the combination of conventional content and formal experimentation in Hippias's *Sunagōgē*, cf. Gray 1998.163–65.

poetry as a stabilization and fixation of the literary system after a period of radical experimentation—that is, the more or less definitive victory of one side in a heated battle over the boundaries and decorum of (written) prose.[10]

I. Sophistic Fables

It is in the context of various kinds of generic and stylistic experimentation that I would situate the Sophists' adaptations and appropriations of humble prose fable. As Ben Edwin Perry and others have argued, in the fifth and fourth centuries, Aesopica or Aesopic fable seems to have been a very loose category, which comprehended jokes, witty comebacks, and comic anecdotes as well as what are now considered "fables" more narrowly defined.[11] But if we take our lead from the Platonic corpus itself, we find two types of fables clearly associated with Aesop: beast fables (as in the fable of the aging lion and the fox to which Socrates alludes in *Alcibiades* I) and aetiological, mythological fables (as in the tale of pleasure and pain Socrates narrates in the *Phaedo*).[12] If we then survey the *Sōkratikoi logoi* of Plato and Xenophon for these two types, we find the following additional examples (all of which have been identified by one or more scholars as instantiations of fable):

1. Beast fables:
   a. The story of the cicadas, told by Socrates to Phaedrus in the *Phaedrus* (259b–d).[13]
   b. The fable of the sheep and the sheepdog, told by Socrates to Aristarchus in Xenophon's *Memorabilia* (2.7.13–14).[14]
2. Aetiological, mythological fables:
   a. Aristophanes' "myth" in Plato's *Symposium* (189d–93d).[15]

---

[10] Cf. Ford 2002.229–71, arguing that the need to set clear rules and parameters for prose writing in the fourth century in turn provoked the first development of a theory of poetry.

[11] Perry 1959.18–20, 1965.xxii–xxx; cf. Dover 1966.42–45, Adrados 1999.37–42.

[12] On these as the only two fables narrated by Socrates that are explicitly linked to Aesop in the Platonic corpus, see Desclos 1997, 2000. The authenticity of *Alc.* I is irrelevant for my purposes, since even if it is not by Plato, scholars generally agree that it is likely to be a fourth-century composition. On the *Alcibiades* in general, how it fits into the *Sōkratikoi logoi* of Plato, and the issue of authenticity, see Denyer 2001.1–29.

[13] In fact, this story combines the two types, since it involves animals but is also aetiological. For this as a fable, see Perry 1959.506–7 (fable no. 470); Karadagli 1981.181–88; van Dijk 1997.327–30; Adrados 1999.381, 402.

[14] For this as a fable, see Karadagli 1981.100; van Dijk 1997.336–40; Adrados 1999.381, 402. For beast fables narrated in the works of other early Socratics, see also van Dijk 1997.321–23, 340–42: he lists in this category a fable of lions and hares told by Antisthenes (alluded to by Aristotle), and another of a boy or prince and a lion cub, narrated in Phaedo's *Zopyrus* (alluded to by Theon and Cicero).

[15] For this as a fable, see Dover 1966; Karadagli 1981.172–77; Adrados 1999.381, 402. Van Dijk 1997.670–71 denies that this is a fable, listing it in his appendix "Non-Fables & Non-Allusions."

    b. Diotima's narrative of the birth of Eros from Poros and Penia in the *Symposium* (203b–4b).[16]
    c. Protagoras's "myth" in Plato's *Protagoras* (320c–22d).[17]
    d. Prodicus's Choice of Heracles, narrated by Socrates to Aristippus in Xenophon's *Memorabilia* (2.1.21–34).[18]

Because of the number of fable narratives in the *Sōkratikoi logoi* of Plato and Xenophon, scholars have been inclined to see this as a phenomenon that arises from a "Socratic" milieu. Thus, for example, Francisco Rodríguez Adrados in his monumental *History of the Graeco-Latin Fable* concludes, "The route by which the fable entered prose, first as an exemplum in the fifth century, then in the collections, was clearly through the Socratic school.... This is not at all strange, given the colloquial and popular tone of the Socratic dialogue."[19] This scholarly reaction recognizes that something new is going on in these texts, but the attribution of the widespread and innovative use of fable in written prose to Socratic circles is ultimately inadequate.[20] For such mere cataloging or listing of examples (as it is usually done) takes no account of the whole literary system, with its intimately interrelated issues of level of style, literary decorum, performance context, and sociopolitical valence, while it also consistently privileges the winning side in what was clearly at the time a hotly contested discursive field. Thus Adrados's assertion that the use of fable "is not at all strange, given the colloquial and popular tone of the Socratic dialogue" simply begs the question, since this choice of "colloquial," "popular" style for the *Sōkratikoi logoi*

---

[16] For this as a fable, see Karadagli 1981.177–81; Adrados 1999.381, 402. Van Dijk 1997.671 denies its fable status.

[17] Protagoras's μῦθος is identified as a fable by Adrados 1999.380, 402; cf. also Aly 1929.70–73 and Dover 1966.42–43. Cole 1991.59–61 treats Protagoras's tale as "rhetorical allegory" or "allegorizing myth" closely related to "Aesopic *ainos*." Van Dijk 1997.669–70 denies its fable status.

[18] For this as a fable, see Welcker 1833.576–81; Grote 1851.VIII.516; Aly 1929.73; Guthrie 1969.277–79; Adrados 1999.380, 402; cf. Cole 1991.58–61. Contra: Van Dijk 1997.673, 683. Finally, note that Socrates' tale of Thales falling down a well and being mocked by a Thracian slave girl at *Tht.* 174a also occurs as a fable about an anonymous "astronomer" in the later Aesopic fable collections; cf. Perry fable no. 40, and see Karadagli 1981.64–65, Cavarero 1995.31–56, Hutchinson 2008.

[19] Adrados 1999.380. Cf. Cole 1991.58–62: Cole does not categorize these as fables, but instead as "rhetorical allegories" or "allegorizing myths"; nonetheless, he insists that these forms develop out of the "Socratic tradition" (p. 60). In my view, he is able to maintain this attribution only by dint of much special pleading: thus (e.g.) Parmenides is Socrates' "spiritual father" and Prodicus is the Sophist "most closely associated with [Socrates] by his contemporaries." (p. 60). A notable exception to this tendency to treat the use of fable as an innovation of the Socratic school is Aly 1929.70–76.

[20] For acknowledgment that this is something new, see Adrados (1999.379), who notes the contrast of the frequent use of fable in *Sōkratikoi logoi* with their complete absence from post-Herodotean history and the speeches of the Attic orators, "whose high tone clearly excluded the fable." To his credit, Adrados also notes, "There are some precedents in the use of the fable, in the same way as the myth, by the Sophists" (p. 380).

itself requires explanation. (This is part of what I will attempt to do in chapter 9.) But such scholarly privileging of the surviving Socratic texts of Xenophon and especially Plato is characteristic, allowing modern scholars to attribute all significant intellectual developments of the fifth and fourth centuries to Socrates and/or the Socratic milieu.[21] I would contend rather that we can track several different appropriations of Aesop (all generically bold and experimental, and all of which confirm in different ways the problematic status of Aesop and humble prose fable for which I've been arguing):

1. First, Sophistic appropriation, which consists in literary elaboration and the pervasive raising of level of style for display pieces (*epideixeis*) on political/ethical topics. The Sophists' stylistic transformation of fable and its linkage to political content and public performance occasion are clarified by juxtaposition with Xenophon's representation of Socrates' contrasting deployment of fable in the *Memorabilia*. Finally, I will suggest, Plato both embeds examples of Sophistic fable and simultaneously debunks them in his dialogues.

2. Second, the Platonic Socrates. At the same time, Plato recognizes the much more radical and subversive potential of Aesopic fable and Aesop more broadly (with his challenge to the wisdom tradition and his characteristic modes of discourse); Plato exploits this subversive Aesopic strand in his doubled competition with older traditions of *sophia* and the Sophists as rival claimants thereto. It is this deadly serious contest of and over *sophia* that (at least partly) provokes Plato's choice of mimetic prose and weird generic motley in the Socratic dialogues.

I will go through each of these claims in order in the remainder of this chapter and in chapters 8 and 9.

In the first place, I would contend that we have a sufficient number of examples to recognize the refined literary elaboration of a fable in artistic prose as a staple (perhaps an invention?) of the Sophists. These literary elaborations of fables seem to have served the Sophists as performance pieces, designed to showcase their skillful and elegant construction of sentences, their fine discriminations of vocabulary, and their artful repackaging of conventional sentiments and values.[22] These high-class adaptations of fables in artistic prose thus repre-

---

[21] This applies more to van Dijk 1997 than to Adrados 1999, since the latter at least attends to the issue of level of style. My objection to Adrados is, then, rather that he has no sense of the necessary interimplication of level of style and sociopolitical issues, nor does he recognize that the "colloquial tone" of Socratic writings is by no means inevitable but is instead a willed choice in the context of fifth-/fourth-century developments of prose. This privileging of Socrates and the Socratic school generally vis-à-vis the Sophists has been critiqued by Kerferd 1981, Mann 2006. My argument here is in fact very consonant with that of Mann 2006—that dialectical argument by question-and-answer is not Socrates' unique discovery, but a prevalent mode of discourse developed by intellectuals (Sophists) of the fifth century.

[22] To my knowledge, the only scholar who has put all these examples together under the rubric of Sophistic adaptations of fable is Aly 1929.70–76 (whose discussion seems to have been almost entirely ignored by later scholars; but cf. Thomas 2000.174–75).

sent an early example of the "domestication" of Aesop and fable that I've suggested occurred repeatedly in the Greek rhetorical and philosophical traditions.[23] At the same time, a couple of references suggest that the Sophists regarded these elaborated fable narratives as particularly appropriate for the education of the young, so that we may see the Sophists as the inventors of a rhetorical tradition still preserved in the late texts of the *Progymnasmata*, of making fable one of the first exercises in the rhetorical training of boys.[24] In fact, before the Sophists of the late fifth century, there is no evidence for the now common assumption that Aesop's fables are mainly intended for the young.

Consider first Prodicus's "Choice of Heracles," in which the personified females Virtue and Vice lay out their respective roads of life for the young hero on the verge of manhood. This composition was famous in antiquity and was summarized at length by Xenophon's Socrates in Book 2 of the *Memorabilia*. Socrates there terms it Prodicus's σύγγραμμα ("prose treatise"), "which he also performs before the largest crowds" (ὅπερ δὴ καὶ πλείστοις ἐπιδείκνυται, *Mem.* 2.1.21).[25] The episode is quite extended and its style high and ornate (as we'll see in a moment). It is difficult to know how closely or accurately Xenophon has quoted or paraphrased Prodicus, but his Socrates ends his rendition of the "Choice of Heracles" with the wry observation, "Thus somehow Prodicus goes through the education of Heracles by Virtue; but he has adorned the sententiae with still more magnificent words than I have now" (ἐκόσμησε μέντοι τὰς γνώμας ἔτι μεγαλειοτέροις ῥήμασιν ἢ ἐγὼ νῦν, *Mem.* 2.1.34).[26] Yet with all the

---

[23] Cf. introduction; chapter 5, pp. 202–3.

[24] The composition, expansion, contraction, conjugation/declension, and critique of fables is offered as one of the first stages of rhetorical education in all the preserved *Progymnasmata*. In the earliest preserved handbook of Aelius Theon (second c. CE) *chreiai* originally came first, then *muthos* (fable); but Theon's text was later rearranged to conform to the practice of later *Progymnasmata* (those of Aphthonius, Hermogenes, and Nicolaus). On all this, see Webb 2001; but Webb also notes that these transformations of fable formed the pivot between the education provided by the *grammatikos* and that of the rhetor; for the same sequencing of fable within rhetorical education, see Quint. 1.9.1–2. This is admittedly something slightly different, since for Prodicus (and, as we will see, Plato's Protagoras) *neoi* are imagined to be the perfect audience, while in the *Progymnasmata*, *neoi* are the ones composing fables as their first rhetorical exercises. But for this kind of reciprocity of production and reception, see Webb 2001.308–10. Jouanno 2006.12–13 offers other evidence for fables as part of the standard education for boys already in the fifth century BCE.

[25] For different interpretations of the relation of Prodicus's written *sungramma* to his oral *epideixis*, see Gomperz 1912.97–99, Nestle 1975.353n. 21, Cole 1991.76–77, O'Sullivan 1996.122 (strongly disagreeing with Cole's model).

[26] Diels-Kranz (II.312) contend, "Der Stil is sicher xenophontisch," but contrast the observation of Spengel, elaborated by Gomperz 1912.101n. 225a, that the "Choice of Heracles" contains a number of passages that play on fine discriminations of meaning of near synonyms (esp. in chs. 2.1.22 and 28). This point, cited with approval by Guthrie 1969.279n. 2, would seem to point to Prodicus and his particular interest in the "correctness of words." For the accuracy of Xenophon's rendition of Prodicus's fable, see Phil. *VS* 1.496: "And why should I characterize the language of Prodicus, when Xenophon has adequately sketched it?" (καὶ τί ἂν χαρακτηρίζοιμεν τὴν τοῦ Προδίκου γλῶτταν, Ξενοφῶντος αὐτὴν ἱκανῶς ὑπογράφοντος;).

elaboration, the "Choice of Heracles" is clearly an allegorical fable, an expansion of Hesiod's fable of the two roads of ἀρετή and κακότης (*WD* 287–92). Indeed, Xenophon's Socrates registers Hesiod's lines as the model, since he quotes them to the same interlocutor, Aristippus, almost immediately before launching into Prodicus's version (*Mem.* 2.1.20).[27] In addition, as B. E. Perry notes, Heracles (along with Prometheus, Zeus, Hermes, and Hephaestus) is a character who figures frequently in fables of the mythological, aetiological type (themselves very prevalent as Aesopic fables in fifth- and fourth-century texts).[28]

But if Prodicus's tale of the youthful Heracles at the crossroads is essentially a fable, it is one that (in Xenophon's rendering) the Sophist has expanded and transposed to high style, full of complex sentences, balanced clauses, and fine discriminations of vocabulary.[29] Or rather, the version we have displays all these stylistic features in its frame narrative and in the speeches of Aretē, while Kakia's clauses and sentences tend to be shorter and simpler. That is to say, the two allegorical females themselves speak in somewhat different styles. Indeed, it is tempting to suggest that the opposition of Virtue and Vice is figured simultaneously as an opposition of (relatively) high and low genres of discourse. For, beyond a somewhat homogeneous patina of elegant style and diction, it is noteworthy that the physical descriptions of Aretē and Kakia diverge precisely in their degree of bodiliness:

καὶ φανῆναι αὐτῷ δύο γυναῖκας προσιέναι μεγάλας, τὴν μὲν ἑτέραν εὐπρεπῆ τε ἰδεῖν καὶ ἐλευθέριον φύσει, κεκοσμημένην τὸ μὲν σῶμα καθαρότητι, τὰ δὲ ὄμματα αἰδοῖ, τὸ δὲ σχῆμα σωφροσύνῃ, ἐσθῆτι δὲ λευκῇ, τὴν δ' ἑτέραν τεθραμμένην μὲν εἰς πολυσαρκίαν τε καὶ ἁπαλότητα, κεκαλλωπισμένην δὲ τὸ μὲν χρῶμα ὥστε λευκοτέραν

---

[27] For the link to Hesiod's allegorical fable, see Welcker 1833.580, Becker 1937.59n. 24, Nestle 1936.165, de Romilly 1992.204–5, O'Sullivan 1992.76–77, Kuntz 1994.169–72 (emphasizing the differences between Hesiod's fable and Prodicus's), Adrados 1999.398. As Nestle, de Romilly, and O'Sullivan note, Prodicus's version acknowledges its source by (among other verbal reminiscences) making ἱδρῶτι the last word of Aretē's first speech to the young Heracles, echoing *WD* 289 (τῆς δ' ἀρετῆς ἱδρῶτα θεοὶ προπάροιθεν ἔθηκαν); indeed, Nestle 1936.164–65 even suggests that Prodicus quoted or paraphrased the Hesiodic lines at the beginning of his fable. For another (implicit) association of Prodicus's "Choice of Heracles" with these same Hesiodic lines (also noted by Nestle 1936.164, O'Sullivan 1992.77), cf. Plato *Prot.* 340d1–5: "And perhaps Prodicus and many others would say the thing according to Hesiod, that it is difficult to become good," whereupon Socrates offers a close paraphrase of *WD* 289–92. For the function of the "Choice of Heracles" in its context in the *Memorabilia*, see below (this chapter).

[28] For the prevalence of the mythological, aetiological type of fables in classical sources, often involving Olympian gods, Prometheus, or Heracles, see Perry 1959.32–35, 1962a.301–7. For a Heracles fable preserved among those of the Augustana collection, see Perry fable no. 111. Kuntz 1994 and Davies 2003 focus on the particular question of why Prodicus might have chosen Heracles as the protagonist of his allegorical fable—an issue both approach through a consideration of mythic archetypes of the hero's quest. I will return to this question—why Heracles?—below.

[29] This last feature is particularly prominent in chs. 22 and 28 of Xenophon's rendition (narrative frame and speech of Aretē, respectively), as noted by Spengel in Gomperz 1912.101n. 225a and Guthrie 1969.279n. 2.

τε καὶ ἐρυθροτέραν τοῦ ὄντος δοκεῖν φαίνεσθαι, τὸ δὲ σχῆμα ὥστε δοκεῖν ὀρθοτέραν τῆς φύσεως εἶναι, τὰ δὲ ὄμματα ἔχειν ἀναπεπταμένα, ἐσθῆτα δὲ ἐξ ἧς ἂν μάλιστα ὥρα διαλάμποι· (*Mem.* 2.1.22)

And two large women appeared to approach him, one fair to see and free in nature, her body adorned with purity, her eyes with modesty, her manner with self-restraint and chastity, with a white garment; the other nourished to the point of fleshiness and softness, with her complexion tricked out to appear whiter and redder than it really was, and her form to seem taller than it was by nature, and she held her eyes wide open, and [she was wearing] a garment from which her youthful charms would most shine through.

From this account it is impossible to derive any specific physical characterization of Aretē, since she is consistently described as "adorned" with abstract qualities—freedom (ἐλευθέριον), purity (καθαρότητι), respect or reverence (αἰδοῖ), and self-restraint or chastity (σωφροσύνη). In contrast, Kakia is all about the body: we register the bulk and softness of her flesh, the colors painted on its surface, the form made to look taller, and the garment that reveals too much of her youthful bloom (ὥρα).[30] Both Kakia's emphatic bodiliness and her shorter, simpler clauses and sentences point to the genre of humble fable, while Aretē's consistent abstraction from the body and magnificent balanced periods suggest high bouleutic oratory or encomium.[31]

Two other features of Prodicus's fable confirm the contrasting genre identifications of his two allegorical female figures. First, note Aretē's introduction to her first speech to the young Heracles: "I will not deceive you with preludes of pleasure, but in the very way the gods have appointed the things that are, I will narrate truly" (οὐκ ἐξαπατήσω δέ σε προοιμίοις ἡδονῆς, ἀλλ' ᾗπερ οἱ θεοὶ διέθεσαν τὰ ὄντα διηγήσομαι μετ' ἀληθείας, *Mem.* 2.1.27). Aretē's emphatic rejection of "pleasure" (ἡδονῆς) in favor of "truth" (τὰ ὄντα, μετ' ἀληθείας) recalls the terms of the opposition I noted in chapter 3 between the indirect, analogical advice of Hdt. 1.27 and the blunt, no-nonsense protreptic of Solon to Croesus at Hdt. 1.31. The pleasure of the former, I argued, belongs properly to Aesop and fable narration, while the commitment to truth of the latter signals the uncompromising integrity of the Seven Sages as political and ethical advisers. Thus here, Aretē aligns with Solon and the other Sages, and Kakia with Aesop and fable.

Second, Kakia's identification with the genre of fable within this literary elaboration of fable is confirmed by the language with which her last speech is introduced:

---

[30] For extensive discussion of these features, see Nicolaïdou-Kyrianidou 1998.83.
[31] Note features that link Aretē's speeches to traditions of encomium: repeated mention of Heracles' noble parentage (2.1.27, 33), and the notion of praise as the highest good (2.1.31, 33). On the "Choice of Heracles" as encomium, see Alpers 1912.12–16; for the overlap of content between advice and encomium, see Arist. *Rhet.* 1.9, 1367b37–9.

> καὶ ἡ Κακία ὑπολαβοῦσα εἶπεν, ὥς φησι Πρόδικος· ἐννοεῖς, ὦ Ἡράκλεις, ὡς χαλεπὴν καὶ μακρὰν ὁδὸν ἐπὶ τὰς εὐφροσύνας ἡ γυνή σοι αὕτη διηγεῖται; ἐγὼ δὲ ῥᾳδίαν καὶ βραχεῖαν ὁδὸν ἐπὶ εὐδαιμονίαν ἄξω σε. (*Mem.* 2.1.29)

> And Kakia taking it up, said, as Prodicus says, "Do you understand, O Heracles, how hard and long the road to enjoyments this woman tells you of? But I will lead you along a short and easy road to happiness."

This is the one and only occurrence of the colloquial fabular formula ὑπολαβοῦσα εἶπεν, not just in the "Choice of Heracles" but in the whole of the *Memorabilia*. And of course it introduces what Kakia imagines to be a decisive objection and final trumping of Aretē's laborious and physically unpleasant proffered path. In fact, this is not the case, as Aretē responds with her longest and most elaborate discourse yet, thereby silencing Kakia and the low genre of fable for good. It is impossible to know whether this playful genre opposition featured already in Prodicus's composition (thereby making it another example of Sophistic generic and stylistic experimentation) or whether it is Xenophon's own handiwork. Still, it is intriguing that it is immediately after introducing the telltale fable formula ὑπολαβοῦσα εἶπεν that Xenophon's Socrates again explicitly attributes the discourse to Prodicus (ὥς φησι Πρόδικος).[32] Is this intended to mark the speech formula as Prodicus's *ipsissima verba*—or even to apologize for the use of such a colloquial expression embedded in an otherwise high-style discourse? The suspicion that this playful genre opposition was original to Prodicus may also find support in the fact that Plato goes out of his way to have Phaedrus (and Eryximachus) mention Prodicus's "Choice of Heracles" in the context of discussing other paradoxical encomia in prose in the *Symposium*.[33]

So much for the style and generic play of the "Choice of Heracles" as we have it. What about its performance context and intended audience? Here Philostratus in his *Lives of the Sophists* (second/third c. CE) adds several useful details to Xenophon's account. In what we might read as his own aetiological fable for the invention of extempore rhetorical performance, Philostratus reports that Gorgias first initiated the practice in reaction to Prodicus's success performing his already-written "Choice of Heracles":

> Prodicus of Ceos had composed a certain pleasant fable (συνεγέγραπτό τις οὐκ ἀηδὴς λόγος) in which Virtue and Vice came to Heracles in the shape of women.... For this story, Prodicus wrote a rather long epilogue (καὶ τοῦ ἐπὶ πᾶσι διὰ πλειόνων συντεθέντος), and then he toured the cities and gave recitations of the story in public, for hire, and charmed them after the manner of Orpheus and Thamyris. For these recitations he won a great reputation at Thebes and a still greater at Sparta, as one

---

[32] Note that this is the only time Socrates interjects "as Prodicus says" within his lengthy presentation of the "Choice of Heracles."

[33] *Sym.* 177b1–4, quoted above p. 267. For the reading of the *Symposium* as an extended critique of contemporary forms of praise and blame, see Nightingale 1995.93–132.

who benefited the young by making this fable widely known (ὡς ἐς τὸ συμφέρον τῶν νέων ἀναδιδάσκων ταῦτα). Thereupon Gorgias ridiculed Prodicus for handling a theme that was stale and hackneyed (ὡς ἕωλά τε καὶ πολλάκις εἰρημένα ἀγορεύοντα), and he abandoned himself to the inspiration of the moment. (Phil. VS 1.482–83, trans. Wright 1968)

Philostratus's account (perhaps based on knowledge of Prodicus's original text?) sheds light on the Sophist's mode of performance and target audience. In reporting that Prodicus "attached a rather long epilogue" (τὸ ἐπὶ πᾶσι) to the "Choice of Heracles," Philostratus suggests a performance akin to a lengthy sermon spun out from an opening parable. Thus it seems that, after the fable proper, with its speaking characters Heracles, Aretē, and Kakia, Prodicus elaborated a long moralizing disquisition that "explained" the fable in nonallegorical terms (much like the "moral," *epilogos* or *epimuthion*, later attached to fables in the rhetorical tradition).[34] Equally suggestive is Philostratus's claim that Prodicus's set piece won him particular honor in Thebes and conservative Sparta "on the grounds that he expounded these things for the benefit of the young" (ὡς ἐς τὸ συμφέρον τῶν νέων ἀναδιδάσκων ταῦτα). This perhaps implies that the literary elaboration of a fable was felt to be particularly appropriate for the young, who might be won over by the pleasure and persuasiveness of narrative, even before their reasoning faculties were fully developed.[35]

We might also note how Gorgias's snide riposte works by belittling and demystifying the genre of fable. Thus Gorgias's "many times said" (πολλάκις εἰρημένα) suggests not just the constant repetition of a written script in contrast to his own improvisatory skill, but also the conventionality and hoary tradition of fable (the same thing Xenophon perhaps implies by quoting the Hesiodic lines right before paraphrasing Prodicus's version).[36] But it is Gorgias's use of the adjective ἕωλα ("stale, day-old") that is really devastating. This word, which occurs frequently in medical and scientific contexts, occasionally in the Attic orators, and then often in Plutarch and Lucian, brings Prodicus's lofty verbal construct down to earth with clinical precision, reducing it to the quotidian,

---

[34] Perry 1940 claims that the "moral" or *epimuthion* developed in a rhetorical milieu (though I would see this happening earlier, if we believe that Herodotus is using *epilogos* in this technical sense already at 1.27—see discussion chapter 3, section I above); for arguments against Perry, based on the continuity from the fable-internal *epilogos* to the fable-external *epimuthion*, see Karadagli 1981.2, 53–71, 116.

[35] It is generally taken for granted by scholars that Prodicus's fable targets young men (as potential students?): thus Welcker 1833.576–81; Grote 1851.VIII.576; Kuntz 1994; Ford 2001.93n. 28. We might compare Hippias's prose *Hypothēkai* of Nestor to Neoptolemus at the sack of Troy, described in Plato, *Hipp. Mai.* 286a5–b6—another artful prose adaptation of a traditional genre (in this case, that of mythological advice poetry), targeted for the education of the young in Sparta (as Plato's Hippias claims).

[36] For a reading of this anecdote that focuses on Prodicean dependence on writing vs Gorgias's extempore oral displays, see O'Sullivan 1992.18–19, 1996.121–24.

bodily level that characterized the humble prose fable before Prodicus had worked his magic on it. Or alternatively, we might say that Gorgias's sneer works by reducing the whole of Prodicus's complex generic amalgam to the low, fabular discourse of the excessively bodily Kakia. We have no way of knowing whether Philostratus's reported quip goes back to the real Gorgias, but it certainly suits the man who asserted that "the opposition's seriousness is to be demolished by laughter, and laughter by seriousness" (quoted with approval by Aristotle, *Rhet.* 3.18, 1419b3).

Finally, we should pause to consider the title of the whole work of which the "Choice of Heracles" formed a part, and what it might signify. We are told that the entire "book" was called *Hōrai*.[37] In 1833, Friedrich Welcker suggested that *Hōrai* referred to "youth" in general, with Heracles as its representative in the allegorical fable.[38] H. Gomperz refined this theory, drawing attention to the plural *Hōrai* and suggesting that the title signified "seasons" of the year or even "times of day" as symbolic correlates to the life cycle of the hero: thus, spring, summer, and winter or morning, noon, and evening would correspond to mythological narratives of Heracles' youth, manhood, and old age.[39] But still the most thorough consideration of the possible contents of Prodicus's work and its title is that of Wilhelm Nestle.[40] Nestle employed the methods of traditional *Quellenforschung* to detect echoes of Prodicus's work in Xenophon's *Oeconomicus* and Themistius's brief fourth-century CE oration "Should One Engage in Farming?" (*Or.* 30). Diels-Kranz had already included a snippet from Themistius's oration as part of their fragment B 5 of Prodicus (*Aus unbestimmten Schriften*):

εἰ δὲ καὶ Διόνυσον καλοῖμεν καὶ νύμφας καὶ Δήμητρος κόρην ὑέτιόν τε Δία καὶ Ποσειδῶνα φυτάλμιον, πλησιάζομεν ἤδη ταῖς τελεταῖς καὶ τὴν Προδίκου σοφίαν τοῖς λόγοις ἐγκαταμίξομεν, ὃς ἱερουργίαν πᾶσαν ἀνθρώπων καὶ μυστήρια καὶ πανηγύρεις καὶ τελετὰς τῶν γεωργίας καλῶν ἐξάπτει, νομίζων καὶ θεῶν ἔννοιαν[41] ἐντεῦθεν εἰς ἀνθρώπους ἐλθεῖν καὶ πᾶσαν εὐσέβειαν ἐγγυώμενος. (Them. *Or.* 30.349a/422 Dindorf)

---

[37] Thus Schol. *ad* Aristoph. *Clouds* 361 = 84 B 1 DK. As Guthrie 1969.278–79n. 2 notes, the scholiast's mention of the title *Hōrai* and of Heracles' final decision (which is not recorded in Xenophon's summary) strongly suggests an independent source for this information.

[38] Welcker 1833.576–79. Welcker's theory was summarily dismissed by Diels in DK, apparently because he assumed that the title could not be original, but was instead a later Hellenistic imposition (he compares the names of the Muses for the nine books of Herodotus's *Histories*). But cf. the critique of Diels by Gomperz 1912.99–100: even if *Hōrai* as a title is a Hellenistic imposition, it must mean something and have some connection to the content of the work, since, unlike the Muses, the Hōrai have no obvious poetic/literary association.

[39] Gomperz 1912.99–100.

[40] Nestle 1936, reprinted in Classen, ed. 1976.425–51; cf. the briefer discussion in Nestle 1975.351–56.

[41] ἔννοιαν is in fact Diels's emendation (unmarked as such) for εὔνοιαν in the mss of Themistius (printed in Downey and Norman's [1971] Teubner text of Themistius). Guthrie 1969.239 and Penella 2000 accept εὔνοιαν. Diels also posits a lacuna after εὐσέβειαν (not reproduced here).

If we should also summon Dionysus, the nymphs, Demeter's daughter [Persephone], the rain-bringing Zeus, and nourishing Poseidon, then we shall be within short range of the rites and add a dose of Prodicus's wisdom to our eloquence. Prodicus makes all of mankind's religious ceremonies, mysteries, festivals, and rites dependent on the blessings of agriculture. He thinks that even the idea of the gods came to human beings through agriculture, and he makes agriculture the guarantee of all piety. (Trans. Penella 2000)

Nestle pointed out that in the sentence immediately preceding the one excerpted by Diels-Kranz, Themistius refers climactically to "all the things the *Hōrai* produce from the earth" (καὶ ὅσα φύουσιν ἐκ τῆς γῆς "Ωραι, Them. *Or*. 30.349a/422 Dindorf) and suggested that, by this collocation of the "seasons" with the "wisdom of Prodicus," Themistius intended to flag his source as the Prodicean *Hōrai*. Then, based on this passage and others in Themistius's oration, Nestle argued that the *Hōrai* actually contained an exposition of Prodicus's anthropological theory that religion, law, and the human sense of justice all derived originally from farming.[42] Finally Nestle argued that the allegorical "Choice of Heracles" provided the climax and end point of Prodicus's treatise.[43]

There is much of value in Nestle's argument: he makes a convincing case that it was, in fact, the text of the *Hōrai* in which Prodicus expounded his anthropological theory of the development of human civilization, religion, and law from agriculture. Where I diverge from Nestle is in his notion that the "Choice of Heracles" formed the climax and culmination of the *Hōrai*, for two reasons. First (and simpler): the large number of ancient references that specifically mention the Heracles fable strongly suggests that it featured early in the work (for we know that the beginnings of texts tend to be the most cited in antiquity).[44] Second (a more complicated argument): Nestle himself suggested that Prodicus in the *Hōrai* explicitly referred to Hesiod's allegorical fable of the "Roads of *aretē* and *kakotēs*"—either paraphrasing or even quoting it before introducing his own fable of Heracles.[45] But structurally, Hesiod introduces this fable addressed to his brother Perses after he has decisively banished the "kings" or "barons" from the poem, as the opening of a hundred-line sequence that leads into the extended survey of the agricultural seasons and their proper work in the second half of the poem (*WD* 286–382).[46] That is to say, in Hesiod this allegorical fable

---

[42] Nestle 1936.153–63 = Classen, ed.1976.427–42. Cf. O'Sullivan 1992.76–77; O'Sullivan is skeptical about many of the details of Nestle's reconstruction as "highly speculative," but he is willing to accept Nestle's thesis that the *Hōrai* had an "agricultural theme."

[43] Nestle 1936.164–70 = Classen, ed.1976.442–51; cf. Nestle 1975.352–53.

[44] For example, in addition to Xenophon's lengthy summary of the "Choice of Heracles" at *Mem*. 2.1.21–34, cf. Plato *Sym*. 177b1–4 (quoted above), *Prot*. 340d1–5, Schol. *ad* Aristoph. *Clouds* 361, Phil. *VS* 1.482–83, 496.

[45] Nestle 1936.164–65 = Classen, ed.1976.443.

[46] For the banishing of the kings and the shift to agricultural advice at this point in *WD*, see Hamilton 1989.57, Nagy 1990a.64–67.

constitutes part of the lead-in to the detailed agricultural prescriptions of the *Works & Days*; so analogically, we might imagine Prodicus's fable introducing his agriculturally inflected anthropology.

And yet it may be objected that Nestle's reconstruction would turn the *Hōrai* into an incoherent grab bag of material; what would connect the heroic fable of the young Heracles with an anthropological treatise tracing the origins of human culture to farming?[47] At the simplest level, we might note that the fable (like Hesiod's) is an *allegory*—and specifically an allegory for the necessity of human toil and effort, one of whose noble (if nonheroic) forms is farming.[48] More speculatively, I would point to an odd moment toward the end of Themistius's brief *Oration* 30 (not noted by Nestle):

> γεωργία δὲ ἀπὸ περιττῶν τοῖς λοιποῖς χορηγεῖ. οὐκοῦν οὐδὲ τῷ βασιλεῖ ὄφελος οὐδὲ ἕν, κἂν Ἀχαιμενίδης, κἂν Ἡρακλείδης, κἂν ὁστισοῦν εἶναι αὐχῇ, εἰ μὴ τοῖς ὅπλοις τὰ τῶν τροφῶν τῆς παρασκευῆς ἁπάσης ἡγοῖτο. (Them. *Or.* 30.351c/424–5 Dindorf)

> Agriculture, from its abundant resources, supplies everyone else. So not even a king has any advantage—whether he is an Achaemenid or a Heraclid or whoever he may boast to be—unless the interests of those who nourish the community take precedence over the whole military establishment.[49] (Trans. Penella 2000)

Themistius insists that even the power of kings depends on agricultural production; but why does he single out for mention Achaemenid and Heraclid kings? In classical (and classicizing) Greek thought, "Achaemenid and Heraclid" signifies the two most conspicuous kingships of East and West, barbarians and Greeks—the royal lines of Persia and Sparta, respectively.[50] Still, perhaps we should see in Themistius's linkage of agriculture and sovereignty, with specific mention of Heraclid kings, one last allusion to Prodicus. Perhaps Prodicus's allegorical fable of the young Heracles at the crossroads pointed forward not just to the hero's own career and personal immortality, but also to Heracles as founding hero and ancestor of royal lineages.[51] Such handling of the Heracles

---

[47] This seems to be the issue that Guthrie 1969.279 with n. 1 has with Nestle and (a fortiori) with Untersteiner's (1954.209, 225n. 74) reconstruction of the *Hōrai*.

[48] For this connection, note especially *Mem.* 2.1.6, 13, 28, where we find emphatic collocations of military preparedness and agricultural effort. Admittedly, agriculture as a paradigmatic form of aristocratic *ponos* is very much a concern of Xenophon himself (on this, see Johnstone 1994, Nikolaïdou-Kyrianidou 1998.93); but this does not preclude its also being a key theme for Prodicus.

[49] Penella deletes τοῖς ὅπλοις from the last clause.

[50] Cf. Penella 2000.188; for a similar collocation of the royal lines of Sparta and Persia, see *Alc.* I 120e6–24b5.

[51] For the possible relevance of kingship to Prodicus's fable, it is worth noting that Dio Chrysostom's adaptation of the "Choice of Heracles" in his First Oration on Kingship transforms the two allegorical females who vie for the young hero's affection into "Kingship" and "Tyranny" (Dio Chr. *Orations* 1.66–84). Equally intriguing: in Dio's account, Basileia is attended by Nomos ("Law"), and also by three female figures—Dikē, Eunomia, and Eirēnē (the Hesiodic Hōrai; Dio Chr. *Orations* 1.74–75). Also highly suggestive is Nicolaïdou-Kyrianidou 1998.82–88, pointing out many ele-

theme, which might simultaneously constitute encomium and a logical connection between kingship and agriculture, could in turn explain Philostratus's assertion (if we can credit it) that Prodicus's "Choice of Heracles" was popular as a performance piece in Thebes (where Heracles was a prominent local hero) and especially in Sparta (still ruled by Heraclid kings).

In any case, I would suggest that both the proposed meanings of the title *Hōrai* might be relevant for Prodicus's text (and that one does not necessarily exclude the other): (1) *Hōrai* referring to "youth" or different "seasons" or "ages" of human life, with the "Choice of Heracles" as the first, for youths on the verge of adulthood; (2) the Hōrai as agricultural goddesses who are also, according to the Hesiodic genealogy, the daughters of Zeus and Themis, Eunomia, Dikē, and Eirēnē (*Th.* 901–3). These divinities would appropriately oversee a treatise that located in agriculture the beginnings of human civilization (including religion and law). Thus, if we may see in the *Hōrai* an anthropological treatise on the origins of human culture, which itself began with the allegorical fable of Heracles at the crossroads, this text would bear striking resemblances in structure and in content to Protagoras's *muthos* in Plato's *Protagoras*, as we shall see a little later.

We find another example of the repackaging and elaboration of Aesopic fable in artful prose among the preserved fragments of the Sophist Antiphon.[52] Thus Stobaeus quotes from Antiphon:

> There is a story (ἔστι δέ τις λόγος) of a man who saw another man getting a large sum of money and asked him to lend it him at interest. But the second man refused. He was the kind of man to distrust others and never help anyone (ἀλλ' ἦν οἷος ἀπιστεῖν τε καὶ μὴ ὠφελεῖν μηδένα). He took the money and stored it away. A third man heard of what he had done and stole it. Some time later the man who had put it away went and failed to find the money. So in great distress at his misfortune, particularly because he had not lent it to the man who had asked him, since in that case not only would he have had the money safe, but it would have earned interest as well, meeting the man who on the earlier occasion had wanted to borrow, he bewailed his misfortune, saying that he had made a mistake and was sorry he had not done what the other man wanted but had refused (ἀχαριστήσαντι), since the money was now quite lost. The first man told him not to worry, but to believe that he had the money in his possession and had not lost it. He should put a stone in the place the money was. "For you made absolutely

---

ments that align Kakia with tyranny in Xenophon's version. As I will suggest below, it may be that Prodicus's original had more to do with sovereignty or kingship (like Dio's adaptation), but that this theme has been deliberately muted in Xenophon's version.

[52] It is irrelevant for my purposes whether there were one or two Antiphons; for recent summaries of the arguments on either side of the question, cf. Gagarin 2002, Pendrick 2002.1–26. On Antiphon's fable, see Aly 1929.75–76 and (with a somewhat different interpretation from that offered here) van Dijk 1997.313–17. Note that Antiphon's use of fable does not figure at all in the account of Cole 1991.58–62, which makes it easier for him to claim something akin to "Aesopic *ainos*" as an innovation of the Socratic tradition.

no use of the money when you had it, so there is no need to think you have lost anything." Indeed, what a man neither uses nor intends to use, it makes no difference whether he possesses it or not, he is not harmed more or less. For if god wishes to bless a man but not without reservation, he gives him plenty of money but poverty of good sense; and by taking away the one he commonly deprives him of both (χρημάτων πλοῦτον παρασχών, τοῦ φρονεῖν ‹δὲ› καλῶς[53] πένητα ποιήσας, τὸ ἕτερον ἀφελόμενος ἀμφοτέρων ἀπεστέρησεν). (Antiphon, 87 B 54 DK, trans. Morrison in Sprague 1972)

A version of the fable that Antiphon presumably adapted and elaborated here is preserved in the Augustana collection:

"The Greedy Man." A greedy man (φιλάργυρός τις) sold his property, bought a lump of gold, and, once he had taken this out and buried it, kept coming back to look at it. One of the men at work nearby saw him coming and going and, guessing what he was up to, removed the gold after he had left. When the greedy man came back again and found the hole empty, he began to weep and tear his hair. Someone saw him in this excess of grief, and when he found out what the reason was, he said to him, "Don't grieve, my friend; just take a stone and put it in the hole and then pretend that's your gold. You didn't use it when you had it, anyhow." (Perry fable no. 225, trans. Daly 1961 slightly modified)

It is worth noting the divergences of Antiphon's retelling from the plain fable version, both in its style and in content and larger purpose. In style, Antiphon's version certainly conforms to Philostratus's characterization of Antiphon's treatise "On Concord" (Περὶ ὁμονοίας), from which it is presumed to come:[54]

A good many of his legal speeches are extant, and they show his great rhetorical power and all the effects of art. Of the sophistic type there are several, but more sophistic than any is the speech *On Concord*, in which are brilliant philosophical maxims and a lofty style of eloquence, adorned moreover with the flowers of poetical vocabulary (ἐν ᾧ γνωμολογίαι τε λαμπραὶ καὶ φιλόσοφοι σεμνή τε ἀπαγγελία καὶ ἐπηνθισμένη ποιητικοῖς ὀνόμασι); and their diffuse style makes them seem like smooth plains. (Phil. *VS* 1.500, trans. Wright 1968)

The narrative is leisurely and expansive (Philostratus's "smooth plains"), and sprinkled with artful coinages and conceits not to be found in the straightforward Augustana version. Thus Antiphon's use of ἀχαριστέω to mean "refuse" or "disoblige" seems to be his own coinage (it earns a gloss in Harpocration).[55]

[53] Word order here follows Pendrick 2002 (for reasons given on his pp. 399–400) vs Diels–Kranz.
[54] Thus DK (87 B 54), Untersteiner 1954.254–55. This presumption is based on both the content and the style of Stobaeus's excerpt. Thus it is partly because the style of this passage conforms so closely to Philostratus's characterization of the style of Antiphon's treatise "On Concord" that modern scholars have assumed that Stobaeus's quotation—offered without title—derives from this source. Cf. Gagarin 2002.93, Pendrick 2002.39–40, both of whom accept the attribution.
[55] For the leisurely and elegant style of Antiphon's fable, see Aly 1929.75 (although he regards it as "volkstümlich"), Gagarin 2002.97–99 (suggesting that the style is more appropriate for oral

Even more striking is the elegant opposition of the fable's punch line, "rich in money, poor in good sense," in which the latter term of the pair perhaps echoes with inversion Hesiod's ironic ἀνὴρ φρένας ἀφνειός ("man rich in plans") of the fool who fantasizes about building his own cart (*WD* 455).[56]

Crucially linked to the shift in stylistic register are the divergences of content, which in turn may point to the broader context and purpose of Antiphon's adaptation. First, as the opening words of the Augustana fable tell us, it's a fable directed against a "greedy or avaricious man" (φιλάργυρός τις), whereas the fault of Antiphon's "second man" is that "he was the sort to distrust and not help anyone" (ἀλλ' ἦν οἷος ἀπιστεῖν τε καὶ μὴ ὠφελεῖν μηδένα). Closely linked to this: Antiphon's version stages an elaborate negotiation between this character and a man who would like to take out a loan at interest. This subplot of the refused loan is entirely lacking from the Augustana's sparer version, which must therefore introduce an innocent bystander (the nameless τις) to deliver the fable's punch line.[57]

All these new plot elements in Antiphon's version presumably serve the larger theme of *homonoia*, for they endorse by negative example the forging of human community and cooperation through mutual trust and willingness to help. Indeed, in this respect, Antiphon's fable closely corresponds to the representation of successful community and its breakdown in the set piece on *eunomia* and *anomia* within the disquisition of the Anonymous Iamblichi (lacking only the vivid particularity of the fable narrative):[58]

(1) An atmosphere of trust is the first result of the observance of law. It benefits all men greatly (πίστις μὲν πρώτη ἐγγίγνεται ἐκ τῆς εὐνομίας μεγάλα ὠφελοῦσα τοὺς

---

presentation/*epideixis* than "On Truth"), Pendrick 2002.45, 397–400. For full references to Harpocration and other late lexicographers dependent on him, see Pendrick 2002.398.

[56] Pendrick 2002.400 notes this echo; see West 1978.273 *ad WD* 455. For the same opposition of literal wealth and metaphorical poverty of understanding, see Eur. *Electra* 371 (cited by West).

[57] This second divergence from the Augustana fable version is noted by Aly 1929.75, Pendrick 2002.395–96.

[58] This parallel is noted by Morrison in Sprague 1972.231. As for the work's title, Pendrick 2002.41–45, 395–97 despairs of finding any meaning in it, insisting that there is no evidence in any of the fragments attributed to "On Concord" for a political or social interpretation of *homonoia* (including B 54). I find Pendrick's extreme skepticism excessive for two reasons: (1) Following much older German critics, the only version he can imagine for political *homonoia* is a very specific topical reference to the oligarchic revolutions in Athens and their aftermath. But Tell (2003.49–106) has collected abundant evidence for Sophistic discussions of political and social *homonoia* as a general theme, and argued that these discussions should not be pinned to particular historical moments of stasis and resolution. (2) Pendrick does not note the parallel between Antiphon's recasting of the fable and the passage from the Anonymous Iamblichi cited in text; but this parallel seems to me to be a very strong argument for the theme of social contract, or of the convergence of individual self-interest and community interest, in Antiphon's fable. For more capacious (though very different) notions of what Antiphon's treatise "On Concord" might have contained, see Havelock 1957.290–94, Nestle 1975.381–88, de Romilly 1992.182–84, Gagarin 2002.93–97.

ἀνθρώπους τοὺς σύμπαντας).... (2) And the changes of fortune which affect wealth, whether good or bad, are most suitably directed by men if they observe the law. Those who have good fortune enjoy it in safety and with no fear of attack; those who have bad fortune receive help from those who enjoy good fortune because of their common dealings and mutual trust (διὰ τὴν ἐπιμειξίαν τε καὶ πίστιν).... (7) but the evils which result from a failure to observe law are as follows: (8) ... [men] hoard money because of the lack of mutual trust and the lack of common dealings but they do not share it (τά τε χρήματα δι' ἀπιστίαν καὶ ἀμειξίαν ἀποθησαυρίζουσιν ἀλλ' οὐ κοινοῦνται), and in this way money becomes scarce, even if it exists in large quantities. (Anonymous Iamblichi, 89 DK 7.1, 2, 7, 8, trans. Reesor in Sprague 1972)

These striking parallels strongly suggest that Antiphon has deployed a stylistically refined version of fable as part (perhaps the beginning?) of a political and ethical treatise on social contract, arguing for the importance of mutual trust and willingness to help for the constitution of successful human community or "concord" (*homonoia*). Indeed, it is even imaginable that, as with Nestle's theory of Prodicus's *Hōrai*, Antiphon's *Homonoia* had an anthropological or diachronic component, tracing out the development of political society.[59]

Prodicus's and Antiphon's uses of fable in turn provide a crucial framework within which to consider Protagoras's μῦθος in Plato's eponymous dialogue. Having been invited by Socrates to offer a display piece (*epideixis*, 320b–c1) on the teachability of *politikē aretē* ("the virtue of citizenship"), Protagoras first narrates a long mythological tale:[60]

"There once was a time when the gods existed but mortal races did not. When the time came for their appointed genesis, the gods molded them inside the earth, blending together earth and fire and various compounds of earth and fire. When they were ready to bring them to light the gods put Prometheus and Epimetheus in charge of decking them out and assigning to each its appropriate powers and abilities. Epimetheus begged Prometheus for the privilege of assigning the abilities himself. 'When I've completed the distribution,' he said, 'you can inspect it.' Prometheus agreed, and Epimetheus started distributing abilities. To some he assigned strength without quickness; the weaker ones he made quick. Some he armed; others he left unarmed but devised for them some other means for preserving themselves. He compensated for small size by issuing wings for flight or an underground habitat. Size was itself a safeguard for those he made large. And so on down the line, balancing his distribution, making adjustments, and taking precautions against the possible extinction of any of the races. After supplying them with defenses against mutual destruc-

---

[59] For a possible anthropological strand in Antiphon's thought (and, in particular, in his treatise "On Concord"), see Havelock 1957.289–90, Guthrie 1969.287–88.

[60] Nestle 1975.282 (followed by Guthrie 1969.63–64n. 3) suggests that Protagoras's treatise "On the Original State of Man" (περὶ τῆς ἐν ἀρχῇ καταστάσεως), including the Prometheus story, would have been performed as a public lecture (*epideixis*); for this, he compares Prodicus's "Choice of Heracles." For this invitation to perform an *epideixis* in the *Protagoras*, see also Mann 2006.

tion, he devised for them protection against the weather. He clothed them with thick pelts, and tough hides capable of warding off winter storms, effective against heat, and serving also as built-in, natural bedding when they went to sleep. He also shod them, some with hooves, others with thick pads of bloodless skin. Then he provided them with various forms of nourishment, plants for some, fruit from trees for others, roots for still others. And there were some to whom he gave the consumption of other animals as their sustenance. To some he gave the capacity for few births; to others, ravaged by the former, he gave the capacity for multiple births, and so ensured the survival of their kind. But Epimetheus was not very wise, and he absentmindedly used up all the powers and abilities on the nonreasoning animals; he was left with the human race, completely unequipped. While he was floundering about at a loss, Prometheus arrived to inspect the distribution and saw that while the other animals were well provided with everything, the human race was naked, unshod, unbedded, and unarmed, and it was already the day on which all of them, human beings included, were destined to emerge from the earth into the light. It was then that Prometheus, desperate to find some means of survival for the human race, stole from Hephaestus and Athena wisdom in the practical arts (ἔντεχνον σοφίαν) together with fire (without which this kind of wisdom is effectively useless) and gave them outright to the human race. The wisdom it acquired was for staying alive; wisdom for living together in society, political wisdom (τὴν δὲ πολιτικὴν), it did not acquire, because that was in the keeping of Zeus. Prometheus no longer had free access to the high citadel that is the house of Zeus, and besides this, the guards there were terrifying. But he did sneak into the building that Athena and Hephaestus shared to practice their arts, and he stole from Hephaestus the art of fire and from Athena her arts, and he gave them to the human race. And it is from this origin that the resources human beings needed to stay alive came into being. Later, the story goes, Prometheus was charged with theft, all on account of Epimetheus.

"It is because humans had a share of the divine dispensation that they alone among animals worshipped the gods, with whom they had a kind of kinship, and erected altars and sacred images. It wasn't long before they were articulating speech and words and had invented houses, clothes, shoes, and blankets, and were nourished by food from the earth. Thus equipped, human beings at first lived in scattered isolation; there were no cities. They were being destroyed by wild beasts because they were weaker in every way, and although their technology was adequate to obtain food, it was deficient when it came to fighting wild animals. This was because they did not yet possess the arts of politics (πολιτικὴν. . .τέχνην), of which the art of war is a part. They did indeed try to band together and survive by founding cities. The outcome when they did so was that they wronged each other, because they did not possess the art of politics (πολιτικὴν τέχνην), and so they would scatter and again be destroyed. Zeus was afraid that our whole race might be wiped out, so he sent Hermes to bring justice and a sense of shame (αἰδῶ τε καὶ δίκην) to humans, so that there would be order within cities and bonds of friendship to unite them. Hermes asked Zeus how he should distribute shame and justice to humans. 'Should I distribute them as the other arts were? This is how the others were distributed: one person practicing the art of medicine suffices for many ordinary people; and so forth with the other practitioners. Should I establish justice and shame among humans in this way, or distribute it to all?' 'To all,' said Zeus, 'and let all have a share. For cities would never come to be if only a few possessed these, as is the case with the other arts. And establish this law as coming from me: Death to him who cannot partake of shame and justice, for he is a pestilence to the city.' And so it is, Socrates, that when the Athenians (and others as well) are debating architectural excellence, or the virtue proper to any other professional specialty, they think that only a few individuals have the right to advise them, and they do not accept advice from anyone outside these select few. You've made this point yourself, and with good reason, I might add. But when the debate involves political excellence (πολιτικῆς ἀρετῆς), which must proceed entirely from justice and temperance, they accept advice from anyone, and with good reason, for they think that this particular virtue, political or civic virtue, is shared by all, or there wouldn't be any cities. This must be the explanation for it, Socrates." (Plato *Prot.* 320c8–23a4, trans. Lombardo and Bell 1997)

Scholars have long debated whether Protagoras's "great speech" on *politikē technē* represents an accurate rendition of the Sophist's own writing or a Platonic pastiche; they have likewise struggled to understand the relation of Protagoras's μῦθος to Platonic myth.[61] To address both these issues: clearly we cannot treat Protagoras's lengthy disquisition as an unmediated representation of his authentic discourse, yet this survey of other Sophistic adaptations of fable encourages us to read Protagoras's "great speech" as precisely the kind of thing we would expect from the eminent Sophist—the lengthy literary elaboration of Aesopic fable. That is to say, Plato has crafted a generically and stylistically appropriate discourse for the great Sophist, even if (as we shall see in the next chapter) this Platonic pastiche emerges as more parodic when juxtaposed with its fabular prototypes.

For Protagoras's μῦθος must be understood as "fable," not "myth" (as it is still conventionally read by many scholars of ancient philosophy). Indeed, in the reading of *Protagoras*, we see clearly the problem of the excessive segregation of disciplinary subfields, for while most scholars of ancient fable have unhesitatingly recognized Protagoras's μῦθος as an aetiological fable, students of ancient philosophy still puzzle over its aberrancy as a sample of Platonic "mythmaking."[62]

[61] On the question of the authenticity of Protagoras's "great speech," Aly 1929.70–73; Guthrie 1969.63–64, 319; Nestle 1975.282; and de Romilly 1992.162 assume that Plato substantially reproduces a Protagorean original; while Havelock 1957.87–94, 407–9 and Cole 1991.59–62 challenge this assumption, seeing much more of Plato than of Protagoras in the speech. For the relation of Protagoras's μῦθος to Platonic mythmaking, see next note.

[62] For the categorization of Protagoras's tale as fable, see Aly 1929.70–73; Adrados 1999.380–82, 402; and cf. Dover 1966.42–43: "Protagoras in Pl. *Prt.* 320cff. offers a story which is philosophically serious, in that it is used as an introduction to an exposition of ethical views which deserve attention, it is systematic, and it is an elegant work of art, but it resembles preliterate myth in represent-

Thus, for example, Mark J. Edwards catalogs the divergences of Protagorean from "Socratic" "myth": the latter does not replace dialectical argument, but only reinforces it (usually afterward); Socratic myth is almost inevitably attributed to another authority; direct speech is rare; the actors are more types than individuals; particular gods are rarely mentioned or involved in the mythic action, and when they are, they do nothing wrong or disreputable; Socratic myth tends to be eschatological, not aetiological. In contrast, Protagoras offers his "myth" in place of reasoned argument, confidently and on his own authority; the tale is aetiological and full of direct speech. Perhaps most importantly, the story's actors (all divine) are distinctly characterized, individual, and fallible. Indeed, it is this thoroughgoing particularity of Protagoras's account that most incurs the philosophical reader's disapproval:

> This order of explanation cannot satisfy a Socrates, however well it may delight the poets. It is indeed the abundance of particulars that prevents the sophist from making any overtures to belief. He is the man who, on another occasion, refused to speak of the gods because he did not know even whether they existed; Plato, who was certain of their existence, would have told him that it was impossible to know anything but good. In this myth the gods appoint one deputy who forgets his trust and another who betrays it; Hermes must deliberate and Zeus himself is subject to anxiety. Speech expresses pride in Epimetheus, ignorance in Hermes and the dignity of the highest god is compromised when he waits for his inferiors to execute, or even prompt the utterance of, his will. These anthropomorphic deities are fashioned after Hesiod and Homer: while the myths of Socrates deify man, the myths of the sophists humanise his gods.[63]

Edwards attributes all these features of Protagorean "myth" to the influence of the poets, but in fact every anomaly in his catalog is characteristic of prose Aesopic fable. Even the particular gods involved and the scenarios in which they participate echo numerous fables preserved in the later fable collections (as we shall see in the next chapter). And yet Edwards is right to insist on poetic influence, for in *style* Protagoras's *muthos* is high and elegant, full of elaborately constructed balancing clauses and periods, and refined diction.[64] Thus, just as

---

ing species of living creatures as being fitted out with their attributes by a supernatural though fallible quartermaster." Note that van Dijk 1997.673 resists this categorization, listing it in his appendix of "Non-Fables & Non-Allusions." For scholars of ancient philosophy treating it as myth, see (e.g.) Wolz 1963, Adkins 1973, Brisson 1975, Miller 1978, Kerferd 1981, Edwards 1992, Ferrarin 2000, Morgan 2000.

[63] Edwards 1992.98. Given the genre of aetiological fable and its characteristic cast of characters here, it also seems somewhat silly to worry (as many philosophical discussions do) about the inconsistency between Protagoras's professed agnosticism and the prominence of gods in this tale. For a reasonable approach to this issue, see Guthrie 1969.63–68.

[64] Many examples of these stylistic features are cited in the commentary of Adam and Adam 1905.108–24; cf. Aly 1929.70–73, Dover 1966.42–43 (quoted above, n. 62).

we have seen in Prodicus's "Choice of Heracles" and Antiphon's adaptation of fable, Protagoras has taken over the content and genre of prose fable, but framed it in a thoroughly elevated style, so as to make it a form suitable for public discourse and display.

Indeed, if we had any doubts, Plato's text teems with generic markers for fable at the moment Protagoras introduces his aetiological tale. This is true not just of the tale's opening sentence (ἦν γάρ ποτε χρόνος ὅτε θεοὶ μὲν ἦσαν, θνητὰ δὲ γένη οὐκ ἦν), but also of the byplay among interlocutors that immediately precedes it:

> ἀλλ᾽, ὦ Σώκρατες, ἔφη, οὐ φθονήσω· ἀλλὰ πότερον ὑμῖν, ὡς πρεσβύτερος νεωτέροις, μῦθον λέγων ἐπιδείξω ἢ λόγῳ διεξελθών;
>
> πολλοὶ οὖν αὐτῷ ὑπέλαβον τῶν παρακαθημένων ὁποτέρως βούλοιτο οὕτως διεξιέναι. δοκεῖ τοίνυν μοι, ἔφη, χαριέστερον εἶναι μῦθον ὑμῖν λέγειν. (*Prot*. 320c2–7)
>
> "I wouldn't think of begrudging you an explanation, Socrates," he replied. "But would you rather that I explain by telling a story, as an older man to a younger audience, or by developing an argument?"
>
> Many of those sitting around answered him that he should proceed in whichever way he wished. "I think it would be more pleasant," he said, "if I told you a story." (Trans. Lombardo and Bell 1997, slightly modified)

There are at least four explicit cues here for fable. First, of course, μῦθος itself can mean "fable," as we've seen from Socrates' usage in the *Phaedo*. Second, in the context of discussion of "fable," Plato's choice of verb for the audience's response to Protagoras's coy question (ὑπέλαβον) is suggestive, redolent as it is of the answering formulae so common in fable encounters of two interlocutors.[65] Third, Protagoras explicitly characterizes *muthos* as what "an elder tells to those who are younger," suggesting that this is a genre that is perceived to be age-specific and appropriately targeted to the young (νεωτέροις).[66] This characterization recalls Philostratus's specification of the intended audience for Prodicus's "Choice of Heracles" (at least according to the Thebans and Spartans): ὡς ἐς τὸ συμφέρον *τῶν νέων* ἀναδιδάσκων ταῦτα. Finally, notice the reason Protagoras offers for opting for *muthos* instead of *logos*: "It seems to me, he said, to be more gratifying (χαριέστερον) to tell you a fable." In χαριέστερον, I would contend, we catch an echo of the characteristic pleasure thought to be

---

[65] For discussion of this characteristically fabular answering formula, see chapter 3, section I, discussion of *Phaedo* in chapter 6, section I above, and Kurke 2010.

[66] We should note that the dialogue as a whole is obsessed with age and age-classes; I count thirteen different references to individuals' ages, age-classes, and relative seniority. In addition, the entire dialogue is framed by references to ὥρα, since it opens with byplay between Socrates and his unnamed interlocutor on whether Alcibiades is now past his "bloom" (ὥρα, 309a2–b2), while it ends with Socrates' assertion that it is time—indeed, past time (ὥρα, 362a2)—for his departure. Is this coincidence, or perhaps a sly reference to Prodicus's *Hōrai*?

generated by indirect fable narrative, even if Protagoras has substituted the more refined and poetic adjective derived from χάρις for the more common characterizations for fabular pleasure through forms of ἡδύς or γλυκύς or verbs denoting the audience's delight.[67]

We might also note that Protagoras's elaborate *epideixis* has very much the same structure that Philostratus attributes to Prodicus's "Choice of Heracles," for the fable narrative itself ends at 322d5 and is followed by a long explanatory exposition (322d6-324d1). Yet it is only at 324d6-7 that Protagoras explicitly indicates a change in mode of discourse, announcing that, for the one remaining problem (why good men don't teach their sons *politikē aretē* or *technē*), "no longer shall I speak *muthos* to you, but *logos*" (οὐκέτι μῦθόν σοι ἐρῶ ἀλλὰ λόγον). G. B. Kerferd, who notes this structural pattern, observes:

> This sentence makes two things plain: the logos begins here only and not earlier at 324a4, and in some sense the discussion of the myth is regarded as continuing right down to this point, 324d1. As the myth proper clearly ends at 322d5, this can only mean that the whole section 322d5-324d1 is regarded as an explanation and application of the myth. The last sentence of the section then, 324c5-d1, must be regarded as summarising the contents of the myth.[68]

With the sole amendment that we should read "fable" for "myth," Kerferd's analysis seems to me to be exactly right, and what he is describing is a fable with a lengthy explanatory epilogue (*epilogos* or, as in Philostratus, τὸ ἐπὶ πᾶσι). Thus, like Prodicus's "Choice of Heracles," Protagoras's aetiological fable is cast in a high, elegant style; it is directed specifically to the young; and it provides the Sophist the occasion or platform for a long explanatory epilogue. In addition, like Prodicus's tale and also perhaps like Antiphon's adaptation of fable,

---

[67] Again, just as with the issue of age and age-classes, χάρις (as a feature of verbal exchange) is an important theme or leitmotif throughout the dialogue as a whole. Thus the χάρις of speaking and hearing *logoi* is foregrounded in the frame dialogue between Socrates and his unnamed interlocutor at 310a, and then referred to repeatedly: cf. 328d8, 335d4-5, 335e1, 344b2, 358a7-9, 360e4, 362a3 (where χαριζόμενος is nearly the last word of Socrates' narrated dialogue). Hence Protagoras's choice of the adjective χαριέστερον participates simultaneously in the dialogue's implicit consideration of what the true forms of *charis* in discourse and intellectual exchange might be, and this perhaps accounts for the substitution of this adjective for other terms for pleasure that are simultaneously more bodily and more conventionally associated with the effect of fable narration on an audience. We should also note that the precise difference in meaning of two verbs denoting "pleasure," εὐφραίνεσθαι and ἥδεσθαι, is thematized by Prodicus at 337c1-4, while at 358a, Socrates playfully suggests to Prodicus that χαρτόν (an adjective derived, like the noun χάρις, from the verb χαίρω) is a synonym or near-synonym for ἡδύ and τερπνόν.

[68] Kerferd 1981.133. Note Kerferd's very interesting suggestion (134-35) that Protagoras's *muthos* and *logos* are *alternative* ways of describing the same phenomena (i.e., they do not have to be reconciled in a single evolutionary time line); cf. Guthrie 1969.65, Cole 1991.60. This idea is particularly interesting and appealing, since it would precisely replicate something like the structure of WD 47-201 (the juxtaposition of the Prometheus-Pandora story and the "myth" of the races—both of which are arguably also fables; cf. Dover 1966.43-44).

Protagoras's elegant and witty tale of Prometheus, Epimetheus, Zeus, and Hermes is offered in the service of a serious disquisition on politics and ethics.[69] Indeed, as we have seen for Prodicus's *Hōrai* and Antiphon's "On Concord," it is just possible that all three of these adaptations of fable derive from works of Sophistic anthropology.[70]

I will return to Plato's *Protagoras* in the next chapter to consider the meaning and implications of Protagoras's represented fable narrative within the dialogue as a whole. But first, I would like briefly to contrast the Sophists' fabular practice with what I take to be the more traditional use of fable as a speech genre by Xenophon. This will entail (among other things) looking carefully at how Xenophon has appropriated and adapted Prodicus's fable for his own purposes in the *Memorabilia*.

II. Traditional Fable Narration in Xenophon's *Memorabilia*

It is noteworthy that all the Sophistic fables and representations of Sophistic fable we have considered thus far involve gods, heroes, and men; we do not encounter a single pure beast fable in the preserved remains or attributed discourses of the Sophists. Of course, given how small our sample set is, it is difficult to know whether this pattern is significant. Is this merely an accident of preservation, or is there in fact a hierarchy perceived even within the category of fable, whereby aetiological fables or fables involving human beings are regarded as higher-class and tonier than their beast-fable brethren? I raise the question because the only beast fable that we find narrated straight through in all of the Sophistic/Socratic material preserved is the "Fable of the Dog and the Sheep" put into the mouth of Socrates in Xenophon's *Memorabilia*. We must take a close look at Xenophon's deployment of fable, for it reveals by contrast what is distinctive and different about the Sophists' strategies.

---

[69] It is worth noting that in the *Life of Aesop*, Aesop also may tell a fable involving Prometheus in the context of his all-important political advising of the Samians (*Vita* G, chs. 93–94). But note that "Prometheus" as the creator of the two roads is Perry's emendation for *Tuchē* in the text of *Vita* G—an emendation accepted by Papathomopoulos 1990 and Ferrari 1997.

[70] Scholars regularly connect Protagoras's fable with his treatise entitled περὶ τῆς ἐν ἀρχῇ καταστάσεως ("On the Original State of Man," as reported by D.L. 9.55) and assume that this was Protagoras's own exercise in anthropology: thus (e.g.) Guthrie 1969.63–68, Nestle 1975.282–89, de Romilly 1992.162–68. One other feature all three sophistic fables may have in common is an explicit affiliation with Hesiod (this is clear for Prodicus and Protagoras; but we have also noted a possible verbal echo of Hesiod's *WD* in Antiphon's fable). Beyond the obvious connection with the Greek didactic tradition, this may have other motivations: (1) Hesiod is strongly associated with the deployment of fables; but also perhaps (2) the choice of Hesiod vs Homer may reflect a particular stylistic choice, akin to the practice of Hellenistic poets. This latter possibility was suggested to me by Mark Griffith; cf. the fascinating discussion of O'Sullivan 1992 on fifth-century precursors for later Greek theories of style.

This is not to claim that Xenophon's own writing is more conventional—less innovative—than that of the Sophists, for Xenophon was himself a master of generic experimentation, as scholars have begun to appreciate. Thus Arnaldo Momigliano hailed Xenophon as "a pioneer experimenter in biographical forms" that combined in complex ways truth and fiction, considering under this rubric Xenophon's *Anabasis*, *Agesilaus*, *Memorabilia*, and especially the *Cyropaedia* as a "paedagogical novel."[71] Specifically in relation to the *Memorabilia*, Hartmut Erbse had already defended the work's unity against older critics who condemned it as an inept and incoherent grab bag of material by pointing out that it is a written text modeled on the structure of a law-court speech—comparable to something like Lysias 16, for a speaker defending himself in a *dokimasia*. For the *Memorabilia* first explicitly refutes official and unofficial charges leveled against Socrates (*Mem.* 1.1-2) and then proceeds to offer a positive account of his life and activities that implicitly continues that work of defense.[72] Vivienne J. Gray in turn builds on Erbse's unitarian argument, but finds still other genres contributing to Xenophon's complex text. For Gray, the *Memorabilia* draws not just on the genre of law-court defense speech but also on much older Greek traditions of didactic poetry and wisdom literature. Like certain Sophistic compositions and more or less contemporary writings of Isocrates, the *Memorabilia* transposes to prose an archaic tradition of poetic didactic, represented by Hesiod's *Works & Days* and the Theognidea.[73] At the same time, it builds on the shorter prose forms of *chreiai* and *apophthegmata*—the pithy, sage words and actions of notable figures that we know circulated already in the fifth century BCE (e.g., Sayings of the Seven Sages and other wise men).[74] Gray exhaustively documents the conventions of *chreiai* at work in Xenophon's construction and framing of episodes in the *Memorabilia*, but also notes the ways in which Xenophon seems to have innovated within this traditional form to capture new, distinctively Socratic discursive features. Thus, in Gray's account, Xenophon has expanded the traditionally brief form of *chreiai* by including Socrates' characteristic dialectic methods of defining terms, proceeding from

---

[71] Momigliano 1971.46–57; quotations from pp. 47 and 55, respectively.

[72] Erbse 1961.

[73] Gray 1998.159–77. In addition to the arguments that Gray offers to demonstrate Xenophon's familiarity with the genre of traditional didactic poetry, we might recall the evidence of Stobaeus, that Xenophon himself seems to have written a treatise on Theognis; see discussion in chapter 5, n. 35 above.

[74] Gray.1998 passim; see esp. 8–16, 105–22, 159–77 (with abundant citation of earlier literature). Gray cites the Sayings of the Seven Sages and a collection of sayings of the Spartan Dieneces referred to by Herodotus at 7.226. For the genre of *chreiai*, see also Sternbach 1963, Gow 1965.12–15, Hock and O'Neill 1986, Kurke 2002. For Sayings of the Seven Sages circulating already in the sixth and fifth centuries, see Snell 1966b, Momigliano 1971.53, Edmunds 1997.41–44, Martin 1998.115–19, and see chapter 2, section I above. Notice also the intriguing suggestion of Goldhill 1998.112n. 25, that individual chapters of the *Memorabilia* might have been read aloud at elite symposia—thus in their performance occasion very similar to something like the Theognidea.

agreed premises, and refutation by question-and-answer (*elenchos*). Finally, Gray suggests, Xenophon has innovated in scale; he has produced the single largest compendium of *chreiai* of a single wise man ever attempted.[75]

Gray also observes that what seems to characterize all identifiable fifth-/fourth-century adaptations of Greek didactic is a combination of formal experimentation and deep conservatism and conventionality of content. This paradox, as she notes, significantly informs and constrains Xenophon's representation of Socrates in the *Memorabilia*.[76] I would concur with Gray's characterization of the *Memorabilia* as innovative in form while largely traditional in content, and would go a step further: of all the extant writers of Sophistic/Socratic prose, Xenophon seems to possess and to respect the boundaries of the most finely developed sense of stylistic and generic decorum and propriety.

We can see this, for example, in his elaborate apology to the reader for introducing personal anecdote into the austere setting of history in his *History of Greece* (*HG* 2.3.56). At the climax of Book 2, chapter 3, Xenophon describes how Critias strikes Theramenes from the list of citizens and unilaterally condemns him to death, inciting the Eleven, led by the brutal Satyrus, to drag him from the altar where he has taken refuge before the eyes of the stricken Boule. At that point, Xenophon continues:

οἱ δ᾽ ἀπήγαγον τὸν ἄνδρα διὰ τῆς ἀγορᾶς μάλα μεγάλῃ τῇ φωνῇ δηλοῦντα οἷα ἔπασχε. λέγεται δ᾽ ἓν ῥῆμα καὶ τοῦτο αὐτοῦ. ὡς εἶπεν ὁ Σάτυρος ὅτι οἰμώξοιτο, εἰ μὴ σιωπήσειεν, ἐπήρετο· ἂν δὲ σιωπῶ, οὐκ ἄρ᾽, ἔφη, οἰμώξομαι; καὶ ἐπεί γε ἀποθνήσκειν ἀναγκαζόμενος τὸ κώνειον ἔπιε, τὸ λειπόμενον ἔφασαν ἀποκοτταβίσαντα εἰπεῖν αὐτόν· Κριτίᾳ τοῦτ᾽ ἔστω τῷ καλῷ. καὶ τοῦτο μὲν οὐκ ἀγνοῶ, ὅτι ταῦτα ἀποφθέγματα οὐκ ἀξιόλογα, ἐκεῖνο δὲ κρίνω τοῦ ἀνδρὸς ἀγαστόν, τὸ τοῦ θανάτου παρεστηκότος μήτε τὸ φρόνιμον μήτε τὸ παιγνιῶδες ἀπολιπεῖν ἐκ τῆς ψυχῆς. (Xen. *HG* 2.3.56)

They led the man away through the agora as he made clear in a very loud voice what was happening to him. One saying of his that is reported is this. When Satyrus said that if he did not keep quiet he would regret it, he replied, "And if I do keep quiet," he said, "will I not regret it?" And when he was actually being forced to die and was drinking the hemlock, they say that he threw the dregs like someone playing *kottabos*, and said "This to the beautiful Critias." I am aware that these quips are not noteworthy, but I find this admirable in the man, that in the face of death neither presence of mind nor playfulness left his soul. (Trans. Krentz 1995, slightly modified)

---

[75] Gray 1998, esp. 121, 178–93. Gray's argument that the *Memorabilia* is built up from the expansion of smaller forms compellingly refutes an earlier scholarly approach to the text as a loose sequence of ineptly shortened and epitomated dialogues composed by earlier Socratics (for this scholarly approach, see, e.g., Gigon 1956).

[76] For this combination, see Gray 1998.121, 159–65, 167, 177, citing Hippias's *Sunagōgē*, Prodicus's "Choice of Heracles," Isocrates, and Xenophon. According to Gray (177), this is both a generic constraint and an effective way for Xenophon to make the historical Socrates' "strangeness" more palatable to his audience by framing him as a traditional sage.

Xenophon acknowledges that the "quips" (ἀποφθέγματα) of Theramenes he records are not "worth mentioning" (ἀξιόλογα)—his standard throughout the *History of Greece* of what merits inclusion in the high genre of history writing.[77] This seems to imply that the private sayings of an individual are not properly the stuff of history. Indeed, this general problem of decorum or level of style is compounded by two particular features of the sayings he attributes to Theramenes in his last moments. In the first place, Satyrus's bullying threat is framed in crude, slangy terms, even if Theramenes transforms those terms in his fearless response. For we find just this use of οἰμώζω (essentially, "you'll be sorry") frequently in representations of low verbal sparring in Old Comedy.[78] Second, Theramenes' combined speech and action of tossing the hemlock lees "for Critias" ironically reference the symposium game of *kottabos*. This reference is at once too frivolous and private, since it transforms a public execution into aristocratic "play," and too intimate, since the dedication "for the beautiful Critias" evokes even as it parodies a form of erotic proposition.[79]

Given Xenophon's own scrupulous regard for the boundaries and hierarchies of genre and decorum, we should perhaps conceive of the *History of Greece* and the *Memorabilia* as occupying complementary generic and stylistic registers in a Xenophontic literary system. The former represents restrained and austere history presented in an elevated style; the latter embraces a looser, more colloquial-seeming style as more suitable to its content of *chreiai* and *apophthegmata* (reminiscences, anecdotes, and sayings) drawn from the life of Socrates. Within this literary system, it is then significant that fable figures only in the *Memorabilia* and only in specific contexts that contrast markedly both with Sophistic appropriations of fable and with Plato's. In contrast to the Sophists, Xenophon's text seems to offer us a deft literary adaptation of the more traditional context, framing, and use of fable as a "speech genre" in social life. In contrast to Plato, Xenophon's text is markedly less ambivalent toward the Aesopic and fabular, finding a positive use for advice via fable as long as its sphere of application is properly circumscribed.

One measure of this difference is that in all of Plato, Socrates nowhere tells a traditional fable associated with Aesop straight through: in the *Phaedo*, he invents an allegorical fable "Aesop would have told, had he thought of it," while in

---

[77] Cf. *HG* 4.8.1, 5.1.4 for this standard and *HG* 2.4.27, 7.2.1 for other moments where Xenophon registers breaches of the prevailing decorum of history. Gray 1998.118–19 also discusses this passage from the *History of Greece* as an example of Xenophon's use of *chreia* and *apophthegma*, but she does not comment on Xenophon's explicit apology for the inclusion of such forms in historical writing.

[78] LSJ s.v. οἰμώζω 2, with numerous passages from Aristophanes listed there.

[79] On *kottabos* in general and the *kottabos* toast in particular as a form of erotic proposition of the *erōmenos*, see Kurke 1999.278–80 with earlier bibliography. Scholars frequently read Theramenes' end here together with Socrates' (thus, e.g., Krentz 1995.139); note the contrast in level of style and decorum, that Theramenes plays *kottabos* with his hemlock, while Socrates wishes to pour a libation to the gods from his cup (cf. *Phd.* 117b6–7).

Alcibiades I, Socrates merely alludes to a well-known beast fable.[80] In Xenophon's *Memorabilia*, by contrast, Socrates is represented narrating what appears to be a traditional beast fable straight through (beginning with the conventional fable introduction, "when the animals could talk"), as a form of practical advice to a beleaguered acquaintance (*Mem.* 2.7.13–14).[81] I will consider the specific context of this fable in more detail below; for now, I would note simply that the occurrences of fable reveal an interesting pattern within the structure and thematic concerns of the work as a whole. For the Aesopic fable elements are noticeably confined or limited within the work only to certain spheres and topics (all of them comprehended by the second Book): bodily pleasures and the relations of private individuals within the household, including the relations of kin and household management.

The first Book of the *Memorabilia* begins with an extended defense of Socrates against the charges on which he was tried and executed by the city (*Mem.* 1.1–2), and then, in the third chapter, launches into Xenophon's reminiscences of how Socrates benefited his companions by word and deed (essentially, a compendium of *chreiai* and *apophthegmata* to illustrate Socrates' universal "usefulness").[82] Xenophon begins his recollections of Socrates with his piety and attitude toward the gods and then turns to the topic of his perfect bodily self-control (ἐγκράτεια, *Mem.* 1.5–6). Book 2 in turn begins with an extended conversation between Socrates and Aristippus that continues this theme, as Socrates tries to convince a recalcitrant Aristippus of the importance of self-control and control of bodily appetites.[83] At the very beginning of the Book, Socrates frames this issue within the broader question of how one ought "to educate [one] who is going to be fit to rule" (παιδεύειν . . . τὸν μὲν, ὅπως ἱκανὸς ἔσται ἄρχειν, *Mem.* 2.1.1), and starts the conversation with Aristippus "from the topic of food just as from first principles" (ἀρξάμενοι ἀπὸ τῆς τροφῆς ὥσπερ ἀπὸ τῶν στοιχείων).[84] We might take these formulations as programmatic for the whole sequence of episodes that constitute Book 2.[85] For here Xenophon

---

[80] For these two as Socrates' only explicit mentions of Aesop and his fables in the entire corpus of Plato, see Desclos 1997.395, 2000. Cf. Rothwell 1995 for parallels for this pattern of avoidance and allusion.

[81] I say "what *appears to be* a traditional beast fable" because a version of it shows up in the corpus of Babrius (no. 356 Perry = Babr. 128), but it may be that Babrius derived it from this passage of the *Memorabilia*.

[82] Cf. Erbse 1961, Gray 1998.

[83] For thematic connections between *Mem.* 2.1 and the topics of the first Book, see Gigon 1956.5–10; Erbse 1961.273–74, 1980.7–10; Gray 1998.123–30.

[84] On the ethical and political meaning of *stoicheion* here, see Erbse 1980.11–12 (contra Gigon 1956.16–17).

[85] It is irrelevant for the argument presented here whether Xenophon himself imposed the book structure within the *Memorabilia* (as Gigon 1956.8–10 thinks) or whether the book divisions are a later, Hellenistic imposition (as Erbse 1980.7–8n. 3 maintains). Either way, I am tracking thematic connections and correlations that do not depend on the book divisions.

shows us Socrates slowly and carefully setting in place the moral and social preconditions—or first principles (στοιχεῖα)—for the proper leadership of the polis that will emerge as the main topic only in the first chapters of Book 3 (1–7). Thus Book 2 works through the individual's control of his bodily appetites (*Mem.* 2.1); the proper relations of son to mother and respect for parents (*Mem.* 2.2); the proper relations of brother to brother (*Mem.* 2.3); the value of friends and how to win them (*Mem.* 2.4–6); and finally, specific examples of how Socrates helped his friends (*Mem.* 2.7–10).[86] As we shall see, it is only in the constitution of these more local and intimate levels of self and community that Xenophon's Socrates deploys fable (more or less framing Book 2 as a whole)—first, his adaptation of Prodicus's "Choice of Heracles" at the beginning of Book 2 and then the fable of the sheep and the sheepdog in specific advice offered to a friend toward its end. In contrast, the sources of Socrates' examples and analogies will be completely different in Book 3, as the arena of discussion shifts from the private to the public and political. In this precise correlation of different speech genres with different levels of content, spheres of performance, and audiences, we can see Xenophon rejecting the Sophists' bold experimentation with fable and reinstating a more traditional system of decorum.

Let us begin with Xenophon's adaptation of Prodicus's "Choice of Heracles." In Xenophon's rendering, Aristippus is the very embodiment of lack of self-control and the indulgence of physical pleasures (*Mem.* 2.1).[87] When Socrates attempts to teach him the value of ἐγκράτεια by asking how he would educate two hypothetical youths, "one to be fit to rule, the other who would never even aspire to rule" (*Mem.* 2.1.1), Aristippus eventually balks at the harsh conditions dictated for those "fit to rule" (ἀρχικούς, *Mem.* 2.1.17) and attempts to replace Socrates' stark binary with a tripartite system:

ἀλλ' ἐγώ τοι, ἔφη ὁ Ἀρίστιππος, οὐδὲ εἰς τὴν δουλείαν ἐμαυτὸν τάττω, ἀλλ' εἶναί τίς μοι δοκεῖ μέση τούτων ὁδός, ἣν πειρῶμαι βαδίζειν, οὔτε δι' ἀρχῆς οὔτε διὰ δουλείας, ἀλλὰ δι' ἐλευθερίας, ᾗπερ μάλιστα πρὸς εὐδαιμονίαν ἄγει. (*Mem.* 2.1.11)

But, said Aristippus, nor do I put myself in the category of slavery, but there seems to me to be a middle way, which I attempt to go, neither through rule nor through slavery, but through freedom, the very [road] which most leads to happiness.

---

[86] For the thematic organization of *Mem.* 2.1–3.7, cf. Gigon 1956.3–4, Gray 1998.128–42. In general, I agree with Gray's account, except that she sees 2.1 simply as the closing episode in a sequence on ἐγκράτεια that begins in 1.5, while she treats 2.2–3.7 as a continuous sequence that develops the positive values of family, friends, and citizens. She does not, however, note that 2.1 sets up the frame of "education in ruling" that is fulfilled only by chapters 3.1–7, after the episodes of Book 2 have established the στοιχεῖα or "first principles" for that sphere of public service.

[87] It deserves emphasizing that this is Xenophon's tendentious version of Aristippus; in contrast, Diogenes Laertius's *Life of Aristippus* suggests a more complex form of reasoned and self-controlled philosophical hedonism (for an excellent treatment of the philosophical logic of Aristippus's lifestyle, see Mann 1996).

Notice that it is Aristippus who introduces the imagery of "roads of life" into the conversation. Socrates responds with a fairly crude version of the argument from nature, insisting that the stronger always seek to dominate the weaker so that, for all his effort to pursue a neutral "middle way," Aristippus will necessarily be reduced to servitude to the strong (*Mem.* 2.1.12–16). Over a hundred years ago, George Grote had already noted how specious and apparently inappropriate for Socrates this argument was, since Aristippus's "middle way" seems to correspond to Socrates' own justification of his (nonpolitical) practice in Plato's *Apology* and *Gorgias*.[88] Indeed, I would concur with Grote's criticism and suggest that the burden of refuting Aristippus's image of the "middle road of freedom" is not borne by this crude and tendentious argument; instead, Socrates ultimately trumps Aristippus's position by replacing his "three roads" with two, by the deployment of a pair of allegorical fables.

But we must first backtrack a little and chart the progressive moves and discursive styles within the conversation. In the first place, when Socrates argues that there is no μέση ὁδός "among men," since the strong always dominate the weak both within communities and in private (*Mem.* 2.1.12–13), Aristippus's response is that he will escape this problem by "not shutting himself up in a *politeia*, but he will be a stranger everywhere" (ἀλλὰ ξένος πανταχοῦ εἰμι, *Mem.* 2.1.13). Socrates responds with withering irony, suggesting that things are no better for strangers now than in the days of the mythical brigands Sinis, Sciron, and Procrustes. He points out that even those in cities make laws, build walls, and acquire allies to protect themselves, while strangers are even more vulnerable (*Mem.* 2.1.14–15).[89] Socrates then tries to draw Aristippus back into analogical question-and-answer, asking how masters treat their slaves—especially how they "chasten" and punish those who lack self-control (*Mem.* 2.1.16). Aristippus, however, refuses to get sucked back into dialectic, responding instead with his own sharp irony. He first characterizes Socrates' proposed program of education as training in "the art of kingship, which you seem to believe is happiness" (βασιλικὴν τέχνην . . . ἣν δοκεῖς μοι σὺ νομίζειν εὐδαιμονίαν εἶναι, *Mem.*

---

[88] Grote 1865.III.536–38: "Though Sokrates, in the Xenophontic dialogue, is made to declare this middle course impossible, yet it is substantially the same as what the Platonic Sokrates in the Gorgias aspires to:—moreover the same as what the real Sokrates at Athens both pursued as far as he could, and declared to be the only course consistent with his security. . . . [T]he argument of Sokrates that no middle way is possible—far from refuting Aristippus . . . is founded upon an incorrect assumption. Had it been correct, neither literature nor philosophy could have been developed." Contra: Erbse 1980.9–10.

[89] Notice Socrates' characterization of Aristippus's life as a *xenos* at 2.1.15: "But you have nothing of these things [sc. the protections available to men in cities], but you spend much time on the open roads, where so many men come to harm" (σὺ δὲ οὐδὲν μὲν τούτων ἔχων, ἐν δὲ ταῖς ὁδοῖς, ἔνθα πλεῖστοι ἀδικοῦνται, πολὺν χρόνον διατρίβων . . .). Thus Socrates first tries to refute Aristippus's image of the *mesē hodos* by replacing it with the literal roads wandered by stateless and vulnerable "strangers." Only when this rhetorical move fails does Socrates resort to two allegorical fables of the choice of roads.

2.1.17). βασιλικὴ τέχνη is an odd expression for Aristippus to use, since he and Socrates thus far have consistently referred only to "ruling" (ἄρχειν, ἄρχουσι, *Mem.* 2.1.1, 1.2, 1.3, 1.6, 1.7, 1.8, 1.9, 1.10, 1.11, 1.12) and "those fit to rule" (τοὺς ἀρχικούς, *Mem.* 2.1.7). Elsewhere in the *Memorabilia*, Socrates himself refers to "true kingship" or βασιλικὴ ἀρετή as that "through which men become statesmen and household managers and competent to rule and helpful to the rest of men and to themselves" (*Mem.* 4.2.11; cf. *Mem.* 3.9.10).[90] Under the circumstances, Aristippus's invocation of βασιλικὴ τέχνη here seems to be heavily ironic, parodying Socrates' own idealistic vision, since he proceeds immediately to reduce that lofty concept to the brute facts of bodily experience:

> ἐγὼ μὲν γὰρ οὐκ οἶδ᾽ ὅ τι διαφέρει τὸ αὐτὸ δέρμα ἑκόντα ἢ ἄκοντα μαστιγοῦσθαι ἢ ὅλως τὸ αὐτὸ σῶμα πᾶσι τοῖς τοιούτοις ἑκόντα ἢ ἄκοντα πολιορκεῖσθαι· ἄλλο γε ἢ ἀφροσύνη πρόσεστι τῷ θέλοντι τὰ λυπηρὰ ὑπομένειν. (*Mem.* 2.1.17)
>
> I don't see what difference it makes if the owner of the skin that's whipped is willing or unwilling, or, in all, the owner of the body besieged by all such things is willing or unwilling—aside from the fact that the one who willingly submits to painful things is also a fool.

Given the possibility we have seen that Prodicus's "Choice of Heracles" engaged with the issue of sovereignty, it is tempting to read Aristippus's reference to the "art of kingship" as a kind of residue of Prodicus's version, which surfaces here in anticipation of the full fable narration. And yet, in Xenophon's version, it is only Aristippus's mockery through the resolute reduction of everything to the body that finally provokes Socrates to resort to allegorical fable in response. Socrates first (briefly) offers arguments for the crucial differences between the willing and unwilling submission to toils and hardships (*Mem.* 2.1.18–19), but soon shifts from argument and dialectic to a much more traditional mode of advice. First, invoking the wisdom of what "good men say" (ὥς φασιν οἱ ἀγαθοὶ ἄνδρες), Socrates quotes against Aristippus Hesiod's fable of the two roads and familiar γνῶμαι from Epicharmus;[91] only then does he launch into Prodicus's famous "Choice of Heracles" (*Mem.* 2.1.21–34), which I have already considered at some length. Prodicus's epideictic treatise (σύγγραμμα), is, as we've seen,

---

[90] Gigon 1956.49–52 notes the oddness of Aristippus's sudden mention of βασιλικὴ τέχνη and offers many useful parallels for the notion in Xenophon and Plato. Unfortunately, in the end, he attributes the sudden appearance of the idea to Xenophon's inept conflation and redaction of two older Socratic dialogues—one concerned with "self-control," the other with "rule" or "kingship." Against Gigon's theory, see Erbse 1980.17 with n. 22, who reads Aristippus's choice of expression here as contemptuous mockery of Socrates.

[91] It is worth noting the observation of Gray (1998.129) that precisely these same passages from Hesiod *WD* and Epicharmus show up together in the context of elaborating a *chreia* on the necessity for toil in education for future success in Hermogenes *Progymnasmata* (II.7 Spengel = Hock and O'Neill 1986.176) and Priscian *De Usu* (Keil III, p. 432.24 = Hock and O'Neill 1986.196). This pattern of occurrence suggests that these are deeply traditional paraenetic quotations.

essentially the extended literary elaboration of an allegorical fable, which Socrates uses to trounce his interlocutor. For the representation of Socrates' conversation with Aristippus ends once Socrates has completed his summary of Aretē's longest speech and earnestly conjured his pleasure-loving interlocutor to "think on these things and attempt to take some thought for your future life" (*Mem.* 2.1.34). As often happens in the reported conversations of the *Memorabilia*, Socrates gets the last word. Thus Aristippus is symbolically defeated and silenced by Socrates' insistent replacement of the three roads of rule, slavery, and freedom by the two roads of "virtue" and "vice," while fable here figures appropriately in lieu of reasoned argument to refute an interlocutor who gleefully reduces all discourse to the level of the body and its experiences.[92]

Indeed, by prefacing Prodicus's fable with Hesiod's allegory of the two roads and Epicharmus's gnomic address to a "wretch" (ὦ πονηρέ), Xenophon's Socrates progressively leeches out of the Heracles tale much of the frame of politics or sovereignty it might have contained. This he accomplishes through the fable's successive transformations of the key term εὐδαιμονία, which Aristippus had linked closely to Socrates' conception of "the art of kingship." In the course of the fable itself, εὐδαιμονία functions as a central contested term, which is thereby progressively pried apart from βασιλικὴ τέχνη and denatured of much of its political association. Thus both Kakia and Aretē in the fable claim to provide *eudaimonia* to their followers (*Mem.* 2.1.26, 2.1.30, 2.1.33). Indeed, the very last words of Aretē's speech and the fable narration as a whole are her promise to Heracles that he will "possess the most blessed happiness" by following her path (τὴν μακαριστοτάτην εὐδαιμονίαν κεκτῆσθαι, *Mem.* 2.1.33). Yet the elements of this "happiness" have come to have little to do with rule or kingship; instead, it consists of the typical Xenophontic triad (here phrased vaguely and in entirely passive terms) that one will be "dear to the gods, beloved of friends, honored by homelands," supplemented by the promise of immortal fame.[93]

It is perhaps the muting of this association with sovereignty that helps account for the oddest element in Xenophon's rendition of Prodicus's fable—the fact that Socrates suspends the narrative without ever telling us what choice Heracles made. We know from other ancient references that Prodicus specified Heracles' preference or choice for "Virtue," but we do not get that "punch line" here.[94] In part this lack of closure better suits the rhetorical context, where

---

[92] See Gray 1998.128–29 for a somewhat different account of the integration of dialectic and traditional *chreia* in this episode; she notes that Socrates' concluding injunction to Aristippus is entirely conventional within the *chreia* form.

[93] Erbse 1980.17 with n. 22 offers a somewhat different interpretation that acknowledges the same general development—the progressive movement inward from a political "art of kingship" to a version of Socratic self-mastery—accomplished by the rendition of Prodicus's fable.

[94] For the specification of Heracles' choice, cf. Schol. *ad* Aristoph. *Clouds* 361 (= 84 B 1 DK): προσκλῖναι τῇ Ἀρετῇ τὸν Ἡρακλέα καὶ τοὺς ἐκείνης ἱδρῶτας προκρῖναι τῶν προσκαίρων τῆς κακίας ἡδονῶν.

Aristippus's choice of lifestyle is still very much unresolved and Socrates emphasizes the need for his ongoing thought and deliberation (notice the present participle ἐνθυμουμένῳ applied to Aristippus at 2.1.34). At another level, the suspension of the fable allows us to read all the separate moral lessons Socrates offers to different interlocutors in the course of Book 2 under the sign of Heracles' as yet unresolved choice. But by suspending the fable, Xenophon's Socrates perhaps also sidesteps the kind of triumphant conclusion we might imagine for Prodicus's version: something like "the young Heracles made his choice and so became a great king and founder of royal lines." Thus, where Prodicus's allegorical fable formed part of a public *epideixis* on ethical and perhaps political topics, Xenophon has transposed it to a private conversation between two interlocutors, muted its political message, and attached it instead to the issue of bodily appetites.

And if the second book of the *Memorabilia* begins with several iterations of the allegorical fable of the choice of roads, it concludes with an animal fable—the fable of the dog and the sheep. Socrates offers this fable in the context of advising his friend Aristarchus on his "*aporia* through physical need."[95] It turns out that Aristarchus is suffering from a surfeit of unmarried female relatives. As he explains to Socrates, since the mass exodus from Piraeus following the brief period of civil war, he has fourteen female relatives crowded into his house, not even counting the slaves. And, since they are well-brought-up gentlewomen, according to Aristarchus, they can do no labor and the whole household is in danger of starvation. Socrates by a series of analogies and arguments persuades Aristarchus to put his female relatives to work, doing "what is considered most noble and most suitable for women" (*Mem.* 2.7.10)—working wool and weaving garments for sale. On Socrates' advice, Aristarchus takes out a capital loan to purchase wool, and, as he proceeds to report triumphantly to Socrates, now all is well: the women are happier because they're busy and productive, and the household has a steady income. The only catch, according to Aristarchus, is that his womenfolk blame him because "he alone of the household eats the bread of idleness" (*Mem.* 2.7.12). Socrates responds, "Then, why not tell them the fable of the dog?" (τὸν τοῦ κυνὸς λόγον):

> For they say, when the animals could talk, the sheep said to the master, "It's strange that to us who furnish you with wool and lambs and cheese you give nothing except what we take from the earth, but to the dog, who furnishes you no such things, you

---

[95] Notice Xenophon's *men-de* contrast at *Mem.* 2.7.1 of two kinds of *aporia*: that "through ignorance" (intellectual *aporia*) Socrates "heals with γνώμη"; *aporia* "through physical want or need" he treats by "teaching [his friends] to help each other according to their capability." It is in the latter category, as opposed to the former, that Socrates also strategically deploys fable; we might take this as Xenophon's version of the traditional opposition of *gnōmē* (explicit advice) vs *logos* (fable). As we have seen, for Plato's Socrates and Protagoras, this becomes a somewhat different opposition of reasoned argument or dialectic (*logos*) vs fable (*muthos*).

give a share of what you yourself have to eat. And the dog, when he heard this, said, "Of course, by Zeus: for I'm the one who keeps you safe, so that you're not stolen by men or ravaged by wolves, since you, at any rate, if I weren't looking out for you, wouldn't even be able to feed for fear lest you be destroyed." And so indeed, it is said, even the sheep agreed that the dog should get preferential treatment. And you also then say to those women that instead of a dog, you are their guard and trustee and, thanks to you, harmed by no one, they work and live safely and sweetly. (*Mem.* 2.7.13–14)

The fable is particularly apposite here because both the female relatives and the sheep are concerned with wool (ἔρια, *Mem.* 2.7.12, 13), while the genders of female "sheep" and male "dog" perfectly correspond to Aristarchus's own situation. But there seems to be more to it than that; there is perhaps the implication that men (like Aristarchus) can handle reasoned argument, but fable is suited to women. And again (as with Prodicus's "Choice of Heracles"), the narrative of the fable ends the chapter and concludes the conversation with Aristarchus; in this case, I think, we are meant to assume that he repeats the fable with good effect to his uppity female relatives and thereby silences them.

It is worth noting the pattern of distribution of fable within the *Memorabilia* as a whole. For Xenophon's text follows a strict decorum, whereby (as we have seen) advice via fable is an appropriate medium within the sphere of individual bodily pleasures and the private disposition of the *oikos*. But notably, as soon as the topic shifts from the personal and domestic to the polis and its affairs (as it does in the pivot from Book 2 to Book 3), the fabular element entirely disappears. Thus the first seven chapters of Book 3 are devoted to Socrates' conversations with various aristocratic, over- and underambitious young men about the proper ways to serve the city as general, cavalry commander, and political orator. Here we find numerous Socratic analogies to crafts and organized group activities, along with deadly serious discussions of tactics, ordering and arrangement of troops, supplies, and ways of improving the city's economic resources—but not a single fable. It is perhaps significant that these opening chapters of Book 3 are also permeated with Socrates' quotations of and allusions to the *Iliad*, especially relating to Agamemnon as a great general and as ποιμένα λαῶν (*Mem.* 3.1.4, 3.2.1, 3.2.2). That is to say, there is a clear generic hierarchy at work, whereby Iliadic references are felt to be appropriate to the most distinguished kinds of public activity—war, generalship, and leading the people.[96] We

---

[96] Cf. also *Mem.* 4.2.10–11, where Socrates' mention that Euthydemus possesses in his library the complete text of Homer leads more or less directly to the idea that what he wants to learn is βασιλικὴ τέχνη or βασιλικὴ ἀρετή. In this light, the claims of Plato's Ion—to have learned generalship from Homer—are not in fact so absurd; cf. Havelock 1963.61–86 and Ford 2002.198–208, who emphasizes the creative adaptation of Homer to the needs and uses of the democratic city.

also find an abundance of historical examples in these chapters, as Socrates cites Themistocles for his fame "even among the barbarians" (*Mem.* 3.6.2) and suggests to the younger Pericles (newly elected general) that he should hearten and encourage the Athenians by reminding them of their past glories (*Mem.* 3.5.8). It is tempting to read this latter choice of interlocutor as a sly Xenophontic joke, for Socrates rehearses for the benefit of the younger Pericles many of the stock themes of the *epitaphioi logoi* in which his father so clearly excelled: the mythical achievements of Erechtheus and Theseus, the glories of the Persian Wars, the Athenians' claim to autochthony, and Athens's role as defender of suppliants (*Mem.* 3.5.9–12).[97] However that may be, Xenophon clearly articulates the pivot from scenes of private domestic advising, bodily pleasures, and women's activities to the public, political sphere in the shift from Book 2 to Book 3 of the *Memorabilia*. And significantly, this shift of topics precisely corresponds to a shift of genres Socrates deploys in offering advice—from Hesiodic didactic, Old Comedy, and fable to Iliadic quotation and historical example.[98]

It is almost as if Xenophon has been reading Aristotle's *Rhetoric* on the proper occasions for the use of fable and historical example (*Rhet.* 2.20, 1393a23–94a8, discussed in chapter 6 above)—or rather, that the two participate in the same system of decorum and the relative weight and solemnity accorded to these two forms of *paradeigma*. In fact, our survey of Sophistic and Xenophontic deployments of fable may help us understand better the strange equivocations in Aristotle's concluding remarks on the proper contexts for the use of fable as *paradeigma*. As noted in chapter 6, Aristotle first offers us extended examples of fable used in bouleutic and dicastic contexts (by "Stesichorus" and "Aesop," respectively, *Rhet.* 2.20.5–6, 1393b8–94a1) and even concludes that fables are δημηγορικοί, "suitable for public speaking," only to backtrack or reverse his

---

[97] Loraux (1986.74, 149) notes the elements of *epitaphios logos* in *Mem.* 3.5. Following earlier scholars, she reads them as a serious attempt "to denigrate Thebes by praising the warrior qualities of Athens in terms reminiscent of Pericles' epitaphios" (quotation from p. 74). It is admittedly very difficult to gauge tone in Xenophon, and yet, no matter how serious the message, there seems to be some humor in the fact that Socrates must rehearse these examples for the *younger* Pericles.

[98] Note that this distribution is not perfect: at *Mem.* 2.6, Socrates briefly cites the historical examples of Pericles and Themistocles for their skill in making the whole polis their "friend" and quotes from the Siren passage in the *Odyssey*. Nonetheless, I would contend that the general pattern of distribution is still significant, since fable entirely disappears after Book 2. I would note one final thematic and structural shift in the *Memorabilia*: in Book 4, Socrates' extended series of lessons to Euthydemus "the fair" is often closely linked to his invocation of Delphi and Delphic wisdom. Thus the *Memorabilia* as a whole charts a trajectory from Aesop to Delphic Apollo—a movement that corresponds to its ascent of topics from bodily pleasures and household management to politics and divine worship, as also of a stylistic progression from fable to political advising and historical exempla to the numinous pithy injunctions (*brachylogia*) of the Seven Sages and the Delphic god himself. Since we find a very similar trajectory in Plato's *Protagoras* and *Alcibiades* I (as I hope to demonstrate elsewhere), as well as in Plutarch's Platonizing *Banquet of the Seven Sages*, we should perhaps regard this as a thematic and structural characteristic of *Sōkratikoi logoi* as a genre.

position in the end: "Examples via fables are thus easier to provide, but examples via historical events are more useful for bouleutic oratory, since things that are going to happen are for the most part like things that have happened" (*Rhet.* 2.20.8, 1394a5–8). Perhaps we should see the odd vacillations or tergiversations in this passage as an attempt to fix and stabilize a system that the Sophists have put in flux by their bold experimental use of high-style fable narrative for public *epideixis* on political and ethical topics. In these terms, Aristotle's attempt to circumscribe and relegate fable in theory corresponds to Xenophon's decorous practice. As we shall see in the next chapter, Plato, too, resists and opposes this Sophistic style of fable narration, but by means more insidious, indirect, and (at least at times) indecorous.

Chapter 8

SOPHISTIC FABLE IN PLATO: PARODY, APPROPRIATION, AND TRANSCENDENCE

WE HAVE SEEN THREE instantiations of Sophistic attempts to appropriate fable for lofty disquisitions on political, ethical, and anthropological topics, and we have considered in turn Xenophon's reinsertion of Prodicus's "Choice of Heracles" into a more traditional advice context. It is time to turn back to Plato, first to examine the range of Platonic responses to Sophistic fable (in this chapter), and then to explore a deployment of Aesop and Aesopic discourse within Platonic dialogue that is at once more insidious and more radical (in the next chapter).

I. Plato's *Protagoras*: Debunking Sophistic Fable

For the first: of course Plato's representation of the Sophists and Sophistic practices is itself never innocent. We cannot therefore simply mine Plato's *Protagoras* for evidence of Sophistic fable narrative without also reckoning with Plato's own purposes in incorporating Protagoras's (or a Protagoras-*like*) voice within his complex text. That is to say, we must consider the function of Protagoras's *muthos* within the dialogue as a whole. In this broader context, I would suggest that Plato represents Protagoras as not merely answering Socrates' challenge about the teachability of virtue, but also simultaneously offering Hippocrates and the other young men in his audience a preview (as it were) of his Sophistic curriculum. Recall that, when asked by Socrates what specifically Hippocrates will learn from him, Protagoras indicates first what he will *not* learn:

> "If Hippocrates comes to me he will not experience what he would if he studied with some other sophist. The others abuse young men, steering them back again, against their will, into subjects the likes of which they have escaped from at school, teaching them arithmetic, astronomy, geometry, music, and poetry"—at this point he gave Hippias a significant look—"but if he comes to me he will learn only what he has come for. What I teach is sound deliberation (εὐβουλία), both in domestic matters—how best to manage one's household, and in public affairs—how to realize one's maximum potential for success in political debate and action." (*Prot.* 318d6–19a2, trans. Lombardo and Bell 1997)

Protagoras here rejects the teaching of arithmetic, astronomy, geometry, and *mousikē* as not useful to the goal at hand, which he explicitly characterizes as εὐβουλία in household and civic affairs. It is also worth noticing Protagoras's account of the traditional education in virtue every child receives in Athens, since this in a sense forms the substrate for his own adapted Sophistic curriculum: as soon as he can comprehend things said, the boy is instructed in *aretē* by "nurse and mother and *paidagōgos* and the father himself" (325c6–d1); then he goes to teachers to learn his letters and cithara playing:

> After this they send him to school and tell his teachers to pay more attention to his good conduct than to his grammar or music lessons. The teachers pay attention to these things, and when the children have learned their letters and are getting to understand writing as well as the spoken language, they are given works of good poets to read at their desks and have to learn them by heart, works that contain numerous exhortations, many passages describing in glowing terms good men of old, so that the child is inspired to imitate them and become like them. In a similar vein, the music teachers too (οἵ τ' αὖ κιθαρισταί) foster in their young pupils a sense of moral decency and restraint, and when they learn to play the cithara they are taught the works of still more good poets, the lyric and choral poets (μελοποιῶν). The teachers arrange the scores and drill the rhythms and scales into the children's souls, so that they become gentler, and their speech and movements become more rhythmical and harmonious. For all of human life requires a high degree of rhythm and harmony. (*Prot.* 325d7–326b6, trans. Lombardo and Bell 1997, slightly modified)[1]

Notice here the clear articulation of learning from poetic models into two stages: first, the reading of poetry by boys when they have just learned their letters (so, poetry that is recited to meter but not sung; presumably mainly Homer). And then, climactically, after they have mastered cithara playing, learning from the "good melic poets" (μελοποιῶν).

Protagoras himself offers a modified version of this traditional curriculum in the discussions he initiates in the two halves of the dialogue. Thus, in the first half, responding to Socrates' invitation to give a display piece (*epideixis*), he deploys fable as appropriate to "an elder speaking to those who are younger" (320c2). We might then understand this as analogous to the style and content of admonition proffered to boys by "nurse, mother, *paidagōgos*, and father himself" in Protagoras's version of the traditional education.[2] Then, in the second half of the dialogue, when Protagoras's and Socrates' question-and-answer exchange threatens to break down, only to be resuscitated by the combined efforts

---

[1] In addition, Protagoras notes, they send them to trainers to train and discipline the body. Finally, once they are men, the city itself takes over their education via the laws (*Prot.* 326b6–e1).

[2] Cf. *Rep.* 2.377b–c on tales told to children by "mothers and nurses" (which includes myths like Hesiod's Zeus and Cronus, but also presumably fables and fairy tales).

of Callias, Alcibiades, Prodicus, and Hippias, Socrates draws Protagoras back into conversation by offering him the role of questioner. At that point, Protagoras renews the discussion thus:

> I consider, Socrates, that the greatest part of education for a man is to be in command of poetry (ἀνδρὶ παιδείας μέγιστον μέρος εἶναι περὶ ἐπῶν δεινὸν εἶναι), by which I mean the ability to understand the words of the poets, to know when a poem is correctly composed and when not, and to know how to analyze a poem and to respond to questions about it. (*Prot.* 338e6–39a3, trans. Lombardo and Bell 1997, slightly modified)

Protagoras's specification here that skill in analyzing and assessing poetry is "the greatest part of education *for a man*" (ἀνδρί) is significant, for it represents an explicit advance on his earlier designation of fable narrative (*muthos*) as apt "for the younger" (νεωτέροις). Notice that this is a development or progression both in style of discourse and in subject matter for Protagoras's potential students: from passive audience to active interlocutors; from Aesopic fable narrative to the analysis of melic poetry.[3]

As other readers of the dialogue have noted, Socrates effectively challenges and subverts Protagoras's implied curriculum, even as he tussles with him for verbal mastery and eventually wins the day.[4] Thus Michael Trapp has observed that, where Protagoras affiliates himself with the "great tradition" of high poetry and Simonides in particular (cf. 316d7), Socrates exposes Simonides as merely an upstart rival of the Seven Sages, thereby also opposing Protagoras's *makrologia* with the Sages' (and his own) *brachylogia*. This is, as Trapp notes, to trump one strand or version of tradition with another.[5] In fact, the recognition that Protagoras's *muthos* is an artful elaboration of Aesopic fable allows us to support and strengthen Trapp's reading of the dialogue as a whole. For, as we have seen from the material reviewed in earlier chapters, Aesop seems to stand in a very close and competitive relationship with the Seven Sages within Greek wisdom traditions already in the fifth century BCE. If this is so, Socrates, by invoking the Seven Sages, is recasting Protagoras's implied pedagogical program (Aesopic fable; then analysis of melic poetry) as a competition in wisdom that the Sages *must* win (Aesopic fable versus Seven Sages' *brachylogia* dedicated to Apollo). This reframing of tradition in retrospect also transforms Protagoras's "great speech" from lofty and expansive Sophistic eloquence to Aesopic slave

---

[3] See Ford 2002.202–3 on the difference between Protagoras's revised Sophistic curriculum and the traditional training in *mousikē* that he rejects at 318e.

[4] See esp. Berger 1984, Trapp 1987, Mann 2006.

[5] Trapp 1987.47–48. Notice that, insofar as Socrates aligns himself with the Seven Sages, this represents a tendentious or disingenuous conflation on his part of two different meanings of *brachylogia*—(traditional) gnomic utterance and (newfangled) dialectical method.

makrologia, which (in Aristotle's formulation) "goes around and around" and "says nothing healthy."[6]

Another way of formulating Plato's sweeping critique of Protagoras's Sophistic curriculum in the dialogue is that he effectively debunks both high and low forms of traditional wisdom as these have been appropriated by the Sophist— both Simonidean lyric and Aesopic fable. For the former: as Wolfgang Mann has argued in detail, Socrates eventually offers a devastating critique of the elite sympotic culture that constituted the conventional performance setting for melic poetry like Simonides' scolion:

> Discussing poetry strikes me as no different from the second-rate drinking parties of the agora crowd (τοῖς συμποσίοις τοῖς τῶν φαύλων καὶ ἀγοραίων ἀνθρώπων). These people, largely uneducated and unable to entertain themselves over their wine by using their own voices to generate conversation, pay premium prices for flute-girls and rely on the alien voice of the reed flute (ἀλλοτρίαν φωνὴν τὴν τῶν αὐλῶν) as background music for their parties. But when well-educated gentlemen drink together, you will not see flute-girls or dancing girls or female harpists (οὔτ᾿ αὐλητρίδας οὔτε ὀρχηστρίδας οὔτε ψαλτρίας), but a group that knows how to get together without these childish frivolities (ἄνευ τῶν λήρων τε καὶ παιδιῶν τούτων), conversing civilly no matter how heavily they are drinking. Ours is such a group, if indeed it consists of men such as most of us claim to be, and it should require no alien voices, not even of poets (οὐδὲν δέονται ἀλλοτρίας φωνῆς οὐδὲ ποιητῶν), who cannot be questioned on what they say. When a poet is brought up in discussion, almost everyone has a different opinion about what he means, and they wind up arguing about something they can never finally decide. The best people avoid such discussions and rely on their own powers of speech to entertain themselves and test each other. These people should be our models. We should put the poets aside and converse directly with each other, testing the truth and our own ideas. (*Prot.* 347c3–348a2, trans. Lombardo and Bell 1997, slightly modified)

As Mann notes, Socrates' ultimate objection here to the interpretation of poetry as a dialectical enterprise is that individual readings are nonrefutable (since the poet himself is no longer present to tell us what he had in mind).[7] But it is also worth attending to the series of analogies Socrates offers along the way to this conclusion. In describing symposia at which hired flute-girls provide the entertainment as those of men who are "base and vulgar" (τῶν φαύλων καὶ ἀγοραίων

---

[6] Cf. Arist. *Rhet.* 3.14, 1415b22–24, *Met.* 14.3, 1091a5–9. It is worth noting that this is very similar to Philostratus's interpretation of Protagoras's "great speech" within the dialogue: "Plato recognized that though Protagoras had a dignified style of eloquence (σεμνῶς μὲν ἑρμηνεύοντα), that dignity was a mask for his real indolence of mind, and that he was at times too long-winded and lacked a sense of proportion (μακρολογώτερον τοῦ συμμέτρου), and so, in a long myth [or rather, a long fable—μύθῳ μακρῷ], he hit off the main characteristics of the other's style" (Phil. *VS* 1.494–95, trans. Wright 1968).

[7] Mann 2006. 181–90.

ἀνθρώπων), Socrates precisely inverts the aristocratic associations of such gatherings, conjuring up through the mention of flute-girls, as Mann notes, the elements of loutish violence, sexual abuse, and hubris that often characterized such elite symposia and especially the drunken rout of the *kōmos*. Mann is right to emphasize all these associations, but in fact we can take the argument further, since there seems to have been throughout the archaic and classical periods a marked articulation of *status* and *gender* in the contrast between song and dance, between the performance of poetry to lyre accompaniment and the playing of the aulos within the sympotic space. That is to say, at the proper elite symposium, the free male participants sing but do not dance; it is a mark of aristocratic breeding and cultivation to be able to perform melic poetry while accompanying oneself on the lyre. Hired slave women, by contrast, provide entertainment by dancing and playing the aulos, an instrument that entirely blocked the mouth and prevented participation in rational speech or song.[8] Thus to assimilate Simonidean lyric poetry to the "alien voice" of the aulos played by a hired flute-girl is to deconstruct or radically undermine the whole system of oppositions that constituted and secured the boundaries of elite male sympotic identity—and, with it, the traditional values of elite *sophia*.

The debunking of Protagoras's deployment of Aesopic fable as a form of *sophia* is more sly and indirect, detectable only when Protagoras's tale is read against its humbler Aesopic models and congeners. These kindred fables fall into two groups: Prometheus fables and fables that involve Zeus and/or Hermes in some kind of distribution of qualities to mankind. In the former category, we find several fables preserved in the late collections where Prometheus fashions living creatures and allots to beasts and men their characteristic attributes. Thus, to give just one example:

> "Prometheus and Men." At the direction of Zeus, Prometheus fashioned men and beasts. But when Zeus saw that there were more of the dumb animals, he ordered him to destroy some of the beasts and make them into men. When he did as he was told, it turned out that the ones who had not been fashioned as men from the start had human form but were bestial in spirit. [The fable has a reproach against men who are wild and wrathful.] (Perry fable no. 240, trans. Daly 1961)

Like Protagoras's fable, this brief tale offers an aetiology for certain human qualities, based on an original division by Zeus and Prometheus.[9] What all the fables

---

[8] On all these oppositions, see Wilson 1999, Martin 2003; on the low or debased status of flute-girls, see also Gilhuly 2009.62–65. As Dover 1980.87, Davidson 1997.81–82, and Rowe 1998.135 point out, there is also the implicit assumption that flute-girls are prostitutes, available to service the symposiasts sexually—an assumption that again undermines the status and values signified by elite sympotic poetry. For flute-girls, see also chapter 9, section II below (on *Symposium*); for the idea that elite male symposiasts should sing but not dance, see Hdt. 6.129, with discussion in chapter 11, section III below.

[9] Cf. Perry no. 100: "Zeus, Prometheus, Athena, and Momus" and, with somewhat less serious point, Perry no. 259, "The Lion, Prometheus, and the Elephant": "The lion often complained to

of this class have in common is that Prometheus is consistently the sole creator of living creatures (even when he works at the behest of Zeus) and the one who endows them with qualities. Indeed, we even find in the second-century CE *Progymnasmata* of Theon, among the list of rhetorical failings or inadequacies for which fables can be criticized, "the thing said contrary to the common conceptions (παρὰ τὰς κοινὰς ὑπολήψεις), for example, if someone should say that human beings were not fashioned by Prometheus, but by some other god" (οἷον εἴ τις τοὺς ἀνθρώπους μὴ πεπλάσθαι εἴποι ὑπὸ τοῦ Προμηθέως, ἀλλ᾽ ὑπ᾽ ἄλλου τινὸς τῶν θεῶν, Theon II.77 Spengel). Notice that this is exactly what Protagoras's fable does, switching the traditional roles of the Titan brothers Prometheus and Epimetheus, and we might read this as Protagoras's clever and showy Sophistic modification of the conventional fable type. But, as Clyde Lee Miller has argued, this role reversal in Protagoras's fable ultimately shows both Titan brothers participating in both qualities—forethought and afterthought— and as such, prefigures the same blend of qualities in Protagoras and Socrates, the dialogue's two main interlocutors.[10] (At this level, it is clearly not just Protagoras opting for a strikingly untraditional version of the fable, but Plato himself, to presage the contest and limitations of both his main speakers.)

Thus we might read the Prometheus-Epimetheus episode in the fable as a testament to the ingenuity of Protagoras (and of Plato). But the *muthos* attributed to Protagoras begins to look more like parody when read against another common set of fables: those in which Zeus and/or Hermes distribute different qualities to mankind. For this is in fact a distinct fable type, which Protagoras's elaborate tale has conflated with or sutured onto a Prometheus fable to account for human possession of both *dēmiourgikē technē* and *politikē technē*, while differentiating them as separate orders of divine gift. As examples of this second type of fable, consider the following:

> "Hermes and the Craftsmen." Zeus directed Hermes to administer a dose of falsehood (ψεύδους φάρμακον) to all the craftsmen. Hermes ground the drug, measured

---

Prometheus that he had made him big and handsome, had provided his jaws with teeth, armed his feet with claws, and made him more powerful than the other animals. 'And with all that,' said he, 'I'm afraid of a rooster!' 'Why blame me?' said Prometheus. 'You have all the advantages I could devise. This is the only soft spot in your make-up.' So the lion lamented to himself and reproached himself for cowardice and finally wished he were dead. While he was in this mood, he met the elephant and stopped to talk to him. When he saw the elephant constantly moving his ears, he said, 'What's the matter with you? Why is your ear never still for a minute?' And the elephant said, as a gnat flew around him, 'You see this little fellow that keeps buzzing? If he gets into my ear, I'm a dead elephant.' And the lion said, 'Then why do I want to die? I'm at least as much luckier than the elephant as a rooster is bigger than a gnat'" (Perry fable no. 259, trans. Daly 1961).

[10] Miller 1978. For this broader interpretation of the dialogue as a whole, Miller notes that Protagoras and Socrates both invoke the virtue or quality of "forethought" at key moments in the discussion (316c5, 361d4), in such a way as to suggest that both of them partake of both qualities. For a similar argument about the mirroring or doubling between Socrates and Protagoras in the dialogue, see Berger 1984.

it out, and administered an equal amount to each. When there was only the tanner left and he still had a good deal of the drug, he took the whole mortar and gave it to him. The result has been that craftsmen have all been liars ever since and tanners most of all. (Perry fable no. 103, trans. Daly 1961)

"Zeus and Men." After Zeus had fashioned men, he ordered Hermes to pour some sense (νοῦν) into them. Hermes measured out equal portions and poured them into each. But the result was that those who were of small stature were filled up by the measure and became wise (φρονίμους), while the potion didn't fill the whole body of the big ones, and they turned out to be less intelligent (ἀφρονεστέρους). (Perry fable no. 108, trans. Daly 1961)[11]

As in Protagoras's fable, both Zeus and Hermes are involved (the latter as servant and intermediary of the former), and as in Protagoras's fable, each narrative crucially turns on the universal, but somehow not precisely equal distribution of qualities among some class of men.[12] At the same time, these two fables suggest a much more jaundiced and down-to-earth view of human nature than that espoused by Protagoras, while both read much more like popular jokes in contrast to the Sophist's lofty disquisition. The same could be said of another fable that features only Zeus, but describes the original distribution of a moral quality, αἰσχύνη ("shame" or "modesty"), itself closely related to Protagoras's αἰδώς (a sense of mutual respect):[13]

"Zeus and Modesty." After Zeus had fashioned men, he immediately inserted all the other sensibilities (διανοίας) into them; the only thing he forgot was modesty (μόνης δὲ Αἰσχύνης ἐπελάθετο). He wondered how he was to get her in and finally told her to go in by the back door (literally, "through the rectum," διὰ τοῦ ἀρχοῦ). At first she refused and stood on her dignity, but when he insisted vigorously, she said, "Well, I'll go, but on this condition, that if anything comes in after me, I'll leave immediately." It is as a result of this that all pathics lack modesty (ἀπὸ τούτου συνέβη πάντας τοὺς πόρνους ἀναισχύντους εἶναι). (Perry fable no. 109, trans. Daly 1961, slightly modified)

If we read the "great speech" in light of these fabular models, it is difficult to take Protagoras's tale entirely seriously, and this may be part of the point. For ancient readers familiar with popular fables like these, there is at least the suggestion that the genre of discourse Protagoras has selected is inadequate to the seriousness of the issues under discussion, while the Sophist's solemn and

[11] This particular fable is cited as a parallel for Protagoras's *muthos* by Dover 1966.43.
[12] Cf. the important point of Kerferd 1981.143–44, that Protagoras's fable specifies universal distribution of *dikē* and *aidōs* to men, but not *equal shares* of the two qualities for each man (as he notes, this distinction is often missed in philosophical discussions of Protagoras's *muthos*).
[13] *Aischunē* is the much more common prose word from the fifth century on, while *aidōs* tends to be mainly archaic and poetic (on both terms, see LSJ s.vv.). Thus "Protagoras's" use of *aidōs* seems consciously archaizing and poeticizing, while *aischunē* is just what we would expect in place of *aidōs* in the late fable collections. (Thanks to Mark Griffith for this point.)

long-winded version exposes him as pompous and self-important in contrast to the crude wit and brevity of his fabular models.[14]

These strategies for undermining both high and low *sophia* present us with a final paradox. By putting fable into the mouth of Protagoras, Plato implicitly casts the Sophist in the role of the slave Aesop who "says nothing healthy." At the same time, the dynamics of the dialogue as a whole implicate Protagoras instead in the role of the pompous and fatuous master, Xanthus, while Socrates seems to take on more and more the verbal wit and interpretative skill that characterize Aesop, the clever slave who constantly outshines his master. Or in other terms: insofar as we have seen Aesop's characteristic stance as challenger, debunker, and parodist of traditional wisdom, the Aesopic role is the perfect one for Socrates the "gadfly" to adopt. I will return to this simultaneous appropriation and disavowal of Aesop for the character and discursive strategies of Socrates within Platonic dialogue in the next chapter; for now, I would like to turn to Plato's *Symposium* to consider the multiple different styles of fable narration embedded within it.

II. PLATO'S *SYMPOSIUM*: RINGING THE CHANGES ON FABLE

I have deferred to the end of this consideration of different Sophistic/Socratic deployments of fable a look at Plato's *Symposium*, for this text contains within its heteroglossic repertoire first a competition between traditional fable and the Sophistic appropriation thereof, limned through the implicit contest of Aristophanes and Diotima, and then the replacement of Sophistic fable in turn by the unique qualities of Socratic discourse. For Aristophanes offers us as the single most compelling account of Eros that precedes Socrates' a traditional allegorical fable on primordial human nature and the origins of erotic desire; Diotima then initiates her erotic education of Socrates with an artful Sophistic fable on the birth of Eros that is intended to counter and trump Aristophanes' fable point by point. Diotima's fable, in turn, gives way to dialectical exchange and lofty *epideixis* that accomplishes the final rout of the particularity valorized by Aristophanes' traditional fable narrative. Only at that point, with the field already cleared (as it were), do Aesopic topoi and discursive features return in Alcibiades' speech to characterize what is unique or incomparable about Socrates and his *logoi*. I will defer detailed discussion of this final move in the dialogue to the next chapter, for a proper exploration of its functions and signifi-

---

[14] For both these points, recall Philostratus's reading of what Plato is up to here (quoted above, n. 6). Cf. also Alcibiades's characterization of Protagoras's obfuscatory *makrologia* at *Prot*. 336c5–d4. Still, I am not insisting that this is the only way to read Protagoras's "great speech," since I myself find it an effective and compelling fable of human progress. Rather I want to suggest that it is nearly impossible to plumb the depths of Platonic irony, so that, as often, Plato gets to have it both ways here. (Thanks to Wolfgang Mann for discussion of this point.)

cance requires contextualization within the broader panoply of the Socratic verbal techniques of analogy and *elenchos*. For the remainder of this chapter, I will focus on the competition between Aristophanes' traditional fable narrative and Diotima's Sophistic version.

But even before turning to consider these two fables and their staged competition, we should note that the entire sequence of symposiastic encomia to Eros is set under the sign of Prodicus's "Choice of Heracles." Thus Eryximachus, in repeating Phaedrus's scandalized complaint that "no one has worthily hymned Eros" (177c2–3), points first to the dearth of poetic celebrations ("hymns and paeans composed by the poets," 177a7), and then adverts also to prose encomia:

εἰ δὲ βούλει αὖ σκέψασθαι τοὺς χρηστοὺς σοφιστάς, Ἡρακλέους μὲν καὶ ἄλλων ἐπαίνους καταλογάδην συγγράφειν, ὥσπερ ὁ βέλτιστος Πρόδικος—καὶ τοῦτο μὲν ἧττον καὶ θαυμαστόν, ἀλλ᾽ ἔγωγε ἤδη τινὶ ἐνέτυχον βιβλίῳ ἀνδρὸς σοφοῦ, ἐν ᾧ ἐνῆσαν ἅλες ἔπαινον θαυμάσιον ἔχοντες πρὸς ὠφελίαν, καὶ ἄλλα τοιαῦτα συχνὰ ἴδοις ἂν ἐγκεκωμιασμένα· (*Sym.* 177b1–4)

But if you wish to consider in turn the worthy Sophists, [isn't it strange] that they compose praises in prose of Heracles and of others, just like the excellent Prodicus— and this is less to be marveled at, but I have already [even] happened upon some book by a wise man in which salt got marvelous praise for its usefulness, and you would see many other such things celebrated.

Notice that the first comparandum (marked emphatically by Ἡρακλέους μὲν) is Prodicus's fable of Heracles at the crossroads. It is intriguing that this ornate and elegant fable is thereby categorized as "praise," in a seeming conflation or fusion of high and low genres (fable and hymn or encomium) within a single discourse that I have already suggested was characteristic of certain Sophistic compositions. Indeed, this implication of deliberate, paradoxical play with the hierarchy of genre and decorum is then immediately reinforced by Phaedrus's bemused reference to "marvelous praise for salt and many other such things."[15] Andrea Nightingale discusses this Sophistic penchant for "paradoxical encomia" and suggests that such compositions work to showcase "the role that rhetoric plays in creating and dismantling 'orthodox' beliefs and values."[16] This is certainly true, but focuses almost entirely on the *content* of such encomia. Within the Greeks' own strict hierarchy of genre, style, and decorum, such literary encomia on modest, quotidian objects must also have produced an effect of a radical misfit in level of style, which would focus attention in turn on the tour-de-force demonstration of rhetorical skills by the speaker/writer. In

---

[15] The commentators (Bury 1969.19, Dover 1980.88, Rowe 1998.136) cite a parallel from Isoc. *Helen* 12, referring to "praises of bumblebees and salt," and suggest that these are references to the fourth-century rhetor Polycrates.

[16] Nightingale 1995.100–102; quotation from p. 102.

any case, it is worth emphasizing that these complex generic mixtures are singled out to serve as paradigms or models for the participating symposiasts' encomia to Eros—and foremost among them, Prodicus's fable of the "Choice of Heracles."

Within this setting, Aristophanes and Diotima compete with different styles of fable narration. That Aristophanes' famous "myth" is in fact an allegorical fable framed and told in a traditional manner was pointed out long ago by K. J. Dover.[17] Thoroughly and meticulously surveying the ancient parallels, Dover concludes, "comparable stories are characteristically Aesopic"; "Plato means us to regard the theme and framework of Aristophanes' story as characteristic not of comedy but of unsophisticated, subliterate folklore."[18] As Dover also notes, such "Aesopic and other unsophisticated stories" are a staple of Old Comedy, but we should not therefore conflate "essence and accident," loosely and sloppily designating Aristophanes' fable as "comedy."[19]

I would concur with Dover's characterization of Aristophanes' speech as a traditional rendition of Aesopic fable and note that, as such, it diverges significantly in style and content from the elegant Sophistic appropriations of fable I considered in the previous chapter. Thus Aristophanes' style is generally simpler, his word order more linear and less "artful," with fewer complex hypotactic or periodic sentences. In addition, his sentence structure feels looser and more colloquial, in contrast to the high polish of Sophistic rhetoric.[20] The same could be said for the particulars of content, since Aristophanes' fable (in contrast to the refined versions of fable ascribed to Prodicus and Protagoras) teems with common, quotidian stuff in vivid images drawn from everyday life. Thus the fable quotes Zeus himself speculating that it might be necessary at some point in the future to cut the halved beings in half again, "so that they hop on one foot, like those playing *askoliasmos*" (a symposium game in which contestants attempted to balance on an inflated and greased wineskin; 190d5–6). The narrative in turn compares the act of cutting to those who cut eggs with hairs to pickle them (190d7–e2), while the divided beings are likened to "fillets of sole or turbot" (ὥσπερ αἱ ψῆτται, 191d4) and (if cut again) to "half-dice used as tallies" (γεγονότες ὥσπερ λίσπαι, 193a7). And when Zeus sets the healing god Apollo to work patching up the poor divided creatures, his efforts are assimilated to the banausic labors of the meanest craftsmen. His instrument is compared to the tool cobblers use to smooth out the wrinkles in skins on the last

---

[17] Dover 1966, 1980.113; cf. Karadagli 1981.172–77, Adrados 1999.381, 402.
[18] Dover 1966, quotations from pp. 42 and 45, respectively.
[19] Dover 1966.41–45, quotation from p. 41.
[20] Note (e.g.) the anacolouthon at 190c3–6. Compare Bury 1969.xxxiv: "In point of style and diction, the speech of Aristophanes stands out as an admirable piece of simple Attic prose, free at once from the awkwardness and monotony which render the speeches of Phaedrus and Eryximachus tedious and from the over-elaboration and artificial ornamentation that mar the discourses of Pausanias and Agathon."

(191a1–3), and he is said to draw the skin of the belly together around the navel "just like those drawstring bags" (ὥσπερ τὰ σύσπαστα βαλλάντια, 190e7–8). Needless to say, all these words find their closest parallels in the teeming, resolutely material, and humble diction of Old Comedy.

In addition, I would contend, Plato explicitly flags Aristophanes' contribution as fable through certain precise dictional cues at its conclusion. Thus immediately before Aristophanes offers his salvific closing words, he pauses to anticipate and deflect a critical intervention by Eryximachus:

> καὶ μή μοι ὑπολάβῃ Ἐρυξίμαχος, κωμῳδῶν τὸν λόγον, ὡς Παυσανίαν καὶ Ἀγάθωνα λέγω—ἴσως μὲν γὰρ καὶ οὗτοι τούτων τυγχάνουσιν ὄντες καί εἰσιν ἀμφότεροι τὴν φύσιν ἄρρενες—λέγω δὲ οὖν ἔγωγε καθ᾽ ἁπάντων καὶ ἀνδρῶν καὶ γυναικῶν, ὅτι οὕτως ἂν ἡμῶν τὸ γένος εὔδαιμον γένοιτο, εἰ ἐκτελέσαιμεν τὸν ἔρωτα καὶ τῶν παιδικῶν τῶν αὑτοῦ ἕκαστος τύχοι εἰς τὴν ἀρχαίαν ἀπελθὼν φύσιν. (*Sym.* 193b6–c5)

> Now don't take it up for me, Eryximachus, and turn this speech into a comedy. Don't think I'm pointing this at Pausanias and Agathon. Probably, they both do belong to the group that are entirely masculine in nature. But I am speaking about everyone, men and women alike, and I say there's just one way for the human race to flourish: we must bring love to its perfect conclusion, and each of us must win the favors of his very own young man, so that he can recover his original nature. (Trans. Nehamas and Woodruff 1997, slightly modified)

Aristophanes' apotropaic gesture here is, of course, disingenuous, since it allows him simultaneously to make and to disavow a pointed joke about the pair Pausanias and Agathon being "cutlets of the male."[21] But I am more interested in the precise genre terms by which Aristophanes has his cake and eats it too. Following Dover, recent translators and commentators interpret κωμῳδῶν τὸν λόγον to mean "turning my speech into comedy," rather than—the looser, nontechnical meaning of κωμῳδέω—"ridiculing my speech."[22] Indeed, we can go even further in seeing in Aristophanes' terms a set of genre-specific designations if we take into account his use of the verb ὑπολάβῃ in this context. Here, as we have seen many times before, ὑπολαμβάνω figures in a competitive dialogue between two speakers (even if only imagined), to designate the verbal quip by which one takes up and turns the other's words against him to end discussion. This is the general semantic field, but here, I would suggest, the verb is meant to evoke the specific context of fable, where ὑπολαβὼν ἔφη frequently marks the final utterance that draws the fable's "moral" or "punch line." For in fact, the trumping quip that Aristophanes disingenuously anticipates—Eryximachus's claim that the story is all about Pausanias and Agathon—would precisely provide a "punch line" for the general fable (τὸν λόγον) that thereby turns it into

---

[21] For the phrase "cutlets of the male," see *Sym.* 191e7. Rowe 1998.159–60 notes how "transparently disingenuous" Aristophanes' statement here seems.

[22] Thus Dover 1980.120, Nehamas and Woodruff 1997.476, Rowe 1998.159; contra Bury 1969.67.

Old Comedy with its specific abuse of named individuals. Thus in order to clarify the full range of genre terms in Aristophanes' formulation, I would translate: "And don't let Eryximachus formulate a punch line for me, thereby turning this fable of mine into comedy, that I mean Pausanias and Agathon. . . ."

Aristophanes recurs to the topic at the end of his speech, in an exchange permeated with several elements we have come to associate with fable narration:

οὗτος, ἔφη, ὦ Ἐρυξίμαχε, ὁ ἐμὸς λόγος ἐστὶ περὶ Ἔρωτος, ἀλλοῖος ἢ ὁ σός. ὥσπερ οὖν ἐδεήθην σου, μὴ κωμῳδήσῃς αὐτόν, ἵνα καὶ τῶν λοιπῶν ἀκούσωμεν τί ἕκαστος ἐρεῖ, μᾶλλον δὲ τί ἑκάτερος· Ἀγάθων γὰρ καὶ Σωκράτης λοιποί.

ἀλλὰ πείσομαί σοι, ἔφη φάναι τὸν Ἐρυξίμαχον· καὶ γάρ μοι ὁ λόγος ἡδέως ἐρρήθη. (*Sym.* 193d6–e4)

"This," he said, "O Eryximachus, is my speech/fable concerning Eros—a different sort from yours. But, just as I asked you, don't turn it into comedy, so that we can hear also what each of the rest will say—or rather, each of the two. For [only] Agathon and Socrates remain."

"But I shall obey you," he said Eryximachus said, "for in fact your speech/fable was sweetly spoken as far as I'm concerned."

Again we find the adjuration, "don't turn my speech/fable into comedy" (μὴ κωμῳδήσῃς αὐτόν, 193d7–8). And strikingly, this leads in response to Eryximachus's acknowledgment of the effects conventionally produced by successful fable narration—pleasure (ἡδέως ἐρρήθη) linked to the persuasion (πείσομαί σοι) of a more powerful or ruling interlocutor (recall that Eryximachus here is playing the role of a somewhat overbearing symposiarch, enforcing the terms of Phaedrus' pet topic).[23]

But if Aristophanes' speech conforms to traditional fable narration, marked as such by these dictional cues at its conclusion, Diotima in turn offers us a high-style Sophistic fable that explains the nature of Eros by giving him a new genealogy. We should note first that Socrates characterizes Diotima as σοφή when he introduces her (201d3), addresses her as σοφωτάτη later when he poses a question in the course of their quoted colloquy (208b8), and tells us that she answered "just like the perfect sophists" (ὥσπερ οἱ τέλεοι σοφισταί, 208c1). Thus Diotima is closely identified with the Sophists, and every aspect of her fable narration corresponds to that identification.[24] In Socrates' account, he and Diotima had in the past played questioner and answerer in a dialectical exchange that precisely paralleled and dovetailed with Socrates' brief dialectical exchange with Agathon. In this re-created past conversation, Diotima compels

---

[23] Cf. Dover 1980.11 and R. B. Rutherford 1995.180 for Eryximachus's adoption of the role of heavy-handed symposiarch and enforcer.

[24] For Diotima as a sophist, see the somewhat different arguments of Belfiore 1984b, Krell 1988.166–69, Rowe 1998.187–88, Gilhuly 2009.77.

Socrates to acknowledge that Eros cannot himself be beautiful and good because he is desire for those things and that, in fact, he is not even a god at all, but a *daimōn*. At this point in the dialectical question-and-answer, Socrates asks, "But who are his father and mother?" and Diotima responds, self-consciously marking a shift in the style of discourse:

> μακρότερον μέν, ἔφη, διηγήσασθαι· ὅμως δέ σοι ἐρῶ. ὅτε γὰρ ἐγένετο ἡ Ἀφροδίτη, ἡστιῶντο οἱ θεοὶ οἵ τε ἄλλοι καὶ ὁ τῆς Μήτιδος ὑὸς Πόρος. (*Sym.* 203b1–3)
>
> It is rather long to narrate, she said. But still, I will tell you. For when Aphrodite was born, all the rest of the gods were feasting and also Poros, the son of Mētis.

Just as Plato's Protagoras shifts from brief question-and-answer to the expansive mode of fable narration once Socrates has licensed him to "give a display speech" (ἐπιδεῖξαι, ἐπίδειξον, *Prot.* 320b8–c1), so here Diotima acknowledges that she is shifting registers from dialectic to narrative and from brief question-and-answer to fabular *makrologia*. And like Protagoras's *muthos* (but very much in contrast to Aristophanes' fable), Diotima's birth story is elegant and polished, full of poetic diction and carefully balanced clauses.[25]

In addition, like Protagoras's characterization of his *muthos* and Philostratus's of Prodicus's "Choice of Heracles," Diotima at one point seems to suggest that her fable of Eros is particularly suited for the young. Thus in the fable itself, she derives many characteristics of Eros from his strange parentage, emphasizing most of all his betweenness (see especially *Sym.* 203c6–e5). Socrates responds to this disquistion by asking, "Who then, O Diotima, are the ones who love wisdom (οἱ φιλοσοφοῦντες), if they are neither wise nor ignorant?" At this point, Diotima loses her patience, snapping back at him with some irritation, "This surely is clear now even to a child (δῆλον δή, ἔφη, τοῦτό γε ἤδη καὶ παιδί), that they are the ones between both of these, of whom Eros also would be one" (*Sym.* 204b1–2). We may take the expression "even to a child" as nothing more than a register of Diotima's exasperation at Socrates' enduring cluenessness; and yet the appearance of this expression immediately after the narration of a fable seems significant. Diotima's implication seems to be, "*Since* I've narrated it in the form of a fable, the point or punch line—Eros's betweenness—ought to be clear even to a child."

Finally, just as Protagoras in Plato's dialogue explicitly articulates the moment at which he shifts the genre of discourse from *muthos* to *logos* (from "fable" to "reasoned argument," *Prot.* 324d6–7), so, too, Diotima marks a shift in discursive mode in response to Socrates' question, "Well then . . . being such, what use does Eros have for human beings?" (*Sym.* 204c7–8):

---

[25] See Bury 1969.101–2, noting several Homeric echoes. Still, Diotima's fable is much more restrained in style than Agathon's flamboyant art prose; cf. Dover 1980.124, noting that nearly all thirty-one cola of Agathon's peroration are recognizable metrical forms. This seems to represent an extreme version (even a parody) of Gorgianic prose.

τοῦτο δὴ μετὰ ταῦτ᾽, ἔφη, ὦ Σώκρατες, πειράσομαί σε διδάξαι. ἔστι μὲν γὰρ δὴ τοιοῦτος καὶ οὕτω γεγονὼς ὁ Ἔρως, ἔστι δὲ τῶν καλῶν, ὡς σὺ φῄς. εἰ δέ τις ἡμᾶς ἔροιτο· τί τῶν καλῶν ἐστιν ὁ Ἔρως, ὦ Σώκρατές τε καὶ Διοτίμα; ὧδε δὲ σαφέστερον· ἐρᾷ ὁ ἐρῶν τῶν καλῶν· τί ἐρᾷ; (*Sym.* 204d1–5)

> This is the very thing, she said, O Socrates, I shall attempt to teach you next. For indeed Eros is such and thus born, and he is [love] of beautiful things, as you say. But if someone should ask us, "Why is Eros [love] of beautiful things, O Socrates and Diotima?" or thus, more clearly: the lover loves beautiful things; why does he love [them]?

Here the articulation of different discursive modes is clearly flagged by the sequence of particles μέν . . . δέ . . . δέ. First Diotima summarizes with a μέν what the fable of Eros's birth has accomplished for the argument; then, with a δέ, she adds the point Socrates had insisted on from the beginning—that Eros is love of beautiful things—as the starting point for the discussion to follow. Finally, with a second δέ that sets this clause in contrast with the μέν clause, Diotima introduces a hypothetical questioner (τις) to ask why Eros is love of beautiful things.[26] The hypothetical questioner is a common strategy for initiating or advancing dialectical question-and-answer in Platonic dialogue, and here it serves to introduce the critical dialectical exchange by which Diotima will redefine Eros as "giving birth in the beautiful" (*Sym.* 204d–9e). Thus Diotima's speech follows the same didactic progression we have noted in Protagoras's *epideixis* and suggested for Prodicus's "Choice of Heracles" and Antiphon's *On Concord*: it begins with an elegant fable, designed to charm and communicate even to the young, and then shifts to reasoned argument as the "pupil" advances in his studies.

But we must finally ask why Plato should incorporate these two fables, each carefully marked as such and articulated as different styles of fable narration, into his complex text? That there is a competition intended between the two fables Diotima herself makes clear when she singles out Aristophanes' account for explicit refutation. Indeed, throughout her lengthy disquisition, Diotima progressively appropriates or refutes much that the earlier speakers had offered by way of praise of Eros, thus retroactively turning all the earlier speeches into mere lower rungs on her philosophical ladder of love.[27] But Aristophanes' speech alone seems to merit explicit mention and rebuttal in the course of her dialectical exchange with Socrates:

---

[26] Cf. Rowe 1998.178 for the structure and relations of these three clauses. Rowe notes that this moment is "the divide between the treatment of Love's character and that of his 'actions,'" as promised in the program of 201d7–e1. Thus the μέν-δέ contrast here articulates simultaneously a shift in *subject* as well as *style* of discourse (just as Protagoras's shift from *muthos* to *logos* does—cf. *Prot.* 324d2–7).

[27] Many scholars have noticed this pattern—e.g., Bacon 1959.426–27; Dorter 1969; Clay 1975; Ferrari 1992.252–53; R. B. Rutherford 1995.185–91; Carnes 1998.108, 118–19; Gilhuly 2009.67–68.

καὶ λέγεται μέν γέ τις, ἔφη, λόγος, ὡς οἳ ἂν τὸ ἥμισυ ἑαυτῶν ζητῶσιν, οὗτοι ἐρῶσιν· ὁ δ᾽ ἐμὸς λόγος οὔτε ἡμίσεός φησιν εἶναι τὸν ἔρωτα οὔτε ὅλου, ἐὰν μὴ τυγχάνῃ γέ που, ὦ ἑταῖρε, ἀγαθὸν ὄν, ἐπεὶ αὑτῶν γε καὶ πόδας καὶ χεῖρας ἐθέλουσιν ἀποτέμνεσθαι οἱ ἄνθρωποι, ἐὰν αὐτοῖς δοκῇ τὰ ἑαυτῶν πονηρὰ εἶναι. (*Sym.* 205d10–e5)

And there is a certain tale/fable told, she said, that those who seek their other half, these are lovers; but my story/account says that love is not of the half nor of the whole, unless, my friend, it happens somehow to be good, since people are even willing to cut off their own hands and feet, if they think they are diseased.

Here Diotima pointedly opposes her own λόγος ("account" but also "fable") to another "fable" that has currency, that lovers are those who seek their other half. In addition, in case we missed the direct reference to Aristophanes' tale, Diotima coolly appropriates his fable's central conceit of our primordial cutting or mutilation and inverts it into an image of the willing amputation of rotten limbs.[28]

But what is it about Aristophanes' fable that requires such explicit refutation? Here I would return to K. J. Dover's analysis of the genre of Aristophanes' speech, when the modern critic explicitly considers Plato's motivation for including such a narrative within the *Symposium* as a whole. Dover notes that Aristophanes is the only one of all the speakers whose account is predicated on the essential singularity and inexplicability of erotic desire. For all the other speakers, one desires an object because it is objectively desirable, containing a certain number of traits that others also desire. On these premises, if one then encounters another object with more such traits, the transfer of desire to that object is inevitable. But Aristophanes' account presents a completely different view of Eros as particular and individual, with nothing rational or objective about it. Dover concludes that Plato works in Aristophanes' speech because it "rests on the values shared by comedy and folklore"—values that in their unwavering commitment to "the individual, the particular and the familiar" are deeply inimical to the pursuit of philosophy as described by Diotima.[29] I would

---

[28] Rowe 1998.181 notes the chronological impossibility or *hysteron proteron* quality of Diotima's discourse here, since of course she supposedly delivered this discourse to a young Socrates years before the symposium at which Aristophanes offers his fable in praise of Eros. And as he also notes, Aristophanes is not fooled, but clearly understands Diotima as a "blind" or "alibi" for Socrates himself when he attempts to raise an objection at 212c4–6.

[29] Dover 1966.47–50, quotations from pp. 47 and 50, respectively. Vlastos 1981 offers a philosophically rigorous version of a similar argument about the nonparticularity and lack of interest in persons of Platonic love. Vlastos's extreme position has sparked much debate and counterargument; see, e.g., Gill 1990, R. B. Rutherford 1995.194–97, Nussbaum 2001.165–99. Thus Nussbaum 2001 contends that we must take into account the concern for the beloved's particularity in Aristophanes' speech and especially Alcibiades', as supplements to Diotima's model, in constructing a full account of Platonic love. Like Nussbaum, I see a concern with particularity as central to Aristophanes' and Alcibiades' speeches, but I do not concur with her argument that the latter speech is about the special privileged knowledge of a *lover* for his unique love object, for the reasons articulated in the

concur with Dover that what most characterizes traditional Aesopic discourse is its commitment to the particular, local, and quotidian, and that this is what makes it the perfect vehicle for Aristophanes' modeling of Eros, unique in this respect among the encomia that precede Alcibiades' eruption on the scene.

In taking over the traditional genre of fable and replacing it with its classier Sophistic derivative, Diotima trumps Aristophanes' tale point by point, thus beating him at his own game. At the most obvious level of content, Diotima replaces Aristophanes' account of Eros as the ultimate fullness and consummation with a fable of Eros's asymmetrical parentage and consequent betweenness. That is, in Diotima's rendering, Eros is all instrumentality—never the end, only the means to get somewhere else. Where Aristophanes' fable is low-class, Diotima's is high-class; where Aristophanes' tale (like comedy itself) gestures toward a pre-Olympian order that threatens the regime of Zeus, Diotima's affirms the sanctity of that Olympian order.[30] And these same contrasts are replayed on the level of form or structure. Comic or popular fable is sufficient unto itself—thus the fable constitutes the whole of Aristophanes' speech. As we have seen, the Sophists appropriated fable in order to make it into the first step of a pedagogical system; fable is used to draw in the young, whose powers of reasoning and arguing are not fully developed, only to be superseded by the forms of dialectical question-and-answer and logical exposition. Just so, Diotima passes from her birth fable to dialectical question-and-answer with Socrates at 204d (as we have seen); then she transitions from question-and-answer to a series of extended monologues (*epideixeis*?) at 206b.[31]

But Diotima's decisive rejection of Aristophanes and the Aesopic particularity his fable valorizes comes in her magnificent last set piece on initiation into the higher "mysteries" of Eros. And indeed it is telling that she feels the need to recur to the refutation of Aristophanes here at the climax of her discourse (albeit implicitly). Diotima has already mapped out for Socrates many stages of ascent through "the correct practice of pederasty" (211b5–6)—from the apprehension of beauty in one body to what is common to all beautiful bodies, to beauty in souls, to beauty in practices and laws, to beauty in kinds of knowledge—when

---

sensible critique of Nussbaum by Gill 1990, esp. 79-83. Instead, I think that Socrates' particularity has different functions within the dialogue and within the Platonic corpus as a whole; for this, see next chapter.

Finally, we might add that Diotima feels all the more need to refute Aristophanes because his fable represents an important new beginning, and lays significant groundwork for Diotima's own model; on this, see Ferrari 1992.250–53, Carnes 1998.107–16.

[30] Cf. esp. *Sym.* 190b5–c1 (where Aristophanes attributes to these primordial spherical creatures the Homeric account of the impious attempt of Otus and Ephialtes against the Olympian gods) vs 203b2–3 (where Diotima seems to refer to the birth of Aphrodite as daughter of Olympian Zeus). For these contrasts between Aristophanes' speech and Diotima's as different styles of fable, see Gilhuly 2009.76–77.

[31] For this structure, cf. Rowe 1998.178.

she pauses to offer a withering critique of the lover's past state of base and small-minded attachment to a single "one":

> καὶ βλέπων πρὸς πολὺ ἤδη τὸ καλὸν μηκέτι τὸ παρ' ἑνί, ὥσπερ οἰκέτης, ἀγαπῶν παιδαρίου κάλλος ἢ ἀνθρώπου τινὸς ἢ ἐπιτηδεύματος ἑνός, δουλεύων φαῦλος ᾖ καὶ σμικρολόγος, ἀλλ' ἐπὶ τὸ πολὺ πέλαγος τετραμμένος τοῦ καλοῦ καὶ θεωρῶν, πολλοὺς καὶ καλοὺς λόγους καὶ μεγαλοπρεπεῖς τίκτῃ καὶ διανοήματα ἐν φιλοσοφίᾳ ἀφθόνῳ, ἕως ἂν ἐνταῦθα ῥωσθεὶς καὶ αὐξηθεὶς κατίδῃ τινὰ ἐπιστήμην μίαν τοιαύτην, ἥ ἐστι καλοῦ τοιοῦδε. (*Sym.* 210c8–d7)
>
> ... [he] gazing now towards a beauty which is vast, and no longer slavishly attached to the beauty belonging to a single thing—a young boy, some individual human being, or one kind of activity—may cease to be worthless and petty, as his servitude made him, but instead, turned towards the great sea of beauty and contemplating that, may bring to birth many beautiful, even magnificent, words and thoughts in a love of wisdom that grudges nothing, until there, with his strength and stature increased, he may catch sight of a certain single kind of knowledge, which has for its object a beauty of a sort I shall describe to you. (Trans. Rowe 1998)

Commentators tend to see in Diotima's contemptuous ὥσπερ οἰκέτης and δουλεύων a reference back to Pausanias's claim that all things are allowed to the Uranian lover in his pursuit of his beloved, including "willingly submitting himself to forms of slavery that not even a slave would endure" (καὶ ἐθέλοντες δουλείας δουλεύειν οἵας οὐδ' ἂν δοῦλος οὐδείς, 183a6–7).[32] This echo is certainly there—and appropriate—since Pausanias at this point limns a stereotypical portrait of the shameful excesses to which a lover mad about a single boy was thought to resort. But this reference back does not fully account for the language of Diotima's sneer, which characterizes the individual erotically attached to "one boy or person or practice" not just as a slave, but also as "base and petty" (φαῦλος ᾖ καὶ σμικρολόγος). In addition, we should note that these two terms are precisely opposed to the "magnificent words and thoughts" (μεγαλοπρεπεῖς) that the one who gazes on the beautiful itself now "brings to birth in ungrudging philosophy" (ἐν φιλοσοφίᾳ ἀφθόνῳ). That is to say, these two sets of terms seem to encode a contrast of genre or type of discourse (note σμικρολόγος versus λόγους ... μεγαλοπρεπεῖς) that is simultaneously figured as a contrast of socioeconomic levels and styles. For φαῦλος, of course, carries powerfully derogatory class/status connotations, especially when (as here) it is opposed to the quintessential traditional aristocratic virtues of "magnificence" and "openhandedness" or "liberality."[33] In order to account for this complex

---

[32] Cf. Bury 1969.126–27, Rowe 1998.197. Bury and Dover 1980.156 also cite the parallel of *Tht.* 172c-3b—a parallel that is very revealing for its grounding of different genres of discourse in markedly hierarchical class/status terms (see below, n. 35).

[33] φαῦλος always carries a strong class/status taint when used of persons; see LSJ s.v. φαῦλος II and (for the use of the term in Plato) Worman 2008.175–76. In contrast, μεγαλοπρέπεια is strongly

play of terms, I would suggest that Diotima's imagery here is also intended as a dismissive reference to the genre of Aristophanes' Aesopic fable as slavish, petty, and low, appropriately conjured up at the moment Diotima rejects the content of Aristophanes' tale with its resolute commitment to the particularity of one "true love"—one's other half.[34]

If this is the case, we should also note the side benefits reaped for the discourse of philosophy by this implicit genre contrast; at the moment Diotima identifies the traditional fable's attachment to particularity as slavish and illiberal, her language appropriates a whole set of associations with wealth, gentlemanly magnificence, and abundance and transposes them to the sphere of philosophy. And even though this ennobling of philosophy is articulated in language that the Socrates of the *Symposium* in his own person could never use (for reasons we'll consider below), Diotima's formulation leaves behind a powerful afterimage or residue of this (newly conjured) philosophy as simultaneously noble and expansive (facing the "great sea of beauty") and entirely raised above any sordid jockeying or competition of genres of discourse.[35]

---

marked in the tradition as an aristocratic "virtue" or disposition—"magnificence" or "munificence" in expenditure. For this traditional meaning of the term, the best source is Arist. *NE* 4.2, 1122a18–23a34; for discussion of the traditional class/status charge of μεγαλοπρέπεια, see Woodbury 1968; Kurke 1991.165–224, 240–56. Plato, who uses words of the μεγαλοπρεπ- family frequently, can deploy it in this conventional sense (e.g., *Hipp. Mai.* 291e, *Meno* 74a, 88a, *Rep.* 2.362c), but more often has Socrates apply it ironically to the grand word choice, magnificent style, arguments, and claims of various Sophists and their pupils (thus, e.g., at *Euthyd.* 303c, *Hipp. Min.* 366e, *Lysis* 215e, *Meno* 70b, 94a, *Sym.* 199c). But most relevant for Diotima's use here in the *Symposium* is a remarkable run of uses of μεγαλοπρεπ- terms by Socrates in *Republic* Book 6 to characterize the true "philosophic nature" (*Rep.* 6.486a, 487a, 490c, 494b, 495d, 503c). Socrates here carefully repurposes this traditional aristocratic virtue as a philosophical one, since he says pointedly at 485e that the philosophic nature is not "interested in money or eager for great expenditure." Nonetheless, throughout this discussion, the philosophical version of μεγαλοπρέπεια continues to have strong aristocratic connotations (perhaps to appeal to his interlocutors, Glaucon and Adeimantus), since Socrates opposes it to ἀνελευθερία and σμικρολογία (486a4–5) and (in analogy) to a short, bald, slave blacksmith who has just come into money and wants to marry the master's daughter (= philosophy!; 495e). Words of the ἀφθον- family occur less commonly in Plato and mainly designate abundance of physical stuff (e.g., water or timber; cf. Bury 1969.127). Still, in the orbit of μεγαλοπρέπεια, it is hard not to hear a traditional class/status resonance in ἀφθόνῳ as well ("ungrudging, generous"); cf. Rowe 1998.197, emphasizing the "donor-recipient relationship."

[34] Cf. Rowe 1998.197: "The general upshot is that the conversion away from the individual—whether lover or beloved?—is an epistemological process, involving the acquisition of that ability to grasp the general/generic which is blocked by too great an attachment to the particular; that is, so the context seems to tell us, to particular, physical instantiations of beauty."

[35] Such a reading of this bit of Diotima's last speech finds support in a remarkable passage in the *Theaetetus* (172c8–176d5), where Socrates takes a spur line off the main track of argument to contrast the way or character of the philosopher with that of the man engaged in political and dicastic affairs in the city. Here the language and imagery of slavery, the necessity of flattery, and the crippling and deformation of the soul (on the analogy of the body) of habitual dicastic speakers are strikingly elaborated in the context of a competition of discursive practices or speech genres, which are thereby figured through a clear hierarchy of socioeconomic class/status.

But even this is apparently not enough, for Diotima returns yet once more to the content and form of Aristophanes' fable at the very end of her visionary account of "the beautiful itself":

ὃ ἐάν ποτε ἴδῃς, οὐ κατὰ χρυσίον τε καὶ ἐσθῆτα καὶ τοὺς καλοὺς παῖδάς τε καὶ νεανίσκους δόξει σοι εἶναι, οὓς νῦν ὁρῶν ἐκπέπληξαι καὶ ἕτοιμος εἶ καὶ σὺ καὶ ἄλλοι πολλοί, ὁρῶντες τὰ παιδικὰ καὶ συνόντες ἀεὶ αὐτοῖς, εἴ πως οἷόν τ᾽ ἦν, μήτ᾽ ἐσθίειν μήτε πίνειν, ἀλλὰ θεᾶσθαι μόνον καὶ συνεῖναι. τί δῆτα, ἔφη, οἰόμεθα, εἴ τῳ γένοιτο αὐτὸ τὸ καλὸν ἰδεῖν εἰλικρινές, καθαρόν, ἄμεικτον, ἀλλὰ μὴ ἀνάπλεων σαρκῶν τε ἀνθρωπίνων καὶ χρωμάτων καὶ ἄλλης πολλῆς φλυαρίας θνητῆς, ἀλλ᾽ αὐτὸ τὸ θεῖον καλὸν δύναιτο μονοειδὲς κατιδεῖν; ἆρ᾽ οἴει, ἔφη, φαῦλον βίον γίγνεσθαι ἐκεῖσε βλέποντος ἀνθρώπου καὶ ἐκεῖνο ᾧ δεῖ θεωμένου καὶ συνόντος αὐτῷ; ἢ οὐκ ἐνθυμῇ, ἔφη, ὅτι ἐνταῦθα αὐτῷ μοναχοῦ γενήσεται, ὁρῶντι ᾧ ὁρατὸν τὸ καλόν, τίκτειν οὐκ εἴδωλα ἀρετῆς, ἅτε οὐκ εἰδώλου ἐφαπτομένῳ, ἀλλὰ ἀληθῆ, ἅτε τοῦ ἀληθοῦς ἐφαπτομένῳ· τεκόντι δὲ ἀρετὴν ἀληθῆ καὶ θρεψαμένῳ ὑπάρχει θεοφιλεῖ γενέσθαι, καὶ εἴπερ τῳ ἄλλῳ ἀνθρώπων ἀθανάτῳ καὶ ἐκείνῳ; (*Sym.* 211d3–12a7)

That, if ever you see it, will not seem to you to be of the same order as gold and clothes, and the beautiful boys and young men that now drive you out of your mind when you see them, so that both you and many others are ready, so long as you can see your beloveds and be with them always (if somehow it were possible), to stop eating and drinking, and just gaze at them and be with them. What then, she said, do we suppose it would be like if someone succeeded in seeing beauty itself, pure, clean, unmixed, and not contaminated with things like human flesh, and color, and much other mortal nonsense, but were able to catch sight of the uniformity of divine beauty itself? Do you think it's a worthless life, she said, if a person turns his gaze in that direction and contemplates that beauty with the faculty he should use, and is able to be with it? Or do you not recognize, she said, that it is under these conditions alone, as he sees beauty with what has the power to see it, that he will succeed in bringing to birth, not phantoms of virtue, because he is not grasping a phantom, but true virtue, because he is grasping the truth; and that when he has given birth to and nurtured true virtue, it belongs to him to be loved by the gods, and to him, if to any human being, to be immortal? (Trans. Rowe 1998)

In this case, commentators and critics have noted the echo of content of Aristophanes' fable in the fleeting vision of those who want nothing else than always to be together with their love object, "if somehow it were possible, to stop eating and drinking, and just gaze at them and be with them."[36] We might add that this echo of Aristophanes—just like the one I have suggested occurs earlier in the speech—is intimately connected with Diotima's decisive rejection of all the particulars of the phenomenal world. Indeed, two references to the mere stuff of the world frame Diotima's echo of Aristophanes' fable, mapping in their

---

[36] Thus Bury 1969.131 and Rowe 1998.200 note the reference back to Aristophanes' speech, esp. to 191a5–b5 and 192c2–e9.

progression the ineluctable triumph of pure philosophical contemplation over mere worldly matter and the discourses that embrace it. Thus her first list consists of "gold and clothes and beautiful boys and young men," while, by the time she gets to her second list, even the physical beauty of individuals has been dissected and disaggregated into its component parts ("human flesh and colors") and finally airily dismissed as so much "mortal nonsense" (φλυαρίας θνητῆς, 211e2).[37] "Mortal nonsense" seems a fit characterization in Diotima's scheme not just for the mundane particulars of the world but also for the speech genre of Aesopic fable that celebrates them.[38] Thus here at the end of Diotima's discourse, traditional fable is utterly routed and disavowed, until (as we shall see), Aesopic discourse and its characteristic particularity return in somewhat different form in Alcibiades' speech.

One final element of Diotima's peroration may support my reading of this as a rout not just of the particularity of the world, but also of the genre of fable where it finds a home. For Diotima concludes that the one who achieves the final ascent—the contemplation of the Form of beauty with the eye of the soul—"brings to birth not [mere] phantoms of virtue (εἴδωλα ἀρετῆς), since he does not fasten onto a phantom, but true [things], since he fastens onto truth." Behind the opposition of "insubstantial images" of virtue (εἴδωλα ἀρετῆς) versus "true" virtue, of course, stands the whole Platonic edifice of the Forms versus the phenomenal world. And, as Christopher Rowe notes, this final opposition discredits in retrospect "all those 'great achievements' referred to in the earlier passage—those of Homer and Hesiod, Lycurgus and Solon— . . . as insubstantial; but so they must be, by implication, in any case, since Homer and the rest lack the vision of true beauty that enables the philosophical lover to procreate true virtue."[39] And yet here also, I want to suggest, we may find a final dismissive reference to fable. I offer this suggestion very tentatively, since it depends on a definition of fable found only in much later sources. The rhetorician Aelius Theon, writing *Progymnasmata* in the second century CE, offers a terse definition of fable (μῦθος) in a mere four words: λόγος ψευδὴς εἰκονίζων

---

[37] Rowe 1998.200 notes that "'gold and clothes' hardly interest the real S." He suggests that Socrates as Diotima's pupil is still playing the role of Agathon, and that this reference is intended for him and the others present. The odd mention of gold here is perhaps intended to contrast with "beauty itself" as Diotima goes on to describe it (εἰλικρινές, καθαρόν, ἄμεικτον)—since these qualities of absolute purity, self-sameness, and resistance to mixture with any other element very much characterize "gold" in traditional Greek culture, especially in sympotic poetry. On the prominence and symbolic significance of gold in Greek sympotic poetry, see Kurke 1995, 1999.41–60.

[38] For the "nonsense" (φλυαρία) of bodily desires, appetites, and emotions that interfere with the soul's pursuit of being, cf. *Phd.* 66c. As Worman 2008.190–91 notes, words of the φλυαρ- family in Plato tend to be strongly associated with *talking* nonsense and with the abusive, iambic discourse of Old Comedy. Notice also that the highly charged class/status term φαῦλος comes up again here at the end, in pointed contrast to the life of the philosophical lover.

[39] Rowe 1998.201.

ἀλήθειαν.[40] I have already suggested that some aspects of rhetorical education as they came to be codified in the late *Progymnasmata* may go back in somewhat looser and simpler form to the practices of the fifth-century Sophists. Likewise here: perhaps we should regard Theon's definition of the genre of fable as a traditional one that has its roots in the Sophistic rhetorical training of the fifth and fourth centuries BCE. For Diotima's final words resonate strikingly with Theon's definition, only substituting the more negative, insubstantial εἴδωλα for Theon's more neutral participle εἰκονίζων, even as she would thereby contemptuously assimilate all the discourses of nonphilosophical others to the humble rank of "fable."[41]

Even if we are not willing to read an echo of Theon's definition of fable into Diotima's closing words, it is clear at this point that the rout of Aristophanes' low comic fable is complete. And it seems that, for this purpose, the Socrates of the *Symposium* needs another speaker or alibi to offer the fancy Sophistic fable that trounces and supersedes traditional fable, as well as to assert the superiority of philosophy in terms that are markedly class/status linked (slavery versus magnificence and abundance).[42] In this way, comic fable is rejected, but the Sophistic appropriation of fable can also be disavowed and superseded, in turn, by a style of discourse that is distinctively "Socratic." For, as Socrates characterizes his own discourse in his brief *captatio benevolentiae* before assuming the mask of Diotima (198d3–199b5), it is anything but the refined, elegant, and "magnificent" discourse we hear from the Mantinean stranger. Socrates insists that he can only speak the truth about Eros (in contrast to the earlier encomia) and can only do so in a style that is entirely artless:

> ὅρα οὖν, ὦ Φαῖδρε, εἴ τι καὶ τοιούτου λόγου δέῃ, περὶ Ἔρωτος τἀληθῆ λεγόμενα ἀκούειν, ὀνόμασι δὲ καὶ θέσει ῥημάτων τοιαύτῃ ὁποία ἄν τις τύχῃ ἐπελθοῦσα.[43] (*Sym.* 199b2–5)

> Consider then, O Phaedrus, if you have any need of such a speech as well, to hear true things said concerning Eros, but with words and such a setting of expressions whatever sort happens to come up.

---

[40] Aelius Theon II.72 Spengel. See the discussion of Theon's definition in Perry 1965.xix–xxiv and introduction, section IIC.

[41] As Richard Martin points out to me, whenever we date Theon's formulation, it draws on a much more ancient topos, familiar from Hesiod's *Theogony* (27–28) and the *Odyssey* (19.203) that fiction as a whole, and at its best, comprises "lies like to true things" (ψεύδεα πολλὰ λέγειν ἐτύμοισιν ὁμοῖα). Note also that there is no more need here for the mediating Eros of the birth fable, since the philosopher seems to achieve immortality for himself. That is to say, Diotima's discourse at this point decisively leaves behind her own "image of truth"—the birth fable of Eros.

[42] This is not at all intended to preclude or invalidate other arguments on why Socrates' alibi here needs to be female; only to supplement those discussions, since surely the choice of Diotima as speaker is overdetermined. Thus, where Halperin 1990 asks, "Why is Diotima a woman?," and Gilhuly 2009.58–97; "Why is Diotima a priestess?," my question might be, "Why is Diotima a Sophist?"

[43] Greek text here follows Dover 1980, Rowe 1998.

ὁποία ἄν τις τύχῃ ἐπελθοῦσα forcefully expresses the seeming chance and randomness of Socratic style, while the omission of any personal pronoun here entirely effaces Socrates' agency from the process. Instead, his haphazard discourse becomes a kind of impersonal, automatic truth speaking that has no regard for style or elegance of composition.[44] This self-description of the (apparent) artlessness of his discourse will be picked up and confirmed by Alcibiades in his extended portrait of Socrates and Socratic *logoi*. There, as we shall see in more detail in the next chapter, themes, images, and discursive structures associated with Aesop return to capture and express a different kind of particularity—that of Socrates himself and his *logoi*. As Alcibiades makes clear, Socrates is profoundly "strange" or "unusual" (cf. τὴν σὴν ἀτοπίαν, 215a2; τὴν ἀτοπίαν, 221d2); in fact, it turns out, he is unique (221c3–d6).[45]

To capture this singularity, Alcibiades tells us at the start of his drunken encomium, he will attempt to praise Socrates "through images" (δι' εἰκόνων, 215a5):

> οὗτος μὲν οὖν ἴσως οἰήσεται ἐπὶ τὰ γελοιότερα, ἔσται δ' ἡ εἰκὼν τοῦ ἀληθοῦς ἕνεκα, οὐ τοῦ γελοίου. (*Sym*. 215a5–6)
>
> And this man will perhaps think it's more for a joke, but the image will be for the sake of truth, not of [getting] a laugh.

Alcibiades here restores us to a lower world of images and likenesses that Diotima had decisively rejected in her account of the final ascent to viewing "the beautiful itself" (211e1, 3, quoted above). And it is striking that his formulation that "the image will be for the sake of truth" (ἔσται δ' ἡ εἰκὼν τοῦ ἀληθοῦς ἕνεκα) almost exactly replicates the terms of Theon's definition of "fable" (λόγος ψευδὴς εἰκονίζων ἀλήθειαν), while his acknowledgment that his audience is likely to take his image "for a joke" also suits the lowly genre of fable. As we shall see, the particular comparison he offers—of *silenoi* morphing progressively into the "hubristic satyr" Marysas—itself has close connections to Aesop as upstart challenger to Apollo. And, as Alcibiades goes on to say, Socrates' *logoi* are also distinctive or unique in their humble and apparently banal and repetitive subject matter (221e1–222a1), and yet at the same time somehow bizarrely democratic or capable of endless replication that preserves their strange power (215b8–d6). As I shall argue, this paradoxical combination transposes distinctive features of Aesopic fable discourse to characterize Socratic analogy. Thus, in Alcibiades' account, Socrates becomes both the subject and the purveyor of Aesopic discourse.

---

[44] For this same sense of randomness or chance in Socrates' style of truth speaking, see *Apol*. 17b7–c2; for the association of this random, "found-object" style with specifically Aesopic, fabular discourse, cf. *Phd*. 61b5–7.

[45] Many scholars have noted the importance of the theme of Socrates' strangeness/uniqueness to the dialogue as a whole: cf. (e.g.) Gill 1990.80–81; R. B. Rutherford 1995.183, 191, 198–99, Nussbaum 2001.184–87; Blondell 2002.69–75; Worman 2008.170.

This final turn on Aesop and fabular discourse in the *Symposium* exposes a paradox inscribed at the heart of Platonic writing. For the closing movements of the *Symposium*—the juxtaposed discourses of Socrates/Diotima and Alcibiades—suggest that Plato wants or needs simultaneously a transcendent model of philosophy as an elevated discourse that has moved beyond particulars, the bodily, and all the dross of "mortal nonsense," and a Socrates who helps him get there through his own (bizarrely Aesopic) particularity.[46] This introduces a kind of irreconcilable tension or necessary rift of literary decorum linked with socioeconomic status within Platonic writing. Comparison with Xenophon helps us appreciate the sharper edge of this paradox within Platonic texts. For on either side, Plato's project seems more extreme than Xenophon's: on the one hand, Plato aspires to a purer metaphysical transcendence; on the other, he somehow requires a more violently and disruptively Aesopic Socrates to get there.[47] This combination of extremes is what generates some of the peculiar quality and effects of Platonic writing in contrast to Xenophon's more moderate and decorous discursive practice.

I will consider this tension or rift as it repeats in other Platonic dialogues in more detail in the next chapter. For now I want to suggest that it is partly this seam within Platonic writing that is being acknowledged and addressed in Socrates' final argument in the *Symposium*, with Agathon and Aristophanes. Here Socrates compels the two drunk and sleepy dramatists "to agree that it belongs to the same man to know how to compose comedy and tragedy, and that the one who is a tragic poet by art is also a comic poet" (223d3–6). As I noted in chapter 6, scholars have found it irresistible to read this as a self-conscious statement of Plato's metaliterary program—on this interpretation, our invisible author thereby characterizes his own multifarious genre-mixing within the dialogue form.[48] I concur with this reading, but I have suggested that in focusing exclusively on the genres of tragedy and comedy, modern interpreters occlude or elide the crucial fact of Platonic *prose*. Instead, I have suggested, we should read this generic binary synecdochically rather than literally, as representing

---

[46] For many Platonic scholars, the paradox is usually formulated as that of writing vs speech (thus, e.g., Berger 1984, Frede 1992, Halperin 1992, Kahn 1996, Nussbaum 2001); this opposition could certainly be conjoined to or mapped on to the Aesopic theme I'm tracing here, since Socrates, opponent of writing, is so strongly identified with the popular *speech* genre of Aesopic fable. But by posing this paradox differently, I want to call more attention to the sociopolitics that inevitably subtends these oppositions in the Greek system. Nussbaum 2001.122–35 also poses this as a different opposition, between the quotidian specificity of poetry/literature and the universalizing of philosophical treatise. In a sense, I am attempting to ground Nussbaum's opposition "literature vs philosophy" in the more historically specific form of Aesop/fable vs the lofty discourses of Sophistic *epideixis* and philosophy.

[47] For a very similar formulation of the tension between transcendence and the particularity of Socrates' characterization in Platonic dialogue, see Blondell 2002.74 and passim.

[48] Thus, e.g., Bacon 1959, Clay 1975, 1994.46, Nightingale 1995.2, 68, R. B. Rutherford 1995.204–5, Nussbaum 2001.194–99.

the whole spectrum of genre and decorum mobilized in the Platonic project—including at its lower end Aesopic discourse and humble prose fable. What I want to add to that argument now is the notion that high and low *genre* are inseparable from high- and low-class *content* within the system of ancient literary decorum, so that in this passage Plato simultaneously acknowledges the weird and volatile unevenness of style and representation written into his dialogues to achieve their final transcendence. One of these is the thread of the Aesopic woven into the representation of the uniqueness of Socrates and his discourses.

Chapter 9

AESOP IN PLATO'S *SŌKRATIKOI LOGOI*:
ANALOGY, *ELENCHOS*, AND DISAVOWAL

LET ME START FROM THE point at which I left off in the previous chapter: from the uniqueness or singularity of Socrates. For it is this most of all that solicits our belief in the world conjured by Platonic dialogue and thereby ultimately draws us into the argumentation that constitutes the main action of Plato's "anti-tragic theater."[1] But how, specifically, does Plato achieve this representational tour de force, crafting an image of Socrates as unlike anybody else, compellingly strange and unique? It is my contention that much of this representation of Socrates is shot through with elements drawn from an older, popular Aesop tradition—elements that borrow for Socrates himself and his distinctive *logoi* the edgy particularity and disruptive social energies of Aesop. Nor should we regard this Platonic borrowing as merely the philosopher's means of accurately representing and thereby paying tribute to his beloved master. For such a naive and sentimental reading crucially effaces the ground of conflict on which Plato constructs the edifice of philosophy. That is to say, on my reading, the Aesopic never figures in Platonic dialogue as an end in itself—as if we might treat this as Plato's magnanimous tribute to Aesop or to Socrates. Instead, Plato always deploys the Aesopic instrumentally, as a set of moves or a mask donned for a deadly serious battle over the cultural prestige and authority of *sophia,* and then, once the territory is won, discarded and disavowed. Thus, in this chapter, I will consider Plato's specific strategies for the appropriation, use, and disavowal of the Aesopic. Close analysis of these mechanisms will help us understand in turn the weird generic motley of *Sōkratikoi logoi* and Plato's choice of mimetic prose as his medium.

In all this, Plato has opted for a set of representational elements that are very different from those of the Sophists, as considered in chapter 7. There I suggested that the evidence we have allows us to identify several different Sophistic attempts to appropriate fable and convert it into an element of high-class public

---

[1] I borrow this phrase from Nussbaum 2001.122–35, along with the point that "debate and discourse are the event" in Plato's dramatic dialogues (quotation from p. 130). For a related argument, see Bakhtin 1984a.106–12, Blondell 2002.37–38. In addition, Blondell 2002.69–80 and passim represents a significant recognition of and meditation on the fact that it is Socrates' compelling richness, particularity, and uniqueness as a literary character that draw us into the philosophical project of Plato's dialogues.

discourse on political and ethical topics. In so doing, the Sophists make fable into a different kind of *makrologia*; in particular, the long explanatory epilogue described or represented in three of our four examples of "Sophistic" fable (Prodicus's, "Protagoras's," and Diotima's) transforms it into a kind of authoritarian, one-way discourse.[2] In addition, the slight evidence we have suggests that the Sophists may have slotted fable in as a first step within an anthropological, developmental narrative and within a carefully structured educational sequence. In contrast to the Sophists, as I will argue in this chapter, Plato opts for *Aesop* rather than *fable*. By this I mean that Plato seems to be drawing on popular or common (largely oral) traditions of the life and adventures of Aesop to inform many aspects of his "unique" Socrates. Specifically, Plato makes use of Aesop's broader subversive relation to the wisdom tradition (which entails also crude or low-class content and style), as well as Aesop's distinctive discursive strategies (which make the interlocutor in Socratic dialogue into a more active participant in the process). In all these respects, we might say, Plato crafts for Socrates an Aesopic character that is distinctly not—or not just—for the young.

I. *Sophia* into Philosophy: Socrates between the Sages and Aesop

In order to understand the status and stakes of Aesopic allusions in the Platonic corpus, we must first recognize that the broader cultural sphere within which the traditions around Aesop operate is the competitive, performative domain of Greek wisdom (*sophia*). Our extensive survey of wisdom traditions in chapters 2–5 suggests the possibility of a more pervasive Aesopic element lurking behind the characterization of Socrates. Or perhaps better: Socrates participates in both the high Sages tradition and the Aesopic debunking thereof. Socrates' location *between* the Sages and Aesop is a phenomenon, I will argue, of the difficult birth of philosophy from an older tradition of prephilosophical *sophia*. At this point, I want to review briefly the elements that connect Socrates with the Sages and high traditions of *sophia*, and then turn to survey in more detail those that link him to Aesop.

Scholars have indeed recognized significant continuities between Socrates and the archaic Sages, while also acknowledging a moment of epochal shift. Thus Richard Martin concludes his account of the Sages with a final nod to Socrates:

> Secularization and "internationalizing" trends transformed Greek sages by an evolution that never affected similar figures in ancient Rome and India, until they turned

[2] For a similar distinction between authoritarian, monologic, or prescriptive pedagogy in the wisdom tradition and a more interactive, dialogic style that engages the interlocutor in active critique, see Blondell 2002.39–52, 95–112.

into philosophers. Socrates, then, provides a sort of endpoint. Against the background I have sketched, of sages who are performers in several spheres, we can certainly see continuities in Socrates' life, in the form of his relationship with Delphi, his role in politics, even his versifying of Aesopic fables. But as he is depicted, all these are marginal activities in Socrates' career. No archaic sage invented the *elenchos*; it was the speciality of a man who constantly broke the frame of the performance by confronting his audience in dialogue and refusing to rely on the power of emphatic, unidirectional self-presentation.[3]

We can elaborate on Martin's suggested connections between Socrates and the Seven Sages from our survey of pre- or nonphilosophical wisdom traditions in chapters 2–4. We noted in chapter 2 Socrates' significant connection with Delphic Apollo through the oracle that "no one was wiser than he" (Plato *Apol.* 20e7–21a7).[4] We might add to that the *Phaedo*'s portrayal of Socrates' composition of a hymn to Apollo and his striking self-characterization later in the dialogue as "fellow slave of the swans and consecrate to the same god," from whom he claims to derive mantic power (*Phd.* 84e3–85b7; cf. esp. 85b4–6: ἐγὼ δὲ καὶ αὐτὸς ἡγοῦμαι ὁμόδουλός τε εἶναι τῶν κύκνων καὶ ἱερὸς τοῦ αὐτοῦ θεοῦ, καὶ οὐ χεῖρον ἐκείνων τὴν μαντικὴν ἔχειν παρὰ τοῦ δεσπότου).[5]

We have also noted that, while the *Crito* tells us emphatically that Socrates never traveled outside of Athens (except once to the Isthmus and on military campaign), Socrates himself in Plato's *Apology* characterizes his quest to find someone wiser than he as "my wandering" (τὴν ἐμὴν πλάνην, 22a6)—a metaphorical evocation, I suggested, of the archaic sage's "wandering" for wisdom.[6] Indeed, this same sequence in the *Apology* represents Socrates' competition in *sophia*, though turned inside out or inverted like a photographic negative. For Socrates seeks out those experts who embody prephilosophical *sophia* as "skilled crafting"—politicians, poets, and *dēmiourgoi*—in order to prove that he

---

[3] Martin 1998.124; see also Ker 2000.327. Note that for Martin, Socrates' "versifying of Aesopic fables" assimilates him to the Seven Sages, who (in Martin's account) are significantly composers of poetry. That is, for Martin, the emphasis is on the process of *versifying*; for me, on *Aesopic fables* as the raw material chosen. In addition, I will argue below that a characteristic Aesopic discourse at least partly enabled "Socrates'" invention of the *elenchos*.

[4] For the oracle as a traditional element in Socrates' life story, trial, and death, see Compton 1990, 2006.154–63; Stokes 1992.

[5] Cf. Plato *Apol.* 23c1, 30a6–7: Socrates' description of his activity cross-examining all those reputed wise as τὴν τοῦ θεοῦ λατρείαν and τῷ θεῷ ὑπηρεσίαν. In addition, Socrates' frequent claim to mantic power in Plato and Xenophon would seem to link his "divine sign" (τὸ δαιμόνιον) with Apollo as prophetic god; on this linkage, see Reeve 2000.

[6] See chapter 2, note 57 and, for Socrates' metaphorical wandering, see also *Hipp. Mai.* 304c2. Cf. *Crito* 52b2–c1, *Meno* 80b4–7, and *Phdr.* 230d1–5, where Socrates acknowledges that he rarely even sets foot outside the walls of the city proper to explore the Attic countryside. Interestingly, in spite of the explicit statement of the *Crito*, Aristotle apparently reported that Socrates went to Delphi (reported by D.L. 2.23); this tradition seems to answer a felt need to have Socrates go on a proper *theōria* to Delphi, like an archaic sage.

is *less wise* than they. And, of course, as it turns out, he wins this inverted contest of wisdom, reluctantly proving himself wiser precisely insofar as he knows his own ignorance.[7]

Another aspect that links Socrates with the Sages (at least in the Platonic representation) is his preferred style of discourse through short question-and-answer—that is, his own version of βραχυλογία and aversion to μακρολογία, the making of long speeches.[8] The power tussle over these two forms of discourse plays an important role in the *Protagoras*, where, of course, it is Socrates himself who strongly identifies the Seven Sages with the art of βραχυλογία (*Prot.* 342a6–43c5).

Finally, I would suggest, we may find echoes of the otherworldly end of the archaic sage in Plato's Socratic dialogues. Recall that, in chapter 2, I argued that there are two characteristic supernatural outcomes for the prephilosophical master of *sophia*: either he descends to the land of the dead as his ultimate voyage to an other place and returns, bearing the esoteric wisdom he's acquired back to the world of the living; or, after a lifetime of mediating between this and the invisible world of the divine, he is finally subsumed into the latter (often while on a *theōria*), so that he receives hero-cult or even divine honors. For the former: it is striking how many Platonic dialogues end with Socrates narrating a myth of the underworld—*Apology*, *Gorgias*, *Republic*, and *Phaedo*. The last three of these the sixth-century CE commentator Olympiodorus designated *nekuiai*, as if, like Odysseus, Socrates had himself descended and returned.[9] And while Socrates is always careful to mark off these accounts as "myth" or tales heard from another, he himself seems thereby to enjoy privileged access to a realm of knowledge his hearers do not possess.[10] For the latter: the suggestion occurs in several dialogues that the true philosopher, through assiduous contemplation of the Forms (*theōria*), is finally liberated from the body and the cycle of bodily reincarnation, and approximates to divinity.[11] Such statements are always hedged round with qualifications and disclaimers; nonetheless, these

---

[7] For the traditional logic of these categories of practitioners of *sophia* in this order, see Kerferd 1976.20; cf. Lincoln 1993. For the contest element, notice especially *Apol.* 22c6–8: "So then I went away from [the poets] thinking I had overcome them (περιγεγονέναι) in the very same way as also the politicians."

[8] Cf. esp. *Alc.* I 106b; *Gorg.* 449b–c, 461d–62a; *Prot.* 335a–336b.

[9] See Westerink 1970.240–41 (I owe this reference to Nightingale 1995.86n. 68).

[10] These myths are often read as Pythagorean and/or Orphic elements in Plato; see, e.g., Burnet 1911.xliii–lv, Dodds 1951. 207–35, Kingsley 1995.79–194. Whether or not these cultic identifications are appropriate, I would simply note that both figures of Pythagoras and Orpheus clearly participated in a broader model or tradition of the sage, in which the element of personal reincarnation played an important part. On the broader tradition, see Scodel 1980 and discussion above, chapter 2, section II and chapter 5, section III.

[11] For the philosopher's liberation from the body and the cycle of bodily reincarnation, see *Gorg.* 524c, *Phd.* 114c, *Phdr.* 249a, *Rep.* 619d–e; for his assimilation to the divine, see *Alc.* I 133b–c; *Phdr.* 248a–d, 249c–d; *Sym.* 212a; *Tht.* 176b–c.

hints of discarnate blessedness represent the philosophical transformation of the ultimate apotheosis of the *theios anēr*, significantly achieved through a new kind of philosophical *theōria*.[12]

We might see all these continuities as philosophy laying claim to or trying to appropriate the cultural authority of the prephilosophical wisdom tradition. To put it in metaphorical terms: philosophy is born trailing clouds of glory from the uncanny or otherworldly realm of prephilosophical *sophia*. But the birth of philosophy, midwifed through the figure of Socrates, is not without its trauma and violence. For Socrates was not unique in affiliating himself with the older wisdom tradition; as we have seen, the Sophists also laid claim to this heritage—hence their name. We recall the venerable genealogy of σοφισταί Plato puts into the mouth of Protagoras in the dialogue that bears his name (cited in chapter 2):

> I say that the sophistic art (σοφιστικὴν τέχνην) is ancient, but that the men of old who had a hand in it, fearing the hatred it caused, made a screen and veiled it, some as poetry, like Homer, Hesiod, and Simonides, others as initiatory rites and the singing of oracles (those around Orpheus and Musaeus). Still others I perceive disguised it also as the gymnastic art—like Iccus of Tarentum and Herodicus the Selymbrian, who, still living now, is a sophist inferior to no one. And your Agathocles has made the musical art his disguise (being a great sophist) and Pythocleides the Ceian and many others. (*Prot.* 316d3–e4)

And while we cannot read these as Protagoras's own words, they are likely to echo (however tongue-in-cheek) something of the Sophists' own self-representation.[13] In this new competition of and over *sophia*, Aesop becomes a symbolic resource mobilized by Platonic philosophy in its doubled work of self-differentiation. For Socrates' occasional Aesopic stance allows a critical or parodic debunking of the high wisdom tradition as well as the Sophistic appropriation thereof.[14]

Thus, like Aesop, Socrates was reputedly ugly, low-class (a sculptor by profession, so, in conventional terms, a laborer or *banausos*), and poor.[15] And the

---

[12] For the transformation of *theōria* from "pilgrimage" and religious "viewing of the divine" to philosophical "contemplation," see Ker 2000, Nightingale 2004. See also White 2000 for a fascinating argument that Socrates received hero-cult worship as a "founding hero" in Plato's Academy, and that the *Phaedo* contains several hints and allusive references to this Socratic heroization.

[13] Cf. Lloyd 1987.92–99; Blondell 2002.96–99, 118, 128–37; Nightingale 2004.29–39; and, for extended discussion of the continuities between traditional sage figures and the Sophists, Tell 2003.

[14] Cf. Jedrkiewicz 1989.114.

[15] For Socrates' ugliness: Plato *Sym.* 215b2–6, *Tht.* 143e; Xen. *Sym.* 4.19, 5.7; frr. of Phaedo's *Zopyrus* (preserved by Cicero *On Fate* 5.7); for Socrates' profession, see *Alc.* I 121a; D. L. 2.19, 21; for Socrates' poverty, *Apol.* 31c2–3. It is also worth noting Duris of Samos's claim (preserved in D.L. 2.19) that Socrates was a slave as well as a stonemason. Blondell 2002.69–79 notes all these unusual qualities of Socrates and also effectively lays out the evidence for Socrates' "ambiguous relationships to his socio-political context" (quotation from p. 75). On all these characteristics of Socrates

330   CHAPTER 9

same ugliness or commonness extended to his *logoi*. For in contrast to the Sophists, who composed epideictic speeches in a highly artificial, poeticizing style (as Gorgias and Hippias did) or even composed poetry that aped the forms and content of traditional *sophia* (as Hippias, Evenus, and Critias did), Socrates is usually represented relying on humble, unpretentious prose. Thus, like Aesop in his opposition to the traditions of high poetry aligned with Apollo and the Sages, Socrates made skillful use of ordinary material that was ready to hand. And it is this debunking power attached to humble, ordinary prose, I suggest, that at least partly accounts for Plato's choice of prose medium for his *Sōkratikoi logoi*.[16] The subversive Aesopic challenge to the old *sophia needs* prose.

II. The Aesopic Bricoleur and the "Old Socratic Tool-Box"

But I would like to push the argument further, and see Aesop as a precursor for two specific modes of Socratic discourse—*epagōgē*, or induction through analogy, and *elenchos*, or the refutation of an interlocutor's position as self-contradictory. Charles Kahn has characterized these two forms as *the* positive and negative arguments that constitute "the old Socratic tool-box." By "the old Socratic tool-box," Kahn means those modes and methods of argument developed and used by the historical Socrates, which he thinks are recoverable from the representation in Plato's *Apology*.[17] As I have noted in chapter 6, I am skeptical that we can derive anything of the historical Socrates from Plato's writing. Instead, I would follow Ruby Blondell's thoughtful analysis of the characterization of what she calls the "elenctic Sokrates," the (more or less coherent) literary character who dominates aporetic dialogues like *Charmides*, *Euthyphro*, *Hippias Minor*, *Ion*, and *Laches*, and who describes his methods in the Platonic *Apology*. For Blondell, this "elenctic Sokrates" is a literary character with distinctive features that differentiate him from the "constructive Sokrates" of what have traditionally been treated as later dialogues (like *Phaedo*, *Phaedrus*, *Symposium*, and most of *Republic*). But, Blondell insists, this is not a matter of the accurate depiction of the "historical" Socrates slowly giving way to a fictional mouthpiece for Plato's own developing philosophy (the traditional model of Socrates within the Platonic oeuvre), but rather of different literary depictions of "Sokrates" tailored to suit different philosophical goals within different dialogues.[18] I am very much in agreement with Blondell's approach, and while

---

as low-class or "iambic," see Worman 2008.157–72; as affiliating him with Aesop, see Jedrkiewicz 1989.113, Compton 2006.156–57.

[16] Cf. Nightingale 1995. 91, Nussbaum 2001.129–34.

[17] Kahn 1996.98.

[18] Blondell 2002.8–14, 115–27. By insisting on these different Socrateses as literary constructs, Blondell also rejects the traditional style-based chronology of Plato's dialogues, which serves in turn to ground a narrative of Plato's philosophical development away from and beyond his master

analogy and *elenchos* are consistent features of all the different "Socrateses" she finds in the Platonic corpus, I will be focusing mainly on Blondell's "elenctic Sokrates." For (as Blondell notes) this character is the one most engaged in an agonistic power tussle with the Sophists and other claimants to *sophia*, and therefore (I would contend) most strongly associated with Aesopic character and discourse features.[19]

In any case, I would like to suggest that Socrates' characteristic positive and negative styles of argument—induction through analogy and *elenchos*—bear a striking resemblance to the positive and negative forms of Aesopic discourse identified in chapters 3 and 4. There I argued that the late *Life of Aesop* can be read as a representation of the life cycle of an archaic sage, but one that over and over again displays Aesop's distinctive popular forms of *sophia*—the skilled crafting or bricolage available to society's abjected and disempowered. The positive version is what I have termed Aesop's implicit advising via fable. In the many fable performances embedded in the *Life*, what is distinctive about Aesop's use of fables—besides their humble and everyday content—is that they achieve their persuasive effects by leaving to the interlocutor (in the *Life* always a person of greater power and status) the work of interpretation. Thus fable works by preserving the interlocutor's illusion of agency and initiative; in contrast to the simple, blunt advising of the Seven Sages, Aesop's indirect advising through little mimetic narratives persuades while it flatters (indeed, persuades *because* it flatters).

Less obviously (as we saw in chapter 4), there is a second, negative form of distinctively Aesopic *sophia* that runs as a leitmotif through the text of the *Life*: Aesop exhibits an uncanny ability to force his (usually more powerful) opponents to incriminate or bear witness against themselves. In all the instances in the *Life*, Aesop is able to leverage a hegemonic opponent's will and power in a kind of martial art of the abjected that cunningly turns the social "weight" of the powerful against themselves. And, as I noted, there is a kinship between these positive and negative forms: Aesop's indirect and fabular style of speaking persuades by allowing its more powerful audience itself to deduce the fable's relevance and point. Where fable works positively, Aesop's coercion of assent or self-incrimination works negatively, but still locates the decisive moment of pivot—of acquiescence—with the interlocutor rather than with Aesop himself. And, as many scholars have noted, it is precisely the same interactive quality that differentiates Socrates' pedagogic method, as portrayed in Platonic dialogue, from the authoritarian, unidirectional style of the Sophists.

It is my contention that Aesop's positive and negative discursive weapons lie behind and help shape the Socratic tools of *epagōgē* and *elenchos*. If these

---

Socrates. Finally, as Blondell notes (p. 11), the "constructive" and "elenctic" or "aporetic" Socrateses tend to coexist in dialogues such as *Crito*, *Gorg.*, *Prot.*, *Rep.*, and *Tht.*

[19] See Blondell 2002.118–19.

suggested affiliations are correct, we can begin to appreciate the enormous serviceability of Aesop and his characteristic styles of discourse to philosophy's refutation of and self-discrimination from older modes of high *sophia* and their Sophistic appropriation. On occasion, I would suggest, Plato even tips his hand, acknowledging the kinship of these elements of the "old Socratic tool-box" to their humbler, practical and embodied versions in the domain of Aesop.

Let me consider each of these methods in turn by focusing mainly on two different dialogues, *Symposium* and *Gorgias*:

Epagōgē ("induction") through analogy.[20] As we saw in chapter 6, Aristotle already recognized that Socrates' use of analogy was closely affiliated with Aesop's characteristic implicit advising via fable, since he categorizes them as two subspecies of invented examples (*Rhet.* 2.20, 1393a23–94a18). Indeed, for Aristotle, both are akin to ἐπαγωγή—persuasion through induction.[21] On several occasions, in fact, Socrates' penchant for humble analogies stands synecdochically as a characterization of all his discourse (each time offered by interlocutors more or less comfortable with his distinctive style of speaking). Thus, in the opening of Xenophon's *Memorabilia*, Critias and Charicles, speaking on behalf of the Thirty, forbid Socrates to engage young men in conversation. When Socrates questions the specific terms of the ban, Critias snaps in exasperation, "Well, Socrates, you'll have to avoid these topics—the cobblers and builders and smiths (τῶν σκυτέων καὶ τῶν τεκτόνων καὶ τῶν χαλκέων); for I think they've already been worn to tatters by your constant chattering about them" (Xen. *Mem.* 1.2.37).[22] Callicles in Plato's *Gorgias* offers a similar list, contemptuously cataloging Socrates' constant topics: "By the gods, you simply never stop talking about shoemakers and fullers and cooks and doctors (σκυτέας τε καὶ κναφέας καὶ μαγείρους λέγων καὶ ἰατροὺς οὐδὲν παύῃ), as if our discussion were about these!" (*Gorg.* 491a1–3).[23]

---

[20] On the forms of *epagōgē* used by Plato (and how they differ from Aristotle's development of the concept and method), see Robinson 1953.33–48, 202–22. In Robinson's terms, I consider here only a subset of *epagōgē*—that conducted through analogy "that passes from case to case without mentioning the universal" (quotation from Robinson 1953.207).

[21] Cf. *Rhet.* 2.20, 1393a26–7, ὅμοιον γὰρ ἐπαγωγῇ τὸ παράδειγμα, ἡ δ' ἐπαγωγὴ ἀρχή, "for the example resembles induction, and induction is a beginning." For the Aesopic influence on Socrates' dialectic method, cf. Gigon 1959.177, 180; Jedrkiewicz 1989.114.

[22] For the connection with Aesop, it may be significant that, in Xenophon's narration, two animal analogies provoke the ban: (1) Critias can't stop rubbing up against Euthydemus like a pig against a rock; (2) it is bad herdsmen who decrease the number of their herd (applied to the murderous activities of the Thirty; *Mem.* 1.2.30, 32).

[23] The fuller is the odd man out here (as John Ferrari has pointed out to me) since neither earlier in the *Gorgias* nor anywhere else in the Platonic corpus is Socrates represented using "fullers" in an analogical argument. I take this to be Callicles' contemptuous transformation of Socrates' "weavers," cited earlier in the *Gorgias* together with cobblers, cooks, and doctors, since, in contrast to the weaver, a fuller does not even make the garment—he just cleans it. (For the fuller's activity of cleaning and the "ridiculous name" of his "art," cf. *Soph.* 227a3–5.)

But the most familiar of these lists, offered by the drunken Alcibiades in Plato's *Symposium*, is also perhaps the oddest (and therefore requires our careful scrutiny). Here I would like to take the opportunity to complete the reading of the *Symposium* offered in the previous chapter. Starting from Alcibiades' somewhat anomalous list of Socrates' constant analogical topics, I would like to consider a whole network of language and imagery Alcibiades uses to characterize Socrates and his exceptional *logoi*. The oddly sorted analogical topics, as well as much of the language and imagery, I would suggest, are borrowed from popular representations of Aesop. And this will bring us back to the topic of Socrates' uniqueness. As I noted at the end of the previous chapter, Alcibiades, proffering an encomium for Socrates, insists that the latter's ἀτοπία means he can praise him only "through images" (δι' εἰκόνων, *Sym.* 215a2–5):

> And this man perhaps will assume that this is more for a joke, but the image will be for the sake of truth, not of laughter. For I say that he is most like those *silenoi* that sit in the workshops of makers of domestic statuary, the ones the craftsmen make holding pan-pipes or auloi, which when opened in two are revealed to have images of gods inside. And I say in turn that he is like the satyr Marsyas. And that you are like these in form at least, O Socrates, not even you yourself could dispute; but that you are like these also in other respects, hear after this. You're an arrogant bastard (ὑβριστὴς εἶ)—or not? For if you deny it, I'll furnish witnesses. But are you not a pipe-player (αὐλητής)? Yes, and much more marvelous than that one too. He on the one hand used to charm mortals through his instruments, by the power from his mouth, and still now, whoever pipes the compositions of that one [charms] (for what Olympus piped, I call Marsyas's, since he taught him). The compositions of that one, as I say, whether a good pipe-player plays them or the meanest flute-girl (φαύλη αὐλητρίς), they alone cause people to be entranced and reveal those in need of gods and initiation rites, on account of their being divine. You, on the other hand, differ only so much from that one, that without instruments, with only bare words (ψιλοῖς λόγοις), you accomplish this same thing. We at any rate, whenever we hear someone else speaking other words, even a really excellent speaker, it is, so to speak, no concern to anyone. But whenever someone hears you or hears another speaking your words— even if the one speaking is a really wretched speaker (κἂν πάνυ φαῦλος ᾖ ὁ λέγων)—we are amazed and entranced, women, men, and youths alike. (*Sym.* 215a5–d6)

Alcibiades then returns to the image of the enclosing satyr at the end of his speech:

> For in fact, this also I left out in the first things I said, that his words also are most like to those *silenoi* opened up. For if someone wishes to listen to Socrates' words, they appear entirely laughable at first—such words and expressions they are clothed in on the outside, just like some hide of a hubristic satyr (σατύρου δή τινα ὑβριστοῦ δοράν). For he talks of pack asses and smiths and cobblers and tanners (ὄνους γὰρ κανθηλίους λέγει καὶ χαλκέας τινὰς καὶ σκυτοτόμους καὶ βυρσοδέψας), and seems always to say

the same things through the same things, so that every foolish and inexperienced man would mock/laugh at his words. But if he should see them opened up and come to know what's inside them, in the first place, he will find that they're the only words that have sense within and then that they are most divine and have the most images of virtue (ἀγάλματ᾽ ἀρετῆς) and to the greatest degree relevant—no, rather entirely [relevant] insofar as it's appropriate for one who's going to be noble and good to consider. (*Sym.* 221d7–222a6)

This is to us perhaps the single most famous and familiar literary representation of Socrates and his characteristic *logoi*, and therefore it is difficult not to succumb to its compelling descriptive authority. (Socrates was just like that.) But we need to defamiliarize this description and notice what is anomalous— what does not in fact fit Socrates as he is characterized elsewhere in the Platonic dialogues or even elsewhere in the *Symposium*. Thus notice in the first passage the claim that Socrates' words, even when repeated by a miserable speaker (κἂν πάνυ φαῦλος ᾖ ὁ λέγων), irresistibly grip and enchant all who hear them— women, men, and youths. But (as a few scholars have noted), we know from the beginning of the *Symposium* that this is not in fact the case; Apollodorus's constant repetition of the words of Socrates has no such compelling effect on his bored and weary interlocutors.[24] We might also note that Alcibiades' hypothetical audience of "women, men, and youths" seems oddly democratic and uncharacteristic of the small intellectual circle Socrates usually aspires to engage.[25] It is also strange and disturbing (though not usually remarked upon) that within the Marsyas-Socrates analogy, the term that parallels the "wretched speaker's" efficacy when he uses Socrates' *logoi* is "the meanest flute-girl" (φαύλη αὐλητρίς). I say disturbing because, within the world of the ancient Greek symposium, flute-girls were usually slaves and generally assumed to be prostitutes (since they were hired entertainment and adept at using their mouths).[26] Thus the alignment of the effective repetition of Socrates' *logoi* with the performance of the "meanest flute-girl" identifies the former with abjected status (both female and slave) and the basest bodily urges.

[24] Thus Halperin 1992.115, Nightingale 1995.120. See also Blondell 2002.108–9, distinguishing between Apollodorus's slavish imitation of Socrates and Plato's own (implicitly more critical and creative) imitation.

[25] Halperin 1992.115–17 notes both these inconsistencies or oddities in Alcibiades' characterization of Socrates' *logoi* and connects them with the theme of writing or inscription. This is a possibility, but such a reading does not account for the other odd elements of Alcibiades' language and imagery here. Cf. *Gorg.* 502d5–8, in which part of Socrates' negative characterization of tragic and dithyrambic poetry as just another form of demegoric rhetoric is that it speaks indiscriminately to an audience of "children and women and men, slave and free [alike], which we do not entirely admire. . . ."

[26] Cf. Aristoph. *Wasps* 1341–50 and the constant visual punning on the aulos case and the erect penis of symposiasts on Attic red-figure vases. On the low status of flute-girls and their ready assimilation to prostitutes, see Dover 1980.87, Davidson 1997.81–82, Rowe 1998.135, Gilhuly 2009.62–5; and see discussion of *Prot.* 347c–48a in chapter 8, section I above.

In the second passage, there is also something a bit odd about Alcibiades' list of Socrates' constant topics, as we can see from comparison with the lists proffered in Xenophon's *Memorabilia* and Plato's *Gorgias*. For this is the only list that contains—in fact, begins with—animals, the humble "pack asses" (ὄνους ... κανθηλίους). Socrates does indeed mention asses (ὄνοι) in analogies seven times in the Platonic corpus, but mainly these passages focus on proverbs or on the breeding and training of asses together with other animals.[27] What differentiates Alcibiades' example from all these other passages is the redundant κανθηλίους, a rare (perhaps comic?) term that appears only here in Plato, derived from the large baskets or panniers on either side of an ass's packsaddle.[28] That is to say, κανθήλιος characterizes the ass (uniquely for Plato) as a beast of burden.

I would suggest that these two anomalies (of audience and of analogical topic) go together, and that they are part of a whole cluster of language and imagery borrowed from traditional representations of Aesop and Aesopic fable. Thus it is characteristic of the humble prose fables of Aesop that they can be told by anyone and appeal to a broad audience, because they achieve their effects not through complex verbal artistry, but through their everyday, easily found content (and this is why, in the later tradition of rhetorical education, fables serve as one of the first exercises for boys). And of course, by beginning his list of favorite Socratic analogies with "pack asses," Alcibiades affiliates them even more closely with Aesopic fables, where perhaps the single most common signification of the ass is as a beast of burden.[29]

Once we notice that these features belong properly to Aesop, several other elements fall into place. For just as Socrates is here characterized by his ἀτοπία— the fact that he is unlike anyone else—so Aesop throughout the *Life* is described as a "wonder" or "prodigy" (τέρας).[30] In addition, both Aesop and his *logoi* are repeatedly characterized in the *Life* in terms of the contrast between humble outer appearance and profound inner worth; thus, for example, in the sequence in which the philosopher Xanthus first encounters Aesop in the slave market of Samos and eventually buys him, Aesop admonishes the foolish philosopher, "Don't look at my form, but rather examine my soul" (μή μου βλέπε τὸ εἶδος,

---

[27] For the breeding and training of asses together with other animals: *Apol.* 27e, *Statesman* 265d, *Gorg.* 516a, *Rep.* 563c; for asses in proverbs: *Phdr.* 260c, *Laws* 701d. In one final instance (*Tht.* 146a), "ass" is the name conventionally given to someone who makes a mistake in a ball game (as an analogy for one who makes a mistake in question-and-answer). On asses in Plato's *Apology*, see Clay 1972.

[28] For the rare term κανθήλιος in comedy, see Aristoph. *Lysistrata* 290, Hermippus fr. 9 KA, Lysippus fr. 7 KA; the term also occurs in Xen. *Cyr.* 7.5.11; Lucian *Pseudologista* 3, *Jupiter Tragoedus* 31.

[29] See Perry fable nos. 164, 179, 180, 181, 182, 183, 185, 189, 263, 279, 357, 411, 458.

[30] *Vita* G, chs. 24, 30, 87, 98; cf. chs.1 (προσημαῖνον) and 10 (τερατῶδές τι πρᾶγμα). Perhaps especially significant for the parallel with Socrates is Xanthus's address to Aesop in *Vita* G, ch. 80 (quoted in chapter 4, section I above): σὺ μέγα δαιμόνιον εἶ.

ἀλλὰ μᾶλλον ἐξέταζε τὴν ψυχήν, *Vita* G, ch. 26). When Xanthus queries, "What is the form?" Aesop responds with an analogy: "At the wineseller's, we see jars that are ugly, but excellent in flavor" (θεωροῦμεν κεράμια ἀειδῆ, τῷ δὲ γεύματι χρηστά, *Vita* G, ch. 26). The *Life*'s most obsessive articulation of the misfit between outer appearance and inner quality is Aesop's introduction of himself to the incredulous Samian demos (who have burst out laughing at the sight of him):

> ἄνδρες Σάμιοι, ‹τί σκώπτετε› ἀτενήσαντες εἰς ἐμέ;[31] οὐχὶ τὴν ὄψιν δεῖ θεωρεῖν, ἀλλὰ τὴν φρόνησιν σκοπεῖν. ἄτοπον γάρ ἐστιν ἀνθρώπου ψέγειν τὸν νοῦν διὰ τὸ διάπλασμα τοῦ τύπου. πολλοὶ γὰρ μορφὴν κακίστην ἔχοντες νοῦν ἔχουσι σώφρονα. μηδεὶς οὖν ἰδὼν τὸ μέγεθος ἐλαττούμενον ἀνθρώπου ἃ οὐ τεθεώρηκεν μεμφέσθω, τὸν νοῦν. οὐ γὰρ ἰατρὸς τὸν νοσοῦντα ἀφήλπισεν ἰδών, ἀλλὰ τὴν ἁφὴν ψηλαφήσας τὴν δύναμιν ἐπέγνω. τὸν πίθον κατανοήσας, γεῦμα δὲ ἐξ αὐτοῦ μὴ λαβών, πότε γνώσῃ; (*Vita* G, ch. 88)

Men of Samos, why do you abuse me, staring intently at me? You ought not to view my appearance, but consider my intellect. For it is strange to censure the mind of a man on account of the shape of his stamp, for many who have the basest form have a sensible mind. Let no one, then, seeing the diminutive size of a man blame what he does not see—the mind. For a doctor doesn't despair of a sick man just looking at him, but having felt his pulse, he comes to know his strength. If you disdain the jar and don't take a taste from it, will you ever know?

The same misfit between the low or humble container and the exceptional quality of "mind" or "soul" within, of course, figures prominently in Alcibiades' portrait of Socrates in the *Symposium*—even using much of the same imagery. Ruby Blondell, commenting specifically on this passage in the *Symposium*, notes that the character Socrates'

> combination of high and low elements.... contributes in no small part to both his uniqueness and to his cultural transgressiveness, especially through the dissonance that it establishes between his inner and outer selves, in sharp contrast to the cultural ideal of inner and outer harmony. There are few literary precedents for this dissonance.[32]

I would contend that Blondell is exactly right here, but that one obvious (sub- or nonliterary) precedent for this characterization of Socrates is Aesop. The sifting of sources in which I engaged in the chapters of part I allows us to posit a common or "little tradition" of Aesop, many of whose subversive or challenging features would go all the way back to oral tales circulating in the fifth century

---

[31] Text follows Perry 1952.62.

[32] Blondell 2002.72. The "literary precedents" Blondell offers are the bowlegged general of Archilochus fr. 114 W, and Odysseus in disguise as a beggar. But intriguingly, she cites in a footnote to this point Papademetriou 1997, a book devoted to *Aesop* as an archetypal hero.

BCE. Indeed, the representation of Aesop in colloquy with a fox in the tondo of a mid-fifth-century cup (fig. 5.1, discussed in chapter 5, section III) proves that Aesop's physical ugliness was already one of his defining features in the classical period. All this justifies us, in turn, in taking the *Life*'s obsessive figuration of Aesop's inside-outside dichotomy as the relic of an ancient tradition.[33]

Thus (to return to the *Symposium*), we might note Alcibiades' progressive specification of the image or statue to which he compares Socrates—"those *silenoi*," then a satyr, then Marsyas himself (215a7–b4). Alcibiades seems to have chosen this last term to enable his comparison of the effect of Socrates' "bare words" (or "prose"[!]—ψιλοῖς λόγοις) to that of the enchanting auletic compositions of the famous satyr. But it is worth noting that in *Vita* G, Aesop himself is compared to Marsyas in the context of his provoking the anger of Apollo (in a passage we have already considered in chapter 4, section II; *Vita* G, ch. 100).[34] And indeed, the image of Marsyas returns to haunt Alcibiades' closing vignette, in which he characterizes Socrates' *logoi* as "clothed in such words and expressions, just like some hide of a hubristic satyr." For, of course, the image of the hide or skin of a satyr evokes the mythic punishment of Marsyas, flayed by Apollo for his hubristic claim to surpass the god in *mousikē*.[35] Marsyas thus figures here, even if unnamed, as the subversive challenger to Apollo's musical *sophia*, and, as such, he has much in common with Aesop. This veiled reference to Marsyas contains a final anomaly; it is rarely noted that Alcibiades' words here subtly transform his original image from the "statue" of a silenus or satyr to a "hide" or "skin." This may seem a trivial difference, but the one other occurrence of the rare word δορά in the Platonic corpus adds a final element. For in the *Euthydemus*, Socrates tells us that the hide of the flayed Marsyas was made into a *wineskin* (ἀσκόν, *Euthyd.* 285c9–d1).[36] The contrast between the ugly container and the taste of the wine is, as we have seen, one of Aesop's favorite

---

[33] Especially if, as I have suggested, this is an allegory within the tradition for the structure and working of fable itself—a form with which Aesop is strongly identified in classical sources.

[34] The comparison with Marsyas, along with the plot strand of Aesop-Apollo antagonism in which it is embedded, is thought by many scholars to be an old feature of the Aesop tradition: thus Hausrath 1913.67, Perry 1936.15, Compton 1990.346. Jedrkiewicz 1989.112–13 and Jouanno 2006.32–37 also note the parallels between Alcibiades' description of Socrates in *Sym.* and elements in the *Life of Aesop* (the contrast between the jar and the taste of the wine; the comparison with Marsyas).

[35] Bury 1969.165 (*ad Sym.* 221e) notes this evocation. For the competition in *mousikē* and Marsyas's flaying as punishment, cf. Hdt. 7.26; Apoll. *Bibliotheca* 1.4.2; D.S. 3.59; Paus. 2.22.9; Ovid *Metamorphoses* 6.382–91, *Fasti* 6.703–8; Hyginus *Fabulae* 165.

[36] It is tempting to suggest that, in a psychologically realistic touch, it is the lurking image of the flaying of Marsyas and the working of his hide into a wineskin that inspires Alcibiades to add "tanners" (βυρσοδέψας) to his list of characteristic Socratic topics, since, in fact, Socrates hardly ever talks about tanners (cf. *Gorg.* 517e2 σκυτοδεψόν; to my knowledge, the only other occurrence of this trade in an analogy in the Platonic corpus). The image of Marsyas's flayed hide turned into a wineskin also suggests a different resonance for the "leathern dialogues" (σκυτικοὺς ... διαλόγους, D.L. 2.122) variously attributed to Simon the cobbler, Phaedo, or the Socratic Aeschines.

images in the *Life* for the gap between his hideous and abject appearance and the remarkable quality of his mind and words.[37] And if we may assume that this imagery is old in the Aesop tradition, Alcibiades' allegorical rendering of Socrates and his *logoi* becomes progressively more Aesopic.

But why represent Socrates and his discourse in terms that are so resonantly Aesopic? And why here, perversely, in a context where Alcibiades has just insisted that Socrates is incomparable—that there has never been anyone like him? We might understand the anomalies in Alcibiades' speech on the level of character and characterization, and argue (with Nightingale) that these are deliberate touches to register Alcibiades' failed or inadequate understanding of Socrates and the philosophic project of his *logoi*. And while Nightingale makes some excellent points about what is odd or inappropriate in Alcibiades' speech, this reading does not explain why his characterization of Socrates should borrow specifically from *Aesop*.[38] I would suggest that we must posit another level, of the author Plato tipping his hand (as it were) to the reader, behind the backs of his unwitting characters. This is not to endorse the sentimental reading that this is Plato's own eulogy for his beloved master, put into the mouth of a character, for there is a very particular context here that motivates this assimilation of Socrates to Aesop and his homely but compelling discourse. Notice that already when he first introduces the image of Marsyas, Alcibiades favorably compares the gripping effect of Socrates' *logoi* with "other *logoi*, even of a really excellent speaker" (καὶ πάνυ ἀγαθοῦ ῥήτορος, 215d2), to which listeners are indifferent. This theme of the "excellent rhetor" reappears with elaboration when Alcibiades returns to his silenus/satyr image at the end of his speech. Immediately before the passage I have already quoted, Alcibiades insists on Socrates' uniqueness:

> There are many other marvelous things someone could mention to praise Socrates. But on the subject of his other activities, perhaps someone could say such things also

---

[37] In addition to the passages already cited in the text, we should note how frequently those who insult Aesop in the *Life* compare him to some kind of container: thus *Vita* G, ch. 14 (χυτρόπους, "a pot with feet or a portable stove"; ἀγγεῖον τροφῆς, "a container of food"), ch. 87 (στάμνος κήλην ἔχων, "jar with a tumor"; λαγυνίσκος εἰκαζόμενος, "likeness of a small flagon"). On the inside-outside or appearance-reality dialectic in the *Life*, cf. Jedrkiewicz 1989.77, 118; Patterson 1991.27–29; Holzberg 1992b.73–75, 2002.83–84, 92; Hopkins 1993.13; Ferrari 1997.11–12; Hägg 1997.186–87; Jouanno 2006.32–37; and see discussion in the introduction, section IIB.

[38] Thus Nightingale 1995.119–27. While I agree with Nightingale's observation that Alcibiades' obsession with asymmetrical power relations, enslavement, and conquest reveals his limitations as a character and a thinker, I do not find her negative reading of the specific image of the silenus or satyr statue opened up to reveal gods persuasive. For here she claims that "Alcibiades thinks he sees some treasure underneath Socrates' philosophical conversations—something different from and better than the *logoi* that Socrates engages in" (123). But this is not what the text says; there are not two sets of *logoi*, but only one, which has a humble exterior (Socrates' lowly analogies) but profound inner meaning. Nightingale here, I suspect, is swayed by her own imagery of hoarding, and "visible and invisible property" applied to philosophic discourse.

about another person, but the fact that he is like no other human being, either of the ancients or of those living now—this is worthy of all wonder. For what sort Achilles was, someone could compare both Brasidas and others, and what sort Pericles [was] in turn, someone could compare both Nestor and Antenor (and there are also others)—and the rest likewise. But what sort this human being is in his unusualness (τὴν ἀτοπίαν)—both himself and his words—seeking, you could find nothing near it, neither of those now nor of the ancients, unless someone should compare him to the things I was saying, to no one of human beings, but to *silenoi* and satyrs, himself and his words. (*Sym.* 221c2–d6)

Here the "excellent rhetor" of the first passage has morphed into the specific Pericles, himself comparable to the sage political counselors of the epic tradition—Nestor and Antenor. Thus this section of Alcibiades' speech carefully stages a competition of high and low modes of public speaking and political advising. For that purpose, the speech (I will not say "Alcibiades") mobilizes echoes of Aesop to challenge and undermine bouleutic rhetoric as a formal skill—a special technique of artful composition that lays claim in its turn to the politically consequential "skilled crafting" of Nestor and Antenor.[39] At the same time, as the additional comparison Brasidas-Achilles suggests, this is a competition of high and low genres (heroic epic and humble fable). But here, very much in contrast to Xenophon's decorous practice (as considered in chapter 7, section II), Alcibiades' speech implicitly inverts the ranked hierarchy of literary forms and performance contexts, to award the crown of competition to the "Aesopic" Socrates.

I have lingered over Alcibiades' speech in the *Symposium* because of its odd characterization of Socrates' favorite analogical topics of conversation. I have detected in Alcibiades' account several anomalous features that seem to derive from Aesop and the peculiar discourses of Aesopic fable—humble content, broad or "common" appeal, repeatability, and alignment with abjected slave status and bodily pleasure ("the meanest flute-girl"). All these Aesopic features are skillfully marshaled in a miniature competition of *sophia* with the high political rhetoric of Pericles and his epic models Nestor and Antenor—and at the same time, their particular linkage with Aesop is just as skillfully elided by Alcibiades' claim that Socrates is unique, like no one else in his *atopia*. This elision of Aesop (in many ways so like the *Phaedo*'s ambivalent treatment of the fable-maker) points us to a significant difference between Aesop's positive act of

---

[39] So, in a sense, this passage in the *Symposium* is comparable to Hdt. 1.27, in that it takes over elements that characterize Aesopic discourse, but represses Aesop and transfers his characteristics to another speaker. If I am correct in seeing the strains of a competition in *sophia* here, staged between Pericles and Socrates and their legendary congeners Nestor/Antenor and Aesop, respectively, we might compare this passage in the *Symposium* to the *Gorgias*, wherein Socrates condemns the "Great Four" statesmen (including Pericles) as mere flatterers of the demos, and claims to be the one and only Athenian who practices "the true political art" (τῇ ὡς ἀληθῶς πολιτικῇ τέχνῃ, *Gorg.* 521d7). But in contrast to the *Gorgias*, this constitutes only a minor theme of the *Symposium*.

implicit advising via fable and Socrates' use of analogy. For the latter, as Richard Robinson observes, always aims at a universal, even when it moves entirely from particular to particular; whereas Aesop's consequential political advising through fables aims at one set of particulars through another.[40] Or, to use the terms of the texts: the *Life of Aesop* defiantly celebrates the unsettling fact that excellent wine comes in ugly jars, embracing that combination as a challenge to traditional high wisdom and its pristine, aristocratic god Apollo. In contrast, the Platonic portrayal of Socrates repeatedly offers us the rude container while assuring us that it is interested only in the universal and divine contents hidden within. This is deftly to shed the humble frame of Aesopic mimetic prose once it has served its purpose, "like the hide of a hubristic satyr."

The negative argument of the *elenchos*. The *elenchos* as practiced by Socrates, especially in the so-called early or aporetic dialogues of Plato, consists in "reducing some stated hypothesis to self-contradiction."[41] Specifically, Socrates repeatedly refutes an interlocutor's stated position through the elicitation by questioning of other premises the interlocutor holds true that eventually lead to a contradiction of the original statement. I am not thereby claiming that Socrates invented the elenctic method entirely on his own; scholars have recognized that he shares with the Sophists the method of dialectical question-and-answer aimed at exposing a self-contradiction within the position of the one questioned.[42] So, for example, in *Protagoras*, Socrates reminds Protagoras of the latter's claim that he himself excels at (and can teach others) both styles of dialectic—abundant long answer and the shortest of short answers (*Prot.* 334e4–35c1). Perhaps the best illustration of the Sophistic version of the elenctic method is Plato's dialogue *Euthydemus*, which represents the two Sophistic brothers Euthydemus and Dionysodorus taking on all comers, claiming that they can refute anyone on any topic through short question-and-answer. If we consider the workings of this method in the *Euthydemus*, it emerges as a fairly crude implement, a procrustean weapon designed for rapid-fire dialogue in which the interlocutor is not permitted to include any qualifications or nuances in his answer.[43] The result of these strict rules and limitations is that all claims and premises are reduced equally and indiscriminately to absurd contradictions or paradoxes, whatever their starting point and whoever the speaker.

[40] Robinson 1953.207.

[41] Brickhouse and Smith 2000.76. For the classic treatment of the Socratic *elenchos*, see Robinson 1953.7–32; for more recent discussions, see Kahn 1983.75–121, 1996.133–42; Frede 1992; Vlastos 1994.1–37; Clay 2000.179–89.

[42] Thus Nehamas 1990.5–6; Mann 2006.

[43] I have found Erler 1986 particularly helpful in understanding the ground rules and protocols of argument in *Euthydemus*. And of course this is not to deny that the representation of Sophistic elenctic in the *Euthydemus* is sharply comic and parodic on Plato's part, as many scholars have noted; see Clay 2000.181, Blondell 2002.119–22, Worman 2008.208–11.

In contrast to this rapid-fire cut-and-thrust of argument, Socrates' version of the *elenchos* feels like a marathon in contrast to a sprint. What precisely differentiates Socrates' elenctic method from that of his contemporary Sophists is a complex question and one still hotly debated within ancient philosophy. This is not a topic I want to take on here, except to point to one particular quality of the Socratic *elenchos* that seems to differentiate it significantly from the Sophistic version: Socrates' *elenchos* is tailored to the interlocutor, and this is what makes it longer, slower, but in the end a finer-grained and more powerful argumentative tool. Socrates adapts the *elenchos* to individual interlocutors—to their positions, situations, and the social pressures under which they labor in public debate. It is this peculiar Socratic adaptation I would like to compare to the distinctive style of Aesopic verbal skill I've identified in the *Life*, whereby Aesop deftly manipulates the will and self-conception of a more powerful interlocutor to compel him to "bear witness against himself" in a form of self-incrimination. I would suggest that the Socratic *elenchos*, while rationalized and technologized, is a kindred form to Aesop's art of self-incrimination (and perhaps adapted by Socrates—or Plato—from this popular figure). The Aesopic quality of Socrates' version becomes easier to see when we recognize that the *elenchos* is not a purely logical form; as practiced by Socrates, it is very much ad hominem. One way this manifests itself is that the additional premises introduced to lead to self-contradiction must win *the interlocutor's* assent, but there is no evidence that Socrates himself is committed to their truth value. (Indeed, at times Socrates seems to use as premises positions he rejects in other dialogues, and some of the arguments used in refutations are patently weak and fallacious.)[44] But the "personal nature of the *elenchos*" goes even further; for, as Charles Kahn has compellingly argued for the *Gorgias*, Socrates' refutation of all three speakers (Gorgias, Polus, and Callicles) turns not on a contradiction between two logical positions simultaneously espoused by each interlocutor, but on a contradiction between a rational position and a form of moral or social pressure exerted on each speaker differently in the particular context of discussion. It is worth summarizing Kahn's arguments briefly, since the *Gorgias* is a veritable Platonic textbook on the nature and workings of the *elenchos*:[45]

[44] The clearest formulations of the ad hominem nature of the *elenchos* are Robinson 1953.15–17; Kahn 1983, 1996.97–98, 110–13, 133–42. Cf. Blundell 1992.131–72, Blondell 2002.113–64, Frede 1992.211–12. Nussbaum 2001.128–29 intriguingly suggests that Plato's representation of Socratic *elenchos* derives from the testing and "cross-examination" of the "ill-sorted beliefs" of characters—and via them, spectators—in Greek tragedy. But notice that Nussbaum's identification of *elenchos* in tragedy is more or less metaphorical, since it is normally the workings of the tragic plot itself, rather than those of a single individual character, that expose another character's confused beliefs, while tragedy does not offer the specific imagery of "bearing witness against oneself" that the *Life of Aesop* and Socratic dialogue share (see below).

[45] I take the phrase "personal nature of the *elenchos*" from Robinson 1953.15; cf. Kahn 1983.75. As Robinson notes in the same context, the *Gorgias* "contains the root ἐλεγχ- over fifty times in its eighty pages" and effectively reveals the personal nature of the Socratic *elenchos*.

a. Gorgias first asserts the value-neutral quality of education in rhetoric (when he claims that teachers of rhetoric should not be blamed or punished for the unjust uses of rhetorical skill by their students), but is then entrapped by Socrates into claiming that, if necessary, he does teach virtue to those who study rhetoric with him. As Kahn notes,

> The curious point, which Polus emphasizes, is that Gorgias is obliged ('out of shame') to make an *insincere* response, since there is good reason to suppose that Gorgias in fact did not propose to teach virtue, and made fun of those who claimed to do so. If Gorgias had answered sincerely, he would have said he did not make his students good men but only effective speakers (*deinoi legein*), and there would have been no direct contradiction with his earlier plea of non-responsibility.... So the refutation of Gorgias is *ad hominem* in a subtler sense: it follows not from his real beliefs but from a claim to teach morality *that he is forced to make because of his position in the public eye*.[46]

b. Polus, Gorgias's younger understudy, is forced by Socrates to contradict his original assertion that "suffering injustice is worse than doing injustice" because he feels obliged to parrot the common opinion that "doing injustice is more shameful." Just like Gorgias (as Callicles notes in turn), Polus is pressured into a self-contradictory position by his sense of shame. Here also, however, this concession is not random, but conforms to Polus's character as represented throughout the dialogue, his social status, and his aspirations. To quote Kahn again, as "an apprentice sophist," he is and needs to be "the faithful mirror of public opinion."[47]

c. Callicles is, in a sense, the most formidable interlocutor because he insists that he will not succumb to the pressure of convention or shame in espousing a strong theory of natural justice. But in the end, he is confounded by the contradiction between his heroic model of the "stronger" as those who are most intelligent and courageous, and his insistence that pleasure is the good (without any discrimination or means of hierarchizing pleasures). Socrates skillfully pries open the implicit rift between Callicles' elitist model of natural justice (rule of "the best") and his egalitarian hedonism by again playing on Callicles' sense of shame. For he conjures the two human types best calculated to offend Callicles' aristocratic, heroic values—the *kinaidos* and the coward—and forces Callicles to acknowledge that, if pleasure is the good, these two represent the height of human blessedness.[48]

---

[46] Kahn 1983.80 (my emphasis on the last phrase); cf. 1983.83: "Given the vulnerability of Gorgias' situation in Athens, he has no choice but to answer as he does."

[47] Kahn 1983.94.

[48] Kahn 1983.97–110. For the *kinaidos* as an abjected "scare figure" within the system of Athenian masculinity, see Winkler 1990.45–70. For the parallel with Aesop, it is worth noting how Socrates here deploys the intrusion of the body against the proud aristocrat Callicles (first through the example of itching and scratching, then through the example of the pleasure of the *kinaidos* as the

Thus, just like Aesop, Socrates uses against each of these speakers their self-conception, vanity, and concern for public appearance as leverage to extort from them public self-contradiction and humiliation. We might compare Socrates' entrapment of these three to Aesop's skillful maneuvering of Xanthus onto the public stage of the Samian Assembly, where the philosopher is forced to give Aesop his freedom so as not to appear petty and greedy before the assembled people (*Vita* G, ch. 90, discussed above, chapter 4, section IV).[49]

In light of these parallels, it is worth noting Socrates' explicit statement in the *Gorgias* of how his *elenchos* differs from the common *elenchos* of the Athenian courts. In response to Polus's repeated appeal to general public opinion, Socrates observes that in the courts, one side believes it has refuted the other (δοκοῦσιν ἐλέγχειν) when it furnishes many distinguished witnesses for its claims, while the opposite side can furnish only one witness or none (*Gorg.* 471e2–7). In contrast, Socrates practices a different kind of *elenchos*:

> ἐγὼ δὲ ἂν μὴ σὲ αὐτὸν ἕνα ὄντα μάρτυρα παράσχωμαι ὁμολογοῦντα περὶ ὧν λέγω, οὐδὲν οἶμαι ἄξιον λόγου μοι πεπεράνθαι περὶ ὧν ἂν ἡμῖν ὁ λόγος ᾖ· οἶμαι δὲ οὐδὲ σοί, ἐὰν μὴ ἐγώ σοι μαρτυρῶ εἷς ὢν μόνος, τοὺς δ᾽ ἄλλους πάντας τούτους χαίρειν ἐᾷς.

> But I—if I do not furnish you yourself as the sole witness agreeing concerning what things I say—I think I have accomplished nothing worthy of report concerning the things we're discussing. And I think it's the same for you, if I don't serve as the one and only witness for your position, and you let all these other [witnesses] go. (*Gorg.* 472b6–c1)

Socrates thus defines the essence of his *elenchos* as compelling one person—one's interlocutor or opponent in argument—to bear witness for one's own position and against himself. This formulation, using the imagery of witnessing, bears an uncanny resemblance to what I noted as a leitmotif in the *Life of Aesop*—Aesop's extorting the assent or acquiescence of the stronger by forcing them *to bear witness against themselves*.[50]

---

logical end point of the former). Thus we might say that Callicles is defeated (in proper Aesopic fashion) by the collusion of *elenchos* and analogy drawn from the lower bodily strata.

[49] On Socrates specifically playing on his interlocutor's vanity, cf. Blondell 2002.119; for a reading of *Hipp. Min.* along similar lines, see Blondell 2002.113–64.

[50] See discussion in chapter 4, section IV above. We might note that, as represented in Plato's *Apology*, Socrates, on trial for his life, calls to witness "the god in Delphi" (μάρτυρα ὑμῖν παρέξομαι τὸν θεὸν τὸν ἐν Δελφοῖς, *Apol.* 20e7–8) and strikingly, although he mentions "the god" twenty-three times throughout the *Apology*, never names him as Apollo (on this, see Reeve 2000). Both the avoidance of the god's name and the protagonist's calling him to witness at the end of his life parallel distinctive features of the *Life of Aesop* (as discussed above, chapters 1 and 4); cf. the end of *Vita* G—Aesop, about to be executed in Delphi, calls to witness "the overseer of the Muses" how he is unjustly executed (ch. 142). Clay 2000.95 notes the odd periphrasis Socrates uses for Apollo instead of naming the god here at *Apol.* 20e; he connects it with Heraclitus 22 B 93 DK.

344   CHAPTER 9

It is no accident, I think, that both Socrates' analogies and his use of *elenchos* tend to look most Aesopic when he is implicitly or explicitly contending with professional "practitioners of *sophia*"—the rhetors and political counselors of Alcibiades' speech in the *Symposium*; the Sophists and Sophists-in-training who lay claim to traditional wisdom in the *Gorgias*. In these contexts of competition against self-proclaimed masters of *sophia*, Socrates' analogies can become aggressively common and bodily (recall the itching, *kinaidos,* and χαραδριός of the *Gorgias*); his *elenchos* edged with the manipulation of public shame, as he deploys all Aesop's demystifying and debunking tricks.[51]

III. Sympotic Wisdom, Comedy, and Aesopic Competition in *Hippias Major*

Having traced out these correspondences between Socrates and Aesop through a piecemeal consideration of a few different dialogues, I would like now to consider the workings of the Aesopic through a more sustained reading of a single Platonic text. I choose for this exercise the *Hippias Major* (henceforth simply *Hippias*). For Socrates' competitive relation to professional practitioners of *sophia* and the Aesopic edge it gives his arguments are nowhere clearer than in this little dialogue. Indeed, the *Hippias* is perhaps the cruelest—and funniest—of all the Socratic dialogues of the Thrasyllan canon, and, for these very reasons, its authenticity was called into question by nineteenth-century (mainly German) scholars who found its "rude levity" and "satiric style" unworthy of Plato. Paul Woodruff in 1982 argued vigorously for the presumption of authenticity and, more importantly, offered a coherent and compelling philosophical and literary interpretation of the text. My reading will build on his but will focus on the elements of prephilosophical *sophia* that permeate Hippias's discourse and that provoke Socrates' Aesopic ripostes.[52]

The dialogue begins with Socrates hailing Hippias and observing that it's been a long time since he visited Athens. Hippias responds that he has been kept busy by his home city of Elis, which is constantly sending him on diplomatic missions, especially to Sparta, where he has also frequently made public performances of his wisdom. Socrates inquires into the sort of thing he performs in Sparta, and this leads eventually to Socrates' asking Hippias to help him against an anonymous heckling questioner who has reduced him to *aporia* by demanding a definition of "the fine" (τὸ καλόν). Hippias responds with three examples

---

[51] Cf. Worman 2008.163–65, making a similar point about the prevalence of "iambic" elements in the dialogues that stage Socrates' confrontation with various Sophists. In addition, Worman usefully suggests that Plato deploys somewhat different tactics and treatment for different generations of Sophists within the dialogues.

[52] I draw the quotations in this paragraph from Woodruff 1982a.94. For the older scholarly position against authenticity, see summary in Tarrant 1928.ix–xvii and Woodruff 1982a.93–106.

of "fine things," each of which Socrates (in the guise of the relentless anonymous questioner) reduces to nonsense by elenctic examination and absurd counterexamples, since they are not definitions of *the* fine, that by which all fine things are fine. About halfway through, Socrates himself takes over and attempts several "proper definitions" of the fine, each of which he then refutes, so that the dialogue ends with Hippias in disgust at the anonymous questioner and Socrates in melancholy *aporia*. My focus will be mainly the first half of the dialogue, rather than Socrates' more philosophical attempts at definition in the second half.

Those scholars who have denied the Platonic authorship of the dialogue cite several elements that are unique to this text within the Platonic corpus: (1) Socrates' thinly veiled disguise as the aggressive anonymous questioner, which is maintained throughout most of the dialogue; (2) a very large number of Platonic *hapax legomena*—words and phrases that seem either comic and colloquial or lofty poeticisms. Finally, these scholars claim that the crudeness of the portrait of Hippias is un-Platonic; how, they ask, can the successful Sophist Hippias be represented as so monumentally stupid as to fail to understand Socrates' request for a definition of "the fine itself," rather than just examples of "fine things," and how can Hippias fail to realize that the anonymous questioner is, in fact, Socrates himself?[53] The great advantage of Woodruff's interpretation is that he addresses all of these issues in a philosophically and psychologically nuanced reading of the interaction of Hippias and Socrates. On Woodruff's reading, Hippias is not at all stupid, but he is (appropriately enough for a seasoned ambassador) a courtly and polite master of forging agreement, and therefore temperamentally inclined to agree with all Socrates' proposals, no matter how absurd they seem. Hippias is, furthermore, perfectly well aware that Socrates is the anonymous questioner, but cooperates with Socrates in maintaining the fiction—a fiction that suits both of them, since it obviates the need for Socrates to insult the Sophist directly, while it allows Hippias to save face and continue the discussion reasonably amicably. At the same time, Woodruff contends, it is not the case that Hippias fails to understand what Socrates is asking for (although Socrates' notion of "proper definition" must have appeared odd and idiosyncratic to his contemporaries); Hippias simply refuses to play Socrates' game and, in fact, never acknowledges that there is anything wrong or inadequate about the examples he offers.[54] Finally Woodruff argues that the dialogue is strongly influenced by comedy—specifically the parodic lambasting of a vain and self-important character by the comic hero (he cites the example of the competitive mockery of the *miles gloriosus* Lamachus by Dicaeopolis at the end of Aristophanes' *Acharnians*). It is this pervasive comic cast that accounts

---

[53] For the stupidity and vanity of Hippias as portrayed in the dialogue, see (e.g.) Tarrant 1928. xxviii–xxx.

[54] Woodruff 1982a.107–12, 123–60. Since, as Woodruff points out, Hippias is not aiming at a complete, exclusive definition of τὸ καλόν, his answers are perfectly successful on their own terms.

346   CHAPTER 9

for the unusual language and style of the *Hippias*, which parodically echoes the historical Hippias's bombastic and ornate poeticizing style and deliberately juxtaposes it to the coarse colloquial idiom of comedy.[55]

While I agree with the main lines of Woodruff's interpretation, I want to focus specifically on the sources and positive content of Hippias's examples of fine things (which have elicited almost no commentary from the philosophically minded scholars who tend to write on the *Hippias*). For these examples and many other features in the characterization of Hippias affiliate him strongly with a prephilosophical sympotic tradition of *sophia* that embraces didactic poetry and lore of the Seven Sages, especially Solon. Hippias's Solonian profile in turn suggests that the nearest model for his almost-slapstick exchanges with Socrates here is the pair philosopher-sage and Aesop, as instantiated in comedy but also in other forms of the common or little tradition.

To set the stage, we should note that the dialogue begins by conjuring up familiar figures of the Seven Sages, whom Socrates compares unfavorably to Hippias himself:

> That is what it is like to be truly wise, Hippias, a man of complete accomplishments: in private you are able to make a lot of money from young people (and to give still greater benefits to those from whom you take it); while in public you are able to provide your own city with good service (as is proper for one who expects not to be despised, but admired by ordinary people). But Hippias, how in the world do you explain this: in the old days people who are still famous for wisdom—Pittacus and Bias and the school of Thales of Miletus, and later ones down to Anaxagoras—that all or most of those people, we see, kept away from affairs of state? (*Hipp. Mai.* 281b5–c8, trans. Woodruff 1982a)[56]

Scholars have noted the patent absurdity of Socrates' assertion that these Sages had nothing to do with political affairs, while Woodruff adds that this whole first section of the dialogue represents a hilarious Socratic parody of characteristic Sophistic claims about technological and scientific progress.[57] But the individual Sages named here also importantly supply the context in which we are meant to read Hippias's wisdom performances throughout the dialogue.[58] For

---

[55] Woodruff 1982a.99–101; cf. Brock 1990.49, who points out that the pervasive comic echoes in *Hipp. Mai.* are, if anything, an argument *for* Platonic authenticity. On the comic or "iambic" qualities of the dialogue, see also Worman 2008.201–4.

[56] I will throughout use Woodruff's translation, except where I must modify it slightly to bring out a different nuance.

[57] For the absurdity of Socrates' claim about the Sages' noninvolvement in politics, see Woodruff 1982a.37, 102, 128; cf. Nightingale 2004.23n. 52, Tell 2010, ch.1. For this as a riff on Sophistic theories of human progress, see Woodruff 1982a.36–37; the joke here, as Woodruff notes, is that "progress" is represented in Socrates' account by Hippias's proper appreciation of the value of money.

[58] In like manner, Socrates makes a point of naming Solon himself early on, when he jocularly observes to Hippias that it's a lucky thing that the Spartans don't want to hear a list of Athenian archons "from Solon on" (*Hipp. Mai.* 285e3–6). Socrates' mention of the native Athenian Sage as

the *content* of Hippias's wisdom is entirely traditional, drawing on lore of the Seven Sages, sympotic τί μάλιστα games, and didactic poetry, even as its *form* of highly poeticized artful prose is innovative. The text makes all this clear to us already when Hippias boasts of the *logos* he recently performed in Sparta, for this is a recasting in prose of the traditional poetic genre of mythological *hypothēkai*. As Hippias describes it, after the sack of Troy, Nestor advises Neoptolemus on "fine practices for a young man" (*Hipp. Mai.* 286a3–b4; notice especially ὑποτιθέμενος, a programmatic term for this genre).[59]

After that preamble, Socrates launches into his question for Hippias: "The fine itself, what is it?" (αὐτὸ τὸ καλὸν ὅτι ἐστί, 286d8–e1; repeated at 287d3 as τί ἐστι τοῦτο τὸ καλόν;). Hippias's first response (which he confidently claims no one will refute "since all who hear will bear witness that you speak rightly") is παρθένος καλὴ καλόν ("a fine girl is a fine thing," 287e4). In the guise of the anonymous questioner, Socrates first ridicules this as an inadequate definition of τὸ καλόν—that by which *all* fine things are fine—and proves this by offering several other examples of "fine things." Hippias is perfectly happy to assent to Socrates' first two examples: "Isn't a fine mare a fine thing?" (θήλεια δὲ ἵππος καλὴ οὐ καλόν, 288b8–9), and "What about a fine lyre? Isn't it a fine thing?" (τί δὲ λύρα καλή; οὐ καλόν;, 288c6). This cluster of καλά reveals the traditional milieu from which Hippias has drawn his answer, for all three resonate with terms found in the Attic scolia and the sympotic elegies of Theognis and Solon. That is, Hippias chooses to understand Socrates' question of definition as an invitation to play the sympotic game of τί μάλιστα; or τί καλόν;—the evaluative ranking of different particular goods in a context of playful competition, which, in the tradition, is strongly associated with the Seven Sages.[60] Thus compare Hippias's and Socrates' exchange here to a pair of Attic scolia preserved by Athenaeus (*Deipnosophistae* 15.695c–d = *Carmina Convivialia* 900, 901 *PMG*), miniature meditations on what is καλόν and what one would wish for:[61]

---

archon implicitly gives the lie to his earlier claim that the sages of old didn't involve themselves in political affairs, but I would contend that the naming of Solon has a broader purpose, signaling his pervasive presence as traditional sage and role model for Hippias throughout the dialogue.

[59] For *hypothēkai* in general, see Friedländer 1913, Martin 1984; for mythological *hypothēkai* in particular, with collected examples, see Kurke 1990.104–7. For Hippias's Trojan *logos* within the context of traditional advice poetry, see also Gray 1998.165 and Blondell 2002.128–34, who links it with conventional educational uses of Homeric epic.

[60] On τί μάλιστα; as a form of wisdom particularly connected with the Seven Sages, see Iambl. *VP* 83, a passage that Burkert 1972.166–70 traces back to Aristotle's treatise on the Pythagoreans; cf. Konstantakos 2004.97, 126–27, 2005.20–21. On τί μάλιστα; as a traditional sympotic form, cf. Burnett 1983.281; for a parallel, cf. Plut. *Banq.* chs. 8–9, 152f–153d.

[61] These are two of the twenty-five Attic scolia (or drinking songs) Athenaeus transmits, which have been taken as relics of archaic sympotic culture. Thus Reitzenstein 1893.13–17 argues that Athenaeus's compilation is based on a collection that was already constituted by the mid-fifth century BCE, with many of the individual poems dating back to the archaic period. On the Attic scolia in general, see also Collins 2004.84–134 (with pp. 122–26 on this pair of distiches in particular).

> εἴθε λύρα καλὴ γενοίμην ἐλεφαντίνη
> καί με καλοὶ παῖδες φέροιεν Διονύσιον ἐς χορόν.
>
> εἴθ' ἄπυρον καλὸν γενοίμην μέγα χρυσίον
> καί με καλὴ γυνὴ φοροίη καθαρὸν θεμένη νόον.
>
> I wish I were a beautiful ivory lyre, and [I wish that] beautiful boys would carry me to the Dionysiac dance.
>
> I wish I were a big, beautiful, unsmelted golden ornament, and [I wish that] a beautiful woman would wear me—a woman who had made her mind pure.

The repeated εἴθε ... γενοίμην and the perfect balancing of terms (ivory and gold, beautiful boys and a beautiful woman) make clear that these two distiches are meant to be a competitive sympotic dialogue, with each repeating forms of the adjective καλός twice in two lines. Hippias's παρθένος καλή corresponds to the second scolion's καλὴ γυνή.

That Socrates knows very well what game Hippias is playing is registered by his second counterexample, λύρα καλή, which opposes Hippias's sympotic reference with an exact quotation from the other scolion of the pair. At the same time, Socrates' first counterexample, ἵππος καλή, adds other sympotic terms to the mix. Thus the segue from a "beautiful maiden" to a "beautiful mare" makes perfect sense in the eroticized context of the symposium, evoking something like Anacreon's "Thracian filly" poem (417 *PMG*). But ἵππος καλή is also a near quotation of the beginning of a Theognidean riddle (Thgn. 257–60) and, more significantly, evokes an elegiac couplet attributed both to Theognis and to Solon (Thgn 1253–54 = Solon fr. 23 W):[62]

> ὄλβιος, ᾧ παῖδές τε φίλοι καὶ μώνυχες ἵπποι
> καὶ κύνες ἀγρευταὶ καὶ ξένος ἀλλοδαπός
>
> Blessed is he who has dear sons and single-hoofed horses and hunting dogs and a guest-friend in a foreign land.

This couplet, too, participates in the same sympotic debate over what is best, since it asserts that it is the possesion of certain καλά (sons, horses, hunting dogs, a foreign guest-friend) that makes a man ὄλβιος.

Hippias's second response continues the game. Socrates presses him, "Do you *still* think that the fine itself by which everything else is beautified and seen to be fine when that form is added to it—that *that* is a girl or a horse or a lyre?" (ᾧ καὶ τἆλλα πάντα κοσμεῖται καὶ καλὰ φαίνεται, ἐπειδὰν προσγένηται ἐκεῖνο τὸ εἶδος, τοῦτ' εἶναι παρθένος ἢ ἵππος ἢ λύρα;, 289d2–5). Hippias responds, entirely unfazed:

---

[62] Text here follows West's version of Solon fr. 23. Plato actually has Socrates quote this couplet in the *Lysis* (212de), so we know he was familiar with it.

But if *that's* what he's looking for, it's the easiest thing in the world to answer him and tell him what the fine (thing) is by which everything else is beautified and is seen to be fine when it is added. The man's quite simple; he has no feeling at all for fine possessions. If you answer him that this thing he's asking for, the fine, is just *gold* (τὸ καλὸν οὐδὲν ἄλλο ἢ χρυσός), he'll be stuck and won't try to refute you. (*Hipp. Mai.* 289d6–e4)

As scholars have noted, Hippias's answer takes literally Socrates' verbs κοσμεῖται and προσγένηται, thus deftly sidestepping the latter's request for the metaphysical "Form" (εἶδος) of "the fine itself."[63] But scholars have not appreciated how richly resonant within the sympotic context is Hippias's answer, "the beautiful is nothing other than gold" (τὸ καλὸν οὐδὲν ἄλλο ἢ χρυσός). Gold, of course, figures in the dueling distiches I quoted above—the "big, beautiful, unsmelted golden ornament" worn by the καλὴ γυνή in 901 *PMG*. Indeed, this context is again implicitly acknowledged by Socrates' first counterexample of the "ivory" used by Pheidias in preference to gold for the countenance, hands, and feet of Athena in his great chryselephantine statue (*Hipp. Mai.* 290b2–8). But we also know of a sympotic scolion that asserted that "all the rest is nothing, except gold" (οὐδὲν ἦν ἄρα τἄλλα πλὴν ὁ χρυσός, 910 *PMG*), attributed to Pythermus (a predecessor or contemporary of Hipponax)—again, presumably, as part of a τί μάλιστα game.[64]

For his third response, Hippias pulls out all the stops. Offering Socrates an answer that will put an end to all discussion and that no one can gainsay, he pronounces:

λέγω τοίνυν ἀεὶ καὶ παντὶ καὶ πανταχοῦ κάλλιστον εἶναι ἀνδρί, πλουτοῦντι, ὑγιαίνοντι, τιμωμένῳ ὑπὸ τῶν Ἑλλήνων, ἀφικομένῳ εἰς γῆρας, τοὺς αὑτοῦ γονέας τελευτήσαντας καλῶς περιστείλαντι, ὑπὸ τῶν αὑτοῦ ἐκγόνων καλῶς καὶ μεγαλοπρεπῶς ταφῆναι (*Hipp. Mai.* 291d9–e2)

I say, then, that it is always finest, both for every man and in every place, to be rich, healthy, and honored by the Greeks, to arrive at old age, to make a fine memorial to his parents when they die, and to have a fine, grand burial from his own children.

Hippias marks this response as his ultimate, climactic version (his own "priamel"?), for he uses not just καλόν, but the superlative κάλλιστον. And it is

---

[63] Thus Tarrant 1928.52, Woodruff 1982a.55–56. These scholars disagree on the degree to which Socrates' question here depends upon the fully worked-out theory of Forms articulated in the *Phaedo*, but this philosophical issue is irrelevant to my argument.

[64] On Pythermus's date, see Athenaeus 14.625c; and notice the similarity of syntax between Hippias's formulation and the preserved snippet of Pythermus's scolion. Cf. also the frequent occurrence of gold in poetic priamels of the "best things": e.g., Pindar O.1.1–3, N.8.37–9, Bacchylides 3.85–92. I would further contend that, in a sympotic context, Hippias's answer is not nearly as crassly materialistic and simpleminded as Socrates makes it out to be, for archaic sympotic poetry is, in general, obsessed with gold as a symbol for the purity and integrity of the noble self. On this elitist symbology of gold, see Kurke 1995, 1999.41–60.

indeed a masterful synthesis of traditional hierarchical rankings of what constitutes the good life, recast in artful rhythmic prose.[65] Thus we might compare Hippias's list of conditions to yet another Attic scolion:

ὑγιαίνειν μὲν ἄριστον ἀνδρὶ θνητῷ,
δεύτερον δὲ καλὸν φυὰν γενέσθαι,
τὸ τρίτον δὲ πλουτεῖν ἀδόλως,
καὶ τὸ τέταρτον ἡβᾶν μετὰ τῶν φίλων.
   (*Carmina Convivialia* 890 *PMG*)

To be healthy is the best thing for a mortal man, but second to be handsome. And third to be wealthy without trickery, and fourth to be young with friends.

That this is an entirely traditional set of terms, always available for scrambling and slightly different ranking, is revealed by a couplet in the Theognidea, which Aristotle informs us was inscribed on the temple of Apollo at Delos (Thgn. 255–56):[66]

κάλλιστον τὸ δικαιότατον· λῷστον δ' ὑγιαίνειν·
πρᾶγμα δὲ τερπνότατον, τοῦ τις ἐρᾷ, τὸ τυχεῖν.

The most just is the finest thing, but the best is to be healthy. And the sweetest thing is to gain whatever one desires.

But these poetic instances still do not provide all the terms of Hippias's consummate definition of what is "κάλλιστον for a man." For that, I would contend, we must turn to the lore of the Seven Sages, especially that of Solon. Recall that in Solon's famous encounter with Croesus, as narrated by Herodotus, the Sage's choice for "the most blessed man of all he's seen" is Tellus the Athenian. When asked by a deflated Croesus, Why Tellus?, Solon explains:

> On the one hand, with his city in good shape, Tellus had fine and noble sons, and he saw children born to all of them and all of them surviving; on the other hand, he was well supplied with property (by our standards) and the end of his life was very glorious (λαμπροτάτη). For when the Athenians were fighting a battle against their citizen-neighbors in Eleusis, he came to aid and, having routed the enemy, died most nobly (κάλλιστα), and the Athenians buried him there at public expense in the very spot where he fell, and honored him greatly (ἐτίμησαν μεγάλως). (Hdt. 1.30.3–5)

While there is some difference in emphasis, many elements here correspond to Hippias's list: wealth, achieving a certain age, children and grandchildren, honor from the Greeks, and magnificent burial.[67] Indeed, the only feature that

---

[65] For Hippias's penchant for artful sound effects here and throughout, see Woodruff 1982a.125–27, 132–33.

[66] See Arist. *NE* 1.9, 1099a25 (where it is termed τὸ Δηλιακὸν ἐπίγραμμα), *Eudemian Ethics* 1214a5. For another version, see Soph. fr. 356 Radt.

[67] The specific differences, I would contend, are due to Herodotus's interest in affiliating Tellus's "blessedness" as closely as possible with his Greek citizen status; thus Tellus receives honorific

finds no parallel in Solon's account is "making a fine memorial to his parents when they die"—the one element Socrates battens onto to refute Hippias's claim for the universal validity of his list by citing as counterexamples heroic children of gods like Achilles and Heracles.[68]

At this point, it is worth recalling the argument made in chapter 3, that behind Herodotus's familiar account of the meeting of Solon and Croesus there lurked a popular oral tradition that imagined all the Sages and Aesop gathered together at the Lydian dynast's court. Indeed, I suggested that Herodotus knew, but (for his own purposes) deliberately suppressed the tradition of a competition in high and low wisdom between Solon and Aesop, adjudicated by Croesus. Fragments of this popular tradition that preexisted Herodotus are preserved, I argued, in such late sources as Diodorus Siculus, Plutarch, and Zenobius commenting on the proverb "Rather the Phrygian."[69] If all this is correct, and if Hippias's crowning definition of what is "finest for a man" is (as I suspect) meant to recall the words of Solon in his paradigmatic encounter with Croesus, then Socrates' obnoxious anonymous questioner is clearly playing Aesop to Hippias's Solon.

Indeed, the text and texture of the dialogue itself support this reading, as Socrates' counterexamples and *elenchos* become progressively more déclassé and Aesopic in response to Hippias's invocation of traditional sympotic and Seven Sages lore. Thus, in order to debunk Hippias's first answer ("a fine girl is a fine thing"), Socrates, after briefly playing along with the sympotic game, abruptly shifts the register. The anonymous questioner, he asserts, will ask, "What about a fine pot? Isn't it a fine thing?" (τί δὲ χύτρα καλή; οὐ καλὸν ἄρα;, 288c10–11). We have seen the prevalent imagery of pots and other humble

---

burial (and perhaps hero cult) from the city rather than from his own descendants. For the markedly civic inflection of Solon's paradigms of the "good life" in Herodotus, see Kurke 1998.153–55, 1999.147–51. Tarrant 1928.57 oddly cites as a parallel Plutarch's abbreviated version of Solon's answer to Croesus (*Sol.* 27), but not Herodotus's account, which is clearly Plutarch's source. Tarrant also cites Isoc. *Evagoras* 71–72, although this passage does not correspond as closely (no mention of burial). For a poetic parallel that offers many of the same terms, see Pindar P.11.50–58.

[68] In fact, we find a parallel even for this idea a little later in Herodotus's account of Croesus. After the capture of Sardis, Croesus, himself now transformed into a sage by the purifying fire, observes gnomically to Cyrus, his conqueror: "No one is so foolish (ἀνόητος) as to prefer war to peace—for in peace, sons bury their fathers, but in war, fathers bury their sons" (Hdt. 1.87.4). Notice that this is another value judgment on what is the best sort of life, asserted through the proper temporal sequence of burial between the generations.

I would also note that there is nothing particularly Aesopic in Socrates' refutation of Hippias's third definition. We do, however, find a striking parallel for Socrates' impious suggestion that Zeus, as father to Heracles and other demigods, would have to be buried by Hippias's definition in the competitive wisdom context of the *Contest of Homer and Hesiod*; cf. *Contest* ll. 121–23, where one poet challenges the other by offering two hexameter lines that describe "collecting the white bones of Zeus dead," which the other must then complete with one more line to deflect that obvious—and impious—construal.

[69] See discussion chapter 3, sections I and II.

containers in the *Life of Aesop*; here Hippias himself marks the vertiginous shift in verbal register from ἵππος καλή and λύρα καλή to χύτρα καλή when he exclaims, "Who is the man, Socrates? What a boor he is to dare in an august proceeding to speak such vulgar speech that way!" (ὡς ἀπαίδευτός τις ὃς οὕτω φαῦλα ὀνόματα ὀνομάζειν τολμᾷ ἐν σεμνῷ πράγματι, 288d1–3).[70]

The same pattern is repeated after Hippias's second response ("the fine is nothing other than gold"), for here the anonymous questioner first counters with ivory and other precious materials, but then reverts to the shabby pot:

> "Then," he'll say, "when someone boils the pot we just mentioned, the fine one, full of fine pea soup, is a gold stirring spoon or a figwood one more appropriate?" (*Hipp. Mai.* 290d7–9)

Hippias again objects to the low and boorish subject matter, but Socrates, unperturbed, elaborates with a hilarious fantasy scenario worthy of Old Comedy:

> Which of the two spoons is appropriate to the soup and the pot? Isn't it clearly the wooden one? It makes the soup smell better, and at the same time, my friend, it won't break our pot, spill all the soup, put out the fire, and make us do without a truly noble meal, when we were going to have a banquet. That gold spoon would do all these things; so I think we should say the figwood spoon is more appropriate than the gold one, unless you say otherwise. (*Hipp. Mai.* 290e5–91a2)

In his argument, Socrates makes properly Aesopic use of ordinary objects that are ready to hand, debunking and exploding Hippias's sympotic and Solonian pretensions by the intrusion of pots, pea soup, and cooking mishaps.[71] At this point, provoked beyond endurance, Hippias simply refuses to converse with a person who would ask such things, and must be cajoled back into dialogue by Socrates.

But why does Hippias react so violently to the mention of ordinary objects? Woodruff, for example, in his commentary is somewhat baffled by the Sophist's explosions of indignation.[72] The key here, I would contend, is the perfect congruence presumed between stylistic and verbal register and the sociological

---

[70] Unsurprisingly, this is the only occurrence of χύτρα in all of Plato; the word is common in comedy (cf. Aristoph. *Acharnians* 284, *Birds* 43, *Peace* 923, *Thesmophoriazusae* 505, *Wealth* 1197); cf. Tarrant 1928.49. On the terms of Hippias's dismayed exclamation here, see Worman 2008.202–3.

[71] For the comic resonances of Socrates' formulation here, see Tarrant 1928.54–55, Brock 1990.44. While there is no exact parallel for Socrates' comic scenario in the *Life of Aesop*, this text is full of cooking mishaps of other kinds: e.g., Aesop deliberately cooks only a single lentil (ὁ φακός), to teach Xanthus about the proper use of mass nouns (*Vita* G, chs. 39–41); Aesop and Xanthus skirmish over the number of pig's trotters boiled in the soup (*Vita* G, chs. 42–43); and Aesop elaborately serves tongues as best and worst (*Vita* G, chs. 51–55, quoted in chapter 5, section 1C above).

[72] Thus Woodruff (1982a.53) on Hippias's strenuous objection to χύτρα καλή: "What is vulgar about the word *chytra*? Apparently, its only fault is that it refers to a household utensil. Gorgias, who

status of speaker and occasion within a culturally pervasive hierarchy of speech forms. This intimate identification or interimplication of style and sociopolitical status is in fact revealed by the various characterizations of the anonymous questioner: Socrates first introduces him by the assertion that he questions ὑβριστικῶς (286c8), while the scandalized Hippias describes him as ἀπαίδευτος (288d1) and ἀμαθής (290e3), and as having "no feeling for fine possessions" (οὐδὲν ἐπαΐει περὶ καλῶν κτημάτων, 289e1–2). These are not merely intellectual failings, but register a lack of culture and of cultivation. Socrates in response confirms Hippias's status-conscious disdain for the anonymous questioner and even carries it further, for he repeatedly associates the imaginary interlocutor with the imagery of dirt or filth. Thus Socrates responds to Hippias's first objection about the use of φαῦλα ὀνόματα, "He's like that, Hippias, not refined. He's garbage (οὐ κομψὸς ἀλλὰ συρφετός), he cares about nothing but the truth" (288d4–5). The use of συρφετός ("sweepings, refuse, garbage") here is distinctly odd, as commentators have noted; elsewhere in Plato it refers to the low-class mob or rabble, but never otherwise to an individual.[73] Socrates continues and elaborates this imagery further in reaction to Hippias's refusal to engage a speaker who would talk about pots, pea soup, and ladles:

> Right you are. It wouldn't be appropriate for you to be filled up (ἀναπίμπλασθαι), when you're so finely dressed, finely shod, and famous for wisdom all over Greece. But it's nothing much for me to mix with him (ἀλλ' ἐμοὶ οὐδὲν πρᾶγμα φύρεσθαι πρὸς τὸν ἄνθρωπον). So help me get prepared. Answer for my sake. (*Hipp. Mai.* 291a5–b2)

Both ἀναπίμπλασθαι and especially φύρεσθαι here carry the implication not just of mixture, but of "defilement" or "infection," the dirtying or tainting of Hippias, in all his self-made finery, with the low-class filth of the anonymous questioner.[74] As a parallel, it is worth noting how frequently in the *Life* Aesop is described or abused in the language of dirt and filth: he is introduced as κακοπινής ("exceedingly filthy," *Vita* G, chs. 1, 16), and repeatedly reviled as ἀπόμαγμα ("dirt wiped off," *Vita* G, ch. 14), κάθαρμα, and περικάθαρμα ("off-scourings," *Vita* G, chs. 30, 31, 69).

---

probably influenced Hippias, was given to noble-sounding euphemisms . . . , and no doubt would have used a more elegant example."

[73] For the anomalous usage here, see Tarrant 1928.lxxx, 50 and Woodruff 1982a.53, 99. Cf. the use of the word for a mob at *Tht.* 152c and *Gorg.* 489c; in the latter passage, Callicles' disdainful dismissal of the many as "refuse of slaves" (συρφετὸς . . . δούλων) makes particularly clear the sociological implications of the term.

[74] For the negative connotations of both verbs (esp. φύρω), see LSJ s.vv.; for ἀναπίμπλασθαι designating contamination or infection, see Tarrant 1928.55. Woodruff 1982a.58 takes φύρεσθαι to be a "metaphor from cooking," but, following on συρφετός, I think it more likely to mean "mixing with dirt or filth." If this is correct, we might also understand Socrates' statement that "It's no matter for me to mix with him" as a metaliterary characterization of the Aesopic or low element "mixed into" Socratic dialogue in general.

We see the same fraught alignment of verbal style and social status in the dialogue, in the ways in which argumentative dueling progressively morphs into the threat of physical beating. Throughout the first half, Hippias suggests repeatedly that the aim in answering is to discredit and publicly humiliate the anonymous questioner—to make him καταγέλαστος, "laughable" or "ridiculous." Socrates picks up this language of dueling public ridicule from Hippias, but suggests that *they* will be shown to be ridiculous by the indefatigable *elenchos* of the anonymous questioner.[75] Finally, at a climactic point after Hippias's triumphant third response, Socrates asserts that the imaginary interlocutor will no longer be content just with mockery and laughter:

> Soc: If he happens to have a stick (βακτηρίαν), and I don't run and run away from him, he'll try to give me a thrashing.
> Hipp: What? Is the man your owner or something? (δεσπότης τίς σου ὁ ἄνθρωπός ἐστιν;) Do you mean he could do that and not be arrested and convicted? Or don't you have any laws in this city, but people are allowed to hit each other without any right? (*Hipp. Mai.* 292a6–b2)

In response to Hippias's query about Athenian law, Socrates confirms that a citizen is legally liable for the unjust beating of another, but comments meekly that in this case, the beating is deserved. Woodruff notes that the prospect of beating another citizen with impunity conjures up the fantasy satisfactions of Old Comedy, while Socrates' suggestion here also recalls Odysseus's beating of Thersites with the scepter of Agamemnon in *Iliad* 2.[76] These parallels are certainly apposite, but they are not merely literary echoes. For, as Hippias's question emphasizes, beating another aggressively asserts his abjected social status in relation to the one who wields the stick. Thus recall that, in *Iliad* 2, Odysseus verbally coaxes and reasons with the other leaders to check their wholesale flight to the ships, but uses the scepter as a weapon only to thrash the uppity commoner Thersites. Likewise, even to lay a hand on a fellow citizen in Athens (much less to beat him) incurs the charge of hubris, the arrogant assertion of one's superiority or, as Demosthenes tersely formulates it, "treating free men as if they were slaves" (Dem. 21.180; cf. 21.185). Thus the threat of a beating vividly exposes

---

[75] For Hippias's suggestion that the anonymous questioner will be made "laughable" or "ridiculous," see *Hipp. Mai.* 288b, 290a, 292a; for Socrates' response that it is in fact he and/or Hippias who will be "laughingstocks," see *Hipp. Mai.* 286e, 289c, 291e–92a, 293c, 297d, 299a, and, on the sheer frequency of the threat of public laughter and humiliation in this dialogue, see Worman 2008.202 with n. 153. Cf. *Life of Aesop* chs. 35–37 (the encounter with the market-gardener, discussed in detail in chapter 4, section I above). In particular, notice the exchange between Aesop and Xanthus when Xanthus has offered a completely banal and lame explanation for the market-gardener's problem, saying "all things are governed by divine forethought": "And Aesop, standing behind Xanthus, laughed. Xanthus says, 'Are you laughing, or are you laughing at me?' (γελᾷς ἢ καταγελᾷς;). Aesop said, 'Not at *you*.' Xanthus said, 'At who then?' Aesop said, 'At the master who taught you.'"

[76] Woodruff 1982a.60, noting "that Socrates was notorious in democratic Athens for quoting the opening lines of this élitist passage from Homer" (= *Il.* 2.188–277); cf. Xen. *Mem.* 1.2.58.

the real-world status staked, lost, and won in the game of words. And yet, oddly, Socrates' beating fantasy inverts the expected alignment of verbal style and social status, as we can see by comparison of the *Hippias* passage with an anecdote told about Gorgias that instates the "proper" analogy between low-class discourse and abjected status. As Philostratus tells it in his *Lives of the Sophists*:

> ἦν γάρ τις Χαιρεφῶν Ἀθήνησιν . . . οὗτος ὁ Χαιρεφῶν τὴν σπουδὴν τοῦ Γοργίου διαμασώμενος· 'διὰ τί,' ἔφη, 'ὦ Γοργία, οἱ κύαμοι τὴν μὲν γαστέρα φυσῶσι, τὸ δὲ πῦρ οὐ φυσῶσι;' ὁ δὲ οὐδὲν ταραχθεὶς ὑπὸ τοῦ ἐρωτήματος, 'τουτὶ μέν,' ἔφη, 'σοὶ καταλείπω σκοπεῖν, ἐγὼ δὲ ἐκεῖνο πάλαι οἶδα, ὅτι ἡ γῆ τοὺς νάρθηκας ἐπὶ τοὺς τοιούτους φύει.' (Phil. *VS* 1.483 = Gorgias 82 A 24 DK)

> And there was in Athens a certain Chaerephon . . . and this Chaerephon carping at [lit., chewing up] Gorgias's seriousness, said, "Why is it, O Gorgias, that beans swell up the belly, but don't put out the fire?"[77] And Gorgias, not at all perturbed by the question, answered, "I'll leave it to you to consider this. But I have known the following for a long time—that the earth bears canes for such men as you."

Here it is Chaerephon's vulgar query about the gaseous effects of beans that provokes and justifies Gorgias's shift from the register of dialogue to the threat of a caning (no matter how jocularly the threat is intended).

And with the inversion of terms (who will beat whom), we get back to Aesop. Notice Hippias's first baffled question, which finds no parallel in the *Iliad* or Old Comedy: "Is he some kind of master to you?" (δεσπότης τίς σου ὁ ἄνθρωπός ἐστιν;).[78] To be sure, the specter of the slave's beating (or more vividly, "flaying," δέρεσθαι) haunts practically every chapter of the *Life of Aesop*, but the *Life* also provides us with a parallel for the role reversal of slave and master. Recall the rueful response of Xanthus when Aesop cross-examines him about urinating while walking, "I hadn't realized I'd bought a master for myself" (ἠγνόουν ἑαυτοῦ δεσπότην πριάμενος, *Vita* G, ch. 28; discussed in chapter 5, section IA above).[79]

But we should also note that this prospect of the "hubristic" interlocutor beating Socrates strangely doubles the roles of befuddled philosopher-sage and Aesopic provocateur. For much of the dialogue, Hippias plays the former and Socrates the latter, but this moment of fantasized beating suggests that somewhere offstage (as it were)—"at home," as Socrates puts it at the end of the dialogue—Socrates himself plays the dimwitted philosopher master constantly

---

[77] There's a pun here on φυσάω that is untranslatable in English, since the verb means both "to swell" or "cause to swell" and "to quench" or "put out" a fire.

[78] For the meaning of τις in this sense, see Tarrant 1928.58.

[79] Xanthus's rueful response here is usually taken to be a borrowing from traditions about Diogenes the Cynic; cf. D.L. 6.29–30, 36 (where Diogenes' new master says the same thing) and see discussion by Adrados 1979, 1999.678; Jedrkiewicz 1989.117–18; Jouanno 2006.21. I am thus suggesting that the role reversal between master and slave might be still older in the Aesop tradition, so as to be familiar to readers of *Hippias* (and perhaps also to influence Cynic traditions?).

shown up by his Aesopic slave. And this doubling is important, both for the sustainability of the dialogue (in which Socrates can represent himself and Hippias as allies against the obnoxious questioner) and for Socrates' ultimate disavowal of the Aesopic "taint" at the dialogue's end.

It may be objected that there is no need to invoke an Aesopic model here; that all the elements I've considered are explicable as influences of comic drama (the parodic lambasting of an *alazōn* by an *eirōn*; the prominent mention of ordinary objects from everyday life; the imagery of filth and scapegoating; and the fantasy of beating an opponent with impunity). But in fact, I would contend, Aesop and comedy are not mutually exclusive alternatives, for it is highly likely that the contretemps of Aesop and his foolish sage master (perhaps Solon?) formed a staple of the comic stage. Thus we know of a play entitled *Aesop* by the fourth-century comic poet Alexis, whose only preserved fragment is a dialogue between Solon and a non-Athenian interlocutor (perhaps Aesop?) about Athenian sympotic practices. This is not to claim that the *Hippias* must allude to this specific comedy (which probably dates to the 350s), but rather to suggest that this was only one of many representations of a parodic competition in wisdom between sage and Aesop on the Athenian comic stage.[80] Such a comic model (or set of models) would ameliorate one weakness of Woodruff's interpretation; notice that the best parallel he can muster for the interaction of Hippias and Socrates from extant Old Comedy is the parodic deflation of the bombastic *miles gloriosus* Lamachus in Aristophanes' *Acharnians*. But if we imagine that Aesop and his sage master may have been as familiar to Athenian audiences as Punch and Judy, Mutt and Jeff, or Bert and Ernie, we have a much closer parallel for the self-important sage and his low-class heckler.

Still, we should not assume that comedy is the *only* medium or genre through which an Athenian audience might have known the Aesop tradition—and this brings me back to the issue of prose. For the dialogue also contains a kind of metaliterary commentary about what is appropriate in prose, and for this Aesop serves as the standard-bearer for a medium that is unpretentious and properly

---

[80] Alexis fr. 9 KA. For the date of the play, see Arnott 1996.18–20, 75; Grauert 1825.28–29 originally suggested that Solon's interlocutor in the preserved fragment was Aesop (a suggestion cautiously accepted by Arnott 1996.75–76, citing abundant earlier bibliography). And although Arnott notes that this is our only attested appearance of Aesop on the dramatic stage, we know of at least two other comedies from the fifth century that put onstage a resurrected Solon: Eupolis's *Dēmoi* (based on a plausible emendation to the Schol. *ad* Aelius Aristides) and Cratinus's *Cheirons*. The former seems to have been a political comedy that brought back to life several great Athenian statesmen of the past, including Solon (for the frr. of the *Dēmoi*, see Eupolis frr. 99–146 KA; for discussion and reconstruction of the play, see Plepelits 1970). The latter, Cratinus's *Cheirons*, seems a much more likely context for the kind of comic competition in wisdom that might include a confrontation of Solon and Aesop, since the play seems to have contained a critique or parody of the Old *Paideia*. For the frr. of *Cheirons*, see Cratinus frr. 246–68 KA. Indeed, given the evidence for a fifth-century tradition of Solon and Aesop, we might at least consider the possibility that the two of them served as models for Socrates and Strepsiades in Aristophanes' *Clouds*.

"pedestrian" (a theme perhaps less likely to have been sounded in the poetic form of comic drama). Thus notice the abuse Socrates imagines the anonymous questioner will heap on him when he repeats Hippias's climactic answer:

> "Tell me, Socrates," you can be sure he'll say, "do you think it's wrong for a man to be whipped when he sings such a dithyramb as that, so raucously, way out of tune with the question?" (ὅστις διθύραμβον τοσουτονὶ ᾄσας οὕτως ἀμούσως πολὺ ἀπῇσας ἀπὸ τοῦ ἐρωτήματος;, *Hipp. Mai.* 292c5–8).

The designation of Hippias's most elaborate response, full of poetic words and artful sound effects, as a dithyramb, with the sneer of the comic deictic τοσουτονί, exposes the absurdity of prose *logos* gussied up as if it were poetry. As Woodruff notes, the dithyramb (at least by the fourth century) was a composition whose "interest derived chiefly from music," but "dithyrambic style" also means a composition full of high-flown neologisms and compounds. In both respects, "dithyrambic" signifies the privileging of ornate or august (σεμνός) style over substance, and this precisely conforms to Hippias's main concern throughout the dialogue.[81] The discourse of the anonymous questioner, by contrast, revels in common, ordinary words and objects (Hippias's φαῦλα ὀνόματα), in the relentless pursuit of "truth." In this context, it is tempting to read Socrates' absurd image of the soup ladle made of gold as an allegory for Hippias's own vacuous and pretentious discourse. Through the idiom of "what is appropriate" (πρέπων), it calls our attention to the comic misfit between precious form and utilitarian function.

This metaliterary clash over what is appropriate in prose helps us understand why this dialogue (at least) deploys the medium. But, as we have seen, the *Hippias* also highlights the status taint attached to the public use of such low forms, and so poses with particular clarity the ideological double bind entailed by Plato's choice of prose medium.[82] And this is precisely why, I would contend, the figure of Aesop, so serviceable in the skirmishes by which *sophia* becomes philosophy, must ultimately be disavowed. In the *Hippias*, this disavowal is effectively finessed by the fiction of the heckling anonymous questioner. For at the very end of the dialogue, Socrates shifts the alliances, observing that he is caught between public abuse by "the wise" (= Hippias) and the private vilification of the anonymous questioner, who "happens to be most nearly related to me and live in the same house" (304d3–4). By this realignment, Socrates' abusive interlocutors, high and low, merge together, while Socrates stands alone to

---

[81] Quotation from Woodruff 1982a.60. Recall that *Hipp. Min.* (368d1) alleges that Hippias wrote dithyrambs among his many other compositions. And cf. *Phdr.* 238d2–3, where Socrates characterizes his first "nympholeptic" speech as οὐκέτι πόρρω διθυράμβων.

[82] Another way of formulating this ideological double bind: while Socrates' stance in Plato generally seems antidemocratic, here in the *Hippias*, his low Aesopic discourse makes him into the democrat in opposition to Hippias's spouting of elitist, sympotic wisdom. On this sociopolitical tension in Plato's portrait of Socrates in general, see Blondell 2002.75–79.

offer the dialogue's final words with a gloomy sigh: "I actually think, Hippias, that associating with both of you has done me good. The proverb says, 'What's fine is hard'—I think I know *that*" (304e6–9). The scholiast to this passage informs us that the proverb "What's fine is hard" (χαλεπὰ τὰ καλά) comes from Solon; thus the Aesopic anonymous questioner first explodes Hippias's sage pretentions, then evaporates at the end, leaving only Socrates as the melancholy Solon, still hoping to learn something in his old age.[83]

As I noted, many scholars have regarded the *Hippias* as so exceptional and aberrant that it must be banished from the Platonic canon. In contrast, I would suggest that even the dialogue's unique ploy of Socrates' sustained ventriloquism of the heckling anonymous questioner simply represents the extreme end—apex, or perhaps nadir?—of an Aesopic spectrum along which a number of Platonic representations of Socrates would find a place. In the *Hippias*, this character, Socrates' crude and spiteful alter ego, in a sense draws off all the spiky competitive energy of the dialogue, so that Socrates can still appear to be the saintly quester after truth, as he is more commonly conceived. Indeed, given the complex work of the rhetorical disavowal of Aesop I've posited for the dialogue's end, we might say, paradoxically, that the modern urge to ban the *Hippias* from Platonic authenticity is a measure of the *success* of Plato's strategy (rather than of Plato's failure as an author). For the dialogue thereby perfectly achieves its goals, like a consummate "self-consuming artifact"; Hippias is stamped indelibly in our memory as a pompous and fatuous poseur, while the rudeness and status taint of Aesop simultaneously guarantee that this cannot really be "our Socrates" or "our Plato."

Still (as I've already intimated in discussion of the *Symposium*), I do not mean to imply by all this that Socrates' and Aesop's procedures are identical; there are clearly significant differences. Most obviously, Aesop's medium is the bodily, the abjected, and the low; thus recall that his first successful self-incrimination of an opponent in the *Life* works entirely through the body, as his slave accusers are forced to vomit up the purloined figs (*Vita* G, ch. 3). Socrates, while he occasionally slums, generally transposes these terms from the bodily to the realm of *logos* and argument. Second, Aesop's methods work only when they take his opponent by surprise: either his interlocutor believes he has formed his own conclusion and decision based on implicit advice via fable, or, in the negative form, the opponent fails to realize that he's been manipulated into "bearing witness against himself" until it's too late. Plato's Socrates, by contrast, is like one of those magicians who tells you how the trick is done as he's doing it (which doesn't necessarily mean he's not still tricking you).

---

[83] Schol. *ad Hipp. Mai.* 304e (Greene 1938.178). Interestingly, according to the scholiast, Solon's quip is itself part of a competition in wisdom, since it is uttered by the Athenian Sage in response to Pittacus's famous dictum "it is hard to be good" (χαλεπὸν ἐσθλὸν ἔμμεναι—quoted in the Simonides poem discussed in Plato's *Protagoras*).

Related to both these differences: on his own terms within the narrative, Aesop succeeds, achieving practical real-world effects, whereas Socrates often fails within the frame of the dialogue. In the *Gorgias*, for example, Socrates never does get Polus explicitly to "bear witness" to the validity of his (Socrates') position, while Callicles' refusal is even more extreme. Callicles grudgingly completes the *elenchos*, as he claims, simply "to gratify Gorgias," and then refuses to speak at all, so that Socrates alone must hold forth with the long final myth.[84] And, of course, it is not just the characters within the dialogue who balk and refuse to submit to the *elenchos*; readers often finish a Socratic dialogue unsatisfied, feeling they could make a better showing than the befuddled interlocutors do, and suspecting that there's something deeply flawed in Socrates' refutation.[85] In fact, even when Socrates succeeds, the *elenchos* is acknowledged to have a purely negative effect. Thus, as articulated by the Eleatic stranger in Plato's *Sophist*, the *elenchos* is cathartic and pedagogic:

> They cross-examine a man's words, when he thinks that he is saying something and is really saying nothing, and easily convict him of inconsistencies in his opinions; these they then collect by the dialectic process, and placing them side by side, show that they contradict one another about the same things, in relation to the same things, and in the same respect. He, seeing this, is angry with himself, and grows gentle toward others, and thus is entirely delivered from great prejudices and harsh notions, in a way which is most amusing to the hearer, and produces the most lasting good effect on the person who is the subject of the operation. For as the physician considers that the body will receive no benefit from taking food until the internal obstacles have been removed, so the purifier of the soul is conscious that his patient will receive no benefit from the application of knowledge until he is refuted, and from refutation learns modesty; he must be purged of his prejudices first and made to think that he knows only what he knows, and no more. (*Soph.* 230b–d, trans. Cornford 1964; cf. *Meno* 84b–d)

Contrast this avowedly negative goal of the *elenchos* with the functioning of Aesop's practical art of self-incrimination. It is perhaps easiest to appreciate the difference by considering the formal or structural point in the narrative at which the opponent is forced to bear witness against himself. This occurs (as I suggested in chapter 4, section IV) (1) with the two slaves trying to frame Aesop at the beginning of the narrative (*Vita* G, ch. 3); (2) with Aesop's successful maneuvering of himself and Xanthus before the whole Samian demos (*Vita* G, chs. 85–90); (3) with Aesop's skillful entrapment of Nectanebo and his counselors in the Ahiqar sequence (*Vita* G, chs. 117–18, 121–22); and (4) with his final

---

[84] Cf. the general observations of Robinson 1953.10–19, Woodruff 1982a.137, and esp. Blondell 2002.125–27 on the persistent failure of the Socratic *elenchos*.

[85] For this readerly response to the Socratic dialogues, witness the whole industry of philosophical readings that consist in ferreting out the fallacies and suggesting better responses the interlocutors might have offered in response to Socrates' elenctic questioning.

summoning of Apollo himself to witness as he's about to be executed in Delphi (*Vita* G, ch. 142). In each case, the opponent's extorted self-incrimination forms the climax of an episode or a whole sequence—(1) Aesop's life as a mute slave before he regains his power of speech (*Vita* G, chs. 1–3); (2) the long Samian sequence that culminates in Aesop's winning his freedom (*Vita* G, chs. 21–100); (3) the Ahiqar sequence (*Vita* G, chs. 101–23); and (4) the Delphic episode (*Vita* G, chs. 124–42). This repeated narrative arc also entails a different structure of readerly engagement and identification; each time we watch Aesop spring the trap, and trick and narrative close together with a satisfying snap. We identify entirely with Aesop and revel in his fantasized success over his opponents, who are mere narrative stooges.[86]

The structure and experience of Socratic *elenchos*, both for the characters within the dialogue and for its readers, could not be more different. And this is perhaps Plato's (if not Socrates') greatest ruse; through the productive use of failure, he conjures "philosophy" as a transcendent form and constitutes it as a sphere of disinterested contemplation beyond all practical competition in *sophia*. This is achieved specifically by constituting dialogue as a reciprocal exchange between cooperating partners (thus notice that Socrates' description of bearing witness for one's opponent potentially goes *both ways* in the *Gorgias* passage quoted above), but, more importantly, by having Socrates fail. Socrates' failure, the negative of the *elenchos*, ignorance exposed, and the *aporia* in which Socrates himself claims to participate as much as his interlocutors—all this produces the permanently open space of philosophy, the provocation to continue the search for "truth" in a privileged domain beyond competition.[87] We might say that the genius of Aesop inheres in his success—his use of practical cunning to trounce his more powerful opponents, while the genius of Plato, contrariwise, resides in his recognition of the positive value of failure and *aporia*. For these transform joke into philosophy; competition into dialogue; and practical bricolage into abstract system, as the narrative particular reaches beyond itself.

---

[86] That is to say, even when there is some character development to Aesop's opponents (as is the case with Xanthus), we do not care whether the opponent/interlocutor *learns* anything.

[87] For the reciprocity of Socratic *elenchos*, see Robinson 1953.9, who takes Socrates' "occasional invitations to reciprocity in elenchos" (including the passage at *Gorg.* 472b6–c1) to be insincere; but on the revolutionary reciprocity of the dialogue form, see Halperin 1992; Nightingale 1995.162–71; Martin 1998.124; Blondell 2002.51, 120–21. For this account of the *elenchos* and the Platonic deployment of *aporia*, I am much indebted to Kahn 1996.88–100; cf. Nehamas 1990 and Woodruff 1982a.118: "But Socrates' chief lesson was the self-induced dissatisfaction . . . that has become the hallmark and mainspring of serious philosophy."

Chapter 10

HISTORIĒ AND LOGOPOIÏA: TWO SIDES OF HERODOTEAN PROSE

> It is time for the student of narrative techniques to consider [the story of the Persian Wars] for what it is—the greatest continuous prose narrative in Greek literature, and a literary masterpiece. So in order to understand Herodotus we must cease to regard him as a historian, and see him as a narrator, whose narrative art is related to that of his sources. Herodotus should be accepted as the creator of a new generic form which only later became identified as history.[1]

AND SO WE COME FINALLY to Herodotus. I set out originally to write a book on Aesop and Herodotus—Aesop in Herodotus—as a way of mapping something of the bizarre, vertiginous shifts in style, genre, and level of decorum that pervade the *Histories*.[2] I slowly discovered that in order to do justice to the topic, I had to go a long way around. But this book was always motivated by a sense of the mystery of Herodotus, so let me start there. It is all too easy for us to take Herodotus for granted. In many ways, it is a simpler task to estrange Plato, since Platonic dialogue is such a weird form when we pause to look at it, whereas we think we know what "history" is. And yet the *Histories* is the earliest monumental piece of Greek narrative prose writing preserved, and it is simply unparalleled in its scope, ambition, control, and capacious inclusion of material. As Arnaldo Momigliano put it long ago, "There was no Herodotus before Herodotus," or, perhaps even more suggestively, "The secrets of [Herodotus's] workshop are not yet all out."[3] Or again, we might quote J. D. Denniston, in his magisterial account of the development of Greek prose style, pausing to marvel at Herodotus:

> Herodotus is an unaccountable phenomenon in the history of literature. He is in the direct line of succession to the logographers: but while they, apparently, had no

---

[1] Murray 2001b.322.

[2] Indeed, the short version or "pitch" for this book would be that I set out to rewrite Aly 1921 with politics.

[3] Momigliano 1960; quotations taken from pp. 31 and 32, respectively. The latter quotation occurs in the context of Momigliano's discussion of Hdt's collection and deployment of oral sources, but it can apply more generally to Hdt's crafting of his rich and mysterious text. For more recent formulations of the uniqueness of Hdt: Lateiner 1989.3–10, 211–27; Fowler 1996.86; Murray 2001b.322; Luraghi 2009.

technique at all, he had a technique at once effortless and adequate to any demands he chose to make upon it. Nor were these demands so small.

. . . .

I have lingered over Herodotus because he is often, as a stylist, damned with faint praise. His achievement, measured by what we know of his predecessors, marks, I believe, a greater advance than any other Greek prose writer achieved.[4]

And though these scholars are writing about different aspects of Herodotus's complex text, a set of questions unites them: Why did Herodotus choose the medium of prose? Where do we locate the precursors for his mimetic narrative art? And how did he get so good at it?

I. History before Prose, Prose before History

Two relatively recent scholarly developments make these questions even more pressing—the complementary realizations that (what we call) history in this period does not necessarily require prose, and that early Greek prose is not necessarily history. For the first: the "New Simonides" fragments discovered and published in the early 1990s—including forty-five lines of an extended elegiac narrative poem on the Battle of Plataea—force us to recognize that Herodotus's choice of prose for his historical narrative of the Persian Wars is neither necessary nor self-evident. In an important article in 1986, Ewen Bowie had argued for a distinctive archaic genre of publicly performed lengthy narrative elegy on historical topics, including the foundations, mythic traditions, and recent history of individual cities. Bowie based his reconstruction on preserved fragments and testimonia relating to such archaic elegists as Callinus, Tyrtaeus, Mimnermus, and Xenophanes, although almost all the texts of this genre of elegy have disappeared, overshadowed by the rise of prose history.[5] The New Simonides fragments in many respects confirmed Bowie's hypothesis and demonstrated that the tradition of historical elegy continued robustly into the fifth century BCE.[6] Indeed, we should recall that, according to ancient reports, Herodotus's own uncle (or cousin) Panyassis composed an *Ionica* in seven thousand verses (what Bowie takes to be not just the history of a single city, but a more ambitious, pan-Ionian narrative).[7]

---

[4] Denniston 1960.5, 8.

[5] Bowie 1986.27–35; cf. Lasserre 1976, Fowler 1996.65.

[6] See Bowie 2001 for discussion of his original theory, problems, and modifications in light of the New Simonides fragments.

[7] Suda s.v. Πανύασις, IV.24–25 Adler; for discussion of Panyassis, see Huxley 1969.177–88; Matthews 1974; Bowie 1986.32, 2001.49–50, 60–61. For the problem of Panyassis's exact relationship to Hdt, see Matthews 1974.9–12, arguing that the tradition that he is Hdt's cousin is more likely to be correct based on the text of the Suda entry on Panyassis.

For the second: there has been a quiet revolution in our understanding of *historiē* (Herodotus's own term for his project, introduced in the opening sentence of the *Histories*). We have come to recognize that ancient history writing in general is a literary and rhetorical genre, and that ancient historians are by no means playing by the same rules as their modern counterparts.[8] But even within the set of ancient historians, Herodotus stands apart, for, as we shall see, his *historiē* is a "predisciplinary" form that invents "history" and is therefore logically and chronologically prior to it.[9] So what did Herodotus himself think he was doing when he did it? And why should he have chosen to write *prose*? This fundamental question is rarely asked, for various reasons. Partly, this is a result of the long-standing division of labor within the field of Herodotean studies between historical and literary approaches (although this division has narrowed somewhat recently, as scholars have become *inter*disciplinary to grapple with Herodotus's predisciplinary text). For generations of earlier historians, their concern was entirely the reliability of Herodotus's factual content and the sources of his information, while prose was taken for granted as the self-evident and transparent medium of truth. In this respect, traditional historians parallel traditional philosophers in their reading of Plato, with "truth value" or "fact" filling the place of philosophical argument, the real "meat" to be extracted from the husk of literary form. But more recently, historical approaches to Herodotus have recognized the need to contextualize him in his contemporary social and intellectual milieus, thereby producing readings analogous to the more situated readings of Platonic dialogue we considered in chapter 6. We have come to realize that "history" is no more an inevitable or transcendent category than "philosophy," but rather the contingent product of a particular historical moment.

Thus Robert L. Fowler and Rosalind Thomas have recently located Herodotus squarely within the intellectual ferment and competition of contemporary Sophistic and scientific practices. Fowler in an important 1996 article challenged Felix Jacoby's still dominant paradigm of Herodotus as the earliest and unique successor of Hecataeus of Miletus, the sixth-century author of two works, a *Periēgēsis* or *Periodos Gēs* and a mythographic *Genealogies*. According to Jacoby, Herodotus only slowly and painfully in his own process of writing invented "history" out of an older tradition of geography and ethnography, only later to be followed by a proliferation of local historians writing in response to Herodotus's panoramic account.[10] In Jacoby's teleological scheme, the development of something akin to modern "scientific" history was a foregone

---

[8] For effective estrangements of the genre of ancient history, see (e.g.) Loraux 1980; Connor 1982, 1984; Woodman 1988.

[9] For *historiē* "before history," see the essays collected in *Arethusa* 20 (1987), Fowler 1996, Thomas 2000. I borrow from Thomas 2000.7, 21–27, 137, 162–63 the notion of Herodotus's text as "predisciplinary"; see further below.

[10] Fowler 1996, challenging Jacoby 1909, 1913.coll. 279–380 (= 1956.44–94). For other recent critiques of Jacoby, see Nicolai 1997; Luraghi 2001a, 2001b; Dewald and Marincola 2006.

conclusion, and the stages of that development completely clear and linear, with each stage represented by a single writer. Fowler notes that, in order to produce such a neat linear development within Greek historiography, Jacoby was forced to downdate a large number of mythographers and local historians whose names we know—many of whom were likely to have been Herodotus's contemporaries over the long span of time in which he researched and composed his *Histories*.[11] At the same time, Fowler observes that, although many of these mythographers and local chroniclers practiced a kind of rationalization of myth, they are in their method of confident but unexplained disagreement with their predecessors not substantially different from earlier and contemporary poets. What sets Herodotus apart from his prose predecessors and contemporaries in Fowler's judgment is his deployment of certain techniques and concepts associated with *historiē*, empirical "inquiry" into such areas as medicine, mathematics, astronomy, natural science, and anthropology—most significantly, the principle of falsifiability and reliance on autopsy.[12] As Fowler puts it:

> The language of Herodotos shows him to be a man of his day. He was not a Sophist, but he was a thinker, and he profited from discussions with other thinkers. He brought the old science of ἱστορίη, critical inquiry, up to date by employing new critical tools, and applied ἱστορίη itself to new subjects.[13]

Fowler concludes that rather than holding Herodotus to the "standards of modern historiography," we should instead see him as engaged in an activity analogous to that of the fifth-century Sophist Protagoras and "allow him to be what any admiring Greek would have called him: σοφός."[14]

More recently, Rosalind Thomas has extended Fowler's project of reinserting Herodotus into his contemporary context.[15] As Thomas notes, there has long been a tendency in modern scholarship to "archaize" Herodotus, partly as a result of Jacoby's model of Herodotus as the single direct successor of Hecataeus, writing at least fifty years earlier, and partly also because of an unconscious assimilation of Herodotus to the oral traditions and archaic history that form much of his subject matter.[16] As a result, Herodotus's approach or

---

[11] Fowler 1996.62–69. Thus Fowler (1996.86 with n. 150), like many other recent scholars, assumes a decades-long process of Hdt's collection of materials, oral performances, and slow composition of the *Histories*, spanning ca. 450 or 440 to 420 BCE. For dates and process, cf. Thomas 1993, 2000.19–21. I will return to the issue of the dating of Hdt at the end of the next chapter.

[12] Fowler 1996.69–80; for Hdt's deployment of contemporary scientific and Sophistic methods, cf. Lateiner 1986.

[13] Fowler 1996.80; cf. p. 86: "[Herodotus] has applied to historical problems the latest methods of other branches of inquiry, making at the same time his own contribution to their development. He did not invent his sources; he discovered the *problem* of sources."

[14] Fowler 1996.87; cf. 80.

[15] Thomas 2000; cf. Thomas 1993, 1997, 2006.

[16] Thomas 2000.4–8. To some extent, this critique applies to many of the readings offered in Kurke 1999, but I would defend my reading practices there on two complementary grounds: (1)

"thought-world" is closely associated with that of sixth-century Ionian philosophers, scientists, and *physiologoi* like Thales, Heraclitus, Anaxagoras, and Xenophanes, while he is kept mainly cordoned off from the Sophistic and scientific milieus of the second half of the fifth century.[17] And yet, as Thomas reminds us, the term *historiē* appears for the very first time in extant Greek in Herodotus's first sentence (Ἡροδότου Ἁλικαρνησσέος ἱστορίης ἀπόδεξις ἥδε . . . , "This is the demonstration of the researches of Herodotus of Halicarnassus . . ."), so that it is a modern anachronism to speak of *sixth-century* Ionian *historiē*.[18] Thus also, in contrast to archaizing approaches that insist on the relevance of the Homeric and archaic meanings of *histor* as "judge, arbitrator, umpire" for Herodotus and his project, Thomas points out that *historiē* is a technical term or buzzword for a whole host of scientific topics of "inquiry" not fully distinguished from each other and sharing a set of distinctive methods in the second half of the fifth century and into the fourth.[19] As Thomas summarizes her argument:

> [H]*istorie* has indisputable associations and connections with far wider kinds of enquiry: the enquiries of natural philosophy, enquiry into nature and into the nature of man, enquiry into the truth about the world through the kind of methods which would by now be associated with natural philosophy and medicine—that is, a critical relation to predecessors, the use of evidence, argument, theoretical ideas about causations and origins, analysis of the process by which you reached the conclusions. So when Herodotus in the opening line described his work as an *histories apodexis*, he was not appealing to the Muse for truth or knowledge, as Homer did; and his claim says something more than Hecataeus' forthright and critical opening. I have suggested that he was signalling to his audience, present and future, that this was a modern

---

The past in oral traditions: as Thomas herself acknowledges, if we take seriously the notion of Herodotus's oral sources, these can represent archaic material stretching back one hundred to two hundred years before the time Herodotus collected his stories (for the time span, cf. Murray 2001a); (2) Continuity of past and present: as I have tried to demonstrate in readings of the Sophists and Sophistic representations in Platonic texts in the previous chapters, there is much more continuity and inheritance from archaic poetry, wisdom traditions, etc., extending into the fifth and fourth centuries than has generally been acknowledged. So perhaps we should not presume such an all-embracing radical break between archaic and classical *Weltanschauungen*; to what extent are we being misled by maverick figures like Thucydides and Plato?

[17] For examples of the close association of Hdt with sixth-century Ionian philosophy, etc., Thomas cites Myres 1953, Immerwahr 1966, Gould 1989.

[18] See Thomas 2000, esp. 161–67; Snell 1924.63 had already noted that the term *historiē* occurs for the first time in Herodotus. Note that Thomas's criticism of anachronism in the application of *historiē* to sixth-century Ionian intellectual trends also applies to Fowler 1996, quoted above ("the old science of ἱστορίη").

[19] Thomas 2000.161–67, 262–74, 283–84, critiquing Lateiner 1989.83–84, Connor 1993, Nagy 1987 (and one should add Nagy 1990b.250–62, 305, 318–22). For an elegant and persuasive reconciliation of the two positions, see Bakker 2002.

work of *historie*—one might be inclined to translate it as 'science'—using the fashionable and significant language of the time.[20]

For Thomas, Herodotus was an active participant and contributor in this context of lively experimentation, intense professional competition, and rapid change that owed at least as much to fifth-century East Greece/Ionia as to Athens.[21] Specifically, Thomas sees many of Herodotus's topics, methods of proof and argument, and rhetorical strategies as characteristic of contemporary fifth-century "science" (*historiē*) and Sophistic—these two, as she notes, not easily separable from each other.[22] Thus Thomas offers detailed comparisons of sections of Herodotus's text (especially in his ethnographic *logoi* and polemical set pieces) with those of near-contemporary Hippocratic treatises and the kinds of Sophistic argument and techniques we find preserved in Plato's dialogues. In the end, for Thomas as for Fowler, Herodotus is best characterized as a profoundly engaged, itinerant intellectual—a *sophos* or *sophistēs*.[23]

Fowler's and Thomas's arguments serve to situate Herodotus squarely within the battles over prose I considered in relation to the Sophists in chapter 7. And this, in turn, has the salutary effect of suggesting that Herodotus's prose form is neither inevitable nor transparent, but, like other Sophistic experiments in prose, innovative, generically multiform, and uneven. Fowler and Thomas thus provide us with a partial answer to the question why Herodotus should choose prose, insofar as they connect his monumental work with earlier and contemporary traditions of mythography, medical writing, natural history, and various other kinds of scientific writing (much of this early prose significantly, like Herodotus's, in Ionic dialect). And yet, as Thomas herself admits, there is much in Herodotus that these affiliations do not account for; in particular, she notes that very different styles and techniques inform Herodotean narrative. For the narrative sections of the *Histories* (which is, of course, a great deal), Thomas, like many other scholars before her, acknowledges Homeric (and other) poetry as a significant influence, seeing Herodotus's work as a daring, at times uneven, amalgam of "old" and "new."[24]

---

[20] Thomas 2000.270. Thomas recognizes as important precursors for this argument Dihle 1962, Lateiner 1986.

[21] See esp. Thomas 2000.9–16 on the vibrancy of fifth-century Ionia and the Athenocentrism of much modern scholarship that plays down or ignores this East Greek milieu on the odd assumption that there was nothing happening in Ionia after the sixth century. In particular, Thomas notes that Hippocrates' homeland, the island of Cos, is almost directly opposite Halicarnassus, and that this may well be significant for Hdt's close intellectual affiliations with the methods of the ancient medical writers.

[22] Thomas 2000, esp. 22–23, 156–58, 250–69, following Lloyd 1979, 1987.

[23] Thomas 2000.8, 162–63, 283–85. In addition to Thomas, other recent work has emphasized the importance of Herodotus's own itinerancy for his *sophia* or *technē*: thus Griffin 1990, Friedman 2006, Munson 2006. I shall return to the topic of Hdt's location(s) at the end of the next chapter.

[24] Thus Thomas 2000, esp. 3, 218, 247–48, 267–74, 284–85; cf. Murray 2001b.323. On occasion, Thomas seems to use "Homer" metonymically for a whole range of earlier Greek poetry. In addition,

And with Homer as an important precursor, let me turn to other, more literary approaches to Herodotus. In the wake of the recognition that Herodotus is "before history," literary scholars, too, have begun to acknowledge the sheer weirdness and uncategorizability of Herodotus's text. Thus Donald Lateiner helpfully argues that Herodotus invented a new genre of literary prose that ultimately found no imitators.[25] Deborah Boedeker has picked up and expanded on Lateiner's insight, noting that Herodotus has crafted a remarkably capacious and variegated new genre (or genres)—a prose text that appropriates and embeds a whole range of earlier poetic forms while also signficantly differentiating itself from the protocols or rules of evidence of these older poetic traditions.[26] This picture of Herodotus's new genre begins to look strikingly like Plato's new invention of the dialogue form, as literary and philosophical scholars have recently characterized it.[27] (Indeed, we might think of both Herodotean history and Platonic dialogue as ancient precursors of the novel.)[28] And yet, while the stakes and purpose of Plato's ambivalent relation to earlier poetic traditions in his "invention of philosophy" seem clear, they are less so in Herodotus's case. Why should Herodotus embed or appropriate so much earlier poetic material, and yet choose the medium of prose? To some extent, scholars still seem to take for granted the self-evidence of the historical project when it comes to this issue. Herodotus just is trying to get at the truth about the past, and in many cases early poetry represents his only available source material as well as his only model for lofty, sustained narrative.

In particular, consideration of the literary form and narrative antecedents for Herodotus's project has focused mainly on the high genres of Homeric epic and Attic tragedy. Thus scholars have identified Homer as an essential model for Herodotus's sweeping and capacious narrative of travels (*Odyssey*) and war (*Iliad*).[29] They have repeatedly pointed out the Homeric resonances in Herodotus's opening sentence, with its goal of preserving the *kleos* of "great and wondrous deeds" and its final focusing on the initial responsibility for a quarrel.[30] They have noted markedly Homeric episodes like the extended catalog of military forces (Hdt. 7.61–99) or the fierce battle over the body of a warrior fallen in combat (Hdt. 7.225).[31] They have cataloged the similarities of Homeric speeches,

---

Thomas alludes to traditional oral tales and folklore as another source for Hdt's narrative art: I will consider this category in more detail below.

[25] Lateiner 1989.14–51, 211–27.
[26] Boedeker 2000.
[27] See chapter 6 above.
[28] For Platonic dialogue as a precursor to Menippean satire and ultimately the novel, see Bakhtin 1981.21–26, 1984.109–12; for Herodotus and the novel, see (e.g.) Tatum 1997; Hornblower 2006.311, 315.
[29] Thus (e.g.) Strasburger 1982, Moles 1993, Griffiths 1995.39–44, Boedeker 2002.98–99.
[30] Thus (e.g.) Stambler 1982.210–11, Nagy 1987, 1990b.217–55; Woodman 1988.1–5; Lateiner 1989.15; Moles 1993; Thomas 2000.218, 260, 267–69; Bakker 2002.6–8; Boedeker 2002.99.
[31] Thus (e.g.) Stambler 1982.210; Erbse 1992.125–27; Boedeker 2002.103, 108.

Homeric narrative structures, and ring composition.[32] Other scholars have pointed to tragedy as a source for moments of Herodotean debate, indirect and elliptical narrative style, and doom-laden tales of human overreaching, hubris, and final peripety.[33] And while these literary strands in Herodotus's text are undeniable and important, the emphasis on epic and tragedy again gaps or occludes the essential diacritic of prose. Indeed many modern discussions imply a dichotomy of prose as "science"/*historiē* versus narrative as "poetic" that runs the risk of reinscribing our modern assumption that prose is the transparent and self-evident medium of truth, and poetry the domain of "fiction." In this respect, this modeling of old and new, poetry and prose in Herodotus bears a striking resemblance to Plato's construction of a blind spot around mimetic narrative prose in the *Republic* (considered in chapter 6 above).[34] At the same time, this implied opposition also occludes moments of Herodotean narrative that are low, comic, or indecorous (and therefore presumably not Homeric in inspiration). For elements like these, scholars generally invoke oral traditions of popular storytelling, but at this point, Herodotus is often strangely collapsed into his sources, or represented as having no choice or control over his material.[35] In addition, the concept of literary form tends to evaporate in scholarly treatments of the low end of Herodotus's generic spectrum, replaced by the largely amorphous categories of "folklore" and "myth."

In relation to the weird, unseemly, or indecorous elements in Herodotus's motley and capacious narrative, we might revive an old idea of Wolf Aly, that

---

[32] Thus (e.g.) Strasburger 1982, Lang 1984.18–51, Lateiner 1989.17–21, Erbse 1992.127–32, Moles 1993, Griffiths 1995, Boedeker 2002.104–5.

[33] Thus (e.g.) Fornara 1971b; Erbse 1992.4, 16–17, 49–55; Saïd 2002. I will return to the affiliation with tragedy at the end of the next chapter.

[34] This alignment of prose with "fact" and poetry with "fiction" is explicit in older scholarship: e.g., Momigliano 1978.2 (quoted in Woodman 1988.1): "As the Greeks had a long tradition of epic poetry before they began to write historical prose, it is tempting to take Homer as a predecessor of the historians.... Herodotus may seem to encourage us in this direction. But the Greeks themselves, and the Romans, knew that there were two differences between history and epic poetry: history was written in prose, and was meant to separate facts from fancies about the past." But it is also implicit in much more recent scholarship: in addition to Thomas 2000, cf. Hartog 1988.340–60 (Hdt as "rhapsode and surveyor"), Moles 1993, even on occasion Nagy 1990b (e.g., 328–29, where "prose" is the medium of an explicit message, "poetry" the medium of *ainos*).

[35] For the former, see Murray 2001a, 2001b; for the latter, see the striking formulations of Thomas 2000.6 (italics added): "It seems likely that many tales and traditions were still in circulation at the time he wrote them down.... Provided one does not take the view that Herodotus made up most of his narrative, it is then possible to say that he may have changed the emphasis, inserted the tales into larger, more meaningful narratives and historical patterning, but to a large extent the repeated story-motifs may be a product of the traditions he picked up rather than his own creation. Anyone recording traditions is liable to change them in the process, even if this is a danger which is consciously being avoided, but it would be going too far to say that they are in any serious sense new 'inventions'. *He must have been at the mercy of his sources to some extent*.... Inevitably they leave their traces in the *Histories*." Another approach is that represented by Griffiths 1995, 2001, 2006, who appreciates Hdt's artistry also in his low or indecorous tales, but treats them mainly as entertainment.

Herodotus draws on and benefits from traditions of popular Ionian storytelling.[36] And one strand within this Ionian tradition is the Aesopic. Traditions about Aesop and the *Life of Aesop* seem to be strongly rooted in East Greece; indeed, scholars have suggested that the first one hundred chapters of the *Vita*, which end with Aesop's celebration and civic honors at the hands of the grateful Samians, might represent a specifically Samian version of the *Life*.[37] Ancient tradition tells us that Herodotus himself hailed from the mixed Greek-Carian city of Halicarnassus in Asia Minor and, when exiled from there, spent a good deal of time on the island of Samos. And, as we shall see, several Aesopic fable elements in Herodotus's text seem to cluster in the Samian stories of Book 3. Is this coincidence?

In any event, I want to focus on the Aesopic because it is at least one element that gives literary form to the low, while also making very clear the necessary interimplication of form and sociopolitics in the ancient hierarchy of genre. It thereby suggests a different dichotomy or opposition that might structure Herodotus's text: not just prose versus poetry as science versus narrative and truth versus fiction, but *historiē* versus *logopoiïa*. By this I mean to designate high versus low prose traditions; new versus old; "science" versus gossip and storytelling, with the idea that Herodotus is fully in control of both forms and has his reasons for including and combining them—reasons that are necessarily not just literary, but entail a potent and risky sociopolitics. So can we find an Aesopic element in Herodotus's work and, if so, what function(s) does it serve? These are the questions I wish to explore in this and the next chapter, as a way of recovering a different strand in the genealogy of ancient Greek mimetic or narrative prose. By focusing on the Aesopic element in Herodotus, I would like to suggest that the beginnings of prose in ancient Greece are not just part of an inevitable, triumphal march from *muthos* to *logos*, following in the train of Ionian *physiologoi*, pre-Socratic philosophers, medical writers, and rationalizing genealogists and geographers. And, as with our discussion of Plato, the possibility of an Aesopic strand within Herodotus's massive text insistently raises the question of the politics of form within the rigid ancient hierarchy of genre and

---

[36] Thus Aly 1921, esp. 15–30, 236–63, 1929.63–76; cf. Griffin 1990, Murray 2001a.32–33. I am not thereby asserting that *all* of Greek popular narrative or the novella derives from Ionia (the full-scale "Ionian Theory" espoused by German critics of the nineteenth and early twentieth centuries; for critique of the "Ionian Theory," see Trenkner 1958.168–77). It should be emphasized that Aly's theory is also quite different from that of Nagy 1987, 1990b.221–24, 325–26, 335, and Evans 1991.89–146. These two latter scholars argue for a very old tradition of oral prose chroniclers or specialized "remembrancers" (Nagy's *logioi*; Evans's *mnamones*). But I am fully persuaded by the arguments of Luraghi (2001a, 2001b, 2006, 2009) that there was no such specialized tradition of prose remembrancers in archaic Greece. For more discussion of Nagy's model of the *logios* as traditional "master of prose," see below in text.

[37] On Aesop traditions in East Greece, see Aly 1921.19–22, Momigliano 1971.35–38, Griffin 1990.64–67; for chs. 1–100 of the *Vita* as a specifically Samian tradition, see Zeitz 1936.253, Nagy 1979.285–86 §8n. 1, West 1984.117–19.

370   CHAPTER 10

decorum. For, I would contend, there is something low, scurrilous, and disreputable about narrative prose insofar as it is the medium of the slave fabulist Aesop, and that Herodotus both acknowledges and disavows this ancestry in the course of his work, even while he uses Aesopic elements skillfully to convey his complex message.

In the next section of this chapter, I will consider the explicit mention of Aesop in Herodotus, and what Herodotus means by *logopoios*, in order to clarify the opposition of *historiē* and *logopoiïa*; then finally, in the last section of this chapter, I will look very selectively at ancient readings of Herodotus that expose the real-world stakes and dangers implicit in Herodotus's bizarre generic motley.

II. Aesop *Ho Logopoios*

But why do I insist on Aesop? As I noted in chapter 6, Herodotus, like Plato, explicitly mentions Aesop as a maker of prose and implicitly acknowledges him as a precursor, while also, like Plato, evincing a certain ambivalence about the low fabulist. In a typical digression in his Egyptian *logos*, Herodotus provides us with the oldest explicit mention of Aesop in all of Greek literature. Pausing from his main narrative to reject a fanciful Greek account that attributed one of the smaller pyramids at Giza to the courtesan Rhodopis, Herodotus offers two counterarguments: first, the sheer expense of a pyramid as beyond the means of even a very successful courtesan; and second, chronological impossibility:

> For Rhodopis existed very many years later than these kings who left behind these pyramids: she was from Thrace in origin, and slave of Iadmon, son of Hephaestopolis, a Samian, and she was fellow slave of Aesop, the fable-maker (Αἰσώπου τοῦ λογοποιοῦ). For in fact, this one [Aesop] did belong to Iadmon, as was demonstrated not least in this way: for when, with the Delphians summoning many times from an oracular command, whoever wished to accept recompense for the life of Aesop, no other appeared, but only another Iadmon, grandson of Iadmon, accepted it—thus it's clear that Aesop also belonged to Iadmon. But Rhodopis came to Egypt when Xanthes the Samian conveyed her, but having come for business, she was freed for a lot of money by a Mytilenean man, Charaxus, son of Scamandronymus and brother of Sappho the melic poet (Σαπφοῦς τῆς μουσοποιοῦ). (Hdt. 2.134–35.1)

Embedded in a digression within a digression, Aesop suddenly pops up, together with a fleeting and tantalizing glimpse of his slavery on Samos, victimization at the hands of the Delphians, and eventual retribution. I have considered in chapter 1 what we may be able to recover of fifth-century traditions about the life and death of Aesop from Herodotus's brief notice; for now I would like to focus simply on Herodotus's designation of Aesop as ὁ λογοποιός (what I've translated as "fable-maker"). By this designation, Herodotus makes clear that for him, as for Plato in the fourth century, Aesopic fables were strongly identified with prose. Whether or not we postulate a much older, native Greek tradition of beast fable in verse (and this is much disputed), by the time such fables get attached to the figure of Aesop (which our evidence allows us to see happening in the course of the fifth century BCE), they are indisputably thought of as prose.[38] Viewed synchronically in a fifth-century context, Aesop is emphatically not a poet, but a prose storyteller (*logopoios*) whose medium is *logos*.[39] For *logos* is Herodotus's standard term for a prose fable (as we shall see), and Herodotus is our earliest source for Aesop. Indeed, if we look again at the digression in which Herodotus first mentions Aesop, we notice that even here, apparently gratuitously for Herodotus's substantive point, a clear structural system is implied, for Herodotus cannot resist opposing Aesop ὁ λογοποιός to Sappho ἡ μουσοποιός.[40]

But there is still more to say about Aesop the *logopoios* in the broader Herodotean context, for it is a curious fact that in all the *Histories* there are only two figures Herodotus designates as *logopoioi*—Aesop (only here) and Hecataeus of Miletus (three times).[41] Because of this conjunction, scholars generally assume that *logopoios* is a neutral designation in Herodotus, specifying only the prose medium while embracing both fictional and factual content (that is, the *logoi* of both Aesop and Hecataeus). Thus, for example, Oswyn Murray observes,

> [Herodotus] uses the word *logos* to refer to the whole (1.5, 95, etc.) or larger or smaller parts of his work (2.38; 5.36), and to individual stories within it. It is hard to resist the conclusion that he would have described himself as a *logopoios*, like Hecataeus (2.143; 5.36, 125) and Aesop (2.134). From these two examples it seems likely that the connotations of *logos* can cover both fiction and factual narrative.[42]

If indeed Herodotus "would have described himself as a *logopoios*" (as Murray asserts), then Aesop is as much a precursor for Herodotus's narrative prose as is Hecataeus. And yet, while an immense amount of scholarly ink has been spilled

[38] For the gradual attachment of beast fables to Aesop as a fifth-century phenomenon, see West 1984. I emphasize Aesop's identification with prose to disagree with Nagy 1979.287–97, 307–8, who consistently refers to Aesop as a "blame *poet*" and to his medium as *ainos*. Nagy is followed by other scholars—e.g., Parker 1983.275, Compton 1990. In contrast, Nagy 1990b.322–26, 335 acknowledges the significance of Hdt's designation of Aesop as *logopoios*. For more extensive discussion of Nagy 1990b, see below.

[39] Cf. M. L. West 1985.94, Murray 2001a.24–25. On fable terminology, see also van Dijk 1997.79–90, Adrados 1999.5–13.

[40] Nagy 1990b repeatedly calls attention to Hdt's juxtaposition of the terms *logopoios* and *mousopoios* in this episode (224n. 54, 325, 335), but he does not consider this an opposition or hierarchy of genres.

[41] Aesop: Hdt. 2.134; Hecataeus: 2.143.1, 5.36.2, 5.125.

[42] Murray 2001a.24–25. For *logopoios* as a neutral (or even positive) designation in Hdt, cf. LSJ s.v. λογοποιός "I.1. *prose-writer, esp. historian, chronicler*"; Powell 1938 s.v. *logopoios* ("maker of *logoi*"); Nagy 1990b.224n. 54, 325, 335 ("speechmaker, artisan of speech"); S. West 1991.145n. 7 ("author").

372 CHAPTER 10

on the extent of Herodotus's debt to Hecataeus, there is almost no discussion of Herodotus and Aesop—with one significant exception. In an extended treatment that seems not to be very well known to many scholars writing on Herodotus, Gregory Nagy makes Herodotus's affiliation with Aesop ὁ λογοποιός central to his reading of the *Histories*.[43] For my purposes, Nagy's treatment is an important one that deserves to be more widely known, even while I have significant disagreements with it. I will thus first summarize the positions my reading shares with Nagy, and then explain in some detail where it diverges from his.

Nagy links Herodotus's stance and activity within the text to those of the *histor*, "judge" or "arbitrator" (as this role functions within archaic poetry and inscriptions), and also identifies him as *logios*, what Nagy translates as traditional "master of oral traditions in prose."[44] At the same time, Nagy notes that Aesop and Hecataeus share the designation *logopoios* (which he glosses "artisan of speech") in Herodotus's text and from that concludes that Aesop as well as Hecataeus is an important precursor for Herodotus.[45] Nagy supports the link between Herodotus and Aesop with a passage from Plutarch's *On the Malice of Herodotus* that I will consider in more detail in the next section.[46] Because of the affiliation he posits between Aesop and Herodotus, Nagy alone of scholars (to my knowledge) reads certain passages of the *Histories* not just with later written versions of Aesopic fables from the fable collections, but also with the *Life of Aesop* tradition represented by *Vita* G, which Nagy assumes goes back to an East Greek/Samian oral tradition that preexisted Herodotus.[47] Thus impor-

---

[43] Nagy 1990b.309–38. The lack of familiarity of Herodotean scholars with Nagy's discussion is again a problem of impermeable boundaries between different subfields. Thus many Herodotean scholars are familiar with Nagy 1987—some even with Nagy 1988; but they do not seem to be aware that four chapters of Nagy 1990b are in whole or in part concerned with Herodotus (this lack of familiarity is to some extent understandable, given that Nagy's title, *Pindar's Homer: The Lyric Possession of an Epic Past*, offers no hint of the extent of its Herodotean subject matter). I do not consider here those scholars who discuss individual fables (implicit or explicit) embedded in the text of the *Histories*—e.g., Meuli 1975a, 1975b; Karadagli 1981. 23, 35–37, 65, 75–79, 84–85, 91; Hirsch 1986; Detienne and Svenbro 1989; van Dijk 1997.270–74; Adrados 1999.401; Svenbro 2002; Griffiths 2006.139—since by and large they do not consider the broader implications of Herodotus's deployment of fable. A notable exception is Ceccarelli 1993; I will consider all these approaches in more detail in the next chapter.

[44] Nagy 1987 (quotation from p. 182), 1988, 1990b.215–24, 314–35.

[45] Nagy 1990b: see especially 224n. 54, 325, 335. In particular, note that at p. 224n. 54, Nagy assumes the equivalence of the two terms *logios* and *logopoios*: "Elsewhere in Herodotus, the word **logopoios** applies to a predecessor of Herodotus, Hecataeus.... It is the likes of Hecataeus that Herodotus had in mind when he used the word **logioi** in the first sentence of the *Histories* proper (1.1.1)."

[46] Nagy 1990b.322–26, 334, citing Plut. *Mal.Hdt.* 871d.

[47] Nagy 1990b.322–25. Note that West 1984.117–18 puts together Hdt. 2.134 with certain elements of the *content* of *Vita* G, but he is not interested in the particulars of the *form* of *Vita* G in relation to the *form* of Herodotus's text.

tant elements of Nagy's approach to which I owe a pervasive conceptual debt are (1) his recognition of the remains of earlier oral traditions sedimented in much later written texts, and (2) his consistent commitment to reading canonical and noncanonical texts with and against each other to produce a richer account of Greek literary and cultural traditions. In the next chapter, I, too, will argue for a connection between certain episodes in the *Histories* and earlier traditions about the life and activities of Aesop preserved in East Greece.

Finally, Nagy argues that Herodotus is engaged in a particular kind of discourse akin to that of Aesop, which he terms *ainos*.[48] For Nagy, *ainos* is indirect or coded communication that offers one meaning on its surface, but another, deeper meaning for those "in the know."[49] On this reading, the model of *ainos* applies to Herodotus's own text, which explicitly names the Lydian tyrant Croesus as *aitios*, "responsible," as a way of implicitly directing that accusation at Athens as *polis tyrannos* in the 420s BCE.[50] In this respect, Nagy sees the Herodotean narrator as a Solon or sage figure offering advice to a tyrant, on the model of the colloquy of Solon and Croesus at Hdt. 1.29–33.[51] There is much in Nagy's reading that I find compelling, especially his notion of Herodotus's coded or indirect style of communication and his political contextualization thereof (although I will argue ultimately for a broader or more diverse audience for Herodotus's coded message). I shall return to both of these aspects at the end of the next chapter to suggest that we might instead see Herodotus as an Aesop figure, offering Aesop's characteristically indirect, analogical style of advice to the powerful.

But we should notice the way in which Aesop progressively disappears from Nagy's account—for this brings me to my disagreements with Nagy. After first identifying Herodotus's text with Aesopic *ainos*, Nagy ultimately elides Aesop in favor of Solon or another sage as Herodotus's avatar or spokesman within the *Histories*. This elision of Aesop is doubly symptomatic. It is first, as I will argue in the next chapter, a typical and understandable response to Herodotus's own ambivalent *fort-da* game with Aesop.[52] But the gapping of Aesop is also simultaneously revealing of certain problems or blind spots in Nagy's own account,

---

[48] Nagy 1990b.309–38. This usage of *ainos* is in fact anachronistic for Hdt, since, as Nagy himself acknowledges (1990b.314), the term never occurs in the text of the *Histories*. As I noted above, Hdt's own term for a fable is *logos*.

[49] Thus Nagy 1979, esp. 235–51, 275, 281–88, 313–16, 1985b, 1990b, esp. 310–38.

[50] Thus Nagy 1990b.305–13, 321–35, following the arguments of Stambler 1982 and Raaflaub 1987 on the relevance of Hdt's message to Athens in the 420s. Notice that for Nagy, Hdt's act of identifying the one who is "responsible" (*aitios*) connects his text simultaneously to a characteristic move of Aesopic fable and to the traditional role of the *histor* as "arbitrator"—in this case, arbitrator of the contemporary quarrel between Athens and Sparta. For further arguments in support of Nagy's linkage of the terms *histor* and *aitios*, see Bakker 2002.13–19.

[51] Nagy 1990b.243–49, 334. Cf. Moles 1996, 2002, making a similar argument but apparently unaware of Nagy 1990b.

[52] Cf. also chapter 3, section I above.

attributable in each case, I would contend, to a method that tends to see only sameness and does not register difference.

In the first place, Aesop disappears from Nagy's account because for Nagy everything is *ainos*. Thus following Karl Meuli, Nagy reads the *ainos*, the tale told by the disguised Odysseus to Eumaeus in *Odyssey* 14, as a coded message designed to be efficacious in a particular social situation.[53] But Nagy then generalizes Meuli's model to all of Homer, Hesiod, Archilochus and archaic iambic, archaic elegy including Theognis and Solon, and finally all of archaic and classical lyric, especially Pindar, while maintaining a link between *ainos* as "fable" and Aesop.[54] All of these then become precursors for Herodotus's *ainos*. But if everything is *ainos*, it ceases to be a useful explanatory category and certainly cannot serve to distinguish a characteristic style of Aesopic discourse from anything else in the tradition.[55]

Another kind of sameness Nagy's account presupposes is sameness through time. This assumption manifests itself in Nagy's claim that Herodotus is one in a long line of *logioi*, "masters of speech" or of "oral traditions in prose." As Nagy puts it, "The word **logios** . . . is a key to understanding the *Histories* of Herodotus as the product of conventions in an oral tradition of prose, related to but not derived from the oral traditions of poetry as represented by the Homeric *Iliad* and *Odyssey*."[56] But in a series of recent articles, Nino Luraghi has effectively dismantled Nagy's model of *logios* as a deeply traditional status or profession of "master of speech" or (as J.A.S. Evans has it) "oral remembrancer." Luraghi argues, based on all the occurrences of the term in Herodotus and other sources, that *logios* is not a status or profession, but an attribute—an adjective, not a

---

[53] Nagy 1979.234–38, following Meuli 1975b (among other scholars). For further discussion of Meuli's argument, see chapter 11, section I below.

[54] For Homer as *ainos*, see Nagy 1979, esp. 222–42; for Hesiod as *ainos*, Nagy 1979.238–41, 1990b.255–56; for Archilochus and iambic, Nagy 1979.238–39, 250, 1990b.149–50; for elegy, Nagy 1985b, 1990b.149–50; for lyric, Nagy 1979.222–42, 1990b.147–50. This generalization of *ainos* is facilitated (1) by Nagy's insistence on synchronic semantic connections among all *ain-* derivatives (*ainos*, verb *aineō*, *epainos*, *ainigma*, *parainesis*, etc.) and (2) by Nagy's argument that *ainos* designates simultaneously "praise" and "blame," based largely on a single one-line fragment of Pindar (fr. 181 SM; see Nagy 1979.250). For arguments against Nagy's interpretation of this fragment, see Kirkwood 1984, Kurke 1991.86.

[55] Indeed, at several points in Nagy's argument, *ainos* comes to be narrowly identified with the embedded poetic element in Herodotus, while the surrounding prose is identified with "the explicit message" (1990b.328); cf. 329, 332: "once the poetry of **ainigma** is quoted, Herodotus can return to a mode of explicit communication, and he therefore reverts to prose." Notice that, once *ainos* is narrowly aligned with the poetic tradition, Aesop the *logopoios* must disappear as a precursor for Hdt; at the same time, these statements of Nagy betray a modern assumption that prose is the default, transparent medium of communication, which therefore itself requires no explanation.

[56] Nagy 1987 (quotation taken from p. 175); cf. Nagy 1988, Nagy 1990b.221–26. Note that Nagy's "archaizing" interpretation of what *histor* and *historiē* mean in Hdt reinforces this idea of Hdt's deeply traditional form and content; hence the extended counterarguments of Thomas 2000 that *historiē* has significant contemporary resonances in the second half of the fifth century.

noun.⁵⁷ For Luraghi, *logioi* are simply the wise, knowledgeable, or authoritative speakers within any local tradition, but precisely insofar as they are nonspecialists, they come to be superseded by the emerging specialization of *historiē*. Thus Luraghi also rejects Nagy's claim that Herodotus would have characterized himself as a *logios*:

> It is true that essentially most of the positive qualities of being λόγιος apply to Herodotus himself: his statements about the gods and human destiny imply a claim to wisdom, and the *Histories* as a whole are a hugely impressive display of knowledge. And yet, it would be wrong to say that he intended to depict himself as a λόγιος. In critically comparing and scrutinizing the traditions of different peoples, he acts as a practitioner of a knowledge that is emphatically non-local and therefore impartial and superior. The authority he claims for himself is based on ἱστορίη, a more comprehensive and complex practice that puts him on a different and higher level than any group of λόγιοι.⁵⁸

Nagy's insistence on a long tradition of *logioi*, masters of "oral traditions in prose," thus begs the question, why Herodotus should choose the medium of prose, and obscures what is genuinely revolutionary about his project.

Finally, although Nagy concerns himself with the entire system of Greek genre (in his terms, "song, poetry, and prose"), he does not generally acknowledge the differentiation of a *hierarchy* of genre, nor does he correlate the generic system with sociopolitics—with a couple of revealing exceptions.⁵⁹ Thus at one point, Nagy notes "a crucial difference between Aesop and Herodotus . . . : whereas the **ainos** of Aesop the slave, in line with Aesop's own social position, is lowly, that of Herodotus is elevated. As such, the implicit **ainos** of Herodotus as **logios** has more in common with the **ainos** of a figure like Pindar, whose epinician lyric poetry overtly refers to itself as **ainos**."⁶⁰ Here Nagy seems explicitly to differentiate Herodotus from Aesop based on the intimate linkage of level of style and social status. But at other moments, Herodotus's relation to Aesop is less clear, as the Herodotean text seems to embrace or contain the whole gamut of what Nagy calls *ainos*. Thus, for example:

> Just as Herodotus parallels the lowly Aesop with themes of **ainos** reminiscent of the fable, so also he parallels the lofty Pindar, again with themes of **ainos**, this time reminiscent of the epinician ode.⁶¹

---

⁵⁷ See Luraghi 2001a, 2001b.156–59, 2006, 2009; cf. also Maslov 2009.10 for arguments against Nagy's interpretation of what *logios* means in Pindar. Against the comparative argument of Evans 1991.89–146, Luraghi contends that there is simply no evidence in archaic Greece for a special status or profession of "oral remembrancer" akin to the African *griot*.

⁵⁸ Luraghi 2009.456.

⁵⁹ For the whole generic system, see esp. Nagy 1990b.17–51.

⁶⁰ Nagy 1990b.326.

⁶¹ Nagy 1990b.337–38; cf. 335: "the parallelisms between the discourse of Herodotus and that of such masters of **ainos** as Aesop on one extreme and Pindar on the other. . . ."

So is Aesopic *ainos* a precursor for Herodotean prose or isn't it? Nagy has it both ways. This confusion or self-contradiction, I would suggest, results from the irreconcilability of two elements in Nagy's argument. On the one hand, Nagy recognizes that there is something low or debased about Aesop and his characteristic discourses, and that there is a fabular or Aesopic element in Herodotus; on the other hand, these recognitions do not consort comfortably with Nagy's model of the *logios* as a high-status and deeply traditional master of oral prose, akin to Homer or Pindar in the poetic tradition. That is to say, Nagy's commitment to making Herodotus the inheritor of a long and distinguished tradition of "masters of oral traditions in prose" makes it impossible for him to see Herodotus's prose as a new, experimental, and uneven form—a complex and not always comfortable amalgam of different elements.

In contrast to this, I would like to linger a little over the connotations of the term *logopoios* in the *Histories*, in order to appreciate better what might be uncomfortable—even risky—in Herodotus's prose form. As I've noted, Herodotean scholars generally take *logopoios* to be a neutral or even positive term, but I am not so sure. For almost all later occurrences of the noun λογοποιός and the verb λογοποιέω suggest the fabrication and purveying of tales of dubious truth value, often by men of low status and/or problematic moral quality.[62] Indeed, by the time of Theophrastus, λογοποιία has become the term of art for unscrupulous gossip and rumormongering (Theophr. *Char.* 8).[63] Scholars have kept these later meanings carefully cordoned off from Herodotus's usage by labeling them as distinctively Athenian or as "belong[ing] to the polemical vocabulary of the orators."[64] Still, I am not entirely persuaded that Herodotus's use

---

[62] For the noun and verb implying fiction or dubious truth value, see Plato *Rep.* 378d, 392a; for the implication of low or degraded social or moral status, see Plato *Euthyd.* 289d; for both together, Thuc. 6.38; Lysias 16.11, 22.14; Andocides 1.54; Isoc. 5.75; Dem. 4.49, 24.15; Theophr. *Char.* 8.1; Polybius 28.2.4; Plut. *Nicias* 30. In fact, the only occurrences of noun or verb I can find that seem to be genuinely neutral (bracketing for the moment Herodotus's usage) are Isoc. 5.109, 11.37 and Arrian *Anabasis* 2.16.5 (Hecataeus as *logopoios*), 3.30.8 (Herodotus as *logopoios*)—but of course it is possible that Arrian is following what he takes to be Hdt's usage. In a sense, these negative implications are not at all surprising given the frequently shifty, unreliable associations of *logos* in usages down through the fifth century (on which, see Lincoln 1997), and the suggestion of (banausic) "fashioning" or "forging" in—ποιός/-ποιέω (on which, see Chantraine 1968–80.2.922–23, Boedeker 2000.103). Thanks to Danielle Allen, who originally called my attention to the negative connotations of the term *logopoios* in later fifth- and fourth-century sources.

[63] Consider in this respect James Diggle's characterization of the *logopoios* in his recent edition of Theophrastus's *Characters*, which bears an uncanny resemblance to the portrait of Herodotus offered by certain modern scholars (e.g., Fehling 1989; S. West 1985, 1991, 2003): "He is an impostor, who spreads news of his own invention and uses a variety of artifices to lend it credibility.... He quotes unverifiable authorities ... and pretends to be moved by the misfortunes he narrates" (Diggle 2004.277). In fact, I would argue that this is exactly how Hdt is trying to represent Hecataeus in his text, and how Hdt himself is represented by some elements of a hostile ancient tradition (for which, see discussion of Plutarch below).

[64] For the former, cf. LSJ s.v. λογοποιός "II. At Athens ... professional speechmaker ... w/ collateral sense of tale-teller, newsmonger." For the latter, see Diggle 2004.277. As far as I can tell,

of *logopoios* does not carry some of the same negative connotations as the later (Athenian) uses, for several reasons. First, notice that the term *logopoios* makes its initial appearance in the *Histories* for Aesop (2.134), and only then, shortly after that, for Hecataeus (2.143). Second, it is striking that of the four times Herodotus explicitly names Hecataeus, in the single instance where he seems actually to be referring to Hecataeus's own writing (6.137), he does not designate him as *logopoios*.[65] In contrast, in each of the other three instances where Herodotus calls Hecataeus *logopoios*, there is arguably something unreliable, improper, or foolish in what Herodotus has given him to say (and this is the most compelling reason for doubt that *logopoios* is an entirely neutral term for Herodotus).[66]

Thus at 2.143, Herodotus offers us the wry portrait of his predecessor Hecataeus boastfully recounting to the Egyptian priests of Zeus/Amon-Re in Karnak his own genealogy, reaching back in the sixteenth generation to a god. The priests respond by exposing the patent absurdity of Hecataeus's arriviste claim by counting off the 345 continuous generations of human-born hereditary priests, represented by 345 wooden statues preserved in the main hall of the temple. Stephanie West has argued persuasively that we should not see a genuine reference to Hecataeus's own writing in this anecdote, but that we must instead read it as Herodotean invention. For West, the story is intended not so much to parody Hecataeus's specific self-important and unlikely claims as it is meant to stage a symbolic confrontation of two different cultures through

---

Aly 1921.18, 212–15 is unique in appreciating how odd it is that Hdt puts Hecataeus and Aesop together in the same class as *logopoioi*. From this, he concludes that Hdt's application of the term *logopoios* to Hecataeus is intended to be derogatory, although, as he also notes, Ctesias (ap. Photius) and Arrian will later designate both together as *logopoioi*. (In Ctesias, we might regard this as defamation of both predecessors, while Arrian is perhaps following what he takes to be a neutral or positive usage by Hdt himself.)

[65] Instead Hdt says, Ἑκαταῖος μὲν ὁ Ἡγησάνδρου ἔφησε ἐν τοῖσι λόγοισι. For this as the only one of the four mentions of Hecataeus likely to be a reference to Hecataeus's own writing, see S. West 1991, esp. 144–45. As Jacoby 1912.col. 2675 (= 1956.190) noted long ago, this is Hdt's one and only explicit reference to an earlier prose text as a source; for a persuasive account of Hdt's reason for this aberration, see Luraghi 2001b.159–60.

[66] Most modern scholars assume that Herodotus is mainly respectful of his Milesian predecessor, while critical of particular details of Hecataeus's earlier accounts (in a way that is characteristic of the bids for authority of ancient historians). For Hdt's relation to Hecataeus, see (e.g.) Diels 1887; Jacoby 1912.coll. 2675–86 (= 1956.190–95), 1913.coll. 341–52 (=1956.75–80); S. West 1991; Hornblower 1994.15–16; Boedeker 2000.107–8. Nicolai 1997 represents an important challenge to older scholarly notions of the unique importance of Hecataeus for Hdt, but still assumes that Hdt treats Hecataeus respectfully when he mentions him. Macan (1895.I.lxvi–vii) interestingly takes a different view: "It is at the expense of Ionians, if at all, that Herodotus betrays a little malice. . . . It is at the geography of the Ionians that the Dorian laughs, and against his own greatest predecessor, and Ionian statesman and historian, that he seems to bear a somewhat special grudge." While Macan's version is cast in the essentializing terms characteristic of his era (Ionians vs Dorians), it is (as we shall see) based on astute observation of particular details in Hdt's text.

exemplary figures (much like Solon and Croesus at 1.29–33).⁶⁷ And yet it seems Herodotus cannot resist a little humor at the expense of his predecessor when he introduces the story:

> πρότερον δὲ Ἑκαταίῳ τῷ λογοποιῷ ἐν Θήβῃσι γενεηλογήσαντι ἑωυτὸν καὶ ἀναδήσαντι τὴν πατριὴν ἐς ἑκκαιδέκατον θεὸν ἐποίησαν οἱ ἱρέες τοῦ Διὸς οἷόν τι καὶ ἐμοὶ οὐ γενεηλογήσαντι ἐμεωυτόν· (Hdt. 2.143.1)
>
> At an earlier time, for Hecataeus the *logopoios*, who had in Thebes genealogized himself and bound his family in the sixteenth generation to a god, the priests of Zeus did the same thing that they [later] also did for me (although I didn't offer my own genealogy). . . .

The wry parenthesis, "for me (although I didn't offer my own genealogy)" is entirely gratuitous for the content of the story and the confrontation of cultures, but it does serve to differentiate the sober Herodotus from Hecataeus as teller of tall tales (*logopoios*), whose aristocratic, heroic pretensions are punctured by the Egyptian priests.⁶⁸

The other two occurrences of Hecataeus's name linked to the designation *logopoios*, 5.36 and 5.125, are both scenes of deliberation and public speaking connected to the Ionian Revolt (and so both partake of the same "oratorical" context in which *logopoios* occurs as a derogatory term in Thucydides and throughout the fourth century). In both contexts, scholars have seen Hecataeus filling the conventional Herodotean role of wise adviser or tragic warner, whose sage counsel goes unheeded.⁶⁹ And yet, in both contexts, there is something a little odd or off about the specific advice Hecataeus is made to proffer. In the first instance (5.36), in a council to discuss whether or not the Ionian cities should revolt, Hecataeus is the lone opposing voice:

> [Aristagoras] then was taking counsel with the rebels, revealing both his own opinion (γνώμην) and the things that had come from Histiaeus. And indeed, all the rest were declaring the same opinion, bidding [him] to revolt, but Hecataeus the *logopoios* in the first place was not allowing [them] to undertake a war against the king of the Persians, cataloging both all the nations whom Darius ruled and his power. But when he was not persuading them, in the second place, he was advising them to act in such a way that they will be masters of the sea. And he said that he foresaw no way that this

---

⁶⁷ S. West 1991.145–54.

⁶⁸ For the aristocratic political interests and motivations of Hecataeus's *Genealogies*, see Nicolai 1997.159–62. If we accept Stephanie West's argument for this story as Hdt's own invention, it produces an effect of vertiginous irony that I'm sure was not lost on Hdt: for Hdt here engages in precisely the kind of unreliable, unsubstantiated gossip that characterizes the *logopoios* (i.e., just what he mocks Hecataeus for).

⁶⁹ For the figure of the sage adviser or "tragic warner" in Hdt, see Lattimore 1939, Bischoff 1965, Immerwahr 1966.72–75, Fehling 1989.203–9; for application of this type to Hecataeus in these two scenes in Book 5, see Lang 1968.29–30, Fehling 1989.209, S. West 1991.154–57, Nicolai 1997.150.

would happen otherwise (for he knew the power of the Milesians to be weak) but only if the property in the temple at Branchidae should be removed, the property Croesus the Lydian had dedicated. In that case, he was holding out great hopes that they would rule the sea, and thus they themselves would be able to make use of the property and their enemies not be able to loot it. (And this property was great, as has been made clear by me in the first of the *logoi*.) Now this opinion was not prevailing, but even so it seemed best to them to revolt.... (Hdt. 5.36.1-4)

Here Hecataeus deploys his considerable geographic knowledge in the service of the argument that it is folly to take on the much more powerful Persians (which does indeed seem to conform to Herodotus's own view).[70] When that argument fails, Hecataeus sensibly predicts that the Ionians cannot effectively resist the Persians unless they make themselves masters of the sea (and this, too, seems eminently correct). But somewhat more problematic is Hecataeus's positive suggestion for how the Ionians might achieve naval hegemony; in proposing that they take and convert to cash Croesus's dedications at Branchidae, he is advocating *hierosulia*.[71] Stephanie West compares his proposal to that of Pericles in Thucydides (2.13), but this comparison elides significant differences.[72] It is not just that Pericles treats this as a loan from the temple that will be repaid afterward, but that in Thucydides, the dedications were made by the Athenians themselves, whereas Hecataeus advocates taking valuables consecrated by someone else—their old enemy Croesus. Herodotus offers no explicit indication of his view of this proposal, but it is at least arguable that he represents Hecataeus the *logopoios* combining his geographic expertise and political savvy with an unscrupulous—even impious—policy suggestion.

Hecataeus's advice at 5.125 is equally problematic, but for different reasons. After the Persian capture of the cities of Ionian Clazomenae and Aeolian Cyme, the troublemaker Aristagoras calls another council:

With respect to these things then indeed, having called together his fellow rebels, [Aristagoras] was taking counsel, saying that it would be better for them to have ready some place of refuge, if they should be thrust out of Miletus, whether he should indeed lead them to Sardinia in order to found a colony from this place, or to Myrcinus in Edonia, which Histiaeus was in the process of fortifying, having gotten it as a gift from Darius. At this point, the opinion of Hecataeus the son of Hegesander, the

---

[70] Cf. S. West 1991.156: καταλέγων τά τε ἔθνεα πάντα τῶν ἦρχε Δαρεῖος καὶ τὴν δύναμιν αὐτοῦ "serves nicely to remind us of Hecataeus' geographical work (just as γενεηλογήσαντι and ἀντεγενεηλόγησαν in the Theban episode call to mind his antiquarian researches)."

[71] As Macan (1895.I.179) recognizes: "Hekataios is one of the tyrant's partisans. This circumstance would not recommend him to Hdt., nor yet his sacrilegious advice.... Hekataios the prosewright is at first in despair and then full of hope, his hopes being bound up with a counsel of despair, if not of impiety." Cf. S. West 1991.156, who also notes the sacrilegious quality of Hecataeus's advice, using it as an argument against the historicity of the anecdote.

[72] S. West 1991.156.

logopoios, was holding [for him] to lead an expedition to neither of these places, but instead, having fortified the island of Leros, to keep quiet [there]; but then later, he could set out from this island and return to Miletus. (Hdt. 5.124.2–125)

Scholars have recognized that, under the circumstances, with the Persians in control of the sea, Hecataeus's plan of fortifying and keeping quiet on the island of Leros is "absurd."[73] Some scholars have therefore suggested that Hecataeus is thinking here only of saving Aristagoras from the ire of the Milesians, and that he serves simply as a stock tragic warner in relation to the foolish Milesian tyrant. For Aristagoras in Herodotus's account fails to take Hecataeus's advice, goes off to Myrcinus in Thrace, and is immediately killed by militant natives.[74] But the fact that Aristagoras's choice is bad does not make Hecataeus's advice good. In fact, Herodotus has embedded in Aristagoras's initial proposal of alternatives the idea of emigration to Sardinia, the very advice the Sage Bias had offered when Ionia was originally conquered by Croesus, which Herodotus himself praises in Book 1 as "most useful" (1.170).[75] Thus here, too, Hecataeus the *logopoios* may know his geography, but his advice is of dubious quality.

All this suggests that the term *logopoios* may already have been a problematic one in Herodotus's time, implying both dubious truth value and disreputable social or moral status, and not therefore a designation Herodotus would necessarily have welcomed for himself. Thus we might follow Rosalind Thomas, who suggests "that when Herodotus talked of his work as *historie* he was deliberately setting it within the milieu of the philosophical and proto-scientific enquiries of his time: a signal to his audience, perhaps, that he was not merely a *logopoios*."[76] Or we might go even further with Stephanie West, who notes "an undeniable tension between the prominence afforded to anecdotes and migratory plots, on the one hand, and, on the other, the resolutely scientific approach to matters of current intellectual debate."[77] I would suggest that West's opposed categories of a "resolutely scientific approach" and "anecdotes and migratory plots" correspond to a tension between Herodotus's roles as *histor* and as *logopoios* that runs through the text of the *Histories*. But in contrast to the implications of

---

[73] The term is Macan's (1895.I.267); cf. S. West 1991.156: "His plan to fortify Leros, Miletus' colony, and establish a base there for an eventual return to the city makes no sense as an anti-Persian tactic."

[74] Thus Lang 1968.33, followed by S. West 1991.156–57. In contrast, Macan 1895.I.267 suggests that Hdt attributes this suggestion in these circumstances to Hecataeus deliberately to make him look ridiculous.

[75] For full quotation of this passage, see chapter 3, section II above.

[76] Thomas 2000.161–67 (quotation from p. 167); cf. p. 163: "What is clear, is that Herodotus calls Hecataeus a *logopoios* along with Aesop . . . —rather than a sophist or a *sophos* or any other possibility—and that his use of *historie* of his own work suggests that he wished to present it in a different light." The negative associations of *logopoios* also strongly suggest that we cannot simply equate the terms *logopoios* and *logios* (as does Nagy 1990b.224n. 54).

[77] S. West 2003.437.

Thomas (and perhaps also West), I assume that Herodotus deploys *both* these modes knowingly and artfully, in spite of the risks involved. I say this because at times this new, contextualized understanding of *historiē* treats the unevenness of the text as an accidental by-product of Herodotean primitivism or "proto-science"—as if Herodotus is trying to be a thoroughly rational scientist, but simply cannot achieve universal application of his scientific principles, forced in the meantime to fall back on story and anecdote as the only available material to fill in historical gaps. But this eminently practical model ignores the issue of *decorum* and the fact that, at least on occasion in his narrative, Herodotus chooses deliberately to rupture or violate a generally high—we might even say Homeric—level of narrative style and tone. We can appreciate this issue of decorum and its deliberate rupture better by recognizing that the role of *logopoios* entails not just a truth but a status taint, and that, even so, paradoxically, it is a role that the Herodotean narrator on occasion assumes.

This paradox emerges clearly in Herodotus's ambivalent treatment of Aesop; indeed, at this point, we can see that Herodotus's designation of Aesop as *logopoios* at 2.134 may itself be a measure of his ambivalence toward this prose precursor. Recall that Aesop shows up only once in Herodotus, contained or cordoned off from the main narrative in a digression within a digression. Even here, we get tantalizing tidbits about his life story, but Aesop is never allowed to speak. Nor does Herodotus ever tell explicit fable as fable in his own voice, but only through the mediation of one of his characters.[78] And yet at the same time, as I shall argue in the next chapter, there are abundant disguised fable narratives and even, on occasion, disguised scenes of Aesopic advising embedded in Herodotus's text. In this respect, there is a significant difference between Herodotus's procedures and those we identified for the Sophists in chapter 7. The Sophists convert Aesopic fable into an appropriate medium for the teaching of the young, while they consistently transpose this humble popular form into stylish artistic prose. Herodotus, as we shall see in the next chapter, preserves the explosive vulgarity of low fable, even as he draws on an older model of Aesop as a sage political counselor.[79] Thus Aesop, I would suggest, is emblematic of all those elements in the *Histories* that make Herodotus himself a *logopoios*, so that by tracking Aesop and his characteristic discourses in the text we

---

[78] Thus, contra van Dijk 1997.270–71, who remarks that it is surprising that Hdt does not attribute the fable at 1.141 to Aesop himself, I would contend that this is not surprising at all, but a matter of decorum. For parallels for the decorous distancing of Aesop and Aesopic fable in the *Histories*, cf. Lang 1984.58–67, who notes that the narrator never speaks proverbs in his own voice, but only attributed to characters, and Griffiths 1995, arguing that blatant derisive laughter or mockery (which the Greeks would have regarded as vulgar) frequently characterizes laughter by characters within the text, but never the narrator's own humor.

[79] Thus on this point, I would disagree with Thomas 2000.174–75, who assimilates Hdt's practices as "story-teller" to Sophistic deployments of fable (following Aly 1929). For this assimilation ignores the use of different types of fable and significant differences in style and decorum of narration.

382   CHAPTER 10

can come to understand Herodotus's embrace of this problematic mode as both narratologically and politically consequential.

III. Plutarch Reading Herodotus: Aesop, Ruptures of Decorum, and the Non-Greek

In order to underscore the issues of decorum involved in Herodotus's deployment of the Aesopic and to appreciate better the real-world sociopolitical stakes of Herodotus's choice of styles and genres, I want to conclude this chapter with a brief consideration of the ancient reception of Herodotus, focusing mainly on Plutarch's treatise *On the Malice of Herodotus*. For, as we saw with the reception of Plato, ancient readings of Herodotus on occasion draw our attention to weird, anomalous, and indecorous elements that modern readers are not always willing or able to come to grips with. We might start by noting that, for ancient as for modern literary criticism, the linkage of Herodotus to Homer was a central topos; thus, for example, the author of *On the Sublime* hails Herodotus as Ὁμηρικώτατος ("most Homeric," 13.3). It is therefore all too easy to read the ancient tradition of Herodotus reception through the lens of modern scholarly preoccupations, assuming that the ancient reception is entirely concerned with historical truth versus fancy or fiction, and that this opposition is identical to our assumed oppositions of prose versus poetry or science versus narrative art.[80] It is true that, on occasion, for ancient as for modern readers, the identification of Herodotus with Homer can refer to literary or narrative artistry; thus Dionysius of Halicarnassus characterizes Herodotus as an "emulator of Homer" precisely in the context of his skillful use of variation in narrative (ποικίλην ἐβουλήθη ποιῆσαι τὴν γραφὴν Ὁμήρου ζηλωτὴς γενόμενος, *Letter to Pompeius* 3). And yet we should not be deceived by this apparent commonality. In fact, ancient readings are often on a skew line to modern approaches, insofar as they are at least equally concerned with decorum as with truth value. For these ancient readers, the identification of Herodotus with Homer is simultaneously a way of registering the decorum and level of elevation considered proper for historiography as a rhetorical genre.[81] By the same token, as we shall see, at

---

[80] In an important discussion of Herodotus reception in antiquity, Momigliano 1960 differentiated between historical and literary-critical/rhetorical responses, and suggested that the text of Herodotus survived mainly as a stylistic model. Murray 1972, Bowersock 1989, and Hornblower 2006, while they disagree with Momigliano's claim that Hdt had no historical imitators, share his basic assumption of a content-style split in the Herodotus reception: (1) ancient historians are concerned only with his truth value; (2) ancient literary critics are concerned only with his style. But I would contend that we must acknowledge the issue of decorum, which crosscuts the content-style or historical-rhetorical divide.

[81] Cf. Woodman 1988 on historiography as a literary and rhetorical genre in antiquity. In addition, Woodman offers the salutary reminder that, for both Herodotus and Thucydides at least, the

least one ancient reader's recognition of the Aesopic in the *Histories* is intimately bound up with disturbingly low elements and ruptures of decorum that taint Herodotus's text and Herodotus himself. For, of course, in the ancient tradition, the concept of decorum is never innocent, but contains a potent sociopolitical element we would do well to be aware of. As I have argued throughout this book, the ancient Greek literary system was founded on a strict hierarchy of genre and decorum that (at least notionally) corresponded to a sociopolitical hierarchy. This combined generic-sociopolitical hierarchy generated in antiquity the opposition Homeric epic–Aesopic fable as one that could do all kinds of ideological signifying work, far beyond the domain we might understand as narrowly literary; we have already encountered this opposition informing the structure and pattern of Xenophon's *Memorabilia*. Thus the hierarchical binary Homeric epic–Aesopic fable could also interact with or map onto other significant oppositions pervasive in antiquity: first, Apollo versus Aesop, where the god is identified with prophetic authority and elite, poetic *sophia*, while Aesop contests and parodies precisely these spheres of power. Second, the same oppostion of Apollo and Aesop is aligned with an opposition between disembodied voice (on the side of Apollo's oracle) over against coarse, excessive bodiliness (the domain of Aesop).

It is necessary to lay out all these overdetermined, shifting oppositions to demonstrate that there is much more at stake than pure literary judgment in ancient assessments of Herodotus. In fact, we can map ancient assessments precisely along a spectrum that runs from Homer to Aesop: insofar as an ancient critic likes Herodotus (for whatever complex reasons of politics, content, and decorum), he assimilates him to Homeric poetry; insofar as an ancient critic dislikes or disapproves of Herodotus, he assimilates him to Aesopic prose. Thus, for example, in a second-century BCE public inscription from Halicarnassus, Herodotus is lionized by the proud Halicarnassians as "the prose Homer" (*Supplementum Epigraphicum Graecum* 48.1330, l. 43: τὸν πεζὸν ἐν ἱστορίαισιν Ὅμηρον).[82] And, as I noted, the author of *On the Sublime* praises Herodotus as Ὁμηρικώτατος, but occasionally censures Herodotus's word choice when he perceives it as too colloquial and bodily.[83] At the other end of the spectrum is

---

Iliad is not fiction but a historical account, so that we cannot simply assume that for the ancients the axis prose vs poetry is isomorphic with history vs fiction.

[82] For discussion of the inscription, see Isager 1998, Lloyd-Jones 1999, Gagné 2006.

[83] For rare criticisms of Hdt's word choice, see *On the Sublime* 4.7 ("frigidity"), 43.1 (terms too common, colloquial, and bodily). Notice also the immediate context in which Longinus characterizes Hdt as "most Homeric": "For many men are carried away by the spirit of others as if inspired, just as it is related of the Pythian priestess when she approaches the tripod, where there is a rift in the ground which (they say) exhales divine vapour. By heavenly power thus communicated she is impregnated and straightway delivers oracles in virtue of the afflatus. Similarly from the great natures of men of old there are borne in upon the souls of those who emulate them (as from sacred caves) what we may describe as *effluences*, so that even those who seem little likely to be possessed

384   CHAPTER 10

Plutarch, in his treatise *On the Malice of Herodotus*. Plutarch has serious objections to Herodotus's *Histories*, not just (as is often said) because of Herodotus's representation of Medizing Boeotians, but also because Herodotus simply does not supply the kind of high, celebratory history of Greek unity and Greek triumph that Plutarch, an elite Greek living under Roman rule, desperately wants.[84] That is to say, this is not just an issue of historical truth, but an issue of decorum that is highly politically charged. In his frustration, Plutarch devotes a great deal of rhetorical energy to debunking or transforming the already-established critical topos that Herodotus is "Homeric" (without ever explicitly acknowledging it). At the same time he works hard to represent Herodotus as Aesopic, thereby undermining Herodotus by refashioning him as a *logopoios* in very much the same terms that Herodotus used to undermine his predecessor Hecataeus. By focusing on just a few moments in this remarkable treatise, I want to demonstrate that Plutarch not only identifies Herodotus with Aesop, but also on several occasions articulates precisely what characterizes Herodotus's discourse as Aesopic. In addition, the imagery and innuendo by which Plutarch discredits Herodotus as an Aesopic *logopoios* in this artful and highly rhetorical text will make particularly visible the concomitant sociopolitics of genre and decorum on which I have insisted all along.

First, Homer versus Aesop. Plutarch begins his treatise by acknowledging the smooth, elegant, and appealing features of Herodotean style (ch. 1/854e). In a sense, this is a necessary starting point, since Plutarch needs to counter the reading of *ēthos* from style that is a pervasive and fundamental tenet of all ancient criticism.[85] He needs to demonstrate that although Herodotus's style gives an impression of ease and geniality, this is simply a cover for genuine malice and mean-spiritedness toward his historical subjects. When Plutarch returns to this same topic of the misfit of style and authorial intent in his peroration, he

---

(οἱ μὴ λίαν φοιβαστικοί) are thereby inspired and succumb to the spell of others' greatness. Was Herodotus alone a devoted imitator of Homer? No, Stesichorus even before his time, and Archilochus, and above all Plato, who from the great Homeric source drew to himself innumerable tributary streams" (*On the Sublime* 13.2–3, trans. Roberts 1935). In this extraordinary conceit, Homer plays Apollo to Herodotus's Pythia, inspiring the Herodotean body with the divine afflatus of Homeric voice.

[84] On the response of Plutarch and the Greek "Second Sophistic" generally to Roman political domination, see Bowersock 1965, Jones 1971, Bowie 1974, Gabba 1982. Note that all modern scholars, whatever they think the precise politics of this relation was, acknowledge that imperial Greek elites set very high store by the glories of the Greek past—especially the Persian Wars of the fifth century BCE. Thus it seems that, across the political spectrum, imperial Greeks wanted a celebratory history of Greek unity and Greek triumph over barbarian invaders. Cf. Momigliano 1960.36: "History was a form of encomium to Plutarch, and evidently Herodotus did not fit into the pattern." Momigliano goes on to speculate that Plutarch's treatise is the only survivor of a once extensive genre of anti-Herodotus tracts (for which we have several titles preserved from the first and second centuries CE).

[85] Cf. Marincola 1994.

includes the sole Homeric quotation in a text that otherwise bristles with learned citations of earlier authors:

> γραφικὸς ἀνήρ, καὶ ἡδὺς ὁ λόγος, καὶ χάρις ἔπεστι καὶ δεινότης καὶ ὥρα τοῖς διηγήμασι· "μῦθον δ᾽ ὡς ὅτ᾽ ἀοιδός, ἐπισταμένως" μὲν οὔ, λιγυρῶς δὲ καὶ γλαφυρῶς ἠγόρευκεν. ἀμέλει ταῦτα καὶ κηλεῖ καὶ προσάγεται πάντας, ἀλλ᾽ ὥσπερ ἐν ῥόδοις δεῖ κανθαρίδα φυλάττεσθαι τὴν βλασφημίαν αὐτοῦ καὶ κακολογίαν, λείοις καὶ ἁπαλοῖς σχήμασιν ὑποδεδυκυῖαν, ἵνα μὴ λάθωμεν ἀτόπους καὶ ψευδεῖς περὶ τῶν ἀρίστων καὶ μεγίστων τῆς Ἑλλάδος πόλεων καὶ ἀνδρῶν δόξας λαβόντες. (*Mal.Hdt.* ch. 43/874b–c)

> The man is an artist, and his tale is sweet, and his narratives have grace and force and freshness. And he has told his story "like a bard, knowingly"—not, but delicately and smoothly. These are the things that simply charm and seduce everyone, but we must beware of his slander and evil speaking just as of a beetle in the roses, cloaked as they are in smooth and soft forms, so that we do not, unbeknownst to ourselves, accept false and out-of-place opinions about the best and greatest cities and men of Hellas.

Plutarch quotes and then strategically negates Alcinous's words of praise for Odysseus's embedded travel tales (*Ody.* 11.368), denying Herodotus true knowledge, while crediting him only with a delicate and smooth bard's style. Plutarch thus acknowledges the preexisting critical commonplace that Herodotus is Homeric at the very moment he transforms its signification, skillfully using it here at the treatise's conclusion to pry apart style and authorial *ēthos*. As several scholars have observed, this is Plutarch at his most Platonic; here, in contrast to Longinus's deployment of Homer as model of sublimity, Plutarch's conjuring of the image of the Homeric bard for Herodotus puts him in the class of lying poets who are to be banished from the ideal polity. That is to say, Plutarch here splices seamlessly from the axis of decorum (Homer = elevated) to the axis of truth (poetry = lying).[86]

By contrast, a few chapters earlier, Plutarch tellingly assimilates Herodotus instead to Aesop. At this point, Plutarch is fulminating against Herodotus's report that the Delphic oracle, consulted after the Battle of Salamis about the adequacy of the Greeks' offerings of *akrothinia*, responded "that he was satisfied with those from the rest of the Greeks, but not with the Aeginetans. But he was demanding as his due from them the *aristeia* of the Battle of Salamis" (Hdt. 8.122). Plutarch, construing this to mean that Herodotus has invidiously deprived the Athenians of the naval *aristeia* through the mouthpiece of Apollo, at this point erupts in a fit of sputtering rhetorical rage:

> οὐκέτι Σκύθαις οὐδὲ Πέρσαις οὐδ᾽ Αἰγυπτίοις τοὺς ἑαυτοῦ λόγους ἀνατίθησι πλάττων, ὥσπερ Αἴσωπος κόρακι καὶ πιθήκοις, ἀλλὰ τῷ τοῦ Πυθίου προσώπῳ χρώμενος, ἀπωθεῖ τῶν ‹ἐν› Σαλαμῖνι πρωτείων τὰς Ἀθήνας.... (*Mal.Hdt.* ch. 40/871d)

---

[86] Thus Lachenaud 1981.258n. 5, Hershbell 1993.154–58. Note that, appropriately enough for a Platonist, what Plutarch specifically denies Hdt is *epistēmē*.

No longer, fabricating his own *logoi*, does he attribute them to Scythians or Persians or Egyptians, just like Aesop to his crows and apes; but now using the persona of the Pythian god himself, he thrusts Athens away from pride of place at Salamis. . . .

By implication, Herodotus's "others" (Scythians, Persians, and Egyptians) are somehow more appropriately identified with the genre of Aesopic fable, both as themselves Aesopic animal characters and (as we'll see when we get to Herodotus) as speakers of fable.[87] On the other hand, the ultimate outrage as far as Plutarch is concerned is Herodotus's co-opting of the Delphic oracle as mouthpiece for his own "fabricated" Aesopic *logoi*.[88] For this is to take the Delphic god, who stands at the apex of the Greek system of prophetic power and elite *sophia*, and reduce him to its nadir, to the figure of Aesop, or worse—to an animal character within an Aesopic tale.[89] Plutarch's priamel of outrage thus implies a view of Herodotus's *Histories* akin to some modern views. On this reading, the first four books, the ethnographic tour of "Egyptians, Persians, and Scythians," is a more acceptable place for Herodotus to "tell tales"—to play the Aesopic fable-maker, while the last five books (the narrative of the Persian Wars proper, starting from the Ionian Revolt) ought to represent high, celebratory history with no low or fabular element.[90] Part of Plutarch's exasperation stems from Herodotus's refusal to play by these rules; though one could make an essentializing distinction (as Plutarch tries to do) between "others" and Greeks, between Eastern exotica and Western history, and map that onto the set of oppositions I've already outlined, Herodotus's text resists and scrambles these overdetermined ranked homologies, even as it maintains an Aesopic element throughout.

Thus, in his polemical attempt to refute the conventional alignment of Herodotus with Homer, Plutarch effectively outs Herodotus as an Aesopic

---

[87] Cf. *On the Sublime* 4.7, where the author offers as some "extenuation" (παραμυθίαν) for a frigid expression at Hdt. 5.18 the fact that the words are spoken by "drunken barbarians" (in this case, Persians) as "characters" (προσώπων) within Hdt's text.

[88] Note how Plutarch's λόγους . . . πλάττων serves as a calque on *logopoios*, with πλάττων tweaking it even further in the direction of fabrication. We might also note that the animals Plutarch mentions are particularly low or disreputable ones within the universe of fable—not lions and foxes, symbols of kingship and cunning, respectively, but the mean-spirited, dirty, and spiteful crows and apes.

[89] Nagy 1990b.322, 334 also quotes this passage of Plutarch as evidence for a strand of Aesopic *ainos* in Hdt; but it is difficult to tell what exactly Nagy thinks Plutarch intends by this statement. At times, Nagy seems simply to equate Delphic oracles and Aesopic fable as instances of *ainos* in Hdt (e.g., p. 322); elsewhere, he implies that Plutarch disapproves of Hdt's too-frequent quotation of Delphic oracles in his history (see esp. p. 334). But this latter claim is not persuasive: Plutarch was himself a Delphic functionary and quoted oracles all the time in his own historical writing. As he does elsewhere, Nagy here simply assimilates different literary and social forms to his overbroad category of *ainos* and thereby collapses or effaces significant cultural oppositions (here: Apollo/Delphic oracle vs Aesop).

[90] This is in some ways comparable to the traditional model of Jacoby (1909, 1913.coll. 279–380 [= 1956.44–94]), and also, at least in relation to Book 2, to Fornara 1971b.1–23.

writer, exposing a side of the Halicarnassian modern readers seem generally unable or unwilling to see. In following Plutarch, I have no desire to endorse his diagnosis—that what motivates Herodotus is "spite" or "malice" (κακοήθεια); nonetheless, I find Plutarch an extremely astute and sensitive reader of Herodotean "symptoms"—those weird or anomalous moments in Herodotus's text often ignored by modern critics.

Nor is this identification of Herodotus with Aesop merely an isolated eruption in Plutarch's text. In fact, throughout his treatise, Plutarch consistently represents Herodotus as Aesopic in his discourse as in his low-class, non-Greek associations.[91] So what, according to Plutarch, characterizes Herodotus's Aesopic discourse? First and most broadly, that it conceals a harsh, malicious, and negative meaning under a smooth and apparently positive surface: like all the forms that Gregory Nagy has characterized as *ainos*, it is a two-tiered communication.[92] More specifically: on several occasions, Plutarch's criticisms of Herodotus strikingly coincide with the ancient stereotypes of "slave talk" that we considered in chapter 3 above. Recall Aristotle's offhand reference to the "*makros logos* of Simonides" in his rejection of the possibility of representing Plato's Forms as numbers in the *Metaphysics*, together with Alexander of Aphrodisias's extended gloss thereon:

> To be sure, all these views are irrational, and they conflict with themselves and with good reasoning, and in them we are likely to have the "long story" of Simonides. For the "long story" occurs, just as of slaves, whenever they have nothing sound to say (γίγνεται γὰρ ὁ μακρὸς λόγος ὥσπερ ὁ τῶν δούλων ὅταν μηθὲν ὑγιὲς λέγωσιν, Arist. *Met*. 14.3, 1091a5–9)

> It will be clear from the foregoing things what the "*logos* of Simonides" is. Simonides in the *logoi* he entitles *Ataktoi* ("Disordered Accounts" or "Miscellaneous Tales"[?]) imitates and says the words that slaves are likely to say when they've tripped up to their masters cross-examining them on why they made these mistakes. And he makes them, in the course of their self-defense (ἀπολογουμένους), speak many long speeches, but nothing sound or persuasive, but everything that comes later the opposite of what was said before. For such (as is likely) is the barbarous and that which is without a share of education (τοιοῦτον γὰρ ὡς εἰκὸς τὸ βάρβαρον καὶ παιδείας ἄμοιρον, Alex. Aphrodis. *Comment. in Ar. Graec*. 1.818.3 Hayduck = Simonides fr. 653 *PMG*)

And recall that Aristotle recurs to this account of "slave talk" in the *Rhetoric*: "This is what those also do who have, or seem to have, a bad case; for it is better

---

[91] This is not to deny the presence of other negative associations (some of them generic) throughout Plutarch's treatise: thus, for example, he assimilates Hdt to unscrupulous false accusers in court, to caricaturists, and to abusive poets of Old Comedy (Cf. *Mal.Hdt.* chs. 6, 7, 27, 33, 35).

[92] Paradoxically, Plutarch's model of surface and depth here inverts the one typically applied to Aesopic discourse (as we have seen esp. in chapters 4 and 9), for the Aesopic is generally characterized as inwardly wise and beneficial, but superficially coarse, humble, and ugly.

to lay stress upon anything rather than the case itself. That is why slaves never answer questions directly but go all round them, and indulge in preambles" (*Rhet.* 3.14.10–11, 1415b22–24, trans. Freese 1982). As I suggested in chapter 3, insofar as Aesop is the quintessential or paradigmatic slave in popular tradition, we might read these characterizations as applying not just generally to slaves, but a fortiori to Aesop.

For his part, Plutarch attributes to Herodotus precisely the same qualities: his discourse is indirect and digressive, "circling round and round" (in general, ch. 3/855b, κυκλούμενος; in particular, ch. 23/860e, οὐκέτι κύκλῳ καὶ κακῶς). Indeed, in relation to Herodotus's recounting of several different stories told about the Argives' nonparticipation in the Persian Wars (Hdt. 7.148–52), Plutarch goes even further, flatly labeling Herodotus's "words" and "poses" as δολερά ("treacherous, deceitful") and, as his rhetorical climax, quoting a line from Euripides' *Andromache*: ἑλικτὰ κοὐδὲν ὑγιὲς ἀλλὰ πᾶν πέριξ (ch. 28/863e = *Andr.* 448, "twisted and nothing sound, but all back to front"). Here we find a striking collocation of many of the same terms Aristotle uses in his two accounts of "slave talk"; Herodotus's words "twist and turn" (ἑλικτά, πᾶν πέριξ) and contain "nothing sound" or "healthy" (οὐδὲν ὑγιὲς). In addition, it is worth noting that this line occurs in the *Andromache* (in typically paradoxical Euripidean fashion) in the context of the Trojan heroine's denunciation of the treacherous Spartan character. That is to say, as Plutarch was clearly aware, this is a characterization of the speech or thought of a hostile, barbarian or quasi-barbarian other, and as such it recalls Alexander of Aphrodisias's final smug and jingoistic tag to his gloss on Aristotle: τοιοῦτον γὰρ ὡς εἰκὸς τὸ βάρβαρον καὶ παιδείας ἄμοιρον. I call attention to these associations, because they will become relevant when we turn to the imagery and innuendo Plutarch deploys against Herodotus throughout his treatise.

But there is still more: just as for Aristotle, the original point of comparison between slave discourse and arguments about the Forms is that both are illogical and self-contradictory, so Plutarch insists that Herodotus's malice "fills his account with confusion and contradiction" (τοσαύτης ἀναπίμπλησι ταραχῆς καὶ διαφωνίας τὸ κακόηθες αὐτοῦ τὸν λόγον, ch. 23/861a). Plutarch repeats this accusation of "confusion" (τοιαύτας . . . ταραχάς) specifically in the context of Herodotus's account of the aftermath of the Battle of Marathon—the treacherous shield-signal, attributed by some in Athens to the Alcmeonidae, and Herodotus's subsequent defense of the Alcmeonids as "tyrant-haters" (ch. 27/862c–63b, discussing Hdt. 6.121–31). Here ταραχή signifies not actual mental befuddlement (as it seems to in Aristotle), but rather deliberate inconsistency, designed to produce a coded discourse of blame masquerading as praise or defense. And in this instance (as in many others), Plutarch proves himself a particularly astute reader of Herodotus, deftly pinpointing "hot spots" or moments of interpretive opacity in the *Histories*. For debate still rages among modern scholars on the degree of sincerity or irony in Herodotus's treatment of this noble Athenian family, and we shall have cause to focus on the so-called Alcmeonid digression when we turn to consider Aesopic elements in the text of Herodotus in the next chapter.[93]

Finally, there is one more characteristically Aesopic discursive feature Plutarch uses to vilify Herodotus—flattery of the rich and powerful. Recall that we find this negative representation of Aesop explicitly formulated in a whole tradition of Solon's and Aesop's contrasting styles of speaking to Croesus, as recounted by Diodorus Siculus and by Plutarch himself in the *Life of Solon*, as well as implicitly in the proverb, "Rather the Phrygian" (see chapter 3, section I above). Thus in the same chapter in which he rails at Herodotus for his ambiguous and self-contradictory treatment of the Alcmeonidae, Plutarch observes that Herodotus has gone out of his way to drag in a mention of Callias and his son Hipponicus, "who was in Herodotus's day one of the richest men in Athens"—for no other reason, Plutarch insists, but "obsequiously to gratify Hipponicus" (ἀλλὰ θεραπείᾳ καὶ χάριτι τοῦ Ἱππονίκου, ch. 27/863b). But we should also recall that alongside the moralizing "Solonian" tradition that saw nothing more than base flattery in Aesop's discourse, there was a different strand of thinking in antiquity that valorized the efficacy of Aesop's characteristically indirect speech. This tradition, represented by the *Life of Aesop* itself and Agathias's sixth-century CE epigram on Aesop and the Seven Sages, construed the distinctive "sweetness" or "pleasure" of Aesopic discourse as an effective means of persuasion. And even as Plutarch clearly rejects this construal of Aesopic flattery throughout his treatise (as in the *Life of Solon*), we may still catch a residue of this contested point in his final grudging concessions about the "charm" of Herodotean style (quoted above, p. 385). For here, Plutarch introduces a term that had not figured at all in his opening praise of Herodotus's style—that of "sweetness," acknowledging καὶ ἡδὺς ὁ λόγος. Taken out of context, this could be read as a perfect characterization of Aesopic "fable" at almost any point in the tradition. And it is hard to resist the suspicion that Plutarch introduces this characterization here climactically, now that he has proven his case for Herodotus as an Aesopic *logopoios* and almost immediately before quoting a Homeric line in order to limit Herodotus's affiliation with Homer to style without *epistēmē*. Thus, I would suggest, Plutarch deliberately juxtaposes the two ends of the generic/stylistic spectrum—Aesopic *logos* and Homeric song—in such a way that they reinforce his rhetorically artful denunciation of Herodotus. Like many other features of Plutarch's treatise, this dialectical juxtaposition of Aesopic and Homeric registers is perhaps a trick he has learned from Herodotus himself, as we shall see when we turn to the *Histories*.

---

[93] For modern debate on how we are to understand the "Alcmeonid digression," see (e.g.) Strasburger 1965.595–97, Fornara 1971b.53–54, Hart 1982.12–16, Thomas 1989.262–72, Griffiths 1995.42–44, Murray 2001a.29–30, Moles 2002.40–42, Fowler 2003, Dewald 2006.150–52, and see fuller discussion in chapter 11, section III below.

390 CHAPTER 10

But we must also attend to the features Plutarch associates with low tales in Herodotus and the imagery and innuendo he deploys implicitly to characterize the earlier writer as an Aesopic *logopoios*. For all these elements reveal with particular clarity the real-world sociopolitical associations that attend the lowest end of the generic spectrum Herodotus has on occasion chosen to include in his variegated and capacious text—associations that were arguably also available to Herodotus's contemporary audiences. Consider first a kind of pause or aside Plutarch makes in the midst of his lengthy rebuttal of Herodotus's version of the Battle of Thermopylae (chs. 31–33/864e–67b). Plutarch has just recounted several edifying "deeds and sayings of the Spartiates" (τολμήματα καὶ ῥήματα τῶν Σπαρτιατῶν) not to be found in Herodotus's text and then draws his indignant conclusion:[94]

> ταῦτ' οὐκ ἄν τις ἐπετίμησεν ἄλλου παραλιπόντος· ὁ δὲ τὴν Ἀμάσιδος ἀποψόφησιν καὶ τὴν τῶν ὄνων τοῦ κλέπτου προσέλασιν καὶ τὴν τῶν ἀσκῶν ἐπίδοσιν καὶ πολλὰ τοιαῦτα συναγαγὼν καὶ διαμνημονεύων, οὐκ ἀμελείᾳ δόξειεν ἂν καὶ ὑπεροψίᾳ προΐεσθαι καλὰ μὲν ἔργα καλὰς δὲ φωνάς, ἀλλ' οὐκ εὐμενὴς ὢν πρὸς ἐνίους οὐδὲ δίκαιος. (*Mal.Hdt.* ch. 32/866c–d)

> For nobody would blame another [writer] who had left out these things. But the one who led together and made mention of the fart of Amasis and the leading of asses by the thief and the gift of the wineskins and many other such things—surely he would not seem to have abandoned noble deeds and noble sayings out of [mere] negligence or oversight, but because he is neither kindly disposed nor just toward certain people.

This passage, entirely concerned with what Plutarch perceives as lapses of decorum in the *Histories*, is revealingly constructed as a series of hierarchical oppositions. Instead of recounting noble *Chreiai* of Greeks heroically facing death in battle, Herodotus has gone out of his way to include low-class—even obscene—tales of disreputable Egyptian tricksters. Nor are Plutarch's two examples chosen at random. The first represents the moment the demotic Amasis changes sides and betrays his master, the pharaoh Apries, sending him a crude message in the language of the body (Hdt. 2.162; for Amasis's low or common status, see Hdt. 2.172).[95] The latter tale expansively celebrates the cunning of another common man, the thief who outwits the pharaoh Rhampsinitus, in the process killing his own brother, who is caught in a trap in the pharaoh's treasurehouse, and then stealing his brother's corpse after cleverly inebriating the men assigned to guard it (Hdt. 2.121).[96] Plutarch's indignant contrast here implies without ever

---

[94] As Bowen 1992.133 notes, many of these "deeds and sayings" are probably post-Herodotean fabrications, but that is irrelevant for the purposes of my argument.

[95] For discussion of several elements in Hdt's Amasis story, including his bodily message to Apries, see Kurke 1995.57–64, 1999.90–100.

[96] Is it coincidence that Plutarch's *Stichwörter* to refer to this tale are "asses" (ὄνων) and "wineskins" (ἀσκῶν)—two terms that we found closely associated with Alcibiades' Aesopic representation

explicitly stating an equation or identification of the Herodotean narrator with the disreputable characters who figure in these tales—an identification cemented by the diction of his last sentence. Just like the treacherous Amasis turning on his sovereign master Apries, Herodotus "deserts" the noble deeds and sayings of the Spartans (the middle προΐεσθαι runs the gamut of meaning from "neglect" to "abandon"), while Plutarch's characterization of Herodotus as neither "kindly disposed" nor "just" aligns him with both Amasis and the unnamed thief. And of course, it is also relevant for Plutarch's insinuations of Herodotean guilt by narrative association that both these crude, disreputable, and low-class figures are Egyptian—barbarian and non-Greek. For the implication that Herodotus himself was of questionable—mixed or barbarian—ethnicity runs insidiously through Plutarch's treatise, finally converging with the Aesopic associations at its rhetorical climax.

Of course, Plutarch famously accuses Herodotus of being a "barbarian-lover" (φιλοβάρβαρος, ch. 12/857a), because he finds the latter's treatment of Egyptians and Persians more positive than that of Greeks, and because Herodotus frequently traces the genealogy of Greek religious practices, heroes, and Sages to non-Greek origins (chs. 12–18/857a–58f; cf. ch. 23/860e). But there are several moments when "barbarian-lover" by implication or association seems to sidle ever closer to the simple "barbarian" in Plutarch's essentializing conception of that category. The first step is taken when Plutarch explicitly raises the issue of Herodotus's own ethnicity, sneering that he was in no position to be so critical of the Greeks who Medized during the Persian Wars:

> ἔδει μὲν οὖν μηδὲ τοῖς μηδίσασιν Ἑλλήνων ἄγαν ἐπεμβαίνειν, καὶ ταῦτα Θούριον μὲν ὑπὸ τῶν ἄλλων νομιζόμενον, αὐτὸν δὲ Ἁλικαρνασσέων περιεχόμενον, οἳ Δωριεῖς ὄντες μετὰ τῆς γυναικωνίτιδος ἐπὶ τοὺς Ἕλληνας ἐστράτευσαν· (*Mal.Hdt.* ch. 35/868a)

> He ought not to have jumped all over those Greeks who Medized, seeing that he is considered a Thurian by some, but himself clinging to the Halicarnassians, who, although they are Dorians, joined the expedition against the Greeks with their harem in tow.[97]

A. J. Bowen takes the first reference to Thurii to be a sneer at the nonparticipation of the Western Greeks in resisting the Persian invasion.[98] But more

---

of Socrates in Plato's *Symposium*? This is not to suggest a specific intertextual link between Plato and Plutarch, but instead that these two terms may signify synecdochically ruptures of proper literary decorum.

[97] I borrow from Bowen 1992.73 his pungent translation of μετὰ τῆς γυναικωνίτιδος, "with their harem in tow." "Harem" is perhaps a bit tendentious as a translation here, since elsewhere Plutarch uses this term to refer to "women's quarters" in a Roman context (*Life of Cato the Younger* 30.4); nonetheless, it does convey something of the shock and non-Greek unseemliness of women involved not as mere camp followers, but as leaders of the Halicarnassian expedition.

[98] Bowen 1992.137.

damning still is Plutarch's reference to Halicarnassus, to which in his rendering Herodotus "clings" with irrational fervor (περιεχόμενον). In relation to Halicarnassus, Plutarch parrots Herodotus's assertion that its people are Dorian (Hdt. 7.99), but immediately calls into question that Greek ethnicity by setting it cheek by jowl with mention of the "women's chambers" or "harem" dragged along (μετὰ τῆς γυναικωνίτιδος). This is clearly a derisive reference to Artemisia, but its negative rhetorical implications extend beyond her. For if the end of the sentence—"made an expedition against the Greeks"—bluntly asserts the Medism of Halicarnassus, γυναικωνῖτις implies something else: that the Halicarnassians are themselves Eastern barbarians, dominated (like the Persians in Greek fancy) by their own too-powerful women.

Plutarch goes a bit further in chapter 39, insidiously associating Herodotus with a specific barbarian ethnicity. After marshaling several dedicatory epigrams to prove the active involvement of the Corinthian contingent at Salamis (against the story Herodotus attributes to the Athenians), Plutarch cites climactically the tradition that the women of Corinth prayed en masse to their civic goddess Aphrodite to "cast lust for battle against the barbarians into their men/husbands."[99] Before invoking the votive statue group and Simonidean epigram that substantiate the veracity of this tradition, Plutarch pauses to adapt a standard topos from the rhetoric of praise:

> καὶ μὴν ὅτι μόναι τῶν Ἑλληνίδων αἱ Κορίνθιαι γυναῖκες εὔξαντο τὴν καλὴν ἐκείνην καὶ δαιμόνιον εὐχήν, ἔρωτα τοῖς ἀνδράσι τῆς πρὸς τοὺς βαρβάρους μάχης ἐμβαλεῖν τὴν θεόν, οὐχ ὅπως ‹τοὺς› περὶ τὸν Ἡρόδοτον ἀγνοῆσαι πιθανὸν ἦν, ἀλλ᾽ οὐδὲ τὸν ἔσχατον Καρῶν· διεβοήθη γὰρ τὸ πρᾶγμα καὶ Σιμωνίδης ἐποίησεν ἐπίγραμμα, (*Mal. Hdt.* ch. 39/871a)

> And the fact that the Corinthian women alone of Greek women prayed that noble and inspired prayer, for the goddess to cast lust for battle against the barbarians into their men/husbands—no way is it believable that a man like Herodotus would be unaware of this, since not even the furthest of the Carians [was unaware of it]. For the matter was talked of everywhere and Simonides composed an epigram....

The idea that some person or achievement is so famous that even non-Greeks at the world's end know of him/it goes back at least to Pindar, and is deployed earlier in the treatise by Plutarch himself, when he asserts that "if there are people on the other side of the world, as some say, inhabiting the underside of the earth, even they have heard of Themistocles..." (ch. 37/869d).[100] Here in chapter 39, Plutarch turns this same topos against Herodotus, using it to prove that the latter could not possibly have been ignorant of the noble prayer of the

---

[99] On the complicated issue of whether these are Corinthian *hetairai* or Corinthian "wives" (the tradition Plutarch's account suggests) and, hence, whether we should translate ἀνδράσι here as "men" or "husbands," see Kurke 1996.73–75.

[100] Cf. Pindar I.6.22–27.

Corinthian women. More interesting, though, is the apparently random invocation of the "furthest of the Carians" as exemplary world's end barbarians. For, to my knowledge, Carians never otherwise figure in this topos—since, of course, they don't occupy the world's end (even from a Greek perspective). Instead, the effect of this alignment of terms, Herodotus-Carian, is to imply (without ever saying) that Herodotus himself is a boorish Carian from the back of beyond.[101]

Finally, Plutarch clinches the implied ethnic slur of Herodotus as Carian in a single mighty sentence that represents the treatise's rhetorical climax and the beginning of its peroration. And here we get back to Aesop and a whole set of negative associations that cluster around the Aesop tradition. Summarizing all the objections he has made to Herodotus's version of the battles of the Persian Wars, Plutarch thunders:

> τεσσάρων δ' ἀγώνων τότε πρὸς τοὺς βαρβάρους γενομένων, ἐκ μὲν Ἀρτεμισίου τοὺς Ἕλληνας ἀποδρᾶναί φησιν, ἐν δὲ Θερμοπύλαις τοῦ στρατηγοῦ καὶ βασιλέως προκινδυνεύοντος οἰκουρεῖν καὶ ἀμελεῖν Ὀλύμπια καὶ Κάρνεια πανηγυρίζοντας· τὰ δ' ἐν Σαλαμῖνι διηγούμενος τοσούτους περὶ Ἀρτεμισίας λόγους γέγραφεν, ὅσοις ὅλην τὴν ναυμαχίαν οὐκ ἀπήγγελκε· τέλος δέ, καθημένους ἐν Πλαταιαῖς ἀγνοῆσαι μέχρι τέλους τὸν ἀγῶνα τοὺς Ἕλληνας (ὥσπερ βατραχομυομαχίας γινομένης, ‹ἣν› Πίγρης ὁ Ἀρτεμισίας ἐν ἔπεσι παίζων καὶ φλυαρῶν ἔγραψε), σιωπῇ διαγωνίσασθαι συνθεμένων, ἵνα λάθωσι τοὺς ἄλλους, αὐτοὺς δὲ Λακεδαιμονίους ἀνδρείᾳ μὲν οὐδὲν κρείττονας γενέσθαι τῶν βαρβάρων, ἀνόπλοις δὲ καὶ γυμνοῖς μαχομένους κρατῆσαι. (*Mal.Hdt.* ch. 43/873e–74a)

> Four battles took place then against the barbarians. From Artemisium he says that the Greeks ran away; and at Thermopylae, while their king and commander risked it all, [he says] that they stayed obliviously at home, celebrating the Olympic Games and the Carneia. And in his narration of Salamis, he has not devoted as many words to the whole naval battle as he has written about Artemisia. And finally, [he says] that the Greeks sitting around at Plataea were ignorant of the conflict up to the very end, just as if it were a battle of frogs and mice, such as Pigres the son of Artemisia wrote in epic verse, playing and speaking nonsense. And of the Lacedaemonians themselves, he says that they were no better in courage than the barbarians, but that they won because they were fighting men unarmed and naked.

Plutarch has already objected to what he regards as absurd and shameful in Herodotus's account of the Battle of Plataea—that the Spartans, Tegeates, and Athenians alone participated, while the other Greek contingents sat idle,

---

[101] It is worth noting in relation to this passage that Plutarch himself assimilates alignment with Carians to a kind of scapegoating at ch. 23/860e, where he characterizes Herodotus's mention that the family of the Athenian Isagoras worshipped the Carian Zeus as his "ritually driving Isagoras to the Carians, just as if to the crows" (εἰς Κᾶρας ὥσπερ εἰς κόρακας ἀποδιοπομπουμένου τὸν Ἰσαγόραν). Such ritual scapegoating is, in turn, precisely what Plutarch accomplishes here in relation to Herodotus.

unaware that the battle had already been joined (cf. ch. 42/872b–73d). What is new here is the rhetorical flourish that this version of Plataea makes it into a veritable *Batrachomyomachia*, a small-scale epic parody narrating a battle of frogs and mice. Not just that: Plutarch interrupts the cascading torrent of this sentence with the apparently gratuitous parenthesis "[the *Batrachomyomachia*], which Pigres the son of Artemisia wrote in epic verse, playing and speaking nonsense." Why this seemingly unnecessary pedantic footnote?

To begin with the *Batrachomyomachia* itself: the comparison of Herodotus's account of the Battle of Plataea with this mock epic completes Plutarch's undermining of the conventional topos that Herodotus is Homeric. For Plutarch thereby implies that while using Homeric form and style, Herodotus has utterly belittled and degraded the content, transforming a victory that Plutarch himself adorns with the resonant Homeric epithet ἀοίδιμος (ch. 41/871d) into the parodic and absurd scuffling of frogs and mice. But there is also a significant connection between the *Batrachomyomachia* and the Aesop tradition, for the provocation to war between the clans of frogs and mice in this hilarious miniepic is identical to one of the last fables Aesop narrates to the Delphians as they're about to execute him in the *Life of Aesop* (*Vitae* G + W, ch. 133; cf. fable no. 384 Perry). In both narratives, the crisis arises from a fatal violation of *xenia* between frog and mouse, when the former invites the latter to dinner at his home in the pond. When the mouse objects that he doesn't know how to swim, the frog offers to bear him on his back through the pond, and both narratives end with the predictable tragic outcome—the mouse drowned, either accidentally or deliberately by the diving frog (*Batr.* ll. 56–98). In Aesop's version, the mouse as he's drowning curses the frog for his death, and is almost immediately avenged by a crow, who snatches up the two animals together and consumes them both. In the *Batrachomyomachia*, the mouse's outraged clan declares war on the frogs for his treacherous death at the hands of the frog king. It is hard to resist the impression, when the two versions are read together, that a traditional Aesopic fable has provided the inspiration and starting point for this playful mock epic of several hundred lines.[102] In any case, Plutarch's climactic reference to this low, parodic synthesis of Homeric form and Aesopic content casts new light on his final sentences, which follow almost immediately. Here, I suggested, figurations of Herodotus as Homeric and Herodotus as Aesopic collude in

---

[102] There are striking dictional correspondences between the *Life of Aesop* version (esp. as in *Vita* G) and the *Batrachomyomachia* that suggest that one has served as source or inspiration for the other. Thus note that both texts use the rare poetic word μόρος ("doom") in the context of the mouse/Aesop's death (*Batr.* 90; *Vita* G, ch. 133), and that *Vita* G's ἐκδικήσω/ἐξεδίκησεν within the fable corresponds to the drowning mouse's invocation of the ἔκδικον ὄμμα of god at *Batr.* 97 (on these dictional correspondences, see chapter 1, n. 104). It seems more likely that the influence or inspiration goes from Aesop to the *Batrachomyomachia*, given how apt the fable is in its context embedded in the *Life of Aesop*; cf. van Dijk 1997.125–26, 137; Holzberg 2002.18; contra Merkle 1992.117–22. As for the dating of the *Batrachomyomachia*, scholars disagree: Lachenaud 1981.257 suggests ca. 480 BCE; West 1984.125 (citing Wölke 1978.46–70) regards it as "late Hellenistic."

Plutarch's ultimate denunciation; we can now see in retrospect that the Homeric has already been transmuted into epic parody.

But even this invocation of the low, Aesopic *Batrachomyomachia* is not enough for Plutarch, for by his pedantic parenthesis, "which Pigres the son of Artemisia wrote . . . ," he aligns Herodotus's narrative with "play" and "nonsense" and Herodotus himself with Pigres and Artemisia. Indeed, Plutarch has already reminded us of Herodotus's excessive attachment to the Halicarnassian queen in his disgusted summary of the account of Salamis: "in his narration of Salamis, he has not devoted as many words to the whole naval battle as he has written about Artemisia." But there is still more at stake here than the association of Herodotus with a topsy-turvy world ruled by women, for in the tradition Pigres, the son or brother of Artemisia, is frequently given the ethnic "Carian." He bears, of course, a Carian name, and the Suda tells us, "Pigres, Carian from Halicarnassus, brother of Artemisia . . . wrote also the *Margites* attributed to Homer and the *Batrachomyomachia*" (Suda IV.127 Adler = *Batr.* Test. 3 Allen). There is in addition an intriguing note appended to the text of the *Batrachomyomachia* in one Paris manuscript: "But some say this is [the composition] of Tigres [*sic*] the Carian" (see Allen's apparatus criticus *ad Batr.* 303). Thus by association, Plutarch utterly traduces Herodotus's own status and ethnicity, implicitly identifying him with women on top, Eastern barbarians, and the low, parodic recasting of beast fable in epic verse. All these same negative associations characteristically cluster in the tradition around the figure of Aesop, as we have seen repeatedly, thereby reinforcing Plutarch's sneaky character assassination of Herodotus by his alignment of the Halicarnassian with the low fabulist.[103]

Thus Plutarch offers us unflinchingly and without sentimentality a clear view of the real-world stakes and sociopolitics of the wide range of genres Herodotus has welcomed into his vast, uneven text (especially those at the low end of the hierarchy of genre and decorum). But, it may be objected, Plutarch occupied a very different world, informed and structured by a much more rigid, xenophobic, and essentializing conception of "the barbarian" than what we

---

[103] Cf. esp. all the associations with Aesop in the passage from Phil. *Apoll.* quoted at the beginning of the introduction. We might connect with this strand of barbarian associations a recurrent image in *On the Malice of Herodotus* of Herodotus as a vandal, tearing down or chiseling out the inscriptions of the glorious monuments of the Persian Wars (e.g., at chs. 34/867f, 42/873d). Surely by Plutarch's time, this imagery of vandalism of monuments and sacred sites is strongly associated with various barbarian incursions into Greece.

It is also worth contrasting *On the Malice of Herodotus* with another Plutarchan work preserved only in fragmentary epitome, *The Comparison of Aristophanes and Menander*. Even in its fragmentary state, this latter work clearly devalues Aristophanes in relation to Menander for reasons that are simultaneously stylistic and political: see Hunter 2000 for an elegant demonstration of the antidemocratic politics that animates Plutarch's vitriolic critique of the Old Comic poet. Intriguingly, Plutarch there also accuses Aristophanes of κακοήθεια ("malice" or "spite"), but his imagery in denouncing the comic poet is completely different: Aristophanes is associated with prostitution and the worst abuses of the radical democracy in Athens, but he is nowhere in the treatise (as we have it epitomated) aligned with the barbarian and the non-Greek.

might imagine in Halicarnassus of the fifth century BCE. For scholars have emphasized the free, easy interaction of Greek and Carian in Herodotus's home city.[104] We are even told that Herodotus's uncle or cousin, who composed an *Ionica* in seven thousand verses, bore the Carian name Panyassis; this suggests the likely intermarriage of Greeks and Carians in Herodotus's own family.[105] And yet it would be naive to imagine that all Greek cities, or even all Greek individuals within each city, shared the same open, cosmopolitan values that seem to prevail in Halicarnassus and in Herodotus's own text. I would suggest that already in the fifth century, it was always available for those so inclined discursively or rhetorically to traduce an Artemisia, a Pigres—or a Herodotus— by identifying them simply as "Carian" or "barbarian."[106]

Indeed, whatever might be true for Herodotus's own ethnicity, the barbarian "other" plays a prominent part in the characterization of fable already in the fifth century BCE, so that in relation to Aesop and fable, it is impossible to limit or confine these associations to a later period. Much of the ancient evidence is collected by Ben Edwin Perry in the testimonia in his massive volume *Aesopica* and succinctly summarized by M. L. West in his 1984 essay, "The Ascription of Fables to Aesop in Archaic and Classical Greece."[107] As West notes, the ascription of fables to Aesop only really begins in the second half of the fifth century BCE; before that, Aeschylus refers to a beast fable as a "Libyan story" (ὧδ' ἐστι μύθων τῶν Λιβυστικῶν κλέος, fr. 139 Radt = Perry *Test.* 86), and Timocreon of Rhodes apparently mentions "Carian" and "Cyprian" *ainoi* in his verse, as well as what "a clever Sicilian man once said to his mother" (Timocreon frr. 4/730, 6/732, 8/734 *PMG*). In Aristophanes' *Wasps*, Bdelycleon recommends to his father "a funny story of Aesop or a Sybarite one" as appropriate symposium fare (Αἰσωπικὸν γελοῖον ἢ Συβαριτικόν, *Wasps* 1259).[108] By the time Aelius Theon writes his *Progymnasmata* in the second century CE, he knows of fables or funny stories "called Aesopic and Libyan, or Sybarite and Phrygian and Cilician and Carian, Egyptian, and Cyprian" (Theon II.73 Spengel = Perry *Test.* 85). And of course Aesop himself seems to be identified as Thracian or Phrygian in the earliest traditions.[109] Amidst this welter of different ethnicities, some late sources attempt to construct a differentiated system: thus a scholiast to Aristophanes'

[104] Thus (e.g.) Matthews 1974.6, 9–10; Gould 1989.5–7.
[105] For testimonia on Panyassis's literary production and his relation to Herodotus, see Matthews 1974.
[106] For a parallel argument for the coexistence within the fourth century of virulently antibarbarian rhetoric with easy, open practices of cultural exchange, see Hagemajer Allen 2003.
[107] See Perry *Test.* 64–65, 85–92, 101 and West 1984.114–16; for more recent discussions of the different ethnicities associated with fable, see van Dijk 1997.105–9, Adrados 1999.14–15.
[108] On the contextual complexities of this recommendation, see Rothwell 1995.249–51.
[109] Heraclides Lembus, summarizing Aristotle's *Constitution of the Samians*, identifies Aesop as Thracian. Aristotle, in turn, may be drawing on the fifth-century local Samian historian Eugeon or Euagon for this detail; see Perry *Test.* 5–6, West 1984.117–18. Many scholars have assumed from Herodotus's reference to Aesop at 2.134 that we are meant to identify Aesop as Thracian, like his

Birds asserts, "Of these fables, the ones concerning irrational beasts are Aesopic, the ones concerning human beings are Sybarite."[110] Theon knows of these attempts at discrimination, but rejects them, observing commonsensically, "they seem to me to conceive it in a silly way, for all the [different] forms occur in all the aforementioned [kinds of fables]" (Theon II.73 Spengel = Perry *Test*. 85).

Thus already in the fifth century, fables and terse punchy anecdotes are predominantly associated with barbarian "others" (Libyans, Carians, Thracians, and Phrygians), with a few distant or marginalized Greek ethnicities thrown in for good measure (Sicilian, Sybarite, Cyprian). And if we can regard something like the Aristophanes scholiast's distinction as current—even if not universally accepted—in the fifth century, we might see the attempt to differentiate between foreign animal fables and Greek tales involving human beings as itself politically and ethnically motivated. For, as I noted in the discussion of Sophistic appropriations of fable, all our examples involve human beings, heroes, and gods, and so raise the possibility that a hierarchy existed even within the genre of fable, according to which allegorical fables were classier than their beast fable brethren.[111] If this is the case, the construction of categories like "Sicilian" and "Sybarite" for fables involving human beings may itself represent an attempt at generic "ethnic cleansing," even if the effort constantly fails within the free-for-all of popular culture and must be constantly renewed.[112] I will return to these speculations in the next chapter, when we come to consider Herodotus's uses of fable. For now, all I want to emphasize is the tremendous risk Herodotus runs with his contemporary audience by incorporating fable into his narrative, given the powerful ethnic or barbarian coding of this lowly genre prevalent at the time. Why would Herodotus take this risk?

"fellow slave" Rhodopis, though this is not explicitly stated by Herodotus; see (e.g.) Zeitz 1936.229n. 2, Perry 1962a.333n. 45, Cartledge 1993.138–39.

[110] Schol. *ad Birds* 471: τῶν δὲ μύθων οἱ μὲν περὶ ἀλόγων ζῴων εἰσὶν αἰσώπειοι, οἱ δὲ περὶ ἀνθρώπων συβαριτικοί; cf. Schol. *ad Wasps* 1259 for the same distinction. The *Birds* Scholia add, "But there are some who say that the short and concise ones are Sybarite, like Mnesimachus in his *Pharmakopōlē*" (Holwerda 1991.80, lemma 471b).

[111] See above, chapter 7, section I.

[112] Thus we should note that the Aristophanes scholiast's distinctions do seem to apply in Timocreon (fr. 8/734 *PMG*) and in Aristophanes *Wasps*, where Philocleon's aggressive "Sybarite" fables all involve human beings (1427–40), whereas his explicit mention of Aesop a bit later introduces a beast fable (1446–49; cf. *Birds* 471–72, 651–53; *Peace* 129). Contra: Nøjgaard 1964.475–76 argues that the categorical distinctions articulated by later rhetoricians and scholiasts are based on just the same ancient evidence we have available and therefore have no validity. Adrados 1999.14–15 follows Nøjgaard; van Dijk 1997.108–9 also rejects these categorical distinctions, insisting that there is too little ancient data to draw any firm conclusions.

Nagy 1990b.325n. 59, 334–35 also cites the Aristophanes scholiast's distinction between Aesopic beast fable and Sybarite human fable, which he connects with Hdt's affiliation with Thurii (the Panhellenic refoundation of Sybaris); he does not, however, conceive of this distinction as entailing a sociopolitical or ethnic hierarchy (as I am suggesting).

Chapter 11

HERODOTUS AND AESOP: SOME SOUNDINGS

> quamquam et apud Herodotum, patrem historiae, ...
> sunt innumerabiles fabulae
> —Cicero, De Legibus 1.1.5

ACCORDING TO GERT-JAN VAN DIJK, there is a single fable narrated in Herodotus's *Histories*: the fable of the aulete and the fish, told by Cyrus to representatives of the Ionian and Aeolian cities in Asia Minor when they come to make terms after his defeat of Croesus (Hdt. 1.141).[1] In contrast, Triantaphyllia Karadagli offers a much fuller list, which, in addition to Hdt. 1.141, includes a whole set of other embedded narratives and communicative performances that Karadagli designates *ainoi dramatikoi* (Hdt. 1.125, 1.158–59, 3.46, 4.131–32, 5.92, 6.86).[2] And while Karadagli explicitly acknowledges that all these latter *ainoi* are not fables strictly defined, she notes that they share many features of communicative situation and even some verbal formulae with other extant fable narratives.[3] Gregory Nagy reproduces Karadagli's list of fables/*ainoi* in Herodotus, without noting her qualifications.[4]

At the risk of sounding like Goldilocks assessing the hospitality of the three bears, I would contend that van Dijk's definition of fable is too snug, and Karadagli's (and Nagy's) too loose. For by defining fable so narrowly, van Dijk misses an essential feature of Herodotean narrative prose, and his account of the meaning of the one and only fable embedded in Herodotus's text can only be local and particular. And while Karadagli's attempt to catch and analyze kindred forms better serves the text and texture of the *Histories*, as fable bleeds into exemplum, *ainos*, riddle performance, and oracle in her scheme, the boundaries become ever blurrier and it is difficult to know where to stop.[5] This critique is

---

[1] Van Dijk 1997.270–74, 536–37; cf. Aly 1921.53; Meuli 1975a.728n. 3, 1975b.744; Griffiths 2006.139.

[2] Karadagli 1981.23, 35–37, 65, 75–79, 84–85, 91.

[3] Karadagli 1981, esp. 3, 36–37, 73. Van Dijk 1997.655–56 energetically refutes Karadagli's categorization of all these *ainoi* as fables in his appendix, "Non-Fables & Non-Allusions." For a minimal definition of "fable," see the introduction, section IIC.

[4] Nagy 1990b.324–25n. 58. In addition, Nagy 1990b.315 adds Hdt. 7.152.2, a passage that he finds "strikingly similar" to Perry fable no. 266, "The Two Packs," but see van Dijk 1997.657 contra Nagy.

[5] Adrados 1999.401 registers something of the same quandary. He lists two fables for Hdt (1.141 and 6.86), but then adds a "Note": "In Herodotus there is an abundance of anecdotes, either purely

particularly applicable to Nagy's adaptation and extension of Karadagli's schema, whereby everything in Herodotus ultimately becomes *ainos*. As I noted in the previous chapter, Nagy's argument is important and I will wind up espousing some similar positions, but I would contend that there might be some value in keeping fable (in Herodotus's idiom *logos*) and *ainos* separate, at least initially. For *ainos* in Nagy's account is a kind of coded utterance that crosscuts genre and even crosscuts the distinction of poetry and prose. Because of this, a too-hasty recourse to this (ultimately all-embracing) category obscures the distinctions, hierarchies, tensions, and sociopolitics of genre that are worth noticing.[6]

Thus I find the interests and approaches of fable scholars too local and those of Nagy too global. At least for the time being, I would like to explore a middle zone and approach the question of fables or the fabular in Herodotus from a somewhat different angle. As we saw in the consideration of Plato, there may be something more to be gained by putting Aesopic fable into the broader context of characteristically Aesopic discursive practices—that is to say, in the context of elements or discourses that we can identify as Aesopic even when Aesop himself is veiled or occluded. From this approach, I hope to demonstrate two broader points relevant to the reading of Herodotus. First, that Aesopic genres of discourse always function as part of a hierarchically organized structural or dialectical system with other genres of discourse. As we have seen particularly in the consideration of Xenophon's *Memorabilia* and Plutarch's treatise *On the Malice of Herodotus*, the conventional Greek system constitutes a generic spectrum that runs from lofty Homeric poetry to humble Aesopic prose, and that provides a code or platform for many other cultural and sociopolitical oppositions beyond the narrowly literary. Thus in the first three sections of this chapter, I want to consider Herodotus's Aesopic moments sorted into three different levels or degrees of the use or appropriation of Aesop. In these sections, we will explore the ways in which Herodotus is himself manipulating and inflecting the

---

novellesque or by way of exempla, which in a certain sense are the same as fables (such as those of Tellus and Cleobis and Biton in I 30 ff.)."

[6] It may be objected that this is just to replace one totalizing term (*ainos*) with another (*logos*), since of course *logos* designates a whole range of different things in Hdt: the smallest narrative unit of "tale" or "anecdote"; much larger narrative building blocks or whole sections (e.g., the "Lydian *logos*" of Book 1, the "Egyptian *logos*" of Book 2); and Hdt's whole work (so, e.g., at 7.152.3); cf. Murray 2001a.24–25. But the fact that *logos* was such a multivalent term does not necessarily mean that the ancients made no distinctions among such categories as beast fable, allegorical fable, historical anecdote, etc. As I have been arguing throughout, we need to consider clusters of formal features, performance situations, and ancient notions of decorum in differentiating among different categories. So for example, in contrast to Adrados (cited in n. 5), I would contend that Leotychides' example at 6.86 (of Glaucus who contemplates breaking his oath) is pointedly *not* a fable, as the beleaguered Spartan king attempts to shore up his shaky authority by deploying the more reputable forms of historical example and Delphic oracle in his speech to the resistant Athenians.

signifying opposition of Homer versus Aesop that we've already seen at work in ancient critical assessments of the Halicarnassian—especially when it comes to his more veiled references to the slave fable-maker. For here we will find Herodotus precisely inverting the terms—resignifying the value and relative status of the opposition low fable–high epic that is more conventionally coded in the later tradition. Herodotus's deliberate inversion serves a characteristically Aesopic purpose, since it allows him to parody and explode the pretensions of Eastern potentates, Greek tyrants, and self-important aristocrats. And this, I hope, will help explain in turn the function of Aesopic elements in Herodotus's text and allow us to see "Aesop" as a real precursor behind Herodotean prose.

Second, as with Plato, I would like to consider the implications of Herodotus's choice of Aesopic discursive strategies for his larger project—not just on the level of content, but also on the level of the narrator's own positioning in relation to his audience. And this will bring me back eventually to the real-world stakes or politics of Herodotus's discursive choices, and to something like Gregory Nagy's theory of Herodotean *ainos*. Thus in the final section of this chapter, I will return to Hdt. 1.27 to consider how the narrator deploys this scene of Aesopic advising framed as fable to teach his audience how to read and understand his complex, coded messages. In the analysis of Plato, we saw how Aesop's distinctive positive and negative discursive strategies both contributed to the "old Socratic tool-box." Nonetheless, we could perhaps say that the negative Aesopic mode is more important for Plato insofar as it helps enable the development of the distinctive method of Socratic *elenchos*. For Herodotus, by contrast, Aesop's positive mode—advising through fable, fictive analogy, and other forms of indirect or coded utterance—will turn out to be the more significant aspect, resonant for the discursive practices and broader projects of the *Histories* as a whole.

Of necessity, this discussion will be selective and incomplete—more a demonstration of possibilities for reading Herodotus than a comprehensive treatment (hence the "soundings" of my title). This necessary limitation results partly from the extremely permeable boundaries of fable (as noted above), and partly from the nature of Herodotus's own vast, complex, and multivalent text. Attempting to write about the *Histories*, I often feel like Alice going down the rabbit hole: suddenly entering a whole world strangely different from our own, with the possibility of never getting out again.

I. Cyrus Tells a Fable

So let me first consider the one and only instance in which Herodotus explicitly narrates a fable designated in the text as a *logos*—Cyrus's response to the belated overtures of the Ionian and Aeolian cities after his defeat of Croesus in Book 1:

Ἴωνες δὲ καὶ Αἰολέες, ὡς οἱ Λυδοὶ τάχιστα κατεστράφατο ὑπὸ Περσέων, ἔπεμπον ἀγγέλους ἐς Σάρδις παρὰ Κῦρον, ἐθέλοντες ἐπὶ τοῖσι αὐτοῖσι εἶναι τοῖσι καὶ Κροίσῳ ἦσαν κατήκοοι. ὁ δὲ ἀκούσας αὐτῶν τὰ προΐσχοντο ἔλεξέ σφι λόγον, ἄνδρα φὰς αὐλητὴν ἰδόντα ἰχθῦς ἐν τῇ θαλάσσῃ αὐλέειν, δοκέοντά σφεας ἐξελεύσεσθαι ἐς γῆν· ὡς δὲ ψευσθῆναι τῆς ἐλπίδος, λαβεῖν ἀμφίβληστρον καὶ περιβαλεῖν τε πλῆθος πολλὸν τῶν ἰχθύων καὶ ἐξειρύσαι, ἰδόντα δὲ παλλομένους εἰπεῖν ἄρα αὐτὸν πρὸς τοὺς ἰχθῦς· παύεσθέ μοι ὀρχεόμενοι, ἐπεὶ οὐδ' ἐμέο αὐλέοντος ἠθέλετε ἐκβαίνειν ὀρχεόμενοι. Κῦρος μὲν τοῦτον τὸν λόγον τοῖσι Ἴωσι καὶ τοῖσι Αἰολεῦσι τῶνδε εἵνεκα ἔλεξε, ὅτι δὴ οἱ Ἴωνες πρότερον αὐτοῦ Κύρου δεηθέντος δι' ἀγγέλων ἀπίστασθαί σφεας ἀπὸ Κροίσου οὐκ ἐπείθοντο, τότε δὲ κατεργασμένων τῶν πρηγμάτων ἦσαν ἕτοιμοι πείθεσθαι Κύρῳ. (Hdt. 1.141.1–3)

As soon as the Lydians had been subdued by the Persians, the Ionians and Aeolians were sending messengers to Cyrus in Sardis, wishing to be [his] subjects on the same terms that they had been also with Croesus. But he, when he heard what they were proposing, told them a fable, saying that an aulos-player, when he saw fish in the sea, played his pipe, thinking that they would come out to land. But when he was cheated of his hope, he got a fishnet, cast it around a great throng of fish, and dragged them out. And when he saw them leaping and twitching, he said to the fish, "Stop dancing, since when I piped, you weren't willing to come out and dance then." Now Cyrus told this fable to the Ionians and Aeolians because, when he had asked them before through messengers to revolt from Croesus, they were not obeying him, but at that time, when these matters were all settled, then they were ready to obey him.

Herodotus's diction here makes clear that his proper term for a fable is *logos*, repeated twice in a frame around the actual fable narrative (ἔλεξέ σφι λόγον, τοῦτον τὸν λόγον ... ἔλεξε). In fact, this same fable appears in slightly different forms in the Augustana collection of Aesop's fables (Perry fable no. 11; first century CE), in Babrius (Babr. 9; first–second century CE) and in Aphthonius (no. 33; cf. Hausrath 1970.I.2.148; fourth–fifth century CE).[7] And while all these collections are much later, it is possible that the tale of the aulete and the fish was already a familiar popular fable when Herodotus composed his *Histories*.[8]

In a seminal 1954 essay, "Herkunft und Wesen der Fabel," Karl Meuli considered this fable among others in terms of its "sociological function." Starting from Odysseus's *ainos* to Eumaeus in the *Odyssey*, Meuli argued that we should understand *ainos* as a coded utterance by which the weak and disempowered expressed themselves indirectly to their social superiors; in the case of Cyrus's fable, Meuli noted, the powerful could also occasionally deploy this same genre

---

[7] This fable is also alluded to in the Gospels: see Matt. 11.16–17, Luke 7.32.
[8] That the fable preexisted Hdt's writing is assumed by Meuli 1975b and acknowledged as possible by Ceccarelli 1993.35–36.

of speaking against the weak, in which case it often assumed "an ironic, threatening tone."[9]

In a separate essay, Meuli argued that Cyrus's fable alluded to the distinctive Persian practice of "dragnetting" a captured city or territory (σαγηνεύειν), and that therefore Herodotus's fable represented the actual response of Cyrus to the Greek ambassadors in the sixth century BCE.[10] This whole issue has been revisited by Paola Ceccarelli in an elegant and thoughtful essay.[11] She notes that by the fifth century BCE, there were abundant Greek and Near Eastern parallels available for the image of fallen enemies or the population of captured cities as fish caught in a net, and that the Greeks themselves consciously registered the connection between the imagery of the fable and the Persian practice of dragnetting (as in Philostratus, *Life of Apollonius* 1.23). From this she concludes not that these were the actual words of Cyrus (which are presumably unrecoverable), but that the attribution of the fable to the founder of the Persian empire therefore had a kind of historical verisimilitude within the "horizon of expectation" of Herodotus's Greek audience.[12]

Ceccarelli furthermore suggests that, if we shift our focus from the first image of the fable (the fish caught in the net) to its second image (the fish dancing), we find a significant echo of Cyrus's fable at the very end of the *Histories*: the portent of pickled fish jumping in the pan that appears to the Athenians and their captive Artaÿctes after the surrender of Sestos (Hdt. 9.120–21). Ceccarelli points out that while Artaÿctes asserts that the portent is directed at him and interprets it as signifying the vengeance of the hero Protesilaus, whose shrine he had plundered, the narrator himself neither affirms nor denies that interpretation. For the Greeks within the narrative and those who constitute the external audience of the *Histories*, the portent may bear an additional signification. For them, if it is connected with the original fable, it could also signify the "resuscitation" of the Ionian and Aeolian cities of the coast and the islands, the "fish" now finally freed from the Persian net and revived.[13]

I find Ceccarelli's arguments for links between 1.141 and the end of the *Histories* compelling and illuminating for several reasons. First, her notion of the multiple possible significations generated from the allusive weave of fable and portent as they apply to different audiences seems very appropriate for Herodo-

---

[9] Meuli 1975b.744. Meuli is followed by Karadagli 1981.23, 65; see also Rothwell 1995 on the power differential that often obtains between the teller of fable and his audience.

[10] Meuli 1975a.

[11] Ceccarelli 1993; the Near Eastern parallels are also discussed by Hirsch 1986.

[12] Ceccarelli 1993.36–49, 55–56.

[13] Ceccarelli 1993.49–57. We should note the refinement or nuancing of Ceccarelli's argument in one respect by Moles 1996.273–74: Moles points out that things are not entirely rosy for the Ionians and Aeolians at the end of the *Histories*, since they are in the process of being *cooked*. On Moles's reading, this points forward to their oppression by the increasingly tyrannical Athenian empire beyond the temporal frame of the *Histories*.

tus's densely coded text; indeed, it is an idea to which I will return in the final section of this chapter. Second, Ceccarelli's argument demonstrates the way in which this single fable carries resonances and proliferations of meaning that extend far beyond its local context, ultimately helping to unify the whole of the *Histories*.[14] Indeed, on her interpretation, the returning image of the fish in Book 9 provides a late (perhaps unexpected) resolution to the fable that alters or inverts our original understanding of it. It may be that such deferred revision of meaning is a characteristic feature available for fable discourse, for we find this technique already in the oldest extant example of beast fable in the Greek tradition—the fable of the hawk and the nightingale in Hesiod's *Works & Days*. The *Works & Days*, as Gregory Nagy has argued, itself stages or enacts the slow emergence of justice (*dikē*) over time that the poet asserts gnomically at one point in the poem (*WD* 217–18).[15] Emblematic of this process is the deferred resolution of the fable of the hawk and the nightingale, which the poet originally tells as an *ainos* addressed to kings "whom he diplomatically presupposes to be *phroneontes*, 'aware' (202)."[16] Occurring immediately after the poet's apocalyptic vision of the complete triumph of hubris over *dikē* in the later Iron Age (*WD* 180–201), this familiar fable seems initially to endorse the same message, as the violent hawk asserts his complete power over the weaker nightingale/singer (*WD* 203–12). But this pessimistic, might-makes-right reading of the fable is revised later in the poem, in words addressed not to the kings, but to the poet's brother Perses:

Ὦ Πέρση, σὺ δὲ ταῦτα μετὰ φρεσὶ βάλλεο σῇσι
καί νυ δίκης ἐπάκουε, βίης δ' ἐπιλήθεο πάμπαν.
τόνδε γὰρ ἀνθρώποισι νόμον διέταξε Κρονίων,
ἰχθύσι μὲν καὶ θηρσὶ καὶ οἰωνοῖς πετεηνοῖς
ἔσθειν ἀλλήλους, ἐπεὶ οὐ δίκη ἐστὶ μετ' αὐτοῖς·
ἀνθρώποισι δ' ἔδωκε δίκην, ἣ πολλὸν ἀρίστη
γίνεται·
(*WD* 274–80)

O Perses, cast these things into your wits and heed justice and entirely forget violence. For the son of Cronus ordained this law for human beings, for fish and wild beasts and winged birds to eat each other, since they do not have *dikē*; but to human beings he gave *dikē*, which is by far the best.

As Nagy notes, these verses offer a revisionary "moral" for the fable of the hawk and the nightingale. Indeed, we might even say that this deferred lesson on the lack of *dikē* among the animals revises the fable by undermining or

---

[14] In this respect, her analysis compares favorably to the more limited interpretation of van Dijk 1997.270–74.
[15] Nagy 1990a.64–75.
[16] Nagy 1990a.65.

deconstructing the basic premise of fable—the analogy between human and animal behaviors—making the fable into a "self-consuming artifact." In any case, as Nagy points out, the corrupt kings of the *Works & Days* have proved themselves too foolish to understand the final implications of the fable; hence they actually disappear from the poem at line 263, never to return, while the fable's deferred moral is addressed instead to Perses.[17] In like manner, on Ceccarelli's reading, the whole of Herodotus's *Histories* becomes a fable with its deferred resolution writ large, ostensibly addressed to different internal audiences (Ionians and Aeolians, Artaÿctes), while offered as an interpretive challenge to an external audience that understands the complex, indirect, multiple meanings encoded in this discursive form.[18]

But at the same time, we must not lose sight of the politics of fable. Ceccarelli's adaptation of Meuli's theory offers persuasive arguments for the appropriateness of attributing this fable to a Persian speaker, given the Persian practice of "dragnetting,"[19] but we should also note that Herodotus has thus credited the one and only explicit fable narrated in the *Histories* to the barbarian—and former slave—Cyrus. So Herodotus's practice here would seem to conform to Plutarch's preference to align or identify fable with "others"—the "Scythians, Persians, and Egyptians" Herodotus makes into speaking fable characters "like Aesop with his crows and apes" (Plut. *Mal. Hdt.* ch. 40/871cd). But we should not be deceived by this into thinking that Herodotus shares Plutarch's essentializing distinction aligning fable with slaves and non-Greek barbarians. For if we attend to scenes of Aesopic advising, we will find the interlinked hierarchies of literary form and status/ethnicity scrambled or inverted. It is to these scenes that I turn in the next section.

II. Greece and (as) Fable, or Resignifying the Hierarchy of Genre

For my second category of the appropriation of Aesop, I would like to consider a pair of scenes where Aesop himself is implicit in Herodotus's narrative—

---

[17] Nagy 1990a.66; for a similar reading of the deferred message of the fable, see van Dijk 1997.128–31, and for the disappearance of the kings from *WD*, see also Hamilton 1989.57.

[18] This reading is in fact very consonant with other readings of the end of the *Histories*; see esp. Boedeker 1988, Moles 1996, Dewald 1997.

[19] Note esp. Ceccarelli 1993.54–55, contrasting Hdt's account with the version of Diodorus Siculus (9.35). According to the latter, the speaker is Harpagus the Mede and he tells an entirely different story drawn from his own earlier experience—as a young man, he had first requested a girl from her father as a bride, but was rejected for a more powerful suitor. Later, the father came back to him and offered him his daughter; he responded that he no longer wanted her as a bride but would take her as a concubine. Thus the story of fish and dragnet seems to be particularly associated with a *Persian* speaker.

scenes of a Greek sage advising an Eastern potentate. One of these scenes I have already discussed at length; at this point, I would like to juxtapose it with another scene from the second half of the *Histories* that shares striking thematic and dictional elements, in order to suggest that there is a characteristic Aesopic shape to these Herodotean episodes. I would contrast this category in particular to the Sophistic adaptations of fable we surveyed in chapter 7; where for the Sophists an elegantly refashioned version of fable is thought to be particularly effective in addressing a large audience of young people, Herodotus seems to be making creative use of an older tradition (perhaps specifically Samian or Ionian?) of Aesop as a wise adviser to Eastern kings and potentates. And here we will begin to see the interaction—even competition—of Aesopic and Homeric genres of discourse.

First, recall the encounter of sage and king at Hdt. 1.27, already considered in chapter 3:

> ὡς δὲ ἄρα οἱ ἐν τῇ Ἀσίῃ Ἕλληνες κατεστράφατο ἐς φόρου ἀπαγωγήν, τὸ ἐνθεῦτεν ἐπενόεε νέας ποιησάμενος ἐπιχειρέειν τοῖσι νησιώτῃσι. ἐόντων δέ οἱ πάντων ἑτοίμων ἐς τὴν ναυπηγίην, οἱ μὲν Βίαντα λέγουσι τὸν Πριηνέα ἀπικόμενον ἐς Σάρδις, οἱ δὲ Πιττακὸν τὸν Μυτιληναῖον, εἰρομένου Κροίσου εἴ τι εἴη νεώτερον περὶ τὴν Ἑλλάδα, εἰπόντα τάδε καταπαῦσαι τὴν ναυπηγίην· Ὦ βασιλεῦ, νησιῶται ἵππον συνωνέονται μυρίην, ἐς Σάρδις τε καὶ ἐπὶ σὲ ἐν νόῳ ἔχοντες στρατεύεσθαι. Κροῖσον δὲ ἐλπίσαντα λέγειν ἐκεῖνον ἀληθέα εἰπεῖν· αἲ γὰρ τοῦτο θεοὶ ποιήσειαν ἐπὶ νόον νησιώτῃσι, ἐλθεῖν ἐπὶ Λυδῶν παῖδας σὺν ἵπποισι. τὸν δὲ ὑπολαβόντα φάναι· Ὦ βασιλεῦ, προθύμως μοι φαίνεαι εὔξασθαι νησιώτας ἱππευομένους λαβεῖν ἐν ἠπείρῳ, οἰκότα ἐλπίζων· νησιώτας δὲ τί δοκέεις εὔχεσθαι ἄλλο ἤ, ἐπείτε τάχιστα ἐπύθοντό σε μέλλοντα ἐπὶ σφίσι ναυπηγέεσθαι νέας, λαβεῖν ἀρώμενοι Λυδοὺς ἐν θαλάσσῃ, ἵνα ὑπὲρ τῶν ἐν τῇ ἠπείρῳ οἰκημένων Ἑλλήνων τείσωνταί σε, τοὺς σὺ δουλώσας ἔχεις; κάρτα τε ἡσθῆναι Κροῖσον τῷ ἐπιλόγῳ καί οἱ, προσφυέως γὰρ δόξαι λέγειν, πειθόμενον παύσασθαι τῆς ναυπηγίης. καὶ οὕτω τοῖσι τὰς νήσους οἰκημένοισι Ἴωσι ξεινίην συνεθήκατο. (Hdt. 1.27)

> When the Greeks in Asia had been subdued to the paying of tribute, [Croesus] next set his mind to building a navy and making an attempt on the islanders. And when all things were ready for the shipbuilding, some say Bias of Priene came to Sardis—others Pittacus of Mytilene. And when Croesus asked if there was any news concerning Greece, [the sage] saying these following things stopped him from his shipbuilding: "O King, the islanders are buying up ten thousand horse, intending to make an expedition against you in Sardis." And Croesus, believing that that man spoke the truth, said, "Would that the gods would put this in mind for the islanders, to come against the sons of the Lydians with horses!" And the other, replying said, "O King, eagerly you appear to me to pray to catch the islanders on horseback on the mainland, expecting the likely outcome. But what else do you imagine the islanders pray for, as soon as they learned that you were going to build a navy against them? Praying [what other thing than] to catch the Lydians at sea, in order to punish you on behalf of the Greeks living on the mainland whom you have enslaved?" And [they say that]

Croesus was overjoyed at the concluding sentence and persuaded by him, since he seemed to speak appositely, he ceased his shipbuilding. And so it was that he made a pact of guest-friendship with the Ionians inhabiting the islands.

As I noted, this episode is filled with anomalies within the text of the *Histories*, for this is the only place in Herodotus where the narrator expresses uncertainty about the identity of a speaker of sage advice and the only place where any of the Seven Sages is credited with a statement acknowledged in the narrative to be untrue. In addition, this little story features several rare expressions and Herodotean *hapax legomena*: ὑπολαβόντα φάναι is an expression that occurs only seven times in the text of the *Histories*, while ἐπίλογος meaning "conclusion" is unique to this episode. I suggested that all these rare features represent the thematic and dictional traces of Aesop, the residue of an oral tradition that preexisted Herodotus of Aesop—perhaps together with the Seven Sages—at the court of Croesus. For here, one or another of the Seven Sages is credited with the kind of indirect advising through fictive analogy that belongs properly to Aesop, and that produces the fabulist's characteristic pleasure and persuasion (κάρτα τε ἡσθῆναι, πειθόμενον). Finally, as I also noted, Herodotus seems oddly to have cast this scene of Aesopic advising as *itself a fable*, through his use of the fable convention of narrative in indirect discourse with speeches in direct quotation and the fable formula ὑπολαβόντα φάναι introducing the utterance of a fable character at the moment he speaks the *epilogos*, the fable's internal "punch line." At this point, I would like to revisit the questions Herodotus's odd framing of this episode raises: Why elide Aesop from this scene of characteristically Aesopic advising? Why simultaneously preserve telltale dictional traces of his occluded presence? And why frame the entire encounter as itself a fable?

But before I can fully address these questions, I would like to consider several other odd dictional features of this episode and juxtapose it with another encounter of Greek sage and Eastern potentate. Notice first the language of Croesus's overjoyed exclamation, which is distinctly heroic—specifically Homeric: αἲ γὰρ τοῦτο θεοὶ ποιήσειαν ἐπὶ νόον νησιώτῃσι, ἐλθεῖν ἐπὶ Λυδῶν παῖδας σὺν ἵπποισι. Αἲ γάρ (instead of εἲ γάρ) is a Homerism that occurs only here in the text of Herodotus, while Croesus's opening words (αἲ γὰρ τοῦτο θεοί) scan as a hemiepes. These heroic resonances of Croesus's opening cadence are reinforced by the lofty periphrasis "the children of the Lydians."[20] In contrast, Croesus's sage interlocutor speaks a language that is resolutely prosaic and pragmatic.

---

[20] By my count, αἲ γάρ occurs thirty-two times in Homer. Λυδῶν παῖδας, though not identical to the Homeric υἷες/υἷας Ἀχαιῶν, still, I think, evokes this heroic periphrasis. Thus How and Wells 1928.I.66, "**αἲ γάρ** (only here in H.) is Homeric. 'Sons of the Lydians' is also poetic"; cf. Asheri, Lloyd, and Corcella 2007.96. (But notice that in Homer this periphrasis is only ever used of the Greeks, whereas here it is transferred to the Lydians.) Aly 1921.36 notes the unusual elevation of Croesus's exclamation compared to the "schlichte Erzählung" of the surrounding narrative. I owe the point about the scansion of Croesus's opening words as hemiepes to Joseph Russo (comment after an oral presentation of this material).

Thus his use of another Herodotean *hapax* συνωνέονται ("buy up") for the islanders' fictive acquisition of cavalry sounds almost bureaucratic, while he consistently opts for standard prose expressions like ἐν νόῳ ἔχοντες and ἱππευομένους in contrast to Croesus's more elevated ποιήσειαν ἐπὶ νόον and σὺν ἵπποισι, respectively.[21] And strikingly, when he gets to his punch line, the Sage's level of discourse sinks even lower: notice the colloquial looseness of construction in the anacolouthon ἀρώμενοι. Thus the Eastern potentate Croesus speaks the language of martial epic, but his Homeric pretensions are immediately deflated by the pragmatic response of his Greek interlocutor, flagged as colloquial and fabular by the formula ὑπολαβόντα φάναι.

We encounter a similar dialogue of Greek sage and Eastern potentate in Book 7, in an exchange Herodotus stages between Xerxes, who has just surveyed his magnificent army, and the deposed Spartan king Demaratus (7.101–4). Xerxes summons Demaratus and asks him: "Now declare this to me, if the Greeks will stand fast and raise their hands against me? . . . I wish to learn your opinion, what sort of thing you say concerning them." At this point, the text continues:

> ὁ μὲν ταῦτα εἰρώτα, ὁ δὲ ὑπολαβὼν ἔφη· Βασιλεῦ, κότερα ἀληθείῃ χρήσωμαι πρὸς σὲ ἢ ἡδονῇ; ὁ δέ μιν ἀληθείῃ χρήσασθαι ἐκέλευε, φὰς οὐδέν οἱ ἀηδέστερον ἔσεσθαι ἢ πρότερον ἦν. ὡς δὲ ταῦτα ἤκουσε Δημάρητος, ἔλεγε τάδε· Βασιλεῦ, ἐπειδὴ ἀληθείῃ διαχρήσασθαι πάντως κελεύεις ταῦτα λέγοντα τὰ μὴ ψευδόμενός τις ὕστερον ὑπὸ σεῦ ἁλώσεται, τῇ Ἑλλάδι πενίη μὲν αἰεί κοτε σύντροφός ἐστι, ἀρετὴ δὲ ἔπακτός ἐστι, ἀπό τε σοφίης κατεργασμένη καὶ νόμου ἰσχυροῦ· τῇ διαχρεωμένη ἡ Ἑλλὰς τήν τε πενίην ἀπαμύνεται καὶ τὴν δεσποσύνην. αἰνέω μέν νυν πάντας τοὺς Ἕλληνας τοὺς περὶ ἐκείνους τοὺς Δωρικοὺς χώρους οἰκημένους, ἔρχομαι δὲ λέξων οὐ περὶ πάντων τούσδε τοὺς λόγους, ἀλλὰ περὶ Λακεδαιμονίων μούνων, πρῶτα μὲν ὅτι οὐκ ἔστι ὅκως κοτὲ σοὺς δέξονται λόγους δουλοσύνην φέροντας τῇ Ἑλλάδι, αὖτις δὲ ὡς ἀντιώσονταί τοι ἐς μάχην καὶ ἢν οἱ ἄλλοι Ἕλληνες πάντες τὰ σὰ φρονέωσι. . . . ταῦτα ἀκούσας Ξέρξης γελάσας ἔφη· Δημάρητε, οἷον ἐφθέγξαο ἔπος, ἄνδρας χιλίους στρατιῇ τοσῇδε μαχήσεσθαι. ἄγε, εἰπέ μοι, σὺ φῂς τούτων τῶν ἀνδρῶν βασιλεὺς αὐτὸς γενέσθαι. σὺ ὦν ἐθελήσεις αὐτίκα μάλα πρὸς ἄνδρας δέκα μάχεσθαι; (Hdt. 7.101.3–103.1)

He was asking these things, but the other said in response, "King, should I use truth [in my answer] to you or pleasure?" And the other was bidding him use truth, asserting that he would be no less pleasing to him than he had been before. And when

---

[21] συνωνέομαι appears to be the technical term in prose for the acquisition of necessary supplies: cf. Lysias 22.6, 12; Xen. *HG* 5.4.56; Plato *Soph.* 224b; Dem. 13.30, 23.208; Plut. *Life of Brutus* 21; P.Oxy. 2106.4. According to Powell 1938 (s.v. νόος), ἐν νόῳ ἔχειν is Hdt's standard term for "intend," which he uses seventeen times; by contrast, ἐπὶ νόον ποιεῖν occurs only twice (here and 1.71.4), both times in contexts of a lofty invocation of the gods. Cf. also 3.21.3, where the king of the Ethiopians uses a similar expression (ἐπὶ νόον τρέπειν) again in the context of divine will, accompanied by the lofty periphrasis "the children of the Ethiopians." Thanks to Boris Maslov for discussion of all these points.

Demaratus heard these things, he was saying the following: "King—since you bid me entirely to use truth saying these things, so as not to be caught out by you later speaking falsehoods—Poverty has always been native to Greece, but Courage is an import, compounded from Wisdom and strong Law. Using her [Courage], Greece fends off both poverty and despotism. Now I praise all the Greeks who dwell around those Dorian lands, but what I'm about to say applies not to all, but to the Lacedaemonians alone: first, that there is no way that they will accept your words that bring slavery for Greece; and second, that they will oppose you in battle even if all the rest of the Greeks join your side.... Having heard these things, Xerxes laughed and said, "Demaratus, what sort of word have you uttered, that a thousand men would fight against so great a force! Come, tell me—you claim that you yourself were king of these men—so will you immediately be willing to fight against ten men?"

At one level, 1.27 and 7.101–4 constitute merely two examples within a much larger series in Herodotus—that of the warner ("tragic" or otherwise) speaking to a figure in authority.[22] And yet certain distinctive features link these two episodes together and separate them from the rest of the series. First, Demaratus's initial response to Xerxes uniquely stages the scene of advising in terms of an opposition of pleasure and truth, an opposition that implicitly also structures 1.27 (cf. ἐλπίσαντα λέγειν ἐκεῖνον ἀληθέα εἰπεῖν, κάρτα... ἡσθῆναι).[23] In addition, just as in 1.27, the Greek wise man's response is introduced with the rare phrase ὑπολαβὼν ἔφη. It must be acknowledged that this speech formula seems slightly out of place here, since it does not mark the witty "punch line" of one speaker that trumps and silences his interlocutor. Instead, I would suggest, the phrase serves here simply to conjure a fable or fablelike atmosphere.[24] At the same time, we recognize by now Demaratus's alternatives—using pleasure or truth—as a topos belonging to the scene of Aesopic advising. In addition to Hdt. 1.27, recall the many references in later Greek texts to the pleasure produced by Aesop's indirect style of advising reviewed in chapter 3 above.

To these passages, I would add one more that demonstrates the association of the opposition of pleasure and truth with fable in a context nearly contemporary with Herodotus. Toward the beginning of the first speech of Aretē in Prodicus's "Choice of Heracles" as Xenophon recounts it in the *Memorabilia*, Aretē solemnly assures the young hero: "I will not deceive you with preludes of pleasure, but in the very way the gods have appointed the things that are, I will narrate truly" (οὐκ ἐξαπατήσω δέ σε προοιμίοις ἡδονῆς, ἀλλ' ᾗπερ οἱ θεοὶ

---

[22] For extended discussion of the figure of the "warner" or adviser in Hdt, see Lattimore 1939, Bischoff 1965.

[23] As noted in chapter 3, section I above, this opposition in 1.27 is reinforced by the contrast with 1.29–33, where we are told first that Solon "did not respond with flattery, but used only the truth" (οὐδὲν ὑποθωπεύσας, ἀλλὰ τῷ ἐόντι χρησάμενος λέγει), and that in the end he did not "please" or "gratify" (ἐχαρίζετο) Croesus by his explicit teaching.

[24] Cf. Karadagli 1981.3, 98–99 for this as one way of reading the effect of specific dictional "fable formulae."

διέθεσαν τὰ ὄντα διηγήσομαι μετ' ἀληθείας). As I suggested in chapter 7, Prodicus's *epideixis* represents the refined rhetorical elaboration of a fable, in which (paradoxically) all the fable elements are attached to the somewhat squalid, disreputable Kakia. So here, Aretē firmly rejects the deception and pleasure that are the hallmarks of Kakia's fabular discourse, promising only the unvarnished truth. In light of these familiar genre oppositions, we can now see that Herodotus stages a turn or variation on this tradition: Demaratus, having offered Xerxes the choice, speaks first *logos*, then *gnōmē* (in Aesopic terms). First, the Spartan king tells what is almost an allegorical, aetiological fable of native Peniē and imported Aretē to explain why the Greeks are the way they are; then he proceeds to calque that fable with an explicit, decoded version ("I praise all the Greeks, etc.").[25]

Commentators have found fault with the logic of Demaratus's allegory: thus R. W. Macan sniffs, "Hdt. however (for it is, of course, Hdt. speaking), rather mixes his metaphors and obscures his argument as in other cases.... If poverty is indigenous (σύντροφος), how is it to be 'warded off,' like the outlandish 'tyranny' (δεσποσύνη)?"[26] But this illogic (I would maintain) is precisely the illogic of a certain kind of fable: consider, for example, Hesiod's fable of *aretē* and *kakotēs*:

> τὴν μέν τοι κακότητα καὶ ἰλαδὸν ἔστιν ἑλέσθαι
> ῥηιδίως· λείη μὲν ὁδός, μάλα δ' ἐγγύθι ναίει·
> τῆς δ' ἀρετῆς ἱδρῶτα θεοὶ προπάροιθεν ἔθηκαν
> ἀθάνατοι· μακρὸς δὲ καὶ ὄρθιος οἶμος ἐς αὐτὴν
> καὶ τρηχὺς τὸ πρῶτον· ἐπὴν δ' εἰς ἄκρον ἵκηται,
> ῥηιδίη δὴ ἔπειτα πέλει, χαλεπή περ ἐοῦσα.
> (*WD* 287–92)

> Inferiority is easy to choose and can be had in abundance; the road is smooth and she lives very near. But the immortal gods put sweat before Superiority, and the road to her is long and straight and rough at first. But when you come to the top, then it's easy, though being difficult.

---

[25] Indeed, once we realize this about Demaratus's speech to Xerxes, it becomes clear that Solon's more familiar and famous advice to Croesus (1.29–33) shares a similar structure. Solon first responds to Croesus's question "whether there is any man you have seen who is the most blessed or fortunate of all?" with two *logoi*—the historical exempla of Tellus the Athenian and Cleobis and Biton of Argos (1.30.3–31). It is only when Croesus utterly refuses to draw his own conclusions about his life from these *logoi* that Solon resorts to a lengthy speech of explicit *gnōmē* (1.32). I owe this point to Elizabeth Irwin, in a response to an oral presentation of this material; cf. Moles 1996.269, Adrados 1999.401 (quoted above, n. 5). Notice that, in these terms, both Solon's advice to Croesus and Demaratus's to Xerxes correspond to the Sophistic pattern of fable narrative and then long explanatory epilogue I described in chapter 7, section I. Here as elsewhere, we might see this as Hdt's synthesis of old and new, since he deploys the Sophistic pattern within the older context of the encounter of sage/Aesop and king.

[26] Macan 1908.I.1.130.

410　CHAPTER 11

Once one attains the summit, the poet assures us, the road of *aretē* "is easy then, though being difficult." We find the same illogic in another version of the fable of the two roads preserved in the *Life of Aesop*:

> When Zeus once commanded it, Prometheus showed to mortals two roads, one of freedom and one of slavery. And the road of freedom he made at the beginning harsh and difficult of access and steep and waterless, and crammed with burrs, entirely risky, but at the end a level plain, having space to stroll around on, in a grove crammed with fruit, well-watered, where it comes to a pause which holds the end of the experience of evils. But the road of slavery he made at the beginning a level plain, full of flowers and having a sweet prospect and much luxury, but in the end difficult of access, entirely hard and precipitous. And the Samians, recognizing what was useful from Aesop's words, all together cried out to [Croesus's] letter-bearer, saying "the harsh road." (*Life of Aesop* chs. 94–95 [*Vita* G])

The Aesopic version playfully elaborates and, by its profusion of detail, makes more obvious the illogic or contradiction in Hesiod's sparer version. At the same time, Aesop's version makes the fable political, transforming Hesiod's two roads of *aretē* and *kakotēs* into those of freedom and slavery. It thereby provides a closer parallel for Demaratus's allegory, since Aesop's *douleia* corresponds to Demaratus's *desposunē*. It is tempting to think that something like the *Life of Aesop* tradition (perhaps as an East Greek oral tradition?) might lie behind Herodotus's staged colloquy here in Book 7. For we might notice, first, that this is the fable Aesop offers the Samians immediately after his generic apologia for speaking *logos* rather than *gnōmē* (quoted in chapter 3, section I above); and, second, that this extended sequence in the *Life of Aesop* occurs precisely in the context of Aesop's advising the Samians not to submit to the demands of Croesus, who has sent emissaries to exact submission and tribute from the Greek islanders. That is to say, Aesop offers his fable in the context of an Eastern threat, when the Greeks must decide whether to submit or resist (precisely the theme of the colloquy of Xerxes and Demaratus in Hdt. Book 7).

Finally, I would suggest that the possibility of this Aesopic tradition behind Herodotus's version might also explain the strange competition of Aesopic and Homeric discourses in this episode, for again (as in 1.27) the Eastern potentate speaks language redolent of Homeric epic. In his response to a Greek adviser whose discourse is marked as fabular by the introductory formula ὑπολαβὼν ἔφη, Xerxes exclaims, Δημάρητε, οἶον ἐφθέγξαο ἔπος. This may appear an unremarkable expression, but in fact it is one of only two occurrences of exclamatory οἶος in all of Herodotus—and the only neuter singular occurrence.[27] And although it is not precisely a Homeric formula, I would suggest that it functions

---

[27] The other occurrence of exclamatory οἶος is 4.3.3 (οἶα ποιεῦμεν); at 5.23.2, Hdt uses the dialect form κοῖον in an exclamation. There is one last occurrence in the interpolated paragraph 6.122 (οἶός τις ἀνὴρ ἐγένετο), but I do not include this in the count. In addition, note κοῖον ἐφθέγξαο ἔπος in Histaieus's question to Darius at 5.106.3.

as a conflation of several different, related Homeric expressions of one speaker's amazement or anger at the words of another. Thus Xerxes' exclamation recalls most nearly οἶον ἔειπες, but also perhaps evokes ποῖον τὸν μῦθον ἔειπες and even ποῖόν σε ἔπος φύγεν ἕρκος ὀδόντων—all of which occur in similar contexts of surprise and reproach.[28] In addition, notice that immediately after his first evocative exclamation οἶον ἐφθέγξαο ἔπος, Xerxes begins his next sentence ἄγε, εἰπέ μοι. This represents the only occurrence of ἄγε as an interjection in all of Herodotus—Herodotean speakers normally use φέρε in this construction.[29] ἄγε is, of course, incredibly common as an interjection in Homeric speeches, even occuring five times in a phrase almost identical to Xerxes', εἴπ' ἄγε μοι.[30] Even so, these may seem small phrases to hang an argument on, but recall that this colloquy of Greek adviser and Persian king occurs right after—indeed, is motivated by—the magnificent catalog of Persian forces that occupies forty chapters of Herodotus's Seventh Book (chs. 61–99). In this sequence, Xerxes is inspired by surveying all his forces to ask Demaratus if the Greeks will dare to resist so great an army. This catalog of Persian forces has generally been recognized as one of the most Homeric sequences in Herodotus's narrative, which interestingly transposes the *Greek* Catalog of Ships to the invading Eastern army. Thus here, as in 1.27, an Eastern dynast with a mighty host speaks in the formulae of Homeric epic, while his Greek interlocutor punctures the dynast's Homeric pretensions by speaking the lowly language of fable. On this reading, we might even recognize Demaratus's famous last words—that the Lacedaemonians will stand fast and fight out of fear of δεσπότης νόμος (7.104.4)—as one final gesture toward allegorical fable.[31]

Thus Herodotus has resignified the hierarchical genre opposition of Homeric versus Aesopic discourse to figure the conflict of East and West and its unexpected outcome in the Persian Wars. In this context, it becomes easier to

---

[28] For οἶον ἔειπες, see *Il.* 7.455, 8.152, 14.95, 16.49, 17.173, 22.170; *Ody.* 13.140; for ποῖον τὸν μῦθον ἔειπες, see *Il.* 1.552, 4.25, 8.209, 462, 14.330, 16.440, 18.361; for ποῖόν σε ἔπος φύγεν ἕρκος ὀδόντων, see *Il.* 4.350, 14.83; *Ody.* 1.64, 3.230, 5.22, 19.492, 21.168, 23.70. Thanks to Joseph Russo for pointing out to me that Xerxes' exclamation may evoke not just οἶον ἔειπες, but this whole set of related Homeric formulae.

[29] According to Powell 1938, s.vv. ἄγω, φέρω, 7.103.1 provides the sole occurrence of exclamatory ἄγε in Hdt, whereas φέρε and φέρετε occur thirteen times.

[30] By my count, ἄγε occurs as an interjection 115 times in Homer (not including plural ἄγετε); for the specific formula εἴπ' ἄγε μοι, see *Il.* 3.192, 9.673, 10.544; *Ody.* 15.347, 23.261. Cf. the formula ἀλλ' ἄγε μοι τόδε εἰπέ, which occurs thirteen times in the *Ody.* and once in the *Il.* What does it mean that Xerxes' word order produces a hiatus avoided by the Homeric formula and a rhythm inadmissible in dactylic hexameter? Are we to read Xerxes as an inept epic composer/rhapsode, or is it simply that in prose, the pressure of normative word order is too strong?

[31] It may also be significant for this pattern of discursive oppositions that Xerxes twice applies the contemptuous verb φλυηρέω to Demaratus's statements at the end of the episode (7.104.1, 5; two of only three occurrences of this verb in all of Hdt). We have seen forms of φλυαρ- in low, Aesopic or fabular contexts already in Plato *Sym.* (211e3; chapter 8, section II above) and Plut. *Mal.Hdt.* (ch. 43/873e; chapter 10, section III above).

understand why Herodotus should choose to write prose that is in some respects Aesopic. For beyond any specific Aesopic allusion, Demaratus's fable of Greek poverty and courage can also serve as a characterization of fable itself, a small, poor, and humble genre that stands in contrast to the sweep, heroic substance, and lavish magnificence of Homeric epic. At the same time, this symbolic resignification of the genre hierarchy may help in turn to explain Herodotus's displacement of Aesop from the scene of sage advising at 1.27. In chapter 3, I suggested that Herodotus elides Aesop from this scene that is properly his so as not to complicate the Greek–non-Greek opposition encoded in the portentous encounter of Solon and Croesus for which 1.27 serves as foil and preamble. At this point, we can see that this is part of a broader strategy that (at least on occasion) symbolically aligns Greece with the humble genre of fable and opposes it to the Homeric magnificence of Eastern powers.

III. FABLE AS HISTORY

As my third and, I suspect, most controversial category of Herodotus's use of Aesop, I would like to consider those instances where Herodotus tells fable as history. A number of Herodotean stories that closely parallel Aesopic fables have been identified by scholars. Thus, for example, Marcel Detienne and Jesper Svenbro have pointed out striking parallels between the failed attempt of Maeandrius to institute *isonomia* on Samos after the fall of Polycrates and the fable of the pleonectic, nomothetic wolf (Hdt. 3.142–43; cf. Perry fable no. 348).[32] Detienne and Svenbro assume that a real sixth-century BCE event generated the beast fable, but I find it hard to imagine exactly how this would occur. Indeed, Alan Griffiths notes that "the very next chapter, in which Maeandrius lures his rivals into his stronghold (and then falls ill) echoes the scheme of The Sick Lion."[33] The presence of this echo (if we accept it) would strongly suggest that the story patterns have traveled in the other direction—from beast fable to the archaic history of Samos. This set of connections is itself intriguing, given that Samos is the island where much of Aesop's life story plays itself out, and (supposedly) the island where Herodotus spent time in exile from his native Halicarnassus.[34]

In any case, Griffiths himself has identified several more such parallels, and I suspect that there are still more than scholars have thus far noticed.[35] But even

[32] Detienne and Svenbro 1989.150–52. For quotation and discussion of this fable, see chapter 3, section II above.

[33] Griffiths 2006.139; the reference is to Perry fable no. 389; cf. Babrius 95, 103.

[34] According to the Suda, s.v. Ἡρόδοτος, II. 588 Adler. Cf. Svenbro 2002, connecting another story in the Samian *logos* with fable.

[35] Griffiths 2006.139–140. And, of course, Detienne and Svenbro 1989, Svenbro 2002, and Griffiths 2006 are considering only *Greek* fables as parallels for Herodotean stories, but note that Grey 2000, in his concordance to the 547 extant Indian *Jātaka* fables, notes Hdtean parallels for ten dif-

when scholars have detected such parallels, they have rarely pursued the larger issues raised by these narrative convergences. In each case, we would like to know in which direction the story traveled—from history to fable or vice versa? If the latter, is this Herodotus's own adaptation of fable as history, or are we to imagine multiforms of a story already in circulation in the oral tradition he inherited? And in cases where it is Herodotus's own transformation, what purposes might it serve? The first two questions may in many cases be unanswerable, but even when scholars have concluded that story patterns have traveled from fable to history, they have usually been content to treat such stories as Herodotean rationalization (as of the related categories of myth and fairy tale) or simply moralizing entertainment.[36] But this is again to occlude or ignore the potent sociopolitics of the lowly form of beast fable and Aesop as its debased purveyor.

I want to consider at some length at least one instance of this phenomenon where the text seems to provide evidence that Herodotus is consciously adapting beast fable as history, and signaling as much to his audience. I will then address the historiographic implications of this conscious choice. Here we will find a confrontation of high and low discourses similar to that in the scenes of Aesopic advising I considered in the previous section. For here, too, the Aesopic or fabular serves to parody and puncture the pretensions of the great. The particular episode occurs as part of the so-called Alcmeonid excursus that follows the account of the Battle of Marathon in Book 6 of the *Histories*. In this sequence in Book 6, Herodotus is ostensibly defending the Alcmeonidae against the charge of showing a shield as a signal to the Persians sailing around from Marathon to Athens after their defeat in battle, and this leads him into a narrative of the sources of the family's wealth and prestige. Thus we get first (briefly) the story of Alcmeon in Croesus's treasury (Hdt. 6.125) and then (more expansively) the wooing of Agariste (Hdt. 6.126–30). In this latter tale, Cleisthenes, tyrant of Sicyon, decides to marry his daughter Agariste to "the best of all the Greeks," so he makes a public announcement at the Olympic Games, inviting all those who "think themselves worthy to be Cleisthenes' son-in-law" to come to Sicyon sixty days hence (6.126.1–2). Herodotus then provides us a lavish catalog of the thirteen suitors who come from all over Greece, including two Athenians—Megacles son of Alcmeon and Hippoclides son of Tisander. Cleisthenes keeps these suitors in Sicyon for a full year, entertaining them lavishly, while he makes trial of them in company and individually, in athletic contests, and at the common meals. Of all the suitors, we're told, he's most impressed with the two from Athens, but especially with Hippoclides "because of his

---

ferent Buddhist Birth Stories [!]. For one of these narrative parallels, see S. West 2003.433–37 (who treats it as a free-floating "migratory motif"). Cf. also Gethin 2006.85, who notes another parallel between Hdt and a *Jātaka* tale not included in Grey 2000.

[36] Thus (e.g.) Griffiths 2006.139–42.

manly courage (ἀνδραγαθίην) and the fact that he's distantly related to the Cypselids of Corinth" (6.128.2). Finally, the big day arrives:

ὡς δὲ ἡ κυρίη ἐγένετο τῶν ἡμερέων τῆς τε κατακλίσιος τοῦ γάμου καὶ ἐκφάσιος αὐτοῦ Κλεισθένεος τὸν κρίνοι ἐκ πάντων, θύσας βοῦς ἑκατὸν ὁ Κλεισθένης εὐώχεε αὐτούς τε τοὺς μνηστῆρας καὶ Σικυωνίους πάντας. ὡς δὲ ἀπὸ δείπνου ἐγίνοντο, οἱ μνηστῆρες ἔριν εἶχον ἀμφί τε μουσικῇ καὶ τῷ λεγομένῳ ἐς τὸ μέσον. προϊούσης δὲ τῆς πόσιος κατέχων πολλὸν τοὺς ἄλλους ὁ Ἱπποκλείδης ἐκέλευσέ οἱ τὸν αὐλητὴν αὐλῆσαι ἐμμέλειαν, πειθομένου δὲ τοῦ αὐλητέω ὀρχήσατο. καί κως ἑωυτῷ μὲν ἀρεστῶς ὀρχέετο, ὁ Κλεισθένης δὲ ὁρέων ὅλον τὸ πρῆγμα ὑπώπτευε. μετὰ δὲ ἐπισχὼν ὁ Ἱπποκλείδης χρόνον ἐκέλευσέ τινα τράπεζαν ἐσενεῖκαι, ἐσελθούσης δὲ τῆς τραπέζης πρῶτα μὲν ἐπ' αὐτῆς ὀρχήσατο Λακωνικὰ σχημάτια, μετὰ δὲ ἄλλα Ἀττικά, τὸ τρίτον δὲ τὴν κεφαλὴν ἐρείσας ἐπὶ τὴν τράπεζαν τοῖσι σκέλεσι ἐχειρονόμησε. Κλεισθένης δὲ τὰ μὲν πρῶτα καὶ τὰ δεύτερα ὀρχεομένου ἀποστυγέων γαμβρὸν ἄν οἱ ἔτι γενέσθαι Ἱπποκλείδεα διὰ τήν τε ὄρχησιν καὶ τὴν ἀναιδείην κατεῖχε ἑωυτόν, οὐ βουλόμενος ἐκραγῆναι ἐς αὐτόν· ὡς δὲ εἶδε τοῖσι σκέλεσι χειρονομήσαντα, οὐκέτι κατέχειν δυνάμενος εἶπε· Ὦ παῖ Τεισάνδρου, ἀπορχήσαό γε μὲν τὸν γάμον. ὁ δὲ Ἱπποκλείδης ὑπολαβὼν εἶπε· οὐ φροντὶς Ἱπποκλείδῃ. ἀπὸ τούτου μὲν τοῦτο ὀνομάζεται. (Hdt. 6.129–130.1)

When the appointed day came for the marriage feast and Cleisthenes' own announcement which [suitor] he would choose from all, he sacrificed a hundred oxen and lavishly feasted the suitors themselves and all the Sicyonians. And when they finished dinner, the suitors were holding a competition over *mousikē* and speeches set in the middle. And as the drinking advanced and Hippoclides held all the rest enthralled, he bid the aulos-player to play a tragic strain, and when the aulos-player obeyed, he danced. And somehow he gratified himself in his dancing, but Cleisthenes, observing the whole thing, was growing suspicious. And after pausing for a time, Hippoclides bid someone bring in a table and, when the table came in, first he danced Laconian dance-forms upon it, but afterwards other ones—Attic dance-moves, and third, propping his head upon the table, he was gesticulating with his legs. Now Cleisthenes, while [Hippoclides] was doing his first and second dances, though disgusted at the prospect of Hippoclides being his son-in-law on account of his dancing and his shamelessness, nonetheless managed to restrain himself, not wishing to explode against him. But when he saw him waving his legs in the air, no longer able to restrain himself, he said, "O child of Tisander, good dancer though you are, you've danced away your marriage!" And Hippoclides said in response, "Hippoclides doesn't care!" And from this incident, this has become proverbial.

Over a century ago, in appendix XIV of his edition and commentary on Books 4, 5, and 6 of Herodotus, R. W. Macan pointed out that the closest parallel for this tale is the Indian fable of the Dancing Peacock, preserved in a Pāli text called the *Jātakas* or *Buddhist Birth Stories*—a written collection of more than five hundred tales that is difficult to date with any accuracy, but that presumably takes over much older pre-Buddhist oral traditions.[37] The *Jātaka* tales characteristically combine prose and verse—prose for most of the narrative, punctuated by a small number of poetic verses that offer the fable's "moral," spoken either by a character within the story whom the Bodhisatta (the one who will become the Buddha) identifies as one of his former incarnations or by the sage Bodhisatta himself outside the frame of the fable. It is generally assumed by Pāli scholars that the poetic verses represent the oldest element in the *Jātaka* fables, many of which go back at least to the fifth century BCE. Around these poetic verses, the prose of the tales has accreted over hundreds of years of oral performances as explanation, expansion, and commentary.[38] Thus in the Pāli tradition (with very few exceptions), only the verses are recognized as canonical and fixed, while the prose paraphrase and expansion would presumably have been slightly different for each performance of the tale over hundreds of years until the tales were committed to writing.[39] And since many of these embedded canonical verses seem to valorize distinctly un-Buddhist and amoral forms of practical wisdom or low cunning, it seems likely that these concentrated story nuggets in poetic form predated their Buddhist appropriation.[40] At the same time, these brief verse narratives more or less require prose expansion and explanation to be comprehensible, so that some Pāli scholars assume that a combined verse-prose form might already have existed in the Ṛg-Veda (ca. 1500–1000 BCE).[41]

As far as I can tell, almost no Herodotean scholars have noticed Macan's parallel or, if they have, have not considered the broader implications of the recasting of Indian beast fable as Greek history.[42] But, in fact, the similarity of

[37] Macan 1895.II.304–311. The parallel between Hdt and the *Jātaka* story had been noted already by Tawney 1883.121 and Warren 1894.476-7.

[38] I am indebted to Rupert Gethin and Alexander von Rospatt for helpful discussions of the *Jātakas* and bibliographic recommendations. For the date range of the *Jātakas* from fifth century BCE (for the verse) to third century CE, see Shaw 2006.xix, l–lii.

[39] Thus Norman 1983.77–78, von Hinüber 2000.54–57.

[40] I owe this point to Alexander von Rospatt (private communication); cf. Norman 1983.79–81, von Hinüber 2000.55.

[41] This is the theory of von Hinüber 2000.56–57, noting that such an early dating is a hotly debated issue within Sanskrit/Pāli scholarship. The particular fable with which I am concerned (the "Dancing Peacock") is carved in bas-relief on a Buddhist relic shrine at Bhārhut that dates to the end of the third or second century BCE, proving that it was already well known before that (on which see Rhys Davids 1880.lviii–lx, cii, 294n. 1; illustrated in Cunningham 1962, plate XXVII no. 11).

[42] As far as I am aware, of scholars writing on Herodotus, only Aly (1921.159), Griffin (1990.73), and McQueen (2000.x–xi, 220) even acknowledge Macan's parallel, but none of them considers the historiographical implications of the transmutation of fable into history. In contrast, scholars of fable in both Indian and Greek traditions seem well aware of the parallel, but this knowledge has not penetrated Herodotean circles; see Chalmers 1895.I.84, Hausrath 1909.col. 1727, Francis and Thomas 1916.32, Schwarzbaum 1968.141.

the two tales is quite remarkable. Here is T. W. Rhys Davids's 1880 translation of the Indian fable (the *Nacca Jātaka*, no. 32 in Fausbøll's text of the traditional 547 *Jātakas*):[43]

> Long ago, in the first age of the world, the quadrupeds chose the Lion as their king, the fishes the Leviathan, and the birds the Golden Goose. Now the royal Golden Goose had a daughter, a young goose most beautiful to see; and he gave her her choice of a husband. And she chose the one she liked the best. For, having given her the right to choose, he called together all the birds in the Himalaya region. And crowds of geese, and peacocks, and other birds of various kinds, met together on a great flat piece of rock. The king sent for his daughter, saying, "Come and choose the husband you like best!" On looking over the assembly of birds, she caught sight of the peacock, with a neck as bright as gems, and a many-coloured tail; and she made the choice with the words, "Let this one be my husband!"
>
> So the assembly of birds went up to the peacock, and said, "Friend Peacock! this king's daughter having to choose her husband from amongst so many birds, has fixed her choice upon you!" "Up to today you would not see my greatness," said the peacock, so overflowing with delight that in breach of all modesty he began to spread his wings and dance in the midst of the vast assembly,—and in dancing he exposed himself.
>
> Then the royal Golden Goose was shocked! And he said, "This fellow has neither modesty in his heart nor decency in his outward behaviour! I shall not give my daughter to him. He has broken loose from all sense of shame!" And he uttered this verse to all the assembly—
>
>> "Pleasant is your cry, brilliant is your back,
>> Almost like the opal in its colour is your neck,
>> The feathers in your tail reach about a fathom's length,
>> But such a dancer I can give no daughter, sir, of mine!"
>
> Then the king in the midst of the whole assembly bestowed his daughter on a young goose, his nephew. And the peacock was covered with shame at not getting the fair gosling, and rose straight up from the place and flew away.[44]

Notice one particular detail in the Indian version: the peacock, as he's dancing, "exposes himself" (and this is the precise point of comparison with the frame tale in the Buddhist version, which explains the shameful self-exposure of a luxurious monk by his having the reincarnated soul of the peacock). Now, of

---

[43] Rhys Davids 1880.291–94. This was the translation used by Macan in 1895 and is still one of the very few English translations of this fable available. Indeed, to my knowledge, besides Rhys Davids 1880, there are currently only two other English translations of the "Dancing Peacock" available: Chalmers 1895.I.83–84 and Francis and Thomas 1916.30–32.

[44] Rhys Davids 1880.292–93.

course, in the Greek version, Hippoclides also exposes himself when he stands on his head and waves his legs in the air—and it is this shocking breach of decorum that causes Cleisthenes finally to snap.[45]

Macan, after noting the striking parallels between the two tales, methodically works through the possible vectors of influence. He concludes that it is much more likely that an Indian beast fable traveled west before the time of Herodotus than that the story of Hippoclides traveled east (perhaps with Alexander, as Macan proposes for the sake of argument) and was eventually transmuted into the "Dancing Peacock."[46] Macan further imagines Greek popular tradition suturing or superimposing the fable of the peacock onto the tale of the wooing of Agariste long before the story reached Herodotus. As he puts it,

> it is evident that the memory of the wedding of Agariste, an historic event fraught with manifold political significance, was obscured, or glorified, by adventitious influences from various quarters, among which may be detected not merely the obvious matter derived from native epic sources, but the remoter workings of oriental fable, transmitted, and transmuted, by long and subtle processes, from Hindustan to Hellas, until what had been a palpable creation of primitive Indian folklore came to pass muster as a serious item in the Hellenic history of the sixth century B.C.[47]

I would wholeheartedly agree with Macan that the story must originally have traveled east to west, rather than west to east.[48] But I am far less ready than Macan to exculpate Herodotus from any conscious knowledge of the story's beast-fable origins, for several reasons. First, it is striking that Herodotus introduces the catalog of suitors by saying, "At that point, however many of the Greeks were puffed up in themselves and their native lands (ὅσοι σφίσι τε αὐτοῖσι ἦσαν καὶ πάτρῃ ἐξωγκωμένοι), were showing up as suitors." The verb ἐξογκόω, here represented by the perfect passive participle ἐξωγκωμένοι, is extremely rare, especially when used—as it is here—metaphorically for those "puffed up" or "swollen" with pride.[49] In fact, this is one of only two occurrences

---

[45] For Hippoclides' self-exposure, cf. Ogden 1997.117. Ogden even sees a pun on ὄρχεις in the rare verb ἀπωρχήσαο, suggesting the translation "you have ballsed up your marriage." This is hardly an American idiom; perhaps we could say instead (forgoing perfect anatomical accuracy), "you've cocked up your marriage"?

[46] Macan 1895.II.307–11. Macan is much preoccupied with the question of when the Greeks might first have been exposed to the peacock as a terminus post quem for the migration of the fable, but he concludes that we cannot assume from the silence of the sources that the Greeks were not familiar with the peacock by (e.g.) the sixth century BCE. On knowledge of the peacock in classical Athens and its strong associations with Eastern-influenced aristocratic luxury, see Miller 1997.189–92. Warren 1894.477 likewise argues that the *Jātaka* tale must be the original; Tawney 1883.121 assumes the opposite vector of influence.

[47] Macan 1895.II.310.

[48] Cf. Aly 1921.159.

[49] Outside of the medical writers (who use the verb literally of physical swellings), ἐξογκόω occurs only twice in Hdt (6.125.4, 126.3) and frequently in Euripides (*Andr.* 703, *Hippolytus* 938, *IA*

of forms of this verb in the *Histories*, both occurring in very close proximity, since Herodotus has just used it to describe the appearance of Alcmeon emerging from Croesus's treasury, grotesquely swollen with gold dust, "like to anything more than a person" (παντὶ δέ τεῳ οἰκὼς μᾶλλον ἢ ἀνθρώπῳ, Hdt. 6.125.4). Macan found the repetition of this rare verb in adjacent stories infelicitous, especially since it is used first literally, then figuratively.[50] But I would contend that the repetition effectively binds the two Alcmeonid tales together, associating both with the distended, grotesque body and the nonhuman. It may also be worth noting that the male peacock literally "puffs itself up" when it "dances" and displays its magnificent tail.

Second, Herodotus seems to preserve the theme of luxury, which is central to the Indian fable but much less prominent in the story of Hippoclides, by displacing it onto the first suitor mentioned, Smindyrides of Sybaris:

ἀπὸ μὲν δὴ Ἰταλίης ἦλθε Σμινδυρίδης ὁ Ἱπποκράτεος Συβαρίτης, ὃς ἐπὶ πλεῖστον δὴ χλιδῆς εἷς ἀνὴρ ἀπίκετο (ἡ δέ Σύβαρις ἤκμαζε τοῦτον τὸν χρόνον μάλιστα).... (Hdt. 6.127.1)

And, in the first place, from Italy came Smindyrides son of Hippocrates, the Sybarite, who was indeed the one man who came to the greatest point of luxury (and Sybaris was most at its peak at this time)....

Herodotus has pulled out all the stops here: the word χλιδή is poetic, occurring only here in the *Histories*, while the superlative ἐπὶ πλεῖστον ... χλιδῆς is reinforced by δή and εἷς ἀνήρ.[51] And since this lavish introduction of Smindyrides as the first suitor occurs almost immediately after Herodotus has characterized the suitors as "puffed up in themselves and their *native lands*" (πάτρῃ ἐξωγκωμένοι), we are encouraged, I think, to notice that Smindyrides hails from Sybaris, "most at its peak at this time" and a traditional byword for luxury.[52] Indeed, I would read all this as a narrative feint: by mentioning Smindyrides first, using a flurry of superlatives associated with his luxurious lifestyle, Herodotus sets us up to expect that the Sybarite will be the front-runner among the suitors—that is to say, the peacock of the fable. (And this is appropriate

---

921, *Or.* 402, *Suppl.* 864) among classical authors. Cf. also Sophocles fr. 942 Radt, οἶκος ... ὀγκωθεὶς χλιδῇ.

[50] Macan 1895.I.381 (*ad* 6.126.12): "**ἐξωγκωμένοι** used in a literal sense c. 125 *supra*, and here rather clumsily repeated."

[51] Cf. Stein 1894.III.219 (*ad* 6.127.3), McQueen 2000.214.

[52] That πάτρη here means "native land" rather than "lineage" is confirmed by 6.128.1, where Cleisthenes finds out the πάτραι of all the suitors and the γένος ("family") of each. In later Greek tradition Smindyrides becomes the very paradigm of Sybaritic luxury, as other writers pick up on and elaborate Herodotus's hints: cf. Aelian *VH* 9.24, 12.24; D.S. 8.19; Athenaeus 6.273b–c, 12.541b–c (citing Chamaeleon and Polemon, respectively). On Smindyrides and Sybarite tales, see also Trenkner 1958.8, 175–76.

enough, since in the Indian version it is a "luxurious monk" whose behavior provokes the story of the dancing peacock.)[53]

But there is still more to say about Smindyrides' ethnic, and this is my third reason for thinking that Herodotus himself was conscious of the story's beast fable origins and expected his audience to recognize them. For, as I noted at the end of the previous chapter, Aristophanes seems to know and abide by a distinction between *Aesopic* beast fable and *Sybarite* fables involving human beings. Herodotus, by placing a Sybarite at the head of his list of suitors, may be said to be signaling thereby the conversion from fabular animals to human characters within the tale.

Fourth: notice that, at the moment Hippoclides responds with his famous quip, his speech is marked with the climactic fabular formula ὑπολαβὼν εἶπε, which we might take as Herodotus winking broadly to an audience that is itself familiar with the fable of the peacock. Indeed, we find striking support for the significance of this speech formula and its low generic affiliations in the Suda entry on the proverb οὐ φροντὶς Ἱπποκλείδῃ:

> παροιμία, ἧς μέμνηται Ἕρμιππος ἐν Δημόταις. Ἱπποκλείδης ὁ Τισάνδρου μέλλων γαμεῖν Ἀγαρίστην τὴν Κλεισθένους τοῦ Σικυωνίου θυγατέρα τοῦ τυράννου ἐν αὐτῇ τῇ τῶν γάμων ἡμέρᾳ ἐπωρχήσατο περιττῶς. μεταβουλευσαμένου δὲ τοῦ Κλεισθένους καὶ Μεγακλεῖ τῷ Ἀλκμαίωνος τὴν θυγατέρα δόντος, πρὸς δὲ τὸν Ἱπποκλείδην φανερῶς εἰπόντος, ὅτι ἀπώρχηται τὸν γάμον τὸν Ἀγαρίστης, ὑποτυχὼν ἔφη· οὐ φροντὶς Ἱπποκλείδῃ. (Suda III. 594 Adler)

> Proverb which Hermippus mentions in the *Dēmotai*. Hippoclides the son of Tisander, when he was going to marry Agariste the daughter of Cleisthenes, tyrant of Sicyon, on the wedding day itself danced excessively. And when Cleisthenes changed his mind and gave his daughter [instead] to Megacles the son of Alcmeon, and said openly to Hippoclides that he had danced away the marriage of Agariste, he responded, "Hippoclides doesn't care."

Whether the comic poet Hermippus, who is more or less contemporary with Herodotus, told the whole story of the wooing of Agariste or simply "mentioned the proverb" that the Suda then calques from Herodotus, we will probably never know. It is possible that Herodotus is alluding to Hermippus, if Hermippus told a parodic version of the wooing of Agariste. It is even possible that Hermippus's comedy explicitly compared the wooing of Agariste to the fable of the dancing peacock. We have already had occasion to observe the close affiliation of Aesop and the low forms of fable with Old Comedy (as in the discussion of *Hippias Major* in chapter 9 above).[54] Theoretically then, the Suda entry could

---

[53] The verse, which is thought to be the oldest core of the *Jātaka* fable, makes it clear that the tale was directed against luxury and frivolity, and this would presumably have been true even before the butt or recipient of the fable was identified as a Buddhist monk.

[54] See also Rothwell 1995.

be following either Herodotus or Hermippus. If the former, the occurrence of the phrase ὑποτυχὼν ἔφη at exactly the same point in the anecdote confirms the equivalence of classical ὑπολαβών and postclassical ὑποτυχών in the same fabular speech formula, for which I argued in chapter 3, section I above. If the latter, the Suda's diction might encourage us to think that the episode was also treated as a fable in Hermippus's comedy.

Whether we take Herodotus or Hermippus to be the innovator or adapter of fable here, or a more general popular tradition, the tale of the wooing of Agariste exhibits the same systematic opposition of high and low genres we have already observed in Hdt. 1.27 and 7.101–4. Admittedly, Cleisthenes in this episode does not speak Homeric discourse, but his actions are permeated with epic resonances. Thus scholars are fond of citing the wooers of Helen as an epic model for the wooing of Agariste, while some have also noted that Cleisthenes kicks off the marriage feast with a Homeric hecatomb (6.129.1).[55]

But what is Herodotus's purpose in this carefully constructed opposition of high and low genres? I would contend that its function in this episode is similar to that of the scenes of Greek sage advising Eastern potentate considered in the previous section. For here, low fable relentlessly demystifies and explodes a tyrant's epic pretensions. To appreciate this effect, we would do well to note certain key differences between Herodotus's narrative and its Indian fable source. First, formal differences. Intriguingly, as I have noted above, the *Jātakas* also characteristically exhibit an interaction of different speech genres—simple narrative prose and archaizing verse—in their narrative structure.[56] But, given the complexities of the long-lived, accretive Pāli text, we cannot be certain whether the characteristic *Jātaka* structure combining prose and poetry preexisted the Buddhist adaptation of older beast fables, or, if it did, whether that formal contrast of genres would have been known to the Greeks who adapted the fable as the story of Hippoclides. What the formal contrast does point up is that the Indian fable tradition also deploys a hierarchy of speech genres to make its point, but here the conventional ranking of poetry as more lofty and exalted than prose obtains, and the Indian fable conveys its message solemnly and without irony. The fact that the Golden Goose, king of all the birds, speaks the versified "punch line" of the fable marks him as the wise character whose moral

---

[55] Scholars who have seen an epic "Wooing of Helen" as model for the wooing of Agariste include Stein 1894.III.219, Macan 1895.II.310, How and Wells 1928.II.117, Murray 1980.202–3, Griffin 1990.73–77 (*Ehoiai*), McQueen 2000.x–xi, Griffiths 2006.136 ("epic cycle"). Contra: Aly (1921.159–60) takes the position that the fable and fairy-tale elements in this narrative preclude any epic resonances, but it is not clear why it has to be either/or; cf. Thomas 1989.269: "But no one origin is convincing when we find both an archaic list of suitors in the grand epic style and the amusing débâcle of Hippokleides' suit." For Cleisthenes' hecatomb, see McQueen 2000.218, and cf. in general on the Homeric aspirations of archaic tyrants Vilatte 1990.

[56] Thanks to David Damrosch, who in his comments after an oral presentation of this material initially called my attention to the significant combination of prose and verse in the Indian fable.

teaching we are meant to accept without question (as indeed does the peacock of the fable, who flies off without a word, finally filled with the shame he had lacked before). Herodotus's version, by contrast, gives Hippoclides the last word, in an exquisite display of nonchalance that earns him a very un-Homeric form of eternal fame in the proverb. And with his response, marked as the punch line of the fable by ὑπολαβὼν εἶπε, the tyrant's pretensions to Homeric grandeur are ironized and exposed as absurd. Thus also a second point of contrast—that of narrative tone and focus of audience sympathy. The Indian version is a solemn fable against vanity and immodesty, which uses the peacock as a negative paradigm. But in Herodotus's farcical version, Hippoclides is the hero, the character we admire and identify with, in his independence and aplomb in the face of self-important tyrannic authority (while we might say that both Cleisthenes and the hapless Megacles are the butts of this joke).[57]

Indeed, there is finally one more element in this narrative that encourages my suspicion that Herodotus is quite consciously deploying beast fable and epic resonances, playing them off against each other for his own thematic purposes. And that is the fact that this little narrative is itself obsessed with the elaboration of hierarchical genre distinctions, which it ultimately *inverts* (like Hippoclides standing on his head). Thus notice that the suitors compete in their final symposium "over *mousikē* and over τὸ λεγόμενον"—that is, song or poetry and prose speeches, in a pairing that precisely replicates the opposition between Sappho ἡ μουσοποιός and Aesop ὁ λογοποιός from 2.134–35 (quoted in chapter 10 above). Next we are told that Hippoclides, who "enthralled all the rest" with his skill in song and speech, shifts the register from vocal performance to bodily movement (a shift already scandalous for a sixth-century Greek nobleman).[58] But then, in a kind of repetition compulsion, generic hierarchy is reinscribed in the sequence of Hippoclides' dance performances. For the first,

[57] Thus Strasburger 1965.596, Thomas 1989.269, Griffiths 1995.43–44. See especially Fowler 2003.313–14: "Hippokleides, not Megakles who wins the bride, is the true hero of the story; the man who beats all those would-be tyrants at their own game, and then shows he doesn't give a fig for the prize. He is the buffoon with whom the audience identifies; positively Aristophanic he is, much like old Philokleon, who even quotes a similar proverb, as he dances merrily and his creditors go begging. The story is a knowing nudge and wink at the expense of the Alkmaionids, in particular Perikles, who was descended from boring old Megakles." It is telling that Fowler singles out Philocleon as the apt Aristophanic comparison for Hippocleides, given that Philocleon tells more Aesopic fables than any other Aristophanic character—precisely in the scene to which Fowler draws our attention.

[58] Cf. Stahl 1987.35, 50–51; Schäfer 1997.25–35. Catoni 2005.149–51 challenges the assumption that dance would in itself have been perceived as inappropriate for a Greek nobleman, arguing that the competition in *mousikē* that Hdt mentions would also allow for dance. But *mousikē* does not necessarily entail dance; for a parallel for Hdt's οἱ μνηστῆρες ἔριν εἶχον ἀμφί τε μουσικῇ καὶ τῷ λεγομένῳ ἐς τὸ μέσον that certainly does not involve dance, see Eryximachus's challenge to Alcibiades at Plato *Sym.* 214b1–2: οὕτως οὔτε τι λέγομεν ἐπὶ τῇ κύλικι οὔτε τι ᾄδομεν, ἀλλ᾽ ἀτεχνῶς ὥσπερ οἱ διψῶντες πιόμεθα; In addition, Catoni's reading ignores Hdt's clear indication that Cleisthenes "becomes suspicious" as soon as Hippoclides starts dancing.

the ἐμμέλεια was, as Aristoxenus tells us, a stately tragic dance, while Hippoclides' second, Λακωνικὰ σχημάτια, were perhaps some kind of war dance or *pyrrhikē*.[59] His third dance, here designated as "Attic," may represent yet another generic and sociological descent, if, as Macan speculates, "the Ἀττικὰ were more distinctly comic (the κόρδαξ?)."[60] Finally, of course, Hippoclides' standing on his head and waving his legs in the air (thereby exposing himself) represents the ultimate intrusion of the comic body, spotlighting the "lower bodily strata" (to use Bakhtin's term).[61]

This obsessive play with genre distinctions and hierarchies makes this episode a parable for Herodotus's own text, which masterfully rings its changes along the whole scale of genre and decorum. On this reading, Hippoclides is a figure for Herodotus himself (as Plutarch registered when he recast the proverb as οὐ φροντὶς Ἡροδότῳ).[62] Like his uninhibited hero, Herodotus blithely uses

---

[59] On ἐμμέλεια, see Stein 1894.III.222, citing Aristoxenus in Bekker's *Anecd.* p. 101: ἦν δὲ τὸ μὲν εἶδος τῆς τραγικῆς ὀρχήσεως ἡ καλουμένη ἐμμέλεια, καθάπερ τῆς σατυρικῆς ἡ καλουμένη σίκιννις, τῆς δὲ κωμικῆς ὁ καλούμενος κόρδαξ. On the likely military nature of "Spartan dance-moves," see Macan 1895.I.385; Legrand 1948.VI.120n. 5; McQueen 2000.219. In contrast to these interpretations, Catoni 2005.151–52 suggests that the problem in Hippoclides' dance is conveyed by the diminutive σχημάτια, which she takes to designate some kind of anthologizing or fragmenting of organized dance structures on Hippoclides' part. But it is difficult to say what the connotation of the diminutive is meant to be here, since this is the one and only use of the diminutive for dance figures in all of Greek. Perhaps the diminutive is simply meant to be derogatory, focalized (as it were) through the perception of the appalled Cleisthenes?

[60] Macan 1895.I.385; cf. Legrand 1948.VI.120n. 5: "Des danses de la Laconie (le pays de la πυρρίκη guerrière) à celles de l'Attique (où fleurissait la κόρδαξ), il y avait déjà progression dans le laisser-aller." Note that Hdt's specification of three different dances before Hippoclides stands on his head and exposes himself also offers a significant contrast to the Indian fable version, in which the peacock seems to engage in a single (generically unspecified) dance. This suggests that the notion of a generic/sociological descent in a sequence of dances is particular to the Greek version.

[61] Cf. Bakhtin 1984b, esp. 368–436. Notice in relation to these last three "dances" the observation of Ogden 1997.117–18 that dancing on a table suggests some kind of early dramatic performance. In addition (intriguingly for the low or inappropriate nature of Hippoclides' sequence of dances), we have a series of Attic red-figure vase representations from the second half of the fifth century of naked dwarfs dancing on tables in what appear to be sympotic scenes. One such scene in the tondo of a cup in Todi (Museo Civico 471, ca. 420 BCE) shows two naked dwarfs on a table, one crawling on all fours and another standing on his head, waving his legs in the air. A stamnos fragment from another such scene of a naked dwarf apparently dancing on a table (Erlangen Kunstsammlung 707, *ARV*² 1039, ca. 450–440 BCE) bears the remains of an inscription –ΚΛΕΙΔΗΣ above the dwarf's head; this scene was already connected with the story of Hippoclides by Lippold 1937 and Beazley 1939 (offering somewhat different interpretations). For this whole series of vases in the second half of the fifth century, see Dasen 1993.230–40, with plates 39.3, 40.2, 47.1 (Erlangen fragment), 50.1–2, 53.2 (Todi cup), 55.1; for interpretation of the Erlangen stamnos scene as a parodic or satiric representation of the Hippoclides episode, see Ogden 1997.118, Catoni 2005.154–61.

[62] Plut. *Mal.Hdt.* ch. 33/867b: "But Herodotus treats Xerxes' savagery towards Leonidas as proof that the Persian was more furious with him than with anyone else on earth, whereas he says the Thebans were branded at Thermopylae though they were medizing, and having been branded, were still medizing enthusiastically at Plataea! I'm reminded of Hippoclides, who danced with his legs on

the lowest forms (comedy and fable) to trump and explode the pretensions of the highest, precisely because these genre axes are identified with and come to represent the oppositions of Greek and Asiatic; private citizen and tyrant; and freedom and slavery within Herodotus's text. Something like this system of complex, overdetermined homologies, I would contend, at least partly accounts for Herodotus's choice of prose as medium and justifies our characterization of him as an Aesopic *logopoios*.

And all this brings me finally to the historiographic implications of Herodotus's transmutation of fable here. Much older scholarship assumed that Herodotus drew his information from "Alcmeonid family tradition" and composed the Alcmeonid excursus as a panegyric on this noble Athenian family. For these scholars, Herodotus was a (somewhat naive and uncritical) adulator of Pericles, and the excursus was motivated by and meant to climax with the celebratory mention of the birth of Pericles himself at its end.[63] Hermann Strasburger long ago challenged such a reading of the Alcmeonid excursus and the larger model of Herodotean sympathy that informed it, pointing out the multiple ironies of Herodotus's narrative in these chapters. As Strasburger noted, neither Alcmeon nor Megacles is very flatteringly portrayed—the former is too greedy and subservient to a barbarian king, the latter an also-ran and nonentity.[64] At the same time, the intimate and advantageous interactions of father and son with the Lydian dynast Croesus and the Sicyonian tyrant Cleisthenes, respectively, undermine or give the lie to what was presumably the family's claim to be *misotyrannoi*, repeated by Herodotus at 6.121 and 123. Strasburger also pointed out that the dream-omen of the lion that presages the birth of Pericles is ambiguous at best, since both within the *Histories* and in other Greek texts, the lion can symbolize sovereignty but also savage, uncontrollable violence and destruction.[65]

Following Strasburger, Rosalind Thomas in her study of the nature and norms of oral tradition offered a thorough methodological critique of the older scholarly notion of Alcmeonid family tradition as the source for all the material in Herodotus's excursus. As she noted, some of the assertions of chapters 121 and 123—including the claim to be *misotyrannoi* and to have been in exile for the entire span of the Pisistratid tyranny—probably did derive from the Alcmeonids, since they conform to the family's entirely positive and democratic self-representation as it is relayed in Isocrates 16, a forensic speech on behalf of the

---

the table: Herodotus seems to be dancing away the truth, and saying οὐ φροντὶς Ἡροδότῳ" (trans. Bowen 1992).

[63] Thus Jacoby 1913.coll. 237–41 (= 1956.23–25), 1949.222–23; see also How and Wells 1928. II.115–20, Myres 1953.12.

[64] Strasburger 1965.595–99; cf. Hart 1982.12–16; Thomas 1989.146–47, 265–72; Moles 2002.40–42; Dewald 2006.150–52.

[65] Thus Strasburger 1965.578, 596–97; for further elaboration of Strasburger's point, see Fornara 1971b.53–54, Stambler 1982.228, Thomas 1989.270–72, McNellen 1997, Moles 2002.41–42, Fowler 2003.314.

younger Alcibiades.⁶⁶ But, Thomas argued, the unflattering portraits of Alcmeon in Croesus's treasury and Megacles' winning of Agariste essentially by default could hardly be imagined to be Alcmeonid family tradition, and were likely instead to be popular stories told *against* the family or for some other purpose entirely.⁶⁷ At this point, in the wake of these critiques and others, the pendulum of scholarly opinion has swung far in the other direction—the majority of scholars now assume that Herodotus was critical of imperial Athens of the post–Persian Wars period, as also of Pericles as her de facto "monarch" and main architect of Athenian empire.⁶⁸

In this context of long-term heated scholarly debate, the recognition of Herodotus's witty and apparently knowing adaptation of fable as history may enable us to advance the discussion. First, we can support Rosalind Thomas's suggestion that there are multiple oral traditions in complex interaction behind Herodotus's Alcmeonid excursus, and perhaps push it even further. For in formal terms, the opposition of positive family traditions versus anti-Alcmeonid popular traditions corresponds within Herodotus's text to high genres versus low. Thomas assumes the free circulation and competition of what seem to be largely amorphous oral tales, although she acknowledges that poetic forms like epinician, scolion, and funerary epigram can occasionally impinge on and interact with this great mass of diverse oral traditions. But even oral tales must have some kind of formal patterning, which tale-tellers use to construct them and make them culturally legible. Herodotus's presentation of material in the Alcmeonid digression and everything we know about the social embeddedness of literary forms in Greek culture suggest that the complex interaction and dialogue of family tradition and popular lore is staged and coded through the competition of high genres like epic, epinician, and tragedy with the low forms of comedy, iambic, and beast fable. And this generic opposition can itself apply at two levels—first, in the heated contest of discourses within the public sphere of the city, then additionally or independently in Herodotus's text. For families like the Alcmeonids and individuals like the tyrant Cleisthenes attempted to control, shape, and propagate their cultural memory through the appropriation of epic forms and the commissioning of high, poetic encomia by professional poets of Panhellenic stature like Simonides, Pindar, and Bacchylides, while popular traditions would tend to embrace the low forms of comedy, iambic, and fable to resist and parody the pretensions of the great.

Thus, for example, we have preserved a Pindaric epinician that celebrates the four-horse chariot victory of Megacles, son of Hippocrates, at the Pythian Games in 486 BCE and uses the occasion to recall all the other family victories

---

⁶⁶ Thomas 1989.144–54, 262–63.
⁶⁷ Thomas 1989.146–47, 265–70.
⁶⁸ Thus (e.g.) Fornara 1971b; Stambler 1982; Raaflaub 1987; Nagy 1990b.303–13; Stadter 1992; Moles 1996, 2002; Pelling 1997; Fowler 2003.

and the magnificent new temple of Apollo at Delphi, constructed with Alcmeonid wealth.[69] But even more significant perhaps in relation to the specifics of the Alcmeonid excursus is the report of the twelfth-century Byzantine scholar John Tzetzes that Pindar narrated the story of Alcmeon in Croesus's treasure-house "in some poem" (*Chil.* 1.8, 18). Since Tzetzes' knowledge of and references to the Pindaric corpus seem to be generally reliable, we need to take this report seriously.[70] But if Pindar did tell this story, it must have looked very different from Herodotus's version. Thus, for example, it is unlikely that Pindar would have applied to Alcmeon the demeaning term συμπρήκτωρ, which occurs elsewhere to designate a slave "helper" or "assistant," or that he would have mentioned Alcmeon's "mouth stopped up" with gold dust and his whole body distended so that he looked "like anything more than a person."[71] These are specific Herodotean dictional choices that significantly alter the tone and message of this tale. Likewise with the next story. We might imagine Cleisthenes and/or Megacles and their descendants attempting to aggrandize themselves by casting the narrative of this dynastic marriage alliance in terms that imitate epic wooing scenes and other forms of high poetic narrative. But against this attempt (if it was made), popular tradition—or Herodotus himself—responds by recasting the tale as fable, thereby valorizing and commemorating instead the irreverent Hippoclides.[72]

This skillfully deployed contest of high and low genres suggests one way in which we might see Herodotean narrative as Aesopic. For Herodotus's narrative

---

[69] Pythian 7, securely dated to 486 by the scholia. For a reading of the poem as enacting a delicate negotiation between the Alcmeonids and the Athenian demos, see Kurke 1991.191–92, Neer 2004.

[70] Based on a Thesaurus Linguae Graecae (TLG) search, I count 43 separate references to Pindaric compositions in the corpus of Tzetzes; of these, 37 refer to 11 extant poems and 2–3 previously known fragments. This leaves only 6 Tzetzes references unidentified (including 2 to "some poem" in which Pindar narrated the story of Alcmeon in Croesus's treasury)—a respectable record for Tzetzes overall. The existence of a Pindaric poem on this subject was noted by Stein 1894. III.217, who then also went on to speculate that the story of the wooing of Agariste may have formed the subject matter of another Pindaric composition. I would like to record here my debt to the late Toni Raubitschek, who first called my attention to Tzetzes' report and told me that he had read through all of Tzetzes and found his Pindaric references generally sound.

[71] For discussion of these negative or parodic elements and others in the tale, see Kurke 1999.142–46, 2003.90–92.

[72] For this anecdote's multiple sources correlated to different generic elements, cf. Thomas 1989.269. In fact, Herodotus's catalog of suitors at 6.127 more than anything suggests parody of the kind of high, encomiastic account filled with aristocratic praise and superlatives one would find in Pindar. Thus notice that only two suitors in the bunch earn superlatives in their own right: Smindyrides of Sybaris (as we have seen) represents the ne plus ultra of luxury, while Hippoclides is said to "surpass the Athenians in wealth and appearance." Of the other eleven suitors, six have no distinguishing characteristics beyond their patronymics and ethnics, while the remaining five are identified merely as sons or brothers of other distinguished or superlative figures. That is to say, these five are also-rans (including, of course, Megacles himself, whom Herodotus characterizes only as "son of this Alcmeon who came to the court of Croesus").

technique in the Alcmeonid digression (and elsewhere) works through a kind of Aesopic bricolage (as I have described it in chapter 4, section IV above). Just as Aesop in the *Life* makes skillful and strategic use of common objects that are readily available in his environment to survive and succeed, Herodotus deploys older *logoi* and oral traditions as "found objects"; but by his canny juxtapositions and creative reuse, he forges new meanings from them.

The second contribution this reading can make to the scholarly debate on the Alcmeonid digression also suggests a second way in which Herodotean narrative might be conceived as Aesopic. And for this, we should pause to appreciate the very intensity of scholarly debate—the fact that different readers can come to diametrically opposed conclusions about Herodotus's position and intent with respect to the Alcmeonids, Pericles, and Athens. For this fact is itself a measure of Herodotus's success in a mode of communication that is distinctively Aesopic: an indirect, coded message to those in power (Pericles, Athens), told in such a way that the surface meaning flatters, but that invites—even demands—further thought and interpretation.[73] And while in this case, as I have suggested, the point of this Aesopic message seems to be mainly critical or parodic, we should not miss Herodotus's broader didactic or bouleutic deployment of this characteristically Aesopic communicative strategy. This will be my topic in the final section of this chapter.

IV. The Aesopic Contract of the *Histories*: Herodotus Teaches His Readers

Having surveyed the passages I've discussed, the reader may be inclined to think that in the end, there is not much Aesop in Herodotus. Why make such a fuss, after all? By way of conclusion I would like to suggest that, as for Plato, there is a sense in which Herodotean narrative is profoundly and pervasively Aesopic, even while it explicitly disavows Aesop or holds him at arm's length. And here again, the link with Aesop and the Aesopic will hopefully help explain Herodotus's choice of prose as his medium.

I would like to locate the influence of the low fabulist and the popular traditions that surrounded him in the quality of indirection that so many readers have identified as central to the Herodotean project. For it is a truism of modern scholarship that Herodotus's narrative art works by indirection and obliquity, challenging its hearers or readers actively to interpret the text for them-

---

[73] Notice that this is precisely how Plutarch reads the Alcmeonid digression in his treatise *On the Malice of Herodotus* (ch. 27/862c–863b). Thus he accuses Herodotus of "pretending to defend" the family, and notices the inconsistency between the claim that the Alcmeonidae were always "tyrant-haters" and the unflattering story of Megacles' brief marriage alliance with Pisistratus at Hdt. 1.60–61. Plutarch's conclusion (as cited in the previous chapter): that this whole sequence in Book 6 is filled with "such great confusions or contradictions" (τοιαύτας ... ταραχάς).

selves.[74] And many scholars have connected this striking feature of Herodotean narrative with Herodotus's contemporary political situation and message. Assuming (as most scholars now do) that Herodotus was actively composing and performing his *Histories* down into the 420s at least, many have argued that his indirect and coded narrative offers a warning to Athens, conceived as *polis tyrannos* in the political catchphrase of the period.[75] Charles Fornara, who, together with Hermann Strasburger, probably contributed the most to the current predominant view of Herodotus's text as deeply enmeshed in the politics of its own time and critical of Athenian empire, identified this indirect narrative style that demanded a high level of audience engagement with that of tragedy. This identification certainly suited Fornara's ultimately tragic and pessimistic reading of the *Histories*, but I would contend that such a literary model misses crucial elements in Herodotean narrative, even as it assimilates Herodotus too much to a profound Thucydidean pessimism.[76] This is not to deny that high poetic genres like tragedy and epic feature in Herodotus's panoply of embedded genres and styles, but simply to suggest that we should not limit the Herodotean narrator to only these resources (especially since these comparanda elide the essential diacritic of prose). Herodotean narrative, as we have seen, accommodates a much wider range of tone and genre than tragedy tolerates,[77] while tragedy specifically does not account for the elements of tact, even flattery, in Herodotus's text. And this latter feature in turn implies a salient sociological fact that structures the Herodotean narrative exchange: there is a significant power differential between narrator and audience, especially if we conceive

---

[74] Just a sampling of scholars who embrace this model of Hdtean narrative: Strasburger 1965; Fornara 1971b.73–74; Stambler 1982.228–31; Raaflaub 1987; Boedeker 1988; Griffin 1990; Nagy 1990b.215–338; Stadter 1992; Dewald 1993, 2006; Moles 1996, 2002; Pelling 1997, 2006; Thomas 2000.3, 247, 285; Fowler 2003; Irwin 2009.

[75] On the dating of Hdt, see esp. Fornara 1971a, 1981. I do not find Fornara's arguments for a date close to 414 for the final "publication" of the *Histories* compelling; like most scholars, I imagine that Herodotus lived and wrote into the 420s, the period of the Archidamian War. On *polis tyrannos* as a political catchphrase of the 450s to 420s, see Knox 1979.87–95; Raaflaub 1979, 1987; Tuplin 1985. On Hdt's indirection connected with a warning or message to imperial Athens, see Fornara 1971b; Stambler 1982.228–31; Nagy 1990b.303–13; Stadter 1992; Moles 1996, 2002; Irwin 2009.

[76] Thus Fornara 1971b, esp. 61–74. Note that, to some extent, Fornara conflates tragic techniques with tragic content or a tragic worldview. Fornara's pessimistic reading of Hdt is enabled and supported by (1) his late dating of Hdt (things look much more "tragic" and irrevocable for Athens in 414 than in the 420s); (2) his developmental model of Hdtean composition, which allows him to dismiss or ignore much of the *Histories*, focusing only on Books 1 and 7–9 as representing the mature Hdtean vision; (3) his importation of certain key concepts from Thucydides to constitute the elements of Hdt's "tragic vision." Thus, for example: "States, like men, were caught in the same net. War was inevitable, if not for one reason then for another. *With human nature as it is*, acts of injustice were inescapable" (Fornara 1971b.77, my italics). Notice how Thucydidean this whole passage sounds, especially the italicized portion; cf. Thuc. 1.22.4, 3.82.2. For other scholars who reject Fornara's tragic Hdt, see Stambler 1982.231; Gould 1989.116–20; Moles 1996, 2002.51–52.

[77] Thus better Moles 1996.264: "the serio-comic is also an essential aspect of the written *Histories*."

Herodotus's audience on the model of imperial Athens as *polis tyrannos*. This power differential again is not adequately paralleled or accounted for by the model of tragedy.

In all these respects, I concur with John Moles's somewhat different account of Herodotus's literary art (offered in the context of a discussion of the Solon-Croesus encounter in Book 1):

> At this point we may pause to register the tact and skill with which Herodotus has conveyed his warning to the Athenians. He emphasises that Solon did not flatter Croesus at all (1.30.3), but at the same time Solon addresses Croesus courteously and answers his question at first obliquely. Similarly, Herodotus' warning to the Athenians is fundamentally parrhesiastic, but obliquely conveyed through the filter of a historical analogy and softened by compliments: he argues against the Athenians through the mouth of a great and revered Athenian, and he uses a heroic Athenian as one of the examples of blessedness. This interpretation is not undermined by Herodotus' extravagant praise of the energising effect which the acquisition of democracy had upon Athens (5.78), or by his insistence, unpopular as it is, that the Athenians saved Greece from Xerxes (7.139.1–5). One can well hold—one should hold—that internal democracy is an excellent thing and incompatible with the suppression of other people's liberty. And frankness towards everybody, Athenians and non-Athenians alike, lends moral authority to specific criticisms. Greek rhetoricians evolved elaborate theories of "figured speech" as a device for conveying advice or criticism to powerful persons or peoples. These included the use of historical analogy and tactful and ingratiating compliment, and they were (arguably) put into practice by skilful poets and orators; but they had nothing to teach Herodotus. Herodotus' use of "figured speech" in this episode already suggests one reason for his resort to "signals" rather than explicit statement: the requirements of tact.[78]

Moles's invocation of "figured speech" seems just right as a characterization of Herodotean narrative, but it is noteworthy that both the theory and the practice of this mode of communication are phenomena of much later antiquity.[79] But, as I have tried to demonstrate throughout, a model closer to Herodotus's own time that perfectly suits Moles's characterization is that of Aesop and his distinctive discursive practices.

This is the Aesop that hides behind Hdt. 1.27, and it is to this episode that I now (finally) return. I have argued that this scene of the effective persuading of Croesus to make terms with the Ionian islanders was attached to Aesop in the oral traditions Herodotus inherited, but that the Halicarnassian has displaced

---

[78] Moles 1996.269–70; cf. Moles 2002.52: "The obliquity with which [Herodotus's] warnings [to the Athenians] are conveyed also signifies: both to provoke thought and to illustrate the relatively safest and best way of warning tyrants."

[79] Thus in his note to this passage, Moles cites scholarship on Roman imperial literature and the *Orations* of Dio Chrysostom (Moles 1996.282–83n. 43).

the low fabulist in favor of one of the canonical Seven Sages as purveyor of this advice. By now, we can see that this displacement is overdetermined: it is dictated first by the decorum of *historiē*/history, which cannot blatantly give the crude fabulist a voice in the text. But there are also, I suggested, multiple reasons for Herodotus to make Croesus's interlocutor into a *Greek* sage. Since this little story serves as foil and preamble for Solon's encounter with Croesus, Herodotus does not want to show the non-Greek and lowly Aesop succeeding where Solon fails, thereby complicating the opposition of Greek polis wisdom and Eastern magnificence so fully mapped out in the succeeding encounter. This is a local reason to replace the Thracian (or Phrygian) ex-slave Aesop with a Greek sage, but I have also suggested that we can detect a pattern that runs through several episodes of the *Histories*, whereby Greek advisers oppose the Homeric magnificence of Eastern potentates with the humble discourse of fable, thus resignifying the hierarchy of genre to represent the clash of East and West that is Herodotus's great theme.

And yet at the same time, Herodotus signals to us (if we care to notice) the Aesopic origins of this tale, for he has included a whole set of verbal traces to mark 1.27 as a scene of Aesopic advising—even to frame the scene itself *as a fable*. Why should Herodotus do this after so carefully excising Aesop? We are now finally in a position to tackle this paradox. I would suggest that Herodotus offers us this early episode of Aesopic advising cast in the form of a fable to teach us how to read his complex text. At the local level, this fable of the encounter of Greek sage and Lydian king sets us up for the multiple coded resonances of the meeting of Solon and Croesus, which follows immediately. Several scholars have seen this more famous sequence as a veiled or indirect warning to the *polis tyrannos* Athens, through the "tyrant" Croesus, to avoid arrogance and overreaching and to "look to the end."[80] The recognition of 1.27 as a fable supports and strengthens this reading: Herodotus signals thereby that the more extended encounter of sage and king is also to be understood as a (didactic or bouleutic) fable, offering coded and indirect advice to the powerful. And of course the same applies to the whole of the *Histories*. This small fable strategically placed early in Book 1 encourages us to understand Herodotus's entire text as bouleutic fable writ large—the ultimate Aesopic *makrologia!*—proffering tales of the past indirectly to advise audiences in his present.[81]

But if we look again at the particular content of 1.27, it will also allow us to nuance somewhat this fabular or allegorizing reading of the *Histories*. Recall that the message the sage conveys to Croesus through fictive analogy in this

---

[80] Thus (e.g.) Nagy 1990b.303–13; Moles 1996.261–70, 2002.35–36.

[81] To this extent, I agree with Fornara 1971b.60: "Thucydides wrote for the future, Herodotus for his contemporaries." And notice how this formulation chimes with Richard Martin's observation about the Seven Sages' "performances of wisdom"—"you have to be there" (Martin 1998.118)—for this quotidian, situational character also applies to Aesopic discursive practices.

chapter is essentially that a land power should not attempt to take on a naval power, buttressing that argument with an almost fablelike commitment to the immutability of those different natures. In the midst of the Archidamian War, this can only be a message for the Spartans, who at least in this instance are figured by the Lydian potentate in the tale. This axis of identification argues against those scholars who read Croesus only as a figure or stand-in for Athens as *polis tyrannos*. One thing the juxtaposition of 1.27 and 1.29–33 should teach us is that such simple one-to-one correspondences are too reductive as a way of reading Herodotus's "figured speech." Instead, as other scholars have argued, we must assume that Herodotus had multiple different (real and intended) audiences throughout the Greek world, and we should recognize that his complex coded narratives work to convey different messages to different audiences simultaneously.[82] Specifically, there are indications throughout the *Histories* that Herodotus is critical of Sparta as well as of Athens, so that we might take Sparta, too, as a great power in need of fabular advising.[83]

But the fabular framing of 1.27 and the *Histories* as a whole has still other implications for the status and situation of the narrator. Several scholars have seen a close affiliation or identification of Solon in his encounter with Croesus and Herodotus, himself also a traveling *sophos* or *sophistēs*.[84] But if 1.27 is framed as a fable, Herodotus the narrator implicitly identifies himself thereby as the fabulist Aesop, spinning tales sweetly and persuasively to the powerful. This identification with the debased *logopoios* Aesop is a risky proposition, for several reasons. If we can trust the later biographical traditions, Herodotus began his life on the mainland of Asia Minor—just like Aesop; crossed to Samos and spent time there—just like Aesop; and then spent much of his life traveling around the Greek world performing his *sophia*—just like Aesop. And of course, as I noted at the end of the previous chapter, since Herodotus derived from a mixed Greek-Carian family from Halicarnassus, it was always available to Greeks from less comfortably ethnically mixed environments to question his Hellenicity, or recast him as a barbarian—just like Aesop.[85] If we are inclined to put stock in biographical explanations (and I'm not sure I am), the parallels between the historical Herodotus and the legendary life of Aesop are perhaps un-

---

[82] Thus (e.g.) Stadter 1992, esp. 783–84, 809; also Thomas 2000.10–12, critiquing the Athenocentrism of many modern readers of Herodotus. For a different model of multiple audiences (internal and external), cf. Ceccarelli 1993 on Hdt. 1.141 (summarized above, section I).

[83] For Hdt (in varying degrees) critical of Sparta as well as Athens, see Strasburger 1965.606–7, Stadter 1992.809, Johnson 2001, Moles 2002.51n. 89 (contra Fornara 1971b.49–50).

[84] On Hdt's identification with Solon, see Nagy 1990b.244–49, 332–33; Moles 1996, 2002; Pelling 2006.105–6. On Hdt as *sophos* or *sophistēs*, see Fowler 1996.86; Thomas 2000.8, 162–63, 283–85.

[85] In this respect, it is perhaps significant that the Suda reports that it was on Samos that Herodotus "practiced his Ionic dialect and wrote his history in nine books" (ἐν οὖν τῇ Σάμῳ καὶ τὴν Ἰάδα ἠσκήθη διάλεκτον καὶ ἔγραψεν ἱστορίαν ἐν βιβλίοις θ´, Suda s.v. Ἡρόδοτος, II.588 Adler). This is an odd assertion, given that the language of public documents set up in Halicarnassus was Ionic—as if Herodotus (like Aesop) had to learn Greek before he could compose the *Histories*!

comfortably close—and this may be another reason Herodotus felt it necessary to transform Aesop into a Greek sage in the significant encounter of 1.27.[86]

But even leaving aside the biographical issues, consider the implications for Herodotus's genre and reception. As Rosalind Thomas has noted, by characterizing his work as *historiē* in his first sentence, Herodotus boldly identifies his project with current "scientific" methods and practices, even while that first sentence combines the scientific project with a Homeric commitment to preserving the *kleos* of "great and wondrous deeds."[87] But Herodotus's narrative portions draw not only on Homeric poetry but also on Aesopic prose, with the Herodotean narrator imitating Aesop as canny political adviser and fabulist (as 1.27 signals to us). Thus Herodotus's "new genre" artfully and deliberately encompasses both *historiē* and *logopoiïa*, as his text combines and integrates scientific "researches" with the narration of fable as history and history as fable. And yet, by opening the *Histories* up to Aesopic *logopoiïa*, Herodotus risks implicating himself and his text in the dubious truth value and status taint that I have suggested may already have attached to that category of storytelling. We have already seen in our consideration of Plutarch's treatise *On the Malice of Herodotus* how a hostile ancient reader could exploit these strange qualities of Herodotean narrative to discredit both Herodotus and his text; even a more sympathetic reader like Cicero seems to register this bizarre generic motley in the words that form the epigraph to this chapter. Although by Cicero's time, the opposed terms have become "history" versus "poetry," neatly aligned in the opening dialogue of *De Legibus* with "truth" (*veritatem*) versus "pleasure" (*delectationem*), we might see behind this the older opposition of *historiē* versus *logopoiïa*, "science" versus tall tales. What Cicero acknowledges is that Herodotus's strange text is compounded of both.[88] But why should Herodotus take these risks and cast himself in this somehow discreditable position? Presumably because he feels his message is an urgent one and this the most effective means of persuading the powerful. Under the circumstances, it is not at all surprising, as Donald Lateiner observes, that Herodotus had no followers in the boldly experimental, hybrid prose genre he created.[89]

---

[86] Alternatively, a hard-core skeptic might suggest that the traditions about Herodotus's life were consciously or unconsciously shaped by the Aesopic qualities of his writing—so that for this reason, he was said to have spent time on Samos (e.g.). I suspect, however, that most modern Herodotean scholars would be reluctant to espouse such a position of radical skepticism.

[87] Thomas 2000, esp. 267–69. For the combination of new and old in Herodotus's first sentence, cf. Bakker 2002.

[88] Indeed, one might be tempted to suggest that Thucydides' sneer at 1.21–22, that his text will not include τὸ μυθῶδες, which characterizes the competitive oral performances of unnamed λογογράφοι, might be intended to include the element of Aesopic storytelling in Hdt. Note especially that Thucydides' contrast is framed in terms of a relative lack of "pleasure" in his text, accompanied by a clear and accurate representation of past events (Thuc. 1.22.4). I have not pursued this argument, however, because I am persuaded by Flory 1990, that by τὸ μυθῶδες, Thucydides means mainly crowd-pleasing patriotic eulogies of Athens and her past triumphs.

[89] Thus Lateiner 1989.13–17, 211–27.

BIBLIOGRAPHY

Acosta-Hughes, Benjamin. 2002. *Polyeideia: The Iambi of Callimachus and the Archaic Iambic Tradition.* Berkeley and Los Angeles.

Adam, J., and A. M. Adam, eds. 1905. *Platonis Protagoras.* Cambridge.

Adkins, A.W.H. 1973. "ἀρετή, τέχνη, Democracy and Sophists: *Protagoras* 316b–328d." *JHS* 93: 3–12.

Adrados, F. R. 1979. "The 'Life of Aesop' and the Origins of Novel in Antiquity." *QUCC* n.s. 1: 93–112.

———. 1999. *History of the Graeco-Latin Fable.* Vol. 1, *Introduction and From the Origins to the Hellenistic Age.* Trans. Leslie A. Ray. Mnemosyne Supplement 201. Leiden.

———. 2000. *History of the Graeco-Latin Fable.* Vol. 2, *The Fable during the Roman Empire and in the Middle Ages.* Trans. Leslie A. Ray. Mnemosyne Supplement 207. Leiden.

———. 2003. *History of the Graeco-Latin Fable.* Vol. 3, *Inventory and Documentation of the Graeco-Latin Fable.* Trans. L. A. Ray and F. Rojas del Canto. Mnemosyne Supplement 236. Leiden.

Albert, Karl. 1983. "*Theoria* und *Thaumazein.*" *Philosophischer Literaturanzeiger* 36: 382–90.

Allen, T. W., ed. 1974. *Homeri Opera.* Vol. 5, *Hymnos Cyclum Fragmenta Margiten Batrachomyomachiam Vitas Continens.* Oxford.

Allen, T. W., W. R. Halliday, and E. E. Sikes, eds. 1936. *The Homeric Hymns.* Oxford.

Alpers, Johannes. 1912. "*Hercules in Bivio.*" Inaug. diss., Göttingen.

Alter, Robert. 1981. *The Art of Biblical Narrative.* New York.

Althusser, Louis. 2001. "Ideology and Ideological State Apparatuses: Notes toward an Investigation." In *Lenin and Philosophy and Other Essays*, trans. B. Brewster, new introduction by F. Jameson. New York. 85–126.

Aly, Wolf. 1921. *Volksmärchen, Sage, und Novelle bei Herodot und seinen Zeitgenossen: Eine Untersuchung über die volkstümlichen Elemente der altgriechischen Prosaerzählung.* Göttingen. [Repr. 1969 with corrections and afterword by L. Huber.]

———. 1929. *Formprobleme der frühen griechischen Prosa.* Philologus, Supplementband XXI, Heft III. Leipzig.

Amandry, P. 1939. "Convention religieuse conclue entre Delphes et Skiathos." *BCH* 63: 183–219.

———. 1944–45. "Note sur la convention Delphes-Skiathos." *BCH* 68–69: 411–16.

———. 1950. *La Mantique apollinienne à Delphes: Essai sur le fonctionnement de l'oracle.* Paris.

Anhalt, Emily Katz. 1993. *Solon the Singer: Politics and Poetics.* Lanham, Md.

Annas, Julia. 1982. "Plato on the Triviality of Literature," in Moravcsik and Temko 1982: 1–28.

Arnott, W. Geoffrey. 1996. *Alexis: The Fragments. A Commentary.* Cambridge.

Arthur, Marylin. 1982. "Cultural Strategies in Hesiod's *Theogony*: Law, Family, Society." *Arethusa* 15: 63–82.

Asheri, David, Alan Lloyd, and Aldo Corcella. 2007. *A Commentary on Herodotus, Books I–IV*. Ed. O. Murray and A. Moreno. Oxford.

Asmis, Elizabeth. 1992. "Plato on Poetic Creativity." In Kraut 1992: 338–64.

Auerbach, Erich. 1953. *Mimesis: The Representation of Reality in Western Literature*. Trans. W. R. Trask. Princeton, N.J.

Austin, M. M., and P. Vidal-Naquet. 1977. *Economic and Social History of Ancient Greece: An Introduction*. Berkeley and Los Angeles.

Avlamis, Pavlos. 2006. "The *Life of Aesop* and Its 'Popular' Element." Unpublished seminar paper.

———. 2010a. "Aesopic Lives: Greek Imperial Literature and Urban Popular Culture." PhD diss., Princeton University.

———. 2010b. "Isis and the People in the *Life of Aesop*." In *Revelation, Literature, and Community in Antiquity*, ed. P. Townsend and M. Vidas. Tübingen.

Babbit, Frank Cole, trans. 1956. *Plutarch, Moralia*. Vol. 2. Cambridge, Mass.

Bacon, Helen. 1959. "Socrates Crowned." *Virginia Quarterly Review* 35.3: 415–30.

Bakhtin, M. 1981. *The Dialogic Imagination*. Trans. Caryl Emerson and Michael Holquist. Austin, Tex.

———. 1984a. *Problems of Dostoyevsky's Poetics*. Ed. and trans. C. Emerson. Minneapolis and London.

———. 1984b. *Rabelais and His World*. Trans. H. Iswolsky. Bloomington, Ind.

Bakker, Egbert J. 2002. "The Making of History: Herodotus' *Historiês Apodexis*." In Bakker, de Jong, and van Wees 2002: 3–32.

Bakker, Egbert J., Irene J. F. de Jong, and Hans van Wees, eds. 2002. *Brill's Companion to Herodotus*. Leiden.

Beazley, J. D. 1939. "Excavations at Al Mina, Sueidia, III. The Red-Figured Vases." *JHS* 59: 1–44.

Becker, O. 1937. *Das Bild des Weges und verwandte Vorstellungen im frühgriechischen Denken*. Hermes Einzelschriften, Heft 4. Berlin.

Belfiore, Elizabeth. 1984a. "A Theory of Imitation in Plato's *Republic*." *TAPA* 114: 121–46.

———. 1984b. "Dialectic with the Reader in Plato's *Symposium*." *Maia* 36: 137–49.

Bell, Catherine. 1992. *Ritual Theory, Ritual Practice*. Oxford.

Belsey, Catherine. 1980. *Critical Practice*. London and New York.

Berger, Harry Jr. 1984. "Facing Sophists: Charismatic Bondage in *Protagoras*." *Representations* 5: 66–91.

Berthiaume, G. 1982. *Les rôles du mágeiros: Étude sur la boucherie la cuisine et le sacrifice dans la Grèce ancienne*. Leiden.

Beschorner, Andreas, and Niklas Holzberg. 1992. "A Bibliography of the Aesop Romance." In Holzberg 1992: 165–87.

Bieler, Ludwig. 1967. *Theios Anēr: Das Bild des "göttlichen Menschen" in Spätantike und Frühchristentum*. Darmstadt.

Bielohlawek, K. 1930. "Komische Motive in der homerischen Gestaltung des griechischen Göttermythus." *Archiv für Religonswissenschaft* 28: 106–24, 185–211.

Birch, C. M. 1955. "Traditions of the *Life of Aesop*." PhD diss., Washington University, St. Louis.

Bischoff, Heinrich. 1965. "Der Warner bei Herodot." In *Herodot: Eine Auswahl aus der neueren Forschung*, ed. W. Marg. Wege der Forschung Band 26. Darmstadt. 302–19.

Bloch, Maurice. 1992. *Prey into Hunter: The Politics of Religious Experience.* Cambridge.
Blondell, Ruby. 2002. *The Play of Character in Plato's Dialogues.* Cambridge.
Bluck. R. S., ed. 1964. *Plato's Meno.* Cambridge.
Blundell, Mary W. 1992. "Character and Meaning in Plato's *Hippias Minor*." In Klagge and Smith 1992: 131–72.
Boedeker, Deborah. 1988. "Protesilaos and the End of Herodotus' *Histories*." *CA* 7: 30–48.
———. 2000. "Herodotus's Genre(s)." In *Matrices of Genre: Authors, Canons, and Society*, ed. Mary Depew and Dirk Obbink. Cambridge, Mass. 97–114.
———. 2002. "Epic Heritage and Mythical Patterns in Herodotus." In Bakker, de Jong, and van Wees 2002: 97–116.
Boedeker, Deborah, and David Sider, eds. 2001. *The New Simonides: Contexts of Praise and Desire.* Oxford.
Bollack, Jean. 1968. "Une histoire de ΣΟΦΙΗ" (Review of B. Gladigow, *Sophia und Kosmos*). *REG* 81: 550–54.
Bonnell, Victoria E., and Lynn Hunt, eds. 1999. *Beyond the Cultural Turn: New Directions in the Study of Society and Culture.* Berkeley and Los Angeles.
Bourdieu, Pierre. 1977. *Outline of a Theory of Practice.* Trans. R. Nice. Cambridge.
———. 1990. *The Logic of Practice.* Trans. R. Nice. Stanford, Calif.
Bowen, A. J., ed. 1992. *Plutarch: The Malice of Herodotus.* Warminster, England.
Bowersock, G. W. 1965. *Augustus and the Greek World.* Oxford.
———. 1989. "Herodotus, Alexander, and Rome." *The American Scholar* 58: 407–14.
Bowie, E. L. 1974. "Greeks and Their Past in the Second Sophistic." In *Studies in Ancient Society*, ed. M. I. Finley. London. 166–209.
———. 1986. "Early Greek Elegy, Symposium and Public Festival." *JHS* 106: 13–35.
———. 1994. "The Readership of Greek Novels in the Ancient World." In Tatum 1994: 435–59.
———. 2001. "Ancestors of Historiography in Early Greek Elegiac and Iambic Poetry?" In Luraghi 2001: 45–66.
Bowra, C. M. 1961. *Greek Lyric Poetry.* 2nd ed. Oxford.
Bracht Branham, R., and Marie-Odile Goulet-Cazé, eds. 1996. *The Cynics: The Cynic Movement in Antiquity and Its Legacy.* Berkeley and Los Angeles.
Braginskaia, N. B. 2005. "'Muzami klianus'!' Kliatvy v literature i avtorskii zamysel 'Zhizneopisaniia Ezopa' (G)." In *V poiskakh "zapadnogo" na Balkanakh*, ed. I. A. Sedakova and T. V. Tsivian. Moscow. 17–29.
Bremmer, Jan. 1983. "Scapegoat Rituals in Ancient Greece." *HSCP* 87: 299–320.
Brickhouse, Thomas C., and Nicholas D. Smith. 2000. *The Philosophy of Socrates.* Boulder, Colo.
Brisson, Luc. 1975. "Le mythe de Protagoras: Essai d'analyse structurale." *QUCC* 20: 7–37.
Broadie, Sarah. 1991. *Ethics with Aristotle.* New York, Oxford.
Broadie, Sarah, and Christopher Rowe. 2002. *Aristotle: Nicomachean Ethics.* Oxford.
Brock, Roger. 1990. "Plato and Comedy." In *'Owls to Athens': Essays on Classical Subjects Presented to Sir Kenneth Dover*, ed. E. M. Craik. Oxford. 39–49.
Brown, Norman O. 1947. *Hermes the Thief: The Evolution of a Myth.* Madison, Wisc.
Bruit, L. 1984. "Sacrifices à Delphes: Sur deux figures d'Apollon." *Revue de l'histoire des religions* 201.4: 339–67.

Burke, Peter. 1978. *Popular Culture in Early Modern Europe*. New York.
Burkert, Walter. 1966. Review of Delcourt, *Pyrrhos et Pyrrha*. *Gnomon* 38: 436–40.
———. 1972. *Lore and Science in Ancient Pythagoreanism*. Trans. E. L. Minar, Jr. Cambridge, Mass.
———. 1983. *Homo Necans: The Anthropology of Ancient Greek Sacrificial Ritual and Myth*. Trans. P. Bing. Berkeley and Los Angeles.
———. 1984. "Sacrificio-Sacrilegio: Il 'Trickster' Fondatore." *Studi Storici* 25: 835–45.
———. 1985. *Greek Religion*. Trans. J. Raffan. Cambridge, Mass.
Burnet, John, ed. 1911. *Plato's Phaedo*. Oxford.
———. 1924. *Plato's Euthyphro, Apology of Socrates, and Crito*. Oxford.
Burnett, Anne Pippin. 1983. *Three Archaic Poets: Archilochus, Alcaeus, Sappho*. Cambridge, Mass.
———. 2005. *Pindar's Songs for Young Athletes of Aigina*. Oxford.
Bury, R. G., ed. 1969. *The Symposium of Plato*. Cambridge.
Buxton, Richard. 1986. "Wolves and Werewolves in Greek Thought." In *Interpretations of Greek Mythology*, ed. J. Bremmer. Totowa, N.J. 60–79.
Bywater, I. 1877. "Aristotle's Dialogue 'On Philosophy.'" *Journal of Philology* 7: 64–87.
Calza, Guido. 1939. "Die Taverne der sieben Weisen in Ostia." *Antike* 15: 99–115.
Campbell, David A., ed. 1967. *Greek Lyric Poetry: A Selection of Early Greek Lyric, Elegiac and Iambic Poetry*. London.
Carnes, Jeffrey S. 1998. "The Myth Which Is Not One: Construction of Discourse in Plato's *Symposium*." In *Rethinking Sexuality: Foucault and Classical Antiquity*, ed. D.H.J. Larmour, P. A. Miller, and C. Platter. Princeton, N.J. 104–21.
Carson, Anne. 1988. "Simonides Negative." *Arethusa* 21: 147–57.
———. 1990. "Putting Her in Her Place: Woman, Dirt, and Desire." In *Before Sexuality: The Construction of Erotic Experience in the Ancient Greek World*, ed. D. M. Halperin, J. J. Winkler, and F. I. Zeitlin. Princeton, N.J. 135–69.
———. 1999. *Economy of the Unlost (Reading Simonides of Keos with Paul Celan)*. Princeton, N.J.
Cartledge, Paul. 1993. *The Greeks: A Portrait of Self and Others*. Oxford.
Cascardi, Anthony J., ed. 1987. *Literature and the Question of Philosophy*. Baltimore, Md.
Cataudella, Quintino. 1942. "Aristofane e il cosiddetto 'romanzo di Esopo.'" *Dionisio* 9.1: 5–14.
Catoni, Maria Luisa. 2005. *Schemata: Comunicazione non verbale nella Grecia antica*. Pisa.
Cavarero, Adriana. 1995. *In Spite of Plato*. Trans. S. Anderlini-D'Onofrio and A. O'Healy. New York.
Ceccarelli, Paola. 1993. "La fable des poissons de Cyrus (Hérodote, I, 141): Son origine et sa fonction dans l' économie des *Histoires* d'Hérodote." *Métis* 8: 29–57.
Chalmers, Robert, trans. 1895. *The Jātaka or Stories of the Buddha's Former Births*. Ed. E. B. Cowell. Vol. 1. London. [Repr. by the Pāli Text Society, 1990.]
Chambry, É. 1925–26. *Aesopi Fabulae*. 2 vols. Paris.
———. 1967. *Ésop. Fables*. 3rd ed. Paris.
Chantraine, Pierre. 1933. *La formation des noms en Grec ancien*. Collection Linguistique publiée par La Société de Linguistique de Paris. Vol. 38. Paris.
———. 1968–80. *Dictionnaire étymologique de la langue grecque*. 4 vols. Paris.
Cherniss, H. 1959. Review of H. D. Saffrey, *Le Περὶ φιλοσοφίας d'Aristote et la théorie platonicienne des idées et des nombres*. *Gnomon* 31: 36–51.

Chin, Tamara. 1999. "Aesop the Signifying Monkey." Unpublished seminar paper.
Clarke, John R. 2003. *Art in the Lives of Ordinary Romans: Visual Representation and Non-Elite Viewers in Italy, 100 B.C.-A.D. 315*. Berkeley, Los Angeles, and London.
———. 2007. *Looking at Laughter: Humor, Power, and Transgression in Roman Visual Culture, 100 B.C.-A.D. 250*. Berkeley, Los Angeles, and London.
Classen, Albrecht. 1995. *The German Volksbuch: A Critical History of a Late-Medieval Genre*. Lewiston, N.Y.
Classen, Carl Joachim, ed. 1976. *Sophistik*. Wege der Forschung Band 187. Darmstadt.
Clay, Diskin. 1972. "Socrates' Mulishness and Heroism." *Phronesis* 17: 53-60.
———. 1975. "The Tragic and Comic Muse of the *Symposium*." *Arion* n.s. 2: 238-61.
———. 1994. "The Origins of the Socratic Dialogue." In Vander Waerdt 1994: 23-47.
———. 2000. *Platonic Questions: Dialogues with the Silent Philosopher*. University Park, Penn.
———. 2004. *Archilochos Heros: The Cult of Poets in the Greek Polis*. Cambridge, Mass., and London.
Clay, J. S. 1989. *The Politics of Olympus: Form and Meaning in the Major Homeric Hymns*. Princeton, N.J.
Cole, Thomas. 1987. "1 + 1 = 3: Studies in Pindar's Arithmetic." *AJP* 108: 553-68.
———. 1990. *Democritus and the Sources of Greek Anthropology*. Atlanta, Ga.
———. 1991. *The Origins of Rhetoric in Ancient Greece*. Baltimore, Md.
Coles, R. A., and M. W. Haslam, eds. 1980. *The Oxyrhynchus Papyri*. Vol. 47. London.
Collins, Derek. 2004. *Master of the Game: Competition and Performance in Greek Poetry*. Cambridge, Mass., and London.
Compton, Todd. 1990. "The Trial of the Satirist: Poetic *Vitae* (Aesop, Archilochus, Homer) as Background for Plato's *Apology*." *AJP* 111: 330-47.
———. 2006. *Victim of the Muses: Poet as Scapegoat, Warrior, and Hero in Greco-Roman and Indo-European Myth and History*. Cambridge, Mass., and London.
Connor, W. Robert. 1982. "Thucydides." In *Ancient Writers: Greece and Rome*, ed. T. J. Luce. Vol. 2. New York. 267-89.
———. 1984. *Thucydides*. Princeton, N.J.
———. 1993. "The *Histor* in History." In *Nomodeiktes: Greek Studies in Honor of Martin Ostwald*, ed. R. M. Rosen and J. Farrell. Ann Arbor, Mich. 3-15.
Conybeare, F. C., J. Rendel Harris, and Agnes Smith Lewis. 1913a. "The Story of Aḥiḳar." In *The Apocrypha and Pseudepigrapha of the Old Testament in English*, ed. R. H. Charles. Vol. 2. Oxford. 715-84.
———. 1913b. *The Story of Aḥiḳar*. 2nd ed. Oxford.
Cook, R. M. 1954-55. "Solon, Fr. 8 (Diehl), ll. 5-6." *PCPS* 183: 3.
Cooper, John M., ed. 1997. *Plato: Complete Works*. Indianapolis, Ind.
Cope, E. M., and J. E. Sandys, eds. 1877. *The Rhetoric of Aristotle with a Commentary*. 3 vols. Cambridge.
Cornford, F. M., trans. 1964. *Sophist*. In *The Collected Dialogues of Plato*, ed. E. Hamilton and H. Cairns. New York. 957-1017.
Cowley, A. E. 1923. *Aramaic Papyri of the Fifth Century B.C.* Oxford.
Cropp, M. J., ed. 2000. *Euripides. Iphigeneia in Tauris*. Warminster, England.
Crusius, Otto. 1920. "Aus der Geschichte der Fabel." In *Das Buch der Fabeln*, ed. C. H. Kleukens. Leipzig. I-LXIII.
Culler, Jonathan. 1975. *Structuralist Poetics: Structuralism, Linguistics, and the Study of Literature*. Ithaca, N.Y.

Cunningham, Sir Alexander. 1962. *The Stûpa of Bharhut: A Buddhist Monument Ornamented with Numerous Sculptures.* Varanasi, India.
Currie, Bruno. 2005. *Pindar and the Cult of Heroes.* Oxford.
Daly, Lloyd W. 1961. *Aesop without Morals.* New York.
Daniel, Robert W. 1996. "Epicharmus in Trier: A Note on the Monnus-Mosaic." *ZPE* 114: 30–36.
Darnton, Robert. 1984. "Peasants Tell Tales: The Meaning of Mother Goose." In *The Great Cat Massacre and Other Episodes in French Cultural History.* New York. 9–72.
Dasen, Véronique. 1993. *Dwarfs in Ancient Egypt and Greece.* Oxford.
Davidson, James N. 1997. *Courtesans and Fishcakes: The Consuming Passions in Classical Athens.* New York.
Davies, M. 1981. "Aeschylus and the Fable." *Hermes* 109: 248–51.
———. 2003. "The Judgements of Paris and Solomon." *CQ* 53: 32–43.
de Certeau, Michel. 1984. *The Practice of Everyday Life.* Berkeley, Los Angeles, and London.
de Falco, Vittorio, ed. 1932. *Demade Oratore: Testimonianze e Frammenti.* Atti della Società ligustica di Scienze e Lettere di Genova, Vol. 11, Fasc. I–II. Pavia.
Degani, E. 1980. Review of M. L. West, *Studies in Greek Elegy and Iambus. Gnomon* 52: 512–16.
Delcourt, M. 1965. *Pyrrhos et Pyrrha: Recherches sur les valeurs du feu dans les légendes helléniques.* Bibliotheque de la Faculté de Philosophie et Lettres de l'Université de Liège 174. Paris.
de Man, Paul. 1983. "Dialogue and Dialogism." *Poetics Today* 4.1: 99–107.
Denniston, J. D. 1960. *Greek Prose Style.* 2nd ed. Oxford.
Denyer, Nicholas, ed. 2001. *Plato: Alcibiades.* Cambridge.
Derrida, Jacques. 1981. "Plato's Pharmacy." In *Dissemination,* trans. B. Johnson. Chicago. 63–171.
Desclos, Marie-Laurence. 1997. "'Le Renard dit au lion...' (*Alcibiade Majeur,* 123A), ou Socrate à la manière d'Ésope." In *L'Animal dans l'antiquité,* ed. B. Cassin and J.-L. Labarrière. Paris. 395–422.
———. 2000. " Le rire comme conduit de vie: l'Ésope de Platon." In *Le rire des Grecs: Anthropologie du rire en Grèce ancienne,* ed. M.-L. Desclos. Grenoble. 441–57.
Detienne, Marcel. 1989. "Culinary Practices and the Spirit of Sacrifice." In Detienne and Vernant 1989: 1–20.
———. 1996. *The Masters of Truth in Archaic Greece.* Trans. J. Lloyd. New York.
———. 1998. *Apollo le Couteau à la Main.* Paris.
Detienne, Marcel, and Jesper Svenbro. 1989. "The Feast of the Wolves, or the Impossible City." In Detienne and Vernant 1989: 148–63, 249–53.
Detienne, Marcel, and Jean-Pierre Vernant. 1978. *Cunning Intelligence in Greek Culture and Society.* Trans. J. Lloyd. Sussex.
———. 1989. *The Cuisine of Sacrifice among the Greeks.* Trans. P. Wissing. Chicago.
Dewald, Carolyn. 1997. "Wanton Kings, Pickled Heroes, and Gnomic Founding Fathers: Strategies of Meaning at the End of Herodotus' Histories." In *Classical Closure: Reading the End in Greek and Latin Literature,* ed. D. H. Roberts and F. M. Dunn. Princeton, N.J. 62–82.
———. 2006. "Humour and Danger in Herodotus." In Dewald and Marincola 2006: 145–64.

Dewald, Carolyn, and John Marincola, eds. 2006. *The Cambridge Companion to Herodotus*. Cambridge.
Diels, Hermann. 1887. "Herodot und Hekataios." *Hermes* 22: 411–44.
Diggle, James, ed. 2004. *Theophrastus: Characters*. Cambridge.
Dihle, Albrecht. 1962. "Herodot und die Sophistik." *Philologus* 106: 207–20.
Dijk, Gert-Jan van. 1994. Review of Papathomopoulos 1989 and 1990. *Mnemosyne* 47: 550–55.
———. 1995. "The Fables in the Greek *Life of Aesop*." *Reinardus* 8: 131–50.
———. 1997. *ΑΙΝΟΙ, ΛΟΓΟΙ, ΜΥΘΟΙ: Fables in Archaic, Classical, and Hellenistic Greek Literature*. Mnemosyne Supplement 166. Leiden.
Dillery, J. 1999. "Aesop, Isis, and the Heliconian Muses." *CP* 94: 268–80.
Dodds, E.R. 1951. *The Greeks and the Irrational*. Berkeley and Los Angeles.
———. 1973. "The Ancient Concept of Progess." In *The Ancient Concept of Progress and other Essays on Greek Literature and Belief*. Oxford. 1–25.
Dorter, Kenneth. 1969. "The Significance of the Speeches in Plato's *Symposium*." *Philosophy and Rhetoric* 2: 215–34.
Dougherty, Carol. 1993. *The Poetics of Colonization: From City to Text in Archaic Greece*. New York.
———. 2001. *The Raft of Odysseus: The Ethnographic Imagination of Homer's Odyssey*. New York.
Dougherty, Carol, and Leslie Kurke, eds. 1998. *Cultural Poetics in Archaic Greece: Cult, Performance, Politics*. Oxford.
Dougherty, Carol, and Leslie Kurke, eds. 2003. *The Cultures within Ancient Greek Culture: Contact, Conflict, Collaboration*. Cambridge.
Dover, K. J. 1966. "Aristophanes' Speech in Plato's *Symposium*." *JHS* 96: 41–50.
———, ed. 1980. *Plato. Symposium*. Cambridge.
Dow, S., and R. Healey. 1965. *A Sacred Calender of Eleusis*. Harvard Theological Studies 21. Cambridge, Mass.
Downey, G., and A. F. Norman, eds. 1971. *Themistii Orationes Quae Supersunt*. Vol. 2. Leipzig.
Drexhage, H.-J. 1997. "Einige Bemerkungen zu Fleischverarbeitung und Fleischvertrieb nach den griechischen Papyri und Ostraka vom 3. Jh. v. bis zum 7. Jh. n." *Münsterische Beiträge zur antiken Handelsgeschichte* 16: 97–111.
duBois, Page. 2003. *Slaves and Other Objects*. Chicago.
Dunbar, Nan, ed. 1995. *Aristophanes Birds*. Oxford.
Eberhard, Alfred. 1872. *Fabulae Romanenses Graece Conscriptae*. Vol. 1. Leipzig.
Edmunds, Lowell. 1997. "The Seal of Theognis." In Edmunds and Wallace 1997: 29–48, 136–43.
Edmunds, Lowell, and R. W. Wallace, eds. 1997. *Poet, Public, and Performance in Ancient Greece*. Baltimore, Md.
Edwards, Mark J. 1992. "Protagorean and Socratic Myth." *Symbolae Osloenses* 67: 89–102.
Ekroth, Gunnel. 2008. "Meat, Man, and God: On the Division of the Animal Victim in Greek Sacrifices." In *ΜΙΚΡΟΣ ΙΕΡΟΜΝΗΜΩΝ: Μελετες εις Μνημην Michael H. Jameson*, ed. A. P. Matthaiou and I. Polinskaya. Athens. 259–90.
Erbse, Hartmut. 1961. "Die Architektonik im Aufbau von Xenophons Memorabilien." *Hermes* 89: 257–87.

———, 1980. "Aristipp und Sokrates bei Xenophon (Bemerkungen zu *Mem.* 2, 1)." *WJA* n.f. 6b: 7–19.
———. 1992. *Studien zum Verständnis Herodots.* Berlin.
Erler, Michael. 1986. "Streitgesang und Streitgespräch bei Theokrit und Platon." *WJA* n.f. 12: 73–92.
Evans, J.A.S. 1991. *Herodotus, Explorer of the Past: Three Essays.* Princeton, N.J.
Fales, Frederick M. 1993. "Storia di Ahiqar tra Oriente e Grecia: La Prospettiva dall' Antico Oriente." *QS* 38: 143–66.
———. 1994. "Riflessioni sull' Ahiqar di Elefantina." *Orientis Antiqui Miscellanea* 1: 39–60.
Fehling, Detlev. 1985. *Die sieben Weisen und die frühgriechischen Chronologie: Eine traditionsgeschichtliche Studie.* Bern, Frankfurt am Main, and New York.
———. 1989. *Herodotus and His 'Sources': Citation, Invention and Narrative Art.* Trowbridge, Wiltshire.
Ferrara, Giovanni. 1964. "Temistocle e Solone." *Maia* 16: 55–70.
Ferrari, Franco. 1995. "Per il testo della Recensione G della *Vita Aesopi*." *Studi classici e orientale* 45: 249–59.
———, ed. 1997. *Romanzo di Esopo.* With translation and notes by G. Bonelli and G. Sandrolini. Milan.
Ferrari, G.R.F. 1987. *Listening to the Cicadas: A Study of Plato's Phaedrus.* Cambridge.
———. 1989. "Plato and Poetry." In *The Cambridge History of Literary Criticism.* Vol. 1, *Classical Criticism,* ed. G. A. Kennedy. Cambridge. 92–148.
———. 1992. "Platonic Love." In Kraut 1992: 248–76.
———. 2005. *City and Soul in Plato's Republic.* Chicago.
Ferrari, G.R.F., and Tom Griffith. 2000. *Plato: The Republic.* Cambridge.
Ferrarin, Alfredo. 2000. "*Homo Faber, Homo Sapiens,* or *Homo Politicus*? Protagoras and the Myth of Prometheus." *Review of Metaphysics* 54: 289–319.
Festugière, R. P. 1949. *La révélation d'Hermès Trismégiste.* II: *Le dieu cosmique.* Paris.
Figueira, Thomas J., and Gregory Nagy, eds. 1985. *Theognis of Megara: Poetry and the Polis.* Baltimore, Md.
Finkelpearl, E. D. 2003. "Lucius and Aesop Gain a Voice: Apuleius *Met.* 11.1–2 and *Vita Aesopi* 7." In *The Ancient Novel and Beyond,* ed. S. Panayotakis, M. Zimmerman, and W. Keulen. Leiden. 37–51.
Fitzgerald, William. 2000. *Slavery and the Roman Literary Imagination.* Cambridge.
Flory, Stewart. 1978. "Laughter, Tears, and Wisdom in Herodotus." *AJP* 99: 145–53.
———. 1990. "The Meaning of τὸ μὴ μυθῶδες (1.22.4) and the Usefulness of Thucydides' History." *CJ* 85: 193–208.
Fontenrose, J. 1960. *The Cult and Myth of Pyrros at Delphi.* University of California Publications in Classical Archaeology. Vol. 4, no. 3.
Ford, Andrew. 1985. "The Seal of Theognis: The Politics of Authorship in Archaic Greece." In Figueira and Nagy 1985: 82–95.
———. 1993. "Sophistic." *Common Knowledge* 1: 33–48.
———. 2001. "Sophists without Rhetoric: The Arts of Speech in Fifth-Century Athens." In Too 2001: 85–109.
———. 2002. *The Origins of Criticism: Literary Culture and Poetic Theory in Classical Greece.* Princeton, N.J.
Fornara, Charles W. 1971a. "Evidence for the Date of Herodotus' Publication." *JHS* 91: 25–34.

———. 1971b. *Herodotus: An Interpretative Essay.* Oxford.

———. 1981. "Herodotus' Knowledge of the Archidamian War." *Hermes* 109: 149–56.

Forrest, W. G. 1957. "Colonisation and the Rise of Delphi." *Historia* 6: 160–75.

Fowler, H. N., trans. 1991. *Plutarch's Moralia.* Vol. 10. Cambridge, Mass.

Fowler, R. L. 1996. "Herodotos and His Contemporaries." *JHS* 116: 62–87.

———. 2003. "Herodotos and Athens." In *Herodotus and His World: Essays from a Conference in Memory of George Forrest,* ed. Peter Derow and Robert Parker. Oxford. 305–18.

Fraenkel, Eduard. 1964. "Zur Form der AINOI." In *Kleine Beiträge zur klassischen Philologie.* Vol. 1. Rome. 235–239.

———. 1977. *Due Seminari Romani di Eduard Fraenkel: Aiace e Filottete di Sofocle.* Sussidi Eruditi 28. Rome.

Francis, H. T., and E. J. Thomas, eds. 1916. *Jātaka Tales.* Cambridge.

Frede, Michael. 1992. "Plato's Arguments and the Dialogue Form." In Klagge and Smith 1992: 201–19.

———. 2004. "Aristotle's Account of the Origins of Philosophy." *Rhizai* 1: 9–44.

Freese, J. H., trans. 1982. *Aristotle in Twenty-Three Volumes.* Vol. 22, *The "Art" of Rhetoric.* Cambridge, Mass.

Friedländer, Paul. 1913. "ΥΠΟΘΗΚΑΙ." *Hermes* 48: 558–616.

Friedman, Rachel. 2006. "Location and Dislocation in Herodotus." In Dewald and Marincola 2006: 165–77.

Führer, Rudolf. 1986. "Zu P. Oxy. 3720 (Life of Aesop)." *ZPE* 66: 19–22.

Gabba, Emilio. 1982. "Political and Cultural Aspects of the Classicistic Revival in the Augustan Age." *CA* 1: 43–65.

Gagarin, Michael. 2002. *Antiphon the Athenian: Oratory, Law, and Justice in the Age of the Sophists.* Austin, Tex.

Gagné, Renaud. 2006. "What Is the Pride of Halicarnassus?" *CA* 25: 1–33.

Gasparov, M. L. 1967. "Dve traditsii v legende ob Ezope." *Vestnik drevnei istorii* 2: 158–67.

Gauthier, R. A., and J. Y. Jolif, eds. 1959. *L'Éthique a Nicomaque.* Vol. 2, *Commentaire.* 2 vols. Paris and Louvain.

Gentili, Bruno. 1988. *Poetry and Its Public in Ancient Greece.* Trans. A. T. Cole. Baltimore, Md.

Gerber, Douglas E., ed. 1970. *Euterpe: An Anthology of Early Greek Lyric, Elegiac, and Iambic Poetry.* Amsterdam.

Gernet, Louis. 1981a. " 'Value' in Greek Myth." In Gordon 1981: 111–46.

———. 1981b. *The Anthropology of Ancient Greece.* Trans. J. Hamilton and B. Nagy. Baltimore, Md.

Gethin, Rupert. 2006. "Mythology as Meditation: From the Mahāsudassana Sutta to the Sukhāvatīvyūha Sūtra." *Journal of the Pāli Text Society* 28: 63–112.

Giannantoni, Gabriele, ed. 1990. *Socratis et Socraticorum Reliquiae.* 2nd ed. 4 vols. Naples.

Gibbs, Laura, trans. 2002. *Aesop's Fables.* Oxford.

Gigon, Olof. 1946. "Antike Erzählungen über die Berufung zur Philosophie." *MH* 3: 1–21.

———. 1956. *Kommentar zum zweiten Buch von Xenophons Memorabilien.* Basel.

———. 1959. "Die Sokratesdoxographie bei Aristoteles." *MH* 16: 174–212.

———, ed. 1987. *Aristotelis Opera.* Vol. 3, *Librorum deperditorum fragmenta.* Berlin and New York.

Gilhuly, Kate. 2009. *The Feminine Matrix of Sex and Gender in Classical Athens*. Cambridge and New York.
Gill, Christopher. 1990. "Platonic Love and Individuality." In *Polis and Politics: Essays in Greek Moral and Political Philosophy*, ed. A. Loizou and H. Lesser. Aldershot, England. 69–88.
Gill, Christopher and T. P. Wiseman, eds. 1993. *Lies and Fiction in the Ancient World*. Austin, Tex.
Gill, D. 1974. "*Trapezomata*: A Neglected Aspect of Greek Sacrifice." *HTR* 67: 117–37.
Ginzburg, Carlo. 1989. "Clues: Roots of an Evidential Paradigm." In *Clues, Myths, and the Historical Method*. Baltimore, Md. 96–125, 200–214.
Girard, René. 1977. *Violence and the Sacred*. Trans. P. Gregory. Baltimore, Md.
Gladigow, Burkhard. 1965. *Sophia und Kosmos: Untersuchungen zur Frühgeschichte von σοφός und σοφίη*. Spudasmata Band I. Hildesheim.
Gluskina, L. M. 1954. "Ezop i antidel'fiiskaia oppozitsiia v VI veke do n.e." [Aesop and the Anti-Delphic Opposition in the Sixth c. BCE]. *Vestnik drevnei istorii* 50.4: 150–58.
Godzich, Wlad, and Jeffrey Kittay. 1987. *The Emergence of Prose: An Essay in Prosaics*. Minneapolis, Minn.
Goins, Scott E. 1989. "The Influence of Old Comedy on the *Vita Aesopis* [sic]." *The Classical World* 83: 28–30.
Goldhill, Simon. 1998. "The Seductions of the Gaze: Socrates and His Girlfriends." In *KOSMOS: Essays in Order, Conflict and Community in Classical Athens*, ed. P. Cartledge, P. Millett, and S. von Reden. Cambridge. 105–24.
———. 2002. *The Invention of Prose*. Greece & Rome: New Surveys in the Classics No. 32. Oxford.
Gomperz, H. 1912. *Sophistik und Rhetorik*. Leipzig and Berlin.
Gordon, R. L. ed. 1981. *Myth, Religion and Society*. Cambridge.
Gould, John. 1989. *Herodotus*. London.
Gow, A.S.F., ed. 1965. *Machon: The Fragments*. Cambridge.
Gower, Barry S., and Michael C. Stokes, eds. 1992. *Socratic Questions: New Essays on the Philosophy of Socrates and Its Significance*. London and New York.
Graefe, Gerhard. 1963. "Der homerische Hymnus auf Hermes." *Gymnasium* 70: 515–26.
Grauert, W. H. 1825. "de Aesopo." Inaug. diss., Bonn.
Gray, Vivienne J. 1998. *The Framing of Socrates: The Literary Interpretation of Xenophon's Memorabilia*. Hermes Einzelschriften. Heft 79. Stuttgart.
Graziosi, Barbara. 2001. "Competition in Wisdom." In *Homer, Tragedy and Beyond: Essays in Honour of P. E. Easterling*, ed. F. Budelmann and P. Michelakis. London. 57–74.
———. 2002. *Inventing Homer: The Early Reception of Epic*. Cambridge.
Greene, W. C., ed. 1938. *Scholia Platonica*. Haverford, Penn.
Greenfield, Jonas C. 1995. "The Wisdom of Ahiqar." In *Wisdom in Ancient Israel: Essays in Honour of J. A. Emerton*, ed. J. Day, R. P. Gordon, and H.G.M. Williamson. Cambridge. 43–52.
Grey, Leslie. 2000. *A Concordance of Buddhist Birth Stories*. 3rd ed. London.
Griffin, Jasper. 1990. "Die Ursprünge der Historien Herodots." In *Memoria Rerum Veterum: Neue Beiträge zur antiken Historiographie und alten Geschichte*. Stuttgart. 51–82.

Griffith, Mark, ed. 1983a. *Aeschylus. Prometheus Bound*. Cambridge.
———. 1983b. "Personality in Hesiod." *CA* 2: 37–65.
———. 1990. "Contest and Contradiction in Early Greek Poetry." In *Cabinet of the Muses*, ed. M. Griffith and D. J. Mastronarde. Chico, Calif. 185–207.
Griffiths, Alan. 1995. "Latent and Blatant: Two Perspectives on Humour in Herodotos." In *Laughter down the Centuries*, ed. S. Jäkel and A. Timonen. Vol. 2. Turku. 31–44.
———. 2001. "Kissing Cousins: Some Curious Cases of Adjacent Material in Herodotus." In Luraghi 2001: 161–78.
———. 2006. "Stories and Storytelling in the *Histories*." In Dewald and Marincola 2006: 130–44.
Grote, George. 1851. *History of Greece*. 2nd ed. 10 vols. London.
———. 1865. *Plato and the Other Companions of Sokrates*. 3 vols. London.
Grottanelli, Cristiano. 1982a. "Aesop in Babylon." In *Mesopatamien und seine Nachbarn: Politische und kulturelle Wechselbeziehungen im Alten Vorderasien vom 4. bis 1. Jahrtausend v. Chr.*, ed. H.-J. Nissen and J. Renger. Berlin. Pt. 2: 555–72.
———. 1982b. "Healers and Saviours of the Eastern Mediterranean in Pre-Classical Times." In *La soteriologia dei culti orientali nell' impero Romano*, ed. U. Bianchi and M. J. Vermaseren. Leiden. 649–70.
Grube, G.M.A., trans. 1997. *Phaedo*. In Cooper 1997: 49–100.
Gulick, C. B., trans. 1980. *Athenaeus, The Deipnosophists*. Vol. 5. Cambridge, Mass.
Guthrie, W. K. C. 1969. *A History of Greek Philosophy*. Vol. 3, The Fifth-Century Enlightenment. Cambridge.
Hagemajer Allen, Katarzyna. 2003. "Becoming the 'Other': Attitudes and Practices at Attic Cemeteries." In Dougherty and Kurke 2003: 207–36.
Hägg, Tomas. 1997. "A Professor and His Slave: Conventions and Values in the *Life of Aesop*." In *Conventional Values of the Hellenistic Greeks*, ed. P. Bilde et al. Aarhus. 177–203.
Halperin, David M. 1990. "Why Is Diotima a Woman?" In *One Hundred Years of Homosexuality and Other Essays on Greek Love*. New York and London. 113–51.
———. 1992. "Plato and the Erotics of Narrativity." In Klagge and Smith 1992: 93–129.
Hamilton, Richard. 1989. *The Architecture of Hesiodic Poetry*. Baltimore, Md.
Hansen, William, ed. 1998. *Anthology of Ancient Greek Popular Literature*. Bloomington, Ind.
———. 2002. *Ariadne's Thread: A Guide to International Tales Found in Classical Literature*. Ithaca, N.Y.
Harmon, A. M., trans. 1961. *Lucian*. Vol. 1. Cambridge, Mass.
Harris, William V. 1989. *Ancient Literacy*. Cambridge, Mass.
Hart, John. 1982. *Herodotus and Greek History*. London and Canberra.
Hartog, François. 1988. *The Mirror of Herodotus: The Representation of the Other in the Writing of History*. Trans. J. Lloyd. Berkeley and Los Angeles.
Haslam, M. W. 1972. "Plato, Sophron, and the Dramatic Dialogue." *Bulletin of the Institute of Classical Studies* 19: 17–38
———., ed. 1980. "**3331**. Life of Aesop." In *The Oxyrhynchus Papyri*. Vol. 47, ed. R. A. Coles and M. W. Haslam. London.
———, ed. 1986. "**3720**. Life of Aesop (Addendum to **3331**)." In *The Oxyrhynchus Papyri*. Vol. 53. London.

———. 1992. Review of Papathomopoulos 1989 and 1990. *CR* n.s. 42: 188–89.
Hausrath, August. 1901. "Die Äsopstudien des Maximus Planudes." *Byzantinische Zeitschrift* 10: 91–105.
———. 1909. "Fabel." *RE* 6, 2. coll. 1704–36.
———. 1913. Review of F. Potente, *Il papiro Golenischeff*. *Philologische Wochenschrift* 51: 65–67.
———. 1937. Review of Perry 1936. *Philologische Wochenschrift* 57: 770–77.
———. 1970. *Corpus Fabularum Aesopicarum*. 2 Vols. Vol. Prius, rev. H. Hunger. Leipzig.
Havelock, Eric A. 1952. "Why Was Socrates Tried?" In *Studies in Honour of Gilbert Norwood*, ed. M. E. White. Toronto. 95–109.
———. 1957. *The Liberal Temper in Greek Politics*. London.
———. 1963. *Preface to Plato*. Cambridge, Mass., and London.
———. 1983. "The Socratic Problem: Some Second Thoughts." In *Essays in Ancient Philosophy*, ed. J. P. Anton and A. Preus. Vol. 2. Albany, N.Y. 147–73.
Headlam, Walter, ed. 1922. *Herodas: The Mimes and Fragments*, ed. A. D. Knox. Cambridge.
Hegel, G.W.F. 1975. *Aesthetics: Lectures on Fine Art*, trans. T. M. Knox. Vol. 1. Oxford.
Helms, Mary W. 1988. *Ulysses' Sail: An Ethnographic Odyssey of Power, Knowledge, and Geographical Distance*. Princeton, N.J.
———. 1993. *Craft and the Kingly Ideal: Art, Trade, and Power*. Austin, Tex.
Henderson, John. 2001. *Telling Tales on Caesar: Roman Stories from Phaedrus*. Oxford.
Heres, Thea L. 1992–93. "La storia edilizia delle terme dei Sette Sapienti (III x 2) ad Ostia Antica: uno studio preliminare." *Mededelingen van het Nederlands Instituut te Rome* 51/52: 76–113.
Herrmann, Léon. 1949. "Une caricature de Phèdre." In *Mélanges d'archéologie et d'histoire offerts à Charles Picard à l'occasion de son 65e anniversaire*. Vol. 1. Paris. 435–37.
Hershbell, Jackson P. 1993. "Plutarch and Herodotus: The Beetle in the Rose." *RhM* 136: 143–63.
Herter, Hans. 1976. "Hermes: Ursprung und Wesen eines griechischen Gottes." *RhM* 119: 193–241.
———. 1981. "L'inno a Hermes alla luce della poesia orale." In *I poemi epici rapsodici non omerici e la tradizione orale*, ed. C. Brilliante, M. Cantilena, and C. O. Pavese. Padua. 183–201.
Hicks, R. D., trans. 1959. *Diogenes Laertius. Lives of Eminent Philosophers*. Vol. 1. Cambridge, Mass.
Hinüber, Oskar von. 2000. *A Handbook of Pāli Literature*. Berlin.
Hirsch, Steven W. 1986. "Cyrus' Parable of the Fish: Sea Power in the Early Relations of Greece and Persia." *CJ* 81: 222–29.
Hock, Ronald F., and Edward N. O'Neil. 1986. *The Chreia in Ancient Rhetoric*. Vol. 1, *The Progymnasmata*. Atlanta, Ga.
Hölscher, Uvo. 1968. *Anfängliches Fragen: Studien zur frühen griechischen Philosophie*. Göttingen.
Holwerda, D., ed. 1991. *Scholia in Aristophanem*. Part II, fasc. III, *Scholia Vetera et Recentiora in Aristophanis Aves*. Groningen.
Holzberg, Niklas, ed. (with the assistance of A. Beschorner and S. Merkle). 1992. *Der Äsop-Roman: Motivgeschichte und Erzählstruktur*. Classica Monacensia. Band 6. Tübingen.

———. 1992a. "Vorwort." In Holzberg 1992: IX–XV.
———. 1992b. "Der Äsop-Roman. Eine strukturanalytische Interpretation." In Holzberg 1992: 33–75.
———. 1993. "A Lesser Known 'Picaresque' Novel of Greek Origin: The *Aesop Romance* and Its Influence." *Groningen Colloquia on the Novel* 5: 1–16.
———. 1996. "Fable: Aesop, Life of Aesop." In *The Novel in the Ancient World*, ed. G. Schmeling. Mnemosyne Supplement 159. Leiden. 633–39.
———. 1999. "The Fabulist, the Scholars, and the Discourse: Aesop Studies Today." *International Journal of the Classical Tradition* 6: 236–42.
———. 2002. *The Ancient Fable: An Introduction*. Trans. C. Jackson-Holzberg. Bloomington and Indianapolis.
Hopkins, Keith. 1993. "Novel Evidence for Roman Slavery." *Past & Present* 138: 3–27.
Hordern, J. H., ed. 2004. *Sophron's Mimes: Text, Translation, and Commentary*. Oxford.
Hornblower, Simon, ed. 1994. *Greek Historiography*. Oxford.
———. 1994a. "Introduction: Summary of the Papers; The Story of Greek Historiography; Intertextuality and the Greek Historians." In Hornblower 1994: 1–72.
———. 2006. "Herodotus' Influence in Antiquity." In Dewald and Marincola 2006: 306–18.
Hostetter, W. H. 1955. "A Linguistic Study of the Vulgar Greek Life of Aesop." PhD diss., University of Illinois at Urbana-Champaign.
How, W. W., and J. Wells, eds. 1928. *A Commentary on Herodotus with Introduction and Appendixes*. 2 vols. Oxford.
Hubert, Henri, and Marcel Mauss. 1964. *Sacrifice: Its Nature and Function*, trans. W. D. Halls. Chicago.
Hunter, Richard. 2000. "The Politics of Plutarch's *Comparison of Aristophanes and Menander*." In *Skenika: Beiträge zum antiken Theater und seiner Rezeption*, ed. S. Gödde and T. Heinze. Darmstadt. 267–76.
———. 2007. "Isis and the Language of Aesop." In *Pastoral Palimpsests: Essays on the Reception of Theocritus and Virgil*, ed. M. Paschalis. Rethymnion Classical Studies vol. 3. Rethymno, Crete. 39–58.
Hutchinson, D. S. 2008. "Thales and the Thracian Wench: Plato versus Aristophanes versus Socrates?" Lecture delivered at UC Davis, May 25, 2008.
Huxley, G. L. 1969. *Greek Epic Poetry from Eumelos to Panyassis*. Cambridge, Mass.
Immerwahr, H. R. 1966. *Form and Thought in Herodotus*. Chapel Hill, N.C.
Immisch, Otto. 1888. "Xenophon über Theognis und das Problem des Adels." In *Commentationes philologae quibus Ottoni Ribbeckio Praeceptori inlustri sexagensimum Aetatis Magisterii lipiensis decimum Annum exactum congratulantur Discipuli lipsienses*. Leipzig. 73–97.
Irwin, Elizabeth. 2005. *Solon and Early Greek Poetry: The Politics of Exhortation*. Cambridge.
———. 2009. "Herodotus' Samian Logos." *The Classical World* 102: 395–416.
Isager, Signe. 1998. "The Pride of Halikarnassos: Editio Princeps of an Inscription from Salmakis." *ZPE* 123: 1–23.
Isenberg, M. 1975. "The Sale of Sacrificial Meat." *CP* 70: 271–73.
Jacoby, Felix. 1909. "Über die Entwicklung der griechischen Historiographie und den Plan einer neuen Sammlung der griechischen Historikerfragmente." *Klio* 9: 80–123.
———. 1912. "Hekataios." *RE* 7, 2, coll. 2666–2769. [Repr. in Jacoby 1956: 185–237.]

———. 1913. "Herodotos." *RE* Supplementband 2, coll. 205–520. [Repr. in Jacoby 1956: 7–164.]
———. 1933. "Homerisches." *Hermes* 68: 1–50.
———. 1949. *Atthis: The Local Chronicles of Ancient Athens*. Oxford.
———. 1956. *Griechische Historiker*. Stuttgart.
Jaeger, Werner. 1948. *Aristotle: Fundamentals of the History of His Development*. Trans. R. Robinson. 2nd ed. Oxford.
Jahn, Otto. 1847. *Archäologische Beiträge*. Berlin.
Jameson, Fredric R. 1981. *The Political Unconscious: Narrative as a Socially Symbolic Act*. Ithaca, N.Y.
Jameson, M. H. 1994. "Theoxenia." In *Ancient Greek Cult Practice from the Epigraphical Evidence*, ed. R. Hägg. Stockholm. 35–57.
Janko, Richard. 1982. *Homer, Hesiod and the Hymns: Diachronic Development in Epic Diction*. Cambridge.
Jedrkiewicz, Stefano. 1983. "Platone e le favole esopiche." *Prospettive Settanta* n.s. 5: 250–64.
———. 1987. "La favola esopica nel processo di argomentazione orale fino al IV sec. a.C." *QUCC* 56: 35–63.
———. 1989. *Sapere e Paradosso nell' Antichità: Esopo e la Favola*. Rome.
———. 1997. *Il convitato sullo sgabello: Plutarco, Esopo, ed i Sette Savi*. Rome.
Johnson, David M. 2001. "Herodotus' Storytelling Speeches: Socles (5.92) and Leotychides (6.86)." *CJ* 97: 1–26.
Johnstone, Steven. 1994. "Virtuous Toil, Vicious Work: Xenophon on Aristocratic Style." *CP* 89: 219–40.
Jones, C. P. 1971. *Plutarch and Rome*. Oxford.
———, ed. and trans. 2005. *Philostratus, The Life of Apollonius of Tyana*. 2 vols. Cambridge, Mass.
Jouanno, Corinne. 2005. "La *Vie d'Ésope*: une biographie comique." *REG* 118: 391–405.
———, trans. 2006. *Vie D'Ésope*. Paris.
Kahn, Charles H. 1979. *The Art and Thought of Heraclitus: An Edition of the Fragments with Translation and Commentary*. Cambridge.
———. 1981. "Did Plato Write Socratic Dialogues?" *CQ* 31: 305–20.
———. 1983. "Drama and Dialectic in Plato's *Gorgias*." *Oxford Studies in Ancient Philosophy* 1: 75–121.
———. 1996. *Plato and the Socratic Dialogue: The Philosophical Use of a Literary Form*. Cambridge.
Kahn, Laurence. 1978. *Hermès passe ou les ambiguïtés de la communication*. Paris.
Kamen, Deborah E. 2004. "Between Slavery and Freedom, Silence and *Parrhêsia*: The Case of Aesop." Paper delivered at Princeton University, April 2004.
———. 2005. "Conceptualizing Manumission in Ancient Greece." PhD diss., University of California, Berkeley.
Käppel, L. 1992. *Paian: Studien zur Geschichte einer Gattung*. Berlin and New York.
Karadagli, Triantaphyllia. 1981. *Fabel und Ainos: Studien zur griechischen Fabel*. Königstein/Ts.
Karla, Grammatiki A. 2001. *Vita Aesopi: Überlieferung, Sprache und Edition einer frühbyzantinischen Fassung des Äsopromans*. Serta Graeca: Beiträge zur Erforschung griechischer Texte. Band 13. Wiesbaden.

Ker, James. 2000. "Solon's *Theôria* and the End of the City." *CA* 19: 304–29.
Kerferd, G. B. 1950. "The First Greek Sophists." *CR* 64: 8–10.
———. 1976. "The Image of the Wise Man in Greece in the Period before Plato." In *Images of Man in Ancient and Medieval Thought: Studia Gerard Verbeke ab amicis et collegis dicata*, ed. F. Bossier et al. Leuven. 17–28.
———. 1981. *The Sophistic Movement*. Cambridge.
Keuls, E. C. 1997. "The Social Position of Attic Vase Painters and the Birth of Caricature." In *Painter and Poet in Ancient Greece*. Stuttgart and Leipzig. 283–92.
Kindstrand, Jan Fredrik. 1981. *Anacharsis: The Legend and the Apophthegmata*. Acta Universitatis Upsaliensis. Studia Graeca Upsaliensis 16. Uppsala.
Kingsley, Peter. 1995. *Ancient Philosophy, Mystery, and Magic: Empedocles and Pythagorean Tradition*. Oxford.
Kirkwood, Gordon. 1984. "Blame and Envy in Pindaric Epinician." In *Greek Poetry and Philosophy: Studies in Honour of Leonard Woodbury*, ed. D. E. Gerber. Chico, Calif. 169–83.
Klagge, J. C., and N. D. Smith, eds. 1992. *Methods of Interpreting Plato and His Dialogues*. Oxford Studies in Ancient Philosophy. Supplementary Volume. Oxford.
Knox, B.M.W. 1979. "Why Is Oedipus Called Tyrannos?" In *Word and Action: Essays on the Ancient Theater*. Baltimore and London. 87–95.
Koller, Hermann. 1957. "Hypokrisis und Hypokrites." *MH* 14.2: 100–107.
Konstantakos, Ioannis M. 2004. "Trial by Riddle: The Testing of the Counsellor and the Contest of Kings in the Legend of Amasis and Bias." *Classica et Mediaevalia* 55: 85–137.
———. 2005. "Amasis, Bias and the Seven Sages as Riddlers." *WJA* n.f. 29: 11–46.
———. 2006. "Aesop Adulterer and Trickster. A Study of *Vita Aesopi* Ch. 75–76." *Athenaeum* 94: 563–600.
———. 2008. *ΑΚΙΧΑΡΟΣ· Η ΔΙΗΓΗΣΗ ΤΟΥ ΑΧΙΚΑΡ ΣΤΗΝ ΑΡΧΑΙΑ ΕΛΛΑΔΑ*. 2 vols. Athens.
Kowalzig, Barbara. 2007. *Singing for the Gods: Performances of Myth and Ritual in Archaic and Classical Greece*. Oxford.
Kraut, Richard, ed. 1992. *The Cambridge Companion to Plato*. Cambridge.
Krell, David F. 1988. " 'Knowledge Is Remembrance': Diotima's Instruction at *Symposium* 207c8–208b6." In *Post-Structuralist Classics*, ed. A. Benjamin. London. 160–72.
Krentz, Peter, ed. 1995. *Xenophon: Hellenica II.3.11–IV.2.8*. Warminster, England.
Kroll, Josef. 1936. *Theognisinterpretationen*. Philologus Supplementband 29, Heft 1. Leipzig.
Kuntz, Mary. 1994. "The Prodikean 'Choice of Herakles': A Reshaping of Myth." *CJ* 89: 163–81.
Kurke, Leslie. 1989. "ΚΑΠΗΛΕΙΑ and Deceit: Theognis 59–60." *AJP* 110: 535–44.
———. 1990. "Pindar's Sixth *Pythian* and the Tradition of Advice Poetry." *TAPA* 120: 85–107.
———. 1991. *The Traffic in Praise: Pindar and the Poetics of Social Economy*. Ithaca, N.Y.
———. 1992. "The Politics of ἁβροσύνη in Archaic Greece." *CA* 11: 90–121.
———. 1994. "Crisis and Decorum in Sixth-Century Lesbos: Reading Alkaios Otherwise." *QUCC* n.s. 47, 2: 67–92.
———. 1995. "Herodotus and the Language of Metals." *Helios* 22: 36–64.

———. 1996. "Pindar and the Prostitutes, or Reading Ancient 'Pornography.'" *Arion* 3rd ser. 4: 49–75.

———. 1998. "The Economy of *Kudos*." In Dougherty and Kurke 1998: 131–63.

———. 1999. *Coins, Bodies, Games, and Gold: The Politics of Meaning in Archaic Greece*. Princeton, N.J.

———. 2000. "The Strangeness of 'Song Culture': Archaic Greek Poetry." In *Literature in the Greek & Roman Worlds: A New Perspective*, ed. Oliver Taplin. Oxford. 58–87.

———. 2002. "Gender, Politics, and Subversion in the *Chreiai* of Machon." *PCPS* 48: 20–65.

———. 2003. "Aesop and the Contestation of Delphic Authority." In Dougherty and Kurke 2003: 77–100.

———. 2005. "Choral Lyric as 'Ritualization': Poetic Sacrifice and Poetic *Ego* in Pindar's Sixth Paian." *CA* 24: 81–130.

———. 2006. "Plato, Aesop, and the Beginnings of Mimetic Prose." *Representations* 94: 6–52.

———. 2010. "Towards a Greek Ethnography of Speaking: The Case of ὑπολαβὼν ἔφη." *Classics@* [Online Journal], Center for Hellenic Studies, http://chs.harvard.edu.

La Penna, Antonio. 1961. "La morale della favola esopica come morale delle classi subalterne nell' antichità." *Società* 17: 459–537.

———. 1962. "Il Romanzo di Esopo." *Athenaeum* n.s. 40: 264–314.

Lachenaud, Guy, ed. and trans. 1981. *Comparaison d'Aristophane et de Ménandre, De la malignité d'Hérodote*. In *Plutarque: Oeuvres Morales*. Tome XII.1. Paris.

Lamberton, Robert. 2001. *Plutarch*. Yale.

Lamedica, Armida. 1985. "Il *P.Oxy.* 1800 e le forme della biografia greca." *Studi Italiani di Filologia Classica* Ser. III, 3. 78: 55–75.

Lang, M. L. 1968. "Herodotus and the Ionian Revolt." *Historia* 17: 24–36.

———. 1984. *Herodotean Narrative and Discourse*. Cambridge, Mass.

Lasserre, François. 1976. "L'historiographie grecque à l'époque archaïque." *QS* 2: 113–42.

———. 1984. "La fable en Grèce dans la poésie archaïque." In *La Fable*. Fondation Hardt pour l'étude de l'antiquité classique. Entretiens 30, ed. F. R. Adrados and O. Reverdin. Geneva. 61–103.

Lateiner, Donald. 1977. "No Laughing Matter: A Literary Tactic in Herodotus." *TAPA* 107: 173–82.

———. 1986. "The Empirical Element in the Methods of the Early Greek Medical Writers and Herodotus: A Shared Epistemological Response." *Antichthon* 20: 1–20.

———. 1989. *The Historical Method of Herodotus*. Toronto.

Lattimore, Richmond. 1939. "The Wise Advisor in Herodotus." *CP* 34: 24–35.

Legrand, Ph.-E., ed. 1948. *Hérodote Histoires. Livre VI: Érato*. Paris.

Lesky, Albin. 1966. "Das Rätsel der Sphinx." *Gesammelte Schriften*. Bern and Munich. 318–26.

Leutsch, E. L. von, and F. G. Schneidewin, eds. 1958. *Corpus Paroemiographorum Graecorum*. Hildesheim.

Lévi-Strauss, Claude. 1966. *The Savage Mind*. Chicago.

Lincoln, Bruce. 1993. "Socrates' Prosecutors, Philosophy's Rivals, and the Politics of Discursive Forms." *Arethusa* 26: 233–46.

———. 1997. "Competing Discourses: Rethinking the Prehistory of *Mythos* and *Logos*." *Arethusa* 30: 341–67.
Lindenberger, James M. 1983. *The Aramaic Proverbs of Ahiqar*. Baltimore, Md.
———. trans. 1985. "Ahiqar." In *The Old Testament Pseudepigrapha*. Vol. 2, ed. James H. Charlesworth. Garden City, N.Y. 479–507.
Lippold, G. 1937. "Zu den Imagines Illustrium." *Mitteilungen des Deutschen Archäologischen Instituts, Römische Abteilung* 52: 44–7.
Lissarrague, F. 2000. "Aesop, between Man and Beast: Ancient Portraits and Illustrations." In *Not the Classical Ideal: Athens and the Construction of the Other in Greek Art*, ed. B. Cohen. Leiden. 132–149.
Lloyd, G.E.R. 1979. *Magic, Reason and Experience: Studies in the Origin and Development of Greek Science*. Cambridge.
———. 1987. *The Revolutions of Wisdom: Studies in the Claims and Practice of Ancient Greek Science*. Berkeley and Los Angeles.
Lloyd-Jones, Hugh. 1999. "The Pride of Halicarnassus." *ZPE* 124: 1–14.
Lombardo, Stanley, and Karen Bell, trans. 1997. *Protagoras*. In Cooper 1997: 746–90.
Long, A. A. 1996. "The Socratic Tradition: Diogenes, Crates, and Hellenistic Ethics." In Bracht Branham and Goulet-Cazé 1996: 28–46.
Loraux, Nicole. 1980. "Thucydide n'est pas un collègue." *QS* 12: 55–81.
———. 1981. "La cité comme cuisine et comme partage." *Annales: Économies, Sociétés, Civilisations* 36: 614–22.
———. 1984. "Solon au milieu de la lice." In *Aux origines de l'Hellénisme: La Crète et la Grèce. Hommage à Henri van Effenterre*. Paris. 199–214.
———. 1985. "Socrate, Platon, Héraklès: sur un paradigme héroïque du philosophie." In *Histoire et structure: à la mémoire de Victor Goldschmidt*, ed. J. Brunschwig et al. Paris. 93–105.
———. 1986. *The Invention of Athens: The Funeral Oration in the Classical City*. Trans. A. Sheridan. Cambridge, Mass.
———. 1989. "Therefore, Socrates Is Immortal." In *Fragments for a History of the Human Body*, pt. 2, ed. Michael Feher with Ramona Naddaff and Nadia Tazi. New York. 12–45.
Lord, Carnes, trans. 1984. *Aristotle. The Politics*. Chicago.
Lucas, D. W. ed. 1968. *Aristotle Poetics*. Oxford.
Luraghi, Nino, ed. 2001. *The Historian's Craft in the Age of Herodotus*. Oxford.
———. 2001a. "Introduction." In Luraghi 2001: 1–15.
———. 2001b. "Local Knowledge in Herodotus' *Histories*." In Luraghi 2001: 138–60.
———. 2006. "Meta-*historiē*: Method and Genre in the *Histories*." In Dewald and Marincola 2006: 76–91.
———. 2009. "The Importance of Being *Logios*." *The Classical World* 102: 439–56.
Luzzatto, Maria J. 1988. "Plutarco, Socrate e l'Esopo di Delfi." *Illinois Classical Studies* 13.2: 427–45.
———. 1992. "Grecia e Vicino Oriente: Tracce della 'Storia di Ahiqar' nella cultura Greca tra VI e V secolo a.C." *QS* 36: 5–84.
———. 1994. "Ancora sulla 'Storia di Ahiqar'." *QS* 39: 253–77.
Macan, R. W., ed. 1895. *Herodotus: The Fourth, Fifth, and Sixth Books*. 2 vols. London.
———. 1908. *Herodotus: The Seventh, Eighth, and Ninth Books*. 3 vols. (I.1, I.2, II). London.

Macherey, Pierre. 1978. *A Theory of Literary Production*. London and New York.
Maier, Friedrich. 1970. "Der σοφός-Begriff: Zur Bedeutung, Wertung und Rolle des Begriffes von Homer bis Euripides." Inaug. diss., Munich.
Mainoldi, Carla. 1984. *L'image du loup et du chien dans la Grèce ancienne: d'Homère à Platon*. Paris.
Malkin, I. 1987. *Religion and Colonization in Ancient Greece*. Leiden.
———. 1989. "Delphoi and the Founding of Social Order in Archaic Greece." *Métis* 4: 129–53.
Manfredini, Mario, and Luigi Piccirilli, eds. 1977. *Plutarco: La Vita de Solone*. Verona.
Mann, Wolfgang-Rainer. 1996. "The Life of Aristippus." *Archiv für Geschichte der Philosophie* 78: 97–119.
———. 2006. *Fighting with Words*. Unpublished ms in preparation.
———. 2009. "A Platonic Conception of Wisdom: *Theaetetus* 172c–77c (The 'Digression')." Paper delivered at the Conference "Wisdom in Ancient Thought," Columbia University, April 3, 2009.
Mansfield, Jaap. 1990. "Cratylus 402a–c: Plato or Hippias?" In *Studies in the Historiography of Greek Philosophy*. Van Gorcum, Assen/Maastricht, The Netherlands. 43–55.
Marc, Paul. 1910. "Die Überlieferung des Äsopromans." *Byzantinische Zeitschrift* 19: 383–421.
Marchant, E. C., trans. 1979. *Xenophon in Seven Volumes*. Vol. 4, ed. E. C. Marchant and O. J. Todd. Cambridge, Mass.
Marincola, John M. 1994. "Plutarch's Refutation of Herodotus." *The Ancient World* 25: 191–203.
Martin, Richard P. 1984. "Hesiod, Odysseus, and the Instruction of Princes." *TAPA* 114: 29–48.
———. 1992. "Hesiod's Metanastic Poetics." *Ramus* 21.1: 11–33.
———. 1996. "The Scythian Accent: Anacharsis and the Cynics." In Bracht Branham and Goulet-Cazé 1996: 136–55.
———. 1998. "The Seven Sages as Performers of Wisdom." In *Cultural Poetics in Archaic Greece: Cult, Performance, Politics*, ed. C. Dougherty and L. Kurke. Oxford. 108–28.
———. 2003. "The Pipes Are Brawling: Conceptualizing Musical Performance in Athens." In Dougherty and Kurke 2003: 153–80.
Maslov, Boris. 2009. "The Semantics of ἀοιδός and Related Compounds: Toward a Historical Poetics of Solo Performance in Archaic Greece." *CA* 28: 1–38.
Masson, Olivier, ed. 1962. *Les Fragments du poète Hipponax: Édition critique et commentée*. Études et Commentaires 43. Paris.
Matthews, Victor J. 1974. *Panyassis of Halikarnassos: Text and Commentary*. Leiden.
Maurizio, Lisa. 1997. "Delphic Oracles as Oral Performances: Authenticity and Historical Evidence." *CA* 16: 308–34.
McCarthy, Kathleen. 2000. *Slaves, Masters and the Art of Authority in Plautine Comedy*. Princeton, N.J.
McNellen, Brad. 1997. "Herodotean Symbolism: Pericles as Lion Cub." *Illinois Classical Studies* 22: 11–23.
McQueen, E. I., ed. 2000. *Herodotus Book VI*. Bristol.
Meiggs, Russell. 1973. *Roman Ostia*. 2nd ed. Oxford.
Merkle, Stefan. 1992. "Die Fabel von Frosch und Maus. Zur Funktion der λόγοι im Delphi-Teil des Äsop-Romans." In Holzberg 1992: 110–27.

Meuli, Karl. 1975a. "Ein altpersischer Kriegsbrauch." In *Gesammelte Schriften*. Vol. 2. Basel/Stuttgart. 699–729.

———. 1975b. "Herkunft und Wesen der Fabel." In *Gesammelte Schriften*. Vol. 2. Basel/Stuttgart. 731–56.

Meyer, Eduard. 1912. *Der Papyrusfund von Elephantine: Dokumente einer jüdischen Gemeinde aus der Perserzeit und das älteste erhaltene Buch der Weltliteratur*. 2nd ed. Leipzig.

Mignogna, Elisa. 1992. "Aesopus bucolicus. Come si 'metta in scena' un miracolo (Vita Aesopi c. 6)." In Holzberg 1992: 76–84.

Miller, Clyde Lee. 1978. "The Prometheus Story in Plato's *Protagoras*." *Interpretation* 7.2: 22–32.

Miller, Margaret C. 1997. *Athens and Persia in the Fifth Century BC: A Study in Cultural Receptivity*. Cambridge.

Miralles, C., and J. Pòrtulas. 1983. *Archilochus and the Iambic Poetry*. Rome.

———. 1988. *The Poetry of Hipponax*. Rome.

Moles, John. 1993. "Truth and Untruth in Herodotus and Thucydides." In Gill and Wiseman 1993: 88–121.

———. 1996. "Herodotus Warns the Athenians." *Papers of the Leeds International Latin Seminar* 9: 259–84.

———. 2002. "Herodotus and Athens." In Bakker, de Jong, and van Wees 2002: 33–52.

Mols, Stephan T.A.M. 1999. "Decorazione e uso dello spazio a Ostia. Il caso dell' *Insula* III x (Caseggiato del Serapide, Terme dei Sette Sapienti e Caseggiato degli Aurighi)." *Mededeelingen van het Nederlands Instituut te Rome* 58: 247–386.

Momigliano, Arnaldo. 1960. "The Place of Herodotus in the History of Historiography." In *Secondo Contributo alla Storia degli Studi Classici*. Rome. 29–44 [= *History* 43 (1958): 1–13.]

———. 1971. *The Development of Greek Biography*. Cambridge, Mass.

———. 1978. "Greek Historiography." *History and Theory* 17: 1–28.

Montiglio, Silvia. 2000. "Wandering Philosophers in Classical Greece." *JHS* 120: 86–105.

———. 2005. *Wandering in Ancient Greek Culture*. Chicago.

Moravcsik, Julius, and Philip Temko, eds. 1982. *Plato on Beauty, Wisdom, and the Arts*. Totowa, N.J.

Moret, Jean-Marc. 1984. *Oedipe, La Sphinx et les Thébains: Essai de mythologie iconographique*. Bibliotheca Helvetica Romana XXIII. 2 vols. Geneva.

Morgan, Catherine. 1990. *Athletes and Oracles*. Cambridge.

———. 1993. "The Origins of Pan-Hellenism." In *Greek Sanctuaries: New Approaches*, ed. N. Marinatos and R. Hägg. London and New York. 18–44.

Morgan, Kathryn A. 2000. *Myth and Philosophy from the Presocratics to Plato*. Cambridge.

Morris, Ian. 1986a. "Gift and Commodity in Archaic Greece." *Man* 21: 1–17.

———. 1986b. "The Use and Abuse of Homer." *CA* 5: 81–138.

———. 1989. "Circulation, Deposition and the Formation of the Greek Iron Age." *Man* 24: 502–19.

———. 1993. Review of J. Ober, *Mass and Elite in Democratic Athens*. *Topoi* 3.1: 271–83.

———. 1996. "The Strong Principle of Equality and the Archaic Origins of Greek Democracy." In *Dēmokratia: A Conversation on Democracies, Ancient and Modern*, ed. J. Ober and C. Hedrick. Princeton. 19–48.

———. 2000. *Archaeology as Cultural History.* Oxford.
Morrison, D. 1994. "Xenophon's Socrates as Teacher." In Vander Waerdt 1994: 181–208.
Morrison, J. S. 1949. "An Introductory Chapter in the History of Greek Education." *Durham University Journal* 41: 55–63.
Most, Glenn W. 1999. "The Poetics of Early Greek Philosophy." In *The Cambridge Companion to Early Greek Philosophy,* ed. A. A. Long. Cambridge. 332–362.
Mülke, Christoph, ed. 2002. *Solons politische Elegien und Iamben (Fr. 1–13; 32–37 West): Einleitung, Text, Übersetzung, Kommentar.* Leipzig.
Munson, Rosaria Vignolo. 2006. "An Alternate World: Herodotus and Italy." In Dewald and Marincola 2006: 257–73.
Murray, Oswyn. 1972. "Herodotus and Hellenistic Culture." *CQ* n.s. 22: 200–213.
———. 1980. *Early Greece.* Stanford, Calif.
———. 2001a. "Herodotus and Oral History." In Luraghi 2001: 16–44.
———. 2001b. "Herodotus and Oral History Reconsidered." In Luraghi 2001: 314–25.
Murray, R. D. 1965. "Theognis 341–50." *TAPA* 96: 277–81.
Myres, J. L. 1953. *Herodotus Father of History.* Oxford.
Naddaff, Ramona A. 2002. *Exiling the Poets: The Production of Censorship in Plato's Republic.* Chicago.
Nagy, Gregory. 1979. *The Best of the Achaeans: Concepts of the Hero in Archaic Greek Poetry.* Baltimore, Md.
———. 1985a. "On the Symbolism of Apportioning Meat in Archaic Greek Elegiac Poetry." *L'Uomo* 9: 45–52.
———. 1985b. "Theognis and Megara: A Poet's Vision of His City." In Figueira and Nagy 1985: 22–81.
———. 1987. "Herodotus the *Logios.*" *Arethusa* 20: 175–84.
———. 1988. "Mythe et prose en Grèce archaïque: L' *ainos.*" In *Métamorphoses du mythe en Grèce antique,* ed. C. Calame. Geneva.
———. 1990a. *Greek Mythology and Poetics.* Ithaca, N.Y.
———. 1990b. *Pindar's Homer: The Lyric Possession of an Epic Past.* Baltimore, Md.
———. 1996. *Poetry as Performance: Homer and Beyond.* Cambridge.
———. 2002. *Plato's Rhapsody and Homer's Music: The Poetics of the Panathenaic Festival in Classical Athens.* Cambridge, Mass., and London.
Neer, Richard T. 2001. "Framing the Gift: The Politics of the Siphnian Treasury at Delphi." *CA* 20: 273–336.
———. 2003. "Framing the Gift: The Siphnian Treasury at Delphi and the Politics of Public Art." In Dougherty and Kurke 2003: 129–49.
———. 2004. "The Athenian Treasury at Delphi and the Material of Politics." *CA* 23: 63–93.
———. 2010. *The Emergence of the Classical Style in Greek Sculpture.* Chicago.
Nehamas, Alexander. 1981. "The Postulated Author: Critical Monism as a Regulative Ideal." *Critical Inquiry* 8: 133–49.
———. 1982. "Plato on Imitation and Poetry in *Republic* 10." In Moravcsik and Temko 1982: 47–78.
———. 1987. "Writer, Text, Work, Author." In Cascardi 1987: 265–91.
———. 1990. "Eristic, Antilogic, Sophistic, Dialectic: Plato's Demarcation of Philosophy from Sophistry." *History of Philosophy Quarterly* 7.1: 3–16.

Nehamas, Alexander, and Paul Woodruff, trans. 1997. *Symposium*. In Cooper 1997: 457–505.
Nestle, Wilhelm. 1936. "Die Horen des Prodikos." *Hermes* 71: 151–70.
———. 1975. *Vom Mythos zum Logos: Die Selbstentfaltung des griechischen Denkens von Homer bis auf die Sophistik und Sokrates*. Stuttgart.
Neudecker, Richard. 1994. *Die Pracht der Latrine: Zum Wandel öffentlicher Bedürfnisanstalten in der kaiserzeitlichen Stadt*. Studien zur antiken Stadt, 1. Munich.
Nicholson, Nigel. 2003. "Aristocratic Victory Memorials and the Absent Charioteer." In Dougherty and Kurke 2003: 101–28.
———. 2005. *Aristocracy and Athletics in Archaic and Classical Greece*. Cambridge.
Nicolai, Roberto. 1997. "*Pater semper incertus*: Appunti su Ecateo." *QUCC* n.s. 56: 143–64.
Nicolaïdou-Kyrianidou, Vana. 1998. "Prodicos et Xenophon, ou le choix d'Heracles entre la tyrannie et la loyaute." In *Kea-Kythnos: History and Archaeology*. Proceedings of an International Symposium, 22–25 June 1994, ed. L. G. Mendoni and A. J. Mazarakis Ainian. Athens. 81–98.
Nietzsche, Friedrich. 1967. *The Birth of Tragedy and the Case of Wagner*. Trans. W. Kaufmann. New York.
Nightingale, Andrea. 1995. *Genres in Dialogue: Plato and the Construct of Philosophy*. Cambridge.
———. 2001. "Liberal Education in Plato's *Republic* and Aristotle's *Politics*." In Too 2001: 133–73.
———. 2004. *Spectacles of Truth in Classical Greek Philosophy: Theoria in Its Cultural Context*. Cambridge.
Nilsson, M. 1906. *Griechische Feste mit Ausnahme der attischen*. Leipzig.
Nøjgaard, Morten. 1964. *La fable antique*. Tome Premier, *La fable grecque avant Phèdre*. Copenhagen.
Nöldecke, Thomas. 1913. *Untersuchungen zum Achiqar-Roman*. Abhandlungen der königlichen Gesellschaft der Wissenschaften zu Göttingen, Phil.-hist. Kl., NF 14, 4. Berlin.
Norden, Eduard. 1915. *Die Antike Kunstprosa*. Erster Band, *Vom VI. Jahrhundert v. Chr. bis in die Zeit der Renaissance*. Berlin.
Norman, K. R. 1983. *Pāli Literature including the Canonical Literature in Prakrit and Sanskrit of All the Hīnayāna Schools of Buddhism*. Wiesbaden.
North, Helen. 1966. *Sophrosyne: Self-Knowledge and Self-Restraint in Greek Literature*. Ithaca, N.Y.
Nussbaum, Martha C. 2001. *The Fragility of Goodness: Luck and Ethics in Greek Tragedy and Philosophy*. Rev. ed. Cambridge.
Ogden, Daniel. 1997. *The Crooked Kings of Ancient Greece*. Trowbridge, England.
Oikonomides, N. 1980. "The Lost Delphic Inscription with the Commandments of the Seven and P.Univ. Athen. 2782." *ZPE* 37: 179–83.
———. 1987. "Records of 'The Commandments of the Seven Wise Men' in the 3rd c. B.C." *Classical Bulletin* 63: 67–76.
Olrik, Axel. 1965. "Epic Laws of Folk Narrative." In *The Study of Folklore*, ed. Alan Dundes. Englewood Cliffs, N.J. 129–41.
O'Sullivan, Neil. 1992. *Alcidamas, Aristophanes and the Beginnings of Greek Stylistic Theory*. Hermes Einzelschriften. Heft 60. Stuttgart.

———. 1996. "Written and Spoken in the First Sophistic." In *Voice into Text: Orality and Literacy in Ancient Greece*, ed. I. Worthington. Leiden. 115–27.

Papademetriou, J.-T. 1980. "Notes on the Aesop Romance New Series, I." *RhM* 123: 25–40.

———. 1997. *Aesop as Archetypal Hero*. Athens.

Papathomopoulos, Manolis. 1989. *Aesopus revisitatus: recherches sur la texte des Vies Ésopiques*. Vol. 1, *La critique textuelle*. Ioannina, Greece.

———. 1990. *Ο ΒΙΟΣ ΤΟΥ ΑΙΣΩΠΟΥ. Η ΠΑΡΑΛΛΑΓΗ G*. Ioannina, Greece.

———. 1999. *Ο ΒΙΟΣ ΤΟΥ ΑΙΣΩΠΟΥ. Η ΠΑΡΑΛΛΑΓΗ W*. Athens, Greece.

Parke, H. W. 1948. "Consecration to Apollo." *Hermathena* 72: 82–114.

Parke, H. W., and D.E.W. Wormell. 1956. *The Delphic Oracle*. 2 vols. Oxford.

Parker, Robert. 1983. *Miasma: Pollution and Purification in Early Greek Religion*. Oxford.

———. 1998. "Pleasing Thighs: Reciprocity in Greek Religion." In *Reciprocity in Ancient Greece*, ed. C. Gill, N. Postlethwaite, and R. Seaford. Oxford. 105–25.

Patterson, Annabel. 1991. *Fables of Power: Aesopian Writing and Political History*. Durham and London.

Pelling, Christopher. 1997. "East Is East and West Is West—Or Are They? National Stereotypes in Herodotus." *Histos* (http://www.dur.ac.uk/Classics/histos/1997/pelling.html).

———. 2006. "Speech and Narrative in the *Histories*." In Dewald and Marincola 2006: 103–21.

Pellizer, E., G. Tedeschi, et al. 1981. "Sei carmi conviviali attribuiti ai Sette Sapienti." *Quaderni di filologia classica* 3: 6–23.

Pendrick, Gerard J., ed. 2002. *Antiphon the Sophist: The Fragments*. Cambridge.

Penella, Robert J., trans. 2000. *The Private Orations of Themistius*. Berkeley and Los Angeles.

Perrin, B., trans. 1914. *Plutarch, Lives*. Vol. 2. Cambridge, Mass.

Perry, Ben Edwin. 1933. "The Text Tradition of the Greek Life of Aesop." *TAPA* 64: 198–244.

———. 1936. *Studies in the Text History of the Life and Fables of Aesop*. American Philological Association Monographs 7. Haverford, Penn.

———. 1940. "The Origin of the Epimythium." *TAPA* 71: 391–419.

———. 1942. Review of A. Hausrath, ed. *Corpus fabularum Aesopicarum*. *CP* 37: 207–18.

———. 1952. *Aesopica: A Series of Texts relating to Aesop or Ascribed to Him or Closely Connected to the Literary Tradition That Bears His Name*. Vol. 1. Urbana, Ill.

———. 1959. "Fable." *Studium Generale* 12: 17–37.

———. 1960. "The Origin of the Book of Sinbad." *Fabula* 3: 1–94.

———. 1962a. "Demetrius of Phalerum and the Aesopic Fables." *TAPA* 93: 287–346.

———. 1962b. Review of Wiechers, *Aesop in Delphi*. *Gnomon* 34: 620–22.

———, ed. 1965. *Babrius and Phaedrus*. London and Cambridge, Mass.

———. 1966. "Some Addenda to the Life of Aesop." *Byzantinische Zeitschrift* 59: 285–304.

Persson, Axel W. 1915. "Xenophon über Theognis." *Eranos* 15: 39–50.

Picard, Charles. 1947. "Autour du Banquet des Sept Sages." ("Nouvelles et correspondance.") *Revue archéologique* 28: 74–75.

Platnauer, M., ed. 1938. *Euripides: Iphigenia in Tauris*. Oxford.
Plepelits, K. 1970. *Die Fragmente der Demen des Eupolis*. Vienna.
Pouilloux, J. 1952. "Promanties collectives et protocole delphique." *BCH* 76: 484–513.
———. 1960. *Fouilles de Delphes ii: La région nord du sanctuaire*. Paris.
———. 1974. "Les décrets delphiques pour Matrophanès de Sardes." *BCH* 98: 159–69.
Powell, I. U. 1925. *Collectanea Alexandrina*. Oxford.
Powell, J. Enoch. 1938. *A Lexicon to Herodotus*. Cambridge.
Preisigke, Friedrich. 1931. *Wörterbuch der griechischen Papyrusurkunden, mit Einschluss der griechischen Inschriften, Aufschriften, Ostraka, Mumienschilder usw. aus Ägypten*. Dritter Band: Besondere Wörterliste. Berlin.
Puttkammer, F. 1912. "*Quo modo Graeci victimarum carnes distribuerint.*" Inaug. diss., Königsberg.
Raaflaub, Kurt A. 1979. "Polis Tyrannos: Zur Entstehung einer politischen Metapher." In *Arktouros: Hellenic Studies Presented to Bernard M. W. Knox on the Occasion of His 65th Birthday*, ed. G. W. Bowersock, W. Burkert, and M.C.J. Putnam. Berlin. 237–52.
———. 1987. "Herodotus, Political Thought, and the Meaning of History." *Arethusa* 20: 221–48.
Radt, Stefan L. 1958. *Pindars zweiter und sechster Paian*. Amsterdam.
Redfield, Robert. 1956. *Peasant Society and Culture: An Anthropological Approach to Civilization*. Chicago.
Reeve, C. D. C. 2000. "Socrates the Apollonian?" In Smith and Woodruff 2000: 24–39.
Reitzenstein, R. 1893. *Epigramm und Skolion: Ein Beitrag zur Geschichte der alexandrinischen Dichtung*. Giessen.
Renehan, R. 1971. "The Michigan Alcidamas-Papyrus: A Problem in Methodology." *HSCP* 75: 85–105.
Rhys Davids, T. W. 1880. *Buddhist Birth Stories*. London.
Richardson, N. J. 1981. "The Contest of Homer and Hesiod and Alcidamas' *Mouseion*." *CQ* n.s. 31: 1–10.
Riginos, Alice Swift. 1976. *Platonica: The Anecdotes concerning the Life and Writings of Plato*. Leiden.
Robert, Louis. 1968. "De Delphes a l'Oxus. Inscriptions grecques nouvelles de la Bactriane." *Comptes Rendus des séances, Académie des inscriptions & belles-lettres*. Paris. 416–57.
Roberts, W. Rhys, ed. 1935. *Longinus On the Sublime*. Cambridge.
Robertson, Noel. 1969. "How to Behave at a Sacrifice: Hesiod *Erga* 755–56." *CP* 14: 164–69.
———. 1978. "The Myth of the First Sacred War." *CQ* n.s. 28: 38–73.
———. 2003. "Aesop's Encounter with Isis and the Muses, and the Origins of the Life of Aesop." In *Poetry, Theory, and Praxis. The Social Life of Myth, Word and Image in Ancient Greece: Essays in Honour of William J. Slater*, ed. E. Csapo and M. C. Miller. Oxford. 247–66.
Robinson, R. 1953. *Plato's Earlier Dialectic*. 2nd ed. Oxford.
Romilly, Jacqueline de. 1975. *Magic and Rhetoric in Ancient Greece*. Cambridge, Mass.
———. 1992. *The Great Sophists in Periclean Athens*. Oxford.
Rose, P. W. 1974. "The Myth of Pindar's First Nemean: Sportsmen, Poetry and *Paideia*." *HSCP* 78: 145–75.

Rosen, Ralph M. 1990. "Poetry and Sailing in Hesiod's *Works and Days.*" *CA* 9: 99–113.
———. 2007. *Making Mockery: The Poetics of Ancient Satire.* New York and Oxford.
Ross, W. D., ed. 1924. *Aristotle's Metaphysics.* 2 vols. Oxford.
———. 1958. *Aristotelis Fragmenta Selecta.* Oxford.
Rothwell, Kenneth. 1995. "Aristophanes' *Wasps* and the Sociopolitics of Aesop's Fables." *CJ* 93.4: 233–54.
Roux, G. 1976. *Delphes: son oracle et ses dieux.* Paris.
Rowe, C. J., ed. 1993. *Plato: Phaedo.* Cambridge.
———. 1998. *Plato: Symposium.* Warminster, England.
Russell, D. A., and N. G. Wilson, eds. 1981. *Menander Rhetor.* Oxford.
Russo, Joseph. 1997. "Prose Genres for the Performance of Traditional Wisdom in Ancient Greece: Proverb, Maxim, Apothegm." In Edmunds and Wallace 1997: 49–64, 143–49.
Rutherford, Ian. 1991. "Neoptolemus and the Paean-Cry: An Echo of a Sacred Aetiology in Pindar." *ZPE* 88: 1–10.
———. 1995. "Theoric Crisis: The Dangers of Pilgrimage in Greek Religion and Society." *Studi e Materiali di Storia delle Religioni* 61 (n.s. 19): 275–92.
———. 2001. *Pindar's Paeans: A Reading of the Fragments with a Survey of the Genre.* Oxford.
———. 2003. "The Prosodion: Approaches to a Lyric Genre." In *Studi di Filologia e Tradizione greca in memoria di Aristide Colonna,* ed. F. Benedetti and S. Grandolini. Naples. 713–26.
Rutherford, R. B. 1995. *The Art of Plato: Ten Essays in Platonic Interpretation.* Cambridge, Mass.
Sachau, E. 1911. *Aramäische Papyrus und Ostraka aus einer jüdischen Militär-Kolonie zu Elephantine.* 2 vols. Leipzig.
Sahlins, Marshall. 1985. *Islands of History.* Chicago.
Saïd, Suzanne. 2002. "Herodotus and Tragedy." In Bakker, de Jong, and van Wees 2002: 117–47.
Salis, A. von. 1947. "Imagines Illustrium." In *Eumusia: Festgabe für Ernst Howald zum sechzigsten Geburtstag am 20. April 1947.* Zürich. 11–29.
Schäfer, Alfred. 1997. *Unterhaltung beim griechischen Symposion: Darbietungen, Spiele und Wettkämpfe von homerischer bis in spätklassische Zeit.* Mainz.
Schauer, Markus, and Stefan Merkle. 1992. "Äsop und Sokrates." In Holzberg 1992: 85–96.
Schefold, Karl et al. 1997. *Die Bildnisse der antiken Dichter, Redner und Denker.* 2nd ed. Basel.
Schmid, W. and O. Stählin. 1929. *Geschichte der griechischen Literatur.* I: Die klassische Periode der griechischen Literatur. 1: Die griechische Literatur vor der attischen Hegemonie. Handbuch der Altertumswissenschaft VII, 1.1. Munich.
Schultz, F. 1866. "Die Sprüche der delphischen Saüle." *Philologus* 24: 193–226.
Schwarzbaum, Haim. 1968. *Studies in Jewish and World Folklore.* Berlin.
Scodel, Ruth. 1980. "Hesiod *Redivivus.*" *GRBS* 21: 301–20.
Scott, James C. 1990. *Domination and the Arts of Resistance.* New Haven, Conn.
Sellars, John. 2003. "Simon the Shoemaker and the Problem of Socrates." *CP* 98: 207–16.

Sewell, William H. 1999. "The Concept(s) of Culture." In Bonnell and Hunt 1999: 35-61.
Shaw, Sarah. 2006. *The Jātakas: Birth Stories of the Bodhisatta*. London, Delhi.
Shipp, George P. 1983. "Notes on the Language of *Vita Aesopi* G." *Antichthon* 17: 96-106.
Sidgwick, H. 1872. "The Sophists." *Journal of Philology* 4: 288-307.
Smith, Nicholas, and Paul Woodruff, eds. 2000. *Reason and Religion in Socratic Philosophy*. Oxford.
Smith, Paul. 1988. *Discerning the Subject*. Minneapolis, Minn.
Snell, Bruno. 1924. *Die Ausdrücke für den Begriff des Wissens in der vorplatonischen Philosophie*. Berlin.
———. 1966. *Gesammelte Schriften*. Göttingen.
———. 1966a. "Die Nachrichten über die Lehren des Thales und die Anfänge der greichischen Philosophie- und Literaturgeschichte." In Snell 1966: 119-28.
———. 1966b. "Zur Geschichte vom Gastmahl der Sieben Weisen." In Snell 1966: 115-18.
———. 1971. *Leben und Meinungen der Sieben Weisen*. 4th ed. Munich.
Snodgrass, A. 1980. *Archaic Greece: The Age of Experiment*. London.
Solin, Heikki. 1972. "Analecta epigraphica XIII: Griechische Graffiti aus Ostia." *Arctos* n.s. 7: 190-99.
Sourvinou-Inwood, C. 1990. "What Is *Polis* Religion?" In *The Greek City from Homer to Alexander*, ed. O. Murray and S. Price. Oxford. 295-322.
———. 1991. *'Reading' Greek Culture: Texts and Images, Rituals and Myths*. Oxford.
Spengel, Leonard, ed. 1853-56. *Rhetores Graeci*. 3 vols. Leipzig.
Spiegel, Gabrielle M. 1993. *Romancing the Past: The Rise of Vernacular Prose Historiography in Thirteenth-Century France*. Berkeley and Los Angeles.
Sprague, Rosamond Kent, ed. 1972. *The Older Sophists*. Columbia, S.C.
Stadter, Philip A. 1992. "Herodotus and the Athenian *Arche*." *Annali della Scuola Normale Superiore di Pisa* ser. 3, 22: 781-809.
Stahl, Michael. 1987. *Aristokraten und Tyrannen im archaischen Athen: Untersuchungen zur Überlieferung, zur Sozialstruktur und zur Entstehung des Staates*. Stuttgart.
Stallybrass, Peter, and Allon White. 1986. *The Politics and Poetics of Transgression*. Ithaca, N.Y.
Stambler, Susanna. 1982. "Herodotus." In *Ancient Writers: Greece and Rome*, ed. T. J. Luce. Vol. 1. New York. 209-32.
Stein, Heinrich, ed. 1894. *Herodotos. Dritter Band, Buch V und VI*. 5th ed. Berlin.
Steiner, Deborah. 2005. "Nautical Matters: Hesiod's *Nautilia* and Ibycus Fragment 282 PMG." *CP* 100: 347-55.
———. 2008. "Be(a)sting a Rival: The Poetics of Fable-Telling in Hesiod, Archilochus, and the Aesopica." Unpublished paper.
———. 2009. "Diverting Demons: Ritual, Poetic Mockery and the Odysseus-Iros Encounter." *CA* 28: 71-100.
Stephens, Susan A. 1994. "Who Read Ancient Novels?" In Tatum 1994: 405-18.
Sternbach, Leo. 1963. *Gnomologium Vaticanum e Codice Vaticano Graeco 743*. Berlin.
Stevens, P. T., ed. 1971. *Euripides Andromache*. Oxford.
Stokes, Michael. 1992. "Socrates' Mission." In Gower and Stokes 1992: 26-81.

Strasburger, Hermann. 1965. "Herodot und das perikleische Athen." In *Herodot: Eine Auswahl aus der neueren Forschung*, ed. W. Marg. Darmstadt. 574–608.

———. 1982. "Homer und die Geschichtsschreibung." In *Studien zur Alten Geschichte*. Band II. Hildesheim. 1057–97.

Studemund, Wilhelm. 1890. "Zum Mosaik des Monnus." *Jahrbuch des kaiserlich deutschen archäologischen Instituts*. Band V. Berlin. 1–5.

Suárez de la Torre, E. 1997. "Neoptolemos at Delphi." *Kernos* 10: 153–76.

Svenbro, J. 2002. "Syloson's Cloak and Other Greek Myths." In *Myth and Symbol I: Symbolic Phenomena in ancient Greek culture*, ed. S. des Bouvrie. Bergen. 275–86.

Swindler, Mary Hamilton. 1929. *Ancient Painting from the Earliest Times to the Period of Christian Art*. New Haven.

Szegedy-Maszak, Andrew. 1978. "Legends of the Greek Lawgivers." *GRBS* 19: 199–209.

Tallmadge, E. R. 1938. "A Grammatical Study of the Greek Life of Aesop." PhD diss., University of Illinois at Urbana-Champaign.

Tarán, Leonardo. 1966. Review of M. Untersteiner, *Aristotele. Della Filosofia*. *AJP* 87: 464–72.

Tarrant, Dorothy, ed. 1928. *The Hippias Maior Attributed to Plato*. Cambridge.

Tatum, James, ed. 1994. *The Search for the Ancient Novel*. Baltimore, Md.

———. 1997. "Herodotus the Fabulist." In *Der antike Roman und seine mittelalterliche Rezeption*, ed. M. Picone and B. Zimmermann. Basel, Boston. 29–48.

Tawney, C. H. 1883. "Indian Folklore Notes from the Pali Játakas and the Kathá Sarit Ságara." *Journal of Philology* 12: 112–26.

Tell, Håkan. 2003. "The Sources of Sophistic Authority: A Sociological Analysis." PhD diss., University of California, Berkeley.

———. 2010. *Plato's Counterfeit Sophists*. Cambridge, Mass., and London.

Temple, Olivia, and Robert Temple, trans. 1998. *Aesop: The Complete Fables*. London.

Thomas, Rosalind. 1989. *Oral Tradition and Written Record in Classical Athens*. Cambridge.

———. 1993. "Performance and Written Publication in Herodotus and the Sophistic Generation." In *Vermittlung und Tradierung von Wissen in der griechischen Kultur*, ed. W. Kullmann and J. Althoff. Tübingen. 225–44.

———. 1997. "Ethnography, Proof and Argument in Herodotus' *Histories*." *PCPS* 43:128–48.

———. 2000. *Herodotus in Context: Ethnography, Science and the Art of Persuasion*. Cambridge.

———. 2006. "The Intellectual Milieu of Herodotus." In Dewald and Marincola 2006: 60–75.

Too, Yun Lee, ed. 2001. *Education in Greek and Roman Antiquity*. Leiden.

Trapp, Michael. 1987. "Protagoras and the Great Tradition." In *Homo Viator: Classical Essays for John Bramble*, ed. M. Whitby, P. Hardie, and M. Whitby. Bristol. 41–48.

Tredennick, Hugh, trans. 1980. *Aristotle in Twenty-Three Volumes*. Vol. 17, *The Metaphysics Books I–IX*. Cambridge, Mass.

Trenkner, Sophie. 1958. *The Greek Novella in the Classical Period*. Cambridge.

Treu, M. 1889. "Griechische Sprichwörter." *Philologus* 47 (= n.f. 1): 193–201.

Tuplin, C. J. 1985. "Imperial Tyranny: Some Reflections on a Classical Greek Political Metaphor." In *Crux: Essays Presented to G.E.M. de Ste. Croix on his 75th Birthday*, ed. P. A. Cartledge and F. D. Harvey. Exeter and London. 348–75.

Untersteiner, Mario. 1954. *The Sophists*. Trans. K. Freeman. Oxford.
———. ed. 1963. *Aristotele. Della filosofia*. Rome.
Usener, H. 1903. "Dreiheit." *RhM* 58: 1–47, 161–208, 321–62.
Uther, Hans-Jörg. 2004. *The Types of International Folktales: A Classification and Bibliography Based on the System of Antti Aarne and Stith Thompson*. 3 vols. Helsinki.
Vander Waerdt, Paul A. 1994a. "Introduction." In Vander Waerdt 1994: 1–19.
———. ed. 1994. *The Socratic Movement*. Ithaca, N.Y.
Vansina, Jan. 1985. *Oral Tradition as History*. Madison, Wisc.
Vernant, Jean-Pierre. 1982. *The Origins of Greek Thought*. Ithaca, N.Y.
———. 1983. "Hestia-Hermes: The Religious Expression of Space and Movement in Ancient Greece." In *Myth and Thought among the Greeks*. London and Boston. 127–75.
———. 1988. "Ambiguity and Reversal: On the Enigmatic Structure of *Oedipus Rex*." In Vernant and Vidal-Naquet 1988: 113–40.
Vernant, Jean-Pierre, and Pierre Vidal-Naquet. 1988. *Myth and Tragedy in Ancient Greece*. Trans. J. Lloyd. New York.
Vilatte, Sylvie. 1990. "Idéologie et action tyranniques a Samos: Le territoire, les hommes." *Revue des Études Anciennes* 92: 3–15.
Vlastos, Gregory. 1981. "The Individual as an Object of Love in Plato." In *Platonic Studies*. 2nd ed. Princeton, N.J. 5–34.
———. 1994. *Socratic Studies*. Cambridge.
Wallace, Robert W. 1998. The Sophists in Athens." In *Democracy, Empire, and the Arts in Fifth-Century Athens*, ed. D. Boedeker and K. Raaflaub. Cambridge, Mass. 203–22, 392–95.
Warner, Rex, trans. 1972. *Thucydides: History of the Peloponnesian War*. London.
Warren, S. J. 1894. "Herodot VI 126." *Hermes* 29: 476–78.
Webb, Ruth. 2001. "The *Progymnasmata* as Practice." In Too 2001: 289–316.
Wehrli, Fritz. 1973. "Gnome, Anekdote und Biographie." *MH* 30: 193–208.
Welcker, F. G. 1833. "Prodikos von Keos, Vorgänger des Sokrates." *RhM* 1: 533–643.
West, M. L. 1967. "The Contest of Homer and Hesiod." *CQ* n.s. 17: 433–51.
———. 1969. "The Sayings of Democritus." *CR* n.s. 19: 142.
———. 1974. *Studies in Greek Elegy and Iambus*. Berlin, New York.
———. ed. 1978. *Hesiod Works and Days*. Oxford.
———. 1984. "The Ascription of Fables to Aesop in Archaic and Classical Greece." In *La Fable*. Fondation Hardt pour l'étude de l'antiquité classique. Entretiens 30, ed. F. R. Adrados and O. Reverdin. Geneva. 105–36.
———. 1985. Review of R. Parker, *Miasma*. *CR* 35: 94.
———. trans. 1988. *Hesiod Theogony and Works & Days*. Oxford.
———, ed. 1989. *Iambi et Elegi Graeci*. 2nd ed. Vol. 1. Oxford.
———, ed. 1992. *Iambi et Elegi Graeci*. 2nd ed. Vol. 2. Oxford.
———. 1997. *The East Face of Helicon: West Asiatic Elements in Greek Poetry and Myth*. Oxford.
West, Stephanie. 1985. "Herodotus' Use of Inscriptions." *CQ* 35: 278–305.
———. 1991. "Herodotus' Portrait of Hecataeus." *JHS* 111: 144–60.
———. 2003. "Croesus' Second Reprieve and Other Tales of the Persian Court." *CQ* 53: 416–37.
Westerink, L. G., ed. 1970. *Olympiodori in Platonis Gorgiam Commentaria*. Leipzig.

White, Robert J., trans. 1975. *The Interpretation of Dreams: Oneirocritica by Artemidorus*. Park Ridge, N.J.
White, Stephen A. 2000. "Socrates at Colonus: A Hero for the Academy." In Smith and Woodruff 2000: 151-75.
Wiechers, Anton. 1961. *Aesop in Delphi*. Beiträge zur klassischen Philologie. Heft 2. Meisenheim am Glan.
Wiersma, W. 1933-34. "The Seven Sages and the Prize of Wisdom." *Mnemosyne* 3rd ser. 1: 150-54.
Wilamowitz-Moellendorff, U. von. 1879. "Phaidon von Elis." *Hermes* 14: 187-89, 476-77.
———. 1890. "Zu Plutarchs Gastmahl der sieben Weisen." *Hermes* 25: 196-227.
———. 1913. *Sappho und Simonides: Untersuchungen über griechische Lyriker*. Berlin.
———. 1916. *Die Ilias und Homer*. Berlin.
———. 1922. *Pindaros*. Berlin.
———. 1925. "Lesefrüchte." *Hermes* 60: 280-316.
———. ed. 1928. *Hesiodos Erga*. Berlin.
Wills, Lawrence M. 1997. *The Quest of the Historical Gospel: Mark, John, and the Origins of the Gospel Genre*. London and New York.
Wilsdorf, Helmut. 1991. "Der weise Achikaros bei Demokrit und Theophrast: Eine Kommunikationsfrage." *Philologus* 135: 191-206.
Wilson, Peter. 1999. "The *Aulos* in Athens." In *Performance Culture and Athenian Democracy*, ed. S. Goldhill and R. Osborne. Cambridge. 58-95.
Winkler, J. J. 1985. *Auctor & Actor: A Narratological Reading of Apuleius's Golden Ass*. Berkeley and Los Angeles.
———. 1990. "Laying Down the Law: The Oversight of Men's Sexual Behavior in Classical Athens." In *The Constraints of Desire: The Anthropology of Sex and Gender in Ancient Greece*. New York and London. 45-70.
Wölke, H. 1978. *Untersuchungen zur Batrachomyomachie*. Beiträge zur Klassische Philologie 100. Meisenheim.
Wolz, Henry G. 1963. "The *Protagoras* Myth and the Philosopher-Kings." *Review of Metaphysics* 17: 214-34.
Woodbury, Leonard. 1968. "Pindar and the Mercenary Muse: Isthm. 2.1-13." *TAPA* 99: 527-42.
———. 1985. "Ibycus and Polycrates." *Phoenix* 39: 193-220.
Woodman, A. J. 1988. *Rhetoric in Classical Historiography: Four Studies*. London and Sydney.
Woodruff, Paul, trans. 1982a. *Plato. Hippias Major*. Indianapolis and Cambridge.
———. 1982b. "What Could Go Wrong with Inspiration? Why Plato's Poets Fail." In Moravcsik and Temko 1982: 137-50.
Worman, Nancy. 2008. *Abusive Mouths in Classical Athens*. Cambridge.
Worthington, Ian. 1991. "Greek Oratory, Revision of Speeches and the Problem of Historical Reliability." *Classica et Mediaevalia* 42: 55-74.
Wright, W. C., trans. 1968. *Philostratus and Eunapius, The Lives of the Sophists*. Cambridge, Mass.
Zafiropoulos, Christos A. 2001. *Ethics in Aesop's Fables: The Augustana Collection*. Leiden.

Zeitlin, Froma I. 1996. "The Dynamics of Misogyny: Myth and Mythmaking in Aeschylus's Oresteia." In *Playing the Other: Gender and Society in Classical Greek Literature*. Chicago. 87–119.
Zeitz, Heinrich. 1936. "Der Aesoproman und seine Geschichte." *Aegyptus* 16: 225–56.
Zeller, E. 1889. *Die Philosophie der Griechen*. 4th ed. Vol. 2, pt. 1. Leipzig.

INDEX LOCORUM

Note: Corpora of inscriptions and papyri are indexed by abbreviations (as in List of Abbreviations, or as in the third edition of the *Oxford Classical Dictionary*); names of authors and titles are given in full.

Aelian
  On the Nature of Animals
    3.9   209n18
  Varia Historia
    2.26   109n43
    9.24   418n52
    10.5   224n52
    12.24   418n52

Aeschylus
  Agamemnon
    468–71, 946–47   122n81
    717–36   243n6
  Eumenides   65
    614–21   61n26
  Myrmidons
    fr. 139 Radt   243n6, 396
  Persians 362   122n81
  Prometheus Bound
    442–506   161–62, 165n13
    454–56, 462–65   165n14
    484–99   168n20
    859   122n81

Aesop
  Fables (Hausrath)
    283   129n11
    288   129n11
  Fables (Perry)
    4   129n9
    7   129n9
    11   145n45, 400–404
    12   129n9
    17   129n9
    19   129n9
    20   129n9, 129n11
    29   129n9, 129n11
    33   129n9
    40   269n18
    62   129n9
    64   129n9, 129n11
    85   223–24
    89   129n9
    93   129n9, 129n11
    100   305n9
    103   306–8
    108   306–8
    109   306–8
    111   272n28
    114   129n9, 129n11
    122   129n9
    125   129n9
    134   129n9, 129n11
    137   129n9
    145   129n9
    154   129n9
    156   129n9, 129n11
    160   129n9
    164   335n29
    175   129n9, 129n11
    179   335n29
    180   335n29
    181   335n29
    182   335n29
    183   335n29
    185   335n29
    189   335n29
    200   129n9, 129n11
    205   129n9
    215   129n9, 129n11
    222   129n9, 129n11
    223   129n9, 129n11
    225   279–82
    227   129n9, 129n11
    229   129n9, 129n11
    236   129n9
    237   129n9, 129n11
    238   129n9
    239   129n9, 129n11
    240   305–6
    242   129n9
    243   129n9
    252   129n9, 129n11
    259   305–6n9
    263   335n29

266	398n4		
279	335n29		
348	152–53, 412		
356	292–93, 297–98		
357	335n29		
384	88, 394–95		
389	412n33		
411	335n29		
458	335n29		

Proverbs (Perry)
107	140n34

Testimonia (Perry)
1	13n35
2	160n3
5–6	202n1, 396n109
21	29–30, 68n43, 71–72, 91, 211–12
23	72n51, 111n49, 137n28, 237n85
24	92, 137n28
25	5, 68n43, 72–73, 90–91, 93, 189, 211–12
26	72n51
27	190
29	62n28
33	32n94, 125–26n1, 137n28, 356
34	104n25, 131, 351, 389
35	32n92, 131, 351, 389
37	137–38, 236n83, 351, 389
45	21, 189–90, 396–97
46	137n28, 190n78
50	32n94, 131–32, 135, 202, 389
53	157n73
57, 58	11n31
62	1–2, 86n94, 395n103
64, 65	14n41, 396–97
70	20–21, 44n132, 397n112
74	21, 44
75	44n133
85–92	43, 135n23, 243n6, 320–22, 396
97	271n24
98	14n41
101	396n107
102	43n130

Agathias
Palatine Anthology
16.332	32n94, 131–32, 135, 202, 389

Alexander of Aphrodisias
Commentary on Aristotle
1.818.3 Hayduck	138–39, 387–88

Alexander Romance   10n24

Alexis
Aesop fr. 9 *KA*   32n94, 125–26n1, 137n28, 356

Anacharsis
Apophthegmata (Kindstrand)
A20A–G	218–19n41
A26A–B, A27A–H	218n40

Anacreon
fr. 417 *PMG*   348

Anonymous Iamblichi (89 DK)
7.1, 2, 8 DK   281–82

Antiphon (87 DK)
B 54 DK   270–71, 279–82, 287–88

Aphthonius
Fable 33 (Hausrath)   401

Aphthonius
Progymnasmata 2.21 Spengel   43n130

Apollodorus
Bibliotheca 1.4.2   337n35
Epitome
5.21	79n71
6.14	79n72

Apuleius
Golden Ass 9.8   171n29

Aratus
Phaenomena 949, 1022   209n18

Archilochus
fr. 114 W	336n32
frr. 172–81 W	88n105

Arctinus
Iliou Persis arg. 13–14 Bernabé   79n71

Aristophanes
Acharnians 1072–1227   345–46, 356
Birds
471–72	20–21, 44n132, 397n112
471–75	43n128
651–53	397n112
837–45, 1125–51	177–78n46

Frogs   114–15
Gerytades fr. 150 Kock   115
Peace 129–31   254n30, 397n112
Wasps
566	157n73
835–62	177n46
1258–59	254n30, 396

INDEX LOCORUM   465

1341–50	334n26	2.20.6, 1393a22–94a1	32n94, 150n56, 202, 255–56
1393–1400	254n30		
1427–40	397n112		
1446–48	3n5, 6–7, 37, 53, 397n112	2.20.7–8, 1394a2–8	156–57, 194–96, 244, 256–57, 299–300
fr. 705 KA	74		

Aristotle
Eudemian Ethics 1214a5	350n66	2.20.9, 1394a9–16	150–51n58
Metaphysics			
1.2, 982a–83a	121–23	2.21, 1394b8–34	130n14
1.2, 982b	120n77	Book 3	267–68
14.3, 1091a5–9	138–41, 303–4, 387–88	3.1.9, 1404a28–35	86n94
		3.14.10–11, 1415b22–24	139n32, 304n6, 387–88
Meteorologica 356b11	254n30		
Nicomachean Ethics		3.18, 1419b3	276
1.9, 1099a25	350n66	fr. 29 Gigon	109n45
4.2, 1122a18–23a34	317–18n33	fr. 487 Rose = frr. 494, 1, 2, 3 Gigon	190n79
6.3, 1139b	115–16	fr. 573 Rose = fr. 591, 1 Gigon	202n1
6.4–5, 1140a–b	116	fr. 862 Gigon	264n55
6.7, 1141a–b	96–97n2, 98n8, 116–20		

[Aristotle]
Athenaiōn Politeia 11.1		112n58

Arrian
9.9, 1170a11–13	216n34	
9.12, 1172a12–14	216n34	
Anabasis 2.16.5, 3.30.8		376n62, 376–77n64

On Philosophy
fr. 8 Ross = fr. 463 Gigon	95–97, 140–41	

Artemidorus
Oneirocritica 5.3		221n43

Athenaeus

Poetics
1, 1447a28–b13	254n31, 257

Deipnosophistae
4.173b–e	74
6.273b–c	418n52
11.504e–9e	258–59
12.541b–c	418n52
14.625c	349n64
15.695c–d	347–48

4.18–19, 1449a23–28	86n94
5, 1449a32–b24	257

Politics
1.2.9–11, 1253a1–18	163–65, 188n72
1.11, 1259a6–19	119, 168
3.13, 1284a15–17	268n14

Babrius
Fables (Perry 1965)	44
9	401
95	45n137, 154–56, 412n33
103	412n33
128	292n81

Rhetoric
1.9, 1367b37–39	273n31
2.20, 1393a–94a	254n30, 255–57, 299–300, 332

Bacchylides
Ode 3.85–92	349n64

Batrachomyomachia
9–121	88n104, 393–95
303	395

2.20.4, 1393b4–8	255–56
2.20.5, 1393b8–22	150, 154, 156, 255–56

Callimachus
Iamb 1 (fr. 191 Pfeiffer) 68n43
  26–28 72n51
  32–77 111n49, 237n85
Iamb 2 (fr. 192 Pfeiffer)
  15–17 72n51, 111n49, 137n28, 237n85

Carmina Convivialia
  890 *PMG* 350
  900, 901 *PMG* 347–48

Cicero
De Legibus 1.1.5 398, 431
De Oratore 2.69.280 171n28
On Fate 5.7 329n15

CID
no. 8 (Phaselis) 56n10
no. 13 (Sciathos) 56, 73

Clement of Alexandria
Stromateis
  1.14.60.3 109n45
  1.15.69 35n103, 177, 182n61
  5.572 216

Comica Adespota
  fr. 460 Kock 56–57n14

Conon (*FGrH* 26)
F 1, l. 42 150n57

Contest of Homer and Hesiod (ed. Allen)
  20–21
  121–23 351n68
  170–71 145n44

Cratinus
Cheirons
  frr. 246–68 KA 356n80

Critias (88 DK) 266–67

Democritus (68 DK)
  A 138 DK 168n20
  B 299 DK 177n44

Demosthenes
Orations
  19.252 142n41
  21.180, 185 354

[Demosthenes]
Orations
  25.40, 26.22 156n72

Dio Chrysostom
Oration 1.66–84 278–79n51

Diodorus Siculus
Bibliotheca
  1.96.2–3 112n57
  3.59 337n35
  8.19 418n52
  9.13.2 111n49
  9.26–28 104n25, 131, 351, 389
  9.35 404n19
  12.11.1 112n57

Diogenes Laertius
Lives of the Eminent Philosophers
Book 1 124n85, 203n6
  1.24, 27, 89, 101 112n57
  1.25 127n3, 142n41, 145
  1.28–33 111n49, 237n85
  1.30 111n53
  1.35–36 104n25
  1.39 113, 120
  1.40 125n1, 131n17
  1.46 142n41
  1.50 112n58
  1.58 145
  1.69 137n28
  1.72 113
  1.75 175n38
  1.77 104n25
  1.79 144–45
  1.82 111n49
  1.83–84 127n3
  1.86–87 104n25
  1.92, 97 235n79
  1.103 218n40, 235n79
  1.104 235
  1.105 218–19n41
  1.106 111n53
  1.110 224n50
  1.117–18 113–14
Book 2
  2.19, 21 329n15
  2.23 327n6
  2.105 258n41
  2.122–23 258, 337n36
Book 3
  3.5 264
  3.9–17 258
  3.18 264
  3.37 264n55
Book 5
  5.50 35n103, 177

INDEX LOCORUM 467

5.80	21, 44		165n14, 168n20
Book 6		348	122n81
6.29, 30, 36	207n14, 355n79	*Trojan Women*	
6.40	139	15–17, 481–83	79n71
6.45	207–8	1106	66n39
Book 8		**Gorgias** (82 DK)	
8.2–3	112n57	A 24 DK	355
8.8, 11, 21	109n43	**Heliodorus**	
Book 9		*Aethiopica*	
9.55	288n70	2.34–3.6	79n71, 82n81

Dionysius of Halicarnassus
Letter to Pompeius 3   382
Roman Antiquities
6.87, 7.16   129n10

Ephorus (*FGrH* 70)
F 181   125n1

Etymologicum Magnum
722.16–17 Gaisford   106n33

Euphorion
fr. 89 Powell   209n18

Eupolis
Dēmoi
frr. 99–146 KA   356n80

Euripides

Alcestis 1135		122n81	
Andromache			
51–53		79n72	
448		388	
1002–3, 1092–95, 1107–8		79n72	
Electra 371		281n56	
Hecuba 23–24		79n71	
Heracles 637–700		115n64	
Ion			
4		66n39	
226–29		56n10, 56n12	
Iphigeneia in Aulis			
313		139n32	
1097		122n81	
Iphigeneia in Tauris			
1115		66n39	
1234–82		64–66, 168n21	
Orestes			
974		122n81	
1656–57		79n72	
Suppliants			
198–213		161–62, 165n13,	

3.10   82n81

Heraclitus (22 DK)
B 93 DK   111, 343n50

Hermogenes
Progymnasmata 2.7 Spengel   295n91

Herodotus
Histories
Book 1

1.1.1	365–67, 372n45
1.11	130n12
1.27	126–36, 147n47, 273, 275n34, 339n39, 400, 405–8, 410–12, 420, 428–31
1.29–33	103–4, 112–14, 136, 147, 350–51, 373, 377–78, 408n23, 409n25, 430
1.29	103–4, 105n32, 126
1.30	134–35, 137, 350–51, 428
1.31	273
1.32	122
1.47–49	57n16
1.50–52	57–58
1.54	58
1.59	120n77, 146–47, 172
1.60–61	426n73
1.65–66	109n43, 113–14, 175n38
1.68	120n77
1.71	407n21
1.74–75	119
1.87	351n68
1.125	398
1.141	130n15, 145n45, 254n30, 381n78, 398, 400–404, 430n82
1.158–59	398
1.169–70	119, 146–47, 172, 174n34, 380

Book 2
2.2   165n12

468 INDEX LOCORUM

2.49	103, 104n26	7.148–52	388, 398n4, 399n6
2.121	390–91	7.225	367
2.134–35	3, 6–7, 15, 47, 53, 76, 91–92, 130n15, 135n24, 242, 370–72, 377, 381, 396–97n109, 421	7.226	298n74
		Book 8	
		8.122	385
		Book 9	
2.143	371, 377–78	9.94	130n12
2.162	390–91	9.120–21	402–4
2.172	390		

Herondas

Mimiambi	8n18
5.14	137n29

Book 3

3.14	91–92
3.21	407n21
3.36	178n46
3.40	122n81
3.46	398
3.139–49	369, 412n34
3.142–43	412

Hesiod

Theogony

27–28	321n41
94–95	108
154–200	248
820–80	65
886–906	100n15
901–3	278n51, 279

Book 4

4.3	127n4
4.76	112n57
4.95–96	103, 105n32
4.131–32	398

Works & Days

47–201	288n70, 289
180–201	287n68
202–12	403
217–18	3, 243, 403–4
263	403
274–80	404
286–382	403–4
287–92	277–78
	147–48, 272, 295–96, 409–10
455	281
618–94	106nn34–35, 107n37
648–62	106, 167
702–3	215n32
724–64	204–12
727–32	205–8
746–47	208–10
755–56	210–12
757–58	205
770–71	108
794–800, 809, 819–20	108n41
fr. 306 MW	98n7

Book 5

5.18	386n87
5.36	371, 378–79
5.78	428
5.80	127n4
5.92	398
5.124–25	371, 378–80

Book 6

6.86	398, 399n6
6.121–31	388–89, 413–26
6.121–23	423–24
6.125	413, 417–18, 424–25
6.126–30	413–23
6.127	418–19, 425n72
6.128	413–14, 418n52
6.129–30	130n12, 305n8, 414–23
6.137	377
6.139	130n12

Hesychius

Lexicon ι 324 Latte	90

Hippias (86 DK)

B 6 DK	267

Hipponax

frr. 5–10 W	85n91, 86, 87n98
fr. 12 W	86

Book 7

7.10	122n81
7.26	337n35
7.46	122n81
7.61–99	367, 411
7.99	392
7.101–4	130n12, 407–12, 420
7.133–37	91–92
7.139	428
7.141–43	172–74
7.147	130n12

INDEX LOCORUM 469

fr. 41 W 87n98
fr. 70 W 86
fr. 118 W 86, 90n111
fr. 128 W 86
frr. 152, 153 W 87n98

Homer
Iliad
2.188–277 354
6.146 69, 72n50, 86–87
12.41–42 151–52
15.411–12 96n1, 98–101
22.8–20 79n73
23.712 96n1
Odyssey
11.368 385, 389
14.457–522 243n5, 374, 401–2
19.203 321n41

Homeric Hymns
Hymn to Apollo (III)
51–60 68–69
131–32 60
165–72 128n5
300–374 65
388–99 67, 73–74n54
453–55 73–74n54
528–37 67–68
Hymn to Hermes (IV)
94–175 2n2
330 73
335 73, 79
494–95 73
511 98n7
528–40 60–61
543–49 73

Horace
Satire I.1.47–49 193n86

Hyginus
Fabulae 165 337n35

***IG* XII.3,** no. 1020 110n47

IK Estremo oriente no. 382 109–10, 180–82

Iamblichus
On the Pythagorean Way of Life
11–19 112n57
30 109n43
83 104n25, 137n29, 347n59
140 109n43

Ibycus
fr. 282a *PMG*, ll. 23–24 107n37, 167

Isocrates
Oration 4 (Panegyricus) 118
Oration 5 (To Philip) 75, 109 376n62
Oration 9 (Evagoras) 71–72 350–51n67
Oration 10 (Helen) 12 309n15
Oration 11 (Busiris)
28 112n57
37 376n62
Oration 16 (On the Team of Horses) 25–28 423–24

Istrus (*FGrH* 344)
F 50 85n91

Julian
Oration 7.207 11n31

Libanius
Defense of Socrates 181 62n28

Life of Aesop
Codex Vindobonensis theol. gr. 128 181–82
Vita Accursiana (= Planudean *Life*, ed. Eberhard 1872)
p. 228 160n3
Vita G (ed. Perry)
ch. 1 4, 353
ch. 2 160, 191
ch. 3 191–92, 196–97, 200n98, 358–60
ch. 4 165–66
ch. 6 62–63, 164n11
ch. 7 4–5, 35–37, 62–63, 135n23, 136, 162–65, 167, 192
ch. 8 164n11
ch. 9 62–64, 163–64
chs. 10, 11 137
ch. 13 63
ch. 14 137, 353
ch. 15 164n11
ch. 16 137, 353
chs. 17–19 192–93
chs. 21–100 5, 12n33, 18n55, 159–76, 360
chs. 22–27 5
ch. 25 224n52
ch. 26 140n34, 335–36
ch. 28 207–8, 354–55
ch. 30 137, 353
ch. 32 137, 149n52, 160–61n4

470 INDEX LOCORUM

ch. 33	61–66, 168	ch. 131	186–87, 213–17, 224
chs. 35–37	38	chs. 132–33	87–88, 188–89, 394n102
chs. 39–41	352n71	ch. 134	37, 193n86
chs. 42–43	352n71	chs. 134–39	88–89
chs. 47–48	223–24	ch. 139	37, 66–67, 188–89, 193n86
ch. 50	140n34	ch. 140	89
chs. 51–55	165n13, 219–23, 352n71	ch. 141	89–90
ch. 62	161n4	ch. 142	18n54, 62, 66–67, 85n91, 92–93, 188–89, 199–200, 343n50, 359–60
ch. 66	139		
ch. 67	235n80		
chs. 68–73	217–18, 353		
ch. 77	66, 168–69, 209–10		
chs. 78–80	38, 66, 169–71, 198, 335n30	*Vita* W (ed. Westermann)	
		chs. 1–100	161, 184n66
ch. 81	142n42, 171	ch. 2	160nn2–3, 191
chs. 81–85	171–72, 174, 198	ch. 3	192n83, 193n86
chs. 81–91	66, 169–74, 189, 192, 197–98, 343, 359–60	ch. 7	37n112, 63n31, 164n11
		ch. 9	164n11
chs. 87–100	33, 38, 137, 172–76	ch. 19	192–93
		ch. 28	207–8
chs. 87–97	142–56	ch. 48	223–24
ch. 88	38, 137, 143–45, 160–61, 174, 184n66, 197–98	ch. 53	162n9, 165n13
		ch. 66	139–40
		ch. 77	209
ch. 90	143	chs. 77a, b	169n22
ch. 93	132, 137, 143, 150, 410	chs. 78–80	169n23, 171n30
		chs. 83–85	13n35, 198n93
chs. 94–95	143, 147–48, 288n69, 410	ch. 89	197
		ch. 90	198n93
chs. 96–97	144, 147–56, 192	ch. 99	134nn20–21
ch. 98	132–33, 144	ch. 100	175
ch. 99	132–34, 137	chs. 101–23	184n66
ch. 100	36, 62n29, 66, 174–75, 337	ch. 110	181
		ch. 124	69
chs. 101–23	5, 33–35, 38, 176–85, 360	ch. 130	213n27
		ch. 132	87–88
chs. 103–4	183–84	chs. 134–39	37, 89n106
chs. 109–10	181, 183	ch. 140	89
chs. 116–22	184, 189, 359–60	ch. 141	89–90
ch. 123	36, 184	ch. 142	5, 67, 92–93, 182n61, 189, 200n97
chs. 124–42	5, 12n33, 37–38, 47, 53–54, 85–93, 185–90, 210–12, 360		
		Vitae G + W	
		chs. 1–100	159–76, 185, 369
ch. 124	69, 72n50, 86, 187	ch. 2	160
ch. 126	70–71	chs. 2–3	191–92, 196–97
ch. 127	62n29, 188n72	ch. 4	165
ch. 130	186, 213	ch. 8	163–65

INDEX LOCORUM 471

chs. 17–19	192–93
ch. 25	224n52
ch. 28	207–8
chs. 34–37	165–68, 354n75
chs. 42–43	193n86
chs. 47–48	223–24
chs. 51–55	165n13, 219–23
ch. 65	18n53, 139
chs. 68–73	217–18
ch. 77	209–10
chs. 81–82	142
chs. 81–90	169
chs. 87–100	33–35, 125, 132–34, 142–56, 159, 179, 197–98
chs. 87–88	133
ch. 93	11n31
chs. 95–96	132
chs. 98–100	127, 142–43
chs. 101–23	14n42, 33–35, 159–60, 176–85
chs. 109–110	180–82
chs. 116–22	198–99
chs. 124–42	29–31, 37–38, 47, 53–54, 85–93, 159–60, 179, 185–90, 210–12
ch. 124	69
ch. 125	69, 86–87, 187
ch. 126	70, 86–87
ch. 127	87
ch. 129	87n99, 187
ch. 130	87, 213
ch. 131	87, 187, 213–17, 224
ch. 133	88, 394
chs. 134–39	7, 53
ch. 138	89
ch. 140	70, 187
ch. 142	92, 185–86n68
Vitae Minores 1	13n35

(For fragments of the *Life* on papyrus, see under *P.Berol.* inv. 11628, *P.Oxy.* 2083, 3331, 3720, *P.Ross.Georg.* I.18, *PSI* II 156.)

[Longinus]
On the Sublime
4.7	383–84n83, 386n87
13.3	262n51, 383–84
43.1	383–84n83

Lucian
Dialogues of the Dead 20.3   109n43
Phalaris II.8   72n50

Lysias
Oration 16   289

Machon
Chreiai   8n18
l. 216 Gow   128n8

Menander Rhetor
Treatise I.353–59   70n46

Moschion
fr. 814 N²   165n13

Nicolaus
Progymnasmata 3.453 Spengel   43n130

Ovid
Fasti 6.703–8   337n35
Metamorphoses 6.382–91   337n35

P.Berol. inv. 11628   7, 17–18, 36n108

P.Oxy. 1800   5, 68n43, 72–73, 90–91, 93, 189, 211–12
P.Oxy. 2083   7, 17, 36n108
P.Oxy. 3331   7, 17
P.Oxy. 3720   7, 17, 180–82, 184n66

P.Ross.Georg. I.18   7, 17, 36n108, 87n98, 88n101, 200n97, 213

P.Rylands 493   44n133

PSI II 156   7, 17
PSI IX 1094   72–73n51

Paroemia Graeca (Leutsch-Schneidewin)
I.18	190
I.122	137–38, 236n83, 351, 389
I.393, no. 94	56
I.393, no. 95	56–57n14
II.193	158n76

Pausanias
Description of Greece
1.4.4	82n81
2.5.5	79n72
2.22.9	337n35
3.16.4	114, 175n38
4.17.4	79n71
10.7.1	79n72
10.24.1	109n44
10.24.6	82n81
10.27.1	79n71

Petronius
Satyricon
47   235n80
111–12   87n99

Phaedrus
Fables   44
Book 1   44n133
Book 3.*Prol.* 33–37   11n31

Pherecydes (*FGrH* 3)
F 64a   76n62

Philodamus
Paean (no. 39 Käppel), ll. 113–14   83

Philogelos   10n24

Philoponus
Commentary on Aristotle's Nicomachean Ethics 1.1   95–98, 101, 140–41n36, 162

Philostratus
Life of Apollonius of Tyana
1.23   402
5.15   1–2, 86n94, 395n103
Lives of the Sophists
1.482–83   274–76, 279, 286, 355
1.494–95   304n6, 308n14
1.496   271n26
1.500   280–81

[Phocylides]
Sententiae 122–31   107n37

Photius
Bibliotheca 252   190n78

Pindar
Isthmian Odes
I.5.28–35   103, 105n32
I.6.22–27   392n100
I.7.18   105–6
I.7.39   122n81
I.8.22–24   82
Nemean Odes
N.7   77–84
N.7.23   105–6
N.7.40–43   80–81
N.7.44–48   81–84
N.8.8–12   82
N.8.37–39   349n64
Olympian Odes
O.1.1–3   349n64
O.1.116   105–6
O.9.38   98n7, 105–6
Paeans
Paean 6   77–84
Paean 6.60–62   82–83
Paean 6.79–86   77–78, 84–85n90
Paean 6.86–111 80n74
Paean 6.109–22 78–80, 222
Paean 7B.20   105–6
Pythian Odes
P.1.12   105–6
P.1.26   120n77
P.4.5–10   57n16
P.4.248   105–6
P.6.49   98n7, 105–6
P.7   424–25
P.8.61–62   58
P.10.20   122n81
P.10.30   120n77
P.11.50–58   351n67

Plato
Alcibiades I   36, 299n98
106b   328n8
120e6–24b5   278n50, 329n15
123a   43n128, 268, 291–92
133b–c   328n11
Apology   111–12, 294, 327–28
17b–c   322n44
19e–20c   266
20e–21a   111–12, 327, 343n50
21a–b   111–12
22a6   112n57, 327
22c6–8   328n7
23c1–30a6–7   327n5
23c1   112n54, 327n5
27e   335n27
30e5   256n36
31c2–3   329n15
39c–d   256n36
39e–41d   328–29
Crito 52b–c   327
Euthydemus   340–41
285c9–d1   337
Gorgias   294, 341–44, 359
449b–c, 461d–62a 328n8
471e2–7   343
472b6–c1   343–44, 360
489c   353n73

INDEX LOCORUM 473

491a1–3	332	241e	260n47
502d5–8	334n25	248a–d, 249a, c	328
516a	335n27	259b–d	268
517e2	337n36	260c	335n27
523a–27e	328, 359	273a	21
Hippias Major	344–58	*Protagoras*	36, 286n66, 279,
281b–c	119, 346–47		282–88, 299n98,
285e	346–47n58		301–8
286a–b	266, 275n35,	316c5	306n10
	347	316d–e	107–8, 303, 329
286c	353	318d–19a	301–2, 303n3
286d–88c	347–48	320b–c1	282, 313
288c10–11	351	320c–24d	1n1, 45, 161–62,
288d	352–53		254n32, 269, 279,
289d–90b	348–49, 353		282–88, 301,
290d7–9	352		305–8
290e–91b	352–53	320c	130n12, 286–87,
291d–e	349–51		302
292a–b	354–55	322a–23a	165n12, 165n14
292c5–8	356–57	322d6–24d1	287–88
304c2	327n6	324d6–7	287, 313, 314n26
304d–e	357–58	325c6–d1	302
Hippias Minor 368c–d	266, 357n81	325d–26b	302
Ion	298n96	326b6–e1	302n1
Laws		334e4–35c1	340
642d	224n50	335a–36b	328n8
698a–701c	260n46	336c–d	308n14
701d	335n27	338e–39a	303
Lysis 212d–e	348n62	339b–47a	122, 358n83
Meno		340d1–5	272n27, 277n44
80b4–7	327n6	342a–43c	328
84b–d	359	343a–b	102n21, 109,
95d6	216		140–41, 235
Phaedo	36, 329n12	343b7	358n83
60b–61b	15, 26, 47, 202,	347c–48a	304–5, 334n26
	217, 242,	361d4	306n10
	251–55, 259–60,	*Republic*	
	263–64, 266n7	Books 2, 3, and 10	247–50
60c	43n128, 268	2.363e6–64a1	248
60c8–9	130n12, 251,	2.366e7–9	248
	253–54	2.377b–c	248, 302n2
61b5–7	196n91, 252n27,	2.377d–78a	248
	322n44	3.392d–e	248–49
66c	320n38	3.393c8–9	249
84e–85b	112n54, 327	3.394b8–c5	249–50
107d–14d	328–29	6.486a–503c	317–18n33
114c	328n11	7.563c	335n27
117b6–7	291n79	8.565d–66a	153n66
Phaedrus		10.595a	250
230d1–5	327n6	10.607b	246, 250
238d2–3	357n81	10.614b–21b	115n65, 328–29

Sophist
  227a3–5   332n23
  230b–d   359
Statesman 265d   335n27
Symposium
  177b   267, 274, 277n44, 309–10
  183a   317
  189d–93d   254n32, 268–70, 310–11, 315–20
  193b–c   130n12, 311–12
  193d–e   312
  199b   321–22
  201d3–5   224n50, 312
  201d7–e1   314n26
  203b1–3   313
  204b1–2   313
  204c–d   313–14, 316
  204d–9e   314–16
  205d–e   314–15
  206b   316
  208b–c   312
  210c–d   316–18
  211d–12a   319–23, 328n11, 411n31
  212c4–6   315n28
  214b   421n58
  215a–d   322, 333–40
  221c–d   322, 338–39
  221d–22a   333–38, 390–91n96
  221e–22b   322–23, 337n35
  223c–d   260, 263–64, 323–24

Theaetetus
  143e   329n15
  146a   335n27
  152c   353n73
  155d25   120n77
  172c–77b   118n70, 317n32, 318n35
  174a   119, 269n18
  176b–c   328n11

[Plato]
  Epinomis
    974e–76c   161–62
    975c6   168n20
  Hipparchus
    228b9   128n7
    228d5–6   251n25
    228e1–3   109n44

Plato Comicus
  fr. 70 KA   93n120, 189–90

Pliny
  Epistle 10.96.10   221–22n43

Plutarch
  Banquet of the Seven Sages 36, 299n98
    146f   218–23
    150a   202–3, 236–37
    151b   217–18
    151d   218
    152f–53d   104n25, 137n29, 347n60
    154d, 155c   104n25
    158c–60c   234–35
  Commentary on Hesiod's Works & Days ad 719 218–19n41
  The Comparison of Aristophanes and Menander 395n103
  Greek Questions
    292e–f   57n16
    296a–b   127n3
  Life of Alexander
    13   149n54
    14   57n16
  Life of Demosthenes
    23.2   149
    23.5–6   148–50, 156
  Life of Lycurgus
    4   112n57
    6.1   113
    29   113n60
  Life of Solon
    2.1   112nn57–58
    4.1–4   110–11, 237n85
    5–6   137n28, 190n78
    8.1–3   142n41
    25.5   112n58
    27   350–51n67
    28   32n92, 131, 351, 389
  Life of Themistocles
    2.6   172–74
    32   175n38
  Moralia
    38b   218–19n41
    113b   129n10

345e	112n57	**Scholia to...**	
506c	218–19n41	Aristophanes *Birds* 471–72	21, 189–90, 396–97
On Isis and Osiris 3/352b	164n11	Aristophanes *Clouds* 361	276n37, 277n44, 296n94
On the Delays of the Divine Vengeance			
556	137n28		
557a	92	Aristophanes *Frogs* 733	86n96
On the Malice of Herodotus	382–96, 399	Aristophanes *Knights* 1136	86n96
		Aristophanes *Wasps*	
ch. 1/854e	384	1259	397n110
ch. 3/855b	388	1446	29–30, 68n43, 71–72, 91, 211–12
chs. 12–18/857a–58f	391		
ch. 15/857f	104n24, 122n81		
ch. 23/860e	391		
ch. 27/862c–63b	388–89, 426n73	Aristophanes *Wealth* 9	110–11
		Callimachus *Iamb* 1	
ch. 28/863e	388	(fr. 191 Pfeiffer), ll. 26–28	72n51
ch. 33/867b	422–23n62	Pindar *Paean* 6.62	83
		Pindar *Nemean* 7	
ch. 34/867f	395n103	58	79n72
ch. 35/868a	391–92	62a, b	81n77
ch. 37/869d	392	62c	82n81
ch. 39/871a	392–93	68a	82–83
ch. 40/871d	372, 385–87, 404	70	80n76
		150a	79n72
		Plato *Hippias Major* 304e	358
ch. 41/871d	394	**Semonides**	
ch. 42/873d	395n103	fr. 6 W	215n32
ch. 43/873e–74a	393–96, 411n31	**Simonides**	
		fr. 542 *PMG*	121–22, 136n25, 303–5, 358n83
[Plutarch]			
Lives of the Ten Orators 848a–b	157–58	fr. 579 *PMG*	148n48
Priscian		fr. 581 *PMG*	136n25
De Usu III p. 432.24 Keil	295n91	fr. 653 *PMG*	138, 387–88
Prodicus (84 DK)		**Solon**	
B 1 DK	276n37, 296n94	fr. 11 W	45n137, 153–56, 244
B 2 DK	147–48, 267, 269, 271–79, 287–88, 293–97, 408–9	fr. 13 W, ll. 51–52	98n7, 105–6
		fr. 23 W	348
B 5 DK	276–77	fr. 29 W	122
Pythermus		fr. 33 W	153n66
fr. 910 *PMG*	349	fr. 36 W	151–53, 244
Quintilian		**Sophocles**	
Institutio Oratoria		*Ajax* 1147–62	156n70, 243n6
1.9.1–2	271n24		
5.11.19	14n41	*Antigone* 332–83	161–62, 165nn12–14
SEG 48.1330, l. 43	383	*Oedipus Tyrannos*	185, 188–89
*SIG*³ no. 1268	110n47, 181–82n59	*Women of Trachis* 35, 357	66n39
St. Paul		fr. 356 Radt	350n66
I Corinthians 10:25, 28	221–22n43	fr. 942 Radt	417–18n49

476 INDEX LOCORUM

Stobaeus (ed. Wachsmuth–Hense)
    3.1.173   110, 144–45, 181n58, 181–82n59
    3.18.25   218n40
    4.29.53   216n35

Strabo
  Geography
    9.3.9   79n72
    10.14.9   112n57
    16.2.39   177n45

Suda (ed. Adler)
    I.161   93n120, 189–90
    II.182–83   93n120
    II.588   412n34, 430n85
    III.543   158nn76–77
    III.594   419–20
    IV.24–25   362n7
    IV.127   395
    IV.657–58   158nn76–77

Synesius
  Praise of Baldness 22.85c   140–41

Syntipas
  Fables 50, 61   129n11

Themistius
  Oration 30   276–79

Theocritus
  Idyll 15   8n18

Theognis/Theognidea   212–17
    1–10   108–9
    11–14   109n42
    19–24   106–7
    27–28   214–15
    31–38   214–16
    255–56   350
    257–60   348
    341–50   115n64
    429–38   215n32
    757–60   109n42
    770   98n7
    783–88, 805–10   113n62
    1119–22   109n42
    1197–1202, 1209–16   113n62
    1225   215n32
    1253–54   348

(Aelius) Theon
  Progymnasmata
    2.72 Spengel   43, 135n23, 320–22
    2.73 Spengel   14n41, 396–97
    2.77 Spengel   306

Theophrastus
  Characters
    8   376–77
    22.4   221n43
  Signs of the Seasons 39   209n18

Thucydides
  History of the Peloponnesian War
    1.21–22   427n76, 431n88
    1.132.2–3   55n8
    1.138.3   173–74
    2.13   379
    3.82.2   427n76
    3.104.5   128n5

Timocreon
    frr. 4/730, 6/732 *PMG*   396
    fr. 8/734 *PMG*   396, 397n112

(John) Tzetzes
  Chiliades
    1.8, 18   425
    5.728–61   86–87, 92

Vergil
  Aeneid 2.469–558   79n71

Xenophanes (21 DK)   108
    B 2 DK, ll. 12, 14   98n7, 105–6

Xenophon
  Cyropaedia   289
    2.2   130n12
  History of Greece
    2.3.56   290–91
    2.4.27, 4.8.1, 5.1.4, 7.2.1   291n77
  Memorabilia   36, 268–70, 288–300
    1.1–2   289, 292
    1.2–12   295
    1.2.9   256n35
    1.2.19–20, 23   216–17
    1.2.30, 32   332n22
    1.2.37   332
    1.5–6   292, 293n86
    Book 2   292–98, 299n98
    2.1.1   292–93, 295
    2.1.6, 13, 28   278n48
    2.1.7   295
    2.1.11   293
    2.1.12–16   294
    2.1.17   293–95
    2.1.18–19   295

2.1.20	272, 277, 295–96		288, 292, 297–99
2.1.21–34	147–48, 269, 271–74, 277n44, 295–97	3.1–7	293, 298–99
		3.9.10	295
		4.2.2	174n33
		4.2.10–11	295, 298n96
2.1.22	272–73	*Symposium*	
2.1.27	273, 408–9	2.4	216nn34–35
2.1.29	273–76	4.19, 5.7	329n15
2.6	299n98	**Zenobius Athos**	
2.7.1	297n95	*Proverbs*	
2.7.10	297	1.47	190
2.7.12	297–98	5.16	137–38, 236n83, 351, 389
2.7.13–14	134, 148n49, 268–69,	5.107	93n120

GENERAL INDEX

Locators for illustrations are indicated in **bold**.

Acharnians (Aristophanes), 345, 356
Adeimantus, 248
Adrados, Francisco Rodríguez, 18, 269
advice, political: Aesop as political adviser, 5, 32, 35, 125, 126–27, 132–33, 142–44, 147, 174, 340; anonymity as political disguise, 11–12; "Choice of Heracles" as political allegory, 278–79; fables as political advice, 131–33, 143–45, 150–56, 373; implicit, analogical style of, 134; indirection or obliquity of message, 11–12; literary genre and, 265; mantic function and, 146–47, 174; as public performance, 144–45, 174–75, 183; Seven Sages as political advisers, 96, 134, 142, 144, 428–30; Sophistic appropriation of Aesop and, 270
Aelius Theon, 43, 320–21, 396–97
Aesop: as alibi or mask, 11–12, 40, 74; Apollo/Aesop antagonism, 47, 59, 60–69, 89n106, 92n115, 174–75, 187, 254n33, 337, 343n50; appropriation of, 270, 326, 329; as "blame poet," 76, 85–86, 242n3; and competitive *sophia*, 5, 95, 122–23, 125, 137–38, 167–69, 200–201, 247; cultural critique and figure of, 12–13, 25–26, 30, 40, 46–48, 53–54, 59–74, 90–91, 96, 211–12; at Delphi (see *Life of Aesop*: Delphic episode); elision of, 125–37, 203, 339–40, 373–74, 406, 412, 429–30; hero cult honors and, 75, 92–93, 175, 189–90; as historical figure, 13–14; as low or abject figure, 1–4, 48, 137, 236, 375–76; mantic ability of, 5, 13, 47, 60–67, 142–44, 168–69, 171–72; as mute (*see* mutism of Aesop); as non-Greek or Other, 136–38, 165–66, 236, 387, 396–97; parody and, 47, 62, 71–72, 77, 85, 93, 176, 203–4, 213–15, 225, 247; as political adviser, 5, 32, 35, 125, 126–27, 132–33, 142–44, 147, 174, 340; prose linked to fable making by, 15, 47–48, 76, 241–42, 247, 251–52; as sage or part of sage tradition, 31–33, 35, 125–26, 131–32, 175–76, 182, 189–90, 202, 303–4; as slave, 3, 5, 13, 61–63, 139–40, 308, 387–88; and subversion of power, 196–201; ugliness or physical deformity of, 3, 61, 132–33, 225–26, 229, 337
Aesop (Alexis), 356
Aesopica (Perry), 16, 18. See also *Vita* G; *Vita* W
Agathias, 131–32
Agathon, 260, 311–13, 320, 323
agriculture: Aesop and civilized, 165–67; Delphi as barren land unsuitable for, 30, 71, 90–91, 92, 211; the *Hōrai* and, 276–79; as skilled crafting linked to *sophia*, 101, 161–62, 165
Ahiqar. See *Story of Ahiqar*
ainos, 43, 243, 267, 373–76, 387, 398–404
Alcaeus, 76
Alcibiades, 216, 303, 308, 316, 320, 322–23, 333–39, 344, 423–24
Alcibiades I, 268, 291–92
Alcinous, 385
Alcmeonid digression, in Herodotus, 388–89, 413–19, 423–26
Alexander of Aphrodisias, 138, 387
Alexis, 356
alibis, 250, 315n28, 321; Aesop as alibi, 12, 40, 74
allegory, 272–73, 278–79, 337n33, 409–10
allusion: to Aesop in Aristophanes, 7, 20–21, 37, 53, 59, 71, 90–91, 189–90, 211, 243, 396–97; to Aesop in Herodotus, 6–7, 59, 128, 381; to fable by Socrates, 291–92; to fables in high genres, 156–58, 244; Solon's deployment of beast fable via, 244
Althusser, Louis, 24
Aly, Wolf, 368–69
ambiguity: indirection or obliquity of message as "political disguise," 11–12; riddles and ambiguity of oracles, 111; in Solon, 151n99
Anacharsis, 218, 235
analogy: Aesop and deployment of, 89, 132–33, 136, 166–67, 188, 193–94, 335–36, 339–40; Aesop and explication of, 89; Aristotle and, 119n72, 255, 257, 259; "the craft analogy," 119n72; Herodotus and, 428; as

GENERAL INDEX 479

Socratic technique, 259, 308–9, 322–23, 330–35, 339–40
Anaxagoras, 119, 172–73, 247, 346, 365
Anaximander, 247
Anhalt, Emily, 151–52
animals: language or speech as attribute of fabular, 133–34, 144, 148. *See also* beast fables; *specific animals*
anonymity: as challenge to scholarship, 17–18; as instrument of appropriation, 119–20; as instrument of political critique, 11–12, 74–75; of interlocutor in *Hippias*, 344–45, 351–58; of *Life* author, 4, 11, 17–19; of murderer of Neoptolemus, 80–82
Antenor, 339
Anthology of Ancient Greek Popular Literature (Hansen), 26
anthropology, Sophistic, 95–102; agriculture and, 165–67, 277–78; evolution of *sophia*, 95–98, 100–101, 159–68; fable and, 287–88, 326; human speech and, 40, 161, 162–65; *Life of Aesop* as, 159–68; mantic expertise and, 168–69; "skilled crafting" model and, 99–102, 161; sociopolitical organization and, 165n12, 279, 282; *Vita* G and, 40, 46–47, 159
Antiphon, 279–82, 288, 314
Apollo: Aesop/Apollo antagonism, 47, 59, 60–69, 89n106, 92n115, 174–75, 187, 254n33, 337, 343n50; as butcher, 79–80; divine infallibility attributed to, 185–86; the doom of Aesop and avenging role of, 200, 343n50; Hermes and, 2, 60–61, 73; high *sophia* and, 108–9; mantic power of, 60–61, 65–66, 187; Neoptolemus as antagonist of, 79–80; as overseer of the Muses, 61–64, 66, 200, 343n50; and ritual antagonism between hero and god, 29, 31, 77–82; Socrates and affiliation with, 111–12, 254–55, 327; tricked into self-incrimination by Aesop, 199–200
Apollodorus, in Plato's *Symposium*, 334
"apology hypothesis," 80
Apology (Plato), 111–12, 256n36, 266, 294, 327, 328, 330
apophthegmata, 289
aporia or the aporetic dialogues, 297, 330, 340, 344–45, 360
appearance vs. reality, 41, 61–62, 86, 133, 137, 193, 197, 306–7, 333–37; *sophia* and disguise, 108

appropriation: of Aesop in contest between Platonic philosophy and Sophists, 329; anonymity as instrument of, 119–20; as instrument of sociopolitical control, 424; philosophy and appropriation of *sophia* tradition, 108, 115–24, 304, 328–29; Plato and appropriation of fable, 286–87, 308–24; Sophistic appropriation of Aesop, 270; Sophistic elaboration and, 270–75, 279, 284–86, 303, 409, 421. *See also* parody
Archilochus, 14, 37, 85–86, 259, 374
Aristarchus, 80n76, 297–98
Aristippus, 269, 272, 292–97
Aristodemus, in Plato's *Symposium*, 260
Aristophanes, 29–30, 74, 114–15, 143, 177, 254, 356, 419; allusions to Aesop in works of, 7, 20–21, 37, 53, 71, 90–91, 189–90, 211, 243, 396–97; as character in Plato's *Symposium*, 260, 308–22, 323; style of fable narration in *Symposium*, 268–69, 308, 310–12, 314–15
Aristotle: on Aesop, 202; on fable as example, 194–96, 202, 244, 299–300; *sophia* as framed and defined by, 115–24; and traditional *sophia*, 115–18
ass-cart, fable of the, 89, 187
asses, 153, 390; analogy to "pack asses," 334–35; ass-cart, fable of the, 89, 187; idiot girl, fable of, 87, 213–16, 224; "the shadow of an ass," 157–58
Athenaeus, 258–59
athletic contests, 55, 113, 155, 413
audience: appeal of fable to, 335; for "Choice of Heracles," 274–76; cross-status identification, 10–11; elites as participants in common culture, 7–9; indirect narrative engagement and, 427; morals or punch lines and, 188–89; oral tradition and collaborative cooperation of the, 28n85; for Plato's *Protagoras*, 301–2; power differential between author and, 427–28; women as audience for fable, 297–98; the young as audience for fable or *muthos*, 271, 286–87, 302–3, 313, 314, 316
Augustana Collection, 44, 280–81, 401
authority: Aesop as challenge to institutions of, 168–69, 187–89, 203–4, 212–15, 223–24, 383; Aesopic critique of, 11–12, 59–71; alibis and critique of, 11–12; as ancestral inheritance, 212–13; Aristotle's framing of *sophia* and, 121–23; as autonomous self-control,

480 GENERAL INDEX

authority (*cont.*)
  207–8, 212; delegation and questionable legitimacy of, 59–64, 63–64, 82–84, 94; Delphi as, 59–64, 83–84, 88, 187; divine origins of, 108, 110–11, 136, 189, 383; of fable, 125, 141–42; gender and, 2; Herodotus and claims of, 375, 377n66; philosophy and appropriation of, 284–85, 329–30; ritual expertise and cultural, 205–6, 223–24; sociopolitical, 99–100, 108, 191, 205; and *sophia* as contested, 125, 135–38, 167–69, 187–88, 325–29; wisdom traditions (*sophia*) as cultural, 95, 98–102, 105–6, 120–21, 125, 140–42, 191, 205
authorship: *Life of Aesop* and multiple, 25; religion or tradition as "author," 31; sole authorship of unitary works, 22, 33; of *Vita* G, 6, 12, 18, 22, 33, 38–39, 42, 69
Avianus, 44

Babrius, 44, 154–56, 401
Babylon, 5, 36n108, 46, 88, 178, 183–84, 188, 198–99
Bakhtin, Mikhail, 262–63
Banquet of the Seven Sages (Plutarch), 20, 36, 203, 217–19, 223, 234
Batrachomyomachia, 88n104, 394–95
beast fables: in Aristophanes, 7, 20–21, 37, 53, 396–97; debate on political freedom associated with, 150–51; in Hesiod's *Works and Days*, 3, 243; in *Memorabilia*, 288, 292–93, 297–99; as political advice, 150–56, 373; Solon's allusion to and deployment of, 151–56, 244. *See also specific animals*
bestiality, 87, 90, 187–88
Bias of Priene, 126–27, 133, 146–47, 172, 218–19, 223, 346, 380, 405
biography, as genre, 252n28
birds: crows, 168–69, 209–10, 394; eagles, 7, 37, 53, 66, 88–89, 142–43, 171–72, 188; mantic interpretation and bird lore, 142–43, 168–69, 171–72, 204, 208–10; peacocks, 416–19, 421
Birds (Aristophanes), 20–21
Birth of Eros, 268–69, 308–9
blame, 89
blame poetry, 76, 85–86, 242n3, 259
Bloch, Marc, 23
Blondell, Ruby, 330–31, 336
the body and bodiliness: Aesop and, 214–15; Aesop as deformed or ugly, 225, **226**, 229; appearance vs. reality and, 41; Aristotle's framing of *sophia* and privilege of mind over, 115–20; comedy and, 422; as "container" of the mind, 333–38; deconstruction of body/soul opposition, 215–17; defecation, 88–89, 207–8, 220, 222, 230–36, 235n80; discourse linked to, 272–74; in fable, 272–73, 292, 298; as low or abject, 125, 203, 272–73, 316–20, 333–34, 383; meat as sacrificial commodity, 219–22; obscenity and bodiliness as parodic deconstruction, 203–4, 212–17, 219–22, 229–36; Prodicus's Kakia and, 272–74; sacrifice and, 224; sage tradition and renunciation of, 234–35; self-control as control of, 235n79, 273, 292–94, 317–18; sex and (*see* sex); slaves and bodiliness, 196–97, 294, 304–5; urination, 206–8; in Xenophon's *Memorabilia*, 293–97
Bourdieu, Pierre, 23
Bowen, A. J., 391–92
Bowie, Ewen, 362
brachylogia/makrologia: Aesop's indirect style as *makrologia*, 139–41; *brachylogia*, 328; and competitive *sophia*, 141, 303–4; Herodotus and *makrologia*, 387–88, 429; as high/low opposition, 140–42; slave speech as *makrologia*, 138–40, 387–88; Socratic dialogue and appropriation of *brachylogia*, 303n5; Sophistic *makrologia*, 280, 303–4; wisdom as pithy or proverbial *brachylogia*, 140–42, 299n98
bricolage: Aesop as bricoleur, 191–93, 196, 252n27; bricoleur as culture hero, 191–94, 196–201; and compilation of *Lives* and fable collections, 45–46; as defined by Lévi-Strauss, 193; "found-object" style and fabular discourse, 322; Herodotus and earlier traditions as found objects, 425–26; as power over ordinary things, 191–92; Socrates as bricoleur, 322n44, 332–40
Burke, Peter, 7, 22
Burkert, Walter, 76, 211–12
butchers or butchery, 74, 77, 79–81, 152

Callicles, 332, 341–43, 359
Calza, Guido, 234
canon, scholarly restrictions of the, 2–3, 5–6, 26, 49, 373
Carians: Herodotus as Carian, 269, 392–97, 430
catabasis, 114–15, 189–90, 328
Cebes, 251–54
Ceccarelli, Paola, 402–4

Certeau, Michel de, 23
Chilon, 113, 114, 146, 147, 172, 231; depiction in wall painting of the Seven Sages, **233**
"Choice of Heracles" (Prodicus), 286; as allegory, 272–73; as fragment of *Hōrai*, 276–79; generic and stylistic experimentation in, 267, 272–74, 309–10; Heracles as figure in, 272; as performance piece, 274–76, 278–79; Plato on, 274; as treatise on self-control, 294–97; Xenophon and, 271–72, 274, 276–77, 294–97
chreiai, 271n24, 289–90, 390
Cicero, 398, 431
Cirrha/Crisa, 30, 70
Clay, Diskin, 259
coherence, narrative: Ahiqar sequence and, 182–85; anomalies as access to cultural and ideological contestation, 25; of Delphic episode, 53–54, 59–60, 75; in the *Life*, 27, 59–60; Sophistic anthropology and, 164–67; "source criticism" and lack of, 27; of *Vita G*, 22, 33–34, 39–40, 46–47, 63–64; of Xenophon's *Memorabilia*, 289
comedy/comic: and the body and bodiliness, 422; clever slave figures in farcical mode, 10–11; fable as content in, 243–44, 310; *Life of Aesop* as comic or parodic, 5, 12n33, 40, 42, 69, 77, 123n84, 198n93; Margites as comic figure, 149n53; mimesis and, 249, 257; mockery in *Hippias Major*, 345–46; New Comedy, 10n26; Old Comedy, 74, 90, 156, 243, 249, 310–12, 344–57, 345–46, 355; in Plato's *Symposium*, 259–60, 263–64, 323–24; as poetic genre, 249; as source for Platonic dialogues, 258–60, 345, 357–60
community, 281–82; and "concord" in Antiphon, 281–82; Delphic oracle and constitution or preservation of social order, 54–55, 113, 144, 205; fable and constitution of local, 293; hierarchy and power within, 294; kin and household management in, 292; narratives as particular to culture or, 28–29; the Other and constitution of, 152, 292; sacrifice and constitution of, 54–55, 57, 152, 187, 212, 221–23. *See also* the polis
comparative reading method, 22–23
competition: ideology and contestation, 24; preservation of narrative as ideological act, 30; speech as, 128–29, 339. *See also* competitive *sophia*
competitive *sophia*: Aesop and engagement in, 5, 95, 122–23, 125, 137–38, 167–69, 200–201, 247; Aristotle/Solon, 122–23; fable and formulas of verbal contest, 253–54; and fable as contested field, 308–20, 314–15; Muses as signal of, 106n35, 167, 184–85, 189; prose writing as contested field, 264–68; riddle of the sphinx as contest, 228–29; the Seven Sages and, 102–8, 137–38, 303–4; theoretical vs. practical *bioi* and, 172; tripod as prize in, 106, 110–11; trumping speech in, 128–29, 253–54, 407–8
contamination: dirt or filth, 353; of the high by the low, 48; of written fable collections, 44
content: "paradoxical encomia," 267, 274, 309–10
Crisa/Cirrha, 30, 70
Critias, 266–67, 290–91
Crito, 327
Croesus: Aesop and, 5, 31–32, 126–27, 130–33, 135–36, 143–44, 147–48, 174–75; in Herodotus, 126–27, 135–36, 146–47, 350–51, 373, 378–80, 398, 400–401, 405–7, 417–18, 423–28; relationship with Delphic oracle, 58; Solon and, 126–27, 131, 135–36, 147, 350–51, 409n25, 412, 428–30
crows, 168–69, 209–10, 394
culture: Aesop and cultural critique, 12–13, 25–26, 30, 40, 46–48, 53–54, 59–74, 90–91, 96, 211–12; competing ideologies within, 23–24, 76–77, 93–94, 99–100, 105; as contested, 23; as dialectic, 23–24; as fluid and permeable, 8, 93–94; narratives as culturally specific, 28–29; parody and critique of, 47; popular culture or "little traditions" as common, 7–9, 22
culture hero(es): Aesop as, 136, 142; bricoleur as, 191–94, 196–201; gods and ancestors as, 100
Cynics, 27, 139, 207–8, 262, 355n79

Daly, Lloyd, 26
dancing, 304–5, 401, 414–19, 422n61
Darnton, Robert, 9, 22
death: Aesop's agency in his own, 5; "eagle and the dung beetle" fable as frame for Aesop's, 7, 37, 66; and resurrection of Aesop, 189–90; theoric death of the sage, 113–15, 186–90, 223
decorum: Aesopic fable and, 76, 269–70, 293–99, 323–24, 369–70, 381–83, 412–15, 428–29; as alternative system to truth value, 386; and elision of subjects or topics in high

decorum (*cont.*)
   texts, 221n43; generic or stylistic experimentation and ruptures of, 265–66, 324, 384–85, 422–23; Herodotus and ruptures of, 381–97, 412–16, 422–23; and hierarchies of genre, style, or content, 2–4, 243–44, 265–66, 290–91, 309–10, 382–83; *Hippias* and decorum appropriate to prose, 357–58; mimetic prose and, 15, 243–44, 265–66, 323–24, 357–58, 361, 369–70, 381–82; rejection of Latinisms in Greek Second Sophistic, 42, 236n83; sociopolitical hierarchies and, 2, 323, 381–82, 383–84, 390–91, 395; Xenophon and, 290–91, 293, 298–99
dedication, 5, 55, 58, 70, 106, 109–11, 174–75, 184, 189
defecation: and demystification of sacrifice, 222; dung beetle's use of shit, 88–89; and parody of wisdom tradition, 220, 222, 230–36; "shitting while flying" as the slave's lot, 207–8; social status and, 235n80
Deipnosophistae (Athenaeus), 258–59
delegation: double agency and death of Neoptolemus, 80–82, 84–85
Delphi, as religious institution: Aesop as challenge to Apollo/Delphic monopoly, 94–95; Aesop's critique of, 47, 59–74, 67–69, 85–91, 211–12; "anticlericalism" directed at, 53–54, 58n19; athletic contests at, 55; "doom" and plague visited upon, 5, 66–67, 188–89; exclusionary ideology, 58–59, 67, 93–94, 212; greed associated with, 56–57, 68–69, 71–73; sacrificial economy of (*see* sacrifice); state functions of oracle at, 55–59; Theoxeny ritual at, 82–84, 94; wisdom traditions connected to, 47
Delphians, Aesopic characterizations of: as agricultural failure dependent on sacrificial economy, 30, 67–68, 71, 90–91, 92, 211; as beasts, 71, 89, 187, 212; as driftwood, 69–70, 86, 87n98, 89; as greedy or stingy or mean, 56–57, 68–69, 71–73; as "slaves of all the Greeks," 5, 68, 70–71, 86–87, 188; theft of sacrificial meat by, 86, 90–91, 211–12; as vegetables, 69, 72n50, 187; as violators of divine law, 88–89, 187–88; as wild or uncivilized, 187–88
Demaratus, 407–11, 412
Demetrius of Phaleron, 21, 31–32, 44, 62, 134, 202
Denniston, J. D., 361–62

de Romilly, Jacqueline, 266
Detienne, Marcel, 57, 79–80, 152–53, 412
dialectics: methodology and, 23
didactic epic, 3, 243
Diels-Kranz, 276–77
Diodorus Siculus, 131
Diogenes Laertius, 44, 113, 139, 145, 153, 177, 235, 258
Diogenes the Cynic, 139, 207–8, 262, 344n79
Dionysius of Halicarnassus, 382
Diotima: Birth of Eros as related by, 268–69, 308–9; contest with Aristophanes, 308–22; style of fable narration in Plato's *Symposium*, 308, 312–15
direct speech, 249
Dodona, 61, 67
dogs, 144, 147–48, 150–51, 177n46, 181n59, 268, 288, 293, 297–98
domestication: of Aesop, 202–3, 236–37, 270–71; of narrative, 12–13
"doom of Aesop," 5, 66–67, 91–92, 188–89
Dougherty, Carol, 55, 112
Dover, K. J., 310–11, 315–16
dreams: interpretation of, 61–62, 64–66, 168, 217, 221n43, 423; Socrates and versification of fable, 251–52
driftwood, 69–70, 86, 87n98, 89
DuBois, Page, 225
dung beetles, 7, 37, 53, 66, 88–89, 188

eagles, 142–43, 171–72; "eagle and the dung beetle" fable, 7, 37, 53, 66, 88–89, 188
East/West: Aesopic/Homeric binary and, 405–7, 410–11, 428–29; East as barbarian Other, 278, 386, 392, 395–96; fable's Eastern origins, 14, 176–78, 396, 410, 414–19; tyranny or despotism as Eastern, 130–31, 137, 149, 400, 429; wisdom as culturally specific, 181
Eberhard, Alfred, 16
education: Aesop's critique of symposium and didactic traditions, 204, 212–17; didactic function of poetry, 214–15, 302, 303, 304–5; fable's role in didactic progression, 271, 302–3, 314, 316, 326; in Plato's *Protagoras*, 301–5
Edwards, Mark J., 285–86
Egypt: Egyptian elements in *Life of Aesop*, 18, 27, 42, 218n38; Herodotus on, 370–71, 378–79, 386, 390–91, 404; Isis as figure in Aesop narrative, 35–36, 62–63, 136n26, 162–63, 208

elaboration, Sophistic appropriation and, 270–75, 279, 284–86, 303, 409, 421
elegy, 3, 105–7, 110, 131–32, 153–56, 212–16, 348, 350, 362, 392
elenchos, 289–90, 309, 327, 330–32, 340–44, 351, 354; reciprocity of, 360; and self-incrimination of the opponent, 359–60; Socratic, 260, 340–44, 400
elision of Aesop: by critics, 373–74; by Herodotus, 125–37, 203, 406, 412, 429–30; Socrates' uniqueness and, 339–40
Empedocles, 47, 114, 190, 247
encomium: appropriate style and content of, 267, 273, 278–79, 322, 333, 384n84; fable as, 309
epagōgē, 330, 332–35. *See also* analogy
Epicharmus, 258, 295–96
epilogos (internal moral or punch line of fable), 130, 135, 275, 406
epilogue, 274–75, 282, 287, 409
Epimenides, 114, 190, 224, 234
Epimetheus, 282–83, 285, 288, 306
Erbse, Hartmut, 289
Eros, 268–69, 308–10
Eryximachus, 267, 309, 311–12
estrangement, 48–49, 241–42, 361–70
ethnicity: Aesop as non-Greek or outsider, 136–38, 165–66, 236, 247, 387, 396–97; Aesop's cultural critique and construction of, 224; of Herodotus, 391–93, 395
Euripides, 64–66, 161, 388
Euthydemus, 299n98, 337, 340
Evans, J.A.S., 374
Evenus of Paros, 266–67, 330
exile, 112–14, 152, 369, 412
experimentation, generic and stylistic: in "Choice of Heracles," 272–74; Herodotus and, 369–70, 376, 421–23, 427–28, 430–31; hybrid or mixed genres, 244, 245, 252n28, 259–67, 260n46, 309, 323, 325; and paradox, 309; Plato and, 260n46, 323–24, 325; prose and, 265–67; and ruptures of decorum, 265–66, 324, 384–85, 422–23; by Sophists, 264, 265–67
extempore rhetorical performance, 274–76

fables: Aesop as "inventor" of, 136–37, 142; aetiological (mythological), 43, 268–69, 308 (*see also* Birth of Eros; "Choice of Heracles"; Pleasure and Pain); aetiology of, 1, 14; *ainos* and, 43, 243, 267, 373–76, 387, 398–404;

allusions to rather than full narration of, 44–45, 156–58, 244, 291–92; ancient terminology for, 43, 130, 132–33, 243, 254–56, 284–87, 320–21, 396–97, 398–401; animals in (*see* beast fables; *specific animals*); Aristotle on use of, 194–96, 244, 299–300; audience for, 271, 286–87, 297–98, 302–3, 313, 314, 316, 335, 339; as barbarian or non-Greek, 14, 176–78, 386, 396–97, 410, 414–19; the body and bodiliness in, 272–73, 292, 298; as bricolage, 194–96; "coded" or indirect style of *ainos,* 373–74, 387, 399, 400–404; as contested genre, 125, 136–37, 314–15, 325–26 (*see also* Diotima: contest with Aristophanes); as critique of Delphi, 87–90; as critique of power, 11–12; definitions and parameters of, 43, 398–99; didactic function of, 271, 302–3, 314, 316, 326, 426–31; diversity of forms in genre, 268, 396–97, 398; as "easy" or pleasurable, 194–96, 256, 286–87; in English literature, 41; as examples or evidence in argument, 150, 156–57, 194–96, 200–201, 202, 244, 255–57, 259, 299–300; features of fables as narrative, 43; as fluid and permeable form, 9–10, 17–18, 28–30, 44–45, 53, 398, 400; formulae signaling, 45, 128–30, 135, 148, 253, 274, 286, 311–12, 314, 398, 406–8, 410, 419–20; indirect discourse and, 131–33, 143–44; *logos* as, 254–56, 371, 400–406; as low form of discourse or literature, 1–4, 136–39, 148, 200–201, 242–43, 256–57, 272–74, 320–21, 412; low social status and, 431; mimetic prose and, 15; morals or punch lines in, 43, 45, 87–88, 130, 135, 189, 275, 404, 406; *muthos* as, 252, 254, 282–88, 284–85, 301, 303; as neglected and isolated in scholarship, 261; as obvious fictions or "false stories," 43, 248, 255, 320–21; Plato and appropriation of, 286–87, 308–24; as political advice, 131–33, 143–45, 150–56, 373; as political critique, 14; Socrates' versification of Aesopic fables, 202, 217, 251–54, 327; as *sophia,* 1–2, 305–6; Sophistic elaborations and elevation of, 270–74, 279–80, 284, 300, 303, 325–26, 409; as a specific event (particularity of), 43; as supplement to reasoned argument, 150; Sybarite, 396–97, 418–19; textual fixation of, 44–45; theory of, in *Life of Aesop,* 11–12; as traditional form, 14; the young as audience for, 271, 286–87, 302–3, 313, 314, 316

failure, productive use or positive value of, 359–61
Ferrari, Franco, 18, 35–40
figs: theft of, 191–92, 197
"figured speech," 39, 428, 430
First Sacred War, 27, 70–71, 75
flattery, 131, 135, 137–38, 318n35, 389, 426, 427
fleas, 255
Flory, Stewart, 130–31
flute-girls, 304–5, 333
Fornara, Charles, 427
Fowler, Robert L., 363–64, 366
foxes: in fable, 88n105, 154–56, 268, 386n88; on red-figure cup, 225–29, **226**
freedom, 11; Aesop's mantic ability and reward of, 13, 66, 143, 144, 169–70; beast fable associated with debate on, 150–51; metaphysics as "free," 122

genres: experimentation with hybrid, 244, 245, 252n28, 259–67, 260n46, 309, 323, 325; Xenophon and experimentation with, 289–90. *See also* hierarchy, generic; *specific genres*
gift exchange, 221, 222n44
god-hero antagonism. *See* hero-god antagonism
Gomperz, H., 276
Gorgias, 266, 274–76, 330, 355
Gorgias (Plato), 258–59, 266, 294, 328, 330, 332, 334, 339n39, 341–44, 359–60
Gramsci, Antonio, 23
Gray, Vivienne J., 289–90
"great and little traditions," 7–9, 423–24
greed, 211; animal images associated with, 152–53; of Apollo, 73; Delphic, 56–57, 68–69, 71–73; fable of the Greedy Man, 280
Grote, George, 294

Hägg, Thomas, 18, 203
Hansen, William, 26
Haslam, Michael, 17, 181
hawk and nightingale, fable of, 403–4
Hecataeus of Miletus, 363, 371–82
hedgehogs, 255
Hegel, Georg Wilhelm Friedrich, 242, 262
Helms, Mary, 99–101, 104–5, 106, 136, 142, 191
Heracles. *See* "Choice of Heracles" (Prodicus)
Heraclitus, 111, 247
Hermes, 1–2, 60–61, 73
Hermippus, 189–90, 259, 419–20

hero cult: Aesop and, 75, 92–93, 175, 189–90; inversion of status, 93; Neoptolemus and, 75, 81–84; *pharmakos* ritual as distinct from, 76; ritual antagonism between hero and god, 29, 31, 77–82; sage tradition and, 114, 189–90, 328; in *Vita* W, 92–93, 189
Herodotus, 11, 125, 134–35, 146–47, 203; Aesop and Aesopic tradition as prose precursor for, 15, 31–33, 42, 47–48, 76n61, 241, 361–70, 371–73, 381–82, 394–95; Aesop as cue to readers of, 426–31; Alcmeonid digression, 413–18, 423–26; allusions to Aesop in, 6–7, 59, 128, 381; analogy as deployed by, 428; assimilation with oral tradition, 364–65; as bricoleur using earlier traditions as found objects, 425–26; characterization of Alcmeonids by, 388–89; "coded" or indirect style and use of *ainos* or fable in, 11, 373–74, 387–89, 399, 400–404, 413–14, 418–26, 426–31; and the creation of history as a genre, 361–70, 376, 431; on Croesus's right to *promanteia* at Delphi, 57–58; dictional traces of Aesop tradition in, 125–37, 406, 429–30; doubling and, 146–47; Egypt as "Other" in, 378–79, 386, 390–91, 404; elision of Aesop by, 125–37, 203, 406, 412, 429–30; as exile or Other, 369, 386–88, 391–93, 395–96, 412, 430–31; explicit mention of Aesop by, 29, 31–32, 47, 53, 91–92, 242, 370–71, 381; generic experimentation by, 370, 421–23, 427–28, 431; Hecataeus and, 363, 371–72, 377–78; history as genre invented by, 48, 361–70, 376, 431; as Homeric, 382–85, 394–95; and inversion of sociopolitical hierarchy, 395; and the Ionian tradition, 145–47, 145n45, 364–65, 368–69, 377–79, 398, 400–402, 405–6, 428–29; and *makrologia*, 387–88, 429; as the Other in Plutarch, 369, 386–88, 391–93, 395–96, 412, 430–31; parody and, 377–78; Plutarch on (see *On the Malice of Herodotus* (Plutarch)); poetry as source material for, 367; prose as understood and deployed by, 370–72, 381–82, 426–31; on Pythagoras and practice of *sophia*, 103; on recompense for death of Aesop, 91–92; risks of generic experimentation by, 369–70, 376, 430–31; and ruptures of decorum, 381–97, 412–16, 422–23; on sages and *sophia*, 102–4, 114, 119, 135–38, 146–47; on Samos, 369, 412, 430–31; as scapegoat, 393; as source, 32–33, 112; tragedy and, 427; truth and, 363,

365, 367–69, 376, 380–82, 385, 407–9, 431; use of fable and oral tradition by, 424
hero-god antagonism, 29, 31, 51, 79–80; Apollo/Neoptolemus, 77–82; appropriation and ideological contestation of, 77; boundary transgression and, 79–80, 82
heroic epic, 3, 242, 394–95
Hesiod, 37, 106, 204–12, 288n70, 289, 403–4; "Choice of Heracles" as elaboration of Hesiodic fable, 272; as fabulist, 14; Socrates on the "false tales" of, 248; *sophia* tradition and, 95
hierarchy, generic, 1–2, 241–44; Aristophanes/Diotima exchange as contest between, 315–20; blame poetry as low form, 259; *brachylogia* and, 140–42, 299n98, 303n5, 328; decorum and relationship of content and style to, 221n43, 263–65, 267, 298–99, 309–10, 323–24, 383–85; examples and, 194–96; fable as low form, 1–4, 136–39, 148, 256–57, 431; and generic interplay in Plato, 254; "great and little traditions," 7–9, 423–24; Homeric/Aesopic binary, 381, 383, 389, 405–7, 410–11, 428–29; inversion of, 339, 421–22; *parabolē*, status of, 255–57; Plato and, 254–55, 259–64, 334–40; poetry vs. prose, 141–42, 242, 420–21; popular culture and interaction of, 2; in scholarly subfields, 261–62; sociopolitical status and, 20, 242, 316–18, 375–76, 390–91, 424; in Xenophon's *Memorabilia,* 298–99
the high/the low: and Aesop as low or abject figure, 1–4, 48, 137, 236, 375–76; contamination of the high by the low, 48; deconstruction of body/soul opposition, 215–17; low or bodily *sophia* of Aesop, 125; mind/body opposition, 115–20, 125, 203, 272–73, 316–20, 333–34, 383; popular culture and interaction between, 2; theoretical *sophia*/practical intelligence, 115–20. *See also* hierarchy, generic; status, sociopolitical
Hippias, 266, 330, 345–46, 367
Hippias Major: competitive *sophia* and, 344, 346–47, 358; Hippias as characterized in, 345–46; as inauthentic or misattributed to Plato, 344–46, 358; mockery as comedic element in, 345–46; as parodic, 345–46; rupture of decorum in, 352–53; Seven Sages and sage tradition in, 346–50, 358; Socratic *elenchos* in, 358–60
Hipponax, 86

historiē, 363, 365–66, 369, 380
Histories (Herodotus), 48; as generic hybrid, 244; as tragedy, 427. *See also* Herodotus
history, as genre: decorum of, 361, 369–70, 382–85, 390–91, 429; Herodotus and creation of, 361–63, 376; as medium for truth, 380–81; poetry as medium, 362; prose as medium, 241–42, 362; as science or scientific, 362–63, 380–81
History of Greece (Xenophon), 290–91
History of the Graeco-Latin Fable (Adrados), 269–70
Holzberg, Niklas, 33–35, 38, 91n112, 185–86, 188, 200n98, 203
Homer, 3, 88, 101, 200, 243, 249; allusion to, 69, 298–99, 354; Homeric/Aesopic binary, 381, 383, 389, 405–7, 410–11, 428–29; mimesis and, 249; Plutarch on Herodotus as Homeric, 382–85, 394–95; Socrates on the "false tales" of, 248
Homeric Hymn to Apollo, 67–68, 71–72
Homeric Hymn to Hermes, 2n2, 60–61, 73, 79
Hopkins, Keith, 10, 25
Hōrai, 276–79
hubris, 185–88, 354–55
hupolabōn eipe/ephē, 128–30, 135, 251–54, 273–74, 286, 311–12, 406–8, 410, 414, 419–20
hupotuchōn eipe/ephē, 129, 419–20
Husselman, Elinor, 4
hybrid forms, 244, 245, 252n28, 259–64, 267, 308–10, 323, 325
hypothekai, 107, 213–14, 266, 347

iambic, 2–4, 14, 85–86, 151–56, 243, 424
ideologemes, 12; Aesop as ideologeme, 41–42
ideology: Aesopic/Homeric opposition and, 383; culture and competing ideologies, 23–24, 76–77, 93–94, 99–100, 105; defined and described, 24; Delphic, 58–59, 67, 84, 93–94, 212; methodology and, 23; preservation of narrative as ideological act, 30; reading methodology and ideological coherence, 25, 46–49, 75–94, 159–60; style and, 42–43, 357, 383
idiot girl (foolish daughter), 87, 186–87, 213–16, 224
Iliad (Homer), 249, 298–99
improvisation: culture as improvisational, 23–24; improvisatory *sophia,* 173–74. *See also* bricolage

GENERAL INDEX

incest, 86, 89–90, 187–88

Indian fables, 414–19, 421

indirection, 201, 286–87; Aesop and indirect fable advice, 133–36, 141; audience engagement and indirect narrative, 427; Herodotus and "coded" communication, 373–74, 387, 399, 400–404; Seven Sages vs. implicit, analogical style of advice, 134; "slave talk" and, 387–88

inside-outside dialectic, 41. *See also* appearance vs. reality

Ionians, 19, 127, 146–47, 172; Hecataeus and the Ionian Revolt, 378–79; Herodotus and the Ionian tradition, 145n45, 364–65, 368–69, 377–79, 398, 400–402, 405–6, 428–29

Iphigeneia in Tauris (Euripides), 64–66

Isis, 4–5, 35–36, 62–63, 136n26, 162–63, 208; Aesop endowed with speech by, 162–65, 192; association of Muses with, 162n9

Jacoby, Felix, 21n65, 363–65

Jahn, Otto, 225

Jedrkiewicz, Stefano, 42, 76n59

Kahn, Charles, 330, 341–42

Kamen, Deborah, 140n3

Karadagli, Triantaphyllia, 129, 398–99

Ker, James, 112–13

Kerferd, G. B., 97–98, 101–2, 173, 287

language or speech: Aesop as garrulous and inclined to lengthy speeches, 139–41; Aesop's acquisition of speech, 4–5, 166; Aesop's tongue as "unshackled," 136n26, 163; direct speech as device, 7, 249, 251, 285, 389; as element in Sophistic anthropology, 40, 161, 162–65; fabular animals and capacity for, 133–34, 144, 148; flute-girls as voiceless, 304; opportunity and deployment of, 144–45; *sophia* as skilled verbal competition, 104–8; tongues as "best and worst," 165n13, 218–22, 235. *See also brachylogia/ makrologia*; mutism of Aesop

La Penna, Antonio, 18

Latin loan words, 18, 42, 236n83

Laws of Manu, 206

Lesky, Albin, 227

Lévi-Strauss, Claude, 193

Life of Aesop: as anonymous, morphing, fluid tradition, 9–10, 17–18, 22, 28–29, 41–42; Assembly sequence in, 171–76, 197; authorship of, 25; bread basket episode in, 192–93; as bricolage or aggregation, 25; as critique, 10, 25, 203; dating of, 6–7; Delphic episode in, 3, 5, 7, 29–33, 37, 53–54, 59–60, 66, 75, 87–88, 186, 191–92, 200n58, 211, 213–17 (*see also* Delphi, as religious institution; Delphians, Aesopic characterizations of); diversity of versions of, 7; grouping and dating of versions of, 16–18; as marginalized or segregated work, 5–6, 26–27; as "metafable," 41; and nonphilosophical sage tradition, 123; as parodic, 12n33, 40, 42, 77, 123n84, 198n93; redactors and shaping of, 8–9, 17, 28–29, 33–44, 42, 47, 62n28, 71, 161, 176; Samian section in, 5, 127, 132–33, 142–44, 147, 165, 174, 197–98, 247, 335–36; textual fixation of, 19–22. See also *The Oxyrhynchus Papyri*; *Vita* G; *Vita* W

Lindenberger, James M., 178–80

lions, 149, 154–55, 268, 305n9, 412, 423

Lissarrague, François, 225

Lives of the Sophists (Philostratus), 274–75

Lloyd, G.E.R., 105

locusts, 133

logopoios, 86, 370–72, 376–82, 384, 389–90, 423, 430–31

logos/logoi: Aesopic, 39–40, 48, 133–34, 241, 369, 371, 389–90, 409–10; *ainos* as distinct from, 399; fables as *logoi*, 254–56, 371, 400–406; *logos/muthos* opposition, 254, 286–87, 297n95, 313–14; prose and, 15, 241, 248n20, 254, 357, 371; Sophistic anthropology and progressive development of, 15, 39–40, 164–65, 241, 369

Longinus, 262n51, 382, 383, 385

the low: abjection, 1–4, 48–49, 137, 236, 333–34, 375–76; Aesop as synecdoche for, 48; bricolage and use of the mundane, 194; and estrangement, 48–49; oral narrative as, 128–29. *See also* hierarchy, generic; the high/the low; status, sociopolitical

Luraghi, Nino, 374–75

Lycurgus (king of Babylon), 5, 46, 184, 198–99

Lycurgus of Sparta, 112–14

Lydia. *See* Croesus

lyric, 3–4, 156, 243, 304–5, 374, 375, 424–25

Lysippus, 131–32, 202

makrologia. See *brachylogia/makrologia*

Mann, Wolfgang, 304–5

manteia. See prophecy or sign reading
marginality: of Aesop in wisdom tradition, 203; Delphi as marginal, 55; interdisciplinarity and, 49; scapegoating and, 86. *See also* the Other
Margites, 117, 149, 395
Marsyas, 174–75, 333–34, 337–38
Martin, Richard, 102–6, 112, 141, 223, 326–27
masturbation, 207–8
maxims, 109–10, 140–41, 280, 289–90; *apophthegmata,* 289
Maximus Planudes, 16
McCarthy, Kathleen, 10
medicine, 99, 118–19, 133, 284, 364, 365
Melissus, 172–73
Memorabilia (Xenophon): the body and bodiliness in, 293–97; fables in, 270, 288, 292–93, 297–99; generic hierarchy in, 298–99; narrative coherence of, 289
Menippean satire, 263
metempsychosis of Aesop, 189–90. See also *catabasis*
Meuli, Karl, 374, 401–2, 404
mice, 88n104, 393–95
Miller, Clyde Lee, 306
mime, 249, 257–58, 262
mimesis: direct speech or impersonation and, 250–51; and emergence of prose, 244; everyday speech vs. poetry, 248; linked to poetry by Plato, 250; poets and deployment of, 248–50; in *Republic,* 247–48; and Socratic philosophy, 244–51
mind/body: body as "container" of the mind, 333–38; as the high and the low, 115–20, 125, 203, 272–73, 316–20, 333–34, 383; intelligence and physical appearance, 193, 197
Miralles, Carles, 85–87, 90n110
Mnesiphilus of Phrearrion, 172–74
Moles, John, 428–29
Momigliano, Arnaldo, 252n28, 361, 384n80, 384n84
morals: Aesop and explicit, 87–88; audience interpretation and implicit, 188–89, 256n36, 404; elision of, 158; as external (*epimuthion*), 45, 130n14, 275; as internal (*epilogos*), 130, 135, 275, 406; as point of fable, 43; trumping speech and, 311–12. *See also* punch lines
Morgan, Catherine, 54–55, 61, 67
Morris, Ian, 55
"Mother Goose" tales, 9

mouse and frog, fable of, 88, 188, 394
Murray, Oswyn, 371
Muses: Aesop's ascent of *sophia* linked to appearances of, 166–68, 184–85; Aesop's relationship with the, 174–75; Aesop's talent as gift from the, 3–4; Apollo's relationship with the, 62, 200; competitive *sophia* and appearance of, 106n35, 184–85, 189; theatrical performance and, 174–75; *Vita* W and elision of, 162n9
muthos/muthoi: fables as, 252, 254, 282–88, 301, 303; as "false stories" or deliberate fictions, 248n20, 255; as first stage of rhetorical education, 271n24; *logos/muthos* opposition, 254, 286–87, 297n95, 313–14; *muthos/logos* progression, 15, 39–40, 164–65, 241, 287, 313, 369; Protagoras's *muthos* in Plato, 279, 285–87, 303, 306
mutism: flute-girls as voiceless, 304
mutism of Aesop, 62–63, 200n98; and demonstration of power over things and people, 191–92, 196–97; and fable making, 201; silence as threat, 198; and slave status, 13, 62–63, 160, 162–63, 185, 191–92, 360; speech as divine gift, 4–5, 62–63, 162–63

Nagy, Gregory, 29, 31, 75–77, 86, 113, 205, 211–12, 372–76, 387, 398, 400, 403–4; *ainos,* 373, 398–404
natural philosophy, 119, 365
Nectanebo, 5, 161, 183–84, 198–99, 359
Nemean 7 (Pindar), 77, 80–84
Neoptolemus, narrative of: Aesop tradition as parodic critique of, 31, 85–94; "apology hypothesis" and, 80; cultural functions of, 77–84; hero-cult honors as warrior, 75; similarities to story of Aesop at Delphi, 31, 75
Nestle, Wilhelm, 276–78, 282
Nestor, 266, 339, 347
Nicomachean Ethics 6, 115–22
Nietzsche, Friedrich Wilhelm, 262–63
Nightingale, Andrea, 121n79, 245–46, 250, 259–60, 309–10, 338
Nøjgaard, Morten, 21

Oeconomicus (Xenophon), 276–77
Oedipus, in the visual tradition, 225–29, **227, 228**
Olympiodorus, 328
"On Concord" (Antiphon), 280–82, 288, 314
On Philosophy (Aristocles), 96

On the Malice of Herodotus (Plutarch), 48, 382–96, 422, 426n73; critique of Herodotus's prose discourse in, 387–89; Herodotus as Aesopic in, 385–89, 391; Herodotus as Homeric in, 382–85, 394–95; insincerity attributed to Herodotus in, 388–89; objections to Herodotus as incomplete or inaccurate historian, 393–94; Plutarch's construction of Herodotus as Other in, 369, 386–88, 391–93, 395–96, 412

On the Sublime (Longinus), 262n51, 385

oracle: Aesop and demystification of, 171–72, 208–10; Aesop as challenge to Apollo/Delphic monopoly, 94–95; contested among Olympians, 60–61; sacrificial economy and controlled access to, 55–58. *See also* prophecy or sign reading

oral tradition, 134; Aesop and, 7, 26–27, 128–29, 336–37; as collaborative cooperation between teller and audience, 28n85; and extempore rhetorical performance, 274–76; fluidity of written text in interaction with, 7, 22, 28–30, 44–45, 53; and Herodotus's use of fable, 424; *Life* as rooted in, 21–22, 26–27; poetry in oral culture, 141–42; selection and adaptation of, 28; textual fixation of, 8–9, 27–28

Ostia tavern painting depicting Seven Sages, 229–36, **231, 232, 233**

the Other: Aesop as non-Greek or outsider, 136–38, 165–66, 236, 387, 396–97; "alien voice" of flute-girls, 304–5; as barbarian, 278–79; community constituted in opposition to, 152, 292; exile and the wanderer, 112–13, 152; fable as non-Greek, 14, 176–78, 386, 396–97, 410, 414–19; Plutarch's construction of Herodotus as, 369, 386–88, 391–93, 395–96, 412, 430–31; sacrificial victim as, 224; underworld as, 115; vulnerability of strangers, 294

"overseer" role: Apollo as overseer of the Muses (*prostatēs*), 61–64, 66, 200, 343n50; Neoptolemus as (*themiskopos*), 81–82, 84; Zenas in Aesop's biography, 62–63, 163–64

The Oxyrhynchus Papyri, 17, 72–73, 77–78, 90–91, 93, 181, 189, 211–12

Paean 6 (Pindar), 77–84
Panofsky, Erwin, 22–23
Panyassis, 362, 396
Papathomopoulos, Manolis, 17, 18

parabolē, 255–57
Parmenides, 247, 269n19
parody: in Aesopic tradition or Aesop as parodist, 47, 62, 71–72, 77, 85, 93, 176, 203–4, 213–15, 225, 247; *Batrachomyomachia* as, 88n104, 393–95; and critique of cultural systems, 47; as critique of oracular authority or sacrificial practices, 62, 77, 85, 93, 169–70; as critique of power, 11–12, 13, 203–4; as critique of *sophia*, 95, 176, 203–4, 213–15; Herodotus and, 377–78; of the high in popular culture, 93–94; narrative mechanisms of parodic critique, 187; of Neoptolemus narrative, 31, 85–94; "original's" relationship with, 77; Plato and, 246, 258–59; of ritual prescriptions, 204–5; of Seven Sages or sage tradition, 212–17, 229–36, **231, 232, 233**; and subversion of philosophy, 203; visual, 224–29

particularity: Diotima and rejection of material, 316–20; fable and, 43, 315–16, 319–20; Socrates and his *logoi* as unique, 322–24

Pataecus, 190
Patterson, Annabel, 41–42
Pausanias, 82n81, 114, 311–12, 317, 320
peacocks, 414–19, 421
pederasty, 214–16, 316–17
performance: *ainos* as, 398–99; "Choice of Heracles" as, 274–76, 278–79; culture as context for constitution of philosophy, 245–46; dance as, 305, 421–22; extempore rhetorical, 274–75; fig episode as public performance of skilled crafting, 192; hierarchy of performance contexts, 141–42, 243, 293, 304–5, 339; oral tradition and fluidity of performed narrative, 28n85, 141, 415; Philostratus on origins of rhetorical, 274–75; political advising as public, 144–45, 174–75, 183; popular culture as public, 7–8; as scene of self-incrimination, 197; Sophists and literary elaborations of fable as, 270–71; status and gender-specific hierarchy of, 304–5, 334; of wisdom, 102, 142, 144–46, 167–68, 183, 191–92, 218–23, 344–47, 429n81

Perrault, Charles, 9
Perry, Ben Edwin, 4, 6, 16, 19–20, 26, 31, 62, 134, 268, 272, 396; dating of fables by, 65; on definition of fable, 43; on textual fixation, 21–22

persuasion: fable as means of, 131–33; flattery and, 389

Phaedo (Plato), 251–53, 255, 291–92
Phaedrus, 44, 209, 225n56, 309
Phaedrus (Plato), 21, 266–67, 268, 274
pharmakos ritual: associated with death of Neoptolemus, 29, 75–76; associated with *Life of Aesop*, 29–31, 75, 85–92; attributes of the *pharmakos*, 86; as competitive activity, 85–94; as distinct from hero cult, 76
Pherecydes, 113, 114
philosophy, Platonic: appropriation of fable as tactic of, 316–18; appropriation of *sophia* tradition by, 108, 115–24, 304, 328–29; as contested term, 329–30; invention of, 244–51, 267n9; mimesis and, 244–51; parody and subversion of, 203; poetry as opposition in Plato's constitution of, 245–46, 250; prose and, 241–42. *See also* Plato; Socratic dialogues
Philostratus, 1–2, 274–76, 280–81, 304n6, 308n, 355
Phrygia or Phrygians, 247, 396, 397, 429
physicality. *See* the body and bodiliness
picaresque, *Life of Aesop* as proto-, 5–6
piety: Aesop as pious, 62–63, 162–63, 185–86, 208, 379; Socrates' self-control and, 292; versification of fables as demonstration of, 253n29
pigs, 219–24
Pindar: death of Neoptolemus in, 77; on poets and the practice of *sophia*, 102
Pittacus, 76, 218–19
plague. *See* "doom of Aesop"
Planudes, Maximus, 16
Plataea, Battle of, 70, 362, 393–94
Plato, 47–48, 107–8; Aesopic tradition and prose of, 241–42, 254, 264, 326; banishment of the poets and constitution of philosophy by, 245–46, 250; generic experimentation by, 260n46, 323–24, 325; mimesis and Socratic dialogues, 244–51; prose as medium of, 325 (*see also specific works*); Protagoras in, 282–88; on the Seven Sages and Apollo, 108–9; Socratic dialogues as generic hybrids, 244, 245, 259–67, 285–86, 308–10, 323, 325
Plato Comicus, 189–90
pleasure: associated with indirect narrative of fable, 131–34, 273, 275, 286–87, 299, 312, 389, 406; audience identification and, 10–11; as bodily experience, 216, 229n64, 235, 292, 293–96, 298, 299, 339–40; as the good, 342;

prose linked to, 44n136; Socrates on pain and, 251, 258; truth/pleasure binary, 273, 407–9, 431
Pleasure and Pain, 251, 268
Plutarch, 48, 131, 203, 217–19, 223, 234, 382–96, 422, 426n73; on Herodotus (see *On the Malice of Herodotus* (Plutarch)); on recompense for death of Aesop, 92
poetry: *brachylogia* as poetic skill, 141–42; didactic function of, 302, 303, 304–5; as medium for history, 362; oracle linked with, 108; prose as challenger to, 266; Socrates on the "false tales" of poets, 248; Socrates' versification of Aesopic fables, 202, 217, 251–54, 327; *sophia* and, 95, 98, 102; as source material for Herodotus, 367
poetry/prose opposition: Aristotle on style and features of, 267–68; and constitution of philosophy, 245–46, 250; Socrates' versification of Aesopic fables, 202, 217, 251–54, 327
the polis, 105; Delphic oracle and constitution of, 54–55, 113, 144, 205; *polis tyrannos*, 373, 427–30; *sophia* as challenge to authority, 108
politics: *sophia* and political skill, 102; *theōria*, political role of, 96, 112–15, 120, 123, 159, 162, 185–201, 328–29; and Xenophon's treatment of "Choice of Heracles," 294–96. *See also* advice, political; status, sociopolitical
Politics (Aristotle), 165
Polus, 341–43, 359
Polycraton, 74
popular culture: "great and little traditions" and, 7–9; interaction of high and low, 2; limited extant record of, 3; parody of the high in, 93–94; reading methodologies to access, 22–23; written texts and elite instantiations of, 21–22
Pòrtulas, Jaume, 85–87, 90n110
Powell, J. Enoch, 130
power: differential between speaker and audience in fable performance, 243–44, 401–2, 427–28; *Life of Aesop* as critique of, 53; parody and, 11–12, 13, 203–4; prose and sociopolitics of form, 261, 264; ritual expertise as means of social control, 205; sacrificial economy and inequities of, 212; slavery and inequities of, 208; and *sophia* as contested, 120–21; symposium tradition and inequities of, 220–21; in Xenophon's *Memorabilia*, 294–94, 294–95

practical intelligence, 115–20, 174
prescriptions or prohibitions, ritual, 204–12
prison: Aesop's conversations while in, 87, 186, 213–17; Socrates' discussion and deployment of fable while in, 251–54
Prodicus. *See* "Choice of Heracles" (Prodicus)
Progymnasmata, 43, 271, 306, 320–21
prohibitions, ritual, Aesop's critique of, 204–12
Prometheus, 143–44, 161, 165n12, 272n28, 282–84, 288, 305–6, 410
prophecy or sign reading: Aesop's mantic skills, 5, 47, 60–67, 94–95, 168–72, 188–89, 197–98; bird lore, 142–43, 168–69, 171–72, 204, 208–10; Delphic monopoly of, 55–58, 187; as divine gift, 62–63; dream interpretation, 61–62, 64–66, 168, 217, 221n43, 423; fables as medium for communication, 188–89; linked to political advising, 146–47, 174; poetry linked with, 108; riddles and ambiguity of, 111, 169–70; Sages and mantic ability, 145–47, 168–69; *sophia* linked to, 95, 101, 102, 142–43, 145–47, 168–74, 188–89
prose: Aesopic tradition and beginnings of, 15, 47–48, 76, 241–42, 247, 251–52; Aristotle on style and features of, 267–68; audience for, 248, 287–88; content appropriate for, 255–56; as contested, 264–68, 356–58; direct speech or impersonation in, 250–51; generic or stylistic experimentation and, 265–67; Hecataeus of Miletus and, 371–72; Hegel on origin of, 242; Herodotus's understanding and deployment of, 371–72; *logopoios* as term applied to, 86, 370–72, 376–82, 384, 389–90, 423, 430–31; as low status or disreputable, 369–70, 376–77, 381; Plato and, 246–47, 262–63, 330; as risky endeavor, 369–70, 376, 430–31; and rupture of literary decorum, 244, 356–57; short prose forms associated with wisdom tradition, 289–90; Socratic dialogues as mimetic, 244–51, 257–59, 262; Sophists and "the battle over prose," 264–68, 265–66; truth and the medium of, 356–57, 363, 365, 367–69, 376, 381; Xenophon and, 241–42
Protagoras, 329; education in, 301–5; fables as *sophia* in, 305–6; *muthos* as fable, 282–88, 301; as parody, 306–8
proverbs, proverbial lore, 140–41, 177–79, 335
"public transcript" vs. "hidden transcript," 11–12, 74

punch lines: elision of, 207–8, 296–97; Herodotus and, 130–31, 406–8, 420–21; in Hesiod, 281; as internal (*epilogos*), 45, 130–31; parodic quality of, 256n36; in Plato's *Symposium*, 311–12, 313; *Vita* W and elaboration on, 89n108. *See also* morals
Pythagoras: associated with Apollo, 109; and practice of *sophia*, 95, 103, 112n57, 114
Pythagorean *acusmata*, 109, 205

Quellenforschung (source criticism), 27–29, 31–33, 38–39, 276–77

reading methodologies, 25–26, 32–33; allusions and reference to fuller versions, 44–45; comparative reading method, 22–23; diachronic approach, 46; Herodotus and use of Aesop as cue to readers, 426–31; ideological coherence and, 25, 46–49, 75–94, 159–60; "regressive method," 22–23; structuralist, 60; synchronic style, 33–35
Redfield, Robert, 7–8
reflectionism, 28
"regressive method," 22–23
reincarnation, 137n28, 189–90, 328–29
Republic (Plato), 246–48, 250–51, 328, 368
resistance: Aesop and, 11–14, 53, 59–71; alibis as instrument of, 11–12, 74–75; culture as scene of, 23–24; to Delphi, 59, 74–75, 187; ideology and, 24; parody and, 11–12, 13, 203–4; of *pharmakos* by Aesop, 85–86; textual, 9, 11–12, 24
Rhetoric (Aristotle), 42, 150, 154, 156–57, 194–96, 202, 244, 259, 299; on fables as examples in argument, 255; on style and features of prose, 267–68
riddles, 111; codes and, 169–71; of the sphinx, 226–29, **227**, **228**
Robert, Louis, 110
Robertson, Noel, 30, 210–11
Robinson, Richard, 340, 360n87
Roman imperial education and rhetorical system, 69–70
Rothwell, Kenneth, 156–57, 243–44
Roux, Georges, 56
Rowe, Christopher, 115n66, 314n26, 318n34, 320

sacrifice: access to oracle, 55–58; Aesop's critique of, 47, 68, 71–73, 187–88, 204, 210–12, 219–22; allotment of sacrificial portions,

83–84; bodiliness and, 224; as brute butchery, 74, 77, 79–81, 152; and constitution of community, 54–55, 57, 152, 187, 212, 221–23; at Delphi, 211; gift exchange linked to, 221; and metaphorization, 222; as parasitic dependence, 67–68, 73; power dynamics of, 212; as problematic, 72–73; selling of sacrificial meat, 219–22; as theft or misappropriation, 90–92; Theoxeny and, 82–84, 94; tripod as utensil of, 111

sage tradition: Aesop and, 137–42, 159–61, 172–76, 189–90; hero cult and, 114, 189–90, 328; life cycle of a sage, 112–15, 123–24, 159–61, 185–87, 328–29; mediation of the divine or otherworldly, 102–3, 114–15, 170–71, 186, 189–90, 203–4, 328; reincarnation of the sage as element of, 137n28, 328–29; theoric death and, 113–15, 186–90, 223; wandering or exile linked to stages of career, 112–14. *See also* Seven Sages

Salmoxis, 103

Samos: and Aesop as political adviser, 5, 127, 132–33, 142–44, 147, 174; Aesop as slave to Xanthus on, 5, 165, 197–98, 335–36; Aesop's sign reading and his bid for freedom, 197–98, 247; circulation of Aesop stories/fable on, 59, 412; Herodotus on, 369, 412, 430–31

sanctuary, violation of, 187–88

"Sayings of the Seven Sages," 109–10, 140–41, 181–82, 217

scapegoat, 27; community as, 92–93; Delphians as, 86–94; Herodotus scapegoated by Plutarch, 393; lone wolf figure as outsider or, 151–53; as sexually transgressive figure, 86, 87, 89–90; theft as attribute of, 86. *See also pharmakos* ritual

Scodel, Ruth, 114–15, 190n8

Scott, James, 11

self-incrimination, 196–98, 200n97, 201, 360; Aesop and extorting of, 343; of Apollo, 199–200; *elenchos* and opponent's, 343–44; in Plato's *Gorgias*, 341–43

Seven Sages: Aesop as associate of, 31–33, 125–26, 131–32, 137–38, 182, 202–3, 303–4; Apollo linked to, 109; as collegium, 126–27, 223; and competitive *sophia*, 102–8, 137–38, 303–4; as Croesus's contemporaries, 1–4, 126–27; maxims and wisdom of, 109–10, 140–41, 180–82, 181–82, 289–90; as mediators with the divine or otherworldly, 102–3,

114–15, 189–90, 203–4, 223; Ostia tavern painting depicting, 229–36, **231**, **232**, **233**; parody of, 212–17, 229–36, **231**, **232**, **233**; poetry and, 141–42; as political advisers, 96, 142, 144, 428–30; sign reading by, 142; Socrates associated with, 326–30; *sophia* tradition and, 95

sex: bestiality, 87, 90, 187–88; flute-girls as prostitutes, 333; in idiot girl (foolish daughter) fable, 87, 186–87, 213–16, 224; incest, 86, 89–90, 187; masturbation, 207–8; pederasty, 214–16, 316–17; scapegoat as sexually transgressive figure, 86, 87, 89–90

sheep, dogs, and wolves, fable of, 144, 147–48, 150–51, 268, 288, 293, 297–98

shipbuilding, 98, 101, 106, 126–27, 405–6

"Should One Engage in Farming" (Themistius), 276–78

sign reading. *See* prophecy or sign reading

silence: muteness of Aesop, 62–63

Simonides, 107, 120–22, 138–40, 147–48, 303–5, 329, 362–63, 387–88, 392

Simon the cobbler, 258

skilled crafting: agriculture as, 101; divine creation as, 306–7, 310–11; fig episode as public performance of, 192; parodies of, 306–7, 310–11; Prometheus as skilled maker, 305–6; *sophia* as, 98–101, 101–2, 105, 112, 123–24, 136–37, 167–68, 191, 327–28

slavery or slaves: Aesop as freed from, 11, 66, 197–98; Aesop as slave, 3, 5, 13, 61–63, 139, 308, 387–88; Apollo as "overseer" of the Muses, 62–64, 66, 163–64; clever slave figures, 10–11, 308; Delphians as servile or slaves "to all the Greeks," 5, 68–69, 70, 71, 86–87; indirect or long story as "slave talk," 138, 139–40, 387–88; *Life of Aesop* as slave narrative, 10, 25; marginalization of, 6n11; mutism and slave status, 13, 62–63, 160, 162–63, 185, 191–92, 304, 360; political advice regarding freedom and slavery, 143–45, 150–51, 407–11; the slave as master or instructor of the owner, 207–8; slaves as lacking self-control, 295, 318–19; in Xenophon's *Memorabilia*, 295

"slave talk," 138, 139–40, 387–88

Smindyrides, 418–19, 425

Socrates: as Aesop figure, 247, 251–55, 259, 323, 326, 329–30, 355–59; analogy as deployed by, 259, 308–9, 322–23, 330–35, 339–40; and artless style of truth telling,

492 GENERAL INDEX

Socrates (cont.)
321–22, 330; as bricoleur, 322n44, 332–40; connection to Apollo, 111–12, 254–55, 327; *elenchos* of, 260, 340–44, 400; as fabulist, 251–55, 290–92, 322; as literary character in Platonic dialogues, 252–53, 270, 291–92, 325–29, 330–34, 358; as low, 329–30; and the Sages or archaic sage tradition, 326–29; as unique, 308, 322–24, 325, 333–36, 338–39; versification of fables by, 202, 217, 251–54, 327; in Xenophon, 288, 290–93

Socratic dialogues: Aesop/Apollo opposition and structure of, 36, 199n98; Aesopic or fabular elements in, 251–53, 260–61, 264, 270–71, 282–86, 301, 323, 326–30 (see also *Hippias Major*; *Phaedo*; *Protagoras*; *Symposium*); colloquial style of, 269–70; as generic hybrids, 244, 245, 246, 252n28, 259–67, 285–86, 308–10, 323, 325; as literary form, 252, 367; as mimetic prose, 246–51, 257–59, 262; politics of form and, 264; as privileged in modern scholarship, 270; tensions or disruption of literary decorum in, 323–24, 354–55. *See also specific dialogues*

Solon, 104–6, 108, 112–13, 122, 126, 145, 151–52, 409n25; Aesop associated with, 32, 131–32, 135–36, 203, 236–37; beast fables deployed by, 142, 151–56, 244, 373; in colloquy with Croesus, 126–27, 131, 135–36, 147, 350–51, 409n25, 412, 428–30; depiction in wall painting of the Seven Sages, 230–34; Hippias and, 350–51, 358; as lawgiver, 113–14; as political adviser, 428–30; *sophia* tradition and, 173, 203, 230, 346–47, 350–52, 356; style of, contrasted with Aesop's, 131–35, 137–38, 389

sophia: appropriation by Sophists, 329, 345–51; Aristotle and traditional, 115–18; chaos/order and, 99; as coherent "wisdom tradition," 95; as competition (*see* competitive *sophia*); as contested, 98–99, 103–5, 120–21; critique of (see *sophia*, Aesop's critique of high); Delphic connections to, 47, 187; as discovery or revelation, 100–101; disguise of, 108; divine origin of, 98–99, 121–23, 136–37; evolution or anthropology of, 95–98, 100–101, 159–68; gods and ancestors as culture heroes, 100; low or bodily *sophia* of Aesop, 125; mantic skills or prophecy and, 95, 101, 102, 142–43, 145–47, 168–74, 188–89; Peripatetic five stages of, 95–98, 111–15, 118; philosophy and appropriation of, 108, 115–24, 304, 328–29; as poetic skill, 95, 105–6; as political wisdom, 95, 105, 118, 119–20; vs. practical intelligence, 115–20; as prephilosophical or nonphilosophical tradition, 104–8; proverbial lore and, 140–41; as ritual expertise, 95, 102, 205–6; as skilled crafting, 98–102, 105, 112, 123–24, 136–37, 167–68, 191, 327–28; travel and, 99, 106, 112–14, 186, 327–28

sophia, Aesop's critique of high, 12–13, 203; and Aesop as ideologeme, 12n32; bird lore, 168–69, 209–10; mantic authority or monopoly, 12n23, 61–62, 66, 168–73, 187, 383; parody as instrument for, 95, 176, 187, 203–4, 213–15, 217–24, 383; ritual prohibitions, 204–12; sacrifice and the sacrificial economy, 47, 59, 68–69, 71–72, 85, 187, 210–12, 221–23; Seven Sages, 135–36, 203–4, 217–24, 247; symposium and didactic traditions, 204, 212–17; Theognis, 212–16

sophistēs/sophistai, 95, 101–4, 107, 364–66; competitive *sophia* and, 105; Herodotus's use of term, 102–3, 104; Pindar on, 103; as poets, 103, 105–6, 105n32; as skilled craftsmen, 99–102

Sophists, 101; appropriation of *sophia* tradition by, 329, 345–51; "the battle over prose" and, 265–66; Diotima's identification with, 312–13; elaboration of fable as device of, 48, 241, 270–75, 279–80, 284–86, 300, 303, 409, 421; fragmentary preservation of works, 261; generic or stylistic experimentation by, 264, 265–67; and sage tradition, 102–15

space: boundary transgression and sacred, 79–80; Delphi and spatial marginality, 55; *sophia* and axes of distance, 99

Spartans, 92, 114, 391, 393, 430

speech. *See* language or speech

status, sociopolitical, 2, 242; age and age-classes as issue in verbal exchange, 287; and allotment of sacrificial portions, 83–84; decorum and appropriateness, 221n43; elites and relationship with "low" culture, 7–11, 21–22; fable linked to low status, 431; familial relationships, 293; flute-girls as abject, 333–34; generic hierarchy and correspondence with, 20, 42–43, 138, 242, 316–18, 375–76, 390–91, 424; Herodotus accused of inversion of, 395; of the interlocutor in *Life*,

331; and mediation of popular culture, 21–22; oracular consultation and right of priority, 58; and participation in common or "little tradition" of culture, 7–9; performance as status and gender-specific, 304–5; *pharmakos*/hero cult and inversion of, 93; among the Seven Sages, 203; Theoxeny and status, 82–84, 94. *See also* slavery or slaves

stele erected to Aesop, 5, 93, 182n61, 189

Stesichorus, 150, 156, 255–56

Stobaeus, 109–10, 181, 216n35, 279–80

Story of Ahiqar, 27, 33–35, 99n96, 176–78, 218n38; Ahiqar section in *Life*, 38, 159–60, 176–85, 198, 199, 202, 359–60; assimilation of Aesop to Ahiqar, 176–85; contest with Nectanebo, 5, 161, 183–84, 198–99, 359; divergence from story of Aesop, 180–85; extant versions of, 176–77; as inspiration for *Vita* G author, 33–35; integration into Greek literary tradition, 177–78; narrative coherence and, 182–85; riddle solving in, 179; self-incrimination in, 198–99

Strasburger, Hermann, 423

structuralist methodology, 24–25

style: Aesop's distinctive discursive, 132–40, 156, 201, 331–32, 341; audience engagement and, 427; colloquial, 2, 6, 20, 128–29, 253, 269–70, 274, 310, 345–46, 383, 407; content and stylistic choice, 261, 265–67, 281, 290–91, 309, 382; dictional traces of Aesop tradition in Herodotus, 125–37, 406, 429–30; and generic hierarchy, 3–4, 242–43, 261, 265–67, 269, 309–10, 382; Homeric/Aesopic binary, 381, 383, 389, 405–7, 410–11, 428–29; as ideological instrument, 42–43, 357, 383; indirect, 133–36, 141, 373–74, 387–88, 399, 400–404, 427; of *Life*, 6, 16, 20–21, 42, 45, 76; Plato's deployment of, 285–86, 345–46; Plutarch and severing of ethos from, 384–85; sociopolitical status and, 20, 42–43, 242–43, 261, 270n21, 353–55; Socratic, 321–22, 328–30, 332, 340–41; Sophists and elaborations of fable, 48, 270–75, 279–80, 284–86, 300, 303, 409, 421; truth and artless, 135, 139, 273, 321–22, 330, 356–57, 407–8

suntomia. See *brachylogia*/*makrologia*

superstition, 204–5

supplication: Apollo as supplicant of Zeus, 64–65; Theoxeny and representatives of communities, 83; violation of supplicant, 88–89, 290–91

Svenbro, Jesper, 152–53, 412

Sybarite fables, 396–97, 418–19

symbols: ideology as symbolic system, 24; texts as symbolic acts, 24

symposium and didactic traditions, 204, 212–17, 223, 234, 346–52

Symposium (Plato), 260, 263–64, 267–69, 274, 332–44, 358; appropriation of fable in, 308–24; fabular formulae in, 311–12, 314; generic hierarchy in, 334–40

synchronic reading, 33–35

Synesius of Cyrene, 140–41

Szegedy-Maszak, Andrew, 112

texts: as contested or negotiated, 24; as symbolic acts, 24

Thales, 112–13, 119–20, 168, 218, 269n18, 365; depiction in wall painting of the Seven Sages, 230–31, **232**

theft: Aesop as falsely accused of, 5, 87–88, 191–92, 200n58, 211; Delphic sacrifice and theft of sacrificial meat, 86, 90–91, 211–12; of figs, 191–92, 197; Hecataeus as advocate of, 378–79; Hermes', of cows, 1–2; *hierosulia*, 86, 90, 211, 378–79; Holzberg and shift from piety to hubris, 185–86; of *sophia*, 107

Themistius, 276–78

Themistocles, 172–74, 392

Theognis, 95, 106–7, 204, 212–17

Theogony (Hesiod), 108–9

theōria (pilgrimage), 96, 112–15, 120, 123, 159, 162, 185–201, 328–29; death of the sage during, 113–15, 186–90, 223

Theoxeny, Delphic ritual and, 82–84, 94

Thomas, Rosalind, 363–66, 368n35, 380–81, 423–24

Thrace or Thracians, 103, 136, 247, 396, 397, 429

Thucydides, 98n5, 128–29, 173–74, 378, 379, 431n88

time, 43, 79n71

tithing, Apolline, 70–71

Tobit, Book of, 176, 183n63

tongues: Aesop's tongue as "unshackled," 136n26, 163; as "best and worst," 165n13, 218–22, 235

tragedy: fable as content in, 156, 243–44, 396; in Greek hierarchy of genres, 76, 156, 249, 263–64, 427; *Histories* of Herodotus as, 368, 427; mimesis and, 249, 257; Plato's *Symposium* and, 263–64, 323–24

translations: of *Life of Aesop*, 26; note on, xv
Trapp, Michael, 303
travel: and the acquisition of wisdom, 113–14; Aesop as traveler, 5, 69, 185–86; as sacred activity, 113–14; *sophia* and, 99, 106, 112–14. *See also under theōria* (pilgrimage)
tricksters, 11–12, 53, 390
tripods, 106, 110–11, 237
truth: Aesop's indirect style and, 139, 273; Alcibiades' use of image as, 333; decorum and, 382, 384; Diotima and abstraction of, 319–20; fable as fiction or deception, 43, 155, 431; fable as medium for, 43, 289, 320–21; Herodotus and, 363–65, 367–69, 376, 380–82, 385, 407–9, 431; in *Hippias*, 353, 358; *logopoios* and, 376, 380–81; oracular, 61–62; plain, direct style and, 135, 273, 321–22, 330, 407–8; pleasure/truth binary, 130–32, 134–35, 273, 407–9, 431; prose as medium for, 363, 365, 367–69, 376; Seven Sages and, 130–32, 134–35, 273; Socratic *elenchos* and, 341, 360
tyranny, 256, 409, 421, 423; advice to tyrants, 146–56, 373–80, 388, 400, 419–20, 428–29; Athens as *polis tyrannos*, 373, 427–30; beast fable associated with debate on, 150–51; fables and, 154–56; as non-Greek or Eastern "Other," 136
Tzetzes, John, 86, 92, 425

ugliness, physical: of Aesop, 3, 61, 132–33, 337; as attribute of *pharmakos* (scapegoat), 86; depictions of Aesop in the visual tradition, 225–29, **226**; and inside-outside dialectic, 41, 133, 137, 193, 197, 333–37; of Socrates, 329–30
underworld: sage and mediation of the otherworldly, 114–15, 189–90; trip to, as *theōria*, 189–90, 328
urination, 206–8

Vansina, Jan, 28, 141
vegetables: Delphians compared to, 69, 72n50, 187; market-gardener episode, 166–67; "wild vegetables" and civilized agriculture, 165–66
ventriloquism, 358; direct speech as device, 251; impersonation of Aesop, 250, 251
visual tradition: Aesop as figure in, 225–29, **226**; Oedipus and the Sphinx in, 226–29,

227, **228**; Seven Sages in, 229–36, **231**, **232**, **233**
Vita G: as anthropology of *sophia*, 39–40, 144–45, 159–65, 183–84; Apollo-Aesop antagonism in, 60–62, 67, 254n33, 337, 343n50; authorship of, 6, 12, 18, 22, 33, 38–39, 42, 69; coherence of narrative, 22, 33–34, 39–40, 46–47, 63–64; dating of, 4, 16, 18, 42; Egyptian elements in, 18; fable logic and narrative in, 189; Latin loanwords and Latinisms in, 18, 42, 236m83; literary allusion in, 6, 69; motto at end of, 189, 194, **195**; Muses in, 136n26, 162–63, 167–68, 174–75, 184; as parodic and subversive, 12n33, 40, 42, 123n84, 198n93; as permeable, fluid text, 22, 38–39; Perry's publication of, 4, 16, 18, 26; as "popular literature," 6–7, 19–22; redactor and shaping of narrative, 12, 17, 33–40, 42, 47, 62n28, 69, 71, 161, 176; synopsis of, 4–5; translations of, 26; *Vita* W's relationship with, 42–43
Vita W, 16–18, 42–43; Apollo-Aesop antagonism elided from, 67–69, 89n106, 92n115; hero-cult honors in, 92–93, 189; Muses elided from, 35–36, 63n31, 162n9, 175; and otherworldly end of the sage, 176, 189–90; "social censorship" and, 198n93; *Vita* G's relationship with, 42–43
Volksbuch theory, 19–22, 27, 30, 68n43
vomiting, 191–92, 358

Wasps (Aristophanes), 29–30, 211
Welcker, Friedrich, 276
West, M. L., 14, 20–21, 59, 204–6, 208–11, 396
West, Stephanie, 377–81
Westermann, Anton, 16
Wiechers, Anton, 29–31, 70, 75–76, 85
Wilamowitz-Moellendorff, Ulrich von, 32n92, 204, 252–53n28
the wild: Delphians linked to, 187–88
Winkler, Jack, 25, 170–71, 203
wisdom traditions: as culturally specific, 181–82; defined and described, 95; Delphic connections to, 47. *See also sophia*
witnessing: self-incrimination, 196–98, 200n97, 201, 359–60
wolves and dogs, 144, 147–48, 150–53, 151–53, 298
women: feminine figures in fable, 87, 186–87, 213–16, 224, 272–76, 296, 409; flute-girls, status and performance by, 304–5, 333–34,

339; sociopolitical hierarchy and role of, 2, 297–98, 304–5, 391–92, 395, 421. *See also* Diotima

"wooden wall" oracle, 172–74

Woodruff, Paul, 344–46, 352–53, 354, 356, 357

Works and Days (Hesiod), 14, 204–12; agriculture in, 277–78; beast fables in, 3, 243, 403–4

Xanthus, 5, 61, 139–40, 142, 143, 166–70, 218; Aesop as master or instructor of, 207–8, 219–21; self-incrimination of, 196–98, 360; as sign-reader, 171–72, 197–98, 209–10

xenia (hospitality), 66, 82, 88–89, 188, 394; Delphic violation of, 187–88; mouse and frog, fable of, 88, 188, 394; Theoxeny, 82–84, 94

Xenophanes, 105–6, 108, 246–47, 362, 365

Xenophon, 270, 276–77; Aesop tradition and prose of, 241–42; fables deployed or recast by, 48, 288–99; Prodicus and, 271–72, 274, 276–77, 294–97

the young: age and age-classes as issue in *Protagoras,* 287n67; as audience, 248, 271, 286–87, 287–88, 302–3, 314, 316; *Hōrai* as youth, 276

Zenas, 62–63

Zenobius, 137, 190